PRODUCTION/OPERATIONS MANAGEMENT

**The Irwin Series in Management
and
The Behavioral Sciences**

Production/Operations Management

FRANKLIN G. MOORE, Ph.D.
Professor Emeritus
Graduate School of Business
The University of Michigan—Ann Arbor

THOMAS E. HENDRICK, Ph.D.
Associate Professor
Graduate School of Business Administration
University of Colorado—Boulder

1977

Seventh edition

RICHARD D. IRWIN, INC. Homewood, Illinois 60430
IRWIN-DORSEY LIMITED Georgetown, Ontario L7G 4B3

The previous edition was published under the title
Production Management.

Seventh Edition

3 4 5 6 7 8 9 0 K 5 4 3 2 1 0 9 8

41495

Lanchester Poℕtechnic Library

ISBN 0-256-01921-5
Library of Congress Catalog Card No. 76–49309
Printed in the United States of America

Foreword to students

THE PURPOSE of a course in production/operations management is to provide you with an insight into how production is brought about. And that is the purpose of this book. It has been designed to portray the conditions under which production takes place and the part managers and workers play in effecting production.

The book will also call your attention to many of the problems faced by managers and to the merits of the different courses of action that are open to them. Emphasis is put on managers as decision makers who continually face alternatives, each having certain advantages, yet at the same time having disadvantages.

This book supplies descriptive material to provide you with the background necessary for understanding the concepts and appreciating the managerial problems presented. Quantitative materials and problems are introduced frequently. These follow the trend in the last several years toward quantifying more and more of the areas of decision making in production and operations management. These problems are confined to small ones of the kind that can be presented and solved in the text. Difficult mathematical calculations have been avoided.

There may be times when you will wish for a definite answer and recommendation in some matter, and find none in the text. This may not be fully satisfying, yet this is how it often is in the real world. If you fly, you generally arrive at your destination quickly, but you don't see the countryside. If you drive on the superhighway, you go more slowly and see more. And if you go on the back roads, you go still more slowly and see much more. Which is best? The answer depends on what you want. The text frequently points out the good and bad things about alternative actions without categorically choosing one as best.

This is the way the world operates. Sometimes it is hard for a manager, even with a considerable array of facts before him, to choose which action will prove to be the best. So don't feel annoyed if the text sometimes weighs pros and cons and does not make a choice. Often the matter being discussed is a little like trying to answer such questions as, "Should I buy a house or rent one?" or "Should I choose this college or that college?" There isn't any one answer which is best for everyone. There are two or more sides to many problems and being aware of them can promote our understanding and help us make better decisions, even if it does make choosing more difficult.

At the end of every chapter you will find several aids that will help you to understand what was presented in the chapter. First, there are review questions. These questions are about matters which you should be able to answer from having read the chapter. If you cannot answer them, it may be well to reread the text discussion on the subject.

It is well to familiarize yourself with new terms introduced in the chapter. If there is any question about the meaning of certain terms, you should consult the index at the end of the book. There you will find references to the pages where the terms are discussed and explained. By referring to the text discussion you will get a better explanation of the term than could be supplied in an abbreviated glossary.

Next are questions for analysis and discussion. These questions relate to the subject of the chapter but often they go beyond it. They have to do with difficult problems and how to apply the ideas in the chapters to actual situations. Many of these questions have been taken from executive training programs. They are questions that mature managers in training classes have asked to apply the ideas presented.

Following the discussion questions are problems or cases or both, depending on the chapter. The problems allow you to apply the techniques introduced in the text to other similar problems to help you fix the method in your mind. The cases are like the analysis and discussion questions in that they relate to the subject of the chapter in a general way, although they are frequently even more far-reaching. These cases, too, are often real-life cases brought up in executive training classes.

Students as well as teachers may want to do further research on the subject of a chapter. For this purpose, selected additional supplemental readings are suggested at the end of each chapter. These are sources where you will find a more thorough treatment of the material. Sometimes these sources will bring up points of view different from those expressed in the text and sometimes they will deal with different aspects of the subjects.

All of these study aids are presented as aids to learning. In a very real sense, a text does not teach, it only helps you to learn.

Preface

PRODUCTION is usually thought of as the making of products. But the production of services has, over the years, become increasingly important. *Production/Operations Management,* a change from the former title, brings the production of services more into focus yet it retains its major thrust in the area of the production of products.

Since the last edition of this book was published, the position of managers, particularly of private organizations and even more particularly of manufacturing companies, has changed. They, along with managers of electric utility companies and mining companies, have come under fire for not being sensitive enough to the safety and environmental protection needs of society. *Production/Operations Management* considers the effects of these matters on managerial practices.

In presenting the material covered in this book the manufacturing firm has been found to be a particularly useful model. It not only represents a large segment of our working population, but it is also the most complex type of organization. Similarly the making of automobiles is used as the illustrative example in several places because the product is familiar to us all and it is easier for students to relate the concept being discussed to its real-life setting when the illustration is of a familiar product.

In this Seventh Edition, a considerable amount of descriptive material has been eliminated in order to provide more space for conceptual matters and to allow for still more emphasis on managerial decision making. Enough descriptive material has been retained, however, to provide a background of information so that students without industrial work experience will not have to discuss concepts and cases in a vacuum. Quantitative materials have been retained but the emphasis is on acquainting students with the existence and availability of the methods of decision making rather than on their developing a high degree of manipulative skill in quantitative areas.

In order to emphasize the managerial decision-making viewpoint, general information is presented first. Following this is a discussion of the problems that managers face in each subject area. Alternative courses of action are considered along with the pros and cons of each. This gives the student both an acquaintance with the various subject areas and their problems, and a feel for the appropriate managerial actions. We have tried to lead the reader along the road to problem solutions so that he or she may develop better skills in this area.

The text has been divided into seven general subject areas, each consisting of several chapters. The suggestions of reviewers of this book helped determine the grouping of subjects and the sequence in which they are presented. Most instructors, however, have personal preferences for the sequence in which they like to present subordinate subjects. It is suggested that where the instructor prefers a different sequence, he adopt the one he likes. Most of the chapters are self-contained enough to allow for their being presented in a different order to suit individual instructors.

The aids to the instructor in the classroom have been strengthened. First, review questions are presented at the end of each chapter. These allow the student to test his own understanding of the subject of the chapter and they can be used in the classroom to further clarify the text material.

Next, questions for analysis and discussion are presented. These relate to the subject of the chapter but often go beyond it. They are often difficult and may have no exact answer. Rather they are intended to generate classroom discussion. Most were originally brought up by mature managers taking executive training programs. They provide an opportunity to relate the subject of the chapter to real-world settings. Usually they generate lively classroom participation, which in turn helps develop better understanding of the subject.

Each chapter has its own problems or cases or both, as may be appropriate. The problems are related to the subject of the chapter and often are similar to the problems explained in the text. It is helpful to have students work such problems since it often happens that their reading about how to do a problem leaves them with less than full understanding. Working problems gives them a better appreciation and a fuller understanding of how the techniques apply.

Some subjects, however, are better explained through cases rather than computational problems. To serve this purpose, cases, some short and some long, are provided at the end of appropriate chapters.

Instructors and students sometimes want to pursue individual subjects beyond what the text offers. To meet this need, at the end of each chapter several "Suggested supplemental readings" are included. These are almost always confined to recent sources because recently published material is usually the most relevant to the current environment.

We want to thank the many instructors who have written to us from time to time offering helpful suggestions. These suggestions help to keep us aware of trends and directions in which the subject of production/operations management is moving, and thus help us to write a better book.

March 1977   FRANKLIN G. MOORE
                                                                 THOMAS E. HENDRICK

Contents

machines. Numerically controlled (N/C) machines. Robotry. Transfer machines. Maldistribution curves and production methods. Machine-use ratios: *Differential housing production line example. Lines and functional manufacture comparison.* Vulnerability of lines to downtime. Automatic assembly.

items used in large volumes. Large special orders. Middle-sized orders. Small orders. Follow-up. Receiving inspection. How much centralization? *Value analysis. Known cost.* Mass production purchasing. How many to buy at one time: *Standard quantities.* Product descriptions. Choosing vendors. Reciprocity. Bidding versus negotiated contracts. Government contracts. Purchase contracts. Discounts. Purchasing problems: *How much price pressure? Gifts.* Miscellaneous functions of the purchasing department.

18 Basic inventory concepts and generalized control systems   424

Raw materials. In-process inventories. Supplies. Enclosed stockrooms. Open stockrooms. Physical inventories. Identification systems. Identifying materials. Materials requisitions. Pricing the materials issued: *Fifo. Lifo. Weighted average cost. Standard cost.* Inventory levels and buying to market prices. Inventory ABC analysis. Maximum-minimum controls. Investment limitation control methods: *Inventory turnover. Dollar limits. Time limits.* Fixed ordering times.

19 Forecasting demand for products and services   448

Top-down forecasting. Bottom-up forecasting. Demand interpretation. Specific item forecasting. Intrinsic forecasting methods: *Trend calculation. Seasonal calculation. Forecast for year 4.* Exponential smoothing (EXSM): *Model 1. Model 2. Model 3.* Measuring forecast errors: *Tracking signals. Adaptive response systems.* The Box-Jenkins method.

20 Master scheduling and material requirements planning   471

Master production schedules: Manufacture to order. Workloads and production capacities. Master schedules: Manufacturing to stock. Production programs. Master schedules: Classes of products. Master schedules: The time period. Master schedules: Basic components. Parts. Assembly orders. Material requirements planning: *Dependent versus independent demand. Lead times. Common use items. Data files for material requirements planning. Product structure trees. "Level" codes. Time "buckets." On-hand stocks. "Netting" and "exploding" orders for end products.* Raw materials requirements. Extraneous demand for parts and components. Priority planning and rescheduling. Lot sizes and the timing of orders.

21 Inventory management: Order points and order quantities   499

Reordering points (ROP). Errors in expectations of use during lead times. Service levels: *Limitations to reorder points based on service levels.*

charts in service organizations. Acceptance sampling. Operating characteristic curves. Single, double, sequential and continuous sampling plans. Average outgoing quality level (AOQL). Degrees of defects in acceptance sampling. SQC in operation.

section one

PRODUCTION AND operations managers carry on their work in a social and economic environment. Society puts restrictions on them as they strive to produce products and services. Their jobs are multifaceted and have to do with managing the organization's resources, people, money, physical property, and the making and selling of products and services.

In this section, Chapter 1 on the Domain of Production and Operations Management presents a brief view of what production and operating managers do. Chapter 2, Basic Management Concepts, and Chapter 3, Basic Economic Concepts, deal with fundamental relationships which managers need to know about as they manage. Chapter 4, Capital Expenditure Analysis, deals more specifically with the financial consequences of investment decisions.

1

The domain of production and operations management

STUDENTS embarking on a course in production and operations management may want to know how the subject relates to the rest of their college courses and to their career objectives. They may have a major interest in manufacturing and production, or their major interest may be in marketing, finance, or government work. They may be looking forward to managing their own small organization, or to working in a manufacturing company such as General Motors, or in a retailing company such as Sears Roebuck. Or they may have in mind a transportation company, such as United Airlines, or working for the government or for some other kind of service organization, such as a bank, motel chain, or hospital.

The purpose of this book is to provide students with a feeling for production and operations management, what it includes, what production and operations managers do, why they do it, and how what they do is related to other areas such as marketing, finance, accounting, and personnel (see Figure 1–1).

SCOPE OF PRODUCTION AND OPERATIONS MANAGEMENT

Production and operations management activities are not confined only to manufacturing. It is true that the production activities carried on in manufacturing companies are the backbone of our consumer society and they produce a broad array of products. Nearly 20 million people work in manufacturing activities or at other activities in manufacturing companies in the United States. But people also do production activities in other kinds of organizations, service type organizations, in particular. In

3

recent years, more and more effort is being directed toward the management of productive effort in the service sector of our economy.

Service organizations such as those in banking, insurance, transportation, hotels, and restaurant businesses produce services much as manufacturing companies produce automobiles, furniture, and ball-point pens. Furthermore, within the service sector, the management of the operations in governmental organizations is receiving more and more attention. The costs of municipal services for schools, police protection, fire protection, trash collection, and so on are outstripping cities' revenues. Costs of hospital services are also increasing rapidly.

Unfortunately, a great many governmental and other nonprofit organizations are poorly managed. According to the Committee for Economic Development, "The greatest opportunity for improved government productivity lies in strengthened management."[1]

Perhaps a helpful way for a reader to get a feel for the kinds of activities, problems, and decisions that make up the work of production and operations management would be to look at some items in the "in-baskets" of some typical production and operation managers. Accordingly, we will present some sample "in-basket" items for the production manager of a small manufacturing company, an assistant city manager, and an operations manager for a commercial bank.

In-basket for Lance Redford

Lance Redford is the production manager for the Zinger Skateboard Manufacturing Company. Zinger sells skateboards worldwide through wholesalers and a variety of retail stores. Redford has just returned from a three-week vacation trip and finds the following items in his incoming mail basket:

1. A letter from the U.S. Labor Department's Occupational Health and Safety Administration informs him that the company is in violation of federal rules regarding permissible noise levels on certain machines in the factory. The letter also reports that the company is not providing adequate safety devices to keep machine operators' hands out of the machines during their "stamping" cycles. The company is also cited for inadequate control of the fumes and dust associated with the vinyl chloride plastics used in the manufacture of certain of their skateboards. The letter from OSHA specifies fines which must be paid by the company and deadlines for clearing up the problems.

2. A memorandum from the director of marketing reads, "As you know, Lance, our market in the West has been increasing substantially, and we should be thinking about building a new warehouse somewhere in

---

[1] *Improving Productivity in State and Local Government,* Committee for Economic Development, 1976, p. 20.

the western states so that we can give better service out there. Would you be able to head up a special study group to consider where we might best locate such a warehouse and how its operations might be correlated with those of our Chicago and Atlanta warehouses?"

3. A note from the supervisor of the machine shop reads, "Lance, I think that the layout and locations of our machines could be improved substantially. We seem to be spending too much time moving parts from machine to machine. I'd like to talk this over with you and see if we could reduce these costs by relocating some of our machines."

4. Fred Cox, supervisor of plant maintenance, has written Redford a note asking if he could meet with Redford soon to discuss some ideas he has regarding the preventing of machinery breakdowns of equipment in use. Cox noted that in the past, "We have followed a policy on most of our machinery of repairing machines only when they break down. Lately this has been causing numerous interruptions to production."

5. Beth Kirkwood, the inventory control manager, has just returned from a week-long seminar where she learned about Materials Requirements Planning (MRP), a relatively new computer based approach to production and inventory control. Her report of these meetings strikes Redford's interest. She reported that, "Some companies are implementing MRP systems on relatively inexpensive minicomputers which are used exclusively for 'on-line real time' control of production, quality, and inventories." Redford has been concerned recently about several orders being delivered late because necessary materials and/or subassemblies were not available when they should have been. He wonders if this MRP approach might be of help here.

6. Bill Hernandez, manager of quality control, asks in a note to meet with Redford concerning the growing proportion of defective skateboards which inspectors have been finding through their statistical sampling procedures. Hernandez says that he is not sure whether the problem is in the use of substandard raw materials, inadequate training of machine operators, sabotage, or just what. Redford has heard from some of the supervisors that recent changes in certain manufacturing operations have made some of the current time standards inaccurate which in turn has caused considerable worker discontent. It may be the proper time to review the work methods and job standards in these areas. This would also be a necessary first step for his other plans to "rebalance" the skateboard assembly line.

7. A letter has been passed on to Redford by the president of Zinger from a lawyer in California who is bringing suit against Zinger on behalf of his client. They are charging that a Zinger skateboard was defective. A thirteen-year-old boy had an accident while going fast down a steep hill when a wheel came off a Zinger skateboard, and he is now paralyzed from the waist down. The president has scribbled a note on the corner of the letter which says, "Lance, meet me tomor-

row morning at 9 A.M. on this matter. Possibly we should stop producing this model and recall those boards which are similar to the one involved in this serious accident. Needless to say, I am very upset."

8. The research and development department has completed its testing of a new product, a skateboard with a small motor powered by a rechargeable battery. Redford must now begin to integrate this new product into existing manufacturing operations. A note in his in-basket reminds him of a meeting next week with engineering, purchasing, and marketing to finalize market forecasts, engineering design specifications, and questions as to which component parts of the new skateboards should be manufactured internally and which parts should be bought from outside suppliers.

9. The last item in the in-basket was a stack of nearly a dozen applications from college students who are looking for jobs in the production and management area. Since he had two openings, Redford thumbed through the stack quickly. One application struck his eye. It was from John Lovell, who was about to graduate from the university. Lovell had majored in production and operations management. From his resume, Redford could see that Lovell had a well-balanced education in this area. His courses included production and inventory control and purchasing. He had also been involved in two "live case" studies with local organizations near the university.

He also noted that Lovell was planning to take the certification examinations sponsored by the American Production and Inventory Control Society. Redford, being a member of this group himself, had heard that the examinations were tough but were designed to examine students' knowledge of academic material and its practical application to the real world of production and inventory management.

Even though Lovell had little experience, Redford decided to invite him for an interview to see if he might fit into one of his openings in the manufacturing division. The opening was that of "assistant production supervisor," where a new person would be responsible, after a training period, for the detailed scheduling and control of one of the skateboard assembly lines. The second opening was in production and inventory control. Redford thought that a man with Lovell's background might be quite helpful in installing an MRP system in the company, if it proved feasible.

Redford looked at his watch and noticed that it was time for him to attend this month's budget meeting. He got out his file which contained his recommendations for capital expenditures for new machinery and additions to plant and warehouse capacity for the next three years. He knew that Jack Karr, the director of finance, would ask about the expected costs and benefits of his recommendations. He was glad that he had prepared his proposals well before he had gone on his vacation.

In-basket for Kristen Thomas

Kristen Thomas is the assistant city manager for Sayerville, a Rocky Mountain city with a population of 250,000. She has a staff of eight budget and management analysts whose job is to help various city departments manage their operations. This staff of eight has a balanced mix of administrative skills; two were trained in political science and public administration; one is a statistician; one an economist; two were trained in urban planning; and two are graduates of business schools with training in production and operations management.

These last two individuals reflect the growing trend of public organizations' need to improve the operations which deliver services to the public. Interestingly, Ms. Thomas's own background was also in production and operations management. She has an MBA in this field and moved into city administration after a number of years in the aerospace industry. In fact, she is currently a part-time instructor in production management at Sayerville City College. The items in her in-basket are:

1. A memo from the city's fire chief reads, "Kristen, I am becoming increasingly concerned about the current locations of our fire stations. As you know, our city has grown rapidly over the past few years, and we have really never done a citywide comprehensive analysis of whether our stations are located correctly in relation to the fire hazards which we must protect. Some of our stations are clustered too closely in the downtown area, while many of our new outlying areas are protected only by distant fire stations. Could you assign someone from your staff to work with us on these location problems?"

2. The telephone rings and it's the director of public works, who says, "Kristen, we are having real problems with controlling our inventories here at Public Works. As you know, we carry spare parts for street lights, for water systems, street paving equipment, and so on. In total we carry more than 10,000 separate items which cost well over $2 million dollars.

   "I have been reading a new book, *MRP: The New Way of Life in Production and Inventory Control,* by Joseph Orlicky (McGraw-Hill, 1975), and I wonder if we could use our computer to help us control our inventories." Kristen, having read the book and lectured on it at Sayerville City College, told him that she thought it was worth looking into and that although her staff was loaded right now with current projects she would see what she could do.

3. An article titled "Work Measurement in Municipal Government" has been sent to her by the director of parks and recreation for Sayerville. The article, by Jerry Bethel of the city of Los Angeles, related how they applied Methods-Time-Measurement (MTM) time standards to work management programs in the Los Angeles Parks Department. She reads: "The department has over 300 facilities located on 217

separate sites which cover 14,000 acres of land and utilize 600 separate buildings. Among these facilities are 144 recreation centers, 71 large parks, 52 swimming pools, 14 senior citizen centers, 13 golf courses, 11. . . ." Kristen notes that they are using MTM time standards to schedule and control the large range of maintenance activities of these facilities.

A note in the corner of the article says, "Kristen, while Sayerville certainly does not have the range of facilities that Los Angeles has, nevertheless, I think we should consider the use of some of these methods. Can you give us some help in this area?"

4. The telephone rings again and it is a city councilman who has a complaint. He says, "I know that we have private companies which pick up our trash here in Sayerville, but doesn't it seem rather wasteful to you, Kristen, for each of the six different companies which are licensed to pick up trash in Sayerville to serve the whole city? Yesterday, for example, I noticed that four separate trucks came through my neighborhood, and each stopped at only one or two houses which were their customers. This seems terribly inefficient to me since the trash trucks must surely spend 80 percent of their time driving around and 20 percent of their time picking up trash. Besides, these trucks are noisy, and they probably get only about six miles per gallon of gasoline. Would you please look into this routing problem, and see what you can do about it?" Kristen said she would.

5. A memo from the police chief of Sayerville reads, "I have just returned from a meeting of police chiefs where I heard about some new police patrol scheduling methods which have been used successfully in cities about the size of Sayerville. These methods would, according to reports, allow us to schedule our patrol beats more efficiently so that they match the 24-hour patterns of calls for police assistance.

"As you know our budget is extremely tight this year and we have been asked to reduce our force by 5 percent. I want to make sure that I schedule our patrol activities in such a way so that we provide the best coverage possible for the citizens of Sayerville, considering our resources. We have a small grant through the Law Enforcement Assistance Act which we can use to implement these methods, but assistance from your office will be appreciated."

Kristen knew of these methods (which were developed under the sponsorship of the United States Department of Housing and Urban Development) and knew that complete users' manuals and computer programs were available at a nominal cost to any city which asked for them. She immediately dictated a letter to HUD requesting these materials.

6. A stack of applications from people who wanted to join the staff came last. Since one of her operations management specialists, Henry Stevens, was leaving to join the Valley National Bank as assistant operations manager, she was looking for someone to replace him.

One application from John Lovell interested her. She could see that his academic background would be a good foundation for the kinds of operational problems which faced the city of Sayerville so she decided to invite him for an interview.

In-basket for Bart Baker

Bart Baker is the operations manager for the Valley National Bank. Valley is a commercial bank located in the city of Hamilton and has 12 branches throughout the state. Bart Baker supervises the operations of the 13 facilities of the organization. In his capacity he is responsible for planning and controlling many of the "production" aspects of the bank. His major responsibilities are in the areas of facilities maintenance, bank security, new branch construction, and inventory control. Baker finds the following items in his in-basket after returning from a two-week "Executive in Residence" program at Hamilton City College:

1. A note from Jim Jones, Baker's assistant, who has been working on methods and job standards for the bank, says that he would like to meet with him and review his progress to date. Jones has been trying to improve the layout of tellers windows so that they will be more effective in serving customers. Hand in hand with this, he has been trying to develop reasonable job standards for tellers so they may determine the capacity of tellers to serve customers and thus arrange the work schedules of the tellers so that they coincide with arrival patterns of customers.

   Jones is also working on how to improve waiting line arrangements at drive-up windows. He would like, of course, to develop something like the single waiting lines used inside the bank but is hampered by the lack of adequate outside parking space.

2. A notice announces a meeting with the capital budget committee next week. Pulling his file from his drawer, Baker saw that he was ready to justify the costs of several capital items. They were:
   a. A new ultrasonic burglar detection system. The slightest motion within the bank jars the system's normal sound pattern, and a disturbance of this pattern activates an alarm.
   b. The installation of plastic card activated cash dispensers on a pilot basis in three suburban branches.
   c. The installation of a telecommunication system between the bank's central computer and the 12 branches.
   d. A new coin wrapping machine which would replace the two machines they currently have and would eliminate the need for one machine operator.

3. A final report from Tom Lopez outlines the plans to open a new branch in the next county. Tom had utilized the scheduling technique called **PERT** (Program Evaluation Review Technique) to coordinate and "time phase" all of the activities which must be completed before

opening day. Included in these activities are the hiring and training of personnel, furnishing of the bank, and the promotional campaign.

4. A letter from OSHA tells Valley that the dimensions of the stalls in the lavatories are in violation of the law.

5. An article has arrived entitled "Designing a Work Measurement Program for Maximum Usability" by Terry J. Abbott, Seattle First National Bank. In this article, Abbott described the applications of MTM based work measurement in the development of over 14,000 time standards for clerical operations in the bank's 140 branches. Baker sends the article on to Jim Jones, who is working in this area.

6. A note from the bank's marketing director asks Baker to evaluate the cost of personnel, facilities, and the like, if bank teller service is extended to 6:00 P.M. on weekdays and until noon on Saturdays. This proposal needs to be evaluated in terms of its possible effects on the other services of the bank.

7. A job application from Mr. John Lovell.

INTERRELATIONSHIPS

The diversity and yet commonality among the items in these three people's in-baskets give an insight into the role of production and operations management in many kinds of organizations. Many more illustrations could have been included. In-basket items could have been presented for other managers, such as for a production manager of a furniture factory, a steel mill, a hospital administrator, or an office manager of an insurance company.

The common thread is that managers have to administer a great variety of activities. In order to do this, they assemble appropriate resources and direct the use of these resources, be they people, machines, or processes, in transforming materials and the time of people into products or services. They direct the inputs so that they produce outputs. Figure 1–1 suggests the universality of production functions.

Successful organizations also have reporting systems which provide current feedback information so that the managers can see whether they are or are not meeting customer demands. If they are not, then, at least in the private business sector, they will lose customers. Consequently, in order to survive, they will have to redesign their products and services. Such changes are likely, in turn, to necessitate changes in internal operations and in the way resources are used internally.

Managers also have to respond to other forces from the external environment, such as government regulations, labor organizations, and local, regional, national, and world economic conditions. Keeping in tune with current conditions is a continuous and a dynamic process.

As Figure 1–1 shows, the field of production and operations management is indeed broad. In general, it deals with the supply side of the work of organizations, whereas marketing deals with the demand side. Other

FIGURE 1–1

Scope of production and operations management

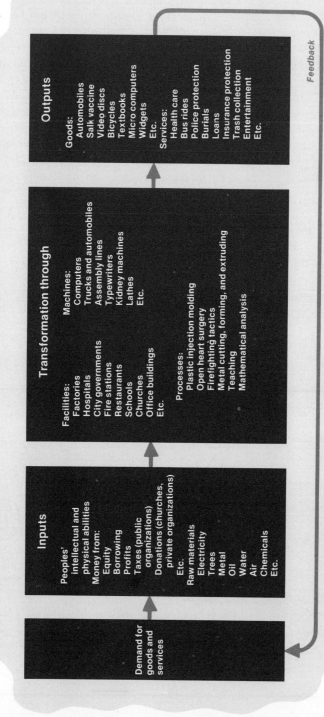

functional people responsible for other areas include finance people who have to do with providing enough money at the right time to pay for labor, materials, and facilities. There are also accountants who are more or less "scorekeepers," controllers, and budget makers; and there are personnel specialists who recruit, train, and develop pay plans for workers. Yet, the work of all of these people is intertwined, and much communication and coordination is required.

The areas of work which are primarily of a production and operations nature and to which this book is largely devoted include those listed in Figure 1–2.

FIGURE 1–2

The domain of P/OM

Subject	Questions dealt with by P/OM
Design of products and services	Are our products safe for consumers to use? What are the best ways to make products or to deliver services, and what machines, labor skills and processes are required? How long a life should our products have before they wear out or become obsolete?
Facilities location and design	Where should facilities be located? How should buildings and equipment be designed to allow work to be done in the most economical manner?
Capacity planning	How much plant, machine, and labor capacity should be provided in order to turn out the desired output? Should we use overtime, a second shift, or subcontract out work?
Capital investment analyses	When should new machinery be bought to replace old machines? When should investments be made in machines in order to economize on labor? What methods of analysis need to be used when making such decisions.
Maintenance	How shall the organization's facilities be maintained and kept in repair? Should repairs be done ahead on a preventive basis or confined to taking care of breakdowns? Which work should be done by inside crews and which should be contracted to outsiders?
Job design	How should people do their jobs so that the work is done efficiently and at the same time provide workers with satisfaction?
Work measurement and standards	How much output can reasonably be expected from workers, how much is being turned out, and how can discrepencies between expected and actual be corrected?
Compensation	How can we decide how much to pay for each job vis-à-vis other jobs? Should workers be paid by piecework, or by the hour, or by salary? Should there be bonuses? What is the proper mix between monetary rewards and nonmonetary incentives?

FIGURE 1–2 (*continued*)

Subject	Questions dealt with by P/OM
Safety	Are our facilities and machines safe for people to operate? Do the processes produce harmful fumes; are they too noisy; are injuries more than rare? How can we and at what cost can we meet federal and state regulations in these areas?
Production scheduling and control	How should work priorities be determined and how should work be assigned to machines and labor so that the capacity is used effectively while at the same time giving customers good delivery service?
Inventory management	How much inventory should we carry of finished products in order to give good customer service? What raw material and work in process inventories should be carried? Should we make or buy component parts? How much should be ordered or produced at a time, and when should it be ordered so materials are available when they are needed?
Purchasing	Who should we buy our raw materials from? How can we tell if their quality and delivery reliability will meet our needs?
Quality standards and control	How can the organization produce products and services of the quality required by the marketing department? How can internal operations be controlled so that unacceptable deviations in quality can be detected, and how can they be remedied?

RESPONSIBILITY OF PRODUCTION/OPERATIONS MANAGERS TO SOCIETY

Our picture so far of production managers in operation has been confined largely to internal organizational matters. This is proper in that this is where most of them operate. Usually only top managers deal with broad social matters.

But high-level managers are in a dual position. They try to serve *their* employers, who are the company's stockholders or legislative bodies. But at the same time they operate in a social system and owe obligations to society. Many of these obligations to society are written into laws, but others in the production area, such as trying to maintain stable employment, to pay fair wages, to serve customers well, and to maintain or increase productivity, are less formal.

Social obligations are not altogether stable but are often dynamic. Recent years have seen a shift and the emergence of a strong consumer consciousness, particularly as it concerns the design of products and services so that they are safe for customers to use and so that working conditions will be safe for employees. Besides this, environmental considerations have also become very important.

Only a few years ago, an enterprising organization could design a product or provide a service in accord with its managers' views of whether or not the market would want it and whether the company could make money doing it. The only considerations were economic, and, so far as quality and safety were concerned, all that was required was to satisfy customers. If they were satisfied, they bought the product or service, and, if they were dissatisfied, they didn't buy it a second time.

Today this has changed. Managers, in both private and governmental organizations, have to pay more attention not only to what their customers might buy, but also to increasing governmental regulation and also to consumer and environmental protection groups. Such groups take them to task if their products or services are unsatisfactory, or if they cause people to get hurt, or if people have their health impaired, or if they do harm to the environment by polluting the air or water, or if they waste scarce natural resources.

Nowadays there are frequent newspaper accounts about lawsuits against manufacturers, doctors, accountants, and transportation companies. And there are frequent stories about a ban on the use of a drug or food preservative or about the recall of a product from the market on orders from the Food and Drug Administration or the Federal Trade Commission.

Much of the criticism in such actions is related to the quality of the product or of the service being rendered. These are areas where the remedial actions to correct the unsatisfactory conditions are often in the domain of production managers and their staff.

PRODUCT SAFETY AND CONSUMER PROTECTION

The great majority of organizations provide us with goods and services which perform as expected, and are of good value, and are safe in use. However, there will always be some goods and services which are unsatisfactory and possibly unsafe in certain applications.

The upsurge in consumer safety consciousness which we are still seeing today had its biggest boost from the publication of Ralph Nader's book, *Unsafe at Any Speed,* which referred to General Motors' subcompact car, the Corvair. This book, published in 1965, in fact, only made the point that small cars are not as safe as large cars. Nonetheless, it shocked the automobile industry and drove the Corvair off the market.[2] Among its immediate effects was the passage of new automobile safety laws which required considerable redesigning of automobiles.

This interest in consumer safety quickly spread out in many directions. Very soon people were calling attention to the hazards in use of any number of other products. Instances were found where toys which children often put in their mouths and chewed on were painted with lead based paint, which could give them lead poisoning. Other toys were found to have sharp edges which could cause cuts, and realistic toy cookstoves were found which could burn children.

---

[2] Corvairs were completely exonerated in 1972 by a government investigation undertaken at Nader's request.

The food industry also came in for attention. Questions were raised over the possible health hazards of artificial coloring matter, of sweeteners, and of preservatives put into foods. Ecologists and environmentalists joined in with their interest in reducing air and water pollution and in the preservation of wildlife.

The public has, on the whole, been favorable and has supported these actions. Consequently, manufacturers and service organizations are redoubling their efforts to comply with the regulations and to improve their products and services.

As a result of this spread in interest in consumer protection, several new laws were passed establishing new governmental agencies with special missions. In 1966, the National Highway Traffic Safety Administration was set up. Its mission was to try to reduce traffic accidents and deaths. It was given the power to set standards for all facets of automobile design which might result in accidents or injuries.

In 1972, the Consumer Products Safety Commission was set up to develop safety standards for consumer products. The commission's general jurisdiction covers more than 10,000 household products from baby cribs to snowblowers. People who use these products have some 4 million accidents a year, of which some 10,000 are fatal accidents. The commission now has over 400 "Product Hazard Indexes" which help it pinpoint trouble areas where improvement of products need to be made.

The National Safety Council's long-time statistics indicate that very few of these accidents are caused by faulty products but rather by unsafe acts by users. (For example, over 1,000 bicycle riders lose their lives annually, largely in accidents with automobiles. Almost never, in such accidents, are the bicycles faulty.) Nonetheless, there are still enough accidents caused by our using these products to justify our trying to reduce the accident rate.

The new laws also give existing regulatory agencies more power. The Food and Drug Administration, for example, can now ban or recall drugs and food items from the market; the Environmental Protection Agency has the power to set standards for vehicle exhaust emissions; and the Occupational Health and Safety Agency has the authority to prohibit the use of equipment and manufacturing processes which it regards as unsafe.

The point to these examples is that the design of products and services is no longer wholly a matter of an organization's managers responding to the needs of the market place, as they see such needs. They have to manage within the framework of the requirements that society imposes on them through government regulations and pressures from consumer and environmental groups.

Negative aspects of regulation

From a managerial point of view, there are two serious negative aspects to the consumer protection wave. First is the cost of complying with the regulations. General Motors reports that today's automobiles each cost $600 more to make because of all of the extras required by emission and safety regulations.[3] Electric power companies spend many millions of dollars for "scrubbers" to keep smoke out of their smokestacks. The government regulators often ask for near perfection when something less would be satisfactory and could be achieved at much lower cost.

The second negative is the wave of lawsuits claiming damages from injuries from products which are claimed to be faulty. These have multiplied in recent years, and juries have been awarding large claims which were not awarded before the consumer protection wave. Today it almost seems that juries take the view that if an accident can happen it is the fault of the maker of the product or provider of the service.

In any case, manufacturers need to do their best to be sure that their products are safe to use, just as service people must try to render good service. Product designers need to use safe materials and to put in appropriate safety guards. Both designers and lawyers should probably decide upon warning labels and look over advertising claims to be sure that they are not misleading in any way and that they include appropriate warnings of dangers. Records also need to be kept of complaints and of responsive actions, and appropriate liability insurance should be carried.

Nor are the makers of products relieved from their obligation to do their best to keep the users of their products from having accidents by the fact that it is really unfair to blame product manufacturers for most accidents. *People* cause accidents far, far more often than products cause accidents. According to the National Safety Council, unsafe practices by people are involved in perhaps as many as 90 percent of all accidents.[4]

People don't get their brakes fixed and then have accidents from faulty brakes. Or *they* drive their cars too fast or after drinking too much alcohol. Or *they* smoke in bed. Or *they* leave open bottles of aspirin around children. Or the *housewife* goes away and leaves the electric iron turned on. Or *people* misuse a product, or use it for purposes for which it was never intended, and then, if it fails, they blame the manufacturer.

None of these acts of carelessness, however, excuse the manufacturers from making the safest product they can. In some cases this means that cheaply made flimsy products will have to be discontinued even if they are in demand since such products are likely to be dangerous in use.

ENVIRONMENTAL CONSIDERATIONS

The 1970s developed into a decade of concern over the impact of our industrialized nation upon our environment. The 1974 Arab oil embargo heightened this concern (it focused attention on our limited oil resources) and caused greater pressure on Detroit automobile manufacturers to design smaller and more efficient automobile engines. The 1970s also produced

[3] See *Business Week,* January 28, 1976, p. 57.
[4] See *Accident Facts,* National Safety Council, annual.

much more widespread support for ecological and environmental protective measures than there was in earlier years.

Like most controversial issues, these pressures have two sides. On the one side, some environmentalists fight strongly for the preservation of our natural resources, almost without regard to the costs which are being incurred along the way and without regard to our needs for oil, coal, steel, copper, and other natural resources.

It is true, of course, that some organizations have damaged our environment by dumping harmful wastes into rivers and emitting smoke and fumes into the air. Strip mining land for coal and leaving it denuded of trees and with unsightly mounds of unleveled overburden used to be common. Today's regulations seek to improve these abuses.

In fairness, it should be said that the managers of most organizations try to do everything economically and technically possible to protect the environment. By no means are they unsympathetic with the objectives of those who want to improve the quality of our lives. It is just that they have to figure out how to do it, and then they have to pay the bills. Everything comes at a cost, and sometimes two or more desirable goals conflict with each other. For example, automobile engines which minimize harmful air pollutants use gasoline wastefully and at a time when we are all trying to save on gasoline.

"Scrubbers" on smoke stacks to get the dirt out of smoke are costing electric utility companies (and subsequently their customers, the public) many millions of dollars. Filtering equipment for cleaning liquid wastes is also costly. Cities as well as companies have to spend large amounts of money to meet the new regulations. Furthermore, much of this extra cost goes to pay for the extra energy used. The same is true in the case of the more stringent land reclamation rules following strip mining of coal. The remedial actions cost more money and consume more energy.

Undoubtedly, these socially desirable goals will continue to have important effects on the design of products and services. And, again, the burden of achieving the goals falls largely on industry. If the managers of industrial companies do not do enough voluntarily, even though doing these things drives prices up, then governmental agencies and nongovernmental pressure groups will be taking them to task. The mandate from the public seems to be "shape up and if it costs more, we will pay."

In general, energy conservation and pollution control are in direct conflict. According to Research Planning Associates, environmental controls will cause the steel industry to use 10 percent more energy.[5] The Environmental Protection Agency disputes this figure and says that it is much too high, while admitting that meeting its standards consumes more energy. Several other industries, among them copper and paper, estimate that meeting antipollution standards will increase their use of energy by 7 or 8 percent.

---

[5] As reported in "Does Pollution Control Waste Too Much Energy?" *Business Week,* March 29, 1976, p. 72.

SUMMARY

The purpose of this chapter has been to set the scene for the study of production and operations management. While there may have been some idealizing in developing the in-basket scenarios for Redford, Thomas, and Baker, they do depict the broad range of activities which production and operations managers face. This provides an insight into the kinds of problems with which people who work in this area deal, and they suggest the sorts of skills which one must acquire through education and experience in order to be effective.

This book deals with the several areas of production practices in which people like Lance Redford, Kristen Thomas, and Bart Baker work. It considers what people in these areas need to know, the problems they face, the merits to alternative solutions, and the decisions they have to make.

REVIEW QUESTIONS

1. Why does the domain of production and operations management include, to some extent, all organizations?
2. What problems and issues do Lance Redford, Kristen Thomas, and Bart Baker have in common? What are the differences?
3. What is the purpose of the APICS Certification Program? (You might contact local members of APICS and ask them.)
4. How does production and operations management generally fit in with other functional activities in organizations?
5. Why are more and more graduates of business schools finding careers in public organizations as well as private organizations?

QUESTIONS FOR DISCUSSION

1. Do cities and banks produce things? What do they produce?
2. Write a short description of the production activities of a manufacturing, service, and public organization.
3. Pick a specific organization (large or small), and identify its inputs, processes, and outputs, similar to those in Figure 1–1.
4. Why get the government into the area of product design? Wouldn't society be better served by letting the marketplace settle the question of quality? Discuss.
5. Almost everyone favors the general objective of cleaning up our air and water. And we are all aware of the need to conserve energy. Yet, it takes extra energy to clean up the air and water. What should managers do? Discuss.

SUGGESTED SUPPLEMENTARY READINGS

Aaker, David A., and Day, George S. "Corporate Responses to Consumerism Pressures." *Harvard Business Review,* November–December 1972, pp. 114–24.

Benningson, Lawrence A., and Benningson, Arnold I. "Product Liability: Manufacturers Beware." *Harvard Business Review,* May–June 1974, pp. 122–32.

Fri, Robert W. "Facing Up to Pollution Controls." *Harvard Business Review,* March–April 1974, p. 26 ff.

2

Basic management concepts

SCHOLARS and managers have long been interested in how best to manage organizations. They have searched for fundamental truths, underlying principles, on which they can rely to help guide them in their actions so that they will be managing effectively. It seems logical that such principles exist since it is obvious that some organizations are managed better than some others. There just must be something that more capable managers know about or do that less capable managers do not know about or do less well.

Years ago much of what passed as knowledge about basic managerial concepts were pronouncements by successful business leaders. These pronouncements were often more in the nature of pontifications and oversimplified authoritarian dogma than they were true principles. Usually they were based on the leader's own experience as he viewed it in retrospect at the end of a successful career. They were not necessarily untrue, but they were often overstated and were only partially true or were only sometimes true.

The social scientists of 25 years ago rejected these generalizations as being of doubtful validity, since they were not based on the findings of carefully organized research. They set themselves out to conduct such research which they hoped would provide more solidly based conclusions.

Not surprisingly, they found it difficult to adapt the methodology of controlled experimentation of the physical sciences to the study of organizational behavior. They could not hold all factors constant for the duration of a study while they studied the effects of variations of one factor; consequently, they could not reliably relate effects to single causes.

They also had trouble with averages and generalizations. Like business leaders, the researchers were searching for generalizations; yet, they had to contend with people being different. No generalization about how people will behave describes us all. The researchers also had trouble generalizing from their samples to other people or organizations. Even if they did find that the 50 people in their study responded in certain ways, this was of little predictive help in showing how 50 million other people would respond. And, unfortunately, from their point of view, the researchers often found that widely accepted beliefs had a great deal of truth to them.

Nonetheless, their continuing studies, which have now gone on for over 25 years, did begin to throw more light on managerial fundamentals. In total, their investigations have sharpened our knowledge of these matters considerably.

LEADERSHIP

The managers of organizations are in positions of leadership in that they have formal authority. Formal authority is the *right* to lead. They are in charge and have the power to hire and fire people, to give directions and assign work, to commit the organization's resources, and to dispense rewards and mete out discipline.

The power of position bestows on managers the right to do these things. When managers use their authority and power and do these things, they are leading in that they cause people to do certain things and not to do certain other things.

This formal power-position concept of leadership is not, however, what scholars or even managers themselves usually have in mind when they talk about leadership. Rather "leadership" has to do with managing in such a way as to win the willing support of subordinates. Managers who lead in this way almost always develop more enthusiastic followers and more effective and more productive organizations.

The research into leadership by scholars has not proven to be as helpful as most people would like because it has shown that leadership is not a simple and easily defined matter. Today's theory concludes that effective leadership *depends* upon successfully matching the characteristics and behavior patterns of the leader with the characteristics and behavior patterns of the followers as they relate to the current situation.[1]

This idea, called "contingency theory," holds that no one single kind of leadership is effective in all cases. It holds that the kind of leadership which will be effective in a given situation is contingent on the matching of the factors mentioned above. There are some situations, for example, where quick authoritarian action is needed. The kind of a leader needed here would be different from that needed in more normal circumstances. Similarly, sometimes the work of subordinates is routine and repetitive

---

[1] The research on the subject of leadership done up to the early 1970s is summed up by Ralph M. Stogdill, *Handbook of Leadership* (New York: The Free Press, 1974).

and there is little need for being "consultative," or "participative," in decision making. Such methods here would waste time and have been known to generate negative reactions in followers.

Generally speaking, however, the research of social scientists on leadership has found that subordinates like to be asked and consulted or at least told ahead about matters relating to their own work. They like to be informed and to be given opportunities to express themselves where their own jobs are concerned. They like to think that the leader is interested in them and their work, and that he is responsive to their ideas, and that he is supporting and helping them.

Many subordinates, but not all, like also to be consulted and told about more important organizational matters, matters which affect the whole organization. This glimpse of larger matters heightens their interest in their doing their own jobs well.

MOTIVATION

Most of us, during our lives, do a good many things that we are not very enthusiastic about doing so we drag our feet. And we also do a good many things that we are enthusiastic about. These we find it easier to work at; we are more motivated to do them. And because of this motivation, we work more diligently to accomplish them.

Managers need to be concerned with the motivation of members of their organizations. They need to try to bring out the best in people and to tap their "interest reserve" and their "effort reserve" in order to get them to make their maximum contribution, thus enhancing organizational effectiveness.

Motivation need not be a matter of overworking oneself. Rather, it can manifest itself by causing people to work more intelligently. Motivated employees are concerned about how effective their contribution is. They see ways to improve the ways things are done, and they exercise initiative and try to do things by effective means. They define their jobs in maximum ways rather than doing only the least they can get by with. If something needs doing, they take it unto themselves to do it. And all of this in addition to applying themselves diligently to their work.

Motivation is in a person's mind, and so naturally it has interested social scientists, particularly psychologists, for a long time. And it interests managers because of their pragmatic desire to have their organization operate more effectively.

In the case of motivation, just as was so in the case of leadership, motivation theory tries to generalize and to say what people will do. And, just as in the case of the followers of leaders, all generalizations need to be used carefully because they overlook individual differences. Below, for example, when we talk about Abraham Maslow's view that money is not a very good motivator, we can agree with his generalization even though we may believe that some people *are* motivated by money.

Nor should we be misled about the powers of motivation. Motivation will cause us to try harder, but it will not make up for all capability limitations. Strongly motivated 6-foot-tall basketball centers are likely to be outgunned by less strongly motivated opposing 7-foot-tall centers.

Motivation theory

Abraham Maslow, who is important partly because of his own ideas and partly because of the stature of certain later theorists who had been his students, was an early motivation theorist.

Maslow felt that people's needs operate according to a hierarchy—physiological, security, belongingness, self-esteem, and self-actualization. He felt that, most important of all, people are motivated to do things in order to eat and to stay alive. An employer could motivate employees to work by paying them enough to meet this need.

But, said Maslow, when this need is met and apparently is going to continue to be met, then physiological needs have very low motivating effect from here on. In their place, the need for security becomes the important motivator. Yet, the need for security, too, diminishes as a motivator as it is met on a continuing basis. Giving a person more security from then on will not motivate him very much.

Next, the desire to belong and to be loved comes into play and will be a further motivator until it too is fulfilled on a continuing basis. Then it declines in importance, and more of it will have little motivating value.

The fourth need is self-esteem and, finally, a fifth need, self-actualization or self-fulfillment, comes into play.

Many well-known social scientists, Douglas McGregor and Frederick Herzberg in particular, got their root thinking from Maslow. McGregor is well known for his Theories X and Y. (Theory X presumes that people are lazy and have to be prodded or given rewards; Theory Y presumes that people want to be productive and, if allowed to have some discretion and control over their job will be motivated and productive.) McGregor said that all too many managers were Theory X managers.

Herzberg says that motivators are of two kinds, satisfiers and dissatisfiers. Improvement in motivation comes only from improving the satisfiers. Improvements in dissatisfiers only lessens dissatisfactions. Herzberg considers money to be a dissatisfier, so he concludes that giving an employee a pay raise makes him less unhappy and does not improve his positive motivation.

Many people think that this is a curiously illogical conclusion. Many of us have had the experience of receiving pay raises which made us more satisfied. According to Herzberg, the way to generate greater positive enthusiasm is to manage in a more participative way and to let people have more opportunity for self-fulfillment and to let them work at their highest capacities.

Rensis Likert is another well-known theorist of the research era of the 1960s. He strongly favored participative decision making. Chris Argyris is another well-known name during the period of development of many theories. He felt that the organizational demands (of conformity) put on individuals served to constrain and constrict their self-development too much. He also, along with many others, emphasized the need to "fuse" the goals of individuals with those of the organization. Individuals could achieve their personal goals if they helped the organization achieve its goals.

Today's theorists on motivation generally agree with their predecessors except that they give more weight to the differences in people and in the complexities of the human mind. They put motivation more on an individual and situational basis, much as does the contingency theory of leadership which we just discussed. There is, however, also a continuing acceptance of the feeling that group behavior strongly influences individual behavior.

Managers' use of motivation theories

On the whole, managers give lip service to the conclusions of motivational theorists, but they still believe that money is a strong motivator. (Workers in many companies, including General Electric and United States Steel, have gone on strikes rather than see piecework pay plans discontinued. Furthermore, piecework is the rule in the making of shoes and clothing.) One wonders how Maslow would explain these things.

Managers also seem to believe that even affluent people may still be motivated by more money because it opens the way for their being able to partake of many of the better things in life, such as leisure and travel. Managers seem to think that subordinates view money not as an end so much as a means to ends.

As for themselves, managers act as if Maslow were wrong. Nearly every large company offers its managers money bonuses for good performance. When General Motors has a good year, its high-level managers get bonuses equal to twice their annual base salary. And few companies offer bonuses of less than a half year's salary to their top managers as a reward for a good year. If higher-level managers believe Maslow, then they think that they are exceptions and that he is not speaking for them.

Motivations of managers at intermediate and lower levels

Nonetheless, pay raise possibilities down within organizations are quite limited. There just isn't enough space salarywise between successive organizational levels to increase the pay within any one level very much so there is need to recognize accomplishment by means other than money. Behavioral scientists all agree in emphasizing the worth of nonmonetary rewards. Managers need to offer opportunities to their subordinates to receive these nonmonetary rewards if they are to motivate them effectively.

Job enlargement and job enrichment

One way to put a little more interest into intermediate and lower-level jobs is to broaden the jobs' activities. Sometimes this is done by just adding duties of a different nature to break up the monotony. In other cases, formerly highly specialized and routinized jobs are redesigned. Instead of five people each doing one task on every product and moving it on the next worker, each one of the five does all five tasks on every fifth unit. In still other cases the worker is allowed to participate in decisions concerning his job. He is told about things that have to do with his job and is consulted and asked to make suggestions. The merits of job enlargement and job enrichment are discussed in Chapter 13.

Organizational development

For the most part, nonmonetary motivations are of the job enlargement or job enrichment kind. Consultative type management, where superiors let subordinates in on what is going on and also consult with subordinates and listen to their suggestions ("open management"), usually helps build positive motivation.

Researchers have found that a healthy atmosphere of back and forth cooperative interchange of information is often hampered by the barrier of managers not being sensitive to what their subordinates and co-equals say and think. They don't listen and they are not receptive to the real meaning of what they hear.

To help them become more aware of the feelings of other people, companies sometimes send their managers to courses in "sensitivity training." These courses, usually two weeks long, bring together small groups of people who try to analyze each other's thinking and the reasons why they have the ideas they have and how people react to them and why.

Most participants in such courses return to their jobs much more aware of the feelings of other people. Yet, when they try to manage differently and in a more understanding way, they are sometimes frustrated because no one else is trying to be different.

Many companies today are trying to retain the benefits that come out of greater sensitivity and a greater willingness to manage in a give-and-take way by extending the general sensitivity training idea, but doing it all "in-house." They are trying to develop a healthy cooperative atmosphere in their organizations, hence the term, "organizational development." Such attempts have met with mixed success since essentially they require so many people to change their personalities. Yet, in some cases, they have been very successful—so much so that many companies now have formal and on-going OD programs.

Motivation through planning and control

Motivational theorists seem to have overlooked one part of motivation that managers can also strengthen. This is the use of controls. Managers should see that plans are drawn up, and that budgets are set up, and that reports of activities and accomplishments are made.

All of these, if used properly, become very effective motivators. Subordinates try to carry out plans and to achieve the goals spelled out. And they try to accomplish results while not overspending the budget. They are *motivated* to do the things that the plans expect them to do. Thus, by requiring such planning to be done, managers motivate their subordinates.

Management by objectives

It is easy, on any job, for a person to become immersed in what he is doing and for him to try to do well what he is doing. There is a danger here, however, that he will not give enough attention to what his work should be accomplishing. A salesman may think that he has done a good job when he calls on a large number of prospective customers even though he hasn't sold much. He thinks in terms of activities and not of objectives.

Management by objectives tries to get him to focus on what his work is supposed to accomplish. MBO is particularly helpful in middle and lower supervisory levels. Superior managers sit down with their subordinate managers and together they work out statements of what the lower managers should be trying to accomplish. Then, and again with the participation of the subordinates, goals, action programs, and progress reports are designed to help the subordinates reach their goals.

Motivation from the use of sanctions

Nor should the motivation growing out of sanctions (negative, punitive actions) be neglected. People who are absent frequently, or who come to work tardy, and who are disciplined for it usually mend their ways and come to work regularly and on time. People who turn out too little satisfactory work and who are disciplined usually improve. Normally, although punitive actions are less effective as motivators than positive actions, they are still far from being ineffective. They do have substantial effects.

STAFFING

The quality of accomplishment of an organization is very much the result of the quality of its people, and these, in turn, are results from earlier recruiting and training practices.

Small organizations are often careless in their hiring practices and also in their later on training work. In contrast, the high-level managers of most large organizations are very aware of the great dependence of the organization's future well-being on the quality of people recruited and with their training.

These two activities, recruiting and training, are closely related. Most recruiting is done for lower-level jobs. Then, when higher jobs open up, the better of the lower people are promoted. Thus, the quality of tomorrow's higher managers depends upon today's selection of people with potential for growth plus their improvement that comes from training and experience and their greater maturity.

Training, however, has to go on throughout the organization, and it needs to be consciously organized training. Many managers do not pay much attention to training their subordinates for advancement. Probably there are many reasons for this. In the first place, it is only human nature not to want to develop a competitor for your own job. And, second, managers don't want to pass part of their own jobs down to subordinates. Third, managers have their regular work to get out and don't like to spend their time training their subordinates.

Probably, however, a fourth reason is the most important. People, managers, and subordinates alike seem to believe that knowledge just rubs off on employees who have been around a while. Anyone who has been around a department for a while has learned how it operates. There is some truth to this; yet, managerial know-how differs from operating know-how and includes knowledge about many things not known by subordinates. The acquiring of this knowledge for those who are promoted should not be left to happenstance to be picked up casually. Rather, it should be supplied for trainees and for promotional prospects through consciously laid out training programs.

Legal requirements

Today's laws also play a part both in selection and promotion of personnel. Our laws require that there be no discrimination on the basis of sex or color. In fact, the law goes farther. "Affirmative action" requirements actually require discrimination in favor of women and racial minorities. An organization without females and minorities in consequential jobs is presumed to have discriminated against them. In order to remedy this situation, the organization will have to discriminate in their favor for a while.

Psychological tests

Ten years ago psychological tests were commonly used to help in both recruiting and in choosing from among candidates for promotion, but they are less common today. It isn't that managers have become disillusioned with them, but that individuals who were not hired or promoted because of low test scores sued in courts, claiming that the tests did not measure anything relevant to the work.

In general, the courts have agreed. So, tests, if used for such purposes, have to be especially designed to test a person's capabilities which are relevant to the job. And, since it is impossible to design separate tests for the hundreds of different jobs in most organizations which have reliable value in predicting a candidate's probable future success, the use of tests has declined.

Appraisal

Obviously, if an organization's best people are to be promoted when openings occur, there must be some appraisal of the past performance of the several candidates which will be helpful in revealing which candidates will perform the best on the job where the opening occurs.

The area of appraisal is one where a great deal of poor work is done. Most middle- and low-level managers are not very good at appraising subordinates who are, in fact, almost always good at some things and not good at other things. Not only that, but managers don't like to appraise at all because not only does it seem to connote their playing God, but the process more or less implies negative criticisms of subordinates. Whenever a subordinate does not get a high rating, there is the implication that the manager should work more closely with such a subordinate to try to help him to improve. A great many managers would rather just shirk appraisal altogether.

Besides, this task is really quite difficult. Appraisal for promotion purposes concerns how well a subordinate will perform on a higher-level job of a kind he has never done before and for which he has no track record, so to speak. If the job is in another department, not under the jurisdiction of the appraiser, he, the appraiser, may not even know what the new job requirements are.

All of this merely says that appraisal is difficult. Nevertheless, it has to be done. Someone gets a pay raise and someone else does not. Someone is promoted and someone else is passed by. And the loser may sue in court claiming discrimination. Managers need to try to be as objective as possible (and to keep records of why they do what they do in selecting and promoting).

ORGANIZATIONAL DESIGN

In all organizations, there has to be some division of labor. Separate groups are set up to perform certain kinds of work. In a manufacturing company, some people make products while others sell them. In a merchandising company, some people buy products, some sell them, and some manage the store. In a hospital, some people take care of patients and some cook meals.

Departmentation

An organization's managers usually have alternative ways in which they can set up subsidiary departments. This is not always evident at any given time since departments are already set up in some particular way and there would be considerable upset if today's managers were to make major changes.

Departments are always set up to take advantage of some kind of specialization. In most cases, this is by the kind of work (by "function"). Each department does one kind of work. A factory's drill press department drills holes in parts; its assembly department puts products together. In a shoe factory, one department cuts out the leather, another department sews the pieces together.

Another common basis for setting up departments is by *product*. In a retail store, one department sells furniture, another sells shoes and another sells cameras. At Zenith, one department makes television sets and another department makes hearing aids.

FIGURE 2–1

Organization chart of a typical manufacturing company

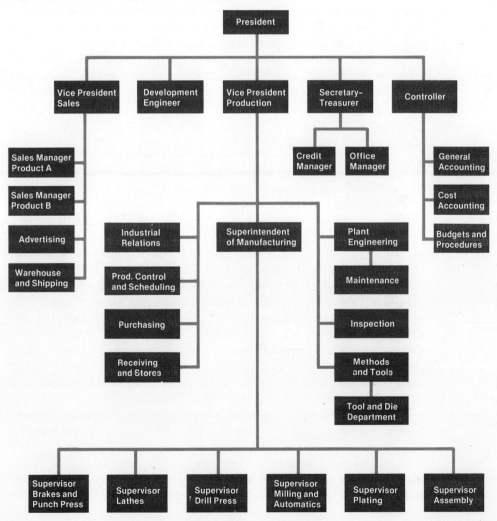

Selling and service organizations often set up their departments on a geographical basis. Obviously, every store and every motel operates in a given area. Other units of the whole organization perform the same kind of work but somewhere else.

Sometimes, too, special departments are set up to deal with certain customer groups. Airplane companies, automobile companies, automobile tire companies, oil companies, and many others have special sales departments to sell to the United States government, to state and city governments, to airline companies, to car rental companies, to bus lines, to trucking companies, and so on.

These several bases for setting departments apart are not always mutually exclusive, and this sometimes causes problems. This is particularly true in foreign operations.

Procter & Gamble makes Camay soap, Puff paper facial tissues, and Folger coffee. These are made and sold by separate departments in the United States. But, how should P & G try to sell to the French market? Should it have a French subsidiary making and selling all three of these products? (Should it let the geographic basis come first?) Or should the Camay, Puff, and Folger product managers in the United States, each one, try to sell his product line in France? (Here the product line would come first.) Managers have to decide quite a few such questions, and often it is difficult to know which is the best choice to make.

Tall and flat organizations

When organizational structures are depicted in chart form, some are tall and narrow whereas others are flat and wide.

The difference is in the "span of control," the number of subordinates reporting directly to a manager. If a president has 20 major department heads reporting to him and each of them has 25 lower-level operatives reporting to him, then there is only one level between top and bottom and only 21 managers and supervisors for an organization of 500 bottom-level operatives. But, if the president has only 5 managers reporting directly to him, then these 5 would need to insert an additional level of supervisors since it would surely be impossible for each of them to supervise 100 operatives effectively. So, if each of these 5 had 10 direct supervisory subordinates and these lower supervisors could each supervise 10 lower-level operatives, the 500 operatives would be taken care of. This arrangement would have a total of 56 managerial personnel and would have two levels between top and bottom.

Sales and service type organizations usually adopt the flat arrangement because the lower units are doing essentially the same thing and it is possible for them to use standard procedures to cover a great deal of their jobs. Furthermore, there is little need for much horizontal cooperation between operating units. The high-level managers of the managers of K-Mart and of Sears stores have wide spans of control.

But, in manufacturing organizations, the diverse work makes closer supervision necessary, and there is a much greater need to coordinate the work of the different departments. Consequently, the usual form of structure is tall or "vertical."

Tall structures utilize more "centralized" control and take care of the need for more supervision and are thought to improve horizontal coordination and cooperation. Promotional opportunities for personnel are more numerous (there are more managerial jobs). Horizontal structures allow subordinates greater freedom through "decentralized" control and so help people develop themselves while the company saves on the cost of managers. Centralization and decentralization will be discussed more fully later in this chapter.

Line and staff departments

An organization's primary work is done by its "line" departments. In a manufacturing company, they make and sell products. In an airline, they fly airplanes, and, in the government's social security department, they take in money and pay out benefits.

Line departments can't, however, do their work without the help of specialized "staff" departments. Staff departments study, analyze, plan, advise, and serve. The personnel department, a staff department, hires people, keeps employee records, conducts training programs, carries on labor negotiations, operates cafeterias, oversees safety, sees that the organization complies with nondiscrimination laws and that it lives up to its labor contract.

Industrial engineers improve jobs, processes, and ways of doing work. Production control makes up and issues work orders for the factory to make products and parts. The maintenance department keeps physical things in shape and operating.

Sometimes there are differences of opinion between line and staff managers. Staffs are there to advise and help, but sometimes line people don't want the help nor do they want to take the advice they get. In other cases, they say they don't get the help that they need but do get help that they don't need. In case they don't want to follow the staff's advice, there is always a question of whether or not they really can refuse; yet, the staff people normally do not have command authority.

Normally, however, both line and staff people appreciate each other's contribution, and they get along well together, working cooperatively and joining together in trying to operate effectively.

DELEGATION

Delegation means assigning work and responsibility to lower-level people in an organization. At bottom levels in an organization this means tell-

FIGURE 2–2

Staff departments in the production area of a typical manufacturing company

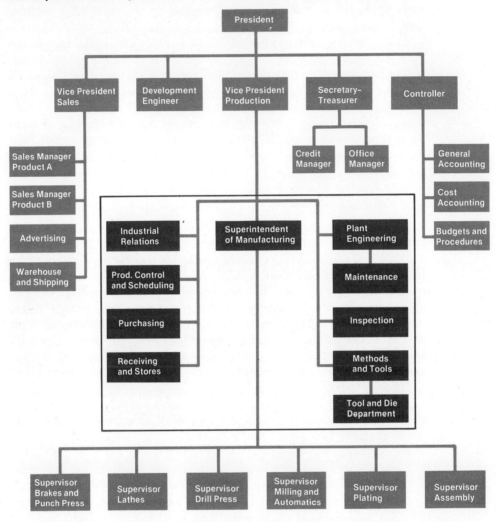

ing an operative what to do. But, at intermediate levels, most of the delegation that managers receive covers work which neither they nor their direct subordinates do. Instead, delegations to intermediate level managers are delegations to *manage* and to direct the activities and accomplishments of still lower people. Much of the delegation that such managers receive is redelegated downward by them.

Delegations to high-level managers are general "mission" type delegations. They don't spell out minor specifics nor individual actions. Marketing managers are to sell products or services. How they do it and what their subordinates actually do are not spelled out in the delegation.

Clarity of delegations

Thus, delegations of responsibility are broad at high levels and narrow and specific at bottom levels. There is a broad area in middle echelons where the recipients of a delegation have "to develop their own job." They have to decide what things should be done, which of these things they should do themselves, and which they should delegate to subordinates to do. They are confined only by their general mission limits and the need for the work in their area to contribute to the work of the whole organization.

Not surprisingly, general delegations sometimes create problems because they are not precise and exact, and the subordinates may be in doubt about what they should do. Nor is their mandate of power always defined clearly. As a result, they may strike out to do what they think they are supposed to do and then find out later on that they are doing things not wanted while at the same time are not doing things that are wanted. Or they may overstep their authority and at other times not move from thinking that they do not have the authority.

Fortunately, such difficulties usually occur only with newly appointed managers. With the passage of time and as the managers gain experience, the general outlines of their missions and of their authority become clarified. They become embodied in the context of mutual understanding and expectancy between superior, subordinate, and co-equals. Managers should, however, always make delegations as clear as possible so that uncertainties and ambiguities will not become problems.

Responsibility

When a manager receives a delegation, he becomes responsible for carrying it out, meaning that he has an obligation to do the work. This responsibility obligation is something the subordinate owes to his superior. Some writers say that a superior cannot delegate responsibility, only authority. Such people would say that responsibility is the inverse of delegation and is an obligation generated in a subordinate's mind when he accepts the authority delegated.

This seems to be more a matter of a play on words than it is a matter of better understanding of the relationships. Yet, proponents of this thinking point to the fact that no manager ever gets rid of *his* responsibility by delegating it to a subordinate. If the sales of a store go down because the clerks are discourteous, it is still the manager's responsibility, even though he may have told them to be courteous. It is true that when a higher manager delegates work he is not freed from the responsibility for its being done.

Joint responsibilities

Many things which need doing lie in the domain of two or more departments rather than in one single department. In order to take care of them properly, the heads of the departments concerned should get together and handle them.

Such matters are often areas of frustration to higher managers because the several subordinates who ought to get together and solve problems do not get together. No one of them feels enough of a sense of responsibility to go ahead, so the matter dangles. Lower-level managers just don't seem to feel free to "encroach" on someone else's domain. They feel responsible for whatever is theirs and theirs alone, but they do not feel any responsibility for moving ahead on matters which are partly their concern and partly the concern of someone else.

Such problems are not serious if the superiors know about them because, if they know about them, they can issue instructions to those of the subordinates who are concerned, telling them to get together and work on these common problems. But often they do not know about them. When this is so, the lack of initiative on the part of the subordinates is unfortunate because the problems are not solved.

Authority

In order to be effective as supervisors, managers need four kinds of authority. Of these, the formal power of position is much the most obvious and is what most people think of as authority. This is the power to assign work, to hire and fire, and to mete out rewards and punishments. Managers need to have this kind of power to be effective.

But managers will be much more effective if they also have three other kinds of authority. First is the authority of knowledge—if they know the work of their subordinates well, they will be respected for their knowledge and they will be more effective. Second, they need to know something about managing and administration, including how to delegate clearly. Third, they will be more effective if they are skillful in human relations since, as a supervisor, they are dealing with people.

Higher-level managers sometimes fail to appreciate the need for subordinate managers having all four kinds of authority. They clothe a subordinate with the authority of position and think that they have given all that is needed, whereas they really ought also to be helping them to develop the other three kinds of authority.

Inequality of authority and responsibility

Ideally, authority and responsibility should go hand in hand. Managers responsible for doing something should have the authority necessary to allow them to do it. When high-level managers delegate a mission or task to subordinate managers, they need to give them authority over the work done by the next echelon down, over the use of machines and equipment, and so on. Without such authority, they can't get the work done.

Yet, in a very real sense, authority can never equal responsibility. A company president has the responsibility for operating the company successfully; yet, there is no end to the things he has no power over—the competition, the prosperity of the economy, tax laws, labor unions, and so on. He also has only very limited power over such things as the company's position in the industry (Chrysler can't displace General Motors), the company's product lines, and the like.

Similarly, lower-level managers must all operate within the framework of constraints about which they can do little. Retail store managers find their location to be a fixed constraint. All managers also have to live with the limitations of their people. Managers, too, even as almost all people do, also have to live within the limits of the money available.

The fundamental inequality of authority and responsibility need not, however, becloud our understanding of these concepts. Surely, we all recognize these limitations. When we say that managers "are responsible for . . ." we recognize that there are limitations. We recognize that they have to try to accomplish results while contending with less than total and complete authority.

Acceptance theory of authority

Managers' actual authority will be nullified if their subordinates don't follow. This idea, called the "acceptance theory of authority," holds that superiors have only such power as subordinates allow them to exercise.

Rarely do subordinates deny power to their superiors, but it can happen. In *Mutiny on the Bounty,* the ship's crew mutinied and set Captain Bligh adrift. In 1776, the American colonies threw off the power of English King George III. And, in 1789, the French beheaded King Louis XVI. In 1974, public pressures forced Richard Nixon to resign the Presidency.

Subordinates in business and nonbusiness organizations practically never rebel, but once in a long time they do. When workers go on a strike, it isn't always for more money. Also, dissatisfied workers sometimes quit.

A greater danger, so far as managing is concerned, is that subordinates who are dissatisfied will drag their feet and go along in a reluctant way. Managers need to manage in such a way as to generate full acceptance and enthusiastic support for the organization's goals if they can.

Unity of command

Today there is a widespread belief that the most effective organizations are those where a friendly cooperative atmosphere permeates the organization.

This should not, however, go so far as to undermine formal lines of authority. Everyone should have his own assigned work to do, and he should be accountable to some *one single* superior for doing his work. (When anyone is responsible to two or more superiors, he may receive conflicting directives, or he may have too much to do. Also, he may, in fact, receive little supervision and actually hardly be responsible to anyone.)

In an atmosphere of extreme cooperation, people work at not only what their superior has told them to do, but they also do things to help other people out—possibly even to the extent of not getting their own assigned work done.

This almost amounts to their reassigning the department's resources (the use of their own time) and of their having two or more bosses. Often such a situation generates conflicts and frustration in the minds of subordinates who are trying to fulfill conflicting directions from two different bosses. A factory supervisor, for example, finds that he has to turn out products which satisfy the quality control people, his workers have to work in such a way as to satisfy safety requirements, and yet he has to try to get his workers to turn out a sufficient quantity of products in order to keep costs within the budget. It is small wonder that the supervisor thinks that he has several bosses.

Centralization and decentralization

Large organizations must, of necessity, be somewhat decentralized. They must be decentralized physically. Possibly, as in the case of chain stores and motels, and even of large manufacturing companies, operations will be spread all over the country.

This matter was touched on earlier in the discussion of departments being set up on a geographical basis or on a product-line basis. Managers have to decide how to divide up activities between separate units and where to put the units.

They also have to decide where certain decisions should be made—at high or at low levels. Major objectives and major policies, for example, need to be set at central offices. But lesser matters can be settled at lower levels. This is what delegation does in operation—it passes down to lower managers the authority to make certain decisions.

Questions such as who should be promoted, Smith or Jones, need to be decided at low levels. So, also, probably should the question of whether a K-Mart should be kept open on Sundays. The decision might best be made to suit local conditions. But whether or not Howard Johnson motels should put on evening entertainment with orchestras and floor shows probably should be determined centrally, just as should the question of whether Amoco Oil Company should make the automobile tires that it sells.

As a rule, lower-level decisions have the advantage of speed and appropriateness to the local situation. They also help low-level managers to grow and develop. But central decisions are better where large money commitments are involved and on matters of major policy.

CONTROLLING OPERATIONS

All organizations have purposes; they exist in order to do something. Union Pacific Railroad transports freight and people; A & P sells groceries; and Boeing makes airplanes. Their organizations have been set up to try to accomplish their purposes.

In order to accomplish organizational purposes, the work of the many subordinate units in every organization needs to be "controlled." The many individual departments need to receive coordinated directives telling them what to do. And they need to have information feedback systems reporting to managers what is happening. Managers then need to compare what has happened with what was supposed to happen and to institute remedial action if accomplishment is falling short.

Plans

Plans try to bridge the gap between organizational purposes—objectives, strategies, and policies—and their accomplishment. Plans formalize vague thinking about goals and concentrate on specifics. They list specific things to be done, and by whom, and by what date, and at what expected cost.

Plans guide and direct activities so that resources and work efforts will be focused and directed toward goal accomplishment. Procter & Gamble's plan, a few years ago, to introduce its new reconstituted potato chip (made from dehydrated potato flakes), "Pringles's New Fangled Potato Chips," included getting supplies out in dealers hands by the announcement date, supplying dealers with store display racks and with potato chips, and all supported by a massive advertising campaign on television and in newspapers to get the new product off to a good start. Money and people were committed to these activities at the proper time to get all of the different things done by the appropriate time.

Some plans are of the small repetitive type. *House and Garden* magazine comes out every month. A great deal of planning of the feature stories, the advertising, and so on goes into the preparation of every issue. Such plans are used up each time and have to be done over again for every issue. The specific plan is used up, but the method of planning is, in a sense, itself a plan that endures.

Similarly, in factories, the manufacturing departments need to receive a continual stream of directives telling them what to make, how many to make, and within what period of time. These directives all flow out from the production control department which receives instructions from the sales department about what products are selling and in what quantities.

Planning is not without its pitfalls, particularly long-range planning. Sometimes it is hard to separate plans from dreams, and, in any case, it costs some money just to do long-range planning.

Far and away the great danger, however, is that the planned accomplishment will not materialize or that it will cost a great deal more than was anticipated—and this is discovered only after a large amount of money has been spent on it. In the case of serious failures, almost all of the money spent in the past will prove to have been lost. Both RCA and General Electric in the mid-1970s gave up making computers, each one after having lost $500 million on computers. They had planned to make a place for themselves in the computer industry, but IBM was too much for them.

The long-time dimension to the fulfillment of long-range plans makes the possibility of loss much greater because not all of the money is committed originally. Rather, the commitments become "creeping commitments." They ever demand more money and then still more money. Always in the background, there is the specter of the loss of all past investments if new commitments are not made.

The French supersonic Concorde airplane ended up costing many times its original expectations.[2] And today's nuclear power plants coming on line are, some of them, costing more than ten times their original estimated costs because of inflation and the very high costs of the extreme protective measures being built in.

This is not to condemn long-range planning. Companies which do not plan are likely to fall behind, and the occasional large losses are the unusual, not the usual thing. Studies made of the results achieved by companies which plan and those which do not plan show that the planners come out considerably ahead.[3]

The need for surveillance

Control starts with plans and delegations, but these are only first steps. In many, perhaps most, cases, performance will fall far short of goals if high-level managers do not exercise continual surveillance.

Surveillance should be showing an interest in, and overseeing subordinates' activities. It should monitor and almost constitute an auditing of the work of the organization.

Surveillance does not imply a lack of confidence in subordinates, but is rather part of the superior's obligation, his responsibility for organizational performance. Even though he has delegated work to his subordinates, he is still himself responsible for what they do, and he should not abdicate these responsibilities to them. Surveillance should not be a furtive undercover activity. Nor should it be a sinister "ready-to-pounce" activity. Rather, it should be cast in the helpful image of "how are we doing? I'm here; what can I do to be helpful?"

---

[2] It cost $3 billion to design and make the first six Concordes. See "How to Reclaim $Billions from Two Gargantuan Boo-Boos," *Forbes, March* 1, 1976, p. 18.

[3] See Zafar A. Malik and Delmar W. Karger, "Does Long-Range Planning Improve Company Performance?" *Management Review,* September 1975, pp. 27–31. See also David M. Herold, Robert J. House, and Stanley S. Thune, "Long-Range Planning and Organizational Performance," *Academy of Management Journal,* March 1972, pp. 91–102.

Superiors often do not exercise as close surveillance as they should. Usually they *do* have confidence in their subordinates, and they themselves have lots of work to do, work which, to them, seems more important and more interesting than digging through reports and trying to see if their subordinates' work is going well.

This tendency to neglect proper surveillance is abetted by the subordinates themselves. Usually they like independence and like to be left alone. Unfortunately, if things are going badly, normally calling this to the attention of the superior is the last thing a subordinate wants to do. One doesn't want to look bad. Managers need to exercise a close enough surveillance to be able to notice unsatisfactory performance, yet not so closely as to deprive subordinates of their jobs.

Control and accomplishment

When one person says that another person can "control" something, usually he does not mean that he has full power to produce results; only that he can do something about the results. A supervisor has "control" over the costs of the products made in his department—that is, he can influence these costs.

The activity of controlling does not therefore always produce results. Managers can only try, and they really have exerted some control if they have, by their efforts, influenced results even if they have not accomplished all that was desired. Many factors beyond their control also affect results so that all that can be expected is that managers, through their efforts, will exert some influence on results.

Appraisal in control

Control implies judging whether or not actions and accomplishments are satisfactory, and it implies that if they are not, remedial actions will be initiated. Obviously, therefore, a manager who is appraising a subordinate's performance has to have standards of accomplishment against which to judge and also reports of performance so that he can compare. Usually the standards are in the nature of plans to be accomplished or are performance standards against budgets.

The matter of accomplishment in the face of difficulties complicates appraisal of results. If everything is against a manager, he may have put in more than normal effort and applied himself diligently; yet, results are far short of earlier expectations. If this is so, he should probably receive credit for effort in lieu of accomplishment. High-level managers should, however, be wary of accepting this explanation from a subordinate. It is *always* offered as excuse for nonperformance, but only sometimes is it a valid excuse.

Appraisers have also to contend with the jobs of almost all subordinates being multifaceted. Subordinates may be supposed to maintain quality, keep quantities up and costs down, train and motivate their subordinates, plan the work of subordinates, and so on. Some subordinate managers are good at some parts of their jobs but not at other parts. Also, some days unexpected things come up, and the subordinate is busy putting out fires. Sometimes what a subordinate does doesn't show.

There is also a problem of weighing the importance of different factors. A manager may be good at one or more important parts of his job but poor at something else, perhaps less important. The important things should weigh most heavily in appraisals. The matter of opportunities may also be important. A manager may have done well on what he did, but he failed to take advantage of opportunities to do better. This, too, needs to be considered in appraisals.

Total accomplishment is a mixture of considerable accomplishment in some directions and on some days and less in other directions and on other days. And it is a matter of doing the important things well and of seeing and taking advantage of opportunities.

Effects of strong controls

Control tries to influence the actions and behavior of subordinates; yet, it is difficult if not impossible to force work out of unwilling subordinates. This fact lies behind much of the emphasis by behavioral scientists on winning the support of subordinates through the use of participative management.

Worse yet, strong pressure from above for accomplishment may cause subordinates to take actions which do harm to the organization in the long run. Rensis Likert feels that strong pressure to perform and to get results will almost always produce more harmful effects than beneficial effects.

Likert holds that pressure for immediate results forces managers to forego forward-looking activities because they cost money today and produce benefits only in the future, not today. He also feels that harm will be done to "intervening variables" by lowering organizational empathy and willingness to cooperate and lowering morale and enthusiasm. These variables are sacrificed in the short run in the drive to accomplish "hard goals" (production quantities, low costs per unit, meeting delivery dates, and the like). Likert says that this harm to the organization will not show up as having hurt the organization's effectiveness for perhaps two years. Then it will show up and will continue to cause lessened effectiveness.

Likert also says that emphasis on short-run hard-goal accomplishment will result in the wrong managers being judged to have done well and that managers who are actually hurting the organization's long-run well-being will be promoted—to the great harm to the organization's future.

Not everyone agrees with Likert. They agree that these things can happen. But there are many good things that can come from pressure controls. In the first place, the sacrifice of forward-looking actions is by no means always serious. Many jobs have very little forward-looking content so this does not apply to them. And forward-looking work is not always merito-rious. Business history, past and current, is full of stories about companies which looked ahead, committed resources and lost hundreds of millions of dollars. Ford Motor's $250 million loss on the ill-fated Edsel car in the 1950s is not even in the top 20 any longer.

Managers under pressure from strong controls often respond by doing a better job of working with their subordinates—and this is almost always a very helpful effect. High-level managers also review the economics of some of their ways of doing things and change them. Several years ago as part of a cost-cutting drive, Ampex, an electronics company, consolidated its advertising and put it all into the hands of one advertising agency. It also weeded out a number of low-volume items from its product line, items which had been losing money. It is very unlikely that these actions did any harm to intervening variables.

Likert's position also seems to contain an implicit assumption that sub-ordinate managers who are not making a good showing meeting hard goals will be discovered to be effective managers tomorrow. But surely a good many of today's seemingly poor managers are just that—poor managers—and they will be poor managers tomorrow as well.

Management information systems

Every means by which a manager learns about what is going on is truly a part of his information system. He may get his information by personal observation, by discussions with other people, or by reading reports. Some of his best information comes from personal contacts, but the bulk of his information he gets from reports.

Reports for control purposes should cover only short periods of time and should be made often so that managers will learn quickly what is hap-pening. They also need to be designed for easy comparison of expected activities and accomplishments and actual activities and accomplishments. They should show up exceptions from normal because the exceptions usually need special attention.

Reports should be made separately for each separate responsibility area. They should show the performance and results in the area under each manager separately. Then it is possible to judge each manager's accom-plishment and to discuss with him what *he* can do to improve things in *his* area. He is motivated to make improvements in *his* department.

One-sided reports

It is impossible to capture the whole of an event or of a performance in words or numbers. So reports covering what is going on and what is being accomplished can never reflect more than part of the situation.

There is the story of the manager of a nail factory in Russia in the early days of the Communists. The central planning office wanted to motivate him to turn out more nails. His reports were made out to show the number of nails produced. So he turned out large numbers of brads and tacks. Since this did not accomplish the purpose, the central planning office put the reports on a tonnage basis. This produced a large surplus of spikes. In both cases quality went down. So, next, the control emphasized quality. This produced smaller volumes of nails that were veritable works of art.

The moral is that subordinates will do whatever makes the report look good. If the report emphasizes quality—quality will be achieved even if at high cost. Emphasize cost and quality will go down. Emphasize no-overtime and there will be too many people on the payroll. Emphasize low overhead ratios and it will be accomplished by letting direct labor go up. Emphasize quick delivery and good customer service, and it will be at the cost of large inventories and air freight. Emphasize low maintenance costs and needed repairs will be postponed.

Obviously, reports should be designed to show not just one thing. If overtime is being avoided by having too many employees, the report should be designed to reveal this. It is, however, actually impossible to design reports to show all of the possible secondary effects of a policy. Managers need to use reports intelligently in order for them to be really useful tools for control.

Budgets

Budgets are the principal control mechanism used in internal control. They show the proposed uses of money in a department and also constitute the plan and the authorization to spend the amount of money allocated.

Normally, budgets are made up by asking department heads how much they will need in order to operate their departments during the coming period. Superior and subordinate go over these requests together and decide on the amounts to be allocated.

It is not surprising that gamesmanship enters into the process. Almost always the total of everyone's requests adds up to more than there is money available so some reductions have to be made. This happens so commonly that everyone expects it and expects to get less than he asks for—so he asks for more than he needs, expecting to get cut back.

This process is probably at its worst in government work where there are no very good units of output by which to measure production or the effectiveness of operations. Governments, federal, state, and city, never have enough funds to allow all of the departments to do all of the things they would like to do. The total funds are limited so if one department gets more, another gets less. Department heads sometimes almost fight each other to get more for their departments.

Gamesmanship does not, however, destroy the usefulness of budgets; it only impairs their usefulness. Everyone learns to live with budgets and they are, in spite of their weaknesses, a very useful tool for control.

The effectiveness of remedial actions

In our discussions of control, it has been suggested that one of its great values is that higher managers find out about unsatisfactory conditions early enough to forestall serious consequences by instituting remedial actions. This implies that superiors can do better than their subordinates, but this is by no means always so. In most cases, the subordinate knows more about his individual area and his problems and what can be done about them than does his boss.

The contribution that superiors can make is usually in focusing extra attention on trouble spots and also causing subordinates to put extra effort into solving the problem. The superior can also assign additional people temporarily to help out. If it is a quality problem, the company's quality engineers can devote time to it.

Often such extra attention improves the situation. The remedial action is effective. But this is not always so. Sometimes the superior's attempts to improve the situation are no more effective than were those of the subordinate. They too are sometimes unable to produce the desired accomplishment through their attempts to control.

REVIEW QUESTIONS

1. What is "contingency theory" and how is it related to leadership styles?
2. How are a person's motivation and capabilities related?
3. A person's needs hierarchy is changing constantly. Discuss this statement.
4. What are McGregor's X and Y characteristics of people's attitudes towards work? Think about leaders you know. Do they seem to perceive people in these two ways? Which perceptions by these leaders seem to be the most effective?
5. What is the essence of Herzberg's theory of motivation as it relates to satisfiers?
6. Is money a positive motivator or not? Discuss.
7. Why is the appraisal of subordinates' work so difficult and often distasteful to managers?
8. Do "affirmative action" programs result in reverse discrimination? Discuss.
9. Why have psychological tests fallen into disfavor in recent years?
10. What are the common ways of structuring an organization?

11. What should determine the span of control in organizational design?

12. Differentiate between line and staff functions in organizations. Is conflict between them healthy?

QUESTIONS FOR DISCUSSION

1. "It is not my fault," said the vice president to the president. "My plant manager made that mistake." Discuss.

2. Should authority and responsibility be equal? Explain.

3. Is there ever a time for having two bosses? Answer fully.

4. Can you justify a wider span of control at bottom than at top levels? Explain.

5. When should departments be set up by type of customer?

CASE 2–1

The Gibson Toy Company (600 employees) makes toys of many varieties but has its biggest volume in toy musical instruments. Gibson holds patents to the use of a loop of rubber tape with bumps on it to play tunes on music box type toys. Some income comes from royalties from other toy manufacturers, but Gibson itself is the biggest maker of such toys.

Gibson does all the metal work, woodwork, assembly, and painting on its toys. But it buys the rubber tape and all plastic parts.

The company is family-owned with no stock outstanding. The board chairman, Bill Gibson, is 68 years old and is not active in the company (he is a great outdoorsman and isn't around the factory much), except that sometimes he feels that the younger men are pushing him into the background. When he gets these notions, he usually makes a big fuss about something they did without asking him and insists that it be changed.

Jack Gibson, 66, his brother, is president. He, too, is not very active (although he is a director in six other companies) and is inclined to let Earl Johnson, executive vice president, run things the way he wants. Johnson and the two Gibsons constitute the board of directors, although the stock is owned 50–50 by the Gibsons.

Johnson found that Gibson's plastics and rubber purchases mounted every year. When they passed the million-dollar mark, he decided to go into the plastics and rubber business. Accordingly, he bought the necessary equipment to make nearly all of the plastic and rubber parts. The manufacturing equipment for plastics and rubber were put in a wing of the factory that had formerly been used for storage.

After a few initial difficulties with the new machines, production began to pick up. And although they showed a loss the first three months, they were clearly "over the hump" and were going to make money. It was at that time that the neighborhood residents circulated a petition, claiming that the odors caused by the new process were obnoxious.

Bill Gibson, on hearing of the petition, was quite upset since he did not know about the plastics and rubber manufacture. He railed about Johnson putting the company into money-losing businesses, spending his money without authority, and making the company a nuisance in the neighborhood. Johnson didn't think it wise to argue with him, but he reminded Jack Gibson that this had been discussed for over two years and that he, Johnson, thought that they had agreed that he should "try out, on a small scale, making our own plastics and rubber."

What, if any, principles of good management (or good organization) have been violated here? What is the real problem here? Recommend a course that will avoid problems of this nature in the future.

SUGGESTED SUPPLEMENTARY READINGS

Bettinger, H. M. "Is Management Really an Art?" *Harvard Business Review,* January–February 1975, pp. 54–63.

Duncan, W. J. "Transferring Management Theory to Practice." *Academy of Management Journal,* December 1974, pp. 724–38.

Sherwin, Douglas S. "Management of Objectives," *Harvard Business Review,* May–June 1976, p. 149–60.

3

Basic economic concepts

GENERAL MOTORS makes automobiles and parts in 120 factories in the United States, and Kresge sells merchandise through 1,000 K-Marts.

All of these facilities require that money be invested, and the wisdom of making such investments rests on economic concepts and economic analyses. In the cases of GM and Kresge, their total investments in buildings, machinery, and equipment comes to $7 billion. Money is also required for inventories and accounts receivable. In these two companies, this comes to a total of $11 billion.

In both of these cases, the company's managers decided, at some time in the past, to make these investments of money. Obviously, they did this only after making a careful economic analysis of each investment; how well would it pay off? How soon? What risks were involved? What alternative investments were available? And what would be their returns?

Such decisions of an economic nature have to be made in all of the areas of production and operations management listed in Chapter 1. The choices made rest on cost/value economic analyses.

PRODUCTIVITY

A person mowing grass with a powered lawn mower is able to mow more grass than he could with a hand-pushed lawn mower. His "productivity," the amount of work he gets done in an hour, is greater. A farmer who puts fertilizer on his fields gets a greater yield, both on a per-acre basis and on a labor-hour basis. His productivity is increased even counting his time putting on the fertilizer. And, in a factory, an employee driving a power-driven fork lift truck can move far more materials at less cost than he can when he uses a nonpowered hand-pulled lift truck.

In all of these examples, there is a money cost, an investment, required in order to make the operator more effective. If this cost is too high, it will not pay to economize on labor. This is where economic concepts come in. (As a generalization, however, it usually pays to mechanize if any substantial volume of production is in prospect. The productivity per labor-hour will be increased by more than enough to pay for the machine.)

In many cases, productivity per labor-hour can be increased just by doing things in different ways—ways which may not cost any more at all. Skilled typists all use all of their fingers, and they are so skillful that they don't have to look back and forth from their manuscript to the keys. The rest of us who use the "hunt and peck" system and use only two or three fingers are much slower and get less done. Our productivity is lower. We turn out less production per labor-hour.

One of the pervasive and enduring objectives of production and operations managers is to improve productivity, thus reducing the costs per unit of output. This, in turn, allows for price reductions or higher wages for workers, or both, and so increases the standard of living in our economy.

During the early 1970s in the United States, productivity per labor-hour after many years of annual increase not only stopped going up, but it actually went down. This, combined with continued wage increases, resulted in severe inflation. Our national Congress, as early as 1971, established a National Commission on Productivity whose mission was to try to improve the nation's productivity.

Whether the commission had anything to do with it or not, the nation's productivity reversed its downward trend in late 1975 and started up again. Much of the gain came from increased efficiency in the production area in factories and the better use of resources in businesses operating in service industries. But some of the improvement came from the more economical use of facilities and resources in the public sector, in schools, and other governmental service departments and agencies.

ECONOMIES OF SCALE

Whenever anything has to be done over and over again, it is almost always possible to become more effective. We learn how to do work at lower cost. This is particularly so where it is possible to mechanize any part of the work.

The economies of scale make it possible to "mass produce" products. Manual tasks can be cut into small tasks to which employees can devote full time, thus becoming very proficient and very productive and consequently reducing costs. This can be observed in any factory. Workers specialize yet can spend their full time at a single task because it has to be done so often.

The opportunities for economies from mass production are almost always much greater in the area of mechanization than just from manual specialization. Large, costly special purpose machines are so productive that they produce goods at very low unit costs *if* the investment can be spread over the production of millions of items over the course of time.

This is why it is possible for Ford Motor to spend $50 million for an automobile assembly plant, or Pacific Gas & Electric to spend $50 million for a power plant, or Exxon to spend $50 million for an oil refinery. These initial costs will be charged off against a million or more cars, or against billions of kilowatt-hours of electricity, or hundreds of millions of gallons of gasoline. The cost per unit is only a few dollars a car, or a few tenths of a cent for a kilowatt-hour, or a few cents per gallon.

The economies of scale are not, however, confined only to manufacturing activities. Heavy research expenditures, for example, are not at all onerous where the volume of the end product runs into big numbers. Years ago RCA spent $75 million developing color television before any sets were sold. But now that hundreds of millions of sets have been sold and with RCA being the largest manufacturer, its original R&D expenditure is now less than $1 a set.

Similarly, the economies of scale operate in advertising. Procter & Gamble spends over $300 million a year advertising its products, principally soap and detergents. But with P&G's enormous volume, the advertising cost per cake of soap is very low.

Diseconomies of scale

The economies of scale are available, however, only if large volumes are in prospect and only after large investments of money have been made.

Several disadvantages are immediately apparent. First, there is the need to invest large amounts of money, some of which will be at risk for a long time. Evaluating this risk means investigating the question of how much the volume will be during the prospective investment recovery period and how long that period will be.

These forecasts of volume and time are also related to selling price since, at a low price, the volume may be high but the investment recovery per unit of product can be only very little. A higher price would reduce the volume but allow for a greater investment recovery per unit.

The disadvantage is the great dependence on the accuracy of the forecasts—which, in fact, sometimes prove to be wrong. In 1975, White Motor, a manufacturer of trucks, wrote off a loss of $30 million when it discontinued the construction of a new factory in Canton, Ohio, to build engines for its trucks. The volume once expected was not materializing and the partially completed factory was sold to Massey-Ferguson at a loss.

Another disadvantage, or diseconomy, is that a "locked-in" investment in plant and equipment makes the company sluggish in responding to changing processes and to changing demand.

American manufacturers of steel, for example, did not adopt the "basic oxygen" process developed in Europe until the 1970s, ten years after its use became common in Europe and Japan. Instead they stuck to their old "open-hearth" process, which was considerably more costly, because of their heavy investments in open-hearth equipment.

Something similar occurred in automobiles. The American companies did not want to change to making smaller cars nor did they move fast in developing good mileage and low air pollution engines. In part, this was caused by their enormous investments in equipment to make larger models and in existing engine-making facilities.

COSTS

All economic analyses and all economic concepts deal with costs. They are concerned with money being spent, and how it can be spent in the most economical way, and how and when it will be recovered out of income.

Fixed costs

Fixed costs are those where amounts cannot be changed in the short run. If an organization signs a five-year lease on a building, the rental costs are fixed for that period of time. If a company buys a plastic injection molding machine on a monthly payment plan, the monthly payments are fixed whether the company finds any plastic injection molding business or not.

Similarly, annual charges made within a company for depreciation are fixed. So are many administrative and financial costs, such as bond interest and insurance costs. Administrative salaries and contributions to pension funds are relatively fixed.

The important thing about fixed costs is that they do not fluctuate with levels of activity. If business goes down, the fixed costs, expressed on a per unit of output basis, may become so high that they are not wholly recovered from sales income. But, if business goes up, the fixed costs *per unit* go down.

Variable costs

Variable costs are costs whose total amount goes up or down when volume goes up or down. The total cost of the meat that goes into Big Mac hamburgers in a month depends upon how many hamburgers are sold. So does the cost of the buns. And so, to some extent, does the cost of labor. More hamburgers mean that more money will be spent for all of these items, and fewer hamburgers mean that less will be spent.

Variable costs, sometimes called "direct" costs or "incremental" costs, vary in total with volume. Their costs per individual unit of production, however, remain almost constant unless economies or diseconomies of scale appear at higher or lower volumes. The cost of the meat in one hamburger is just about the same whether few or many are sold. The way in which fixed and variable costs relate to each other lies behind "break-even" analyses (which are discussed later in this chapter).

Opportunity costs

Opportunity costs are the profits which a "foregone" choice of actions would have earned but which are lost because another choice is made. Obviously, the profits from the choice made should be greater than the foregone profits or else the choice is a poor one.

A person who keeps his money in a mattress instead of investing it in a savings account or in some other investment incurs a cost from having made this choice. He has foregone the earnings the investment would have brought him.

In the mid-1970s, Volkswagen introduced its very successful "Rabbit" model to the American market. The demand was greatly in excess of the company's anticipations, and the cars supplied to the dealers promptly sold out. Dealers estimated that they lost several million dollars of sales before adequate supplies became available. Had the company, initially, invested more in manufacturing capacity, it would not have lost these sales and incurred these opportunity costs.

It is rarely possible to put an accurate monetary value on an opportunity cost because one can rarely know what might have been. For example, what is the opportunity cost of not going to college? If young people invest four years of their life and several thousand dollars of money in an education, on the one hand they are foregoing the opportunity to earn a salary during those four years. On the other hand, if they do not invest in a college education, their lifetime earnings will probably be substantially lessened. The logic is easy to follow, but the numbers needed for comparisons and their probabilities can never be reduced to exact numbers.

Sunk costs

Sunk costs are investments made in projects from which normally the money cannot be recovered except gradually through their costs being charged to continued production and operations. They are not like the inventories of a bankrupt store from which part of the money can be recovered right away through a liquidation sale. The money spent by an apartment owner putting in an elevator cannot be recovered by a liquidation sale of the elevator shaft and the elevator. (Often, however, even illiquid assets, such as a factory building, can be sold at some price or other, thus recovering some, possibly all, of the investment.)

Sunk costs are not at all synonymous with lost investments. They are only money tied up and illiquid except as it may be possible to release it by means of continued operations or by a bargain sale. If, however, it proves impossible to recover the money in the future, then sunk costs are sunk in the most literal sense. A wildcatter who drills for oil and comes up with no oil, only salt water, has lost the money he spent drilling the well.

The importance of the sunk cost idea is in its nature as a more or less permanent irrevocable investment which was made in the past. In most economic analyses of future projects, money spent in the past on related projects, and which is now a sunk cost, is irrelevant to future decisions. "What's done is done."

TIME VALUE OF MONEY

The concept of the time value of money is related directly to the concept of opportunity costs, presented above. This concept, the time value of money, says that $1 on hand today is worth more than $1 to be received at some time in the future. How much more? The amount that today's dollar could earn, if invested, between today and the date in the future when the other dollar would be received.

Conversely, the present value of $1 to be received in the future is less than $1. Both figures, the future worth of today's money and the present value of future money can easily be calculated.

The future value of present money

If we were to invest $100 today at a rate of 10 percent a year and let the interest earnings accumulate and also to earn interest ("compounding" the interest), the total value at the end of any given time period can be found by using the following formula:

$$F = P(1 + i)^n$$

where:

F = future value
P = present amount
i = interest rate as a decimal per period
n = number of periods

For our example, and assuming a period of three years,

$$F = \$100 (1 + .1)^3 = \$133.10$$

The present value of future money

If someone is to give us $100 at the end of three years and if interest rates are 10 percent, the present value of that $100 can be found by using this formula:

$$P = \frac{F}{(1 + i)^n}$$

For our example,

$$P = \frac{\$100}{(1 + .1)^3} = \$75.00$$

The need to calculate the present value of money (or to "discount" it to today's value) to be received at different times in the future will become apparent in the problems on page 85 on capital investment analysis methods. (See also Appendix A, page 723.)

PROBABILITY IN DECISION MAKING

When managers have to decide under uncertain conditions, often they can use probability analysis to help them arrive at the best decision. To do this, they would need to list several possible results, stated quantitatively, and then assign a probability (a percent likelihood) to each result. Suppose, for example, that the managers see the folowing possibilities:

Profits	Probability	P x P
100...............	.20	20.0
150...............	.50	75.0
200...............	.25	50.0
250...............	.05	12.5
Total...........		157.5

The question is what should they really *expect* in the way of profits. For planning purposes they need to think and act as if the *expected profits* would be one number. Probability analysis allows them to calculate such a number simply by multiplying the two data columns and adding up. In our example, the managers should then proceed to use 157.5 as the expected profits, since this represents the composite of their judgments about the probabilities of the different levels of profits occurring. If the *expected* costs (which can be similarly calculated) of producing these profits were likely to be less than 157.5, then they could go ahead, otherwise not.

BREAK-EVEN ANALYSIS

Break-even analysis is a helpful tool used in analyzing managerial economic problems. It shows how much sales volume (in units or dollar sales) a company needs to have in order to break even financially. It also shows how much profit the company would earn or the loss it would suffer at various volumes above and below the break-even point.

Most manufacturing companies must operate above 60 percent of their capacity to break even. Normally most companies operate at a little more than 85 percent of their capacity, although they would like to operate at about 92 to 93 percent. Above 92 to 93 percent, efficiency usually drops off due to the disappearance of all slack. Hold-ups anywhere are likely to hold up other departments right away. (This is a "diseconomies of scale" situation.)

In order to calculate break-even points, it is necessary to determine fixed and variable costs for various sales volumes. This can be done for overall operations and sometimes for individual projects.

When break-even analysis is used in machinery buying decisions, the fixed costs are the machine's depreciation (which estimates its amortized capital cost) and such other fixed costs as insurance. Variable costs are almost wholly made up of materials and direct labor costs and are "incremental" in that each additional unit of production causes an added increment of cost.

Break-even analysis allows us to ask "What if" questions. For example, *if* the selling price for a new solar heating panel is $100 per unit, and direct materials and labor costs are $80 per unit, and fixed costs per month are $20,000, *then* break-even analysis will show how many units will have to be sold in a month in order to break even. This occurs when the total revenue equals the total cost. In formula form this becomes:

$$P \times Q = F + (V \times Q)$$

where

P = price per unit
Q = quantity
F = fixed costs
V = variable costs per unit

Since Q, the quantity, is the unknown we want, it helps to restate this formula as follows:

$$Q = \frac{F}{P - V}$$

In our example, which is shown graphically in Figure 3–1, the unit sales required to break even would be:

$$Q = \frac{\$20,000}{\$100 - \$80} = 1,000 \text{ units}$$

"Contributions" to Overhead or Profits

The term $(P - V)$ is called the "contribution." It is the amount by which the selling price per unit exceeds the variable cost per unit (or total revenues exceed total variable costs). In our example, the sale of one solar heating panel contributed $20 toward offsetting fixed costs up until the break-even point, 1,000 units, was reached. Above 1,000 units this $20 would be a profit.

FIGURE 3–1

Break-even chart

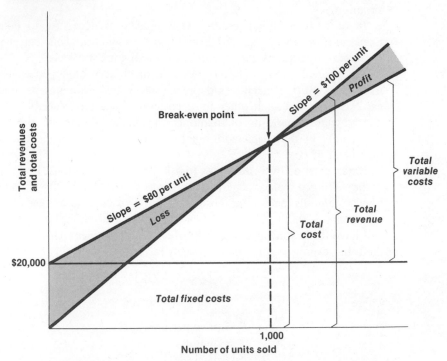

These relationships can be used by managers in their planning. They can determine, for example, the effects on profits (or losses) of changes in sales quantities. If they want to know at what volume the profits would amount to $5,000, all they have to do is to divide $5,000 by $20 and find that 250 more units, or 1,250 in total, would have to be sold.

The total number of sales needed, put in formula form is:

$$Q = \frac{F + \text{desired profits}}{P - V}$$
$$= \frac{\$20,000 + \$5,000}{\$100 - \$80} = \frac{\$25,000}{\$20} = 1,250 \text{ units}$$

To be realistic, however, the company's managers should allow for income taxes because all profits generated by sales above the break-even point are taxed. The tax rate is something a little less than 50 percent, the exact figure depending on how much profit the company earns. If, in our example, it is 40 percent, then each $20 of profit will shrink to $12. Therefore, in order to earn $5,000 after taxes, 417 units ($5,000 ÷ $12) above the break-even point, or 1,417 units in total, will have to be sold instead of 1,250.

The formula for the total number needing to be sold now becomes:

$$Q = \frac{F + (\text{desired profit} \times \dfrac{1}{1 - \text{tax rate}})}{P - V}$$

$$\frac{\$20,000 + (\$5,000 \times \dfrac{1}{1 - .4})}{\$100 - \$80} = \frac{\$20,000 + (\$5,000 \times 1.67)}{\$20}$$

$$= \frac{\$20,000 + \$8,333}{\$20} = \frac{\$28,333}{\$20} = 1,417 \text{ units}$$

One can see that by manipulating the variables in the equations many "What if" questions can be answered. What if, for example, direct material costs were to increase by 12 percent? What would happen to the break-even point? Or, what if competition forced us to cut our price from $100 to $90? Answers to such what if questions can be calculated.

"CONTRIBUTION RATIOS" OR "PROFIT VARIATIONS"

For some purposes it is useful to know the "contribution ratio" or, as it is sometimes called, the "profit variation" for individual products. This ratio measures the product's contribution as a percent of its price per unit. The formula for its calculation is:

$$\text{Contribution ratio} = \frac{P - V}{P} \times 100$$

Using our earlier example:

$$CR = \frac{\$100 - \$80}{\$100} \times 100 = 20\%$$

Low contribution ratios come from labor and material costs making up most of the cost, thus using up most of the income. Changes in total volume do not affect profits very much because the variable costs are so high relative to the selling price. Conversely, if fixed costs are a bigger part of total costs, then the contribution ratios of individual products are higher, and volume changes cause greater swings in profits.

These relationships are important since, once a manager knows the contribution ratios of his products, he can push the ones which contribute the most and perhaps remove those from the product line which have low CR's and thus high opportunity costs. These ratios can also help a manager if he has to decide whether to take on jobs at prices which cover variable costs but only part of fixed costs.

An example will illustrate how important different contribution ratios can be in determining overall results. Suppose that a company makes three models of typewriters, each of which has a different contribution ratio as follows:

	Total sales	Contribution ratio	Contribution	Fixed costs	Profit
Portable manual........	$1,000,000	25%	$ 250,000	$200,000	$ 50,000
Portable electric........	1,000,000	35	350,000	200,000	150,000
Regular electric........	1,000,000	45	450,000	200,000	250,000
Total..............	$3,000,000		$1,050,000	$600,000	$450,000

If a sales increase of $1 million comes from selling more portable manual typewriters, this would increase profits by $250,000. But if a $1 million sales increase comes from selling more regular electric models, it would add $450,000 to profits. Obviously, the greater sales effort should go into selling regular electric typewriters.

Often it is more meaningful to express contribution values on a per labor-hour basis. In our example it might be that portable manual typewriters sell for $100 each and take 10 hours of labor. Portable electrics might cost $200 each and take 15 labor-hours while regular electrics sell for $300 each and take 25 hours of labor. Unit sales in our example would be 10,000, 5,000 and 3,333, respectively. The contribution per unit is $25, $70, and $135. The contribution per labor-hour comes to $2.50, $4.67, and $5.40 respectively. This bears out the above conclusion that regular electric typewriters should be pushed; but it would not always come out this way. If, for example, it took 35 labor-hours for each regular electric typewriter, the contribution per labor-hour would be $3.85. In such a case it would pay to push portable electrics instead.

BREAK-EVEN ANALYSIS AND DECISION MAKING

Break-even concepts can be applied as an aid to managerial decision making in a number of areas. The few examples presented here are intended only to provide a "flavor" for the use of this tool.

Mechanization decisions

Suppose that a new glass-cutting machine would decrease the amount of glass breakage and labor required in the manufacture of our solar heating panel. What would happen to the break-even volume if such a machine were purchased? It would have a monthly fixed charge of $3,000 and would reduce variable costs to $75 per unit. If we carry over all other figures from our previous example, the new equation would be:

$$Q = \frac{\$23,000}{\$100 - \$75} = 920 \text{ units}$$

The installation of this machine would reduce the break-even volume down to 920 units and thus would be an improvement, and the machine should be bought.

Choices among processing alternatives

Break-even analysis can also be used to aid in making choices from among alternative processes by comparing the relative advantages of each. In a manufacturing situation, for example, processes requiring simple machines which are easy to set up are usually slow and costly to operate. On the other hand, larger volumes of output may allow the use of faster machines which are costly to set up but which, once set up, are less costly to operate. Often there are several alternative methods, each of which may be the most economical for certain ranges of output. The method which should be used depends upon the expected volume of output.

The making of a small bushing illustrates such a choice from among alternatives. This bushing can be made on an ordinary general purpose lathe which is easy to set up but not very efficient in production. The bushing can also be made on a turret lathe which is more costly to set up but which produces at lower unit costs once it is set up. Neither of these machines can compete, however, with automatic screw machines when volume begins to count. Setup costs are much higher, but operating costs are much lower.

In the case of the bushing, it costs $2.50 to set up an ordinary lathe, after which the operating cost is 45¢ per unit; turret lathes cost $5.00 to set up and 20¢ per unit for operating costs; and automatic screw machines cost $15.00 to set up but only 4¢ per unit for operating costs.

The cost formulas for making this bushing on these three kinds of machines are (with x being the quantity to be made each time the machine is set up):

Lathes.............................	$ 2.50 + $.45$x$
Turret lathes........................	5.00 + .20x
Automatic screw machines..............	15.00 + .04x

Figure 3–2 shows graphically how the costs of making the bushing on these machines compare. Lathes are the least costly for very small quantities, then turret lathes, and then automatic screw machines for all large quantities.

Sometimes a chart is all that a manager would need for deciding which method to use because the size of the order is not near a crossover point on the chart. But if it is necessary to know the exact crossover points (points A, B, and C in Figure 3–2), these can be calculated very simply. It is only necessary to set the equations for the two methods being compared as equal to each other and solve for x. The comparison of lathes to turret lathes, for example, is:

$$\$2.50 + \$.45x = \$5.00 + \$.20x$$
$$.25x = \$2.50$$
$$x = 10$$

FIGURE 3–2

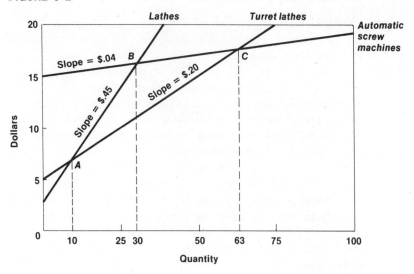

Thus, point A on the chart, the point of indifference between these two methods, is at a volume of 10 units. Similar calculations comparing automatic screw machines to lathes and to turret lathes show that points B and C, the other crossover points in Figure 3–2, are at 30 units and at 63 units.

So, for orders under 10 units, a lathe should be used, for 10 to 63, a turret lathe, and above 63, an automatic screw machine. If the turret lathes are all tied up on other work and not available, then a lathe should be used up to 30 units, and automatic screw machines for orders of more than 30.

Crossover charts can also be used in new equipment purchase choices. The lines on the chart would compare the costs of doing the work in the present way against what they would be if a machine were bought.

Make-buy decisions

The break-even concept can also be useful in "make-buy" decisions, those cases where a company's managers are choosing between making a part inside or buying it already made from the outside.

Make-buy questions can come up at any time. Should the company have idle capacity when such a question comes up then, at least for the moment, the decision to make is almost automatic since the cost of machines does not need to be considered (the cost of the capacity goes on whether the choice is to make or buy).

The real make-buy questions come up when making would involve the purchase of more equipment. It is here that break-even analyses can help. To illustrate, we will suppose that our solar panel manufacturer is making a decision about whether to make or buy a part.

If we invest $3,500 in a new die, we will be able to make this part ourselves for an added cost of $1 per unit in variable costs. If, however, we buy the part, the vendor has quoted two prices to us, $1.55 each for quantities up to 10,000 units and $1.30 each for all orders of over 10,000.

Because of the price reduction if we purchase over 10,000 units, we need to calculate two break-even points, one comparing each purchase price with our inside manufacturing costs. These two formulas are:

$$\$1.55x = \$3,500 + \$1x$$
$$\$.55x = \$3,500$$
$$x = 6,364 \text{ units}$$
$$\$1.30x = \$3,500 + \$1x$$
$$\$.30x = \$3,500$$
$$x = 11,667 \text{ units}$$

Because there is no start-up cost involved and no machine to buy, buying the part would always be less costly for all small quantities. But

FIGURE 3–3

Make-buy decisions

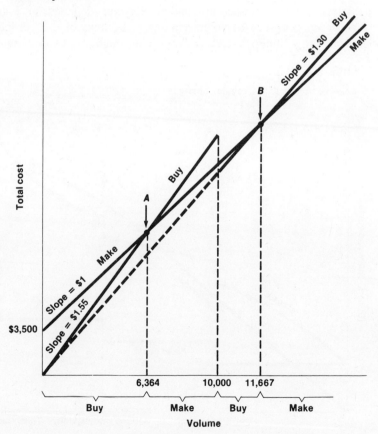

our formulas tell us that although buying would be less costly up to 6,367 units, making is less costly thereafter.

The volume price cut at the 10,000 mark complicates matters. For quantities just over 10,000, again it pays to buy but only up to 11,673 units, after which it again is profitable to make. All of these relationships are depicted in Figure 3–3.

CAUTIONS IN THE USE OF BREAK-EVEN ANALYSIS

Break-even analyses should be used with discretion because of the many assumptions which are made. First, it is difficult to separate fixed costs from variable costs in many operations; often these are only rough estimates. Secondly, variable costs per unit are not always as constant over a range of volumes as the straight lines on break-even charts indicate. Sometimes economies of scale cause variable costs to be less per unit as the volume increases. At other times, diseconomies of scale work the other way and cause variable costs per unit to increase as volume increases. Fixed costs, too, may not stay constant over the full range of volume under consideration. And, finally, greater volume may be in prospect but only at reduced prices.

These several interacting relationships are depicted in Figure 3–4. Fixed costs may rise as volume increases because of the need to add to capacity in a "lumpy" sort of way. This might be caused by the need

FIGURE 3–4

Break-even chart with irregular changes

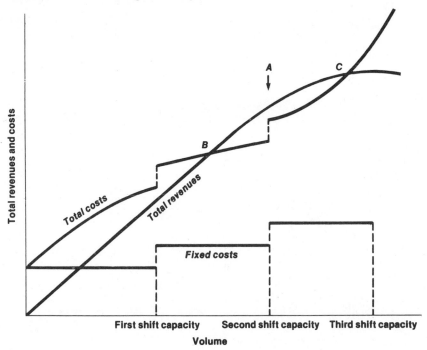

to buy more machines to support the added volume. Similarly, the addition of a second shift increases the salaries of supervision and other indirect labor which are relatively fixed costs.

Nor is the variable cost line a straight line. Because of the economies of scale, their total may go up more slowly than volume until near capacity levels. Then they go up faster than does volume because it is usually quite costly to get out the very last possible units of production.

And, lastly, neither is the income line such a nice straight line as we have depicted. As a firm tries to increase its volume, it may have to cut prices on some items in order to sell more. This has the effect of flattening out the income line on the right side of the chart.

If one were to look at Figure 3–4 and accept the cost and revenue figures shown there at face value, the volume which would produce the greatest profits would be just below point A. That is the point of greatest spread between income and outgo. However, a manager looking at this chart and knowing the inexact nature of the figures that went into its make-up would probably conclude that it would be most profitable to produce at a volume somewhat above point B but somewhat less than point C's volume but not necessarily just below point A.

TRADE-OFF ANALYSIS

Many managerial decisions rest on another managerial economics concept, "trade-off analysis." "Waiting line" problems are of this sort. If a large airport had only one landing strip, then airplanes coming in would have to queue up and fly around in the air waiting their turn to land. Similarly, airplanes wanting to go up would have to wait their turn. This would be costly. But more landing strips would be costly too, and, if there were several such strips, then they would be idle some of the time and that too would be costly. Somewhere there is a proper trade-off point between the cost of more landing strips and the cost of airplanes waiting.

Figure 3–5 depicts the way these opposing costs are related and depicts the point of minimum combined cost. As the cost of airplane

FIGURE 3–5

Trade-off relationships

A.

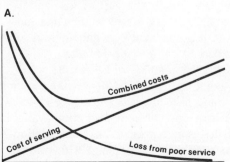

B.

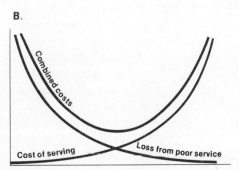

idleness goes down, the cost of idle landing strips goes up. When these two costs are added together, we develop a "total incremental cost curve" whose low point is the most economical trade-off point, and the airport managers know how many landing strips to provide.

This concept of there being an optimal trade-off point between two opposing sets of costs has many applications. The scales along the two axes of the two diagrams in Figure 3–5 could be for a retail store where the attempt would be to balance off the costs of idle clerks against the loss of customers from having too few clerks. Or it could be the costs of carrying larger inventories balanced off against the loss of business from being out of stock of certain items. The diagram would be the same. Only the scales would change.

In a factory a trade-off diagram could be depicting balancing off the waiting time of maintenance employees against the costs of production delays from having to wait for machine repairs when there are too few maintenance people. Or it could be the matter of parts lots order size. Large infrequent lots hold down setup and paper work costs—but at the expense of having larger average inventories and the costs that these inventories entail.

Figure 3–5 shows two types of trade-off relationships. Diagram A reflects the relationships when the cost of providing services varies on a straight-line basis, as would occur in the case of carrying larger inventories in order to reduce the losses from being out of stock. The same relationship would occur in a retail store where the matter would be relating the number of clerks to the prospective losses from customers not waiting when the clerks are all busy.

Sometimes, however, the costs of providing the service are curvilinear, just as are the savings possibilities. This situation, depicted in diagram B, would often occur where quality is concerned. In this case, the horizontal scale would be measures or degrees of quality. Not only does better quality cost more in almost all cases, but almost without exception higher and higher degrees of quality cost disproportionately more. This is indicated by the cost of the quality line curving upward on the right of diagram B.

Although the concept of trade-off analysis is quite useful in conceptualizing problems, it is sometimes hard to work out exact numbers. We have spoken of "the cost of idle clerk time," "the cost of lost business," "the cost of idle maintenance people," "the costs of waiting machines," and so on. These costs are real; yet, it is almost always difficult and sometimes impossible to get exact numbers to put into a calculation.

Nonetheless, the concept and even the numbers which can be gotten do provide managers with a starting point as they try to answer the question, "Which costs will go up or down and how much if I do more or less of something? What is the point of least cost when two or more variables are concerned?" The curves which result represent an accumulation of changes in cost behavior of several variables which change with volume.

FIGURE 3–6

Some important trade-off decisions in manufacturing

Decision area	Decision	Alternatives
Plant and equipment	Span of process	Make or buy
	Plant size	One big plant or several smaller ones
	Plant location	Locate near markets or locate near materials
	Investment decisions	Invest mainly in buildings or equipment or inventories or research
	Choice of equipment	General purpose or special purpose equipment
	Kind of tooling	Temporary minimum tooling or "production tooling"
Production planning and control	Frequency of inventory taking	Few or many breaks in production for buffer stocks
	Inventory size	High inventory or a lower inventory
	Degree of inventory control	Control in great detail or in lesser detail
	What to control	Controls designed to minimize machine downtime or labor cost on time in process, or to maximize output of particular products or material usage
	Quality control	High reliability and quality or low costs
	Use of standards	Formal or informal or none at all
Labor and staffing	Job specialization	Highly specialized or not highly specialized
	Supervision	Technically trained first-line supervisors or nontechnically trained supervisors
	Wage system	Many job grades or few job grades; incentive wages or hourly wages
	Supervision	Close supervision or loose supervision
	Industrial engineers	Many or few such engineers
Product design engineering	Size of product line	Many customer specials or few specials or none at all
	Design stability	Frozen design or many engineering change orders
	Technological risk	Use of new processes unproved by competitors or follow-the-leader policy
	Engineering	Complete packaged design or design-as-you-go approach
	Use of manufacturing engineering	Few or many manufacturing engineers

FIGURE 3–6 (continued)

Decision area	Decision	Alternatives
Organization and management	Kind of organization	Functional or product focus or geographical or other
	Executive use of time	High involvement in investment or production planning or cost control or quality control or other activities
	Degree of risk assumed	Decisions based on much or little information
	Use of staff	Large or small staff group
	Executive style	Much or little involvement in detail; authoritarian or non-directive style; much or little contact with organization

Source: Wickham Skinner, "Manufacturing–Missing Link in Corporate Strategy," *Harvard Business Review*, May–June 1969.

REVIEW QUESTIONS

1. What are economies and diseconomies of scale? Give examples.
2. There are several different classifications of cost. What are they?
3. Why is it difficult to estimate "opportunity" costs?"
4. How does the interest rate affect the future value of present money? The present value of future money?
5. Explain how the contribution ratio and the break-even point are related.
6. List the ways that managerial decisions might change the break-even point and show how it would be changed.

QUESTIONS FOR DISCUSSION

1. How can the break-even volume be calculated for specific products?
2. The president looks at the break-even chart which his controller has just constructed and asks: "How can we lower the break-even point?" How should the controller answer him?
3. Is a break-even chart reliable enough as a managerial tool for a manager to rely on it in making a major business decision? Discuss.
4. Would the cost line on a break-even chart provide a reliable projection of costs if volume decreased by, say, one third? Justify your answer.
5. Suppose that some variable costs prove not to be wholly variable, particularly as volume decreases and some fixed costs prove not to stay wholly fixed, particularly when volume goes up. What would

this do to break-even analyses? How often are either of these possibilities actual factors in real situations?

6. How do income taxes affect break-even points?

7. Discuss the limitations and cautions which should be taken in using break-even analysis.

PROBLEMS

1. What is the value of $1,000 invested today at the end of two years if the interest rate is 10 percent?

2. What is the present value of someone's promise to pay $1,000 at the end of two years if we value money at 10 percent per year?

3. Farnsworth Manufacturer has $50,000 in assignable fixed costs to a new electronic pest repeller designed for backyard use which utilizes high frequency sound. It will wholesale for $20.00 and has a variable cost of $12.43. What is the break-even point?

4. Farnsworth (see problem 3) wishes to have a profit of $25,000 this year on the pest repeller, and their tax rate is 48 percent. How many units must they sell?

5. At a sales volume of $125,000, Fred's Income Tax Service has variable costs of $60,000, fixed costs are $50,000, and profits are $15,000. What is its dollar sales break-even point? How much sales volume does it take to produce profits equal to a cost reduction of $500?

6. Variable costs are 40 percent of the sales price of $10 per unit for Modern Products, Inc. With fixed costs of $200,000, what is the break-even point? Assuming that sales have been exactly at the break-even volume, should Modern cut the price to $8 if this would boost sales volume to 50,000 units?

7. Superior Western's fixed costs are $20,000, and variable costs are $50 per unit. In order to improve profits, it has been proposed that the company spend $30,000 plus $50 per unit to improve the product and change the price as well. The marketing staff has made the following estimate of the effects of these actions:

Price per unit	Annual sales without improvement	Annual sales with improvement
$400	5	40
350	15	125
300	40	200
250	100	375
200	250	600
150	500	1,000
100	900	2,000

What action will yield the greatest profit for Superior?

8. The Atlanta plant has a capacity of 50,000 units per year, has fixed costs of $240,000, and variable costs of $3 per unit. The Boston plant makes the same products. It has a capacity of 75,000 units per year, fixed costs of $260,000, and variable costs of $4 per unit. The present production rates are for Atlanta, 22,000 units, and for Boston, 45,000 units a year.

a. What are the unit costs of production in each plant at present production levels?

b. What would they be at capacity?

c. For most economical production costs, how should the present 67,000 units be divided between the two plants?

d. Assuming that sales will, in the future, come to 75,000 units a year, how should this production be divided between the two plants?

9. Using a one-shift operation, Joyce, Inc., is selling its maximum output (except for overtime) of 4,000 units at $175 each. Fixed costs are $300,000, and variable costs are $360,000 for capacity operation.

It would be possible, however, to boost sales to 4,500 units by using overtime. This would increase variable costs to $400,000. (Some of the variable costs do not go up and down in direct proportion to output.) It is also possible to raise prices to $180 and still sell 4,100 units.

For greatest profit, what should be done?

10. For the past period, Bishop Recreational Products has operated at capacity with the following distribution between products:

Product	Volume (units)	Contribution per unit	Labor-hours	Contribution
A...........	10,000	$10	10,000	$ 30,000
B...........	12,000	12	20,000	35,000
C...........	6,000	20	20,000	30,000
D...........	4,000	10	15,000	20,000
E...........	3,500	25	17,500	30,000
			82,500	$145,000

Business is expected to increase 10 percent in the next period, but it will not be possible to expand labor beyond 85,000 hours. What products should Bishop push? What should the product distribution be to use the 85,000 hours to best advantage?

11. Downing Press' plant has a capacity of 200,000 books per year with fixed costs of $450,000 and variable costs of $3 per unit. It can probably sell 100,000 units in its home market at $13 each. It can probably sell the other 100,000 books it could make in foreign markets at $7 per unit. What are the profits prospects from the home market alone? What might they be if the company produced at capacity and sold the second 100,000 abroad?

12. The Link Company, a large chain store company, makes the following proposal to a vendor. Link proposes to pay $4 for each product. Labor and machine costs come to $7.50 per hour for the vendor. Factory overhead is 125 percent of labor and machinery costs. General and ad-

ministration costs are equal to 20 percent of factory costs. Materials cost will be $.50 per unit. The cost of tooling may be neglected since Link will pay separately for it.

For small quantities, the total product time for labor and machines is 10 minutes per unit for up to 1,000 units. This production time will be reduced by 10 percent by the time 5,000 are produced, 12 percent at 10,000 and 15 percent at 50,000.

a. What should the supplier's price be if his profits are to be 10 percent of the selling price—for 1,000, 5,000, and 50,000 units?

b. At what point will the $4 price allow the vendor to earn $.40 on each unit?

13. With fixed costs of $30,000 and variable costs averaging $4 per unit, Gem Lawn Mowing has been mowing 6,000 lawns per year at an average of $10 each. What profit has it been earning? Would it be wise for it to spend $10,000 for advertising if advertising would raise the volume to 7,500 units? Assuming that the advertising has no carryover benefits into future periods, how much better or worse off will the company be if it spends the $10,000?

14. Continuing problem 13, suppose that Gem believes that a $5,000 advertising expenditure would raise the volume to 7,500 units, but its managers don't feel very sure about this. They feel that a $5,000 expenditure for advertising will be likely to increase volume as follows:

Volume	*Probability*
6,300	.05
6,600	.10
6,900	.15
7,200	.18
7,500	.25
7,800	.17
8,100	.10

Should the company advertise? What is the probable payoff (or loss)?

15. Suppose that the company that owns the three kinds of machines referred to on page 57 got an order for 100 products. As we saw on page 58, this work should be done on automatic screw machines, but the automatics are busy, so the work has to be done on turret lathes or regular lathes. How much extra would it cost to do this work on either of the two less efficient kinds of machines?

SUGGESTED SUPPLEMENTARY READINGS

Heenan, David A., and Addleman, Robert. "Quantitative Techniques for Today's Decision Makers." *Harvard Business Review,* May–June 1976, pp. 32–62.

Jarrett, Jeffrey E. "An Approach to Cost-Volume-Profit Analysis under Uncertainty." *Decision Sciences,* July 1973, pp. 405–19.

Kim, Chaiho. "A Stochastic Cost-Volume-Profit Analysis." *Decision Sciences,* July 1973, pp. 329–42.

4

Capital investment analysis

PRODUCTIVITY does not result from manual work alone, but rather from the work of people using facilities. They use simple hand tools or they operate highly sophisticated machinery and equipment, and both they and the facilities they use are housed in appropriate buildings.

These facilities always cost money, often a great deal of money, and it must all be invested before production occurs. In several industries in the United States, the steel industry for one, these investments come to over $50,000 per employee. When they run this high, the investment is equal to an employee's wages for several years. Obviously, the commitments of such large sums of money are made only after careful economic analyses of the payoff prospects.

THE NEED FOR CAPITAL EXPENDITURES

The need for capital expenditures comes from several sources. First, fixed assets (other than land) are continually wearing out. Machines are always, figuratively, marching down the road to the junk heap, and some reach the end of the road every year. Sometimes the end of the road is economic; a machine is obsolete even though it may still be operable.

The first and usually the biggest need for capital investment is to keep the productive facilities operating efficiently. Existing machines and equipment can be overhauled or rebuilt, or they can be replaced. Of these, the replacement of existing facilities is the big item so far as money needs are concerned.

The second need for capital investment is for expansion. Our country is growing, and most companies grow year after year, so they have to keep buying more plants and equipment year after year. Growth needs may, however, be somewhat irregular, and normally their money needs are smaller in amount than expenditures made for replacing assets.

A third need is for money for socially desirable projects, such as equipment to reduce air and water pollution and to carry forward other activities for the benefit of society. Costly equipment sometimes has to be installed for worker safety and health.

A fourth need might be said to be sustaining projects, such as a new vault for keeping records.

The money a company has (from its cash flow) and the money it needs don't always match. Almost always the total cost of requested projects exceeds the money available. The chairman of U.S. Steel's finance committee once said that he had to make up his annual $500 million capital expenditure program out of department heads' "Christmas lists," which usually asked for more than double what was available.

Top managers should not, however, regard the capital investment proposals of their subordinates as "Christmas lists." Nearly all of these proposals are for projects which will produce more income, either directly or through reductions in costs. Nor should top managers start with the idea that only a certain amount of money is available. Rather, they should consider how productive the new equipment promises to be, and, if the proposals are money-saving proposals, how much money they can save. Individual projects should be studied on their own merits, regardless of how much money they take and how much money is available.

Only after all of the promising proposals have been looked over should a decision be made about what to do. Ordinarily, only as many projects as can be paid for with the money at hand will be approved, but a company might approve more proposals if they look so good as to justify borrowing money or selling more stock. Possibly, too, the new equipment proposed could be leased or bought on the installment plan.

Discovering machine needs

When does a machine need replacing? When does an old automobile need replacing? Neither machines nor automobiles wear out all at once, in which case people would know for certain when they need replacing. Actually, it is possible to keep old machines or old automobiles running for years by continuing to repair and rebuild them. But repair costs are usually high for old machines, just as they are for old automobiles. Obsolescence, too, occurs. Every new and more efficient model of a machine makes it a little less economical to continue to operate the old one.

The point is that uneconomical operations have to be searched out. Lower-level managers have to watch for the point of uneconomical operations of old machines. Single-spindle lathes that are over 50 years old can turn out considerable quantities of products which would cost less if they

FIGURE 4-1
Typical large company capital expenditure decision-making model

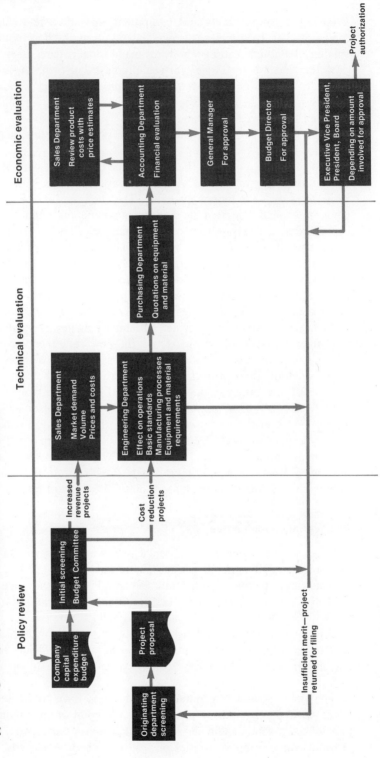

Source: American Management Association.

were made on newer automatic screw machines. The fact that an old machine still operates and can be kept busy does not necessarily mean that it is economical to use it. It is also necessary for lower-level managers to search out places where money needs to be spent to reduce noise, smoke, or water or air pollution, as well as to make conditions safer for workers.

Major projects

In contrast to what we have been saying about the need for lower-level managers to discover machinery replacement needs, major improvement proposals do not originate in and come up from the shop. Only minor shop project requests start near the bottom and go up to top management for review. The need for whole new factories and for million-dollar projects, in contrast, is first seen in the front office. Often such projects are so big that special task forces of high-level people are set up to do the planning and later to oversee the project's construction.

CHOICE OF PROJECTS

Since there are nearly always many more economically worthwhile projects and more socially desirable projects than a company has money for, its managers have to choose from among them. Normally, the projects which promise the highest rate of return on the investment are approved. But this can't be the only guide because sometimes no-rate-of-return socially desirable "must" projects, as well as sustaining projects needed to carry on the business, also need to get a share of the money.

In addition, various projects which are not very certain to pay off might be approved if they might some day pay off very well. An electric power company might, for example, build a nuclear power plant which is not expected to pay very well but is expected to serve as a pilot project which will help pave the way for better paying nuclear power plants in the future. The probability of higher later payoffs needs to be considered in the analyses of projects.

Nor are capital expenditure decisions always clear and distinct from operating decisions. A company could, for example, spend money for research and for advertising. But it could also save on research and advertising and buy more machines. Top managers often have to choose between operating costs and capital investments.

MARGINAL RETURNS AND OPPORTUNITY COSTS

Sometimes one project might be chosen over another because of marginal differences which in Chapter 2 were called "opportunity cost" situations. (When there are two or more ways to do something which will cost different amounts or which will yield different returns, there is an opportunity to save money by using the least costly way or by investing in the most advantageous way.)

Suppose, for example, that project A will return 15 percent on an investment of $50,000 and project B will yield 18 percent and would cost $40,000. If the decision were to invest in A, its extra $10,000 investment would produce a little extra income in spite of the lower rate, but the extra contribution would not be large. Project A's total return would be $7,500, B's would be $7,200; so the extra $10,000 invested in project A would bring in only $300, or 3 percent. But if B were a 12-percent project, B would bring in only $4,800 against A's $7,500. This time the extra $10,000 required for A would produce $2,700, or 27 percent, on the extra investment.

A manager probably would not calculate opportunity costs when comparing two projects such as these because the choice is so obvious. Opportunity costs could, however, be very important if C, a completely unrelated project, required $10,000 and would yield 20 percent. Suppose, for example, that there is only $50,000 to invest and only these three projects to consider. The best choice would be to choose B and C, the two highest returning projects. But, if B were a 12-percent project, the choice should be A with its 15 percent rate, even though this means foregoing both B and C—in spite of C's being a 20-percent project. A will yield $7,500; B and C combined will yield $6,800. Here is a case where a manager ought to pass up a 20-percent project in favor of a 15-percent project because the opportunity cost of choosing B and C over A is $700.

SAVINGS AND ALTERNATIVES

It costs money to buy machines and buildings, and it costs money to use them. Yet, we say that a proposed project will save money if it costs less than the alternative ways for doing things.

This introduces a curious difficulty into the process of calculating savings. A project's savings depend on the relationship between its own cost of operation and on the cost of the existing method to which it is being compared. So, the worse the present method, the more a new project can save! (Actually, any time a new project will save a great deal, the improvement probably should have been made earlier. Costs have been allowed to creep up higher than should have been permitted.)

Overhead savings

Capital investment project analysts should be quite conservative in claiming savings in overhead costs. Overhead charges, as calculated by the accounting department, are rarely less than 100 percent, and they may be 250 percent or more of the direct labor cost.

Almost never should a project's prospective savings estimate include saving that much overhead, because savings in direct labor seldom cut overhead expenses very much. Every project should be credited with saving any overhead that it really will save, but most capital investment projects don't, in fact, save much overhead. On the contrary, because they create more depreciation, they may cause overhead to go up.

CASH FLOW

Most of the money to pay for new machines, new equipment, and new buildings comes from companies' cash flow, although companies sometimes also sell stock or borrow money to finance capital expenditures.

A company's cash flow is the money it could have left over each year. This is not, however, the same as a company's profits for the year. When customers buy products and pay their bills, a company has a gross cash income. The customers are, in effect, paying all of the company's bills. They are giving it—today—money to cover the payments the company made some time ago for the electricity bill, the tax bill, the pay of employees, the cost of materials, the wearing out of the machines and buildings, everything—and probably a little more which is left over as profit (See Figure 4–2). Normally, most of every company's gross cash inflow goes right out again as it is used to pay today's bills for electricity, taxes, to buy replacement machines, to build buildings, and so on.

The gross cash flow not only pays all of a company's day-to-day expenses, but also includes money which recovers the decline in the value of machines and buildings because of their wearing out. A company's net cash flow, then, is equal to retained profits after taxes and dividends, plus depreciation on machines, equipment, and buildings, plus any income from the sale of fixed assets.

FIGURE 4–2

Cash flow system of a manufacturing organization

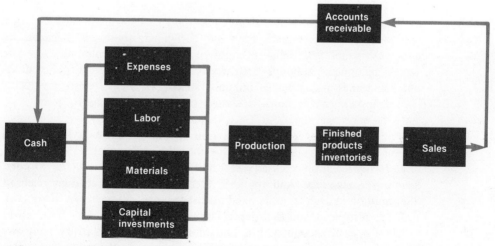

Source: American Management Association.

This does not mean that a company will have all of its net cash flow left over at the end of a year. A good bit of this cash, perhaps all of it, will be spent for new machines or other new capital investment projects as the year goes along. The point is that during the year certain monies, free of immediate commitment to current bills, come into the company and its managers get to decide how to use them.

Since the net cash flow provides most or even all of the money used for capital projects, its size has much to do with capital investment decisions. The part of the cash flow that comes from depreciation provides most of the money for machinery replacement purposes. It ought to provide all of the money needed for replacement machines, but today's new machines always seem to cost more than the ones they replace, so companies sometimes have to use part of their profits for replacement projects. And, of course, all of the money for expansion has to come out of the profits part of the cash flow, or else the company will have to sell more stock or borrow money.

Cash flow is usually equal to more than 15 percent of a company's fixed assets, and sometimes it goes up to 25 percent or more. In 1974 General Motors' net cash flow of $1.8 billion amounted to 29 percent of its $6.2 billion of fixed assets. Almost half, $850 million, of General Motors' cash flow came from depreciation. This was equal to 14 percent of GM's equipment and plant value. U.S. Steel's 1974 depreciation of $385 million was 9 percent of its $4.17 billion investment in equipment and plant. Besides this, retained profits in U.S. Steel produced another $635 million, so its cash flow came to $1.02 billion, or 24 percent of its fixed assets.

DEPRECIATION

Depreciation cash

It has been shown that depreciation produces part of a company's cash flow. But accountants don't like the word "produces" because the company is not any richer because of it. Nor do accountants like the word "generates," although both words are used in financial publications and sometimes in companies' annual statements.

Perhaps either the word "releases" or "recovers" is more descriptive. After a year's operation and if a company did not buy any more machines or buildings, the effect of depreciation would be to move money from the machines and buildings accounts into the cash account. As we saw, in 1974 depreciation released $850 million of cash from General Motors' fixed asset accounts. And for U.S. Steel in 1974, depreciation released $385 million in cash from its fixed asset accounts.

It has also been said that depreciation cash probably never turns up in full in the cash account at the end of the year because every company has to keep buying new machines and buildings all the time. But, when it buys new machines and buildings, it gets to make choices about how much to spend and what to buy.

Reinvested depreciation cash does not necessarily go into the same kind of assets that it came from. In fact, it usually goes into different kinds of machines and equipment—those which will be most useful in the future.

Depreciation methods

Pointing out that depreciation is complicated solves no business problems. Businessmen still have to show on their accounts a money value for depreciation every year. And the way that businessmen keep their accounts must satisfy the U.S. Internal Revenue Service. This is because of the tie-in between the calculation of costs (including depreciation), profits, and income taxes.

The Internal Revenue Service wants everyone to depreciate everything over its full life. But because no one really knows how long equipment will last, business practice is to write machinery investments off on a minimum —not a maximum—life expectancy. This means claiming that machines will not last very long and claiming full depreciation in just a few years. If a company doesn't do this, it will sometimes end up showing an asset on its books—as still being worth money—when in fact it is valueless. Not every machine lasts as long as was originally expected. The government often allows these fast writeoffs as incentives to invest in new capital equipment to maintain a healthy economy.

Straight-line method   Historically, the straight-line method has been much the most common method for figuring depreciation. This method starts with a machine's installed cost, minus its expected scrap value at the end of its expected useful life. This number is divided by the number of years it will be used. A $10,000 machine, expected to last ten years and then to be worth $1,000 as scrap, will have a $900 depreciation every year.

Declining balance method   In the declining balance method, an item is depreciated by a certain *percentage* of the balance every year. A $10,000 machine which is expected to last ten years can be depreciated at a 20-percent depreciation rate. Twenty percent of $10,000, or $2,000, is the first year's depreciation. At the beginning of the second year, the machine is carried on the books at $8,000. Twenty percent of that, $1,600, is the second year's depreciation. The third year's depreciation is 20 percent of $6,400, and so on.

The declining balance method allows for heavy depreciation in the early years of an asset's life and then less and less as time goes on. This method never depletes all the values, so users of this method, near the end of an item's life, switch over to straight-line depreciation.

The examples above used 10 percent of the expected loss in value for straight-line depreciation and 20 percent of the remaining value for the declining balance method. In general, a company can use, as the declin-

FIGURE 4–3

**Comparison of straight-line, declining balance, and
sum-of-the-years' digits
depreciation methods**

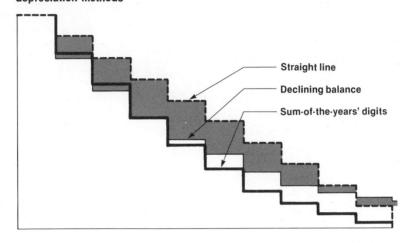

ing balance rate, a rate double that of the straight-line method, except
that it is not allowed to go over 20 percent, and in the case of some classes
of assets the allowable limit is less than double the straight-line rate. So,
in our example, the company could not go over 20 percent, but it could
use any other lower percentage if its managers cared to. A company does
not have to depreciate at the highest allowable rate.

Sum-of-the-years' digits Another method is the sum-of-the-years'
digits. If we take a 5-year-life item and add $5 + 4 + 3 + 2 + 1$, we get
15. In the first year we depreciate the item $\frac{5}{15}$ of its cost, next year $\frac{4}{15}$,
and so on. For a 10-year item the sum of the digits is 55, so the first year's
depreciation would be $\frac{10}{55}$ of its cost. Although it is not particularly
complicated, this method is not commonly used.

Variable or unit depreciation Variable or unit depreciation is becoming more popular. This method requires an estimate of the number
of units a machine will produce during its lifetime (these units can also
be expressed as hours of operation). Depreciation is then figured on a
unit basis and charged to accounting periods according to the number of
units produced in the period. The amount charged to any period, therefore, depends on the asset's use in the period. Many accountants feel that
this method gives a better picture of the amount of depreciation which
should be charged than do other methods.

Group depreciation In practice, probably no large company depreci-
ates every machine separately. Instead, except for big items where considerable money is involved, machinery investments are grouped into life
groups. All machines with ten-year life expectancies are put into one class
in the company's accounts. Every time a new ten-year-life machine is

bought, its cost is added to the total for all ten-year-life machines. Every year 10 percent of this total is charged off as depreciation.

This makes it necessary to have separate accounts for several life classes: 5 years, 10 years, 15 years, and so on. But there is no need for thousands of separate depreciation accounts—one for every machine. The effect of depreciating by groups is to put depreciation largely on a straight-line method of depreciation which neglects salvage value.

Other methods There are still other methods of depreciation, but the five that have been described here are the only ones commonly used by manufacturing companies. The sinking-fund method, for example, sometimes used by utilities and railroads, is possibly unknown in manufacturing.

INFLATION

Inflation complicates normal depreciation practices. An example of how this works would be a machine with an expected life of ten years which was bought in 1975 for $10,000. If the company sets aside the $1,000 depreciation cash each year, the machine will be worn out by 1985, and the company will have its $10,000 for a replacement machine. But, by 1985, the replacement will surely cost more than $10,000, perhaps as much as $20,000. Thus, the company had better have laid aside some extra money because it will have to spend perhaps $20,000 to buy another machine. Part of the apparent profits over the years has disappeared.

Because of continual inflation, companies would like to depreciate on the replacement cost of a machine, but the government will not allow this for tax calculation purposes. Actually, even depreciating on a replacement-cost basis fails to recover enough cash. In the example above, if the replacement machine's price went up $1,000 every year and if the government allowed depreciation on a replacement-cost basis, then depreciation cash would have been $1,000 for the first year, $1,100 for the second, and so on. But this practice, if carried on for ten years, would produce only $14,500, not $20,000.

Borderline decisions

If, in the long run, it appears to be a toss-up as to whether to put in new machines or not, it is often better to install them. There are several reasons for this.

First, if a new machine will almost pay for itself based on today's calculation, then after another year of wear on the old machine, a new one will even more surely pay out. But by then the new machine will cost even more. It would have been better to have bought it sooner.

Second, wage savings are usually underestimated. Wages seem always to go up even more than was expected, which means that future savings of wages are usually underestimated.

A third reason is the short life of the machine that is assumed in the calculations. Nearly all machines last longer than the life expectancy used in depreciation calculations. Consequently, the depreciation used in the calculations proves to have been exaggerated, which has the effect of underestimating the savings.

Fourth, the quality of the product is usually improved and scrap rates will usually decrease. These gains, though real, are not measurable and therefore usually left out of savings calculations.

The arguments in favor of mechanizing when the figures show it to be of borderline wisdom seem strong, but there is a negative side. First, machines cost substantial amounts of money which, once spent, is usually at risk for a long time. So, it is necessary both to produce the money and to be willing to invest it in what will essentially be a sunk cost which cannot be recovered except in the long run through continued operation.

Second, there is an increase in fixed costs. A new machine's use is usually expected to reduce direct labor costs by more than its depreciation cost at expected operating levels. The investment substitutes a relatively low fixed cost per unit for a higher variable cost per unit. But because the investment is a fixed cost, it raises the company's break-even point. It takes more business volume to break even after buying machines than it did before. Even though the investment will produce better profits in the future when high volumes are produced, it results in less profit or even causes greater losses from low-volume production.

Third, because of the heavier fixed costs and the higher break-even point, the company is more vulnerable to loss. Low sales volume results in greater losses than would have taken place without mechanization.

Still another disadvantage—and this in spite of the claims made above—is that new machines don't always come up to expectations. Of course, no one expects them to do as well as the machinery maker says they will, but, even after allowing for this, the machines sometimes produce less than was expected. They get out of order too often, turn out too many poor products, need more repairs, wear out tools faster, and so on, than was expected. Particularly, there is likely to be trouble at the start since it takes time to debug new equipment. Because all of these things add to the cost, they should be put into the estimates but often not enough is allowed for.

Knowing these things, officials sometimes turn down projects which—on paper—show considerable promise. They do not always go ahead and buy machines even in promising situations, to say nothing of toss-up situations.

INCOME TAX CONSIDERATIONS

Federal income taxes are high for companies which make large profits. In 1974, General Motors earned $1.68 billion but paid out $730 million of it to the government as income taxes. No one is required to carry on business in such a way as to pay the utmost in taxes, so when there are choices, as occurs with depreciation methods, the tax angles should be considered.

In the case of depreciation, all machines ultimately become fully depreciated (or sold) no matter what method is used. Yet, the depreciation method that is used affects when taxes are paid. Some methods allow a company to retain more cash earlier in an asset's life than other methods. If the company can put this money to work profitably right away, this is an advantage.

We will use a one-machine factory, the Northern Company, as an example to show how the straight-line, declining balance, and sum-of-the-years' digits depreciation methods operate. Straight-line depreciation is a slow depreciation method whereas both of the other two methods recover depreciation faster.

Northern has a new machine which cost $10,000 and has an expected life of ten years and an expected resale value at the end of that time of $1,000. This machine reduces operating costs by $2,000 a year, in addition to recovering the $900 of depreciation claimed to have occurred in the straight-line depreciation method. The machine thus produces a pretax relative cash flow of $2,900.

Here is how taxes and cash retention would work out in the first year with these three methods of depreciation:

	Straight-line	Declining balance	Sum-of-years' digits
Claimed depreciation...................	$ 900	$2,000	$1,636
Savings (or pretax profits)...............	2,000	900	1,264
Income taxes (48% of profits)............	960	432	607
Cash retention.......................	1,940	2,468	2,293

By using declining balance rather than straight-line depreciation, the company gets to keep $528 more in the business for the time being. The sum-of-the-years' digits method lets it keep $353 more than with straight-line.

One could wonder why the government allows the use of fast depreciation when this deprives it of taxes for the time being. The government allows it because it wants to encourage, rather than discourage, new machinery purchases since this increases the nation's productive capacity and promotes economic growth. Also, later on, as the machine gets old, the remaining depreciation is small and taxes will be higher. The effect is to change the timing of paying the tax. Businesses gain because they can put the retained extra cash to work. In billion-dollar companies the extra retention amounts to millions of dollars. Fast depreciation also provides protection against unexpected obsolescence.

Income tax considerations in other areas

Maintenance is another area where taxes affect decisions. During lean years with no profits, a company probably will not fix or repair anything it doesn't have to. It would probably do this to conserve cash, regardless of income taxes. But income taxes constitute another reason for under-maintenance in bad years, because all maintenance costs in years when a company loses money come out of the company's pocket. But, in good years if money is not spent, it takes the form of profits, and the government takes nearly half of it. So it is well to do maintenance work in good years because nearly half of the expense is saved in taxes.

Many research costs are similar to those for maintenance. In good years a company might go ahead with research which may not pay off, but it should not go ahead with this kind of research in poor years.

Because capital investment is wholly a forward-looking matter, it is highly important to try to calculate how productive new facilities will be and how much it will cost to operate them. But, since these matters lie in the future, they, like all forecasts, are likely to be somewhat inaccurate. No method for analyzing capital expenditure proposals, whether elegant and sophisticated or not, will insure good decisions. It is like trying to figure out whether to trade in an old car this year or next year. There is no way to tell for sure that one decision is better than another decision. Yet, because today's machinery and equipment is very specialized and not easily reconverted into cash, good analyses are more critical than ever.

ANALYSIS METHODS

Most companies use one or all of the following three methods in their calculations for capital equipment buying decisions:

1. Return on investment.
2. Payback.
3. Discounted cash flow.

None of these methods is perfect. Return on investment and payback are easy to figure but are not very incisive. Discounted cash flow requires more involved calculations but more truly reflects the relative merits of alternative choices.

Before we consider these methods individually, one fundamental difficulty inherent in all methods should be pointed out. Whether a new machine should or should not be bought depends upon what its cost to operate will be compared to what it will save. And, as was said earlier, what it will save depends as much upon the company's present methods as it does on the costs of the proposed method. Thus, in replacement problems, there can never be any absolute measure of the profitability of the investment. It depends as much on how inefficient the present method is as on how efficient the proposed method will be.

INVESTMENT AND INCOME FLOW PATTERNS

Capital equipment projects always cost money during their construction period. As construction moves along, more and more money is paid out. Then, when a project comes on-line (which is, for a steel mill, perhaps three years after expenses start), it starts to generate an income flow. After an early shakedown period, during which minor troubles keep costs high and which may last for several months, the flow of savings usually is high for several years. Thereafter, as the project "ages," its savings flow lessens.

The pattern of total money going out and coming back is likely to be something like that depicted in Figure 4–2. The money keeps flowing out until the project comes on-line. Thereafter, the savings flow first recoups the investment and then produces a net earning.

Sometimes, however, prospective savings flows have different patterns. This would happen if a company builds more capacity than it needs in the near future. Even after such a project comes on-line, its savings or income flow will start out small and grow later, as the excess capacity begins to be used. A few years ago, for example, the John Deere Company built a farm equipment machinery factory in France even though the company expected to lose money for five years before sales would be enough to generate profits.

In any case, in profitability calculations, the analyst should use whatever income flow pattern the project is likely to generate because the time and shape of earnings streams have much to do with a project's profitability. For simplicity's sake, in the examples used here, a regular even flow for all the years of a machine's life will be assumed.

PAYBACK

The payback method for analyzing the merits of capital investment projects, which tells how long it takes to get the investment back, is widely used. Most executives want to know how long their money will be at risk before they approve a project. The payback period should always, of course, be shorter than the asset's expected life.

The calculation to get the payback period is one of finding out how long it will be until a project's gross after-tax cash flow equals its investment.[1] If the prospective cash flow is constant year after year, the calculation is to divide the investment by the annual cash flow and get the payback period expressed in years.

In payback, all interest is centered on the near-future cash flows of the

---

[1] In these calculations the cash flow is calculated as being the project's savings, minus the income tax on the savings, plus depreciation. This differs from a company's overall net cash flow because this cash is not diminished by any dividends paid out.

project and not on its ultimate returns or long-term cash flows. Payback pays attention to how long the investment is at risk and, as a method, overemphasizes liquidity. Payback pays no attention to the economic life of the asset beyond the payback period, nor to its salvage value, or its postpayback cash flows. Thus, it neglects the most important part: How much a company will end up earning on the investment.

Some companies turn down projects which will not pay off quickly. As a policy, this is probably unwise because it may result in a company's becoming very inefficient before it mechanizes. A new project can pay off in two or three years only if the present method is quite inefficient. Mostly, companies should not wait until present methods become so inefficient.

Yet, because the amounts involved are small, most minor tooling and cost-saving devices are approved only if they will pay out in a year or so. Small machines, where neither costs nor savings are great, are allowed two or three years. Large, expensive, heavy-duty, durable machines may be allowed more time. This could occasionally take up to five years or more.

RETURN ON INVESTMENT

Some companies call their method for judging an investment's probable return the "return on investment" (ROI) method. Yet, in fact, there is really no one method which everyone calls the "return on investment" method.

First-year return

Companies which call their method "return on investment" often look only one year ahead and compare a prospective machine's savings to its required investment. They divide its first year's after-tax savings by the average investment for the year and get its rate of return on the investment. This method is commonly used for evaluating small projects.

Full-life return

On bigger projects, companies commonly divide the average annual after-tax savings expected during the future years of a project's life by its average investment over this life. Again, the answer is regarded as the return on investment.

Calculating the return on investment in either of these two ways is not very satisfactory for evaluating long-life projects because it puts distant years' returns on the same basis as the returns from near-future years. In fact, however, near-future returns are worth much more than distant-future returns. Using full-life expected income in this way does not consider the time-value of money.

DISCOUNTED CASH FLOW

The discounted cash flow method, often referred to by other names, such as the "discounted rate of return," or "present value," for analyzing capital equipment investments is commonly, yet not universally, used.

The essence of the discounted cash flow method is simple. All expected costs and all incomes expected to be generated by a project are reduced to their present value and compared. Discounted cash flow, in effect, assumes that all the savings a machine will make in the future are available to the company right now but discounted to their present value. And it assumes that—right now—the company pays fully for the project and for all its future expenses (again discounted to their present value), including repairs and income taxes on the machine's savings. Then the method compares the total to see how profitable the project may be.

Although the discounted cash flow idea is simple, its calculation is somewhat complicated because of the need to express future incomes and outgoes in today's dollars. A second complication comes from the fact that a project's savings are savings only as they are compared to something else (probably to continuing to use a machine the company already owns). A third complication arises when the existing machine will last fewer years than the proposed new one (and this is common). It is really not possible to speak about savings beyond the life of the machines being displaced.

A fourth complication, and a serious one, is that many of the figures needed for discounted cash flow calculations are simply not available. No one knows what the future costs of repairs will be nor how fast tools will wear out and what their replacements will cost. Nor does anyone know how much a project might save in the years ahead. A project's actual "income flow" will depend on business levels and how much time the machine will be used on the various jobs that can be done on it. The lack of solid data on which to base calculations is one reason why on-the-job analysts are less enamored with discounted cash flow than are academicians.

Discounted value in machine economy studies

Discounting puts everything on a current dollar basis. It uses the concept of the present value of money which was explained on page 51. If a company buys a ten-year-life machine today for $10,000, its cost is in 100-cent dollars. During the first year it gets back $1,000 depreciation. (To simplify the problem it will be assumed that the company gets no depreciation money back until the end of the year, and then it gets the whole $1,000.)

Getting $1,000 a year from now is the same as having $952, or $900, or $870, or $833 (or some other figure) now; it depends on the interest rate. Actually businessmen usually use 20, 25 or 30 percent interest in their calculations. These numbers seem high, but things don't always work out well. There are risks. Also, machines may become obsolete before they wear out. And, if new machines save money, there will be more profits, almost half of which will go into income taxes.

Before applying the discounting idea to a problem, it is well to see how the problem works out if no attention is paid to discounting. We will consider two alternatives:

Proposal A	*Proposal B*
1 machine	2 machines
$20,000 installed cost	$10,000 installed cost ($5,000 each)
8 years of life	10 years of life
No scrap value	No scrap value
$5,000 per year to operate, including labor, repairs, and all other items (*but not depreciation*)	$7,000 per year to operate

Since the life of proposal A is only eight years, the comparison will be made only for eight years even though the machines in proposal B will last ten years.

Proposal A		*Proposal B*	
Depreciation in 8 years........	$20,000	Depreciation in 8 years.......	$ 8,000
Operating costs for 8 years....	40,000	Operating costs for 8 years....	56,000
Total cost.................	60,000	Total cost.................	64,000
Average cost per year.........	7,500	Average cost per year.........	8,000

On the basis of this analysis the company should purchase the machine in proposal A rather than the two machines in B. A final decision should wait, though, until the answer obtained from the discounted cash flow method is available.

In using the discounted cash flow method, everything is reduced to today's dollars. Starting with proposal A (see Figure 4–4), we see that this machine is paid for with 20,000 of today's dollars. There is no discount on today's dollars; thus, today's value of this payment is $20,000.

Next, it will cost $5,000 to run the machine for one year. Rather than getting mixed up with some costs coming soon and some coming late within the year, we will assume that none of the $5,000 is paid until the year end and then it is all paid at once. A 20-percent discount rate is used.

Appendix B, page 000, shows precomputed discount figures. Looking at the 20-percent interest column there, we find that $1.000 due to be paid in a year from now—at 20 percent—has a present value of $.833. So $5,000 a year from now is worth today .833 × $5,000, or $4,165.

Similar calculations are carried through for other years. The results are shown in Figure 4–4. The present value of all cash outflows for project A is $39,180, or an average of $4,898 per year. Similar calculations for B show that the present value of its eight-year costs comes to $36,385, or an average of $4,548 per year.

This time the choice is B and by a margin of $350 per year! Yet in our calculation above it looked as if A were better. But that analysis, which

FIGURE 4–4

	A One machine	B Two machines	Discount factor at 20 percent	Present value A	B
First cost................	$20,000	$10,000	1.000	$20,000	$10,000
Operating cost during:					
Year					
1....................	5,000	7,000	0.833	4,165	5,831
2....................	5,000	7,000	0.694	3,470	4,858
3....................	5,000	7,000	0.578	2,890	4,046
4....................	5,000	7,000	0.482	2,410	3,374
5....................	5,000	7,000	0.402	2,010	2,814
6....................	5,000	7,000	0.335	1,675	2,345
7....................	5,000	7,000	0.279	1,395	1,953
8....................	5,000	7,000	0.233	1,165	1,631
Credit for remaining value of machines at end of 8 years...............		2,000	0.233		−467
Total.................				$39,180	$36,385
Average...............				$ 4,898	$ 4,548

used undiscounted dollars, gave too little consideration to the fact that choosing A would require the paying out of $10,000 extra, and right away. The discounted rate of return analysis shows that the company will be better off not to invest that extra money in proposal A—that is, if a 20-percent return is desired. The added investment in proposal A will not produce a 20-percent return.

The actual rate of return

One might ask, however, what rate of return the investment of an extra $10,000 in project A will produce. In our problem, this proves to be 9.3 percent. The method of calculating this actual rate of return requires trial discounting at different rates of return and interpolation. It is worked out in Appendix C.

BOOK VALUE OF OLD MACHINES

Some people see the book value or "sunk costs" of old machines as a problem in machine economy studies. Sunk costs, discussed on page 50, are expenditures already made and not directly recoverable. They embody the effects of past decisions which are irreversible and are, therefore, not relevant to the present decision.

A company may, for example, buy a ten-year-life machine for $20,000, use it for six years, depreciating it on its books at $2,000 a year, and then consider replacing it. The accounts show it still to be worth $8,000. Suppose that it has a value today of $3,000 if sold and that it will probably be worthless in four more years.

At this point there is a proposal to buy a new machine. In the analysis comparing continuing to use the old machine against buying the new one, should the costs of using the old machine include $2,000 of depreciation for each of the next four years? One might say, of course, that this is consistent with what the company has been doing. It is what the government would require for tax purposes if no new machine were bought.

Why even think of not listing $2,000 depreciation every year? The reason is that the machine is actually worth only $3,000, not $8,000. From here on—in machine economy studies—the depreciation every year should be $750 (one fourth of $3,000), not $2,000 (one fourth of $8,000). The past should not be considered with the future, and accounting practices should not be allowed to confuse the issue. Past depreciation charges have, in fact, been too low, and this produces a wrong picture of the future if these past mistakes are carried into machine economy studies.

The hard point to accept is that if a new machine is not bought, the regular depreciation schedule of $2,000 per year carries on, and in four years $8,000 of depreciation is recovered. There seems not to have been a loss of $5,000. Yet, if a new machine is bought and the old one is sold for $3,000, this would establish a $5,000 loss on the company's books. What has happened, though, is that the company has already suffered an unrecognized loss of $5,000. If it does not buy the new machine and it continues to recover $2,000 "depreciation" annually, it is actually recovering $750 of depreciation and $1,250 of unrecognized profits. In the next four years this unrecognized profit will total $5,000 and will offset the $5,000 unrecognized loss that the company has already suffered. Normal depreciation practices cover up all of this, and, since it washes out in the end, it goes unseen.

Writing down the old asset to its present used-machine value makes it hard for a new machine to make a good showing. The old machine's future depreciation is now shown to be very low ($750 in our example instead of $2,000); this holds down the calculated cost of keeping it in operation.

Book life of old machines

Just as the analyst should not use the book value of old machines in machine economy studies, neither should one use book life. If the accounts say that a machine has three more years of life but it now appears that it will last five more years, by all means the five-year figure should be used in the calculation.

BAYESIAN ANALYSES

Bayesian analysis is a method which helps in capital investment decisions by bringing probability into the calculations of expected returns.

A Bayesian analysis allows managers to convert nebulous and vague intuitive judgments into quantitative numbers which can be more precisely analyzed, equated, and compared. The gain is not that the vague judgments converted into numbers are improved, but, assuming that they are the best that can be obtained, the relationships between them can be calculated and not left to further intuitive evaluation.

A brief example will illustrate the method. We will assume that the Cox Company is going to introduce a new product for which it has to build a new addition to its plant. The new product may catch on and sell well, or it may not sell well. If it sells well, the company's managers would like to have built a large addition. But, if sales prove to be low, they would prefer to have built only a small addition. The monetary consequences of these actions are:

FIGURE 4–5

Profit prospects (thousands of dollars)

	Sales	
Plant addition	High	Low
Large...........	+280	−180
Small...........	+ 70	− 20

At this point it is not at all clear what Cox's managers should do. Here is where it is necessary to bring the managers' intuitive ideas of probability into play.

Suppose that they decide that there is a 30-percent chance of high sales and a 70-percent chance of low sales. The next step, therefore, is to multiply the +280 possible profits from a large addition by .30 to get +84 and the −180 possible loss from a large addition by .70 to get −126. Summing up: +84 + (−126) = −42. Doing the same for the small addition: +70 × .30 = +21; −20 × .70 = −14. +21 + (−14) = +7.

The choice is now clear as between these particular choices. If the 30–70-percent probability figures are reasonable, the large addition has an "expected monetary value" of −$42,000 and the small addition of +$7,000. At these probabilities, the small addition is the choice.

The "expected monetary value" is not a forecast of the probable results but is rather the expected average result which would occur if the managers faced 100 identical problems and chose the small addition each time. Although it is true that managers do not get to make 100 such decisions and so average out, this is still the most logical choice to make, given the information available, even for one choice.

Bayesian analyses in actual practice are, of course, far more complex than is our simple example and would include more alternatives.

DECISION TREES

When a person comes to a Y in the road, he has to choose which branch to take. Having chosen one, it opens up a whole set of possibilities while cutting off another set. And, having chosen one road and pursuing it for a distance, he comes to another Y. Again he has to choose, and again he opens up certain possibilities while closing off others.

Managers of organizations often have to make similar decisions. As they look ahead for a given time, they see that they have to make a choice, and, having made it, they open up certain future possibilities while at the same time closing off other possibilities. And, having gone down the selected road, other choices have to be made again and still again.

FIGURE 4–6

Decision tree model

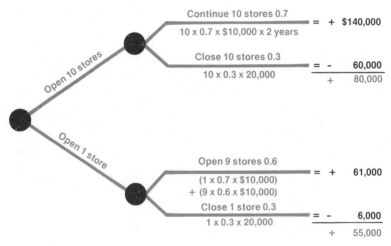

If the possibilities were depicted graphically, they would look like Figure 4–6. Starting from a single point on the left, the lines branch out and split into numerous lines on the right, hence the name, "decision tree."

To be useful in decision making, a decision tree needs to have the projected payoffs for each end-line as well as the probabilities of each one occurring set along each end-branch of the tree.

To illustrate, we might picture McDonald's considering going into a new area with its fast food stores. Its managers are considering putting in one store to try out the area, or putting in ten stores, the number which they believe the area really should have. In either case, after one year, they plan to review the situation. If they start with one store, they will either open up nine more and go up to ten or they will close the one. If they start with ten, they will either continue them all or close out all of them.

Figure 4–6 depicts these choices as a decision tree which is extended out for two years. The payout estimates, the probability estimates, and the calculations are shown along the lines.

We will say that McDonald's has decided that a return of $10,000 per year per store is satisfactory. Less return would mean that McDonald's could invest its money better elsewhere, but it would cost $20,000 per store in loss for each store closed up. The managers estimate that there is a 70-percent chance of the new stores coming up to the $10,000 desired return objective; except that if they start with only one store and go up to ten a year later, the chances are only 60 percent because competition may become better established within the first year.

The calculations are indicated in Figure 4–6. They show that, on a two-year calculation basis, that McDonald's should open up all ten stores right away. At the end of two years its expected profits will be $25,000 greater than if one store were opened first and then nine more added later.

REVIEW QUESTIONS

1. Who in an organization should normally see the need for a capital expenditure project and so originate a request?
2. What is a company's "cash flow"? What is it made of? How is it related to capital expenditures?
3. Why is depreciation important in a company's capital investment program?
4. Explain the most commonly used depreciation methods. Which recover the investment the quickest? Which the slowest?
5. How do the return on investment and payback methods differ from each other?
6. Explain how the discounted cash flow method operates.
7. Explain how the "expected monetary value" column in a Bayesian analysis is arrived at. How is it used?
8. How do decision trees differ from Bayesian analyses? When would a decision tree probably be better?

QUESTIONS FOR DISCUSSION

1. What good does it do to have divisional and central office staff groups study machinery buying proposals carefully? How can they, 1,000 miles away, tell if the proposals are sound or not?
2. Division heads know their new machine needs best. Why not let them have the final say on what they get?
3. The employees have been complaining about poor locker room facili-

ties. Explain how to calculate the rate of return on the prospective investment required to modernize these facilities.

4. Should the analyst always, sometimes, or never include overhead and sales and administrative costs in the calculation of break-even points for individual projects, such as one machine? Why? If sometimes, when and why?

5. Some people say that it is impossible for a company to increase its cash account in years when it loses money. Can it? Explain.

6. Will using the sum-of-the-years' digits depreciation method instead of straight-line depreciation give a company more or less protection against inflation? (This relates to the matter of normal depreciation providing inadequate funds to buy replacement machines.)

7. How can sum-of-the-years' digits depreciation be handled by a company using group depreciation?

8. The text says to mechanize if the figures show it to be a toss-up so far as saving money is concerned. What justification is given? Is this sound? Discuss.

9. Do income taxes encourage or discourage the making of capital investments? Why?

10. Calculating the rate of return by comparing a new method to an existing method makes the new method look good or bad, depending on how bad the old method was. How can the badness of the old method properly have anything to do with the goodness of a new method? Why not do away with comparisons to the past and calculate the absolute rate of return on new proposals?

11. "The future's not ours to see." Try to forecast the number of miles you will drive your car next year and the amount you will spend on gasoline and repair bills. What is the good of trying to forecast a machine's productivity and operating costs?

12. Some people say that in cost saving calculations made when comparing new machines with old machines, the prospective loss in book value of old machines to be discarded if a new machine is bought should be disregarded. Do you agree or disagree? Why?

13. Aren't decision trees rather worthless in that the organization finally ends up going down one and only one path? What good does it do to know all about what might have been?

PROBLEMS

1. Suppose that $500,000 is available for investment in capital projects. Which projects from among the following shall be chosen?

a. Which projects should be chosen and what would be the average rate of return?

b. In this solution has any project been selected which has a lower return than any omitted project? If so, what would be the effective rate of the high-return project if it were put into the list of approvals at the expense of dropping a project to make room for it?

Project	Capital requirement	Expected rate of return
A........................	$300,000	18%
B........................	50,000	25
C........................	350,000	15
D........................	175,000	15
E........................	100,000	20
F........................	100,000	30
G........................	Invest excess in 5% bonds	5

c. If the company could borrow $50,000 more at 15 percent, should this be done? What projects should be approved, and what would their average rate of return be? (Do not forget the interest charge as an offset to the income.)

2. A company buys a machine for $6,000 and uses a 20-percent declining balance method of depreciation. Maintenance costs are expected to be $300 in each of the first two years and then to go up annually as follows: $500, $700, $1,000, $1,400, $1,900, $2,500. When should this machine be replaced?

3. Some years ago TRW bought a Warner & Swasey lathe for $18,000. It was depreciated on a 12-year basis. Last year, at the close of the 12th year, it was fully depreciated on TRW's books and the $18,000 had been recovered. The lathe, although practically worn out, still had a resale value of $2,000.

A replacement lathe to do the same work is priced at $34,000, but, since today's work is more exacting, the proper lathe to buy (attachments included) costs $48,000.

If, over the 12 years, the depreciation cash had been put to work each year earning 15 percent and if income taxes were 50 percent of profits:

a. How much extra money would TRW now have to find in order to replace the machine with the $48,000 machine?

b. How much extra sales would it have taken to generate this extra amount of money (TRW would get a pretax profit of 20 percent of the sales price on these products)?

c. Suggest a solution to the problem that TRW faces.

4. Compare the following two alternatives:

	Machine A	Machine B
Installed cost................	$8,500	$14,000
Estimated life................	10 years	12 years
Salvage value at end of estimated life........................	$2,500	$ 1,000
Annual operating cost..........	$3,500	$ 2,000
Interest cost.................	15%	15%

a. Using first-year costs only, which investment is better?

b. Is the answer to (a) influenced by the depreciation method used? Show the figures for straight-line, sum-of-the-years' digits, and declining balance methods for the first year.

5. The question is whether to replace an existing machine with a new machine. The new machine will cost $12,000 and will have an expected life of 12 years, with an expected salvage value of $1,500 at the end of 12 years. This machine will recover its straight-line depreciation each year, and when compared to using the old machine will show a $2,500 pretax savings besides. The company is in the 50 percent tax bracket and can earn 15 percent (pretax) on alternative investments.

Should this machine be bought, and, if it should, what is its payback period?

6. Because of the lack of sensitivity of the weigher, a company's automatic coffee can-filling machine is set to put 16¼ ounces of coffee into the cans so that no can will contain less than 16 ounces.

This weigher cost $3,000 five years ago and ought to last for ten more years. The machinery salesman offers a new, more sensitive weigher which could be set at 16⅛ ounces. He will allow a $400 trade-in on the old weigher against the new machine's purchase price of $8,000. The new machine ought to last ten years. Neither it nor the present weigher will have any final salvage value. Coffee costs $1.60 a pound. Interest is 10 percent.

How many 1-pound cans of coffee must be sold per year to pay for the new weigher?

7. Assume the following data:

Cost of a new tool	$800
Expected life of new tool	5 years
Interest rate on invested funds	10 percent
Insurance and repairs per year	$80
Number of times used per year	10
Setup cost per time used	$10
Estimated labor cost savings per unit from using new tool	$.05
Increased material cost per unit	$.015

Using the first-year performance method:

a. Compute the volume required to break even (include a savings in overhead at 100 percent of direct labor).

b. What would the break-even volume be if the overhead savings were omitted?

c. What would the true break-even point probably be?

8. A heavy duty ten-ton truck can be bought for $15,000. It should last eight years, at which time its salvage value ought to be $2,000. Maintenance will probably cost $1,200 a year. Besides these costs there are other costs, exclusive of the driver, of $30 a day. A similar truck can be rented for $55 a day (without a driver). Interest is 10 percent. How many days a year will the truck have to be used in order to justify buying instead of renting one?

9. There are two proposals for making new products. Method A equipment costs $250,000, will last 10 years, and will have a salvage value of

$25,000. Method B equipment costs $450,000, will last 15 years, and is expected to have a salvage value of $45,000. Each method should produce a $150,000 annual revenue.

Besides the original investment, method A will cost $90,000 a year. Method B has annual added costs of $60,000. The company wants to get 15 percent on this kind of project.

    a. How big a rate of return will method A yield?
    b. How big a rate of return will method B yield?
    c. What rate of return will the extra investment in B yield?

10. According to Bayesian analysis, which action will be best in the following case? An all-out cost reduction program will produce a gain of $500,000 if it is highly successful, $200,000 if it is moderately successful, or will lose $100,000 if it works out poorly. A less extensive program would produce $250,000 or $75,000, or lose $25,000. On a business-as-usual basis, the prospects are $100,000, $25,000, and 0. The chances of excellent results are .30, mediocre results, .55, and poor results, .15. Which action should be taken?

CASE 4-1

The Fry Company has been considering several capital investment projects on which various rates of return appear to be in prospect. The accountant who has prepared the figures has been careful to point out that the anticipated returns have been reduced to half because of income taxes. (If projects save money, presumably it will show up as a profit and be taxed at 50 percent.)

There has been a question about how to evaluate the cost of borrowed capital. The bank will lend money at 8 percent. The accountant carried this cost in the calculations at the full 8 percent. This had the effect of reducing the effective rate to 4 percent since, if the company were to use its own money, the whole 8 percent would show up in profits and be taxed at 50 percent. Since this is the normal situation, it is therefore customary to regard the true cost of borrowed capital as half of the stated interest rate.

The Fry Company has earned no profits during the last two years and therefore has paid no income taxes. The question the president raised with his accountant is about this matter of considering the interest on borrowed money as costing only half of its actual rate, considering the fact that Fry is currently paying no income taxes.

The president saw even more to this problem, however. He asked: "If it is proper to say that costs associated with capital equipment invest-ments ought to be thought of as costing only half because of income taxes, then why should we not say the same about labor and materials? These costs, too, are deductible for tax purposes, so let's consider them to have a net cost of only half of their actual cost.

There seems to be some kind of a problem here. What is it? Is there usually something wrong in considering interest to cost only half of its rate? What *is* the true interest rate?

CASE 4–2

The Daisy Company has asked for a review of its practice of making its own gunstocks (the part of the gun which fits against the shoulder) out of wood or whether it should buy gunstocks made out of plastic. Historically, all were made from wood and all were made by Daisy. In recent years cheaper plastic gunstocks have become available and have been used in increasing number on low-price BB guns.

Daisy figured that it made a $.30 profit on each wooden gunstock it made and $.10 on each plastic gunstock it bought. The volume of purchased plastic gunstocks has grown to 1 million a year. It is expected that this volume will grow steadily to 2 million in five years and hold steady at that level for the next five years. This analysis is to concern only the next ten years.

Daisy is considering several choices: (1) continuing the present practice and buying all plastic gunstocks, (2) continuing to buy for five years and then change to making, (3) buying enough plastic-making equipment to make 1 million gunstocks a year, (4) after five years expanding this plastics operation to an annual capacity of 2 million gunstocks.

Alternative 2 will require an investment at the end of five years of $3 million, which will have to be written off in the next five years. There is a 20-percent chance that operating costs will be $2 million in the first year and $600,000 per year for the last four years. There is an 80-percent chance that first-year operating costs will be $1.2 million, and $600,000 per year for the last four years.

Alternative 3 will require the immediate purchase of $2 million worth of equipment (which will be worthless at the end of ten years). There is a 75-percent chance that the first year's operating costs will be $1.5 million and $700,000 a year for the remaining nine years. There is a 25-percent chance that operating costs will be $1.2 million the first year, and $600,000 a year for the remaining nine years.

Alternative 4 will cost another $1 million at the start of the sixth year. Additional operating costs associated with operating the expanded operations have a 60-percent chance of being $700,000 a year for all five remaining years and a 40-percent chance of being $500,000 a year.

What should Daisy do? Why? What profits prospects do the various alternatives offer?

SUGGESTED SUPPLEMENTARY READINGS

Dyckman, T. E., and Kinard, J. C. "The Discounted Cash Flow Criterion Investment Decision Model with Accounting Income Constraints." *Decision Sciences,* July 1973, pp. 301–13.

Petry, G. H. "Effective Use of Capital Budgeting Tools." *Business Horizons,* October 1975, pp. 57–65.

Powers, W. J. "How Government Policies Affect Capital Investments." *Nation's Business,* November 1975, p. 67.

section two

DESIGNING OUTPUTS

NEW PRODUCTS and new ways to serve people are being developed continually. Neither the managers of factories or service organizations can safely rest on their present products or methods of serving for their organizations' future well-being.

It is necessary to put resources into searching for new and better ways of doing things so that one's own company, rather than a competitor, will bring out the new product or introduce the new way of serving that will someday replace today's products and service methods.

Research and development, the subject of Chapter 5, differs from most of the other subjects in this book in that the work being discussed is not production in the usual sense. Often the end product is more knowledge. And sometimes it is not obvious how this new knowledge can be incorporated into the organization's products or services. Chapter 5 considers research as the searching for new knowledge. Then the discussion turns to development, the means by which this knowledge is incorporated into improved products.

Development shades off into product design, the subject of Chapter 6. Designers, however, have to be more practical and earthier people than researchers. They have to work within two very important constraints. First, they have to consider customers and what the customers want and what they don't want. And second, there is always a cost limitation. Products must not cost too much, or else they will not sell.

In addition to these two constraints which engineers have always had to be concerned with, there is one more, and, where it applies, it is of overriding importance. This is the need to comply with all laws and obligations to protect consumers and to meet all antipollution standards.

Besides these operating constraints, designers are concerned with such technical matters as explaining their designs to the factory (by means of drawings, specifications, and tolerances) and standardization and simplification.

5

Research and product development

ALL ORGANIZATIONS have purposes. They try to make and sell products or to render certain services. Business organizations have to be ever alert to see that the design of the products and the kind of service they render are what customers want, lest they lose their customers and go bankrupt. Public organizations such as government agencies also try to carry out their missions so as best to serve the public. One of the most important of all managerial functions in all kinds of organizations is to see that the inputs of the organization's resources result in properly designed products and services, or "outputs," which suit the customers' desires.

Products and services come into existence because someone believes that there is need either for a product which no one is making or a service which no one offers or which has been costing too much. In fact, this is the way, some day in the past, today's products and services came into existence. Someone, at some time in the past, saw a need and moved to fill it.

Managerial imagination is usually needed because opportunities are often not readily apparent. Ten years ago, Kentucky Fried Chicken uncovered an enormous market for prepared food that no one realized existed. And it took years of greater and greater sales in the United States of small foreign compact cars to convince Detroit that a great many Americans wanted small cars. The managers of America's automobile companies just did not believe that very many Americans wanted small cars. They let Volkswagen and Toyota sell millions of cars. Then, paradoxically, in 1976 when Detroit gave in and supplied small cars in variety and quantity, the American public opted for bigger cars again.

So it is that managers need always to be on the lookout for new products and new services which they might provide. One need only to walk through a department store to imagine how much effort goes into the design of new products and the redesign of old products. Similarly, one has only to open the yellow pages of the telephone book to see the broad array of services which have been developed to meet our every need.

The first part of this chapter will deal with designing products, while the latter part will consider matters relating to the development of services.

RESEARCH AND DEVELOPMENT

Everything in old movies looks out of date because it is out of date. Old products are continually being redesigned, and new products are continually being developed.

Research has produced the scientific knowledge that lies behind the development of television, jet airplanes, electronic computers, seawater desalting plants, nylon stockings, wonder drugs, insecticides, nuclear power plants, laser beams, microcomputers, videodiscs, and thousands of other things. And today a great deal of research effort is being directed at solving air and water pollution problems, product safety problems, and health services.

Research payoffs

The bloom is off the rose, however, so far as big quick payoffs are concerned. New discoveries and innovations are harder to come by, even though occasionally there is a new major scientific breakthrough which creates whole new products which have substantial impacts on existing products, possibly making them obsolete overnight.

But, even in these cases, competition usually holds profits down to nominal amounts. Hand-held pocket-sized calculators for under $20 drove older type desk-top mechanical calculators off the market in only two or three years. Then the competition among the little calculator makers themselves drove almost all of them out of business.

Acrylic-type fibers have taken away most of wool's former near monopoly in carpets. And today most of the clothes we wear are made almost wholly from synthetic fibers and not from cotton or wool. All of these innovations have come out of research; yet, because of competition, the makers of these products have earned only nominal profits.

Product design improvements growing out of research
in microcomputers

But even though bonanza payoffs from research are now rare, further improvements continue to be made all the time. One of the most important in the 1970s was developments in microcomputer technology.

Figure 5–1 shows a greatly magnified "chip" (sometimes called a "computer on a chip") which contains memory and logic units, transistors, diodes, and electrical circuitry, all so small that the whole chip could be covered by only four of the grains of salt which are shown, also greatly magnified, in Figure 5–1, lying around the chip. Such a chip will perform work formerly done by equipment bigger than desk size. Yet these chips will soon be mass produced and will sell for only a few dollars apiece.

Microcomputer technology is already being adapted to uses which many people would feel is quite far out. Some of these applications have been made by newly established small companies by scientists and engineers

FIGURE 5–1

A microcomputer chip with its circuits etched on compared to grains of salt, indicating the extent of miniaturization

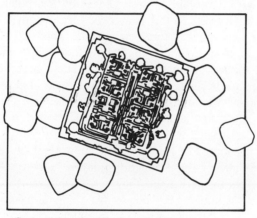

Source: International Business Machines.

who saw new application possibilities.[1] Thematic Corporation, a new small company, has introduced an advanced and very fast new blood-chemistry analyzer. Telesensory Systems, another small new company, has introduced a talking calculator for the blind. It can receive a limited number of verbal instructions, and it reports results verbally.

Microcomputers are expected to become common in the late 1970s as they replace electromechanical control systems in such home appliances as ovens, refrigerators, dishwashers, and washing machines. Already they are being used to keep scores in bowling alleys and to measure out drinks in bars as well as to control liquor inventories. In automobiles, their introduction will probably eliminate sparkplugs and other electrical circuitry

---

[1] A number of unusual applications of recent microcomputer advances are described in "Here Comes the Second Computer Revolution," *Fortune,* November 1975, pp. 138 ff.

and make hard winter starting and engine tune-ups a thing of the past. Ford Motor reports that microcomputer controls can add 20 percent to gasoline mileage.

And, although electronic controls of large complex machinery are not new, they are becoming more sophisticated and are replacing machine operators' judgments. In some cases this reduces the years of training formerly needed to develop skilled machine operators and allows less skilled people to operate the machines.

SOURCES OF IDEAS

Although research provides the base from which new innovative applications can be developed, innovative ideas come from many sources rather than just from researchers. Marketing people see the need for something their customers want. Production people see opportunities to improve methods and processes. Everyone in an organization is a potential source of ideas. In order to try to tap this source of ideas, many firms try to generate a creative environment for their people. They tell them about technical advances and ask for ideas about how they can be incorporated into products and services. And they tell them about areas where new products or services are needed. Often they have suggestion systems and give awards for worthwhile improvement suggestions.

Sometimes new products and services are developed by individual people who are not associated with any company at all. Most of us never become aware of this source of ideas because most small-scale inventors have neither the capital nor the production nor the marketing know-how to bring their products to market. So they sell their ideas to companies, something which is not hard to do, since most companies are always on the lookout to buy the rights to marketable innovations.

Developing a climate favorable to innovation

In spite of what has just been said, however, a great deal of innovation comes from researchers. Other employees have their regular work to do and don't get to spend much time innovating. The desirable "creative environment" which can be so helpful can have the most far-reaching effects if it exists in the research area itself. *Business Week* describes the practice at 3M (formerly Minnesota Mining and Manufacturing) as follows:[2]

> At 3M, a researcher who prefers to get lost in a lab can spend his career there and be well rewarded for his work, but the ambitious inventor is free to move on. Managers are always promoted from within, and promotions are frequent. It is just as common for inventors as it is

---

[2] "How Ideas Are Made into Products at 3M," *Business Week*, September 15, 1973, pp. 224–27.

for marketing and production men to ride upstairs with their products, to become product managers, then heads of departments, and keep going from there. . . .

One such inventor, A. G. Bush, the father of Scotch tape, went on to become chairman of 3M. . . . When an engineer conceives a product, he is encouraged to make a prototype before discussing it with his superiors. Then, if he really does have something, he, the engineer-inventor becomes part, and often the leader, of a development team. (The team also usually includes a production man, and—at this early stage of a product's life—a marketing expert.) If the product continues to show promise, the division can authorize a pilot production run. Only in the next phase, where higher production and test marketing begins, do officers at the group and corporate levels become involved.

The research climate at 3M allows engineers and inventors to go out on a limb without being afraid of damaging their careers or losing their jobs. One idea, an attempt to farm oysters under controlled conditions, failed miserably, but no one was criticized for trying to develop the idea. It was not known to be a failure until it was tried out.

Some innovative products are of the "Why didn't I think of that?" kind. For example, years ago, lacing up and later unlacing ski boots was a tiring and bothersome job. Then someone invented the buckle boot and so changed the whole ski boot industry. Similarly, McDonald's and Kentucky Fried Chicken perceived that people wanted simple foods served quickly and at low prices. The result has been the billion dollar fast foods industry.

Probably very few people ever thought that they needed an electric toothbrush, or a hot lather dispenser, or an electric carving knife, or a telephone answering service. But, when given a chance to buy them, millions of people bought. Imagination often pays off in product creation and service improvement.

RESEARCH RISKS

Only after the research on a project is done and money spent on it can it begin to save money or produce income. RCA had $50 million invested in color TV before its color sets reached the American living room and had $125 million invested in it before it began to pay off.

Currently, RCA, Holland's Philips, MCA, and other electronic firms have invested over $200 million in developmental costs for "videodiscs." (A videodisc is a victrola record-like disc on which a half-hour of a movie has been recorded. Played on a record player connected to a television set, the movie, sound, color, and all comes out through the TV set.)

While color TV has certainly paid off for RCA and the whole TV industry, enthusiasts for videodiscs think that the payoffs here could be even more. They think that the sales of videodiscs could reach half a billion dollars annually by 1980 while the sales of accompanying accessory items might amount to half as much more.

Unfortunately, research does not always pay off. Du Pont spent $25 million over 25 years developing Corfam (artificial leather) before putting it on the market in 1964. Six years later, after losing $100 million on Corfam, Du Pont stopped making it. Polaroid spent over $350 million on its SX–70 camera, but initial sales were much less than expected.[3] Later on, after price cuts, SX–70 sales improved. General Motors developed and successfully tested a new gas-turbine truck engine and had firm orders for a substantial number of these engines from Greyhound Bus Lines. Yet GM backed off from starting into mass production because of its expected $200 million start-up costs.[4]

Unfortunately, risks are not always limited to the research expenditures themselves. If a company does not do research, it risks losing out to its researching competitors.

The dilemma is even worse, however, because competition is inter-industry. Plastics have taken over part of paper's position in wrappings. And paper has taken away part of wood's market for containers. Nuclear power plants are cutting in on coal in electric-power generating plants, and perhaps some day solar heaters will cut into the sales of furnace manufacturers as well as the business of heating oil and natural gas suppliers.

Probably the biggest risk in research lies in the high mortality rate of research projects. RCA estimates that 90 percent of its research ideas are useless. Du Pont reports that one third of its chemical research projects prove unfeasible while still in the laboratory. And even after succeeding in the laboratory, most of the rest prove impractical in production and in the marketplace, as was the case with Polaroid's SX–70 camera until extensive changes were made in its production processes.

Even technical successes sometimes go sour. Plastic pipe, made from vinyl, styrene, and polyethylene, grew from nothing to a $100 million a year business some years ago. Plastic pipe was a great success, but everybody got into the act. Within a few years, none of the 80 manufacturers of plastic pipe was making much money out of it because of price competition. Similar experiences occurred in the mid-1970s in the hand-held calculator industry.

Yet, since everyone knows that research payoffs are hazardous and that few projects pay off, one might ask why do almost all companies of any size carry on research. Aside from having to research in order to keep up, it is still true that some of the successes pay for themselves several times over. In general and in total, research usually pays off.

Furthermore, if a company does not do research, then income taxes will take nearly 50 percent of its profit dollars—nearly half of what is left over

---

[3] "The SX–70 Camera Deglamorizes Polaroid," *Business Week,* November 30, 1974, p. 90.
[4] "Why the Turbine Engine Stalled at GM," *Business Week,* August 25, 1975, pp. 40–44.

—so tax savings pay for almost 50 percent or more of research costs. The question is not, "Is research worth its cost?" but, "Is research worth 50 percent of its cost (or less if some of the retained earnings would have been paid out in dividends)?"

DESIGN BY IMITATION

The first firm to bring a new product to the marketplace almost always has an advantage from being first. But, at the same time, this company is exposed to a new risk, and that is that a later entering company will imitate the product, or, worse yet, improve upon it and possibly capture a large share of the market.

In fact, the greatest "newness" in many companies' products come not from innovation but from imitation. This is only natural since a company cannot possibly be first with everything new in its industry. Part of most companies' product development programs is usually directed at developing imitative equivalents of someone else's successful products. Procter & Gamble brought out its Puff facial tissues only after Kimberly Clark's Kleenex and Scott Paper's Scotties had proven to be successful.

Sometimes imitative design is done through "reverse engineering." A competitor simply buys a product, takes it apart to see how it works and how it is made, and then makes its own almost alike product. Russian automobiles and airplanes are usually almost carbon copies of certain specific automobiles and airplanes made by Western nations.

Also, and unfortunately, there have been cases where designs have been shamelessly stolen through "industrial espionage," or by employees who quit and then join a competing company, or who start their own company, where they use product designs or processes developed by their former employing company.

Most imitative product development is, however, aboveboard. No automobile is remarkably different from another, and no refrigerator is wholly unlike others. Competing companies are largely just trying to do the same job a little better than their competitors.

Companies which adopt imitation as a policy can sometimes be the "second with the most." It is true that imitators start a step behind, but often they can move faster than the original innovator since they have his designs and market success to look at. In the 1950s Sperry Rand had the first computers, but IBM soon had most of the market. In the 1960s, 3M's Thermofax method unearthed the big paper-copying market (which A. B. Dick's mimeograph had never revealed), but then Xerox moved in and took it away. Now IBM and Kodak are threatening Xerox with their new copiers just as Kodak is threatening Poloroid with its new instant camera.

The obvious gain from following instead of innovating is the saving of research and development money that the leaders spend on failures and on debugging their new products. Yet, this saving is made at the risk that an early start will pay off well and quickly and generate a permanent lead.

The imitators of Procter & Gamble's Pampers have, none of them, been able to dislodge P & G from its leading position in disposable diapers.

PRODUCT LIFE CYCLES

Most new products that are offered to the public go through a life cycle. First, when products are very new, they do not always work very well, and they are high priced. Only the venturesome consumer buys at this stage. The market for the product has to be developed. Next comes the second stage: The product is improved and standardized, becomes dependable in use and lower in price, and consumers buy it with little urging. It sells in much larger quantities as it comes into common use.

In the third stage, the product is mature, dependable in performance, reasonably priced, and does not change much from year to year. Sales volume may even fall off because everybody now owns one so sales are largely dependent on replacements or on population gains. Automobiles, radios, television sets, and kitchen appliances all have gone through these stages. Industries based on important innovations seem to take up to 30 years to reach maturity although the pace is sometimes quicker, as has recently occurred in the cases of semiconductors and microcomputers.

Finally, most products come to a fourth stage, the decline in demand. They are supplanted by new products. Admittedly, this does not happen to all products. Knives and forks have been around for a long time as have been scissors and paper clips. Nor have newer products, electric carving knives and electric scissors displaced them. Nonetheless, because

FIGURE 5–2

Typical product life cycle

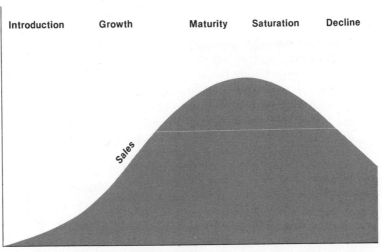

so many products keep coming to the end of the line, companies have to work continually at developing new products to take their places.

Merck Company reports that, as a normal thing, 70 percent of its pharmaceutical sales come from products introduced within the last ten years. And, year after year, RCA consistently gets 80 percent of its sales from products introduced in the preceding ten years. It is little wonder that so many companies spend so much on research and development.

Sometimes products go on the market too soon. Often it takes from three to five years or more to perfect complicated products—to get all the bugs out—but venturesome customers don't want to wait. Customers hear about new things and how they will help them with their problems so they want them right away—even before they are fully developed.

International Business Machines always has orders for new designs of computers before they are fully engineered and long before they go into production. (This has, in fact, caused problems for IBM. IBM's competitors have complained that IBM competes unfairly by "leaking' information about new products ahead of time so that the customers will wait for IBM's next model instead of buying the competitor's currently available computer.)

But is it too soon, after all, to go to market with an incompletely engineered product? Actually no product is ever fully engineered. It just is not possible to wait until a product is perfect before starting to sell it. Sewing machines have been with us for over 100 years, and even telephones are now 100 years old, but they keep changing for the better. And the automobiles and airplanes of 50 years ago were, by today's standards, crude and not well engineered. But they were produced and sold, and they rendered good service to the buyers. Generally firms should not wait for final permanent designs before they offer their products to the public, so long as they provide reasonable value and are safe to use.

The important question is: When is a product well enough developed to sell it? Somewhere along the line it should be offered for sale, and, at this point, its design has to be "frozen"—so far as manufacturing is concerned—long enough to allow production to proceed. Engineers rarely get to do as much design perfecting as they would like before their product goes to market. They do get their chance, however, to make further improvements as new models are introduced later on.

MATERIALS DECISIONS

In many cases designers can choose from among different materials to use. Just as a carpet can be made of wool, cotton, flax, rayon, nylon, or other synthetics, so can industrial products be made from different materials. A gear can be made from steel, iron, brass, aluminum, nylon, or other plastics. Wrapping and covering materials can be made of cloth, leather, paper, or hard or soft plastics.

In making the choice from among the possibilities, the designer needs always to keep in mind (a) the performance requirements of the product or part, (b) the relative material costs, and (c) the relative processing costs.

Often, since each of the alternative materials will perform well, the real choice depends on the relative costs of the materials and on their processing costs. And by no means does the low cost material always win out. Many small metal parts, for example, are made out of copper or brass instead of steel—even though steel costs less than one tenth as much per pound—because copper and brass can be machined so quickly that their processing costs are far less. Similarly, in spite of its costing at least five times as much as steel per pound, zinc is often used for small intricately molded parts because it works so well in die casting, which is a low-cost way of making high-volume intricate items. (Today, however, zinc is losing out to molded plastics because plastic materials now cost less and can be die-cast even more readily than zinc.)

When materials contribute to a product's final appearance, the designer can sometimes have the better of two worlds. A walnut cabinet makes an attractive television set, but walnut is very costly and is not as durable as steel. Today, however, very low-cost and very realistic simulated vinyl coatings can be put on metal surfaces. The television set can be made of durable steel yet have an attractive simulated walnut finish.

The decision of what material to use is usually an enduring one but not always. If the price of one metal goes up and that of the alternative comes down, it may become economical to reverse the choice. In its early days, plastics cost too much for general use, but now, since their costs have come down, plastics compete successfully with various metals. Similarly, in the mid-1970s, when the third-world raw materials producing countries raised the price of copper, many users turned to aluminum.

The choice is sometimes related to the prospective volume. For low volume, costly but easily worked raw materials are often the best. Small low-cost general purpose machines can handle easily worked material such as brass or bronze, but they are not very economical for working hard materials such as steel. For high volumes, on the other hand, expensive machines can handle hard-to-work materials economically. A purchasing department should always be alert to price and volume changes which might justify changing materials.

VALUE ENGINEERING AND VALUE ANALYSIS

Value engineering (usually done by design engineers) or value analysis (usually done by the purchasing department) means that everything that is made or bought is thought of as being made or bought to serve a purpose. Before deciding to make or buy parts, if substantial amounts of money are involved, engineers and buyers should consider what purpose these parts serve. Would another lower-cost design work as well? Could another less costly item fill the need? Would less expensive material do the job? And, on purchased items, are the vendors' prices as low as they could be?

In a great many cases there are different ways of getting work done. If two parts have to be fastened together, the design engineer should not think first of how to design a low-cost bolt. Rather, he should think first about making the two pieces as one. If this cannot be done economically, then he might consider riveting the pieces together, or welding or gluing them, or making the parts interlock like pieces of a jigsaw puzzle. If he still thinks that a screw or bolt is the best solution, then—and only then —should he consider the bolt's size and shape and whether it should be made inside or bought.

Design engineers also need to be conscious of trade-offs. Silver wire, for example, conducts electricity better than copper, but it is rarely used in place of copper because it costs over 100 times as much per pound. Silver's extra conductivity is not sufficient to offset copper's lower price, unless the weight saved from being able to use thinner wires, as well as extra reliability, is extremely important as, for example, in a spaceship's electrical system.

Sometimes value analysis has to step into the background and give way to other considerations. In the early 1970s, automobile designers had to redesign automobile bumpers. Until then, bumpers had been made as low-cost items and were made from relatively thin steel. They were more for looks than for use and were actually largely ineffective as protection devices.

Then new laws intended to provide the public with greater safety were passed. These laws, plus concern by consumer groups about the high cost of repairing the damage caused by minor front-end accidents, made it necessary for the companies to redesign the bumpers and to build more protection and durability into them even though at a higher cost and at a higher price to consumers. Value analysis was overruled.

Value analysis, particularly in purchasing, sometimes saves considerable money rather than just minor amounts. At General Electric, a screw of special design had been costing 15¢, but value analysis found a way to make it for 1.5¢, producing annual savings of $20,000. A hand-made gasket, costing $4.15 each at GE, was found to cost 15¢ when bought from an outside gasket maker. General Motors' Frigidaire division reported this savings: For aluminum doors bought for an evaporator, three vendor quotations ranged from $2.40 to $2.70. Frigidaire's estimate of what it should pay was $2.05. The final price was $2.10, for annual savings of $27,000.

Both engineers and purchasing people should try to avoid setting unnecessarily high specifications. In one plant the purchasing agent found that its engineers had specified that certain parts be made to very exact measurements—although the parts were later enameled before they were used. After enameling, the measurements were much less exact, but the parts were still quite suitable for the purpose. Loosening the part's dimension tolerances cut the purchase price. Before this the company had not been getting full value for its money since it had been paying for a close fit which it did not need and actually did not get in the finished part.

In spite of what has just been said, there are times when value analysis should *not* be used. A man can use a paper clip to hold his necktie instead of a $5 tie clip, and it would do the job satisfactorily. Buttons can be used in place of cuff links. Where esthetics and price economy clash, designers and buyers need to decide which should rule. Value analysis generally focuses on function, not on esthetics.

THE METRIC SYSTEM AND PRODUCT DESIGN

Within a few years, Americans will probably adopt the metric system. It will take some getting used to. The milkman will leave a one-liter bottle of milk (1.05 quarts), and a husband may be asked to buy 450 grams (1 pound) of hamburger on his way home for supper where his wife, size 91–72–91 centimeters (36–28–36 inches), will greet him. When the customer at the gas station says, "Fill 'er up," he may end up buying 60 liters of gasoline (15.8 gallons). And the air pressure in his tires ought to be kept up to 12.7 kilograms (28 pounds).

When a man steps on a scale he will find that he weighs 68 kilograms instead of 150 pounds. Instead of being 6 feet tall, he will be 1.83 meters tall. Pike's Peak in Colorado will be 4,301 meters high instead of 14,110 feet. And an 8½ x 11 inch sheet of paper will be 21.6 x 27.9 centimeters.

A city lot 60 x 150 feet will become 18.29 x 54.86 meters. A farmer who used to own 200 acres of land will have 81 hectacres. Whereas it used to be 10 miles to town, it will become 16.1 kilometers. The speed limit will be 86 kilometers an hour instead of 55 miles per hour. And the distance from New York to Chicago will change from 840 miles to 1,351 kilometers.

Summers may seem cooler, though, when the thermometer gets up to only 35 degrees (centigrade) instead of 95 degrees (Fahrenheit). Winters may, however, seem colder. Instead of 14 degrees above zero, the thermometer will show 10 degrees below.

It all sounds confusing to an American's ear, but the changeover is already slowly underway. It may be comforting, however, to look at the clock and calendar. Three P.M. will still be 3 P.M. and Monday, March 20, will still be the same since there is no metric time system.

Why should we change?

The metric system for measurements is a more rational system than the English system which the United States has always used. An inch was first defined in England to be the length of four dried barley corns (grains of barley) laid end to end. Other measurements in this system, such as quarts and pounds, similarly grew out of traditional measurements, none of which have any orderly relationships to each other as does our decimal monetary system where ten cents equal a dime, ten dimes equal a dollar, and so on.

The metric system is also a decimal system with relationships between various units being based on powers of the number ten. A meter is formally defined as one millionth of the distance from the equator to the North Pole and is slightly longer than our yard (39.4 inches). For units smaller than a meter, the prefixes are deci (tenths), centi (hundredths), and milli (thousandths). So, a tenth of a meter is a decimeter; a hundredth of a meter is a centimeter; and a thousandth of a meter is a millimeter. On the other side of a meter, ten meters is a dekameter, one hundred meters is a hectometer, and one thousand meters is a kilometer.

The other basic measurements in the metric system are the liter (which is about 5 percent more than a quart) which is used to measure volume, and the gram which is the basic unit for measuring weight. A kilogram (1,000 grams) is about 2.2 pounds. The same prefixes (deci, centi, and so forth apply to these units as well. (A minor disadvantage of the metric system is the need to use symbols exactly as the system specifies, lest there be confusion. For example, "k" means kilo, but "K" means Kelvin; "m" means mill, but "M" means mega.)

The metric system, which is also known as "SI" or "System International," is used by every large country in the world except the English speaking countries, and even these, except for the United States, have been changing to metric. Our being out of step has occasional disadvantages in international trade.

Legislation

Back in 1971, it was seriously suggested in Congress that we convert from the English system to the metric system. Legislation relating to changing has developed only slowly, however, because in some areas changing is so costly. The National Bureau of Standards has estimated that these costs will come to at least $6 billion and could possibly end up going up to several times this amount over the next decade or two.

Hard versus soft conversion

We can convert to metric in either of two ways. First, the so-called soft conversion is just changing all existing measurements which are in inches, pounds, and so on into their metric equivalents. The other, more costly approach is the so-called hard conversion. Hard conversion gives up our characteristic sizes and substitutes metric sizes. Such changes would be more costly because they would, in some cases, require extensive changes in equipment.

In soft conversion, a 12-ounce glass of Coca Cola would merely be restated as .34 liters. In hard conversion, the 12-ounce bottle would disappear and be replaced and become a ¼ of a liter bottle or a ½ liter bottle. Such changes would mean new bottle-making machines which are very costly. Container sizes would also have to be changed. Such changes would be wasteful and would produce little or no gain.

There are difficulties in other areas also. Workers have to be educated to use the system. And during the changeover period there would be need for dual dimensioning (showing inches and centimeters) on drawings and machine dials. There would be extra costs from keeping track of two separate inventories of the items which were actually being changed in size. And there would be problems of reconciling past and present cost accounting and statistical information which would have to be collected by both methods during the changeover. Miles per gallon will, for example, become kilometers per liter.

Going metric may also put a severe burden on smaller firms. They are usually short of cash, and the extra costs of changing would weigh heavily on them. There would be problems, too, for a small company which provides parts for one customer who wants his parts to be in metric units whereas other customers want their products in inches.

Advantages to going metric

We would not be going metric, however, unless there were consequential advantages. Its greater convenience has already been mentioned, and this is itself important, but there are other advantages. Many American manufacturers are already providing items based on the metric system. Often this requires them to have two production facilities, one for the American market and the other for the rest of the world. The saving from consolidating these facilities would be substantial.

Design engineers would also welcome the change. Most engineers are already well versed in the metric system and find it much easier to use. Boeing estimates that savings in drafting time in the aerospace industry alone will exceed $1 billion a year!

Also, educators believe that they could save an estimated $1 billion in teachers' salaries because the metric system requires about 25 percent less time to learn than the English system. It does away with the need for most fractions. No longer would students have to calculate ¾ of 1½ pounds of a product.

One of the biggest advantages, however, is the simplicity and in the interrelationships between the basic measurement units in the metric system. The seven listed here are: length, volume, weight, temperature, power, pressure, and energy. Engineers work with all of these measures, but most people would be concerned with only the first four. Figure 5–3 shows the relationships:

FIGURE 5–3

Element being measured	American units	Metric units
Length	Inch, foot, yard, mile	Meter
Volume	Pint, quart, gallon	Liter
Weight	Ounce, pound, ton	Gram
Temperature	Fahrenheit degree	Centigrade degree
Power	Horsepower, watt	Watt
Pressure	Pounds per square inch	Pascal
Energy	Foot pound, British thermal unit, calory	Joule

In all cases, the metric system shows differences in measurements between very small and very large by using powers of ten. There is only one single basic unit. But, in our English based system, this is not so. It takes 12 inches to make a foot, 3 feet to make a yard, and 5,280 feet or 1,760 yards to make a mile. All the way up and down the line, greater or lesser size measurements are not multiples of ten nor are they sequenced logically.

And, although it is of no importance to most people, the basic metric units are interrelated in a coherent way that helps engineers and scientists. For example, one kilogram accelerated one meter per second, produces a force of one newton. (Measures of force were omitted from our list above because they are not significant to most of us.)

Some American companies started to go metric in the early 1970s and so have already made some of the necessary changes. Ford Motor began manufacturing automobiles to metric specifications in one factory in 1973. Other auto manufacturers are also making similar changes as are Caterpillar Tractor, International Harvester, IBM, and many others.

Ford Motor estimates that in the fastener area alone (nuts, bolts, screws, and rivets), the conversion to a single international measurement system for these items would save American manufacturers a half a billion dollars a year. Unfortunately going metric is not enough here because there are matters not only of the number of threads per inch or per centimeter and the diameters and lengths of bolts and screws, but also of angles and pitches of threads. The American and European standards are different on all of these. Restating measurements into metric units is not enough. So far, little progress has been made in reconciling the two sets of standards.

REVIEW QUESTIONS

1. What impact is the microcomputer industry having on product design?
2. Where do new ideas for new products and services come from?

3. What are the stages in the life cycle of most products? Of what significance are these phenomena in research and development?
4. Since the costs and risks of research are so great, why would it not be a good idea for a company to cut out research and let other companies do it and then either develop something similar very quickly or pay the other company a royalty for using its idea?
5. What role do materials play in product design?
6. Describe the objectives of value engineering and value analysis.
7. What is the logic of the metric system that allows measurements to be simplified?
8. What is hard versus soft conversion to the metric system?
9. What are the advantages and disadvantages of our switching to the metric system?

QUESTIONS FOR DISCUSSION

1. How can a value analysis analyst do a very good job when he really does not know what it costs to do things in other companies? Besides, he doesn't know how "hungry" other companies are for business and what prices they might, under pressure, quote. Without such knowledge, isn't he limited in what he can accomplish?
2. Since a high proportion of research projects are failures, can most companies really justify spending 2 percent of their gross income on research? Discuss.
3. Should research departments be set up according to fields of science (such as chemistry, metallurgy, and the like), or by product lines (such as automobiles, refrigerators, and the like), or some other basis. What might be the advantages and disadvantages of each choice?
4. A scientist develops an improvement for a carburetor. This improvement has value for cars and for the company. How might a top manager go about judging the value of this contribution from research?
5. Should a product designer pay more attention to form design (what the product looks like) or to functional design (how it operates)? Why?

PROBLEMS

1. It is anticipated that a company will make 800,000 units of product A in a year and will have a factory cost of $2.50, of which $.95 will be spent for materials. The rest of the factory cost is for processing. Redesigning product A should save 2 percent of processing costs and 5 percent of materials costs. There is a question, however, about how much the redesigning will cost. The designers think that a $25,000 budget will do the job.

a. If it is required that the $25,000 be recovered out of savings in one year, should this expenditure be approved?

b. Suppose that the $25,000 is approved and has been spent but that the improvement is still far from finished. If it is cut off now, no gain at all would be realized, and the $25,000 would all be lost. The design engineer, however, is very enthusiastic and feels sure that for an additional $50,000 budget he can be certain of getting the savings originally expected. Should the top manager approve this additional $50,000? (Assume that he agrees with the designer's expectation of success.)

2. A part weighing three pounds can be made from steel or copper. In the case of steel, half of the original material is used up as cutting waste. For copper, a fourth of the original material becomes cutting waste. To machine the part from steel takes 25 minutes per unit, whereas copper takes 15 minutes. Steel costs $.15 a pound and copper $.65 a pound. Steel scrap is worth $.05 a pound and copper scrap is worth $.30 a pound. The machine and the operator together cost $10 an hour.

a. From which metal should the part be made? How much will this choice save vis-à-vis the other method?

b. What would the comparison be if copper went up in price to $.90 a pound (and scrap went to $.40 a pound)?

c. If the price of steel remains constant, what would be the price of copper at the break-even point between steel and copper? (Assume that copper scrap is still worth $.30 per pound.)

3. Two kinds of paint are being considered. A gallon of brand A costs $6 and will cover 300 square feet of surface. It will last about three years and can be applied at 75 square feet an hour. A gallon of brand B costs $10 a gallon and will cover 400 square feet of surface. It goes on at a rate of 90 square feet an hour. Painters cost $7 an hour.

How long will brand B have to last to be competitive with A?

4. The Day Company is bringing out a new product, the parts for which can be bought or made. If bought, they will cost $2 per unit for the 10,000 units expected to be made.

a. Making these parts will cost $5,000 for tooling plus $1.30 per unit variable cost. Should Day buy or make these items?

b. Day can go more automatic and spend $15,000 for machines, which would reduce variable costs per unit to $.60. Should Day buy or make these items and, if it should make them, by which method?

5. From what we hear, many television viewers resent loud and blatant commercials: The Arp Company, a television manufacturer with national distribution, has had an occasional request from a dealer for a remote control cutoff with an automatic timer. A viewer could push a button on the cutoff box and it would turn off the speaker (or the picture also, as the viewer chooses) for one minute. Then the program would turn on again automatically.

Arp's analysts estimate that it will cost $25,000 to develop such a "Hush Button" and $40,000 more to get it into production. Besides this, it will take a $50,000 advertising campaign to introduce the product to the market.

It is proposed, in the future, to supply Hush Buttons without added charge on all sets retailing for $250 and up. For lower price sets, it is to be available as an "extra" for $25. Owners of any make TV can buy a Hush Button and have their sets modified for its use for $40.

It is estimated that Hush Buttons will cost $3 each in variable costs to produce. Besides this there will be an extra fixed cost of $30,000 in the first year. It is proposed to sell Hush Button units to dealers for $20. It is expected that the Hush Button will boost the sales of sets priced at over $250 (where its cost will be included in the set's price at no extra charge) enough to offset the cost of providing it on all such sets.

With this cost-price structure, how many Hush Buttons will Arp need to sell in order to recover all its initial expenses out of profits during the first year?

6. Sales are $10 million a year. Fixed costs are $5 million (which includes $300,000 now being spent annually for research). Variable costs come to $4 million a year. The research director wants to double the research expenditures, claiming that this will boost sales. After talking it over with the sales department, the following estimate was arrived at concerning the sales probabilities if the research expenditures are doubled:

Sales (millions of dollars)	Probability
10	.50
11	.30
12	.10
13	.05
14	.03
15	.02

Should the research expenditures be doubled? On a nondiscounted basis, what is the answer? What would it be if future incomes were discounted at 15 percent?

7. The New Company finds that because a competitor has brought out a new product it is lagging behind, but it can probably catch up if it starts immediately on a crash design program. Doing this will probably get New's new product out in six months. Less expenditure will still produce results, but more slowly. A crash program will cost $1.5 million instead of the $800,000 a slower program would cost. The hurry-up job also opens the door to a .1 probability that the design will be faulty, in which case another $300,000 will have to be spent, and it will take six more months to correct the trouble.

If the crash program succeeds, New will not only catch up but its managers think that New will have a six-month lead on its competitors. This will mean profits of $400,000 during that period. Besides this, there will very likely be a continuing advantage to New for the five remaining years of the product's life. The payoff prospects for the next five years in total are:

With crash program		*Without crash program*	
Profits	*Probability*	*Profits*	*Probability*
$2,000,000............ .50		$2,000,000............ .20	
1,500,000............ .30		1,500,000............ .30	
1,000,000............ .15		1,000,000............ .35	
500,000............ .05		500,000............ .15	

What action should be taken?

8. Visit a manufacturing firm which is changing to the metric system. Report on the problems they are experiencing and what advantages they have found.

CASE 5–1

According to Peter Drucker, consumerism means that the consumer looks upon the manufacturer as "somebody who is interested, but who doesn't really know what consumer realities are, and who has not made the effort to find out." Perhaps Drucker is right, so far as what many consumers think. But whether this is what consumers think or not, consumerism seems to have gone even further. Manufacturers are often held liable for injuries even when consumers use products wrongly.

A woman bothered by bugs bought a can of insecticide, but, instead of spraying it on the furniture or in the air, she sprayed herself. She had a violent allergic reaction and sued and collected from the manufacturer.

In another case, a man who was injured in an accident while riding in a 13-year-old car sued the manufacturer. When he was thrown against the gear shift, the knob on top broke apart, and he was impaled on the shaft. The knob was made of white plastic, which over the 13 years had oxidized and developed hairline cracks. The man sued the company, claiming that the company had made the car with faulty materials, and won his suit. So did the woman who plugged a 115-volt vacuum cleaner into a 220-volt plug, causing the sweeper to "blow up." It is hard to see how a motor burning out could "blow up," but somehow the woman got hurt in the process.

In all three of these cases there seems to have been no negligence on the part of the manufacturers. These accidents did not occur because the manufacturers were remiss in their concern for consumer needs.

In another case, a man was injured when the steering wheel of the car he was driving came off in his hands in an accident. The car was so badly damaged that it was not clear whether the steering wheel had been faulty or not. Nonetheless, the manufacturer was held liable. Today's consumerism seems almost always to hold manufacturers liable regardless of their culpability.

Hundreds of cases of extreme consumer protectionism can be quoted. In the vacuum cleaner case the court said the label should have warned that plugging it into a 220-volt line would be disastrous.

Since manufacturers have only one source of income from which to pay for both greater safety and liability claims, these costs must be added to the costs of products for everyone.

What really should the answer be? How far should a manufacturer have to go to protect everybody against highly unlikely accidents? How much should *all* consumers be required to pay for such protection for the few who have trouble?

SUGGESTED SUPPLEMENTARY READINGS

DeSimone, D. V. "Moving to Metric Makes Dollars and Sense." *Harvard Business Review,* January–February, 1972, pp. 102–12.

Dhalla, Nariman K., and Yuspek, Sonia. "Forget the Product Life Cycle Concept!" *Harvard Business Review,* January–February 1976, pp. 102–12.

"Microcomputers Challenge the Big Machines." *Business Week,* April 26, 1976, pp. 58–63.

6

Designing products and services

CHANGING markets, new technologies, and other factors are always creating new trends in the design of products. Some of today's trends promise to have substantial impact upon the kinds and arrays of products we will see in the future.

Narrowing product lines

Raw materials scarcities, fear of price controls, the energy crunch, and other economic conditions are causing many companies to reduce variety and to discontinue making items in their product lines which are only marginally profitable. For example, in the mid-1970s General Electric discontinued making food blenders, electric fans, heaters, humidifiers, and vacuum cleaners. Between 1970 and 1975, the number of automobile models was reduced from 375 to 300. Banks and savings and loan associations economized by cutting back on some of their services, and brokerage companies reduced their research aimed at finding stocks of undervalued companies.

Product simplification

In addition to reducing variety in end products and services, many firms are trying to simplify their products by redesigning parts and components so that fewer pieces will do the job. By making parts do double duty, Chrysler cut the number of parts in a car by 20 percent between 1970 and 1976. Ford Motor has a formal program which it calls "complexity reduction," which is given credit for reducing the number of emission control component parts by 56 percent in 1975 and 1976.[1] International Harvester also reports substantial reductions.

Other organizations are also streamlining their products. Addressograph Multigraph has reduced the number of cylinders in its duplicating machines by over 75 percent. National Cash Register has simplified its products by making them out of "families" of components which may be used interchangeably in such diverse products as computers for the medical profession and for automatic bank tellers.

In the semiconductor field, Texas Instruments redesigned its digital watches down to only five parts, far fewer than competitor's watches. Now TI's watches can be assembled in a few minutes compared to over a half an hour for competitors' watches.

Automobile companies work continually at simplifying and reducing the weight of their cars. Lighter weight cars get better gasoline mileage, and this became important in the mid 1970s. In its 1976 models, Chrysler trimmed 184 pounds off its Duster and Dart lines by going more to lightweight materials. Forty-seven pounds of weight were saved through substituting aluminum for steel in bumper reinforcing bars. Another ten pounds saved came from using thin high strength steel for government required crash protection beams inside car doors, and so on.

Curiously the way the government's Environmental Protection Agency's regulations operate provides an extra incentive for car manufacturers to reduce weight. For test purposes, cars are grouped into 500-pound weight groups. Cars weighing under 3,000 pounds have to meet certain standards, those weighing from 3,000 to 3,500 pounds have to pass slightly more rigorous tests. By reducing the weight of the Duster and the Dart to under 3,000 pounds, Chrysler saved having them classed in with bigger cars.[2]

STANDARDIZATION

When you buy a light bulb, you know it will screw into the socket because light bulb bases are standardized (only a few kinds of bases are made). But an American light bulb will not fit into a socket in Europe, or vice versa, because their bases are different. Or, if you buy a new hose to sprinkle your lawn, you don't have to wonder if it will screw onto the water faucet because the size of the pipes and screw threads are standard.

Also, most people probably never think about a light bulb's voltage because, in the United States, 110 volts is standard in homes. But again, Europe is different; several voltages are used there. An American traveler in Europe using an electric shaver has to buy an adapter.

We have used the word "standard" as meaning that only certain specific sizes are made and sold. Some people prefer to call this process of limiting

[1] "Product Streamlining Picks Up as Companies Are Pressed to Cut Costs," *Wall Street Journal*, October 23, 1975, p. 1.

[2] "How Auto Engineers Find New Ways to Up Car Gas Mileage," *Wall Street Journal*, October 20, 1975, pp. 1 and 19.

the number of sizes "simplification." "Standardization," these people would say, is something else; it is the process of *specifying* the size, shape, performance, and other characteristics of the items being made. These two concepts are so closely related, however, that we will use them here as being nearly the same.

Standardization (including simplification) usually means that non-standard items will not be made—except when a customer orders them specifically (and pays extra for them).

Sometimes standards have been enacted into law for safety or health reasons. Automobile windshields, for example, must be made of safety glass (which does not shatter and make jagged edges on impact). Although standardization has largely been voluntary in the past, today's product safety laws are making it mandatory in many areas. The glass now used in eyeglasses, for example, must now be very resistant to breakage. It is standardized at a high-quality level.

Most industries, even those producing consumer products where there are no legal regulations, can and do standardize extensively on a voluntary basis. This holds true in the setting of shoe sizes, photographic film, automobile tire sizes, nails, pipe, and even razor blades.

Advantages of standardization

Standardization reduces the kinds, types, and sizes of raw materials which have to be bought and the variety of items to be made inside. Since the total quantities to be bought or made are distributed over fewer varieties, larger quantities of each are bought or made. This results in lower costs per unit for bought items and for items made inside, in fewer patterns, tools, jigs, fixtures, and setups, all of which contribute to lower costs.

Disadvantages of standardization and simplification

Some manufacturers, especially those making assembled products, do not accept industrywide standardization because they find that using "the perfect part" is better for them than using a standard part that is not quite so well suited to their particular use. A company making power lawn mowers may not want the same engine which is used for chain saws, or motorcycles, or outboard motors on boats. Instead, it may be better for this company to use an engine designed especially for power-driven lawn mowers.

Manufacturers using large volumes of nuts, bolts, wire, valves, bearings, electric motors, switches, and other such items also frequently find that "the perfect part" for a particular purpose is cheaper to use, even if it should cost a little more to make, than to buy a standard part.

There are other reasons why industrywide standardization programs often are only partially successful. Standardization tends to favor large, well-known companies because small (or new) companies can rarely get much business by making and selling the same things and at the same prices as larger companies. They often survive by offering something different at the same, or close to the same, price as large companies charge for standard products.

Manufacturers of "style goods," such as women's clothes, do not standardize very much because women want "something different." They do, however, abide by industrywide size standards which need to be consistent.

From the social point of view, there is a potential danger in standardization. If new products are standardized too soon, before their design is fairly mature, standardization may become an obstacle to progress. Color television, for example, appeared in Europe later than in the United States. This permitted European television to incorporate more advanced technology and to use 160 lines to the inch instead of the American 120 lines to the inch; consequently, their pictures are sharper. American television was standardized before some of this advanced technology was developed.

Typewriter keyboards, too (many years ago), were frozen too soon, and this has stood in the way of improvement. They have a poor arrangement of letters (60 percent of the work load falls on the left hand, whereas most people are right-handed). We know how to arrange them better but can't make the change because millions of typists are trained to use the present keyboard—to say nothing of our having millions of typewriters with the bad key arrangement.

Improvements which call for different nonstandard products must always be made if progress is to continue. A standard should, therefore, be in a sense more a prevailing style than it is a permanent standard. Standards should not be permitted to "freeze" or be kept only for their own sake.

MODULAR DESIGN

With repair labor being just about as costly in a factory as it is in a home and with breakdowns being costly in both cases, designers are turning to modular construction with products being made of easily detachable subassemblies or sections. When a single item fails, the whole module (of which the item is a part) is removed and a new module is put in. Later the removed module can be repaired and put into replacement stock or it can be thrown away.

Electrical printed circuit boards (or "cards") and integrated circuits are usually components of this sort. Plug-in bases are made as integral parts of such boards, thus allowing for their easy removal. If a transistor or diode fails, the whole card on which it is mounted along with other diodes, condensors, and the like, is removed and replaced by a replacement card.

Modular design is used extensively in computers, both in the microminiature and circuit board way, but also in a larger way. Standardized major components are made with their physical dimensions and electrical systems compatible so they can be hooked up in different combinations to make what are essentially different computers. In computers, for example, the units which store information, the units which "read in" information to the calculating section, and the units which print out results are available in several sizes and with varied capabilities. They can be connected with any combination of other major units.

RELIABILITY

As a person sits in a comfortable chair in the evening reading the newspaper, the light bulb in the reading lamp suddenly burns out. Designers can rarely design, nor can manufacturers make, products which will not finally fail. Nor can they design or make products which will last for an exact length of time—no more, no less.

A product's length of life is dependent upon its design, upon the degree of manufacturing perfection, upon the conditions under which it is used, and upon chance. Usually the longer a product is supposed to last, the more costly it is to make.

Reliability is the probability that a part or a product will last a given length of time under normal conditions of use. Thus, one aspect of reliability is expected length of life. In the case of a light bulb, the goal could be 1,000 hours or it could even be 2,000 hours. (Ordinary light bulbs have a "rated" or "expected" life of 1,350 hours.) Obviously even ordinary light bulbs are very reliable up to 1,000 hours, perhaps with a reliability of 0.98, meaning that only 2 bulbs in 100 will probably fail within 1,000 hours. But very few bulbs will last 2,000 hours; possibly here the probability might be 0.05. If someone wants bulbs which will usually last for 2,000 hours, he will need to order special bulbs.

A second aspect of reliability is the condition of use. A light bulb of the usual design is unlikely to last even 1,000 hours if it is continually bumped around. But flashlights sometimes get bumped around, and so flashlight bulbs need to be sturdier than reading lamp bulbs because they are expected to work in spite of a few bumps.

Sometimes the conditions of expected use are most extreme. Many of the parts that go into space vehicles sometimes have to operate at temperatures of more than 200 degrees above zero and also at other times at temperatures of more than 200 degrees below zero.

Parts, therefore, need to be designed to have the desired reliability under their expected conditions of use. For most consumer products, conditions of use are not extreme although everyone recognizes that some products, such as automobiles or motorcycles, are sometimes misused and not well maintained. And, while the reliability of most consumer products is satisfactory to most users, we have all had "lemons" of one product or another.

Third, reliability has to do both with individual parts and whole products. Whole products fail when *any* critical part fails, so the reliability of whole products is much less than the reliability of individual parts. The more critical parts there are, the less the reliability of the whole product. Sewing machines, power lawn mowers, and automobiles all have a good many parts whose failure individually would cause the product to fail. And computers, space vehicles, and other exotic products have thousands of parts whose operation is critical to the operation of the whole product. Back in the 1960s it took the United States 13 tries to get a space vehicle to take the first close-up pictures of the moon; the first 12 tries were failures. Several years ago, the United States submarine *Thresher* sank, and 129 men lost their lives because one pipe joint—out of 8,000—failed.

A system of 100 interacting parts, each of which has .9999 (or 99.99 percent) reliability, has an overall reliability of 0.9900 (or 99 percent); a system with 1,000 interacting parts has 90 percent reliability; 3,000 parts have 75 percent; and 10,000 parts have 37 percent. The Telstar communications satellite has more than 10,000 electronic parts, and even though these parts do not all interact, and not all are of critical importance, extremely high reliability had to be built into Telstar's parts to get it to operate in the first place and to keep it operating in the years since it was put into orbit in 1963.

A fourth matter is how serious is failure? If an automobile steering mechanism fails, it can cause a wreck, but sometimes the failure of a part is not critical. If a lamp bulb in a reading lamp fails, little harm is

FIGURE 6–1

System availability as a function of component reliability and the number of components

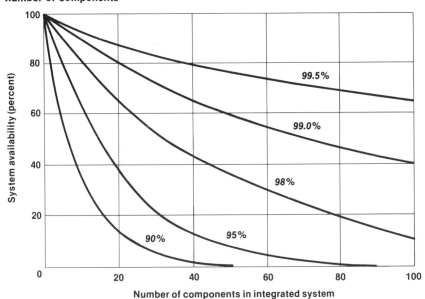

done. Or, if a person drops a telephone and the plastic casing cracks, the casing has "failed" but the telephone still works.

Point five is a corollary of point four: How quickly can a part failure be fixed, and how big a job is it to fix it? Indeed, the seriousness of a failure often depends upon how quickly and how cheaply it can be fixed. Quick maintenance gets the system back into operation right away so that little harm is done. When a storm knocks out the electric power for part of a city, the potential harm is great, but usually the actual harm is much less because the power company gets the power restored so quickly. And, of course, when the light bulb in a lamp burns out, we can unscrew it and put in another. When replacement is simple and fast, product reliability is less important.

Unfortunately, points four and five sometimes don't apply because there is no chance to fix or replace a critical part that has failed. The United States missed taking pictures of the moon the first 12 tries because the parts that failed were critical and there was no way to fix them in outer space. And broken steering mechanisms in automobiles can cause accidents before there is any chance to fix them. Faulty electronic components in computers can cause wrong answers, and possibly no one will know that they are wrong (although several checks for accuracy are built into today's computers). In such cases, a high degree of reliability is very important even if it costs a good bit more money.

A sixth point is that usually the reliability of systems can be improved by making products out of more perfect parts, parts which are made to fit more exactly or which are made out of special long-wearing materials. But, as almost always, the greater the reliability, the higher the cost.

An example from Texas Instruments illustrates how greater reliability requirements caused costs to skyrocket. TI sold one kind of transistor for consumer and industrial use for $.25 each with no guarantee of its reliability. But for its use in military systems, it had to give reliability guarantees, so the price was $.85 for the same (but more carefully processed and tested) transistor. But when it came to spaceship use, its very careful manufacture and testing, which were required to insure its high reliability, shot the costs of this same transistor up to $10.

Fortunately, greater quality does not always cost very much more money. Parts which might fail can often be "overdesigned" at nominal cost. A handle or a hinge on a suitcase can easily be made far stronger than it needs to be at very little extra cost. So can a door hinge on an automobile. Added strength in these cases costs very little.

The discussion so far might lead one to think that reliability is a black-or-white matter: A product works or it doesn't. Often, however, failure is not like that. This leads to point seven, the degree of failure. If a television tube sometimes goes zigzag or gives snowy or fuzzy pictures, has it failed? Has there been a failure in an automobile if the brake pedal has to be pushed farther down than formerly? Poor performance is often a matter of degree, with absolute failure as the final stage. In a practical sense, failure occurs when performance is so poor that there is a decision to repair or replace the part.

There is also the question of performance expectations. When a television picture tube fails, the customer regards it as a failure, whereas if it lasted ten years before failing, it is not—in the eyes of the manufacturer— a failure at all.

Point eight is that reliability is closely tied to maintenance, particularly preventive maintenance. A reading lamp will probably never burn out while someone is reading if the old bulb is taken out and a new one is put in every 800 hours. Normally, preventive maintenance can result in high reliability for a product even where long-term reliability is not engineered into the parts of the product. It is only necessary to replace parts before they have been used enough to become unreliable. If a person buys a new storage battery for a car every two years, the car will probably always start in the winter. Unfortunately, however, preventive maintenance costs money, so it is only a different (and usually somewhat costly) way to increase the reliability of products.

We have said that the failure of a noncritical part often does not affect the whole product's operating performance. This is, however, sometimes a misleading statement because the failure of one part may hasten the failure of other parts. A broken telephone case lets dust and dampness into its inside, and in due time this will probably make trouble. Or an automobile will run when one cylinder is not firing, but, if it is continued in operation with one cylinder missing, it is hard on the car's bearings and will make them fail sooner.

REDUNDANCY

Where the failure of a part or subsystem is critically important, engineers often add a redundant part or subsystem as insurance. It is like wearing a belt and suspenders at the same time or having a backup quarterback. The extra is not used at all unless the regular part fails. Should the regular component fail, then the total system automatically switches over and uses the standby.

The need for redundancy depends primarily on the seriousness of a failure and secondarily on its cost. The specter of a nuclear explosion coming from nuclear electric power generating plants having an accident frightens us all. Because of this, nuclear power plants are being designed to withstand the worst earthquakes, floods, or other "acts of God" ever recorded in their areas. Every piece of equipment has to meet the stiffest quality controls anywhere in civilian industry. If any component fails, layer after layer of "redundant" safety features are ready to be activated. M.I.T. scientists estimate that the way today's nuclear plants are built, even 100 such plants, considered together, would have a probability of an accident involving 1,000 or more deaths only once in a million years.[3]

---

[3] "The Great Nuclear Debate," *Time,* December 8, 1975, p. 36.

Redundancy for safety's sake is actually quite common. Every auto-mobile, for instance, has a mechanical hand brake as well as its regular hydraulic brake system which itself has a redundant system built into it. If the foot brake fails, the driver is not without a brake. Aircraft have in-dependent ignition systems and can fly quite safely (except for single engine airplanes) if one of their engines dies.

Today's electronic computers have two sets of every subsystem whose failure would be critical to their operation. And, with minicomputers being so inexpensive, some computer users are actually using two computers where one could do the work. The second is merely backup if the first one goes out. Cities and state police are also doing this where critical informa-tion needs to be kept "on-line" and right up to date as is the case with information about fugitives and stolen cars.

In industry, we hear most about redundancy in exotic products such as space vehicles where every critical subsystem is backed up by a second emergency system. In smaller ways, however, the redundancy idea is used a good bit in everyday products. Men's shirts are usually sewn with double seams where one really ought to be enough. Or, in a factory, if two pieces of steel have to be welded together with four spot welds and there has been trouble with the welded spots not holding, it is easy to specify six spot welds instead of four. Then it won't matter if one or two of them don't hold. This can be done wherever the extra cost of welding two extra spots is nominal.

Even nature believes in redundancy. We all start with two eyes, ears, lungs and kidneys, but we can get along with one. Nature's redundancy, however, usually calls for the regular use of both components, whereas industry's redundancy is usually a first-unit-use, second-unit-standby ar-rangement.

Redundancy economics

Redundancy economics can be quite complex, but a simple problem will illustrate the principles. Suppose that a system has two components, A and B, which operate as in Figure 6–2. The probability of A's being operative for as long as the normal life of the system is 0.90 and B's is 0.95. Since both have to operate, and either can fail, the system reliability is $0.90 \times 0.95 = 0.855$.

Suppose that a failure costs $1,000. The probability of failure during the system's normal life expectancy is therefore $1 - 0.855 = 0.145$ and the long-run average expected cost of failure is $0.145 \times \$1,000 = \$145$.

To make the system more reliable, it is proposed to put in a second A unit, together with a switch, so that if the first A unit is inoperative, the

FIGURE 6–2

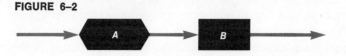

FIGURE 6–3

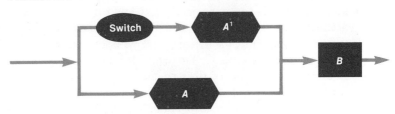

second (A′) will switch on automatically—a system like that shown in
Figure 6–3. Should such a redundant system be put in at a cost of $300
if the switch has a reliability of 0.98 and the reliability of unit A′ is 0.90?

If called into use, the redundant system will be operative $0.98 \times 0.90 =$
0.88 of the time. The redundant system will then take care of 88 percent
of the expected 10 percent failures of part A. So the reliability of the A–A′
part of the system becomes $0.90 + 0.10 \times 0.88 = 0.988$. B, however,
has not been improved; so the whole system's reliability has now become
$0.988 \times 0.95 = 0.939$. The probability of failure is $1 - 0.939 = 0.061$.
Now the expected average failure cost will be $0.061 \times \$1{,}000 = \$61$.

Expected average failure costs are now reduced by $84 (from $145 to
$61), but the protection cost $300 so the total cost is $361. Without the
redundant system, the average expected cost of failures was $145; so the
redundant system will not pay for itself. It would be better to take the 14.5
percent chance of having a $1,000 failure than to spend $300 to reduce
the risk to a 6.1-percent chance of having a $1,000 failure. It would pay
in the long run only if the cost of the redundant system were reduced $84.

DESIGN BY COMPUTERS

Computers are being used more and more in design work and in the
actual making of engineering drawings. The movement is not rapid, however, because most automatic drafting machines cost $100,000 or more.
When they are hooked up with computers, several engineers can all
be using one computer at the same time. Where companies have them,
automatic drafting machines can take a computer's calculations describing
the direction and curvature of lines and draw the lines at rates of 200
inches or more a minute. Old drawings can also be called up and modified
to make new drawings.

General Electric uses computers to design electric motors. I-T-E Circuit Breaker uses them to design custom-built transformers. Allis Chalmers
uses them to decide the best shapes for drying kilns. General Motors uses
them in automobile design. And airplane companies use them to compute
the contours of wings as well as to design integrated circuits.

When there are several ways to do anything, a computer can quickly
make all the comparisons and pick the best way, whereas, without a com-

puter, an engineer cannot make all the comparisons and would have to rely on judgment. Once the computer has made its calculations, it can have the automatic drafting machine make the drawings while the computer itself proceeds to produce all the manufacturing instructions needed for making the product including instruction tapes for directing "numerically controlled" machines (discussed in Chapter 10). Alternatively, before the final design decision is made, the designer can have several different designs drawn up for his inspection. These can be put on paper or can be projected alongside each other on a cathode ray tube or "scope."

A computer can also project, on such a tube, a drawing which it has made from the design instructions put into its memory by the designer. Then, after looking at it, if he wants to eliminate a line or draw in a new one, he can do it on the scope with an electronic pen connected to the computer. The computer will change its memory instructions so that it will thereafter project the revised drawing. The computer can also enlarge a picture or turn it so that it can be seen from another angle, such as left front, rather than from front. And it can also pair up mating parts to see how they fit.

As if this were not enough, this process is now well enough developed so an engineer can even draw a preliminary design on the scope with his electronic pen and the computer will reproduce it on call. It will even straighten out lines, smooth out curved lines, and reproduce the improved sketch on call.

DESIGN CONFLICTS

Production, engineering, marketing, and finance people in organizations often have different objectives, all or any of which may affect the final design of products and which may be in conflict with each other.

Figure 6–4 humorously depicts some of the possible differing viewpoints about design. Everyone sees the product differently. In actual practice at the one extreme, production people want to make only a few kinds of products and with few variations so that they can have long production runs. And they want changes, if any have to be made, to be simple so that they can be made easily.

On the other hand, design engineers usually want to build durability into products so that they will serve well for a long time, even if this means using more costly materials or processes. Marketing people almost always want a wide variety in the product line so they can attract the customer's eye and have something different for every customer. And, in order to follow what the market wants all the time, marketing people want frequent redesigns of existing products.

Finance people have still other objectives, such as high profitability, fast cash flow, rapid inventory turnover, and a quick return on the investments in plant and equipment.

Even personnel people sometimes have a say through their concern

FIGURE 6–4

The factory designs a swing for the children

As proposed by the marketing department.

As specified in the product request.

As designed by the senior designer.

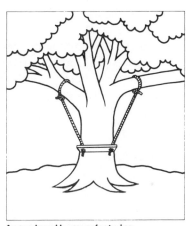

As produced by manufacturing.

As used by the customer.

What the customer wanted.

with how workers' jobs are set up. They want jobs to be designed so that boredom for workers is lessened. This is usually possible through job enlargement, but it comes at the expense of losing some of the gains from specialization. Often an economical trade-off can be worked out.

DESIGNING SERVICES

For a long time, the service sector of our economy has been growing at a faster rate than other sectors. Today well over half of the employed people in the United States are engaged in rendering services rather than in producing products. Employment in government work, education, transportation, health care, finance, and other service type organizations exceeds that of the production type industries, manufacturing, construction, mining, and farming.

Lines of services offered

The concept of designing, or developing, services is much more elusive than that of designing products. Services are not something one can hold in one's hand, and they are usually perishable and cannot be stockpiled. A service not rendered today cannot be saved up and added to the services to be rendered tomorrow.

Service organizations must decide how wide their lines of service shall be. Should an insurance company, for example, offer both life insurance and property and casualty insurance? Should it have its own claims adjusters, or should the company use independent claims adjusters? Colleges and universities have to decide whether to offer a broad range of courses or to confine their efforts to fewer areas and to do them in greater depth.

Cities also have to make decisions about what services to offer their citizens. Should they provide free trash pick-up or should they let private companies provide this service at a charge to its citizens? Should a city provide day care centers, job training programs, and extensive public health services? Or should these services be provided by private or nonprofit organizations? Do cities have an obligation to provide bus transportation for the few people who need it since it is not profitable enough to be done by private companies?

In many organizations these decisions are not open choice decisions. Few organizations have enough money to do everything that they deem worthwhile. In the face of costs rising faster than tax income, many cities have had to curtail the services formerly offered. Day care centers, rehabilitation programs and such activities are cut off when money is short.

We could go on but these examples illustrate some of the problems faced by service organizations. Nor are there easy answers to most of these questions because they depend on how widespread is the demand, how willing are people to pay for the service, and what skills capabilities the organization's people have, and what its physical equipment is suited to do. Essentially, the providing of a service or the addition of a service to an existing organization's programs needs to be analyzed just as carefully as a manufacturer analyzes the matter of adding a new product to the product line.

Level of service

The level of service which an organization provides for its customers has to do with balancing its ability to supply the services wanted by customers against the need to operate economically at the same time. The problem that the managers of service organizations face is how to operate economically and yet give customers good service when service calls are irregular. Sometimes there are many service calls in a short time, and sometimes the service wanted takes a long time. In order to give good service there have to be enough service people to meet these calls, yet during slack periods they don't have enough to do. The manager has to strike a proper balance point between the cost of waiting customers and waiting employees.

Sometimes the need for quick service is so critical that sufficient capability to meet unusual demands should be available almost on a standby basis. A city ought to have enough fire fighting equipment, and it ought to be located where it can respond to fire calls in minutes. Similarly, a police department's squad cars should be able to respond to a robbery call in minutes. In contrast, a wait of half a day is not too long to wait until a trash collection truck comes along and picks up the trash. These concepts are discussed more fully in Chapter 26, on waiting lines and simulation.

Manufacturing companies have similar problems. A factory should have first aid facilities capable of handling emergency injuries. And in the selling end, there is the question of the "service level," meaning how big a stock of products to carry in finished products inventory so that customers' orders can be filled off the shelf. A "95 percent service level" means that the company is able to fill 95 percent of customers' orders from items already carried in inventory.

Service availability

When designing services, managers need to consider when the service needs to be available (eight hours a day? twenty-four hours a day? five days a week? seven days?).

There is also the question of where to locate facilities in order to provide good service and of whether to have only one centrally located facility or to decentralize and have several satellite facilities spread around in the area to be served. The current trend is to provide decentralized service facilities, such as neighborhood health clinics, state unemployment offices, and branch banks. In a factory, there are usually several decentralized production control and quality control offices. Maintenance crews, too, are usually at least partially decentralized. These are all responses to the general goal of putting services closer to where the need is so that, on the one hand, people do not have to travel long distances to receive the services and, on the other hand, service people do not have to go far to render their services.

"Servicing what we sell"

An important part of many manufacturing firms' "total product" concept is servicing the products that they make and sell. For these firms this is one of the strongest competitive advantages they may have. In the computer industry, where products are extremely technical and complex, one of the major competitive advantages that large firms like IBM, Burroughs, and Control Data have is their extensive network of service engineers who are *always* available to respond to a call of a customer whose computer has "gone down." Of course, the service engineers actually spend most of their time doing preventive maintenance so that stoppages in service rarely occur.

Not all firms service what they sell. Rather, they rely on local dealers to handle all "after sale" matters. Companies making typewriters, refrigerators, washing machines, and any number of other items find it more satisfactory to rely on local repair firms who may even also handle competing lines, because the volume of repair work is not enough to justify a company-owned chain of service outlets.

We return now to the question of what are the differences between designing products and designing services. In a service organization, the service it renders is really its "product." Actually, in many ways, producing services and producing products are not altogether different, although the design of services is a much "fuzzier" activity than the design of products.

When a *product* is designed and manufacturing commences, "What you see is what you get." But *services* are usually less subject to exact definition, and the emphasis is placed upon the people needed to perform the services and their training and on the facilities they will need in order to render the service.

Service organizations are usually more flexible and can change their activities more readily than can manufacturers because most of the time they do not have heavy investments in equipment. If they change their activities, their office space can be changed to the new uses rather easily. And, if changes in personnel are needed in order to change the nature of the activities, this would be the same for both manufacturing and service organizations. Admittedly service companies sometimes have heavy investments in equipment, as in the case of airlines and hospitals. But, in most cases, it is easier for service companies to change the nature of the services they offer than it is for manufacturing companies to change to quite different products.

REVIEW QUESTIONS

1. Should a manufacturer standardize his products? Why?

2. What are the dangers to society from standardizing too soon in the development of a new product?

3. Reliability is a trade-off between product life and cost. Discuss.

4. How does the reliability of a product's individual component parts affect its overall reliability?

5. Summarize the text discussion of reliability but from the point of view of the consumer.

6. How does redundancy relate to reliability?

7. What does the probability of failure have to do with redundancy economics?

QUESTIONS FOR DISCUSSION

1. The designer for a nut and bolt manufacturer has been selected by his company to be a member of an industrywide committee on standardization. What should he want to know and how will he be able to decide what is good for the industry, his company, and the consumer?

2. An administrator says, "Why can't technical people think less about abstractions and more about end products with real market potential?" What can an administrator do to develop a realistic attitude in the minds of his company's scientists?

3. Some companies "expense" their research costs, meaning that they regard them as part of the costs of doing business today. This is in contrast with some other companies which "capitalize" part or all of today's research costs, in which case they regard the capitalized portion of these expenses as an increase in a new capital asset (the partly developed hoped-for new product). Which is the better way to handle such costs? Why?

4. Would you pay more for a hand-made product? Why? If you would, how has mass production failed?

5. Oscar Mayer is famous for weiners. How should a specification writer for this company go about writing specifications for a weiner? What problems would be involved? Is a specification worthwhile here?

6. Who is in the best position to decide whether certain parts and components should be made inside or bought outside? Would a committee help? Who should be on it?

7. How are tolerances usually set? Is there a better way? What should a company do to try to have its tolerances set as reasonably as possible?

8. In automobiles, "soft" springs make for a smooth ride at low speeds. But at high speeds soft springs cause more swaying. And, when

heavily loaded, cars with soft springs ride very low. What kinds of springs should be put into cars?

9. Design is always a compromise, a trade-off of quality versus cost. How can a designer know where to set the performance level? If a company makes carpets, should it make them to wear for 40 years of heavy traffic? Or to wear out in 5 years of light traffic? Should the company go for the $15- or the $30-a-yard business?

10. Make a freehand sketch of the parts of the chair you are sitting on and show dimensions and tolerances. Discuss the problems involved.

11. An airplane crashes because its altimeter (a purchased part for measuring how high up the airplane is) gave a wrong reading. Who is responsible? The altimeter manufacturer? The airplane maker? Suppose that the altimeter had been in use for a long time; does this affect the answer? Discuss.

12. How do companies manage product safety design?

PROBLEMS

1. Visit a manufacturing or service organization, and write a short report on their approach to designing safety into their products or services.

2. Modular components are designed so that although each module contains several parts, a module can be put in or taken out as easily as if it were just one part. Almost always the modules are small, and their component parts are quite small—so much so that if one of the small parts fails it does not pay to repair the module. Instead it is removed, like a burned-out light bulb, and thrown away. This means that when one component fails, several good components are thrown out. It costs too much to disassemble the module in order to save the good parts.

We are dealing with a module whose parts have the following probability of failure rates in 2,000 hours of operation. A: .003; B: .012; C: .004; D: .009; E: .020; F: .011; G: .006; and H: .012. Assume that these parts, separately, cost as follows: A: $.19; B: $.72; C: $.04; D: $.22; E: $.11; F: $.19; G: $..38; and H: $.30.

These parts have to operate sequentially, but they can be split into two modules between any two components; for example, between A and B, B and C, C and D, and so on. Assembly work costs $.10 more if the parts are split into two modules. Should they be made as one or as two modules? And if the choice is two modules, which parts will go into each module?

3. The Amrine Company offers to deliver five small machines for $1,700 each and guarantees a mean time between failures (MTBF) of 1,000 hours and a useful life of about 5,000 hours. The Phillips Company bid is $2,500 per machine with a guaranteed MTBF of 1,500 hours and a useful life of about 7,500 hours. Breakdowns cost $50 each for repair time and lost production. Replacement parts of the kind needed for the Amrine machines

will normally cost $25 per repair. Parts for Phillips machines come at $50.

    a. Which machines should be bought?

    b. How many machines of each kind would operate a year without a breakdown? To answer this question, divide 2,000, the operating hours in a year, by the MTBF. Use the answer as an exponent and raise the fraction 1/2.72 to the power indicated. If, for example, the exponent is 1, then 1/2.72 is simply 0.37. This is the probability that one machine will operate for a year without failure. Multiply this probability by the number of machines to answer this question.

    4. The ABC Company pays a royalty of $.60 a unit on a product it manufactures. Royalties are paid at the end of the year and will have to be paid for five more years before the patent runs out. Production for this year and the next five years is expected to be 7,000, 8,000, 10,000, 12,000, 12,000, and 11,000, respectively.

    The patent holder has offered ABC the opportunity to pay $25,000 in lieu of all future royalty payments.

    Assuming that money is worth 8 percent to ABC in other uses, what should it do? Show the figures.

    5. In the case of the redundancy example in the text, what would the answer be if part A had a reliability of .94 and part B .92, with all other figures remaining the same?

SUGGESTED SUPPLEMENTARY READINGS

Mullick, Santinder K., and Haussener, Donald. "Production Decisions for New Products." *Management Accounting,* August 1974, pp. 27–32.

Norquist, W. E. "How to Increase Reliability of Consumer Products." *Mechanical Engineering,* January 1973, pp. 25–28.

Rao, Vithala R., and Soutar, Geoffrey N. "Subjective Evaluations for Product Design Decisions." *Decision Sciences,* January 1975, pp. 120–34.

section three

DESIGNING PRODUCTION FACILITIES

EVERY KIND OF production requires physical facilities in the form of buildings, machines, and equipment. These have to be so designed and arranged as to allow for the economical production of products and services.

These facilities should be located advantageously, considering the sources of the company's physical inputs, such as materials, labor, and other costs, and its outputs, considering freight costs and the location of markets. Chapter 7 considers locations and the interactions of the various factors which bear upon the proper location of an organization's production facilities.

Chapter 8 introduces the concept of capacity and relates the productive capacity provided to the capacity which future operations seem likely to call for. Methods for calculating the capacity of a production facility are discussed. So also is the matter of employee work hours and their probable output as it relates to the hours of work. The effect of the learning curve as it changes capacity is considered.

The buildings which house operations need to be so designed as to facilitate economical production. They need to provide for housing the facilities used directly to produce products or services and to keep these assets in operable condition. Chapter 9 deals with the kinds of buildings and their internal services. The arrangement of production facilities within a factory to allow for economical production is also considered in Chapter 9. The merits of various layout patterns are presented. Methods for moving products from operation to operation are also considered.

Chapter 10 continues the study of arrangements of machines and equipment so that production will be facilitated and carried on in the most economical way. Chapter 10 also considers the nature of metal working operations. Then it turns to the possibility of using lines of machines.

Chapter 11 continues the discussion of the overall designing of factory operations for economical production. This chapter is devoted to the designing of manual jobs along assembly lines—the kind of work we all associate with mass production. This is where large numbers of workers have adjacent work stations through which products pass from one to the next until the products emerge at the end of the line as finished products.

Chapter 12 concerns the maintenance of the organization's physical facilities so that they will continue to be productive. It also takes up the problem of materials handling and the physical movement of materials throughout the plant.

7

Location of facilities

CONTRARY to what we might intuitively think, a plant's exact location is not always of great importance. Nearly all giant companies have production facilities in many locations around the country, and many of them are relatively equal in efficiency.

Yet there are differences, and there may be advantages or disadvantages because of location factors. It is even possible for negative factors to be critically important. Several years ago the National Seating and Dimension Company went to Varney, West Virginia, for low-labor rates but went bankrupt trying to train coal miners to be good wood workers. And over the last half century, most New England textile companies that did not move South, where costs are less, went bankrupt. Most furniture companies, too, have had to move South in order to remain competitive. So, although a plant's location is often not highly important, there are cases where it is very important.

Some locations are better, sometimes decidedly better, than other locations; yet, good locations are not scarce as is evidenced by the diverse location of the American manufacturing industry. Steel mills are found in Pennsylvania, Ohio, Indiana, Illinois, Alabama, California, and other states. There are shoe factories in Massachusetts, New York, Maryland, Ohio, Illinois, Wisconsin, Missouri, and California. Many other industries show similar dispersions, many with international locations in Europe, Japan, Canada, Mexico, and South America. The world is shrinking too, with more and more industries competing in world markets rather than national or regional markets.

There are other examples. Years ago General Electric built its Appliance Park (for household appliance manufacture) at Louisville. Why

FIGURE 7–1

Location of steel production facilities in the United States

Source: American Iron and Steel Institute.

Louisville, instead of Cincinnati, St. Louis, or Indianapolis? Many other companies have built plants in these cities. And years ago automobiles developed in Detroit, tires in Akron, airplanes in Los Angeles and Seattle, General Electric in Schenectady, National Cash Register in Dayton. In most of these cases, the original choice of where to locate, made many years ago, was largely pure happenstance.

PITFALLS IN LOCATION CHOICES

Companies sometimes make mistakes in choosing locations. One firm accepted a community's offer of a free site and then found that subsoil conditions were so bad that it had to spend several times a good site's cost on foundations. Another company turned down an in-town site at $20,000 an acre and bought outlying land at $4,000 an acre. Then it ran into two years of zoning problems and had to buy two extra lots for "protection," only to have sewer problems. It finally cost $25,000 an acre, plus the delay.

A third company accepted a town's claims that glossed over a poor labor picture. Six months after it moved in, it had labor problems. A fourth company located where there was only one means of transportation—whose charges promptly went up because of the lack of competition. A fifth located in a nice industrial park, then found that it was four miles out of the free city pick-up and delivery zone. It is paying a penalty of more than $60,000 a year for this oversight. A sixth put up a $15 million paper mill but didn't buy enough space for the disposal of waste chemicals. Now its five-acre lake of waste liquid is filling up, and there is no more land for reservoirs.

Plant location specialists have no end of such stories. The common thread is that some one thing, overlooked, turned out to be seriously disadvantageous. Location choice is perhaps as much avoiding all seriously negative features as it is choosing the most positive factors.

Rarely does an organization locate a new facility today without careful study. Every attempt is made to choose the best location and, in particular, avoid faux pas. When Chrysler was choosing a place to put a $50 million assembly plant (which opened some years ago in Belvidere, Illinois), it went through a computer analysis of 20 locations. Among the considerations were inbound and outbound freight rates; direct and indirect labor costs; the anticipated percentage of sales in each of 459 economic zones all over the United States for three years and five years ahead, and other factors designed to yield a dollars-and-cents estimate on such things as freight backhauling versus overtime operation.

In the service sector, considerably more effort is also being spent in properly locating branch banks, retail stores, fire stations, community health centers, to name a few.[1]

LOCATION AS AN INDIVIDUAL MATTER

The examples just given of unfortunate location choices would have been unfortunate for any company. But, because most companies are more careful and make better analyses, such mistakes are probably few.

It is more probable that a location is good or bad because of the way its merits relate to the needs of the particular organization concerned. For one organization it may be most important to be located near the organization's customers. But it may be more important to another organization to be near the sources of supply of materials and component parts. Still other organizations may find that the most important thing is to locate where there is an adequate labor supply of the kind needed by the organization. Nor can transportation be forgotten. These are high where products are heavy and bulky.

Thus, the biggest reason why organizations choose varied locations is that their needs differ. Consequently, it takes different locations to meet these different needs. So, although the discussion in the remainder of this chapter is in general terms, a good location is an individualized matter. This is called a "situational" or "contingency" approach to decision making—stated simply, "It all depends."

---

[1] See Chapter 26 for a detailed description of a fire station location analysis.

ECOLOGY AND ENVIRONMENTAL VALUES

Manufacturing plants often produce waste in the form of polluted water, air, or solid wastes, and often they are noisy. For the most part noise is within the plant, so its reduction is related to worker safety and comfort more than to community well-being.

Not many years ago, polluted air and water were accepted as facts of life about which nothing need be done, and, indeed, as things about which nothing *could* be done, but not today. Public sentiment, backed by federal and local laws, is putting pressure on managers to improve these conditions. (The ecology wave is not confined to the United States; Sweden, Japan, Russia, and many other countries also have antipollution laws.)

Federal law prohibits companies, and municipal governments as well, dumping waste into navigable waterways without a permit, and such permits are now almost impossible to obtain. Companies and cities which have been dumping effluents now have to clean up.

The contaminants are of many kinds. A steel mill, for example, routinely flushes cyanides, phenols, suiphides, and ammonia into adjacent rivers. Electric power plants and many factories return hot water to rivers (thermal pollution). There is apparently no good way to get rid of heat except by means of expensive and gigantic cooling towers. Today's regulations say that warm water discharged into a river may not raise the stream's temperature by more than 5°, or above 87° in any case. (The sun does better than 87° in many places, so there are places where this regulation is unrealistic.) Sometimes this water contains too much oxygen and is harmful to fish. Steel plants usually emit sooty smoke and sulphur dioxide fumes into the air.

The job of cleaning up is by no means easy, nor can it be done at low cost. Union Carbide, for example, has been spending $40 million a year trying to stop its air and water pollution in West Virginia. And even at this rate it will take several years to do the job well. Riegel Paper Company spends $10 million a year on cleaning up. Kansas City Power & Light has invested $45 million in a "scrubber" system which is supposed to remove the ash, soot, and harmful gases from the smokestacks of its coal-burning electricity generating plant.

It is estimated by the President's Council on Environmental Quality that it will cost some $5 billion annually throughout the 1970s to reduce emissions and solid wastes to a satisfactory level. Some 20 percent of the cost will be required for air pollution control, 40 percent for water pollution control, and the other 40 percent for solid waste disposal. Industry will not have to pay all of this cost, however, since sewage, waste, and trash disposal are included in the figures, and these are largely costs to local city governments.

Managers of some factories say—perhaps correctly—that the costliness of meeting all the antipollution standards is too great and that they will have to close down some operations. No doubt such statements are for the most part exaggerations, but, nonetheless, they will prove to be true in some individual cases.

If, in an individual case, it comes down to relaxing the standards or closing a facility down, some communities seem ready to let the factory close down and do without the industry and its jobs. This is a most difficult question for a community. Almost certainly the people who would lose their jobs if this occurred would rather have jobs and dirty air or water than clean air and water and no jobs.

Yet, with today's regulations, the choice is often not their's to make. Employers sometimes find that the added cost for a plant which is already somewhat uneconomical to operate is too much. Faced with regulations that would force operations at a loss, the decision is to close up. Not only the employees but communities, too, may not have the power to relax state and federal regulations, even if they are willing to endure the old conditions.

Industry gets some tax relief from the financial burden incurred for alleviating pollution situations. The costs of antipollution equipment receives special tax consideration (in both federal and state income taxes) in the form of faster write-offs and tax reductions to offset part of the expense. And local tax rates on the value of antipollution equipment are often very low. There may be other benefits. The recovered (and reusable) effluent itself, particularly from chemical plants, is sometimes worth enough to offset part of the cost of staying clean.

Besides these positive incentives to clean up, a number of possible punitive actions face organizations which do not comply with the regulations. Penalties that would deny government contracts to noncomplying companies seem likely to be enacted into law. And noncomplying city governments may be denied government grants. It is even possible for the responsible managers to be sued by outsiders, or to be fined, or even jailed. All of these possible penalties may backfire, however, because they make it more certain that old facilities will just be closed down.

Quite a few people believe that this represents overkill and that government regulators are asking for too much too fast and imposing restrictions which can be met only at high cost, which, of course, has to be passed on to the public.

Employees, and frequently their unions, are objecting to the severity of restraints which may result in their losing their jobs. In a few cases, the regulations have been relaxed. The energy crisis of the mid 1970s caused the relaxing of some standards. Prior to this crisis, many electric power generating plants were switched from coal to oil and gas as a means for complying with antipollution standards (to get rid of the coal smoke). Now, many have been given permission to go back to coal in order to save on oil and gas.

Some of the biggest adjustment problems are faced by city governments which have to contend with sewage and trash disposal. A great many communities cannot afford to build the facilities needed to meet the state and federal regulations. Some communities, however, are building prototype plants which recover reusable materials from trash and which produce methane gas which can be used in place of coal or oil to power electrical generation plants. These attempts have, so far, not proved to be financially attractive.

RELOCATION

Several years ago PPG (formerly Pittsburgh Plate Glass Company) built a mile-long modern addition to its glass plant outside Cumberland, Maryland. It was built to use a new process which floated molten glass on a bed of molten tin, a process that was developed in England for producing plate glass at low costs. When the new plant came into production, the company's old Ford City, Pennsylvania, plant went on short hours. Essentially PPG relocated its production and moved it from Ford City to Cumberland.

Whenever an existing organization makes location decisions, they involve either the relocation of existing facilities or expansion by opening facilities in new geographical areas.

Plant relocation is common with the trend being from cities to suburbs or occasionally across country, usually from East to West, or North to South. Some of the causes for this migration are lower taxes, less crime, more recreational activities, and a more relaxed life. Other reasons include the need to expand and increase capacity, to open new markets, or to be closer to raw materials or suppliers.

The relocation of the PPG facilities referred to above was for still a different reason. PPG would have liked to have built its new glass factory at Ford City. It did not want to move, but the labor union at Ford City wouldn't allow this process there, hence the expansion at Cumberland.

Curiously, if business gets either better or worse, there may be need to relocate. If it gets better, the company's managers have to decide where to build the added facilities. Or, if business gets worse, perhaps the poor location of one or more of its facilities has been a contributing cause of the difficulty.

Actually facility relocations probably should be more common than they are. Many plants are in locations which become more obsolete every year; yet, each year their managers put off moving. Sometimes they even expand production or service facilities in wrong locations because they are already there. They really have a relocation problem, but they don't recognize it, or they don't have the courage to face the task of building a new plant. Examples can be seen in retail stores "hanging on" in decaying core areas of cities; of fire stations built 75 years ago and mislocated with respect to the current hazard characteristics of the city. A&P grocery's rejuvenation program of the mid 1970s consisted of closing down supermarkets in poor locations.

Sometimes the poor location of facilities can be disasterous. Two of the major reasons for the failure of retailing giant W. T. Grant in 1975 were its rapid expansion a few years earlier into poor locations and their reluctance to close many old stores which were located in what had become poor locations.

THE COMMUNITY VIEWPOINT

Most communities are anxious to attract industry because of the jobs and the money industry brings into the community. Besides this, the taxes industry pays helps lower the burden on individuals. People need jobs, and communities without businesses are rarely prosperous. The United States Chamber of Commerce says that 100 new factory workers in a community will make 110 new households and will create 75 more jobs in the community in other lines. One hundred new factory workers in a community also means nearly $1.5 million in annual personal income and $1 million more in bank deposits in the community.

In fact, so many communities want industry that even a minor objection by anyone in one community can be enough to cause a company to choose another community. Several years ago Columbus lost a new Ford factory to Lorain, Ohio, because a college professor objected to the rezoning of a small part of the site. Columbus lost 2,000 jobs to Lorain.

At the same time, most communities are quite demanding. They want industry but no "dirty" industry, only clean service or light manufacturing industry. They want it to be staffed entirely with high-paid childless executives. And they want the factory to look like a park with no smoke, noise, nor rail nor truck traffic in and out. It is not easy to satisfy all their demands.

Actually, in the 1970s, the ecology and antipollution wave really did dampen the enthusiasm for new industry in some communities. In 1970, residents of the small town of Congers, New York, picketed the site of a future $3 million Reynolds Metal Company plant. They were afraid that it would pollute a nearby state park. So Reynolds built its plant elsewhere. Later, the people of Beaufort, South Carolina, demonstrated against a proposed $100 million chemical plant to be built by BASF, a large German chemical company. They were afraid it would cause air and water pollution. This plant, too, was not built there.

Such opposition to new industry (and there have been other such cases) would never have occurred a decade earlier. But in the 1970s and stimulated by student age groups (who were not very job-conscious), many people became aware of potential dangers to the environment, and this feeling frequently played a part in facility locations.

By no means are all people united in such viewpoints. In 1971, the Sierra Club, the United Automobile Workers, and several other groups objected to the building of a nuclear power plant in Midland, Michigan. Whereupon, 15,000 Midland citizens held a football-style rally supporting its construction.

In all three of these cases, the local unemployment rate was probably

FIGURE 7–2

Winner, New Stanton, Pa., gets the new Volkswagen plant and the loser, Brook Park, Ohio

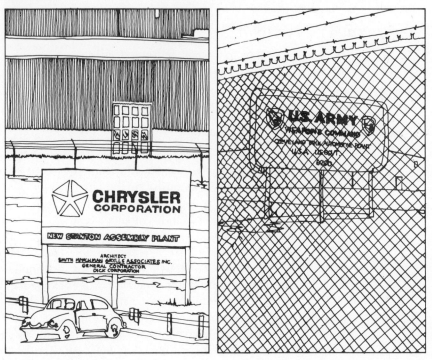

Source: *Business Week*, June 21, 1976.

over 7 percent at the time. Turning away new jobs is surely not what everyone wants. The unemployed in Congers and in Beaufort would almost surely feel the same way as did the citizens of Midland. Given a chance they would have chosen jobs.

In 1976 when Volkswagen was deciding where to put its new assembly plant in the United States, dozens of communities tried to get it to locate there. The choice finally made was New Stanton, Pennsylvania, where VW bought from Chrysler a partially completed assembly plant (see Figure 7–2). Because the plant would add 5,000 jobs, the state of Pennsylvania put up nearly $50 million to help VW buy the property and to improve upon rail and roadway connections. The state also agreed to see that $150 million more would be made available for borrowing. VW was to invest $50 million of its own money.

Communities as places to live

Over the years, companies planning new factories are paying increasing attention to the nature of the community as a place to live. Employees, including company executives, probably do better work when the community is a pleasant place in which to live. Adequate schools, recreation, cultural, and sports activities are an important part of this decision. At the same time, companies avoid many big city residential suburbs because taxes will probably be high there.

COMMUNITY DOMINATION

Most companies prefer not to put a plant anywhere where it would dominate the community. General Electric does not like to put a plant anywhere where it will hire more than one eighth of the people working in the area. GE has more than 100 factories, so this policy would rule out many locations where GE already is, including Schenectady. Such policies are in agreement with most community objectives; they too do not want single-company or single-industry domination.

Seattle, dominated by Boeing Aircraft, is a case in point. In the early 1970s Boeing's business was down, and several thousand employees were laid off. Consequently, Seattle had a double depression. The whole country was in a depression, and on top of this Seattle had its own extra local depression. Things became so bad that a group of laid-off engineers rented a freeway billboard at the edge of Seattle which said, "Last one to leave Seattle, please turn out the lights."

Another General Electric policy is not to locate a small plant in a big metropolitan area where its corporate voice would be muffled or lost.

Still another policy is not to put plants too close together. Ford Motor Company likes to have its plants 15 miles or more apart (although its Detroit plants are not that far apart). Westinghouse says 20 miles. These reasons are tied in with the above reasons, but a company also avoids having two of its plants drawing from and competing for the same labor pool.

LABOR LAWS AND RELOCATION

When a company relocates and closes down its old plant, it may have a legal obligation to offer jobs in the new location to employees in the closed-down plant. Laws and court decisions are ambiguous on this matter, but they are moving in the direction of giving employees in a plant that is being closed down a vested right in a similar job in the new plant.

Companies should clarify this matter by spelling out in their labor contracts what, if any, obligation they have in case of plant relocations. Practically speaking, this usually means that they agree to offer either (1) employment in the new plant, and possibly some moving expenses, or (2) substantial severance pay to employees who are not offered jobs in the new location. Retraining programs are often set up for severed employees. Also, employees near retirement age can retire early on liberal pensions.

If employees are given a chance to move with the relocation, the number of employees who accept drops off sharply with the distance of the move, and even more sharply if the new plant's pay rates will be less. Several years ago, when Armour closed its Sioux City, Iowa, meat packing plant (1,200 employees), it gave three month's notice and set up both an employment and retraining office. One hundred displaced workers who were more than 55 years old and had 20 years' service retired. Six hundred others took severance pay equal to about $125 per year of service. Only 400 asked to be transferred to Armour jobs elsewhere. And at an earlier plant closing at Fort Worth, Texas, only 155 out of 1,000 asked for transfers. The geographic choice of relocation, of course, can make a difference. When Western Electric, a few years ago, relocated one of its plants from New Jersey to Colorado a substantial number of employees made the move.

LABOR

Wherever a company goes, it must have employees, so an ample supply of labor is essential. It helps if the available labor is already skilled, but for most companies this is not necessary. Most companies expect to train new employees because jobs are so varied and so highly specialized that a company will never find very many new employees who already know how to do most of its jobs.

For regular factory or office jobs the work habits and attitudes of prospective workers are much more important than the skills they already have. People in some areas are just better workers than those in some other areas. Absentee rates differ, and so does the willingness to work.

If a company moves to a new location, it may have to move a few of its skilled workers and some supervisors, but it will usually recruit most of its new work force from the area of the new plant. If it moves to a lower wage area, this can often cause problems about what pay rate to use for transferred workers. If they are paid their old high rate, they are out of line with the new workers. But, if they are to get the local area rate, they take a pay cut, which of course they do not like.

An effective new labor force cannot be recruited quickly. When a factory moves into a community, it will take time to build up a good work force. Good workers are rarely out looking for jobs in great numbers. In fact, it is well to build up employment slowly and thus not to have to hire too many marginal people.

One should also pay attention to quantity and distance. The personnel planners for a new factory should not plan to hire more than 5 percent of the area population or 20 percent of the eligible labor force. Nor should they plan to recruit beyond 20 miles from the new plant. If there are not enough people to fill the factory's needs within 20 miles, it will probably have trouble finding employees. It is possible, however, that in the future, employers may not be free to make this decision. In 1976, the government's Equal Employment Opportunity Commission ordered Timken (maker of bearings) to go out 25 miles. In Bucyrus, Ohio, where Timken has a factory, there were very few blacks, so the EEOC wanted Timken to go 25 miles away and hire blacks who lived in Mansfield.

FREIGHT COSTS

Freight costs as a location factor are of little consequence for companies making small high-value products such as watches or cameras. Their freight costs (which is often air freight) amount to only 1 or 2 percent of their total costs. So far as freight costs are concerned, it doesn't matter where they locate. But for larger, heavier products it matters more. In rare cases (cement, plaster, gypsum), freight costs are much higher. Johns Manville and U.S. Gypsum spend close to 20 percent of their sales dollars for freight.

For most companies, freight cost differentials are not as important as wage differences. If wages in one location are noticeably lower than in another, it will pay to go there even if freight costs are a little higher.

So far as freight costs are concerned, one might think that a plant should be located where total freight costs are the least. But this is easy to say and hard to do. Companies buy thousands of different raw materials from suppliers in many locations. And they sell nationwide. It is hard to discover the location where freight cost is least. Besides, in ten years' time suppliers will not all be where they are today nor will a company's customers. So the rule to locate where freight costs are the least is usually not too helpful.

Freight costs cannot be eliminated no matter where a factory is located because, in one form or another, the product has to be moved from the raw material producer to the final user; thus, a facility should be located somewhere between the raw material source and the market. Locating near raw materials reduces raw materials freight, but freight costs for delivering products increase. Locating near the market saves on finished products freight but increases on raw materials freight costs. Being near the supply source, however, is not always important because vendors often "equalize" or absorb freight differences. They pay all freight costs above the cost from the customer's nearest competitive supplier. Sometimes they pay all the freight costs, in which case a company might as well locate its factory near its market.

NEARNESS TO MARKET

Being near the market lets an organization give better service to customers, and it often saves on freight costs. Of these two advantages, giving better service is usually the more important.

But, as we have noted, a facility can't always be near its market—its whole market—because this market is too widespread. It may be nationwide or international. Large companies with worldwide markets may put plants in many parts of the country or the world to get close to these markets. Bucyrus-Erie, which manufactures gigantic earth-moving equipment for the coal mining industry, recently opened a new plant in Pocatello, Idaho, to be near the vast coal reserves in Idaho, Wyoming, and Colorado.

Smaller companies must either give up the idea of being close to all their customers or must concentrate their selling in the area near their factory so that they can be close to their market. Small plants in New England serve the northeastern states; those on the West Coast serve the Pacific states. Most small plants are started close to the owner's home, and, as they grow, they develop their market nearby. In many cases, the location of a facility determines its market area more than the market area determines the facility's location.

In the service sector, the market area is usually determined by travel time of customers to the facility (banks, recreation facilities, restaurants, hospitals) or of travel time of servers to customers (fire trucks and ambulances to houses, telephone installers, appliance repairers).

NEARNESS TO RAW MATERIALS AND SUPPLIERS

Being near its raw materials allows a company to get better supplier service and to save on incoming freight. But—like being close to the market—this is not always possible. No one facility can be close to 5,000 suppliers. General Motors buys from 50,000 suppliers in at least 1,000 different locations. On the other hand, no matter where a factory is located, it can probably find nearby suppliers for most of the things it buys, so every factory can be near many of its suppliers. General Motors' buying is spread out primarily because its own manufacturing is spread out. Its plants are near most of their suppliers.

Companies that use iron ore or other materials which create a lot of waste often locate near their raw materials so they can minimize the transportation of the heavy, bulky waste. Similarly, where finished products are heavy, bulky, and of low value, freight costs limit the area the companies can serve. Cement plants, for example, mostly serve local areas and are found in many parts of the country.

NEARNESS TO OTHER PLANTS AND WAREHOUSES

Companies usually try to locate new plants where they will complement their other plants and warehouses. The best location for a facility, therefore, might depend on where its other facilities are. New locations should fill a hole where the company has no facility and where its markets are now not adequately served or are being supplied by costly long-distance hauls.

The location of competitors' plants and warehouses also need to be considered. Each company should develop location strategies where they will have the advantage over competitors both in freight costs and fast customer service.

WATER

Some companies need a great deal of water—more than is available at low costs in some places. U.S. Steel's Fairless Works uses 250 million gallons of water a day, and only a large river (the Delaware) could supply this much.

For industries that need such large quantities of water, most locations cannot be considered. Industries which need large amounts of water include paper, sugar refining, steel, rubber, leather, chemical, rayon, food processing, aluminum, and nuclear power plants. Producing a ton of synthetic rubber requires 60,000 gallons of water, a ton of aluminum takes 300,000 gallons, a ton of rayon 200,000 gallons, and steel 40,000 gallons per ton. Water is used directly in the processes, or for cooling products or machines, for condensing steam, or for washing, cleaning, quenching, and for air-conditioning.

Companies that use these quantities of water need to be very sure that future supplies will be ample for their needs. This becomes a more critical factor in plant location year by year because the use of water is increasing, and environmental pressures are more and more stringent on the use and pollution of water.

Water used in these processes is often contaminated, or it is hot after its use and needs to be decontaminated or cooled before it can be returned to rivers or lakes. Since nearly all cities and states have laws against dumping waste of harmful nature into waterways, the costs of returning water to its natural state are often very important factors into any location decision.

LAND COSTS

Land costs and local taxes are sometimes deciding factors in factory location choices, although on the whole they are relatively unimportant. The total cost of a site, including taxes and landscaping, may be as little as 3 percent and is usually less than 10 percent of the total cost of a facility. Of this total, the land itself is often less than half. Since it is only a one-time cost, it is usually relatively unimportant in the choice of a location. In fact, it is sometimes such a minor factor that communities wanting industry often donate land (or offer it at a reduced price) to an organization which it would like to have locate in the area. Often they rezone the land to accommodate the user.

LOCAL TAXES AND LOCATION INCENTIVES

Local real estate and property taxes also are usually relatively unimportant, and, except where other considerations are nearly equal, neither should be the deciding factor in the choice of a location. Most manufacturing companies have investments in plant and equipment and inventory of $10,000 or more per employee. (General Electric's investment in plant and inventories is $12,000 per employee, National Cash Register's is $13,500, General Motors' is $17,000.)

Large cities usually have tax rates of from 2 to 6 percent of the value of property, so it would seem that taxes might be anywhere from $200 to $800 (or more) per year per employee. But rarely are taxes as high as, say, 6 percent because assets are almost never appraised at their full value (although legally they are usually supposed to be appraised at full value). A company usually ends up paying perhaps 2 percent of its assets' real value. This amounts to somewhere around $300 per employee, with differences between areas rarely being more than $100 per employee per year. This could be important, but, taken by itself, it is seldom a decisive factor, particularly since low tax rates often don't stay low.

This generalization, that taxes should count little in location choice, does not always apply, however. U.S. Steel has investments in plant, equipment, and inventories of $26,000 per employee. DuPont's total plant, equipment, and inventory investment comes to $32,000 per employee. To them even small tax rate differences are of consequence.

Communities that furnish free sites or even rent- and tax-free buildings to new companies for a period of years usually get new companies. Generally these "incentives" are for limited periods, after which a company pays regular rent and taxes (or even more to support incentives for others). Companies should not allow temporary inducements to overshadow the basic merits of alternative locations. If they do, they may find themselves located where, in the long run, overall costs are higher.

Most large companies regard location free offers as a relatively minor factor. By no means, however, are they opposed to accepting such offers, and they frequently do accept them. They do so, however, only where the other factors for alternative locations are more or less equal.

FOREIGN LOCATIONS

With domestic production costs increasing and foreign markets expanding rapidly, many American companies are locating facilities abroad. Most of these are primarily to supply foreign markets; however, some of these are to take advantage of lower labor costs (especially in countries such as Mexico, Korea, and Taiwan) to produce products for the American market. The movement is slowing down, however, because wages in almost every part of the world have gone up faster in recent years than in the United States.

But in the very low wage-rate areas, the wage savings overseas are great enough so that, in spite of the many difficulties caused by learning local customs and complying with local laws and the great distance, it is still likely that labor-intensive items will be made abroad in the years ahead.

URBAN, SUBURBAN, AND SMALL-TOWN LOCATIONS

The movement away from the cities is still on so far as many facility locations are concerned. Today there is hardly a small town that does not have one or two factories. But—and this is sometimes not appreciated—most manufacturing is still done, and most new buildings are still being built, close to cities. Today's trend is to moderately small factories, so small towns with small labor pools are suitable. But new plants, large and small, are also being built on the outskirts of big cities.

Wage rates in small towns are usually a little lower than in cities, although not so much lower as they used to be. Even so, they are sometimes as much as one fifth lower. Often, too, labor relations are better in small towns since they are less influenced by other companies' labor problems.

Small towns have some disadvantages, but most of them are minor. It takes a while—possibly a year or two—to train unaccustomed new workers to get used to manufacturing activities. Inventory investments are likely to be larger, particularly for spare parts for maintenance. And the company will need to have a fairly complete maintenance department because it cannot draw on outsiders. Fire insurance rates may be higher. Absenteeism during hunting season will be greater.

Many companies, wishing to leave congested city locations, go only as far as the suburbs and not to rural locations. If they move to a nearby suburb, they may not have to hire very many new employees. Suburban locations usually give a company most of the advantages of both city and country. Labor is plentiful and the plant is not far from the market provided by the city, which, in the case of small plants, is often its main market. Land for present and future needs is usually available at reasonable prices and taxes are generally a little lower than in cities.

Suburbs usually have better rail and truck connection than small towns—almost as good, in fact, as those of cities. Suburban plants are also close to service industries. Located in a suburb, a company does not need to have so many of its own maintenance people—electricians, plumbers, and so on—as it would in a small town.

ORGANIZED INDUSTRIAL DISTRICTS

Factories, stores, and homes don't mix very well; they ought to be in separate areas. Factories need railroads and superhighways, and they create truck traffic. Among other things, they need high-power electric lines. All these things are undesirable in residential areas. Whole industrial districts—of factories and only factories—constitute a happy solution to the problem of mixed areas. To meet this need, some 2,000 industrial parks have been set up in the last 20 years.

The advantages of industrial parks include lower construction costs, because preliminary site work is done, and site preparation pitfalls are few because the land is already prepared. Financial and transportation services are close. The site is already favorably zoned, and it is in a prestige area where land values are likely to go up because of the controlled programs.

On the negative side is the small acreage available for expansion (usually 5 acres and rarely more than 25 acres). The facility also becomes part of a community and may have to submit to control of its architecture, design, and construction, or even to using a "suggested" contractor. It has close neighbors whose labor problems may spread to other organizations in the industrial park. Traffic flow in and out of the park and from and onto roads and highways may be congested during rush periods, although some of this can be eliminated by staggering shift times.

Space requirements

Inasmuch as the amount of floor space needed in a new plant varies a great deal between industries, a company's old operations will suggest how much space is needed. Here are some general guides: compact operations, not much extra space anywhere; 200 square feet per worker (this includes all floor space, not just the space at a person's workplace). Ordinary manufacturing, with ample aisles and storage areas, needs perhaps 500 to 700 square feet per worker. Spread-out manufacturing might require up to 1,500 square feet per worker.

When a company is building a new factory, it should prepare for the future and choose a site with more space than it needs for the present. Westinghouse Electric uses a 5-to-1 or 50-acre rule, whichever is greater. It tries to get a site 5 times as big as its present-building floor space requirements, ar at least 50 acres. Some companies use even a 10-to-1 ratio. If they end up not requiring all the land, they may want to control the land next to their new facility to minimize the build-up of hot-dog stands, bars, loan companies, gasoline stations, and small stores, which add to the traffic congestion. Excess land can usually be sold or leased at a profit to other organizations which compliment the parent organization.

Most companies acquire enough land to let them double their initial capacity. Actually, a 4-to-1 ratio will often provide enough land for this much expansion.

The mid-1970s saw a reversion away from such substantial provision for the future. Many companies found that they had been wasting their money by investing in real estate that they did not need at the time and not in the future either. Often, too, the companies that did need to expand found that because of changed conditions they wanted to expand somewhere else and not where they had bought extra land 10 or 20 years earlier.

SITES

Choosing the general area is the real job in selecting a location, but the site within the area must also be suitable. It must have, to some extent, all of the characteristics already discussed. It probably should be near a residential area where workers can live. And it should be near main streets or roads and be served by the public transportation system. Often land that has been zoned for industrial use is the poorest available; it is sited on an old dump, or it is swampy or subject to floods, or it is inaccessible.

Land for a site should be dry and able to carry the building's weight without much settling. The site must be zoned for industrial use, and it needs to have good police and fire protection.

If the facility's operations unavoidably creates smoke or fumes, it should choose a site so that the prevailing winds will carry them toward the open country—although a company may have to put in antiair pollution equipment to stop smoke and fumes even in rural locations. If the plant's processes produce large quantities of waste which have to be carried away by water (common in chemical companies), the site must be next to a river or some other large body of water. And again antipollution regulations also must be met.

The cost of alternative sites will be important only if there is a great difference in the prices and little difference in the merits. Besides the cost of the land, some sites will require more filling, grading, and expensive foundations, or more costly connections to utilities than other locations.

It is desirable to have a railroad siding and a truck dock, and, for some companies, a dock for ships. Being near a superhighway is also very desirable and may be more important than being near a railroad. (Half of everything Ford Motors buys comes in on trucks and half of Ford's finished cars leave by truck.)

There should be enough room for the present buildings, for future expansion, and for parking employees' automobiles. In size, the parking lot may approximate the total area of the plant itself; however, a good public transportation system (often with fares subsidized by the company) reduces this need and this cost.

Any company that is planning to build a new facility should not look only at communities that are aggressively going after new industry. Communities that are not actively seeking industries may have greater advantages than those which try to attract new plants. And both "active" and "passive" communities will often, if asked, make concessions equal to those offered by other places. Parke-Davis wanted to build a research facility in Ann Arbor, Michigan, on a site which would require new sewer construction, and when the company objected to bearing the nearly $100,000 charge, the city cut it to less than half. When Chicago Pneumatic Tool Company was thinking of moving from its Cleveland plant, Utica, New York, was its choice until the company found that New York tax laws were unfavorable. When Utica's city leaders went to Albany and in two days got the laws changed, Chicago Pneumatic found the new laws satisfactory and moved to Utica.

When the search for a new location gets down to picking the exact site, it is well to have either expert consultants or real estate brokers do the final investigating of good and bad points of different sites. Better yet, they should first get an option on the most likely site. The point is that the company needs to keep its identity secret. Any time a well-known company becomes interested in a plot of ground and people find out about it, its price skyrockets. Options protect a company against price gouges.

MAKE-BUY ALTERNATIVES IN NEW FACILITIES DECISIONS

Obviously a new facility need not be built if an existing facility is available whose size and other characteristics fit the organization's requirements. In fact, many organizations begin their operations, relocate, or expand by buying or leasing an existing facility. W. T. Grant, which went bankrupt in 1975, sold over 100 of its empty stores to Kresge, Sears, and J. C. Penney. The new Bucyrus-Erie facility in Pocatello, Idaho, mentioned earlier, in which Bucyrus-Erie planned to make large earth-removing equipment, was actually an existing plant. It had been built in World War II to manufacture huge battleship guns. In another case, the Michelin Tire Co. purchased an empty Gates Rubber plant in Denver rather than building a new facility.

In these times of inflating building costs, this is often the most advantageous thing to do. Since empty facilities (especially large ones) have few alternative uses and their carrying charges are substantial, the owners of such buildings (often including specialized equipment) are usually willing to sell or rent them at very reasonable prices.

COMPARING ALTERNATIVE LOCATIONS

An analysis of location alternatives should consider both objective factors (such as taxes, labor, transportation, and material costs, and market potentials) and subjective factors (such as schools, recreation, labor union activities, political climate, and even weather conditions).

Companies needing new locations often set up search teams to seek out and evaluate location alternatives. When A. H. Robins (chemical manufacturer) decided to expand its capacity for producing chemicals, it set up a task force of two teams; one to consider the building of a new facility and the other to study buying an existing plant. Because of other considerations, the search was to be limited largely to the state of Virginia.

The "build" team had an engineering firm make a preliminary design of the plant. Then it asked the state of Virginia's industrial development department to help choose a site. The search soon narrowed down to 9 possible locations. Meanwhile the "buy" team narrowed its search to 20, of which 3 became serious candidates.

Robin's first decision was to build a new plant. But, one of the three final candidates for buying was a company which was interested in merging with Robins, and this is eventually what happened. Robins expanded its capacity through this merger and did not build after all.[2]

Rating location alternatives

A simple method which can be used to aid in choosing among location alternatives is to have decision makers evaluate the relative desirability of each location on a number of factors and to evaluate the relative importance of each of the factors in the location decision. For example, suppose the following sites are being considered in terms of the five listed factors. For each factor, each of the team members distributes ten points among the alternative sites in terms of their relative merits. These several point distributions are then averaged to get a composite distribution. Figure 7–3

FIGURE 7–3

	Labor cost	Market potential	Taxes	Water supply	Recreational opportunities
Seattle	3	2	3	5	4
Denver	3	5	2	1	4
St. Louis	4	3	5	4	2

shows one company's composite ratings for Seattle, Denver, and St. Louis.

The figures in Figure 7–3 could be added horizontally to get a total score for each city, but, if this were done, it would impute equal weight to each of the five factors. Actually, in this analysis, the company decided to assign weights, as follows: labor costs, 20 percent, market potential, 30 percent, taxes, 10 percent, water supply, 30 percent, and recreational opportunities, 10 percent. The ratings in Figure 7–3 were accordingly multiplied by the weights, producing the numbers in Figure 7–4.

FIGURE 7–4

	Labor cost	Market potential	Taxes	Water supply	Recreational opportunities	Total
Seattle	60	60	30	150	40	340
Denver	60	150	20	30	40	300
St. Louis	80	90	50	120	20	360

When the weighted point credits for each city are added horizontally, we find that St. Louis has the edge.

The method illustrated here uses the composite of the judgment of several people. Obviously such a mechanical procedure would not be used as the sole criteria for making a decision. Rather, the panel of people asked to participate in the analysis sits down and discusses other factors

---

[2] The story of this merger is told in "Planning a Plant: How a Drug Firm Decided to Build a Chemical Facility," *Wall Street Journal,* October 22, 1975, p. 1.

not included in this calculation before arriving at a decision, or they use the results of the calculation as a basis for further discussion and rating. This approach is sometimes called the "Delphi" method.

THE TRANSPORTATION METHOD IN LOCATION DECISIONS[3]

The transportation method is an operations research technique which can be helpful in making factory and warehouse location decisions. When a company has several plants and several warehouses and is thinking either of putting in added capacity in one place or another or of reallocating the territories served by each factory, this method can be used.

It is easier to understand the transportation method if we start with a reallocation problem, where it must be determined which factories should supply which warehouses and with what quantities. The assumption here is that both factories and warehouses are already in existence. Later the method can be switched to the question of whether or not to build new facilities and where.

In its initial form, the transportation method assumes that each warehouse should be supplied from the nearest factory. There will be times, however, when individual plant capacities and nearby warehouse needs do not match up, and shipments have to be made from more distant plants. The transportation method will show the most economical pairing up of capacities and demands.

The transportation method is suitable for both small and large problems although, of course, all large problems would be handled on computers.

---

[3] Technically, transportation problems are special cases of linear programming problems (described on pages 608–17). Alternative methods to the one described here for solving transportation problems are called the modified distribution method (MODI) and Vogel's approximation method (VAM). Both of these methods are described in operations research books.

Stated in mathematical terms, the transportation method is as follows: There are m plants and n warehouses to which a given commodity is to be shipped. The ith plant has an amount, s_i, of the commodity ($i = 1, \ldots, m$) and the requirements are such that the jth warehouse will get the amount r_j ($j = 1, \ldots, n$). X_{ij} is the quantity of the commodity to be shipped from plant i to warehouse j. C_{ij} is the cost of shipping one unit of the commodity from plant i to warehouse j. The problem becomes:

$$\text{Minimize} \sum_{i=1}^{m} \sum_{j=1}^{n} c_{ij} x_{ij}$$

Subject to

$$(1) \quad \sum_{j=1}^{n} x_{ij} \leq s_i$$

$$(2) \quad \sum_{i=1}^{m} x_{ij} \geq r_j$$

$$(3) \quad x_{ij} \geq 0 \text{ for all } i, j$$

It is assumed also that $c_{ij} > 0$, $r_j > 0$, $s_i > 0$ and $\sum_i r_j \leq \sum_i s_i$.

FIGURE 7–5

Plant	Capacity	Warehouse	Quantity needed
A.................	200	1...................	150
B.................	100	2...................	300
C.................	400	3...................	100
D.................	400	4...................	200
		5...................	300
Total...............	1,100		1,050

A company such as H. J. Heinz, for example, might use it to control tomato canning and the shipment of canned tomatoes. Heinz could determine which canning factory should ship what quantity to which of its many warehouses, or from which of its many warehouses to customer companies, and make these assignments in such a way that shipping costs are minimized. Cities can also use this method to determine how to "ship" trash to alternative land fills.

The transportation method is a trial and error process—but with certain rules to follow. It does not, at first, produce the optimal answer. Rather, it first produces a feasible answer and then improves on it until the best solution is found. The method is an "algorithm" since it consists of several recurring mathematical steps which finally allocate the supply to the demand at the lowest cost while meeting the individual warehouse needs without exceeding any factory source limitations.

Often transportation method problems consider only relative freight costs, but, if different factories produce at different costs, then the two (factory costs and freight costs) can be added together to get relative delivered unit costs for use in the problem.

To illustrate this method we will assume that the Goodride Tire Company has four plants and five warehouses and is concerned with only one line of tires. Any plant can ship to any warehouse, but the costs are different. The costs used in this example include each factory's unit cost *and* the freight costs per unit for shipping products to each warehouse. Daily plant capacities and warehouse demands are shown in Figure 7–5. Factory costs plus freight costs from the plant to each warehouse are shown in Figure 7–6.

When a problem of this kind is solved manually and without a computer

FIGURE 7–6

From plant	To warehouse				
	1	2	3	4	5
A.................	$22	$30	$25	$20	$24
B.................	20	29	21	25	20
C.................	24	30	24	24	24
D.................	23	28	24	22	23

FIGURE 7–7

From plant	To warehouse				
	1	2	3	4	5
A...................	2	10	5	0	4
B...................	0	9	1	5	0
C...................	4	10	4	4	4
D...................	3	8	4	2	3

(large problems would always go on a computer), normally the first step is to subtract the least cost figure ($20 as shown in Figure 7–6) from every cost figure, thus producing Figure 7–7. This is not an essential step and is taken only to make the numbers small (so that the analyst can see the differences more readily) and to hold down the size of the numbers used in later manipulations.

Partial matrix A is then set up. The cost differences are put into small boxes in the upper right corner of each box in partial matrix A. A column to show the plant capacities is added at the right. Similarly a row showing total warehouse needs is added at the bottom (the added column and row figures are sometimes called "rim conditions").

Partial matrix A also contains an added column for "warehouse 6" because of the fact that the four factories can supply more product units than are needed (their total capacity is 1,100, whereas the demand comes only to 1,050 units). Warehouse 6 is an imaginary or "dummy" warehouse, which would receive the 50 units the four factories can produce but which are not needed. In the final allocation of orders to factories, one of the plants will not have to supply all the products it could. This will show up as an allocation of 50 units of this plant's capacity to the imaginary warehouse 6.

Partial matrix A

From plant	To warehouse						Supply
	1	2	3	4	5	6	
A	2	10	5	0	4		200
B	0	9	1	5	0		100
C	4	10	4	4	4		400
D	3	8	4	2	3		400
Demand	150	300	100	200	300	50	1,100 Total

Solving the problem begins by arbitrarily allocating warehouse needs to plants such that the demand and capacity constraints are met. Starting at the upper left, plant A is first assigned 150 units from warehouse 1. This is all that warehouse 1 needs. So the remaining 50 units of plant A's capacity go to warehouse 2. But warehouse 2 needs 300 units altogether. So plant B's entire capacity of 100 is also allocated to warehouse 2. Warehouse 2's remaining needs, then, are to be furnished by plant C.

This arbitrary allocation process continues down each column, moving from left to right, until everything demanded is allocated. As it happens, the number of squares which will have units assigned to them both in the initial and in all subsequent improved allocations will always be equal to one less than the sum of the number of plants and warehouses. In this case, this is $(4 + 6) - 1 = 9$. If this is not so, then there is an error in the calculation.

The way we have started to solve the problem is called "the northwest corner method" simply because it starts in the upper left corner (the northwest corner on a map). With this allocation, matrix A is complete. Demands and capacities are matched in a feasible way, although alternative allocations almost surely exist which produce lower costs.

Matrix A

From plant	To warehouse						
	1	2	3	4	5	6	Supply
A	2 / 150	10 / 50 ⟶ 0	5 / ⟶ 0	0 / 0	4 / 0	0	200
B	0 / 0	9 / 100	1 / 0	5 / 0	0 / 0	0	100
C	4 / 0	10 / 150 ⟵	4 / 100 ⟶	4 / 150	4 / 0	0	400
D	3 / 0	8 / 0	4 / 0	2 / 50	3 / 300	50	400
Demand	150	300	100	200	300	50	1,100 Total

Since no attention has been paid to the costs of this allocation, the next step is to multiply the cost differentials in each little corner box by the quantity allocated and then add them up. The calculation is $(150 \times 2) + (50 \times 10) + (100 \times 9) + (150 \times 10) + (100 \times 4) + (150 \times 4) + (50 \times 2) + (300 \times 3) = \$5,200$. This allocation therefore entails total costs of \$5,200 in excess of the base \$21,000 $(1,050 \times \$20)$, which would be the inescapable minimum.

It is obvious from looking at matrix A that some allocations have been made to high-cost blocks whereas lower-cost blocks are available. So the next step is to set about improving this first tentative allocation.

Looking first at plant A's allocations, can we see any shifts that can be made that would save costs? It costs zero excess dollars to ship from plant A to warehouse 4, whereas this initial allocation of plant A's capacity to warehouses 1 and 2 entails excess costs of $2 and $10 respectively. Is it possible to ship warehouse 2's allocation of 50 units to warehouse 4 instead and save $10 excess costs per unit? Yes, but to do so we must somehow reduce the amount allocated to warehouse 4 so its amount remains at 200. This can be done by transferring either 50 units of plant C's allocation to warehouse 4 to warehouse 2 or 50 units of plant D's allocations to warehouse 4 to warehouse 2. Either transfer would, in itself, lose $6 per unit transferred. (Block C–2's cost is $10 per unit minus block C–4's cost of $4 = $6; similarly, the $8 unit cost in block D–2 less D–4's cost of $2 = $6.) But the $10 savings from shifting plant A's allocation to warehouse 2 to warehouse 4 would result in a net savings of $4 ($10 − $6) for every unit so shifted. Accordingly, as shown in matrix B, the 50 units from plant A are shifted from warehouse 2 to warehouse 4 and 50 units from plant C are shifted from warehouse 4 to warehouse 2. (The alternative shift of 50 units from block D–4 to D–2 could have been made instead; the decision was arbitrary since the savings both equal $4 per unit transferred.)

Matrix B can now be made by incorporating these changes in the original allocations.

Since 50 units were shifted at a savings of $4 each, the total costs are reduced $200.

From here on, the procedure is repeated by evaluating each empty block to see if more cost savings can be made. There prove to be several other changes which will still reduce the costs still further. The inter-

Matrix B

From plant	To warehouse						Supply
	1	2	3	4	5	6	
A	2	10	5	0	4	0	200
	150	0	0	50	0		
B	0	9	1	5	0	0	100
	0	100 ——— 0 ——— 0 ——▶ 0					
C	4	10	4	4	4	0	400
	0	200	100	100	0		
D	3	8	4	2	3	50	400
	0	0 ◀——— 0 ——— 50 ——— 300					
Demand	150	300	100	200	300	50	1,100 Total

Final matrix

From plant	To warehouse						Supply
	1	**2**	**3**	**4**	**5**	**6**	
A	2 / 0	10 / 0	5 / 0	0 / 200	4 / 0	0	200
B	0 / 0	9 / 0	1 / 0	5 / 0	0 / 100	0	100
C	4 / 150	10 / 0	4 / 100	4 / 0	4 / 100	50	400
D	3 / 0	8 / 300	4 / 0	2 / 0	3 / 100	0	400
Demand	150	300	100	200	300	50	1,100 Total

mediate matrices are not shown, but in due time the final matrix emerges. This final matrix reduces the total cost to $4,100 above the $21,000 inescapable minimum.

This solution shows that plant C, with a capacity of 400 units, will actually ship only 350 and will either not produce the other 50 that it could produce or will hold them in inventory for the time being.

Had the warehouses needed more than the factories could produce, we would have had to put in plant E, an imaginary factory, instead of imaginary warehouse 6. Allocations of products to be shipped from plant E would actually be shortages and would tell us which warehouse would have to do without and how many units it would be short of its total needs.

Other applications

Our example of how to use the transportation method has been confined to how best to use existing facilities. This same method can also be used to weigh the merits of expanding one plant as against another. All that is necessary is to work out the problem as if the expanded capacity were already in existence and to use cost figures that are appropriate to what the actual costs would be.

The transportation method can also be used to weigh the merits of building a new factory versus expanding some existing facility.

Finally, it can also compare building new factories in different locations. All that is necessary is to work through the calculations as if the new facilities were in existence and operating at their probable costs.

For example, if plant A, B, and C exist, plant D could be one of the candidates under consideration. After the analysis is complete, D would be replaced with another candidate with its costs and capacities, and the analysis repeated. The resulting costs of the two analyses would then be compared.

REVIEW QUESTIONS

1. How stringent are antipollution laws? Will they, in fact, cause companies to do anything which they would not otherwise do if there were no regulations?

2. What part do labor laws and union contracts play in factory relocation decisions?

3. Both nearness to good transportation and the availability of an adequate labor supply are almost always listed as musts in discussions about location. Yet, if these are so important, how does it happen that industry is so spread out across the United States?

4. How important are local taxes in the choice of locations? How much do they come to in total?

5. What advantages should a company expect to gain if it locates in an industrial park? What bad features might there be?

6. What characteristics should an ideal site have? What should the relationship be between the size of the building and the size of the site?

7. When they build a new factory, many companies buy 50 acres or more of land. Why do they waste money buying so much land they don't need?

8. Could the operations research transportation method be used if demands exceed capacity? How? Could it be used to help decide whether or not to put up a new factory? How?

QUESTIONS FOR DISCUSSION

1. How could a company go about picking a location which would be good over the years? Explain.

2. How could a city or other governmental agency go about picking locations for fire stations, health clinics, or state employment offices?

3. How can one location be much better than others if it takes a computer to figure out which one is better?

4. Each year *Factory* magazine surveys new plant construction in the United States; the results of its studies are reported in the May issue each year. As part of this activity the reporters ask company officials why they put their new factories where they did. There is no general agreement, and the most popular reasons given one year shift a bit from those of the year before. Why do experts differ so widely on the relative importance of location factors?

5. If a company moves to a lower wage area, should it offer its former wages to employees who are invited to move, or should those who are invited to move be offered wages comparable to those in the area where the new operations will be located?

6. If a company happens to locate in an area where the labor attitude is poor, is there anything its managers can do about it?

7. How do labor laws affect location choices?

8. How can location be so important if a college professor's objections are enough to cause a company to choose a location 150 miles away? (See page 143.)

9. If a small town gave a company a free site and tax exemption for ten years, should the company accept? Discuss fully.

10. A small toy manufacturer, who sells nationally and is located in the Chicago area, is thinking of moving his plant to Fayetteville, Arkansas. Advise him and support your position.

11. A location consulting firm has produced the following analysis comparing six alternative locations for a company which will have 1,000 employees.

	A	B	C	D	E	F
Hourly cost of labor....	Low	Moderate	Very low	Moderate	High	High
Productivity of labor...	Moderate	Moderate	Moderate	Low	Moderate	Moderate
Freight cost..........	High	Moderate	High	Moderate	Moderate	Low
Labor supply.........	Adequate	Adequate	Plentiful	Plentiful	Adequate	Plentiful
Union activity........	Moderate	Active	Negligible	Active	Active	Significant
Living conditions......	Good	Very good	Rural	Very good	Excellent	Good

If the company were to choose on the basis of this evidence, which location should be chosen? Why? If more information is really needed, what information?

PROBLEMS

1. Minimize the shipping costs in the following situation. The numbers in the body of the table are the shipping costs per unit.

From factory	To warehouse				Factory production
	D	E	F	G	
A..........................	$9	$12	$5	$ 9	300
B..........................	8	8	6	12	400
C..........................	6	11	8	6	500
Warehouse needs.............	200	600	100	300	1,200

2. Suppose that in problem 1 (above) competition between trucks and railroads reduces shipment costs from plant C to $4, $8, $6, and $4 respectively. What is the solution to the problem?

3. The Sun Company has plants in Cleveland, Chicago, Houston, San Francisco, and Seattle. It ships product A from these plants to warehouses in Los Angeles, Denver, Omaha, St. Louis, and Atlanta. In the table below are given the freight costs per unit for shipping product A from each plant to each warehouse.

| | *Warehouse* | | | | | |
Plant	*Los Angeles*	*Denver*	*Omaha*	*St. Louis*	*Atlanta*	*Quantity available*
Cleveland..........	$14	$10	$9	$ 7	$ 7	800
Chicago............	12	8	5	5	7	200
Houston...........	9	7	8	6	6	600
San Francisco.......	4	7	9	9	15	100
Seattle............	8	9	9	10	16	400
Quantity needed....	300	500	300	400	600	2,100

From which plant should products be shipped to each warehouse? What is the total freight bill?

4. If, in problem 3, Sun enlarged its Chicago factory so that it had a capacity of 500, how should the shipment pattern change? How much freight costs would Sun save? If these were weekly savings, how long would it take freight savings alone to pay for the Chicago factory's $5,000 expansion cost?

5. Sales have been increasing in areas distant from Sun's present plants in Chicago and New York, so the company is considering putting a third plant in Denver or Dallas. After study it has reduced the pertinent remaining data to the following:

| | *Distribution costs per unit* | | | | *Expected annual demand units* |
| | *From existing plants* | | *From proposed plant* | | |
To warehouses	*Chicago*	*New York*	*Denver*	*Dallas*	
Washington................	$ 1.62	$ .92	$ 2.71	$ 2.51	24,000
Atlanta....................	1.78	1.95	2.12	1.72	18,000
New Orleans...............	2.05	2.41	1.93	1.17	27,000
San Francisco..............	3.22	4.69	1.67	2.14	17,000
Los Angeles................	3.32	4.78	2.25	2.38	22,000
Plant capacity (units)........	40,000	45,000	25,000	25,000	
Production cost per unit......	$ 3.66	$ 3.79	$ 4.19	$ 4.13	

Where, on the basis of these figures, should Sun put the new plant, in Denver or Dallas?

CASE 7–1

The Costello Company, with 1,500 employees and located in Terre Haute, Indiana, makes hinges for all kinds of doors, from house doors to automobile doors. It also makes related hardware items such as door latches and catches. Business has been good and the company has to expand. Several members of the board of directors favor moving all automobile parts to a site near Detroit in Mt. Clemens, Michigan. Several key personnel man, however, don't want to move their families to or near a big city.

They propose, instead, moving to Jackson, Michigan—75 miles from Detroit. Labor rates would be 10 percent lower, but extra freight costs would offset half of this gain. Also favoring Jackson is relative freedom from labor troubles. Satisfactory sites and ample labor supplies are available both in Mt. Clemens and Jackson. Transportation is also satisfactory in both places.

What should be done? Why?

CASE 7–2

A few year ago the Fisher body division of General Motors decided that it needed to put up a factory east of Chicago, west of Pittsburgh, and north of the Ohio River. This was to be Fisher's tenth and, at the time, largest factory.

Fisher picked Kalamazoo, Michigan—150 miles east of Chicago and 150 miles west of Detroit. At the time the head of Fisher said that Kalamazoo was picked because of "its progressive business climate. We took a good look at Kalamazoo and its people, and we liked what we saw."

What characteristics give a community a "progressive business climate"? How might a mayor of a city go about helping to create a climate which will attract business? Could a company's management *create* a favorable attitude in its new employees? What makes a community appeal to a prospective employer so that he "likes what he sees"?

CASE 7–3

In the past decade the movement out of big cities has extended to large company home offices as well as factories. Literally hundreds of major companies have deserted the U.S. major cities for surrounding suburban areas. Among others, for example, American Can and U.S. Tobacco have moved to Greenwich, Connecticut, and Pepsico has moved to Purchase, New York, Olin Corporation to Stamford, Connecticut, and American Cyanamid to Wayne, New Jersey.

Yet all is not well, and now a different tune is often played. Working in suburbia is not all it was cracked up to be. Executives miss the excitement and stimulating contacts of the city. They complain about being company captives and smothering in a cocoon of paternalism in suburbia. "You get awfully tired of seeing those same faces every day, and all day, and evenings too."

Once many large home offices move into a small town, it soon begins to develop big-city problems. Crime rates rise, 5 p.m. traffic jams develop, pollution often becomes a problem, and green trees and open spaces turn into parking spaces and big buildings. The local labor supply is frequently inadequate, and almost always the company has to hire almost a whole new office staff since its former staff people will neither commute to a distant new location nor will they sell their houses and move to the new location. Should they want to move, their problem is made worse by the high housing costs in nice suburbs.

The company officials too are somewhat isolated. They are not close to lawyers, bankers, accountants, consultants, and advertising agencies.

As a result of all these factors working together and at the same time, there has been a slowing of the exodus, and, in fact, a slight reversal of the outward movement. This has been stimulated by rising office rental rates in suburban locations and lower rates in the big cities.

Yet Caterpillar operates successfully in Peoria, Illinois. The same is true of Maytag in Newton, Iowa, and Kellogg in Battle Creek, Michigan.

Discuss the merits of being located "where the action is."

SUGGESTED SUPPLEMENTARY READINGS

"Greyhound Corporation's Many-Sided Game Plan for Site Selection." *Industrial Development,* July 1974.

"New Trends in Plant Site Choices." *Nation's Business,* October 1975.

Speir, W. B. "Pollution and Plant Site Selection." *Factory,* July 1971.

8

Capacity planning

When Florsheim builds a plant to produce shoes, its managers have some idea of the number of pairs of shoes the plant will be capable of turning out. When General Motors builds an automobile assembly plant, its managers have certain expectations concerning the number of cars the plant will be able to produce. A hospital is built to house a specified number of beds, and a school's enrollment is limited by the number and size of classrooms. These facilities are all built to a size that has certain "capacities."

THE CONCEPT OF CAPACITY

The capacity of a factory is an ambiguous concept. It is not like the capacity of a milk bottle which will hold one quart of milk and no more under any circumstances.

Capacity is a *rate* of output, a quantity of output in a given *time,* and it is the highest quantity of output that is possible during that time. Yet, capacity is at the same time a dynamic concept which is subject to being changed and managed. To some extent, it can be adjusted to meet fluctuating sales levels.

The unit of output

One problem with the concept is the unit of output. An automobile tire factory turns out tires, but tires come in many varieties. A tire factory can turn out more of some kinds and sizes of tires than other kinds and sizes. So its capacity when expressed in the number of tires is ambiguous.

In a one-product factory there would not be this kind of ambiguity, but single-product factories are almost unknown. Even a Kellogg's corn flake factory turns out several kinds of breakfast cereals. Oil refineries turn out different kinds of gasolines and oils. Book printing companies turn out large books and small books and in various quantities. Fire departments put out big fires and little fires. It is possible to express a refinery's capacity as so many barrels or gallons of oil or gasoline, and it is possible to express a book printer's capacity as so many books, but neither would be wholly accurate because the number would differ according to the mix of the kinds of products being made. The units of production are not homogeneous.

The matter of product mix is important when planning for the future. Sometimes, when a company's top administrators approve plans to spend money for added capacity, they express the new capacity only in terms of dollars' worth of sales. They leave it to the industrial and process engineers to develop a prospective product-mix breakdown. After doing this, these same engineers then have to calculate the kind and number of machines needed to produce the expected dollar volume for the mix they anticipate.

Time

Time poses another problem. A person talking about capacity is talking about a quantity of output in a given amount of time, but how much time? Some kinds of manufacturing processes require continuous operation. A steel mill must operate continuously, 24 hours a day, or not at all. When it is not operating, the furnaces cool down (unless extra money is spent to keep them hot though idle), and they must be relined with new fire bricks at high cost. The only way a steel mill can change its scale of operation is to open up or close down furnaces. When talking about the capacity of a steel mill, a manager probably would be thinking about the total amount of steel it can turn out while operating all of its furnaces 24 hours a day, 7 days a week. On the other hand, the capacity of a ski lift would probably include only daylight hours.

Most operations do not operate around the clock; instead, they operate from 8 to 5 daily, Monday through Friday. Their capacity is regarded as being their normal output in a 40-hour work week. But a 40-hour week is not their maximum capacity. It is usually possible to work more hours a day or more days a week. In most cases, the maximum possible capacity is considerably more than the 40-hour output.

CAPACITY, INVENTORIES, AND STEADY PRODUCTION RATES

Capacity should never be considered by itself but rather as part of a bigger picture. Often, because of sales volume variations, a company has to choose between increasing or decreasing its production levels or carrying inventories, both of which are costly. Christmas is a time of heavy sales in department stores, spring is a busy period for automobiles, and bathing suits sell well in the summer. But sales dip for many items in off seasons. Such variations make it difficult to operate efficiently.

If a facility's managers were to expand and contract production with sales, their plant's capacity would have to be big enough to take care of peak sales, but the plant would not work at top capacity very much of the time. Operating this way is usually impractical because it is impossible to keep an efficient work force with off-and-on employment. A factory's normal production capacity probably should be set at a point well below its peak needs.

Operating steadily is fine from the production point of view, but, if sales are irregular, other costs must be considered. Management could choose to produce at low volumes continually and pass up the extra sales during high sales periods. This might be a costly solution to the problem because of the sales which would be lost. Another alternative would be to produce at a higher level, but this would probably cause inventories to build up during slack periods. But carrying inventories can also be costly.

In the case of automobiles, for example, the late fall and winter months are low months, followed by heavy demand in the spring. It would be very expensive for Chevrolet to make 50,000 extra cars in October, November, and December just to keep producing steadily. By the end of December it would have 150,000 extra cars on hand. Even at $3,000 each, $450 million would be needed to carry the inventory. By the first of April the inventory might be up to 200,000 cars and $600 million. Farms and fair grounds would be needed as parking lots for all of these cars.

Besides the staggering investments, there is a danger of a poor sales year. If car sales in the spring did not come up to what was expected, production would have to be cut back. Such miscalculations can bankrupt companies. Stockpiling finished products is dangerous because no company knows for sure just what volume it will sell in the future.

There are, however, some things a company can do to regularize production. It can change its capacity by increasing or decreasing work hours. And, although it is not a happy solution, the organization can change its capacity by hiring extra employees or laying off people as sales go up and down. And it can change its capacity by subcontracting more work during peak periods and doing all the work itself in slack periods. (IBM uses this approach to maintain its "no-layoff" policy.) It can also do a little stockpiling and try to stimulate sales in off seasons. Possibly, too, it can try to hold back some peak-season business, promising later delivery and hoping that business will not be lost. And, as a long-run policy, a company can try to diversify into related product lines whose seasonal demands are opposite to that of existing products.

No one of these measures can, by itself, be carried far enough to eliminate all changes in production rates. A little of each, however, carried on at the same time, will accomplish quite a bit of leveling out of production.

Finally, it is well to note that idle plant capacity is a tremendous incentive to try to increase demand. It might stimulate sufficient extra sales effort to generate enough added demand to alleviate much of the problem.

PLANNING OVERALL PRODUCTION LEVELS

In order to adjust a factory's capacity up and down to respond to the demands of the marketplace, it is necessary to forecast sales expectations and to plan for the needed capacity changes. Otherwise changes are likely to be sudden and drastic and, consequently, costly to make.

Forecasting (which is the subject of Chapter 19) is particularly important where products are made to be stocked rather than to fill customers' orders already on hand. Almost all makers of products that are sold to final consumers make them to stock. Products are made for expected sales, but they are neither ordered nor sold until after they are made and put into finished goods stock.

It is necessary to forecast, at least roughly, the sales of every important product and of groups or classes of minor products and to do this month by month. This has to be done in order to tell the factory what to make and to check the future capacity demands against the capacity available. The problem is to foresee what and how many products the customers will buy (and customers are, for the most part, an unpredictable lot). This is an area where computers are being very helpful even though they do not produce perfect forecasts.

In addition to the unreliability of forecasts are the equally important irregularities of sales. It could easily be, for example, that a sales forecast would show that the sales of product A for the next three months will be in the range of 15,000, then 25,000, and, finally, in the last month, 10,000. Almost always it would be uneconomical to make the necessary capacity adjustments to match such an extremely irregular demand pattern. At the 25,000 level, the plant would probably be on a 10-hour, 6-day week schedule, whereas, at a 10,000 rate, it would be on short hours, would have some people laid off, and the plant would be half idle. Managers have to try to operate more steadily than this.

Yet, if operations are steadier, this will mean that there will be times when more products are being produced than are being sold, so inventories will build up. There will be other times when the reverse happens, and inventories are drawn down. The existence of inventories allows production and sales to be "decoupled" so that production can be carried on economically while at the same time the irregular demands of customers are taken care of by filling orders out of stock. Inventories cushion differences between production and sales.

This is one situation where optimizing one factor, in this case inventories, should *not* occur. Optimal inventories, considered by themselves, almost always are small inventories. But holding down inventories often neglects the total picture and would sometimes be poor inventory control from the total operations viewpoint.

Capacity as a lower-limit constraint

The discussion so far has emphasized how a factory's lack of capacity sets top limits to production schedules. But capacity also serves as a lower-level constraint. During slow sales periods it is almost always desirable to produce more products than are currently being sold because it is so uneconomical to reduce capacity drastically when it is highly probable that sales will soon again pick up.

Capacity as a limiting constraint to production schedules at the low end is different from the way it works at the upper end. At high levels it becomes a very positive limiting factor. No more can be produced. At the low end it is a managerial decision constraint. Physically, it is possible to stop production altogether, but this would usually be so uneconomical that managers impose a managerial decision constraint requiring a certain amount of production even when some of the production is not needed and has to go into inventories.

OVERTIME FOR EXPANDING CAPACITY

Although workers in the automobile industry almost always work short hours in the winter, in the spring they are usually on overtime. Management plans it this way. Yet, when we say that management plans it this way, we do not mean that management wants the short hours. We mean that companies plan for overtime in the spring rather than planning to hire large numbers of extra employees who would soon have to be laid off. Similar decisions are also common in other industries with large seasonal variations in sales.

Planned overtime to meet seasonal peaks has many advantages. It increases the employee's pay and usually more than offsets the lowered earnings during seasonal lulls, so most of the employees like it. It minimizes the need for hiring more people and laying them off later. Jumping employment up and down usually results in low productivity. Besides, this would increase unemployment taxes when the new workers were laid off. And sometimes a company cannot find enough people with the right skills to hire anyway.

Furthermore, in autos, steel, and many other industries, full work crews are needed for many of the operations. It is not possible to get, say, 10 percent more output by adding 10 percent more workers. Longer hours for regular crews is often the only way to get 10 percent more output. Also, much of the work is paced by conveyors or by equipment work cycles. Consequently, fatigue from the long hours does not result in lower output (quality, however, might suffer).

Overtime is not, however, without its problems. One is that workers' incomes go up and down because the overtime is not regular and continued. Another problem is the lowered production pace when the work is not machine or paced by fixed-speed conveyors. Obviously, if production drops off drastically during overtime hours, labor costs during these hours become prohibitive.

Important, too, is the drop in a worker's pay when overtime stops. A cut from a 50-hour week to a 40-hour week pares a person's pay 28 percent (from 55 to 40 hours' pay). Most workers would not like 28 percent pay cuts. So, if they have any notion that operations are going down to 40 hours and if they are not machine paced, they sometimes drag out their work. It may be necessary to continue the overtime just to get a normal 40 hours of work done.

We are saying that workers want to work overtime because of the quite high pay. Sometimes this is so. When only a few people are asked to come in on Saturday and work overtime, workers frequently use their seniority to be among those chosen.

Yet, in some cases, the reverse happens. Workers do not want to work overtime. If they have been working overtime for a long time, they may prefer shorter hours. In particular, they often object to surprise decisions, such as a foreman asking them at 3:30 in the afternoon to work until 8 or 10 P.M.

Normally, workers can be disciplined for refusal to do the work assigned, so it is not surprising that the question of being allowed to refuse to work overtime is covered in the labor contract, meaning that managers are not wholly free to make overtime decisions. Today's labor contracts often give workers a right to refuse to work overtime unless they are told ahead of time and unless the whole department works extra hours.

This has a curious effect on assembly line work. If it is decided on short notice to work a line overtime, some of the workers will surely say no. Then the foreman has to recruit people from other jobs for the overtime on the line. He ends up with a mixed crew of workers, some of whom are on jobs strange to them. Yet, production continues because of the fixed pace of the line. If these jobs are difficult to learn quickly, quality may suffer. On the other hand, if the tasks are relatively simple, quality is usually not affected.

Overtime and operating efficiency

Long workweeks are fatiguing, so gains in output from long hours are not proportional to the extra hours because hourly output slides off. And since overtime hours cost an extra half in pay, the direct labor costs of the extra units produced by the overtime are quite high.

No studies seem to have been made in recent years of the effects of long hours on productivity; however, scattered reports from industry support

FIGURE 8–1

Hours per week	Hours, percent of 40	Output as percent of 40-hour production	Index of hourly production
40.................	100	100	100.0
48.................	120	117	97.5
56.................	140	121	86.4

the results reported in studies made a number of years ago. The results of the studies are found in Figure 8–1.[1]

These figures are, of course, only approximate and cannot be used as exact relationships. The actual decline in any specific case would depend on a great many things. The decline is more pronounced on heavy than on light work, more pronounced for women than men, more after weeks of overtime than at first, more on employee-paced work than on machine-paced work, and more when workers are paid by the hour than when they are on piece work. Absenteeism and accidents also increase a little with continued long hours.

For men, according to the BLS studies, total output reaches its peak at about 56 hours (less on heavy jobs). Above 56 hours the drop-off in hourly output from fatigue more than offsets the production in added hours, so total production goes down. For women, the peak is somewhere around 52 hours.

FIGURE 8–2

Hours per week	Production per hour	Total production in week	Labor cost: $7.00/hr. regular $10.50/hr. overtime	Average cost per unit	Extra production	Extra costs	Cost per unit for extra products
40........	100	4,000	$280	$.070	0	0	0
48........	97	4,656	364	.078	656	$ 84	$.128
56........	86	4,816	448	.093	816	168	.206

For low labor costs per unit, a company probably should stick to 40 hours. Figure 8–2 shows how much more the production from the added hours can cost. It shows that by going from 40 to 48 hours a week, total production (in a hypothetical case) might be expected to go from 4,000 units to 4,656, but, because of overtime costs and slightly lowered hourly output, the unit costs for the extra units are much higher.

---

[1] *Hours of Work and Output*, Bulletin no. 917 (Washington, D.C.: U.S. Department of Labor, Bureau of Labor Statistics).

The extra 656 units produced by going from 40 to 48 hours cost $.128 each (direct labor costs only) or nearly double the $.07 unit cost for production in a 40-hour week. And the extra 816 units produced by working 56 hours are obtained at a labor cost of $.206 each, nearly 3 times the labor cost of the units produced in 40-hour weeks.

Figure 8–2 does not, however, tell the whole story. It exaggerates the costs of production during overtime because certain other costs, such as the company's hourly contribution to the supplemental unemployment benefit fund and other costs of fringe benefits, do not go up 50 percent for overtime hours as does the direct pay for hours worked. Nor do workmen's compensation taxes. Also, social security taxes are based on only the first $15,000 of a person's earnings. Should workers' earnings go above that there is no further social security tax for the year.

But, even more important, some charges, such as for general plant overhead, *do not go up any at all*. They are taken care of in the 8-hour a day operating costs. If they amount to as much as 50 percent of direct labor costs (and this is common), then the costs of overtime hours are about the same as for regular hours. The only extra costs are those stemming from fatigue-caused lower production. Thus, the total costs of producing on overtime may not be nearly so much as Figure 8–2 suggests.

It is possible also that working long hours today will not cause as much decline in productivity as was found in the older studies cited above. The pace of work in today's factories is less demanding than it used to be. Affluent workers, who can easily get jobs elsewhere, often do not push themselves very hard. Absentee rates, for example, are higher than they used to be and may even go to 10 percent or more on Mondays and Fridays. When this is so, the work pace during the regular 40 hours may be leisurely enough that long hours may not result in any substantial reduction in hourly output.

In fact, it is now customary in many organizations to have a few extra "floaters," (employees to fill in for absentees). It is not unknown for such workers to come to work and be kindly told to "get lost." On days of excellent attendance there is simply nothing for them to do. In a sense these floaters are an "inventory safety stock of labor." If they are not needed, then idle "labor inventory" costs are incurred.

It is interesting to note that during the recession of the 1970s, many organizations retained skilled employees rather than lay them off even when they had little for them to do. Because of this (and other reasons) national productivity figures went down.

CAPACITY AND THE 40-HOUR WEEK

A small plant, operated day and night, can turn out just about as much as a larger plant operating only one shift. So, when a company plans its operations, it can choose whether to put up a small plant and use it intensively or a larger plant and use it less intensively.

Most manufacturing companies can operate 8, 16, or 24 hours a day. A plant operating 8 hours a day needs to be nearly 3 times as large as one in 24-hour operation in order to produce the same daily output. Similarly, operations can be carried on for 4, 5, 6, or 7 days a week. The fewer hours worked, the more physical plant capacity is needed for a given output.

At first, operating a small plant long hours looks like the best arrangement because the overhead costs per unit of product are reduced. Most of the time, however, it costs less to operate a larger plant fewer hours. Common practice is to have a plant large enough to take care of normal needs when it operates 8 hours a day and 5 days a week.

Although single-shift production requires a larger plant and more machines than 24-hours-a-day production, equipment depreciation costs per unit of product may, in the long run, be about the same either way. Three-shift operations permit one machine to produce almost as much as three machines would produce in one shift, but a machine that is used 24 hours a day lasts only about one third as long as a machine that is used 8 hours a day. Over the years, a company may have to buy about the same number of machines in either case.

Many overhead expenses, such as building depreciation, insurance, taxes, interest on investment, and obsolescence of machinery, are reduced when a small plant is used intensively. But three-shift operation has certain costly disadvantages which often more than offset the gains. Second- and third-shift employees get higher hourly pay rates (commonly 5 percent extra on the second shift and 10 percent on the third shift). And unless they are paced by production lines, night shift workers are a little less productive than first-shift workers. Night shifts often have more new employees than day shifts because most people like the day shift, and, as soon as they can, they use their seniority to transfer to first-shift work. There is also usually a little more turnover and more absenteeism among night-shift workers. Also, night-shift people often do too many things during the day and come to work tired, and so are less productive.

In any case and as a consequence of all these factors, night-shift workers may be no more than 90 percent as efficient as their day-shift counterparts. Products made on the night shift are likely to cost 10 percent more than products made on the day shift, depending, of course, on how important labor costs are in total manufacturing costs.

Maintenance is also easier with one-shift, five-day operation than with three-shift, seven-day operation. In the former case, most repairs can be done in off hours with no interference to production. Less intensive use of the plant also permits production to be expanded during peak periods with little increase in overhead costs because adequate plant capacity is already available.

Many companies use parts of their plants intensively (16 or 24 hours a day) and other parts extensively (8 hours a day) at the same time. They buy the smallest possible number of very expensive machines and operate them two or three shifts, while other machines work only the normal first shift.

Detroit's auto companies, GM, Ford, and Chrysler, usually plan for their automobile assembly factories to operate, during their busy periods, 53 hours a week (five 9-hour days plus one 8-hour day). They do not plan to use second shifts even during seasonal peaks because there are just too many problems and costs involved in hiring large numbers of people for short periods of time. And the auto companies have found that work-weeks of more than 53 hours cause too much absenteeism. People just don't show up for work.

Automobile companies do not, however, put in enough capacity to handle their peak sales volumes in 53-hour weeks. Rather, they set the 53-hour capacity at 75 to 80 percent of their peak needs. This means that they are not able to fill all orders from new production during sales peaks. So during peak seasons, some customers have to wait. To avoid losing too many sales, the companies do a little stockpiling ahead of the peaks, and they try to get their dealers to do the same. By setting capacity production below their peak needs, they can operate at capacity for a good portion of the year.

Yet everybody has seen automobile plants lighted up and operating at night, so there is obviously some second-shift operation. This, however, is usually confined to parts-making departments, where machines are costly. In such cases, normal parts-making "capacity" is the output of two shifts. The capacity of second-shift parts-making plants equals the one-shift needs of the assembly plants.

BREAK-EVEN CHARTS AND CAPACITY

When a factory is operating at or below capacity, the relationships among costs, sales, and profits are as they are shown in the break-even chart in Figure 3–1 (page 54).

But there are times when demand exceeds capacity. If such an excess demand appears to be temporary, capacity should probably be expanded by working overtime in spite of the extra costs. Such a company's break-even chart would change from that shown in Figure 3–1 to that shown in Figure 8–3. So long as the new profit spread, "A" in Figure 8–3, exceeds the old "B" profits in Figure 8–3, this would be a paying action.

Should, however, the larger sales volume appear to be permanent, then perhaps the capacity should be expanded by adding more machines rather than using overtime. Such a change would result in a new break-even chart: Figure 8–4. The new higher level of fixed costs would move the break-even point a little to the right (a higher volume would now be required). But since considerably higher volume is expected, the profit spread should be greater than before.

Even if today's above-normal-capacity demand is only seasonal, it may

FIGURE 8–3

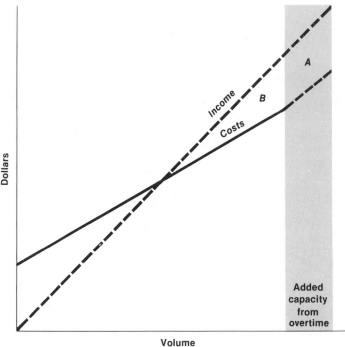

still pay to make the permanent additions to capacity indicated in Figure 8–4. This would be true, for example, if the extra amount of available profits, even though available for only part of a year, were greater than the reduction in profits during the rest of the year when operations return to the old capacity level. Whether or not such permanent capacity should be added can be calculated.

Let us say that:

Old profits at old capacity are P_o.
New profits at new capacity are P_n.
Profits with new capacity but at old capacity levels are P_r.
The fraction of the year when operations will be at new capacity are F_1.
The fraction of the year when operations will be at old capacity are F_2.
Then the new capacity should be installed any time that

$$(P_n \times F_1) + (P_r \times F_2) > P_o.$$

Although it may not often be wise, another choice open to managers when demand exceeds capacity is to raise prices and so hold volume down. Such an action would raise the income line but would decrease the volume. The proper decision would depend on the expected profits at the two different volume levels.

FIGURE 8–4

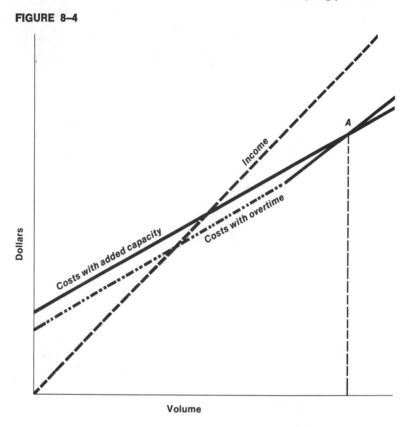

WORK FORCE CAPACITY

We have been making the point that it is quite uneconomical to increase and decrease the work force with every sales increase and decrease. This might sound as if we were saying that a given number of employees is a fixed capacity resource.

But this is far from true. Substantial adjustments can be made without having to resort to hiring more people and then having to lay them off.

An example will show how this could work. Suppose that the labor requirements needed to make all of the company's products while working a normal 5-day, 40-hour week produces the following expectation of employee needs:

June	300
July	400
August	600
September	450
October	400

The labor load in August is double that of June. Actually, however, the figures on the number of people needed are for "equivalent employees." There is a need for the work that this number of employees would do in a 40-hour week. But, as we have suggested earlier, the hours per week can be changed, and so can the amount of work sent to outside contractors. And, by doing a little stockpiling, some of the work from peak months can be transferred to earlier months, as shown earlier.

Here is a feasible plan for factory work hours to take care of the sales needs while holding the work force constant.

Month	Number of people	Hours a week	Equivalent people contracted outside
June....................	350	34	—
July.....................	350	46	—
August..................	350	58	92
September..............	350	51	—
October.................	350	46	—

Whether to go to overtime, or to vary the work force more, or to send out more work, or to build inventories are obviously largely managerial decisions (except where the labor contract provides otherwise) and depend, as before, on the relative costs of the alternatives.

Our example demonstrates that a factory's capacity, so far as labor power is concerned is susceptible to considerable change without the need either of hiring more employees or laying people off.

Labor power planning has many more minor facets which need to be allowed for. We did not, in our example, allow for any loss in production from fatigue during long workweeks, which would probably be substantial during the 58-hour workweeks planned for August. Nor have we allowed, in our example, for any stockpiling with inventories to be carried over.

Nor are all months alike. Some have as few as 20 and some as many as 23 work days. So a given workload *per month* is not the same employee load in different months. Absences also need to be figured in. It takes at least 105 people on the payroll to keep 100 people on the job. And it takes even more in the summer when everyone takes vacations (presumably, because of its summer sales peak, employees in this company would take their vacations at other times during the year). Labor turnover may also need to be considered. There is always a loss in production when an employee leaves and is replaced, so if there is a significant turnover this needs to be allowed for.

Indirect labor to support the work of direct workers needs to be planned just as much and perhaps more than direct labor. This is partly because some "indirect" people are technical employees and are sometimes hard to find and partly because it is hard to know just how many indirect workers are needed. Most companies try to get an idea of how many indirect workers they need by using some kind of a ratio of indirect workers to direct workers or to the factory's work load. They do not, however, continually increase and decrease indirect employment in proportion to factory work load changes.

MACHINE CAPACITY BALANCE

For companies that make varied products, the mix of products shifts all the time, and this places unequal loads on different machines and work centers. Also, some machines are slower than others; consequently, some equipment will always be working full time while other equipment is sometimes idle. Some work centers will be working overtime while others are on short hours.

Long-term trends cause part of the problem because yesterday's products often required machines which are not needed as much today. At the same time, today's products call for heavy use of certain other machines. About all that can be done is to add more machines where today's demand consistently required costly overtime work and where this demand seems likely to continue. Old machines—those no longer used—can be retired. By making such changes continuously, a reasonable balance of capacity for doing various kinds of work can be maintained.

It is also possible to work on controlling the demand side. If some department is not busy, the sales force can try harder for the kind of business which will use its machines. Or, if departmental capacities are out of balance, jobs formerly sent out to subcontractors can be brought back in-house, as is IBM's policy. Similarly, work in overloaded departments can be sent outside or delivery dates to customers can be changed.

Bottleneck limitations

When machine capacities are out of balance with needs, it is the bottle-necks which hurt because they limit what can be done. Often a bottleneck can be loosened by improvisations which expand the capacity of bottleneck machines temporarily. They can be operated through lunch periods and they can be worked overtime. Normal overhauls can be postponed by running the machines until they break down. Or they can be speeded up and run as fast as they will go, even if this is hard on the machines and tools. Two or three people, instead of one, can be assigned to do setups and repairs to speed them up.

The supervisor can also try to get people who operate bottleneck machines to hold down their coffee breaks. And, if a person has to be away from the machine during the day, the supervisor can have someone else keep the machine running. Also, it is not unknown for supervisors to "roll up their sleeves" and pitch in and help—if union rules allow it, that is (usually they don't). Finally, it may be possible to supplement the bottle-neck machine's capacity by doing some of the work on older, less efficient machines. Or perhaps part of the work can be sent out to other companies.

Most of these improvisations are only expediencies, however, and they do not solve imbalances between operations permanently. And because individual machines' capacities differ and the work loads generated by sales keep shifting, there will always be a few bottleneck spots.

A plant's capacity is therefore limited by the capacity of its bottleneck operation. If this operation can be changed, this single change affects the capacity of the whole plant or department. It may even be economical to redesign the bottleneck machine so that it will run faster, or maybe a second machine of this kind should be bought.

The gain in total capacity, however, will not be equivalent to the improvement in the bottleneck operation. If the latter's capacity is increased by 25 percent, the increase in a department's capacity might come to, say, only 5 percent, because now some other operation becomes a bottleneck. This will be illustrated in our discussion of machine use in Chapter 10. Capacity expansion becomes a matter of handling a succession of bottlenecks.

LEARNING CURVES AND CAPACITY

An organization's capacity for doing work is usually a changing characteristic. As time passes, equipment is added where it is needed or taken out of service where it is not needed, thus creating new levels of capacity.

The capacity of the human side of organizations changes, too, and not only because of additions to or subtractions from the workforce. People learn and acquire competence, thus increasing the capabilities of the organization. It is possible, when operations are new, to anticipate the degree of improvement which learning will produce and thus to calculate with some degree of accuracy the size of the work force as well as the cost of doing work both early in a new work experience and later on after learning has occurred.

This is the essence of the "learning curve" concept. This concept assumes that practice leads to improvement: People need fewer labor-hours for producing a given quantity of work. Learning, with its reduced labor-hour input implications is always at work in manufacturing. Most experience at making anything can always lead to more economical methods.

Airplane and electronics manufacturers have found that the learning curve concept operates when they make products in large numbers. Knowing about the curve and the expected rates of improvement allows their managers to project the need, later on, for fewer labor-hours per unit of product as well as lower costs per unit. All airplane and electronics makers therefore use the learning curve (on all government contracts for such products, in fact, the government requires them to expect lower costs per unit as quantities mount) in estimating the cost of direct labor and in scheduling, planning labor needs, and for budgeting, purchasing, and pricing.

Mostly these companies use an 80 percent curve or something very close to it. An 80 percent curve means that every time the production quantity doubles, the average amount of *direct labor* for all units produced up to that point goes down to 80 percent of its former level. This is an average for all units and not just the direct labor-hours put into the last unit. Thus, if the first 10 units require an average of 100 direct labor-hours per product, the first 20 units (including the first 10) will average 80 labor-

FIGURE 8–5

Typical learning curve for airplanes

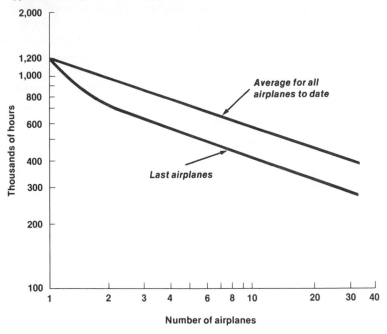

hours per unit of product. Airplane companies plot their figures on double-logarithmic paper, which makes the curve become a straight line.[2]

Learning curves in decision making

An example will illustrate how the learning curve can help in managerial decision making. The Strand Company has a contract for 1,000 units of

---

[2] The formula for the line is:

$$\log Y = S \log X + \log C$$

where S is the slope, X is the number of units of product, and C is the direct labor-hours required by the first product. Y is the average number of labor-hours. The formula for the slope of the line is

$$\text{Slope} = \frac{\log \% - 2}{\log 2}$$

For an 80 percent curve the formula becomes:

$$\frac{\log 80 - 2}{\log 2}$$
$$\frac{1.90309 - 2}{.30103}$$
$$-.322$$

The slope of the line is always negative since the method assumes that hours per unit go down as volume goes up.

product A. Labor is $8 an hour, and the contract is taken with the idea that the labor cost should average out at 10 hours or $80 per unit.

Strand has now been producing for six months on this contract and the president asks for a report. He wants to know (1) what is the average labor cost per unit for all of the products to date; (2) what did the last unit produced cost; (3) at what volume will the average labor cost go down to $80 per unit; (4) will the company make or lose money on the labor part of the contract, and by how much; (5) what learning curve percentage is operating and what is its slope.

Here are the production records:

Month	Units produced	Direct labor labor-hours
March...................	14	410
April.....................	9	191
May......................	14	244
June.....................	18	284
July......................	20	238
August..................	38	401

First, it is necessary to figure the cumulative production, the cumulative labor-hours, and the average labor-hours per product:

Month	Total production to date	Total labor-hours to date	Average labor-hours per unit
March.................	14	410	29.3
April..................	23	601	26.1
May...................	37	845	22.8
June..................	55	1,129	20.5
July..................	75	1,367	18.2
August................	113	1,768	15.6

The easiest way to get answers to the president's questions is to start by plotting the average labor-hours per unit on a double-log chart, as is done in Figure 8–6. The horizontal scale is the accumulated production and the vertical scale is the average labor-hours per unit. After plotting

FIGURE 8–6

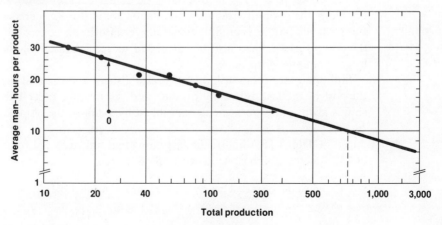

the points, the next thing is to draw in a straight line that best fits the location of the dots. (Usually this line can be drawn by inspection, but such a line could also be calculated by the least squares method.)[3] This line is the learning curve that is operating.

Most of the president's questions can be answered by looking at this line of best fit. What is the average labor cost for all of the production to date? To answer this, it is not necessary to use the chart at all since the actual data are available and were used in calculating the average labor-hour figures. As of the end of August the products have averaged 15.6 hours; so, up to now, the direct labor cost has averaged $125 per unit.

At what volume will the average labor cost go down to $80, or 10 hours? To answer this question, it is necessary to extend the line in Figure 8–6 downward to the right and read the quantity below the point where the curve crosses the 10-hours line. Although this is too fine a measure to be read off such a small chart as Figure 8–6, the answer is actually 604 units. Will Strand make or lose money on the labor content part of the contract? At 1,000 units and at the rate labor utilization is improving, labor will be down to 8.65 hours, or $69.20 per unit. So Strand stands to earn $10.80 per unit, or $10,800 in total, on the labor part of the contract. This is in addition to the profit originally expected and included in the price for each unit of product.

Strand's analysts were also asked for the slope of the line. To find this they should insert (in Figure 8–6) a point 0 anywhere below the curve. Then they should measure from point 0 horizontally to the right to where it intersects the learning curve line. (In Figure 8–6 this measures 1.75 inches.) Next they should measure vertically up to the curve (.49 inches on Figure 8–6). The next step is to divide the vertical measurement by the horizontal measurement and thus get the slope of the line. In our example this slope proves to be −.28.

Strand's president also asked the percent at which the improvement curve is operating. The analysts can get this by doubling any quantity and reading off the gain. For example, at 20 units the curve shows 26.6 labor-hours; at 40 it is 21.8 labor-hours. Dividing 21.6 by 26.6 shows that doubling the quantity reduced the labor-hours to 82 percent of their former level. So this is an 82-percent curve. (Both the slope of the line and the curve's percent can also be calculated more accurately mathematically by least squares procedures.)

Still one other relationship can be established: the relationship between the cost of the last individual product and the average cost. This relationship is always the average cost multiplied by 1 minus the slope of the line. In this case it is $1 - .28$, or .72. Since the average time of all units produced to date is 15.6 hours, the last individual unit uses $.72 \times 15.6$ hours, or 11.23 hours of labor, which cost $89.84.

---

[3] The equation for such a line by the least squares method is:

$$\log Y_c = \log C + S \log X$$

Learning curves in nondefense industries

Outside the airplane and electronics industries, learning curves are rarely used because of certain limitations. One difficulty pertains to carry-over knowledge of the work force, because new products usually are not wholly new. Even new airplanes are not wholly unlike earlier models. And each year's new automobiles are much like last year's. Even a new industry, such as television was in 1950, depended on electronic tubes and circuitry which were familiar to radio makers. When manufacturers turned to making TVs they already knew a good bit about how to make them. Such carryover knowledge makes it difficult to set a starting point for learning curve calculations.

Another limitation is that the curves are concerned only with manual work. Where machines are heavily involved, an 80-percent curve calls for more improvement than can probably be realized, and it may be necessary to use an 85- or 90-percent curve. The problem is deciding, for the case at hand, what curve to expect—80, 85, 90 or what?

Still another problem is that curves may exaggerate labor savings. In order to achieve reductions in direct labor costs, it is necessary to put industrial engineers, tool engineers, supervisors, and others to work trying to make improvements. But these specialists are indirect labor, and their costs are usually not shown as offsets against the gains in direct labor costs, but rather they go into overhead. Many firms, however, do try to account for this by charging specialists' time to particular jobs. This is not only good cost accounting procedure, but often government contracts require this to be done.

Still one more difficulty is that companies that are not used to using learning curves are likely to misinterpret the expected savings unless they change the way they keep their cost records. To use the curve correctly, setup and preparatory costs incurred before the contract starts should be kept apart and excluded from the calculation. If these are charged to the contract and later incorporated into a cost calculation for the first units produced, the first units will appear to cost a great deal.

Similarly, all work hours should be charged to the products which get the benefit of the work. If some of the hours worked in March are for units of products to be finished in April or May, these hours should be charged to April's or May's products and not to March's products. Proper charging is easy for giant complex products such as airplanes but is less feasible for stoves or refrigerators. If a company's regular cost accounting records are not separated this way (so that direct labor costs throughout production are charged to the specific products that got the benefit of the work done), it will have to change its recordkeeping procedures so that the charges are made properly.

REVIEW QUESTIONS

1. Why is it so difficult to know the capacity of a production facility?
2. What helpful adjustments can production schedule planners make in order to bring the capacity available to meet sales demands into reasonable balance?
3. Overtime is commonly used as a way of temporarily expanding capacity. How costly is it?
4. How might variations in workloads be handled without changing the size of the work force? Discuss these possibilities.
5. How are hours of work related to output? What changes in quantities ought a manager expect from longer or shorter hours? Discuss.
6. Is it better to have a small plant and work second and third shifts or to have a larger plant and to work one shift only?
7. How much reduction in direct labor cost per unit should an airplane company expect if it produced 100 airplanes instead of 50 and if an 80-percent curve were in operation? Explain how this concept operates.
8. When the learning curve is used, what is the relationship between the direct labor cost required for the last individual unit and the average for all units to date? Is this relationship always the same?
9. If companies that make household appliances were to try to use the learning curve, what adjustments would they need to make in their accounting procedures? Why?

QUESTIONS FOR DISCUSSION

1. The president of a company asks his analyst to make up an "index of capacity" for the plant. He wants the analyst to reduce the company's various products to some kind of common denominator so that he can compare the capacity requirements of schedules to the plant's capacity to produce. How should the analyst go about making some kind of a measure of "standard units" output which would serve this purpose?
2. The analyst has just reported to the general manager that his figures show that the company should not expand its capacity right now because this would mean idle capacity during future low periods. The president decides to expand anyway. He says that an idle plant is a tremendous spur to the sales department to get out and sell. Discuss.
3. If shorter workweeks boost hourly production and cut unit costs, why not work only 30 hours instead of 40? Discuss.
4. "It is illogical for the learning curve line to do down forever." Discuss.

PROBLEMS

1. A company with a capacity of 1,000 units a month has fixed costs of $2,000 a month and labor costs of $6 a unit. Materials costs are $2 per

unit. The company has been producing at 80 percent of capacity and selling its product for $12. What is its net income? What would it be at 100 percent of capacity?

What would its net income be at 120 percent of capacity if it is assumed that 20 percent more products could be produced on overtime at an extra $3 labor cost per unit for all production above 100 percent? What would the net income be if production declines by 2 percent per hour because of the long hours? Should the company accept a contract which will call for 120 percent capacity for an extended period of time if the price is $12 and if the company could not otherwise operate at 100 percent of capacity?

2. There are five products to be made on six types of equipment. The table below shows the operating times (in decimal hours) and the job setup times for each operation. In each block there are two times: The upper number is the job setup time and the lower number is the operating time per unit.

Omitting a consideration of machine-use rates, how many of each kind of machine will be needed if the plant works a 40-hour week?

Equipment	Job number				
	1	2	3	4	5
Mult-Au-Matic..............	.670		.761		.073
	.036		.078		.097
Vertical mill.................		.543	.790		.870
		.097	.102		.105
Turret lathe.................		.732			.839
		.019			.021
Forging machine..............	.521	.434			.768
	.017	.049			.057
Centerless grinder.............			.087	.161	
			.036	.016	
Simplex mill..................	.617	.614	.911	.658	
	.053	.073	.081	.077	
Quantity needed per month.....	700	2,300	1,400	100	300
Manufacturing lot size.........	300	200	500	200	400

3. The production schedule for a certain part calls for manufacturing 1,500 units per week. While there is some fluctuation in this requirement, the fluctuation is very small. Production of the part calls for five operations performed on five different machines. The time requirements for each of these operations are as follows:

Machine	Time per unit (hours)	Machine-use ratio	Operator efficiency
1.........................	.045	.84	110
2.........................	.101	.77	130
3.........................	.089	.91	90
4.........................	.049	.69	105
5.........................	.050	.81	130

Calculate the number of machines required for these operations if the plant works 40 hours a week. (See Chapter 10 for a discussion of machine use ratios and Chapter 15 for a discussion of operator efficiency.) If you feel that more information is needed before it is possible to decide how many machines will be needed, what information is lacking?

4. Machines A, B, and C characteristically lose .3, .7, and .2 hours each day for maintenance. Besides, frequent rush orders have in the past taken up .5 hours each on these machines. In planning work it is necessary to allow for such orders. The department works 8 hours a day. Operators on these machines are usually 110, 135, and 120 percent efficient respectively.

How many hours will it take for an order to be produced which calls for 20, 15, and 25 standard hours of work on each machine, respectively?

5. In the following example, should one machine be bought and operated 24 hours a day or should three machines be bought and operated 8 hours? The machines cost $100,000 each and have a normal life of ten years with no salvage value. Interest on investment is figured at 20 percent a year.

Twenty-four-hour operation is really only 21 hours because of lunch periods and the loss of production at shift changes. But it is necessary to pay for 24 hours of operator time. First-shift operators get $5, second-shift operators $5.20, and third-shift operators $5.25 per hour. Production on the second and third shifts is only 98 percent of the first shift.

With regular one-shift production the company does not pay for lunch periods, and it gets 8 hours' work for 8 hours' pay. Since the plan is to work only 5 days a week, there is plenty of time in either arrangement for major repairs, so this matter need not be considered.

6. It is required to make 3,000 units a month of a part which requires grinding machine time. The standard time for this operation is .17 hours per unit.

a. How many machines will be needed if they work 8 hours a day for 20 days a month at 100 percent efficiency and there were no scrap losses or lost machine time?

b. What is the answer if the company gets only 80 percent machine utilization from the machines and the operators are 105 percent efficient?

c. How many items should be started into production if the scrap rate is .07? And how many machines (using the production expectations arrived at in b) will be needed?

7. The up-to-date figures on the TAP Company's contract for making 500 small airplanes show the following:

Number of airplanes	Direct labor-hours per pound
10	21.0
15	19.5
25	18.9
35	16.2
50	15.8
100	15.3
150	14.3
200	13.9
250	13.2
350	12.3
450	11.9

The contract price anticipates that the average direct labor-hours per pound will be down to 10.5 by the time the contract ends.

a. Will the average be down to 10.5 at the end of the contract?

b. Suppose the contract includes an expected $10 per labor-hour cost (the airplanes weigh 3 tons each), $300,000 for materials and bought components, $400,000 overhead, and 8 percent on all costs for profit. What is the price per airplane?

c. What is the cost of the 450th airplane?

d. At the rate things are going, how much profit will the company make or lose on this contract?

e. Negotiations are being started for a second contract for 100 more of these airplanes. What should the new price be if all arrangements are carried over from the first contract but the achievements to date of the learning curve are recognized?

CASE 8–1

The production manager of the Par Company was considering the unusually large backlog of orders with early promise dates. Quite a few of the company's best customers were wanting quick delivery.

Just then he got a call from the sales manager about one of these orders. The sales department had promised delivery last Friday, but because of the factory's heavy load it had not been shipped—and was, in fact, not finished on Tuesday, when the sales manager made his call.

"I thought that order went out days ago. I promised that we would get it to them by last Friday. What is happening? What can I tell them now? Tomorrow for sure?"

"Wait until I check on today's reports. According to my reports, that order won't get shipped until Friday of this week. We've got a 'rush' tag on it, but everything that has to go through the gear hobbing machines is rush, so a good many orders are going to get behind. And you want all of those other orders, too, don't you?"

"Yes, we do; it has taken us a long time to land two or three of those new orders, and it is very important for us to give good service if we are to get any more orders from them. And we can't let our regular customers down either; they depend on us. I think you ought to be working overtime."

"Well, I asked about that for last Saturday and the superintendent turned me down. He said no—that you had to bid pretty low to get most of those jobs and the price just won't stand the added cost of overtime work. I'll ask him again, and maybe you ought to call him too. If he still says no, then maybe we can send a few jobs out to other shops. That would help the schedule, but we don't make much money sending work out."

"OK, but how about giving me a call tomorrow morning so I can tell the customer something? And something he can rely on, too."

Almost immediately, another call came through to the production manager—from the general manager. He, too, wanted to know about one of the late orders because he had had a call about it from the customer company's president.

Discuss this case.

SUGGESTED SUPPLEMENTARY READINGS

Abernathy, W. J., and Wayne, Kenneth. "Limits of the Learning Curve." *Harvard Business Review,* September–October 1974, pp. 109–19.

Belt, B. "Integrating Capacity Planning and Capacity Control." *Production and Inventory Management,* 1st quarter 1976, pp. 9–25.

Schemenner, R. W. "Before You Build a Big Factory." *Harvard Business Review,* July–August 1976, pp. 100–104.

9

Facilities design and layout

FACILITIES DESIGN CONSIDERATIONS

THE MANAGEMENT of production and operations includes providing and maintaining the buildings and services needed to house and serve the people and machines used to make products and provide services. Most of the time buildings and services are probably regarded as merely being present and not needing managerial effort. Yet, they constitute part of the productive asset base of every manufacturing and service organization and require a great deal of managerial input when they are constructed. And they continue to call for a considerable amount of ongoing managerial attention to keep them operating so that they contribute to effective operations.

The main job of facilities is to house manufacturing and service operations. But they must also house a multitude of supporting services, which may take up to half of the total space.

There need to be aisles, elevators, stairways, offices, a cafeteria, a dispensary, stock rooms, tool rooms, dispatching stations, timecard racks, locker rooms, washrooms, and toilets. There is need for telephones, intercom systems, computer data input and printout stations, electricity of various voltages, hot and cold purified water, unpurified water for processes, compressed air, high- and low-pressure steam, natural gas, lights, heat, ventilation, and probably air conditioning. Some of these services need wires, pipes, or ducts. Out of doors there is need for shipping and receiving docks for both rail cars and trucks. Also needed are a parking lot for cars and storage space for coal or other materials. The list is long.

Facility services are much like services in a house—no one thinks much about them so long as they work well. But let them be poorly arranged or out of order, and they become very important. Buildings and their services are sometimes so poorly arranged as to interfere with efficient operations. High buildings with several floors or weak floors, low ceilings, columns too close, elevators off in corners, inadequate or poorly located storage areas, and so on all interfere with efficient production and boost material handling costs.

Productive facilities should be flexible and easily adaptable to changes in operations. Built-in flexibility is the best way to make changes easily. Some things which help are: (1) wide bays (open areas between rows of posts or walls); (2) ceilings high enough for overhead conveyors, or mezzanines, whether they are needed now or not; (3) space (or installed wires) for high-voltage electricity for areas that do not need it today; (4) heavy duty floors; and possibly (5) machines (in some areas) on easily detachable mounts so that departments can easily expand.

TYPES OF BUILDINGS

Single-story buildings

Single-story buildings are the most common kind today. They can be as wide or long as needed and can easily be expanded. Single-story buildings have no stairs, elevators, elevator wells, or ramps to connect floors. There are few posts to interfere with overhead cranes or to reduce light. It is easy and inexpensive to move materials from job to job because all the moving is horizontal, not up and down. Heavy equipment can be put on separate foundations.

There are some disadvantages though. Single-story buildings require more ground space. Also, if there is a flat roof and no glass skylights, it is necessary to use artificial light in most of the plant. Also, a forced ventilation or air conditioning system will usually be required.

Architecture and styling

A facility's architecture can have an important impact upon its fixed and variable cost structure, as well as upon the attitudes of the people who work there. Because of the nature of many industries and because of heavy fixed investments in a physical plant, many organizations have historically taken a utilitarian approach to the appearance and design of their production facilities. The industrial sections of many communities have consequently been less attractive (to say the least) than residential sections.

However, things are changing. Many organizations are spending much more money on the design of their facilities trying to make them at the same time both economical functionally and architecturally attractive.

Westinghouse, in the mid-1970s, built a new plant to make electrical transformers at Jefferson City, Missouri. This 570,000 square foot facility was built on a 100-acre site at the foot of a high bluff. It was designed to blend into the area where the state capital buildings and an expensive residential area (on the bluff above the plant) are within view. Its contemporary design contains extensive landscaping (including an eight-acre lake which doubles as a storm drainage basin) and a relatively uncluttered roof—for the benefit of the residents on the bluff.

The plant is also designed to appeal to employees, with higher motivation and productivity being the objective. The trapezoid-shaped office areas have attractive views of the lake, capitol, and a nearby river. And there is an extensive use of carpeting, wood, and coordinated color schemes in the offices. The plant was also designed for expansion, should extra capacity be required. Westinghouse believes that this plant will be one of their most productive facilities.

The Cummins Engine plant in Walesboro, Indiana, as another example, is almost entirely underground. The 600,000 square foot facility (which employs some 2,000 people) is placed in a 320-acre wooded site. All that is visible to passersby is a parking lot which is on the roof of the facility and a 28-foot high glass tower which serves as a high rise storage area. This storage area is served by computer controlled stacker cranes. A stand of trees covers a buried set of tanks which contain chemicals used in production.

These two plants are characteristic of a trend which has been going on for some time toward college campus-type facilities. Such plants have well-kept lawns, patios, and even pools, and several buildings rather than one. Campus-type factories have a pleasant, leisurely feel, but they need ample ground space and they are expensive to build. This kind of plant is best suited for light, heavily engineered products. And they are more suitable in warm, dry climates, although there are a good many such plants in other parts of the country. There is also a trend in the warmer areas to have interior patios, open at the top, and with a pool surrounded by lounging areas for use during coffee breaks and at lunch time.

Although new buildings make the best show, a great deal of plant remodeling is always being carried on. For example, the huge 560 building Dow Chemical plant complex at Midland, Michigan, has been undergoing extensive refurbishment for several years. Dow is trying to change its plant appearance from a fortress-like structure to one which its employees will find more pleasing, as well as one which will encourage the cleaning up of adjacent areas which have, over the years, become blighted.

Prefabs of one sort or another also continue to be popular, and they too are now designed more attractively. Sometimes a prefab is a whole prefabricated steel building and sometimes only interior components, as when movable office partitions have been prefabricated. They can be designed as modular units that can be put together in varied ways to give variety in shape and form. The units are made to blend well with masonry, brick, and glass. The metal or wooden parts of prefabs come prepainted in various colors, so there can be attractive combinations. Not only are prefabs low in initial cost, but usually they can be expanded easily or disassembled and moved to other places.

Some rather unique experiments are also being tried in modular construction. For example, a $200-million fertilizer processing plant in the Kenai Peninsula, Alaska, has been constructed of modular units built in the state of Washington and transported by barge over 1,000 miles of waterways to the plant site.

Also, DuPont has been developing "containerized" factories. The plant facilities (machines and the like) for a new Australian explosives plant were shipped in containers which were themselves then used as part of the factory building. DuPont used containers made of plywood which had doors and windows installed in them and special connecting hardware which allowed them to be used first as containers and later as modular parts of the building.

BUILDING COSTS

A new facility's cost depends on what is required. In 1977 a simple building with a 10-foot ceiling might be built for about $15 a square foot. But it would be necessary to go above $30 a foot to get very many "trimmings." Costs vary, of course, in different parts of the country. Size also affects the square-foot unit cost. Large facilities can cost a little less per square foot than smaller ones. Worker density also affects the costs. Less space per worker often means more machines per foot, more electrical connections, and more of all of the accessories that equipment requires. And at the same time, greater worker density requires more locker rooms, cafeterias, entrance ways, and so on. These things increase the cost per square foot.

A new factory building's cost can be estimated rather easily. If, say, 400 square feet per employee is needed and a new building costs $15 per foot, then the initial investment in the building will be about $6,000 per employee. If depreciation is calculated on a 40-year basis, depreciation will be about $150 a year per employee. Interest at 9 percent of $6,000 comes to $540. So depreciation and interest will probably approximate $690 per year for near-future years. Taxes, insurance, and other costs will probably bring the total cost to $900 per employee per year. This would be not far from 10 percent of the payroll or a little more than 3 percent of the sales dollar. A company can probably save more than this from the economies it incorporates into a new plant.

Leasing is an alternative to buying. One year's rent is likely to cost more than one tenth of the total cost of a new building (including land) or probably well above the $900 per employee per year in the example above. Normally it costs more to rent than to own.

Companies that build new plants usually try to build improvements into their new plants. They usually end up with lower costs for (1) handling (down 20 percent or so), (2) supervision, (3) maintenance,

(4) inventory, (5) shipping, and (6) insurance. Lighting usually is improved so much that it costs a little more. Employee morale and product quality usually both go up. Output per employee-hour nearly always goes up, so labor costs per unit of product decrease.

ENERGY COSTS

When the Arab nations took over all foreign oil operations in their countries in the mid-1970s and tripled the price of oil, this not only made energy cost more, it also dramatized our fundamental shortage of oil in the United States as a source of energy. Companies now are designing new facilities and refurbishing their current ones with energy saving in mind.

General Electric estimates that about two thirds of the energy consumed in its manufacturing facilities is for "plant environment" (such as heating and air conditioning) and only one third is for manufacturing activities or processes. If GE is typical, it is very important to design facilities which use energy efficiently.

The possibility of using solar energy for heating is getting a lot of attention in sunny parts of the country. Some firms are already using heat-collecting panels built on the roof or sides of their plants. General Electric is pioneering in using the sun's heat in the North. At its Valley Forge (Pa.) Space Center, GE installed 5,000 square feet of heat-absorbing solar panels on the roof. On sunny days these provide enough heat for the plant's 200,000 square foot cafeteria and most of the heat for all of the plant's hot water needs as well. The heat panels, installed at a cost of $300,000 were installed as a precommercial test of feasibility.[1]

The Northrup Corporation is taking an easier and less expensive approach to using the sun's energy. In one of Northrup's California plants it has gone back to skylights (glass-covered openings in the roof) to allow sunlight to illuminate and heat the factory area. The sunny California weather provides about 80 candle feet of light, the same as electric lights, which are now turned off during many of the daylight hours.

Other organizations are implementing computer controlled energy use systems. For example, Bowling Green State University in Ohio is using a small IBM computer to control the heating and cooling of its 95 buildings. The system monitors these buildings so closely that their monthly peak electrical consumption is down from 14,000 to 9,000 kilowatts, which means an annual savings of $350,000.

COMMUNICATIONS SYSTEMS IN THE PLANT

Factories, though normally beehives of activity, would stop the minute communications stopped. People talk to each other, giving and receiving

---

[1] See "GE's Solar Heat," *Business Week,* April 21, 1975, p. 38.

directions, and they send and receive written directions and reports. Besides the internal telephone system, most organizations also have public address systems with speakers in all departments so they can page anyone. And, if papers have to be sent back and forth, there might also be pneumatic tubes. Electrically transmitted facsimile reproduction is also found occasionally. Work orders, documents, and drawings can be sent by wire from one department, or even from one plant, to another.

Computers may also be wired directly to various reporting stations or even among plants on leased telephone lines. People who have finished jobs on their machines insert their job cards into card reporting boxes (called "transactors") which tell the computer that these jobs are completed. The same thing happens with stock withdrawals from storerooms and with inspectors' reports. The central computer then updates its records and, if need be, prints out a report. This instantaneous reporting keeps the computer's records up to the minute.

On-line consoles for computers are now the rule in big manufacturing facilities. Consoles with direct input and output access to the central computer are located in various departments around the plant. Thus, each department can have immediate computer use.

Radio and television are sometimes used. Radio (including citizens' band units) is very good for directing truck drivers and maintenance people who usually are away from their home departments. Television (not broadcast TV but closed-circuit TV) is in a class by itself as a way of monitoring impossible-to-watch spots—say inside a furnace, or to watch freight yards, plant fences, or emissions from smoke stacks. And videoscopes of processes in operation can be studied at leisure or even in blown up size and in slow motion.

General Electric in one of its plants televises drawings to assemblers who are doing complex wiring jobs. Hughes Aircraft has a complete closed-circuit TV system so that its people in central offices and those out in the plant offices can both talk to each other and see each other. TV is also used for sales meetings. People from the West Coast do not have to be brought to New York; they can get together in West Coast cities and be part of a two-way TV meeting.

SECURITY

Facilities have always needed fences and a certain amount of outdoor floodlighting to hold down thievery and vandalism. This need has become greater in recent years since crime rates, bomb scares, and the possibility of civil outbreaks are greater. Visitors are no longer allowed to wander around inside the premises, and even outside service repair people and vendor salesmen are escorted to and from their work, and their tool boxes and briefcases may be inspected before they leave.

Television has proved to be a great help here. From a central location, it is possible to monitor parking lots, loading docks, storage yards, fences, and entrances. Television cameras also help discourage vandalism and illegal harassment during strikes. People are often reluctant to cause trouble if they know they are being photographed in the act. Pictures become irrefutable evidence of offenses.

Electric-eye systems with alarms and scanning moving picture cameras have been added in interior areas which are vulnerable to theft or sabotage. Other more sophisticated devices are also available. For example, the John Meyer Company, a Connecticut sportswear designer and manufacturer, has installed a combined electronic and ultrasonic surveillance system.[2]

Doors are equipped with photoelectric intrusion devices which, when tripped, signal an alarm to the monitor board and to the local police station. Inside the plant, an ultrasonic detection system detects any motion equal to that of a person taking 30 steps in any direction. More locks and barred windows and fewer entry and exit doors are also now provided. And records are kept of the people who have keys to security doors.

Meyer's system is also particularly effective against "lock-in" burglaries. A thief gets into the plant disguised as a repairman or truck driver; then he hides until after hours, and, after his burglarizing activities, he hides again till he can leave the next day during regular hours. Many plants are also reducing the thievery by putting up signs warning people of security measures. Seeing the signs, only the most dedicated criminals, and "Mission Impossible" vandals will not be dissuaded.

Protecting designs, formulas, and secrets

Thievery of physical items can be insured against, but almost always these are of minor consequence compared to the possible harm that can come from the theft of trade secrets and prototype designs of new products. The theft of even such things as pricing strategies and new product release dates can cause serious loss to an organization. Such losses usually cannot be insured against.

The president of one public relations firm says that companies he has worked for have had employees pose as customers, shareholders, and securities analysts to get into competitors' plants and ferret out information about their market share, new product introductions, shipping dates, and so on. At one chemical company, a cleaning woman segregated certain papers out of her trash hamper and sold them to a competitor. The buyer was after a batch formula, and he got it.

IBM found that its plans and the hardware for a new direct access storage unit had been stolen and had gotten into the hands of competitors who had made and sold them under their own names. Although a ring of

---

[2] Meyer's system is described in "An Alarming Plant," *Factory,* January 1975, p. 43.

11 employees were arrested for conspiracy, this did not make up IBM's loss.

Actually, although "bugging" telephones and stealing information are rare, they are, nonetheless, persistent practices. Companies with technical secrets now, as a routine matter, make periodic "sweeps" to detect electronic bugs. And they are as careful about shredding and burning important thrown out papers as the government is with worn out paper money. They are also compartmentizing development programs more. Then very few people know about the whole activity.

Precautions don't always work, however. Acoustic Research unveiled one of its new "Pi-One" speakers at a trade show in Chicago. To ship it back to the factory, they disguised and mislabeled the packing case. But thieves correctly selected the mismarked case and stole the demonstration speaker.[3]

Fire protection

Internal fire protection is also an important security consideration. Some firms which use flammable materials like rubber, magnesium, or petroleum in the products have their own internal fire department or fire brigade with special chemical fire fighting equipment and fire retardants. Others, and this is commonly required by law, install extensive smoke detectors and sprinkler systems. These devices usually also report alarms instantly to the company's internal fire department (and to the community's municipal fire department as well) which is trained to handle the kinds of fires which might occur in all major hazard areas.

FACILITIES LAYOUT CONSIDERATIONS

A plant's internal arrangement of facilities, its layout, should be designed to permit the economical movement of materials through processes and operations. Travel distances should be as short as possible, and picking up and putting down products or tools should be held to a minimum— as should paper work and instructions to operators and truckers. This should result in the minimization of handling and transportation costs, as well as holding down inventories in process and machine idle time.

The never-ending struggle to keep the productive capacity of operations in balance with current needs means constantly adding machines in some places and taking out old machines in other places. Because businesses grow, more machines are usually added than are removed. In any case, the layout of machines often must be rearranged and materials handling systems must be redesigned.

Since the advantages of good layout are so great and so obvious, a person might wonder why any company would put up with any other

---

[3] This experience was described in "Business Sharpens Its Spying Techniques," *Business Week,* August 4, 1975, p. 63.

kind. There are several reasons. One is that management doesn't always know that its layout is inefficient. In other cases the managers recognize that their layout is poor, but it costs money to change it, so nothing is done.

Other reasons (and very important ones) why many companies do not have efficient layouts is that a good layout does not just happen, nor does a good layout, if unchanged, stay good very long. Most companies make many products, each of which follows a different route through the plant, so a good layout for one product may be a poor one for another. Changes in the product mix sometimes change efficient layouts into poor layouts. These new mixes often mean that the former layout is now really inefficient. If the new product mix is likely to endure, then the layout of machines and processes should be changed. A good layout must therefore be a changing layout. It must be flexible enough to be changed quickly, inexpensively, and with few disruptions to operations.

SPACE REQUIREMENTS

Machine space

Machines need floor space plus space for their electric motors and control panels, as well as for their operators and conveyors (if they are used). They also need space for the storage of materials before and after the operations have been performed. Furthermore, maintenance and machine repair people need enough room to work. There is also need to consider the shapes of the machines. Some are long and narrow, others are round, and some are nearly square. Some extend upward ten feet or more above floor level; others have beds or foundations extending several feet below floor level.

In total, machines will usually require more space than the total of their separate space needs because these spaces never dovetail exactly. Storage spaces, however, rarely need to be of any particular shape, so they provide a certain amount of flexibility in layout. The actual placing of machines is generally decided after experimentally placing machine templates (paper cutouts or even three-dimensional models made to scale) in position on a floor plan.

Product space

In most organizations the space allowed for storage, machines, conveyors, and aisles provides enough room for products in process, but companies that make large assembled products, such as locomotives, freight cars, or airplanes, need extensive assembly or erection floors. Acres of floor space are sometimes needed as, for example, for assembling airplanes.

Usually, large products are partially assembled in one part of the assembly area and then moved to another area where more work is done to them. Each area needs to be large enough to hold several products at a time. Often, too, the space will need to be high and free from posts or other obstructions so that partially assembled products can be moved by an overhead crane.

For smaller products it is usually necessary to provide point-of-use temporary storage areas next to the machines. In assembly line production, it is a good idea to make such spaces large enough so that material can be taken directly from the receiving point to the production line and stored there, thus saving its going into and out of a separate storage area.

Service area space

Service areas—washrooms, locker rooms, restaurants, medical facilities, offices, tool rooms, stock rooms, and storage areas, as well as weighing scales, elevators, stairs, and aisles—are important support facilities to manufacturing operations. They should be close to work areas where they can be most useful, yet not be where they will disrupt production.

Some companies with unused overhead space put locker rooms and wash rooms on balconies. But service areas should not be shunted off into leftover corners without regard to their proper functional location. Convenience is a part of the service. Also, attractively placed, well-maintained cafeterias can contribute to job morale. Utility services, such as power, light, water, and so on, also take up space, and the layout

FIGURE 9–1

Mock-up of a plant layout

Source: Westinghouse Electric Corp.

should put them where they can serve to best advantage and where they can be gotten to quickly in case emergency repairs are needed.

Overhead space

Overhead space, as well as floor space, should be considered in layouts because overhead space saves floor space (and floor space costs more than overhead space). Overhead conveyors and cranes can take materials directly to work places, which is something that trucks operating in aisles cannot always do as easily. Also, overhead conveyors are often used for the temporary storage of materials between operations, which will cut handling costs considerably and free floor space at machine centers.

Today's high-stacking lift trucks allow for the economical use of floor space. They can, despite narrow aisles, stack materials up to 20 or 30 feet at almost no cost above that of setting loads on the floor. Floor-space requirements are thereby reduced drastically.

EFFECTS OF MATERIALS HANDLING EQUIPMENT

The kinds of materials handling equipment that are used affect machine arrangements. Hand or powered trucks, for example, require wider aisles than are needed by conveyors. Fork lift trucks require wider aisles than other types of indoor trucks. Sloped ramps from one floor to the next are needed if trucks are used and if elevator capacity is limited. Overhead cranes, on the other hand, require open spaces that are free from supporting columns.

LOT VERSUS CONTINUOUS PRODUCTION

Many companies make finished products which are assemblies of separate pieces or components. Raw materials are first made into parts which are later assembled into finished products. In this kind of manufacturing, products can be made continuously or in lots. This applies to individual parts as well as to finished products. A company uses "lot production" when it makes up, as one order, enough products or parts to meet the needs of, say, one month. Then it turns to other products, which also are made in lots. When the supply of one kind of part or final-assembled product is nearly used up, another lot is processed and the stock is replenished.

When parts or products are made in lots, there are several decisions to make. How many units should be made at one time as one lot? Only a few at a time and frequently? Or larger lots less frequently? These are important questions because they result in different unit costs. If the lots are too large, they result in excess inventory costs; if they are too small, they result in too many small reorders. The number that should be made in order to produce the lowest unit cost is called the "economic lot size" and is discussed in Chapter 21.

Here we are not interested in the size of the reorder lots or with lots as such, but with the fact that lot production and continuous production need different layouts of machines and equipment. Lot production requires a "process" layout whereas continuous production requires a "product" layout.

LAYOUT PATTERNS

There are four basic patterns of layout. First, "process layout" refers to the grouping of similar machines into departments where only certain kinds of work are done. Second, "product layout" refers to the grouping of machines required to make certain products along lines down which the products move continuously as in an assembly line. Departments are places where particular products are made.

Third, "group layout," sometimes regarded as a separate kind of layout, is really just one kind of product layout. In group layout, parts and components being made are grouped into "families," and areas or departments are set apart to work only on such parts and to do everything needed to make them complete.

Fourth, "fixed position layout" applies to complex assembled products being put together on one spot. Most companies use predominately one or the other of these layout patterns.

Departments making parts for assembled products do not need to use the same pattern as that of the assembly department. Parts are often made in process departments whereas subassembly and final assembly are more often arranged on a product basis.

PROCESS LAYOUT

Process layout (sometimes called "functional" or "job lot" layout) is a grouping together of machines and people to do similar work. Grinding is done in a grinding department, painting in a paint department, and so on.

Advantages of process layout

Process layout makes the best use of the specialization of machines and people. Functional departments are also flexible and are able to handle a variety of products. The machines are general purpose machines, which are usually less costly than special purpose machines. Products requiring diverse operations can easily follow diverse paths through the plant as can be seen in Figure 9–2.

Process layout plants are less vulnerable to shutdowns than product layout patterns. If a machine breaks down, its next assigned work can be transferred to a nearby similar type of machine, and the delay will rarely

FIGURE 9–2

Layout patterns

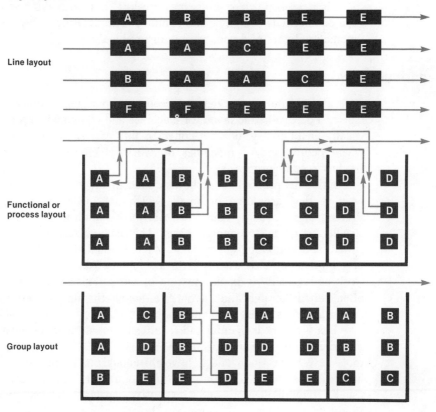

interfere with the progress of other orders through the plant. If the products are varied and are made in small quantities, costs are lower with process layouts than with product layouts. And since the machines and workers are somewhat independent of each other, this method is suitable for incentive pay systems.

Disadvantages of process layout

A process layout has certain disadvantages. General purpose machines usually operate much more slowly than special purpose machines, so operation costs per unit may be higher—often much higher. Work routing, scheduling, and cost accounting are costly because these things have to be done separately for every new order. Materials handling and transportation costs are high. Since different products follow different routes through the plant, it is usually not economical to use conveyors, so truckers have to haul materials in process from machine center to machine center.

Materials usually move slowly through the plant. Consequently, the inventories of materials in process are high and a large amount of storage space is needed. Orders sometimes are lost. It is also difficult to keep a good balance between labor and equipment needs. Process layouts are best for small volumes of a wide variety of products.

PRODUCT LAYOUT

Product layout means that the product's operation requirements dominate and determine the layout of machines and equipment. Products move, usually continuously, down a conveyor line past successive work stations where people and/or machines do work which results in the finished product (see Figure 9–2).

Continuous production is the best kind of layout pattern for products, whether they are large or small, which are made in large quantities. Products are moved by conveyor from work station to work station either steadily or on a stop-and-go basis. This is how television sets, kitchen stoves, and automobiles are made. At individual work stations the work may be manual as it usually is in assembly work, or it may be machine work as it usually is in the making of parts. This kind of production is often called "straight-line layout," although the line sometimes turns a corner and goes on in another direction.

When the work is manual and requires tool assistance, as most assembly line jobs do, the operator usually works with portable tools. Because these tools have to be small and lightweight enough to be portable, they have limited capabilities. In contrast, the continuous manufacture of *parts* usually requires larger, more expensive, special purpose machines to stamp, forge, shear, drill, bore, tap threads, plane, grind, hone, or otherwise give a piece of metal the shape, size, contour, or surface it needs to have. (Product layout lines are the subject of Chapter 11.)

Advantages of product layout

The main advantage of a product layout pattern for continuous manufacturing is its low cost per unit, provided there is enough volume and standardization. Low costs result from the use of automatic fast-production equipment, and, because of the use of fixed routes for materials, almost everything can be moved and moved quickly and at low cost by conveyor. Materials handling costs, travel distances, inventory in process, and storage space can be reduced substantially. Production-control paper work is also simplified. And the comparatively simple machine-tending jobs simplify the training of new workers. Supervision is also easier since the jobs are routine and supervisors can oversee larger numbers of subordinates. In economic terms, these advantages usually far outweigh the disadvantages of lines.

Disadvantages of product layout

There are, however, several possible disadvantages. The large invest-ment in special purpose machines requires high volume in order to achieve low unit costs. Furthermore, a product layout with continuous manu-facture is vulnerable to stoppages because there is usually only enough storage room for small supplies of products between operations. When work stops at any point, everything stops quickly. Also, the rate of output is quite inflexible. The only way to get more output is by working the entire line overtime or by putting on more shifts. To get less output, every-thing goes on short hours.

Product design changes often cause problems. Such changes change op-erations and operation sequences. They may reduce or eliminate the work of some work stations or they may add to the work of other stations. The whole line may have to be restructured. Because this is costly, desirable changes in the design of products may not be made as often as they should.

Continuous production does not handle product variety easily. Variety upsets the exact work assignments at work stations. Some automobiles are to have radios installed, others not. Some Samsonite luggage has brown covers, some red. Some automobiles have tinted glass windshields, others not; some have blue wheels, some white, and so on. Even small variations in finished products make a great deal of extra production control work. The continual inflow of parts and components to the assembly line must be carefully directed and monitored. The flows of parts and components to assembly lines have to be carefully coordinated, not only as to quantity, but also as to type, kind, and sequence.

Parts must also fit. It is not possible to rework parts along an assembly line. And even laying aside a nonfitting part and using the next one is often not possible because the exact sequencing of arrival of parts would be upset.

The capital investment is usually high in product layouts because of the special purpose machines and conveyors. Also, even though a machine may only be needed part of the time, it is often necessary to commit an entire machine, even though similar machines are also used part time elsewhere in the plant. And because entire sets of operations are tied to-gether, line production is often not suitable for incentive pay systems, unless the incentive is tied to the performance of the entire group working on the line. Samsonite does, in fact, use a group incentive pay plan for the workers on its luggage assembly line.

There can also be problems with labor. Absenteeism is hard to handle since every work station *must* be staffed and with one or more employees who can keep up even though the task may be new to the replacement employee. It is necessary to anticipate absenteeism by having a few extra employees on the payroll just for fill-ins.

The highly repetitive work along assembly lines also does not appeal to everybody. And most of the jobs are machine paced, which some workers find objectionable. There are, however, several possibilities for designing assembly line jobs which "enlarge" or "enrich" them and make them a little more interesting. These alternatives are discussed in Chapter 13, "Job Design."

Behind-the-scenes labor costs are also generally high. The operators who tend the machines are relatively few, but they are only a part of total labor costs. Machine designers, methods engineers, setup, materials supply and maintenance people, and others add substantially to these costs.

GROUP LAYOUT

Group layout sets apart areas and groups of machines for making "families" of parts which require similar processing. Each part is made complete in this small specialized area with the entire machining sequence being done there.

Advantages claimed for group layout are a saving in handling costs; parts do not have to be hauled to far corners of the plant. And it is easier to know where each lot is. Delivery times can be estimated more precisely and scheduling is simplified. Setup costs can often be reduced since next operations on machines may be much like preceding operations, thus making it possible to use part of the former setup.

FIXED POSITION LAYOUT

Fixed station layout is often used for large, complex products, such as factory machines themselves, hydroelectric turbines, locomotives, airplanes, and ships. The product may remain in one location for its full assembly period, as in the case of a ship. Or it may stay in one area for a long time, perhaps several weeks, while considerable work is done on it. Then it is moved to another assembly area where more work is done. In total, it may be moved only four or five times.

There really are few economic advantages to the fixed work station method except that it avoids the prohibitively high costs which would be entailed if the product were moved from one work station to another very often. Indeed, the fixed station arrangement is probably the only feasible way to put these large products together.

However, because some workers don't like paced moving assembly lines with their small repetitive tasks, some manufacturers are experimenting with fixed position assembly layouts. Hewlett Packard's assemblers of desk calculators, for example, work at benches where they do a number of tasks on each unit, including their own testing. Their total assignment can take an hour or more. When one worker completes his assigned tasks, the product is moved on to the next bench where another worker has another large collection of assembly tasks to perform, and so on.

This approach requires a bank of one or two partially completed calculators at each work station to "decouple" assemblers from each other so delays will not hold up later assemblers. Unfortunately, most experiments of this sort increase assembly costs rather than decrease them as compared to the costs of regular assembly lines. It is not clear that the higher morale and fewer problems of absenteeism and turnover are enough to offset the less efficient method of production.

This method of lengthy individual job assignments is also flexible so far as design changes are concerned. It is also usually possible to shift the sequence of doing things if materials or tools don't arrive or if people are absent. Because the job assignments are so long, there are always several people doing the same set of tasks on other units of the product.

LAYOUT METHODS

Companies that build new facilities often spend two or three years in preliminary work, part of which goes into searching for improved methods to use in the new plant. The building of a new plant provides an excellent opportunity to make far-reaching improvements. With a new layout, it is possible to eliminate many wasteful practices. Suppose, for example, that in a present plant, two people are operating a truck when one is enough. Cutting down to one would prabably produce objections. But with a new factory in a different location, a conveyor—requiring no workers at all—can be put in, thus eliminating the problem and improving the method.

One way to begin a layout analysis is to start with an assembly diagram (or process chart) that shows the way the finished products are made from subassemblies and how the subassemblies are, in turn, made from parts. Next, lists of the operations required to make the parts should be obtained from the engineering department. These lists show the sequence of machines needed for successive operations. If the layout is to be product oriented, the lists provide a pattern for setting up work stations for people and for placing machines.

A second way to begin a new layout is to consider products from a materials handling point of view. Are the products heavy and dense (castings, forgings) or bulky and light (hollow sheet metal items)? How about their shape? Are they long and slim, or floppy, or readily stackable? What about the risk of damage? Are they easily broken or marred, or dangerous or hard to contain (acids), or are they immune to harm (scrap iron)? Are they covered with oil and grease, or are they dry and clean?

Next, the quantities of each product need to be considered. If the expected volume requirements will justify it, a product layout for the hard-to-handle items can be developed. But, if the volume is small, it may be necessary to stay with a process arrangement. In any case, cutting the transportation cost of hard-to-handle items is an important consideration in layout.

A third way to begin a layout analysis is to begin with floor space drawings showing all permanently or semipermanently fixed items—everything that cannot be changed or moved easily. Then, all proposed new machines and equipment can be marked in at their ideal positions. Almost certainly, some permanently fixed features (posts, stairways, elevator wells, and the like) will be in the way, so it will be necessary to make adjustments. Part of the ideal layout will have to be given up as the proposed locations of machines are juggled around until a reasonably good layout, yet one which respects the fixed factors, is found.

THE TRAVEL CHART OR LOAD-PATH MATRIX METHOD
FOR PROCESS LAYOUT

A quite different way to solve a process layout problem is to focus largely on trying to reduce the transportation of in-process materials from department to department.

The "travel chart" method tries to juxtapose departments between which there will be an expected heavy flow of products. A simple example will show how this works.[4] We assume that a factory which makes nuts and bolts is to be laid out and that, in total, the factory will produce 100,000 pounds of nuts and bolts every week. There are a variety of paths the various nuts and bolts may take through the different departments, depending upon the item.

First, it is necessary to construct a "from and to" matrix showing the flow of materials from department to department. These figures would come from order routing sheets and from projections of the quantities of products to be produced in the future. Figure 9–3 shows this expected volume of flow.

Next, an initial schematic diagram is developed showing the sequence of departments through which the materials will have to move. Ideally, the ultimate solution should be the one where most materials would move along a line drawn directly from the first department to the last department. If this were possible, then a product layout would be more appropriate.

In Figure 9–4 (our first attempt to develop such a schematic diagram), the numbers in the circles are department numbers. The numbers along the connecting arrows are the pounds (in thousands) of products which go from one department to the other. In Figure 9–4, the circles have been drawn in a uniform grid, but this will be changed later as departmental

---

[4] This method can be stated mathematically as one which minimizes $\sum_i \sum_j N_{ij}$ D_{ij}, where i and j are the "to" and "from" departments. N_{ij} is the number of loads going from department to department and D_{ij} is the distance between departments i and j. For complex layout problems, computers can be programmed to carry through all of the necessary interaction calculations. Four somewhat different computerized programs that are available for arranging layouts are described in Thomas R. Hoffmann, *Production Management and Manufacturing Systems* (Belmont, Calif.: Wadsworth Publishing Co., 1971), pp. 242–46.

FIGURE 9–3

Thousands of pounds from departments	Thousands of pounds per week to departments											
	2	3	4	5	6	7	8	9	10	11	12	13
1	90									10		
2		75	15									
3				20	45	5					5	
4							13				2	
5									5	12	3	
6								35		10		
7									5			
8							3		5	5		
9									18	20		
10										33		
11												90
12												10

square footage requirements are considered. As can be seen in Figure 9–4, there are many situations where material leapfrogs several departments to get to its destination. Whenever this happens, it usually results in long costly movements of materials.

The next step is to reconstruct Figure 9–4 by moving departments around to reduce the long hauls where the traffic is heavy. Departments between which there is heavy traffic should end up being placed next to each other in as many cases as possible. As Figure 9–4 is drawn, adjacent departments (short hauls) are those between 1 and 2, 1 and 5, and 1 and 6.

FIGURE 9–4

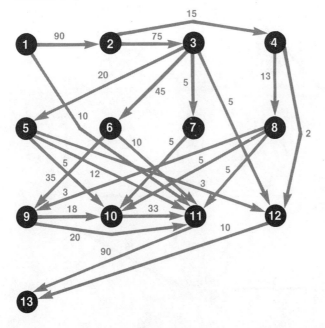

Nonadjacent departments (long hauls) are 1 and 11, 2 and 4, 3 and 11 and 11 and so on.

In an example as simple as this one, an analyst can soon arrive by trial and error at a reasonably good rearrangement of departments to meet this objective. One obvious improvement, for example, would be to move department 13 to the right so that it is below department 11. However, after trying other combinations (and there is a very large number of them), this move may later be discarded.

It took us five stages of improved layouts to arrive at Figure 9–5, in which all solid lines are transportation routes to adjacent departments and are therefore short hauls. The dotted lines are wasteful long hauls among nonadjacent departments. Figure 9–5 still shows 35,000 pounds going by long hauls, but this is low compared to the 499,000 pounds going by short hauls.

Having arrived at the schematic arrangement of departments, our next step is to consider each department's size. This has been done in Figure 9–5

FIGURE 9–5

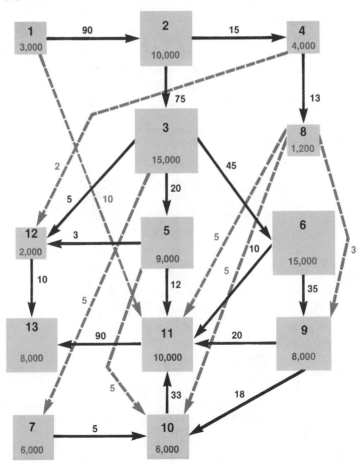

FIGURE 9-6

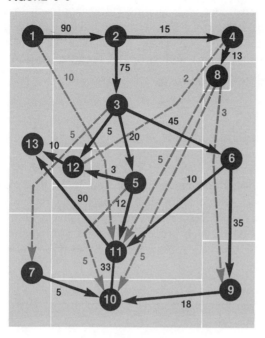

where the sizes of the blocks is in accord with each department's required square footage. It is not necessary, however, that departments be square in shape. So the next step is try to fit the departments into a building, either an existing building or a new one. If the building is to be new, then the departmental requirements will determine its size and have a part in determining its shape. Figure 9–6 shows how the 13 departments in our example might fit into a 560-by-700-foot floor plan.

The travel chart method does not consider all of the problems that engineers face in layout analyses since it pays attention only to the flow of products between departments and not to transportation within departments. It also pays attention only to the material which has to be moved, but only as loads. And implicitly it assumes that distance and costs vary together. There may also be other things which are important, such as bulk, fragility, the need for departments to be close together in order to help coordination, their need for common service and supporting facilities, or the isolation of noisy or hazardous operations.

COMPUTERIZED LAYOUT METHODS

Because of the large number of combinations of departmental patterns which must be considered in larger more realistically sized problems, computer programs have been developed to aid in this analysis.

Perhaps the best known of these is CRAFT, which stands for Computerized Relative Allocation of Facilities Technique. CRAFT uses a heuristic (trial and error but with guiding rules) approach to determine a solution, much as we did in our example but without a computer. CRAFT requires essentially the same information (plus the cost of handling between departments) and an initial feasible solution layout on which it tries to improve.

LAYOUT IN SERVICE ORGANIZATIONS

Banks, restaurants, hospitals, and offices face many of the same layout problems as do manufacturing organizations. For the most part, the same layout methods can be used. Instead of loads moving among departments, the analyst must consider the movement of people (who is required to work face-to-face with whom more than others), and the movement of paperwork. In the cases of restaurants, it is the movement of raw materials (uncooked food) through processing centers (refrigerators, stoves, ovens, and the like), and the movement of finished products (cooked foods) to customers.

REVIEW QUESTIONS

1. If a company's estimates show that it can probably save 10 percent of its direct labor costs if it builds a new factory, should it go ahead and build or not? Why?
2. When a company is planning to build a new factory, should it make improvements in the old plant or should it wait until it gets into the new plant?
3. Obviously a new factory is built only if it will allow for more effective operations. Where do these savings come from?
4. What trends are taking place in the design of facilities?
5. What things can organizations do to provide security to their facilities? Their processes and formulas?
6. What are the four basic layout patterns for facilities? What are the advantages of each? When should each be used?
7. How should a company's practice of producing by lots or continuously be related to the layout pattern used in the factory? Why?
8. How should layout engineers go about devising a factory's layout if they use the travel chart method?
9. How does it happen that many companies do not really know what it costs to move products around and to handle them?

QUESTIONS FOR DISCUSSION

1. The engineer for the construction company which wants to sell a company on building a new plant has just looked over the present

layout. "Your layout is very poor and is no doubt resulting in your costs being from 8 to 10 percent more than they should be," he tells the company president. How can anyone tell if the layout is poor?

2. If the engineer in question 1 says the present layout is quite inflexible as one piece of evidence that it is poor, how important is this? Does inflexibility matter today? He says that if his compay were to build a new plant, it would build in flexibility. How does one "build in" flexibility?

3. Under what conditions should the layout be based on moving the workers and not the products? What diseconomies would this method cause?

4. When, if ever, should a factory's offices be put on mezzanines rather than on the ground floor?

5. How should an analyst go about his task if he is told to produce an estimate of the costliness of a company's materials handling?

6. Suppose the analyst in question 5 is also asked to develop a program for reducing the costs of materials handling. How should he go about this assignment?

7. Should there be a central materials handling department or not? What would be the advantages and disadvantages of having such a department?

PROBLEMS

1. A company needs to expand and is considering a metal prefab, a wooden building, and a cinder-block building. The figures are as follows:

	Metal prefab	Wood building	Cinder-block building
Initial cost.....................	$10,000	$12,000	$25,000
Years of expected useful life.......	10	20	30
Annual maintenance.............	400	300	150
Carrying charges................	18%	18%	18%

Which type of construction should be chosen, and how much will this type save as against the other methods?

2. What would it cost to build a factory for 750 workers who need 450 square feet of space each (service areas take additional space equal to 40 percent of the space needed per worker)? There is no need to build a building with many fancy trimmings, but on the other hand there is need for something better than the simplest construction.

3. Suppose, in problem 2, that land costs were extra and were $3,000 per acre (43,560 square feet) and that the company wants a 4-to-1 ratio (land space total is to be 4 times the new building space). What will the real estate tax be on the land and building (not including machinery or in-

ventories) if appraisals come to about 40 percent of the costs and the rate is 3 per $100 of valuation?

4. Suppose, in problem 3, that land costs $6,000 an acre and the tax rate is $3.25 per $100 of valuation (valuation being 50 percent of true market value). Labor costs $8 an hour in both cases, but in the second case labor is more efficient. How much more efficient would labor have to be to make these two choices equal so far as taxes are concerned?

5. An air conditioning company estimates that it will cost $2 a square foot to install air conditioning and $1 per square foot a year to operate it on the days when it will be needed. The equipment will have a 10-year life. Money is worth 15 percent.

This company claims that air conditioning will cut labor turnover by half (it is now 25 percent per year, and each turnover is estimated to cost $500). The air conditioning company also claims that labor productivity will go up 5 percent.

At the Roy Company workers earn $5 an hour and are provided wtih 350 square feet per worker. People work 2,000 hours a year.

a. On the basis of these figures, should Roy put in air conditioning?

b. Roy's managers suspect that the air conditioning company is exaggerating and that the savings will come to only half of those claimed. If this were so, what should the answer be?

c. Suppose, on the other hand, that Roy's managers believe they will get the gains but that air conditioning will cost 50 percent more than they have been told. Is the answer the same? Show the figures.

d. If the savings estimates are accepted but the turnover reductions are not believed, how much productivity gain will be required to break even on installing air conditioning?

e. Because business is picking up, Roy is hiring more workers and expects soon to have one worker for every 250 square feet. What would the answer be for this worker density?

6. The following departments are to be fitted into a 200-by-300-foot building which is being bought. The building has a railroad spur along the west side, the long side, of the building. Along the tracks is a loading platform for both rail and truck traffic. It is outside the building and not part of the space allocation problem. The layout has to meet the following space requirements inside the building:

Department	Space (square feet)
A Receiving..................................	750
B Raw materials storeroom.....................	1,500
C Manufactured parts storeroom................	1,250
D Subassemblies storeroom.....................	3,000
E Finished products storeroom..................	3,750
F Supplies storeroom..........................	1,000
G Machine shop I.............................	200′ × 30′
H Machine shop II............................	150′ × 45′
J Bench operation............................	50′ × 45′
K Subassembly I.............................	150′ × 45′
L Subassembly II............................	70′ × 50′
M Final assembly*............................	245′ × 50′
N Packing and shipping........................	2,500
P Production and engineering office.............	1,200
Q Factory manager's office.....................	400
R Cost accounting office.......................	1,700
S General accounting office....................	1,700
T General offices.............................	2,400
U Secretary and treasurer's office...............	300
V Vice president and general manager's office.....	400
W President's office...........................	600
X Sales office................................	1,100
Y Purchasing and traffic office.................	825
Z Personnel.................................	625
AA Reception room for departments Y and Z......	750

* Includes 3,000 square feet for subassembly storeroom department D.

Lay out the departmental arrangement on a scale of 1 inch = 40 feet.

7. The new engineers, recently hired, are crowded for office space. It has been necessary to put them five to an office. Since the offices are only 16 by 20 feet, they are somewhat crowded. The average salary of these engineers is $14,000. More space can be built for $20 a square foot. Newly built space would have a life of 25 years and would then be worth 10 percent of its original cost. Taxes, insurance, maintenance, and interest cost 10 percent a year. Janitor service, heating, and lighting cost $1.50 per square foot.

How much would the productivity of the men have to increase to justify assigning four, three, two, or one man to a 16-by-20-foot office?

8. Three alternative plans for a revised layout show the following expected results:

	A	B	C
Cost.....................	$8,000	$10,000	$13,000
Annual saving............	2,200	2,600	3,200

The new layout will probably be used for five years before it will be changed. Interest on investment is 12 percent.

a. Which plan should be chosen?

b. How much higher a rate of return will the selected plan yield than the other two alternatives?

9. The Stevenson Company needs a new layout which will meet the following conditions. The problem is to suggest a general pattern and arrangement of departments. Department sizes are to be approximately as follows:

Department	Size (square feet)	Department	Size (square feet)
A......................	3,000	D......................	2,500
B......................	7,500	E......................	3,500
C......................	6,000	F......................	4,500

On the average, the loads of work that go from one to the other department every day are as follows:

From	To	Number of loads	From	To	Number of loads
A..........	B	22	C..........	A	1
A..........	C	11	C..........	B	6
A..........	D	1	C..........	D	6
A..........	E	5	C..........	E	3
A..........	F	6	C..........	F	9
B..........	A	4	D..........	E	1
B..........	C	15	D..........	F	10
B..........	D	6	E..........	B	2
B..........	E	7	E..........	F	12
B..........	F	2	F..........	B	2
			F..........	C	3

Draw a proposed plant layout for a rectangular building that can be nearly square but should not be long and narrow.

Indicate how many loads will have to pass between nonadjacent departments. Don't, however, make departments into corkscrew shapes just so they will touch many other departments.

10. The analysis of work loads at the Exo Company has proceeded to the point where the area requirements for each work center have been established. These space needs are:

Work center	Department number	Square feet
Centering..................	1	1,000
Mill........................	2	5,000
Lathe......................	3	6,000
Drill.......................	4	3,000
Arbor press.................	5	1,000
Grinder.....................	6	2,000
Shaper.....................	7	2,000
Heat treat..................	8	1,500
Paint.......................	9	1,000
Bench assembly..............	10	1,000
Inspect.....................	11	500
Pack.......................	12	1,000

Production in those departments is confined to the following seven products, which will move through these departments in the sequence shown:

Units per month	Units per load	Product	Sequence
500	2	A	4,7,8,10,11,12
500	100	B	1,3,8,4,6,2,11,3,10,12
1,600	40	C	1,2,4,6,3,11,10,12
1,200	40	D	4,10,2,12
400	100	E	4,6,10,5,12
800	100	F	3,9,10,12
400	2	G	1,2,3,4,5,6,7,8,9,10,11,12

Using the method described in this chapter, develop a proposed arrangement and layout of departments for the new plant expansion. Aim for a rectangular plant.

SUGGESTED SUPPLEMENTARY READINGS

Mutner, R., and McPherson, K. "Four Approaches to Computerized Layout." *Industrial Engineering,* February 1970.

Naghabat, F. "An Efficient Equipment-Layout Algorithm." *Operations Research,* May 1974, pp. 662–68.

Parsons, J. A. "A Technique for Suboptimal Solutions to the Facilities Layout Problem." *Journal of Systems Management,* July 1974, pp. 42–43.

10

Production processes and machine systems

ONCE PRODUCTS and services are designed their specifications must be translated into specific processing systems which create the product or provide the service. For example, in manufacturing a new model typewriter, it is necessary to determine what processing methods to use for making its component parts. Some may be stamped from sheet steel; others may be die-cast from aluminum or they can be plastic parts formed by plastic injection molding.

Decisions must be made about the kinds of machines to use to perform these operations. Questions have to be answered, such as, will "general purpose" machines (such as drill presses, lathes, and stamping machines) be sufficient to do the work? Or can "special purpose" machines (perhaps computer controlled) be justified because of the high prospective volume of parts and products to be made?

How should the typewriters be assembled? Should one worker assemble an entire typewriter, or should assembly be broken down into a number of stages where each worker repetitively performs only one or a few steps? Should the products move down an assembly line, or should they be assembled complete at one assembly station? At what stages of the process should inspection or testing take place to insure the desired quality level?

These and other similar questions have to be answered by manufacturing engineers and systems analysts who work closely with production and operations managers as they develop the necessary production processing systems.

Nor are these activities peculiarly and only associated with factory production. Service organizations, such as airlines or even city governments have to develop services appropriate to their work.

FIGURE 10–1

Model of information flow from product design to production

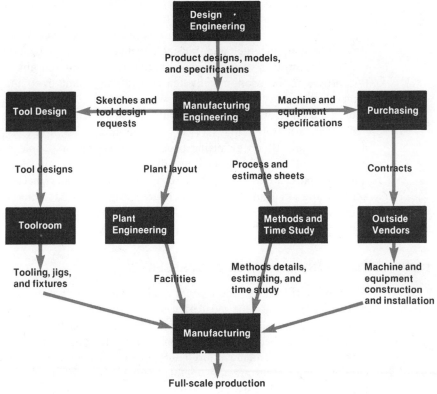

Source: Richard C. Vaughn.

Figure 10–1 shows the kinds of information flows which are needed in order to translate product design specifications into processing instructions.

PRODUCTION PROCESSING SYSTEMS

Every manufacturer and every service organization already has processing systems for producing its goods and services. These were developed in the past. And, although these usually do not change fast, there is almost always a slow evolutionary process of change going on. Sometimes, however, big changes do come quickly. The steel industry, for example, was revolutionized some ten years ago by the introduction of the basic oxygen process, which makes higher quality steel at less cost than other processes.

Sometimes, too, a company has to invest large amounts to install up-to-date methods which have been developing over the years but require extensive change to use to their fullest. Chrysler did this in 1975. It built a new $2 million automatic welding system for welding together the body shells for its newly introduced Volare and Aspen small cars. In about 6½ minutes, a "team" of 13 robot welding machines (6 on each side of the assembly line and 1 overhead) perform 504 spot welds on each body shell as it travels along a 140-foot track.

Some cities are now building prototype plants to process garbage and trash into methane fuel and burnable pellets to use in generating electricity. The process also recovers limited amounts of reusable metals. If this proves to be economically feasible, garbage and trash may not be something to bury but something which, when recycled, has a market value and which will improve our utilization of scarce natural resources.

Systems for delivering services can be just as complex as those in manufacturing. Blood cleansing processing systems for people whose kidneys are not functioning (kidney dialysis machines) are, for example, quite complex. So also, mountain resorts catering to skiers need to provide ski-lifts and ski trail systems which are designed to accommodate skiers with differing abilities. The ski lifts need to be safe, yet fast enough to transport skiers up the mountain at rates which keep waiting at a minimum.

BASIC METAL TRANSFORMATION PROCESSES

So many of today's products are made from metal, that metal processing methods are perhaps the most pervasive of all systems in modern day production operations. Consequently they merit attention here.

After having been abstracted from ore, metal processing usually starts with molten metal being poured into ingots or sometimes "pigs." In the case of gold or other precious metals the ingots may be roughly a foot long by some four inches by four inches in size. Pig iron pigs are larger. Steel ingots are much larger, perhaps as large as two feet by three feet by ten feet and weighing several tons.

Ingots and pigs are later reheated and processed into specific items. Ingots can, while hot and soft, be rolled between squeezing rollers into billets, bars, sheets, or other standard semifinished forms. Billets and bars can be cut by shearing, sawing, or flame cutting into smaller pieces which can be pounded into rough shape for forging. In forging, the metal is heated to a soft state and then pounded into final shape (the head of a hammer is made this way).

Metal can also be rolled out into sheets which can be sheared or stamped into pieces and then folded or bent into desired shapes (the outside of a stove or refrigerator is made this way). Pieces of sheet metal can also be "drawn," or pushed between two dies, to make them take on the desired shape (an automobile fender is shaped this way).

Metal is sometimes made directly into its final shape by casting, which means pouring it, while molten, into molds, which usually are made of sand. Sometimes molten metal is forced into water-cooled metal molds of intricate shapes. This method, called die casting, is used to make many trim and decorative parts out of zinc or plastic. Knobs on television sets, type-writer keys, electric plugs, and a host of other items are made this way.

There are also other less common processes such as extrusion. Metal, particularly aluminum, can be extruded through an orifice which gives it a certain cross section, such as are used in aluminum window and door frames. Another less common process is sintering, where powdered metal is compacted in a forming die to the desired shape. Later this compacted part is baked at close to the metal's melting point, which causes it to fuse into a solid piece.

Or sheet metal can be "spun" (dished aluminum platters and bun warmers are often made this way). A flat piece of metal is put next to a semiball form and rotated, and, as it rotates, force is applied to push it against the semiball. In the end, it will have taken the shape of the semi-ball form. Another somewhat uncommon process is "coining," where a forming surface contour is forced against a piece of metal (our coins are made this way).

Most metal forming, however, starts with a rough piece which is over-sized, and then the excess is removed, much as a sculptor "exposes" a statue in a stone. The excess metal can be removed in many ways. It can be ground off; it can be drilled out or, with thin metal, punched out; it can be chipped, or sheared, or shaved off.

Of these processes, shaving off the excess is much the most common. Except for grinding, which is done by an abrasive grinding wheel, the tool is almost always a steel tool with a carbaloy tip which is harder and tougher than the metal being cut. Usually this process generates consider-able heat and requires that a stream or coolant liquid be directed at it constantly.

Sometimes the material being machined is rotated against a stationary cutting tool, as in the case of lathes. One form of lathe is the turret lathe; another is the automatic screw machine. Both of these machines can per-form two or three operations on a part in sequence or simultaneously. The cutting tool may be stationary or may rotate in a fixed spot while the ma-terial is passed back and forth against the tool as it shaves or chisels off a little more metal at each pass. This is called "milling" or in some varia-tions, "shaping."

If the tool rotates and makes a hole, it is "drilling," but, if the tool is stationary and the work is rotated around it to make a hole, it is "boring." Sometimes a hole is first drilled to rough size and then finished to more exact size by using a "broach." A broach is a slightly tapered mandrel with sharp ridges at each size expansion, and, as it is pulled through the hole, it enlarges it by gouging off the required amount of metal and making the hole the right size.

A different way to remove excess metal is with chemicals, which eat away the unwanted metal. To control the process, the areas that are not to be thinned down are covered with a chemical resistant coating. The chemical eats away the exposed surfaces, leaving the remaining areas untouched. Later the coating is removed, and the piece has the high and low areas as designed.

Hewlett-Packard, which make calculators, computers, and other sophisticated electronic devices, uses such a process for manufacturing printed circuit boards. The entire process is monitored by a minicomputer which automatically moves the boards through the proper sequence of dips into the various chemicals (acids, neutralizers, water, and so on). The system can handle several different types of circuit boards at the same time. The computer "remembers" which vat each board is in and how long it is supposed to stay there. At the proper time an automatic conveyor moves down the line of vats and arrives at the vat at just the right time to remove the board and take it on to the next operation.

Other important processes include heat-treating parts for hardening. The parts are heated close to their melting point and then are quenched quickly in a cool liquid. This process hardens the surface. In other cases, just the reverse is done: Castings are heated up close to their melting point and allowed to cool very slowly. This "annealing" process relieves the internal strain originally set up by thick and thin areas cooling at different rates. The unequal cooling rates, by causing the castings to shrink unevenly, creates internal strain. If these are not relieved by annealing the casting will crack more easily. Water glasses which have not been properly annealed will break very easily.

MACHINING PROCESSING SYSTEMS

Year by year, more and more work once done by people continues to be transferred to machines. Machines respond very quickly to control signals and can apply great force smoothly and precisely. They can do several operations at the same time, and they can handle repetitive and routine tasks well. More and more machines are also being developed to do things which people never could do, such as refine oil or to make chemicals or plastics. And in almost all cases the equipment is becoming more fully automatic. (Machines are vastly inferior to people, however, when it comes to reasoning, exercising more than minimal judgment, or at developing new methods.)

Today's more advanced equipment is being designed to include closed-loop feedback systems. Machines control themselves. They inspect their own output, and, if they are turning out poor work, they reset themselves.

In order to do these things, they contain minicomputers which contain built-in memory units which allow them to remember what they are supposed to do, sensor units which monitor their output, reporting and judging systems which they use to compare the quality of the work they are turning out with what they are supposed to be turning out, and correction effectuators which reset the machine whenever this is needed (see Figure 10–2). All of this is done quickly and accurately since the com-

FIGURE 10–2

A process control system

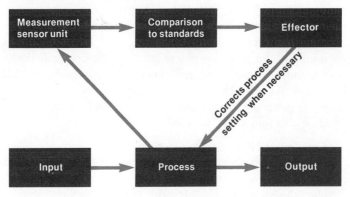

puter can store vast amounts of information and can calculate virtually instantaneously.

Automated process controls are now widely used in oil refining, chemicals, steel making, cement, and other "process" industries. (Process industries may be contrasted with fabrication industries which assemble products from component parts.) Materials in process industries are processed inside tanks, vats, pressure vessels, and the like and materials flow from one processing step to another in pipes and ducts. The processing, the rates of flow, temperatures, mixture ratios, and so on are controlled largely by minicomputers. In the case of oil refining, complex mathematical models "optimize" the way crude oil (which is by no means always homogenous and, depending on its source, differs in chemical make-up, viscosity, volatility, specific gravity, and so on) is refined into various finished products, such as premium and regular gasoline, jet fuel, and heating oil.

GENERAL PURPOSE VERSUS SPECIAL PURPOSE MACHINES

The best way to make a product depends upon how many are to be made, because machines can be designed to do most manual operations. Such machines sometimes are very costly; yet, they are so productive that they cost very little per unit of product if a large volume is produced. Thus, the prospective volume determines the proper "depth of tooling," or the extent to which managers should mechanize or automate. In fact, specialized machines are so costly that they are sometimes made in sections so that product model changes will obsolete only part of the whole machine. Automobile fenders, for example, are formed in huge presses that have removable dies. When models change, the companies take out the old model dies and put in the new. They still have a specialized machine, but they do not have to buy a whole new press for every model change.

For low volumes, the big investments in special purpose machines cannot be justified, so general purpose machines which are designed to do one kind of work rather than one job should be used. Usually these machines are not costly, and they are suitable for performing a wide range of operations. The machines, however, require highly skilled machinists both to set them up as well as to operate them, and they are relatively slow in operation. Special purpose machines also require skilled people to set them up, but, because many are automatic, they can be operated by semi-skilled or unskilled labor.

In using general purpose machines, a number of things usually have to be done either manually or automatically:[1]

1. Move the workpiece to the machine.
2. Load the workpiece onto the machine in the right position and affix it rigidly and accurately.
3. Select the proper tool and insert it into the machine.
4. Establish and set machine operating speeds and other conditions.
5. Control machine motion, enabling the tool to execute the desired function.
6. Sequence different tools, conditions, and motions until all operations possible on that machine are complete.
7. Unload the part from the machine.

In the operation of traditional general purpose machines, lathes, milling machines, drill presses, and so on, all seven of these activities are performed by the operator. But with automated machines, the machines do numbers 3 to 7 of the above activities, and they do them faster and as well or better than the most skilled operator can do them.

As volume goes up, it is possible to justify the use of specialized gadgetry attachments on a machine, such as magazine feeds, special tool guides, and material holding devices ("jigs and fixtures"). These items speed production and lower operating costs.

NUMERICALLY CONTROLLED (N/C) MACHINES

Today a great many, and it may soon become the majority of, metal cutting machines used to make parts are "numerically controlled." These machines are ideal for small- and medium-sized lots but not for large lots where "transfer machines" are more effective. Essentially, numerically controlled machines (which may also be classified as general purpose machines) automate steps 3, 4, 5 and 6 listed above.

Instead of an operator getting instructions to plane a surface, mill a slot, or drill a hole in each item of a lot of 50 steel castings, the directions go directly to the machine. The machine is told, by means on instructions on electronic tape or punched paper tape, to advance its planing tool to the surface of the casting and to plane its surface to a set thickness for a

---

[1] Nathan H. Cook, "Computer-Managed Parts Manufacture," *Scientific American,* February 1975, p. 26.

certain width. It is then told to change to a tool for cutting a slot, to cut the slot, and then to drill a hole, and so on. Once a tape has been programmed and the machine set up with the proper tools in place, all the machine operator has to do is fasten the unfinished casting in place and remove it when the work is done.

The term "numerically controlled" comes from the fact that a machine's instruction program is based on mathematical relationships which tell the machine how far to advance its tools, how many cuts to take, to what depth, and the like. Where necessary, these directions cause the machine to make several coordinated motions at the same time (see Figure 10–3). These directions come from each machine's minicomputers, which may not always be wholly independent but may be satellites of a central computer and receive part of their instructions from the central computer. Local tape controls can even be eliminated in "direct numerical control" (DNC).

Numerically controlled machines do work much faster and more accurately than skilled operators in manual operations. And, although it takes high skills to program machine instructions from a drawing and to design a machine's setup, once this is done, production is almost fully automatic and little labor is required. Both the tapes and the design of the machine setup can be kept for repeated use in the future.

N/C machines can be expensive; most of them cost at least $100,000. Numerical control attachments put on older machines are likely to cost $50,000 or more. Machine programmers are also needed, and castings and forgings can't have as much minor size and shape variation as with conventional machines. (Castings made in sand molds are only "more or less" identical in size and shape.)

Another disadvantage of N/C machines is that they often require complex and frequent maintenance. Because they operate so effectively, they remove metal a large part of the time they are running, and, consequently,

FIGURE 10–3

System for direct control of numerically controlled machines

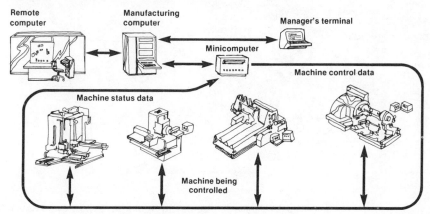

Remote computer

Manufacturing computer

Manager's terminal

Minicomputer

Machine control data

Machine status data

Machine being controlled

they wear out tools and their own operating parts more rapidly. Also, in order to operate correctly they need to be adjusted to close tolerances. Their downtime during operations is likely to run over 4 percent, which is higher than for less sophisticated machines.

All of these requirements mean that N/C machines require a substantial amount of highly sophisticated maintenance. Often jobs are so complicated that the machinery manufacturing company's troubleshooters must be consulted to aid in programming the instructions for the part to be processed.

ROBOTRY

It is usually possible to develop mechanical robots ("iron men") to do most highly repetitive manual jobs. Only their cost stands in the way of more of them. Curiously Japan (where labor pay rates are lower than in most other developed countries) apparently has gone farther in this direction than any other country. For example, Kawasaki (motorcycles) in Japan has developed robots which can assemble motors and gearboxes.[2] The development of robots in Japan may have been caused by its rapid industrial development in the 1960s which created a severe labor shortage. Although in the mid-1970s Japan's labor shortage appeared to be in the past, their present forecasts anticipate another labor shortage before the 1980s.

FIGURE 10–4

Individual robot on an automobile assembly line

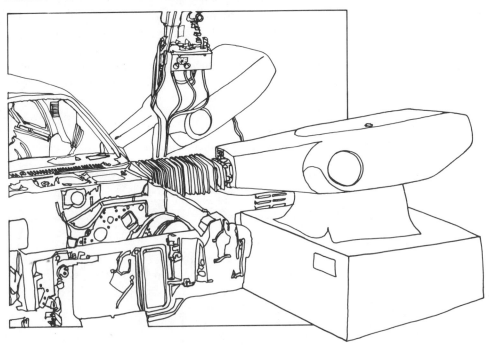

---

[2] As described in James S. Albus and John M. Evans, Jr., "Robot Systems," *Scientific American*, February 1976, pp. 77–86.

FIGURE 10–5

PROGRAMMING AN INDUSTRIAL ROBOT is frequently done by using a hand controller to guide the robot through a sequence of operations. The successive positions of all the robot's joints are stored in a memory. By switching from the "teach" to the "playback" mode stored positions are repeated. The robot is now ready to take its place on production line.

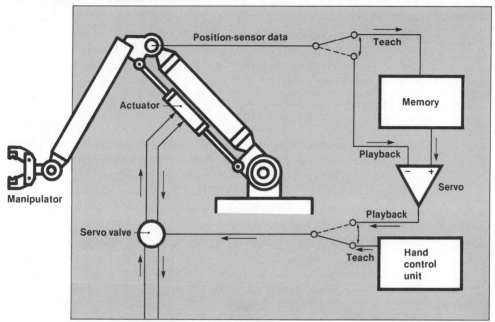

Source: *Scientific American*, February 1976, p. 79.

In the United States, robotry is uncommon except in the automobile industry. A robot costs $25,000 or more and is considered to be worthwhile economically only if it can substitute for one person on each of two shifts, or where the work is particularly dangerous or arduous.[3] Operating costs, however, are usually low, running between $1 and $2 an hour.

Robot makers estimate that ultimately they can make robots that can do half of the jobs done in factories by blue-collar workers.[4] Even after one discounts these optimistic estimates by robot makers, the possibilities are still enormous.

Robots are more general purpose in application than automated machines since they, like general purpose machines, can be reprogrammed rather easily. Typically they are programmed by having a technician "tell" the robot what to do. Figure 10–5 shows graphically how this is done. Robots are, however, both blind and stupid; they cannot do "scene analysis." If a robot is supposed to pick up something, it does so whether

---

[3] See Tom Alexander, "The Hard Road to Soft Automation," *Fortune*, July 1971, p. 97.

[4] In General Motors' heavily automated Chevrolet Vega factory in Lordstown, Ohio, robots do 95 percent of the spot welding (there are over 9,000 spot welds in a Vega car body). At one point, two robots make 130 spot welds in 4½ seconds.

anything is there or not. Parts and products have to be presented to them "just so," (left side front, standing on end, or what not) and, if they are not, the robot doesn't know it and proceeds to act as if they were.

Industrial robots are an important means for releasing human beings from dirty and onerous labor. They eliminate drudgery. They don't take coffee breaks, don't belong to unions, and they work around the clock. They show up for work every day and quickly learn reasonably complex work. They don't get hurt and never complain about dust, fumes, heat, or cold. And they can do a great variety of jobs with only a change in program and gripper hand (large mechanical tweezers).

TRANSFER MACHINES

For large volumes of metal parts transfer machines are superior to numerically controlled machines. Transfer machines do many operations on a part rather than just one or two. And, although their setup costs are high, the setup cost per part is low because of the volume.

Transfer machines, illustrated in Figure 10–6, have almost reached the automation stage in metal working. An unfinished part, say a steel casting or a forging, is fastened to a conveyor which moves on a stop-and-go basis from one machine to the next. The part stops long enough at each machine to have one or more operations performed on it. Separate machines, performing successive operations, are lined up on each side of a conveyor, and, as the conveyor stops, each machine automatically reaches out and performs its operation on the part. As the operating parts on the various

FIGURE 10–6

Transfer machines

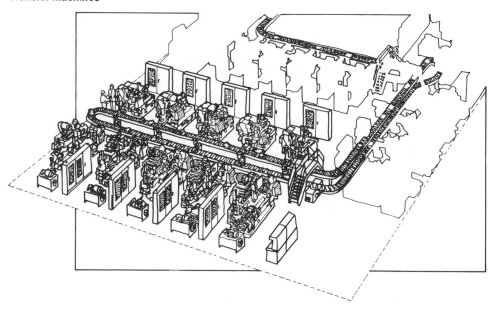

machines move back and out of the way, the conveyor moves another step, and the performance is repeated on the next units. The machines, though actually separate, operate together as if they were parts of a very complex single purpose machine. Such machine groupings eliminate all product handling except the little that is needed before the first and after the last operation.

An interesting problem arises when one operation takes considerably longer time than others. In such a case the operation must be considerably speeded up or else that particular operation must be broken into two parts. If it is a hole, one drill may drill it only part way, and another drill, at another work station, may drill it the rest of the way. This allows individual operations to be in balance.

MALDISTRIBUTION CURVES AND PRODUCTION METHODS

Most companies make a wide variety of products, some of which sell in large volumes and others in small quantities. Production lines are usually the most efficient way to manufacture high-volume products but not small-volume items.

It is possible to use a Pareto maldistribution curve to get an idea of which products to make on lines. The Pareto maldistribution concept holds that in many situations there are a "vital few" and a "trivial many" groups of items. It is not uncommon for a company to find that 20 percent of its products are responsible for 80 percent of its volume. In fact, this concept applies to so many things that it has become known as the 20–80 rule.

To construct a Pareto curve, the first step is to list all of a company's products and the sales volume of each. Next, it is necessary to rank them in order of their sales volume. Then the sales volumes of the ranked items are added cumulatively and converted into percentages of total sales. Finally, the paired percentages (percent of sales and percent of products) are plotted on a chart.

A simplified example will illustrate how to develop a Pareto maldistribution curve. Let us say that the Gripper Wrench Company sells many kinds of wrenches, of which the following 20 are representative. Their volumes (in thousands of dollars) are:

Annual volume

1,000	5,000
44	30
300	73
56	200
3,800	600
900	140
115	105
2,100	1,600
87	50
100	100

Sales in order of magnitude	Cumulated sales	Percent of cumulated sales	Items	Percent of items
5,000	5,000	30.5	1	5
3,800	8,800	53.7	2	10
2,100	10,900	66.5	3	15
1,600	12,500	76.2	4	20
1,000	13,500	82.3	5	25
900	14,400	87.8	6	30
600	15,000	91.5	7	35
300	15,300	93.3	8	40
200	15,500	94.5	9	45
140	15,640	95.4	10	50
115	15,755	96.1	11	55
105	15,860	96.7	12	60
100	15,960	97.3	13	65
100	16,060	97.9	14	70
87	16,147	98.5	15	75
73	16,220	98.9	16	80
56	16,276	99.2	17	85
50	16,326	99.5	18	90
44	16,370	99.8	19	95
30	16,400	100.0	20	100

When all of the paired percentages have been plotted and connected by a line as is done in Figure 10–7, they will make up a distribution curve (it is called a maldistribution curve because it departs so much from a diagonal line).

Figure 10–7 is curved, showing that the company's volume is heavily concentrated in a few of its products. If in Figure 10–7 we read across the bottom scale to 20 percent and then go up to the curve and left to the

FIGURE 10–7

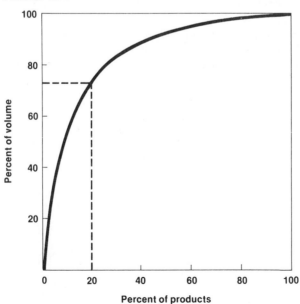

vertical scale, we arrive at approximately the 75 percent mark. If we assume that our sample was representative of all the company's products, then the best-selling 20 percent of all of Gripper's wrenches produce 75 percent of the company's sales volume. These are its big bread-and-butter products. Reading across the bottom to 50 percent and going to the curve, we find that the best 50 percent of the products produce 95 percent of the volume. The remaining 50 percent produce the remaining 5 percent of the volume and, thus, don't amount to much.

This information can help a manager decide whether to go to line production and for which products. If the company ought to go to line production for any products at all, those products will be in the 20 percent group which produces 75 percent of the business. Quite possibly, several of these big selling items should be made by line production. Considering the other end of the chart, a company probably should not use line production methods for making the 50 percent of its products which bring in only 5 percent of the volume. Perhaps some kind of special production facilities, short of line production, would be best for the middle 30 percent of the products which produce 20 percent of the volume.

In the real-life situation from which this example was taken, the company involved, after seeing that its chart was quite maldistributed, went to line production for its high-volume items and saved 17 percent of its manufacturing costs.

MACHINE-USE RATIOS

Owning a machine for eight hours and getting eight hours of work out of it are two different things. Setup time, repair time, operator personal time, not enough work to keep machines busy, and other causes all result in machine idle time. This reduces a machine's operating time and its realized capacity. Machines along production lines might be utilized up to 90 percent of the time. But rarely does one keep machine-use ratios this high in functional departments such as the drill press, automatic screw machine, grinders, and similar departments which specialize in one kind of work.

In functional departments, 60 percent utilization of machine time (meaning that such a machine is actually running 288 minutes in a 480-minute day) is quite good, and 40 percent is common. If it is assumed that machine use in functional departments is 50 percent, and if it would be possible (by installing a line) to increase this to 60 percent, the gain would be very worthwhile. The extra 20 percent in production would be free so far as extra machine investment is concerned.

An example will show how volume helps boost machine-use ratios. The discussion will assume that the line arrangement, where an entire line of machines is devoted to making one item, is responsible for the gains.

If a company has high volume and limited variety, it might be able to have reasonably high machine-use ratios even in functional departments.

But with high volume and limited variety, it would probably be better to utilize lines anyway to earn the gains from low handling and low inventory costs. Thus, high machine-use ratios and lines go together.

Differential housing production line example

This example assumes that a company makes a differential housing for automobiles which is needed in large quantities and requires seven machining operations. Figure 10–8 lists the machines and each machine's hourly output capacity. In addition, Figure 10–8 shows the number of machines of each kind which would be needed for various production levels. The company has to have one of each machine in order to produce any products at all. And, of course, the machines will not be very busy at low levels of output. As the quantities produced go up, the machine-use ratios go up until production reaches 40 units per hour, which is the internal grinder's output limit. At 40 units per hour, the internal grinder is operating at 100 percent of its capacity; all seven machines combined are averaging 58 percent.

If more than 40 units per hour are needed, the company will have to buy another grinder. As production continues to go up, when requirements pass 57 units per hour, it will be necessary to acquire a second automatic screw machine. If the requirements go still higher, another maximum capacity is reached at 62 units per hour at which point a second polishing jack for the exterior will be required.

Figure 10–8 shows how, as production rates go up, one bottleneck after another arises. At each point another machine of some kind will be required. Figure 10–8 carries this example's analysis up to 120 units an

FIGURE 10–8

Kind of equipment	Units per hour	Units of output per hour							
		40	57	62	63	79	80	114	120
		Percent of capacity of 1 machine at various production rates per hour							
Automatic screw machine.....	57	70	100	109	111	139	140	200	211
Surface grinder..............	156	26	37	40	40	51	51	73	77
Drill press..................	128	31	45	48	49	62	63	89	94
Centerless grinder...........	63	63	90	98	100	125	127	181	190
Polishing jack for exterior.....	62	65	92	100	102	127	129	184	194
Internal grinder.............	40	100	143	155	158	198	200	285	300
Polishing jack for interior.....	79	51	72	78	80	100	101	144	152
Total of percents..........		406	579	628	640	802	811	1,156	1,218
Number of machines (before adding one)..............		7	8	9	10	11	12	13	14
Average utilization (percent)..		58	72	70	64	73	68	89	87
Average utilization after buying next machine (percent).....		51	64	63	58	67	62	83	81

hour, by which time the company will need two or more of all but two kinds of machines.

In constructing Figure 10–8, the average utilization of each of the seven kinds of machines was calculated for every production level at which it became necessary to buy another machine; hence, the columns headed 40, 57, 62, and so on. In each column, the percent use of each kind of machine at that production level is listed. Then these use percentages were added, and the total was divided by the number of machines to determine the average utilization percent.

At the first bottleneck point where the production rate was 40 units an hour, the seven machines' average utilization rate is 58 percent of the time. But buying a second grinder brings the total up to eight machines, so the average utilization rate drops to 51 percent. No more machines are required until production reaches 57 units per hour. At 57 units, average machine utilization is 72 percent, requiring the company to buy a second automatic screw machine, thus dropping utilization to 64 percent.

The utilization ratios in Figure 10–8 have been plotted in Figure 10–10. The line is jagged but generally moves upward toward the right, since the higher the volume, the greater the average use of all machines.

Theoretically it is incorrect to average the use ratios of a $16,500 machine with another which costs $350. A better approach would be to analyze the use of the investments in machines. Attention should be centered on each machine's investment; high or low rates of use of expensive machines are more critical than differences in the use of inexpensive machines.

The investment utilization ratios are shown in Figure 10–9 and are plotted in Figure 10–10. In Figure 10–9, for example, at an output rate of 40, 100 percent of the $8,700 cost of an internal grinder is utilized.

FIGURE 10–9

	Installed cost of 1 machine	Units of output per hour							
		40	57	62	63	79	80	114	120
		Machine value used at various production rates per hour							
Automatic screw machine..	$16,500	$11,550	$16,500	$18,000	$18,300	$22,950	$23,100	$33,000	$ 34,800
Surface grinder...........	8,275	2,150	3,050	3,300	3,300	4,200	4,200	6,050	6,350
Drill press	650	200	300	300	300	400	400	600	600
Centerless grinder	6,000	3,800	5,400	5,900	6,000	7,500	7,600	10,900	11,400
Polishing jack for exterior ..	350	200	300	350	350	450	450	650	700
Internal grinder..........	8,700	8,700	12,450	13,500	13,750	17,250	17,400	24,800	26,100
Polishing jack for interior..	350	200	250	250	300	350	350	500	550
Total value used........		26,800	38,250	41,600	42,300	53,100	53,500	76,500	80,500
Investment before adding 1 new machine...........		40,825	49,525	66,025	66,375	72,375	72,725	81,425	97,925
Investment utilization (percent)...............		66	77	63	64	73	74	94	82
Investment after adding new machine..........		49,525	66,025	66,375	72,375	72,725	81,425	97,925	106,625
Investment utilization (percent)..............		54	58	63	58	73	66	78	75

FIGURE 10–10

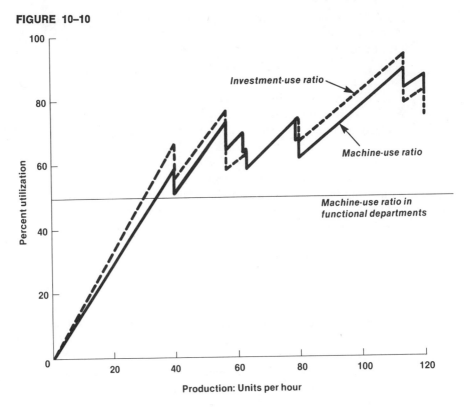

But only 70 percent of the cost of an automatic screw machine is utilized ($16,500 × .7 = $11,550).

To investigate this matter, we calculated both the average machine-use ratios and the average investment-use ratios. These are both plotted in Figure 10–10. It is surprising that the investment-use ratios are almost the same as the time-use ratios. Actually these two ratios will probably always be close together if there are several machines even though the investment in individual kinds of machines varies quite a bit.

Lines and functional manufacture comparison

The question our example poses is: Should the company go to line production to make the differential housings or not? (The assumption is that high machine-use ratios mean that a line will be economical. And by "high use ratio" is meant anything higher than the 50 percent use which might be possible in functional departments.)

Figure 10–10 shows that the machines will be busy 50 percent of their time at a production rate of 35 units per hour or more. Since 35 units an hour is 6,000 a month, then if volume is expected to stay above this level, the company should utilize line production.

Putting in a line should be economical. To estimate how much a line might save, assume a monthly sales volume of 13,000 gear casings (75 per hour). The chart shows that at 75 units per hour, the machines will operate about 67 percent of the time. They will probably be about 67/50 as productive as the productivity usually obtained from machines in functional departments. In our example, this will require $70,000 worth of machines to produce 75 units an hour. Were the machines in use only 50 percent of the time, the company would probably need 67/50 as many machines, worth $94,000, to reach this level of output.

This could result in a capital investment savings of $24,000. This estimate would, of course, depend upon how well the company could utilize the machines in functional departments. With a volume of 13,000 a month, functional departments might increase their utilization ratio halfway from 50 to 67 percent, reducing the cost advantage of a line to about $12,000. Savings in handling and inventory costs would most likely be more important than this investment savings.

VULNERABILITY OF LINES TO DOWNTIME

Lines virtually eliminate most work-in-process inventories. As soon as one operation is finished, the product moves to its next operation. The product deadtime between operations usually amounts to seconds, not hours, and often only 1 or 2 items wait between operations—not 50 or 100 as in functional job shop work arrangements.

Yet, it may be dangerous to have many sequential operations tied closely together. If one machine fails, they all stop, causing extensive costly idle time. For example, assume that four machines of equal capacity are doing successive operations on a part made in large quantities. When the machines are operated individually, products slide down a chute at each machine into a tote box on the floor. When the box is full, the operator dumps it into the next machine's feed hopper.

Suppose that it is possible to hook these four machines together by adding, say, $800 worth of conveyors. Then each machine will dump its products onto a conveyor which takes them directly to the next machine's feed hopper. This saves labor, eliminates almost all the inventory of partly made products in process, and moves products through the production faster.

This all sounds very good, but it may be unwise. Each machine is subject to occasional breakdowns because tools become worn or get out of adjustment, and the machines have to be stopped in order to correct the problem. Suppose that each machine in Figure 10–11, when run separately, is down 10 percent of the time from worn tools or for minor repairs. This rarely holds up the others because of the between-machine supplies of products. As a result, close to 90 percent utilization of the machine group can be achieved.

It would appear that if these four machines were connected, their

FIGURE 10–11

Separated operations

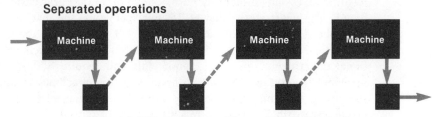

Unit availability 90 percent and line availability 90 percent

Conveyorized operations

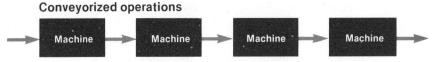

Unit availability 90 percent and line availability 69 percent

utilization ratio would be $.90^4$, or .65. This is not true, however, since such a calculation implicitly assumes that any machine not in operation has the same likelihood of breaking down as it has while operating. In order to correct for this, it is necessary, first, to calculate the ratio between the idle time of individual machines and their operating time. This ratio is: $.1 \div .9 = .11$. The utilization ratio for all four machines is then calculated as follows:

$$U_4 = \frac{1}{1 + 4r} = \frac{1}{1 + 4\,(.11)} = \frac{1}{1.44} = .69$$

Thus, the expected utilization ratio is .69 or 69 percent. And the line would be expected to be out of operation 31 percent of the time.

Whether successive machines should be hooked together in this fashion depends upon the expected downtime for the line. In Figure 10–11, for example, suppose that when the between-machines tote pans of material were eliminated, this reduced the investment in inventory by $400. At an inventory holding cost of 20 percent a year, this saves $80 per year. And suppose that there will be additional savings of $1,000 in hopper-tending labor each year by the installation of the conveyor system.

Considering the $800 cost of installing the conveyors, the proposed new arrangement seems to gain $280 the first year ($1,000 + $80 − $800) and $1,080 each year thereafter.

But these calculations have not considered expected downtime. If each machine is worth $3 an hour in operation, the extra loss of 21 percentage points of one year's time (because the machines now run only 69 percent of the time instead of 90 percent) comes to 420 hours per machine (assuming a 2,000-hour year), or 1,680 hours in total, with an expected loss of $5,040 per year. Under these considerations, the company should not conveyorize and hook these machines together until this downtime can be reduced.

Automated installations of all kinds require that individual machines be highly reliable. Chrysler's Plymouth division, for example, uses 1,800 solenoid switches in one section of an automated assembly line in its engine factory. If one such switch fails, merely finding it is often a difficult task. Such failures just cannot be allowed to happen often, or the losses will be staggering. (To keep this from happening, the equipment needs to be designed to be largely trouble free, and parts need to be replaced before they fail.)

If a line is held up, it idles all the machines and all the employees working on the line, which is very costly. In a heavily automated steel mill, interferences which stop the mills are estimated to cost at least $1,000 a minute! Production is lost, and possibly products or equipment are ruined. Losses can occur just as easily in food production, chemicals, glass, rubber, and other industries. If a line stops during the production of these items, almost surely both the products in process and the machinery will be damaged because heated materials being processed cool and congeal mid-process.

Paradoxically, managers of highly mechanized production lines should not be too concerned about keeping the few employees who serve such lines busy all the time. On the contrary, it usually pays to have maintenance mechanics available on a standby basis to repair the line should it break down. However, when the line is running well, these mechanics usually have little to do.

AUTOMATIC ASSEMBLY

In manufacturing, one of the last frontiers of handwork is assembly, and putting finished pieces together is still handwork in most industries. Assembly lines for putting shoes together, suits of clothes, automobiles, typewriters, adding machines, stoves, refrigerators, radios, television sets, and so on are characterized by *people* putting things together.

Nevertheless, automatic assembly is slowly becoming more common, although its high first cost and lack of flexibility stand in the way of faster acceptance. Automated assembly requires costly magazine feeds, indexing turn tables, robot fingers, hands, and arms, and all the electronic equipment (electric eyes, solenoid switches, electronic circuitry, and so on) that goes along with it. IBM assembles many of its electronic panel units automatically. Parker Pen assembles ball-point pens automatically. Gabriel Company assembles 2,000 valves an hour automatically. McGraw-Edison assembles 1,500 roller skate wheels an hour. Sara Lee puts cakes and pies together automatically.

Here, in general, is how automatic assembly operates. A supply of every part is loaded into a hopper (or magazine feed) located above an assembling machine along a conveyor or around a Lazy Susan revolving table. The first assembling machine automatically picks out one of the frame parts of the product and fastens it on the conveyor. Then the conveyor "indexes" or moves it to the next work station (a foot or so away). There the next assembling machine puts its part into place in the frame. Then the conveyor indexes again and moves the frame to the next station, where part two is attached. Then more moves and more parts are added. Besides placing the parts, the machine fastens them, so that finished assemblies come off at the end of the line.

Here is what goes on at each of the 16 work stations of an IBM automatic machine for assembling wire contact relays:

Station 1 feeds molded plastic frames into the left side of a turret fixture. A vibrating feeder positions the frames, which move down inclined rolls to a loading platform. An air cylinder drives a horizontal reciprocating plunger, which pushes frames along a platform one at a time. Jaws lift a frame and place it in the left side of the fixture. A photoelectric cell watches the frames on rails and cuts off the feed if the frames back up. Frames pass through a fixture which stops those with misaligned or bent terminals. If one stops, the frames back up to a photoelectric detector.

Station 2 is the same as station 1 except that it feeds frames into the right side of the turret fixture. Between stations 2 and 3 an inspection device checks the loading of frames in their holding fixtures.

Station 3 probes for the presence and location of holes in the frames, and absence of dirt or "flash" in the holes. If the probe is impeded, work on the frames stops.

Station 4 countersinks holes in the frames for guide pins.

Station 5 taps holes for set screws.

Station 6 cleans chips from holes with an air blast.

Station 7 ejects frames found substandard at station 3. A memory pin, extended at station 3, closes an electric circuit at station 7, actuating rams that remove the frame from its work-holding fixture.

Station 8 examines tapped holes with photoelectric cells for broken taps. Clogged holes stop the light and this stops the machine. A signal light shows the operator the trouble spot.

Station 9 inserts rubber bumpers into threaded holes. Vibratory hoppers feed these bumpers in the correct position. Nozzles lift the bumpers by suction and transfer them to holes. When bumpers are seated in the frame, the air flow in nozzles automatically reverses from suction to pressure. Bumpers are released and pushed into position by air pressure.

Station 10 checks with photoelectric cells for the presence of bumpers. When a frame lacks one or both bumpers, the machine stops and a red light signals the operator.

Station 11 inserts a set screw into a tapped hole in the relay frame in the left side of the holding fixture. A vibratory feeder positions screws for driving. An automatic screwdriver sets screw at the right depth.

Station 12 inserts a set screw into frame in right side of the holding fixture.

Station 13 inserts guide pins into frames. A transfer arm picks up pins by vacuum and moves them by mechanical linkage to location where it inserts the pins into the frames.

Station 14 flares guide pins to secure them in frames.

Station 15 performs final inspection. It probes for guide pins and checks for high, low, or missing set screws.

Station 16 removes all relays. Those that have passed all inspections slide down a track into a container. Memory pins locate faulty relays, and, when they find a faulty one, they close an electric circuit, which shifts the track so that it drops the rejected relay into a reject box. This station also probes the fixtures to make sure all relays have been ejected.

So far, no one puts whole automobiles or any other big product together automatically, although General Motors' Lordstown, Ohio, factory approaches automated assembly. Probably industry will never assemble many whole, complex products automatically, but the possibilities are great for small electrical products, such as light bulbs, switches, telephone transmitters and receivers, transistors, radios, condensers, electric circuit panels, and the like. Also, small mechanical products, such as scissors, wrenches, staplers, can openers, and a host of others, could be assembled automatically.

Again, the Japanese are leaders in this area. Their government is supporting a large research and development program directed towards developing a fully automated unmanned factory.

REVIEW QUESTIONS

1. In metal cutting operations in factories is it, in general, better to have the material or the cutting tool move? Or is this not revelant? Why?

2. Is it possible to get the benefits of costly special purpose machines, which produce low unit costs for high-volume items, yet avoid most of the risks of loss if product designs change before the machines have fully paid for themselves? Explain.

3. Why do numerically controlled machines operate so economically?

4. How can the 20–80 law be helpful in decisions concerning the depth of tooling?

5. How much improvement in machine-use ratios ought to be achieved when a company changes from lot production to line production? What conditions would make this an economical move?

6. Is it more important, when comparing machine-use ratios of machines under different production situations, to compare the machines' hours of use ratio or dollars' investment-use ratio? Why?

7. Is there anything that managers can do to reduce either (a) the probability of a production line's having to stop or (b) the duration of the downtime when a stoppage occurs?

QUESTIONS FOR DISCUSSION

1. Machine tool builders should know the capabilities of their machines better than anyone else, so their recommendations about speeds and feeds ought to be the best. Yet many companies feel that they can do better and so figure out their own speeds and feeds. Why is there this discrepancy? Discuss.

2. How can machine design engineers do a proper job of setting the most appropriate depth of tooling when market forecasts of sales volumes of products are often off by 50 percent or more?

3. Why is it that interest in robotry seems to be more general in Japan, where wages are relatively low, than in the United States, where wages are high?

4. Since high volume makes it possible for a company to use production lines which are so economical, how can companies with lower volumes get along?

5. If a company has several machines, each doing its job in sequence on the product, would conveyors probably cause production to go up or down? Why?

6. Isn't the maldistribution idea largely a textbook concept since every company ought to know which products are its biggest sellers? Discuss.

7. There is a good bit of acceptance of the Pareto maldistribution curve. Would its principle hold true for the products sold in a K-Mart or Sears store? If the answer is no, doesn't this suggest that maldistribution curves do not have such universal application?

PROBLEMS

1. Suppose that the following is a fair sample of the variety in sales volumes of all the items made by the Rio Company. Construct a maldistribution curve and read from it about what percent of the company's best-selling products produce 80 percent of its sales.

Product	Annual sales	Product	Annual sales
1	$315,000	9	$110,000
2	25,000	10	5,000
3	110,000	11	275,000
4	9,000	12	190,000
5	17,000	13	13,000
6	60,000	14	60,000
7	450,000	15	125,000
8	8,000		

2. A company is introducing a new product which it plans to price at $100 per unit. It is considering five alternative ways to make this product, each having different tooling-up costs and different variable costs, as follows:

Method	Tooling cost	Variable cost per unit
A......................	$10,000	$75
B......................	15,000	50
C......................	25,000	30
D......................	40,000	20
E......................	50,000	16

The prospective volume estimates are:

Quantity	Probability
1,000...........................	.15
1,500...........................	.20
2,000...........................	.25
2,500...........................	.18
3,000...........................	.13
3,500...........................	.06
4,000...........................	.02
5,000...........................	.01

Which manufacturing process should be chosen?

3. Suppose that in the example given in the text on line processing (p. 232) the productivity figures are as follows:

Kind of equipment	Units per hour
Automatic screw machine...	22
Surface grinder...........	180
Drill press...............	90
Centerless grinder........	20
Polishing jack for exterior...	175
Internal grinder..........	75
Polishing jack for interior...	200

Draw up a machine time-use chart similar to Figure 10–9. Should the company go to line production (assuming that this should be done at the point where the machines will be 55 percent busy on average) if production will be 10 units per hour? 20, 30, 40, 50 units? Where is the crossover point—where should the change be made to line production?

The company doesn't have a very good idea of what the demand for this product will be, but the market forecasters have made the following estimates:

Hourly output	Probability
10...........................	.05
20...........................	.15
30...........................	.20
40...........................	.30
50...........................	.20
60...........................	.05
70...........................	.05

Should a line arrangement or a functional arrangement be installed?

4. In the text's example of chaining successive machines together (p. 236) we found that the losses outweighed the gains. Suppose we had six machines with the following normal downtimes: .02, .06, .07, .03, .05, .10. This means that machine one runs 98 percent of the time, machine two, 94 percent, and so on. (The machines are of equal capacity.)

By spending $10,000 for equipment, which will last five years, we can reduce the inventory between operations by $3,000 and also save $10,000 in labor (in a year) picking up and putting down materials. Inventory carrying costs are figured at 20 percent per year. The plant operates 2,000 hours a year, and we'd like to keep these machines operating; in fact, we lose $8 an hour on every machine for every hour it does not operate.

Should we go ahead and mechanize? If we do, how much will we gain or lose? Note: Generally for "n" machines with equal or unequal down-time proportions the formula used is,

$$U_n = \frac{1}{1 + \sum\limits_{i}^{n}\left(\dfrac{\text{Downtime proportion}_i}{1 - \text{Downtime proportion}_i}\right)}$$

5. The engineers have decided that volume is sufficient to justify setting up a small work center to work continuously at making part A. This particular job is a drilling operation, and 120 pieces per hour are wanted.

It takes ¼ minute to unload the drilling machine, ½ minute to load it, and 1½ minutes to drill the hole. The work is done by a machinist whose hourly rate is $6. But the unloading could be done by a $4-an-hour helper. Machine time is calculated to be worth $10 an hour. During the 1½ minute of drilling time the machinist could be doing other work, such as loading another machine.

Set up this work station so as to minimize the costs of producing 120 pieces per hour.

SUGGESTED SUPPLEMENTARY READINGS

Ansley, A. C. *Manufacturing Methods and Processes.* Philadelphia: Chilton Book Co., 1968.

Dooley, A. R., and Stout, T. M. "Rise of the Blue-Collar Computer." *Harvard Business Review,* July–August 1971.

Pritchard, H. S. "New Approaches to Computer Control of Conveyor Lines." *Factory,* November 1971.

11

Designing assembly line production systems

MAKING ASSEMBLED products out of parts is largely manual. People attach parts and components, doing it all manually or with the aid of simple portable hand tools. As we said in an earlier chapter, production lines save labor because products are moved by conveyor and are not carried around by people. Also, the direct movement of products from one operation to another almost eliminates in-process inventories. And it eliminates a great deal of paper work because it is not necessary to tell production workers and material handlers what to do.

Perhaps the most important problem in line production is to align the jobs so that they all require almost identical times to perform because the output of a line is limited to that of the individual work station which takes the most time. If one assignment takes more time than the others, its rate of output will determine the line's maximum production. Workers at other work stations with shorter work assignments will be underutilized. It becomes highly important, therefore, to try to develop equal work assignments for every work station.

AUTOMOBILE ASSEMBLY JOB DESIGN

In General Motors' Willow Run plant outside Detroit, Walter Jones, at work station 15, picks up a long, slender metal tube which is bent into an odd shape. Jones fastens this tube with four clips to the underside of a Chevrolet automobile body that is hanging from an overhead conveyor as it slowly passes over his head. The tube is part of the Chevrolet hydraulic brake system, and the bends in it allow it to follow the contours of the underside of the car.

Jones does not, however, fasten either end of the tube to anything because this is not part of his job. Fastening the ends is part of someone
else's job, because either (1) Jones already has all the work he can handle
(this is true in any case, because if Jones fastened the ends he would *not*
do some of the other work he now does), or (2) the parts that the hydraulic tube is to be fastened to are not on the car yet, or (3) Jones's
working position would make it hard or awkward for him to do the
fastening, whereas this will not be so for some other worker farther down
the line.

Jones has a collection of small tasks to perform on every car that
comes along (at the rate of one a minute). His collection of tasks adds
up to enough to keep him busy for about one minute (probably a little
less, but definitely not more than one minute).

Jones does not have the work station to himself; he works only on the
left underside of Chevrolets. Jack Hamett, who works at the same station,
works only on the right underside of Chevrolets.

Neither Jones nor Hamett is hurrying with his tasks, yet each works
steadily. The duties which make up each man's one-minute job package
were selected to add up to almost one minute's work when he works
steadily yet not at a rapid pace. (Employees on a typical automobile assembly line are allowed two 23-minute paid breaks per 8-hour shift
besides the 30-minute lunch break which is unpaid. Besides this, relief
workers—one for each seven on the line—fill in from time to time.)

A visitor walking along this assembly line would find everybody working at about the same pace. At every work station people, sometimes
one, sometimes two, perform their near one-minute collection of tasks on
the cars that keep coming along. And as the conveyor moves, the Chevrolet becomes more nearly a car as more parts are put on. Somewhere along
the way, someone fastens one end of the hydraulic brake tube to the car's
master brake cylinder, and someone else fastens the other end to the
brake for a wheel.

RATE OF OUTPUT AND NUMBER OF WORK STATIONS

To justify the use of assembly lines for production, the demand must
be rather high. If, for example, there is need for 2,000 assembled products
a week, they probably should be produced by the line production method.
The line could be planned to turn out about one unit a minute. (Although
there are 2,400 minutes in a 40-hour week, some time is lost for rest
breaks and starting and stopping each day.)

Both the people and the machines along the line would be geared to
work one minute on each unit of product, so that the total work to be
done would have to be broken up into one-minute jobs. If, in total, it took
120 minutes to assemble a product, this work might well be divided into,
say, 130 slightly less than 1-minute jobs. The plan, then, could be for a
line with 130 work stations. (Each person's assignment would have to be

for a little less than one minute's work because the bits and pieces of work which are to average one minute or less, won't come out even because their work time will vary a little.)

The matter of line speed and job cycle time is discussed later in this chapter; here, however, it should be said that line production usually is not very satisfactory for low production—say 25 units per week. In such a case each person would have nearly an hour-and-a-half job assignment on every unit. Proficiency at doing all of the minute tasks in this hour-and-a-half assignment would probably be low. It would be better to use lot production for only 25 units a week rather than set up an assembly line.

A first step in determining work station assignments is to determine the workload of the line. The number of units required per hour, multiplied by the labor-hours required per unit, gives the total labor-hour workload per clock hour. So, if it takes a total of 2 labor-hours, or 120 labor-minutes of assembly time per unit of product, and 60 units an hour are required, something like 130 employee-hours (the extra 10 hours allow for delays) must be provided along the line every hour.

Cycle times and number of work stations

It is also necessary to determine the cycle-time and number-of-work-stations (or work zones) relationships. If 60 units an hour are required in the example above, 65 work stations through which 1 unit of product moves every minute would do the job, provided that there were 2 people at every work station each with almost a 1-minute collection of duties.

But a 65-work station arrangement is not the only alternative to the 130-work-stations with 1 employee at each. Another choice would be to have 80 or 90 stations with 1 worker at some stations and 2 workers at others. Or the line could have 45 stations with 3 people at most of them. Or, if the assemblers would not get in each other's way, there could be fewer stations with more people.

It is also possible to change the cycle time. There could be 2 lines with 30 units coming off each line per hour. This would double the amount of specialized equipment needed, but it would open up other possibilties of line speed, number of stations, and number of people at each station. In any case, there are many possible choices and not just one or two.

When the cycle-time and number-of-work station relationships have been decided, this automatically sets both the line speed and the amount of space which will be needed along the line. If the products are automobiles and 1 per minute is required, it may be necessary to provide as much as 25 feet per work station along the conveyor. If so, then the conveyor will have to move at a rate of 25 feet per minute. And since all assemblers have close to 1-minute jobs, each station (with 2 workers per station) will have to be 25 feet long or longer. In total, at least 65×25 feet, or 1,625 feet of work space, will be needed for the work stations along the line. This is a minimum.

If a line normally moves 25 feet during the minute it takes the workers to do the work, it is a good idea to allot a little more than 25 feet to the station. Then, if one of the assemblers needs to stay with the product a little longer, he can do so. This gives him a little latitude in balancing out his long and short work cycles. It also gives the job designer the opportunity to assign employees work packages which contain almost a full minute's work instead of something less. Normally, since a worker can stay with the product for only a minute, his work package has to be sufficiently less than one minute to allow for occasional work cycles greater than one minute.

Space between stations may also be needed to provide for between-jobs storage banks or for other reasons. But, if there are no such reasons, it is well to put work stations in as little space as is required—25 feet in our example.

The discussion so far has assumed that the number of work stations and the space required can be determined as the first step in setting up a line. This is not always the case, however, because the exact number of work stations and the number of assemblers needed must await the development of "work packages" for each employee. Possibly these can be developed so that on the average they contain .85 minutes of work for each worker. But the work content of any one assembler's assignment might end up being a little higher or a little lower. But, whatever it is, the final number of workers and work stations depends on how the work tasks are combined into work packages. We will see later that there can be complications here, depending upon the sequence in which the assembly tasks must be performed.

Desirability of a single line

It might seem that when a total assembly job is made up of a thousand or more small bits of work which add up to 120 minutes there would be an almost limitless number of combinations of how these bits can be made into work station assignments.

At one extreme, one person could do the whole job. In this case it would seem that 130 or so assemblers could be working at the same time, each assembling a complete product. At the other extreme, 130 or so people (or even more with still shorter assignments) could each be doing just about one minute's work on each product as it passes a work station. Between these extremes there could be any number of combinations. There could be, for example, 24 people each doing 5 minutes of work on every 24th product in one place along the line, or there could be individual workers doing 2 minutes of work on every second unit, or there could be only 40 assemblers along a line, each doing 3 minutes work on every third product, and so on.

A moment's thought, however, reveals how impractical almost every other possible combination is when compared to a line with each person

FIGURE 11–1

Assembling refrigerator and freezers at Whirlpool, where the minor tasks add up to nearly full use of the operators' time (average 82 percent)

(a) Putting insulation on cold plate tubing
(79.2 percent)

(b) Driving 3 screws in shelf and liner
(94.8 percent)

(c) Installing crisper pan
(85.5 percent)

(d) Positioning suction line in clips
(69.3 percent)

doing about one minute's work. Other arrangements usually multiply both materials handling costs and tooling costs, and this must be considered when evaluating more complex line configurations.

If 130 people each made whole products, supplies of the hundreds of parts would all have to be brought to each of the 130 work stations. At each work station, therefore, there would have to be bins for each of these hundreds of parts, and they would have all to be replenished from time to time.

Each worker would also need every tool that would be required for

FIGURE 11–2

A loop-type assembly conveyor and work stations

each bit and piece of the whole job. He would need nut and bolt tighten-ers, soldering irons, riveters, and everything else. If any operation needed special work area conditions, such as heat removal from welding, each work place would have to have this too. One hundred and thirty sets of everything would have to be provided!

Truckers would also have to truck away finished units: 1 every 2 hours from 130 different work stations, or else let them pile up. In any case, the inventories of parts and finished products and the materials handling costs would be exorbitant.

When all of these factors are considered, the *economical* choice is al-most always one production line, with each worker doing a part of the total work and doing it on every unit. No one else does this work, each bit of work belongs to a single employee's work assignment. However, other considerations such as "job enlargement" or "job enrichment" programs (which are discussed in Chapter 13) sometimes make it necessary to make some concessions in order to reduce extreme boredom and monotony.

HEURISTIC LINE BALANCING

Years ago it was a tedious task for engineers to determine the balance between assembler's assignments along production lines so that they were equally busy and so that everything was kept moving evenly. The engineers had to make out long lists of minor parts (5/100 and 10/100 of a minute parts, not 2- and 3-minute parts) called "elements" of the total task of assembling a car. Then, mindful of the sequence in which elements had to be performed (the windshield trim cannot be put in place until the windshield is installed) and how long the minor tasks took, they developed work packages of close to one-minute duration for the assemblers who were to work along the line.

Today this method has not changed, but it is no longer the tedious task it used to be because computer programs are available to analyze as many as one wants of the millions of possible combinations which exist in assembling a complex item like an automobile.

Computers do not, however, search out every possible combination of the thousands of minor tasks before settling on certain collections of tasks which become the job assignments along the line. Instead, they search for near perfect collections or "bundles" of elemental tasks. This is called a "heuristic" (trial and error with guiding rules) approach. In a heuristic approach, once the computer finds a near perfect set of tasks, it sets these tasks apart as the job assignment for work station 1, then it does the same for work station 2, and so on down the line.

The computer does not just take the first duties it comes to which add up to less than or equal to the limit time which, in our example, is 1 minute. If these happen to add to .65 minute and the next element considered takes .40 minute, it would reject the .40-minute element for the moment because this element would make the work package exceed 1 minute. The computer does not "close" the package at .65 minutes because this would leave the work station with .35 minutes of idle time. Instead, the computer sets the .40 minute activity aside momentarily while it searches for other short-time elements to bring the work assignment for work station 1 up to or close to a minute. When it can find no more elements which fit within a minute, it regards work station 1's assignment as complete and sets it aside. Next the computer comes back to the .40-minute activity and uses it as the first part of the assignment it will develop for work station 2.

In heuristic procedures the computer is programmed to follow logical rules, such as element A must come before B, work on the frame of the car must be done before the body shell goes on, work on the top of a car should not be combined with work on the bottom, the total time in a job assignment cannot add up to more than a minute, and so on. The computer is given all of these instructions; then its job is to find combinations of duties which fit the restrictions.

Electronic calculator assembly example

The assembly of a small hand-held calculator will illustrate how job packages are developed. A listing is first made of the assembly task elements, their required time, and their assembly precedence requirements.

These are shown in Figure 11–3. There it shows that element 1 takes .2 minutes and has no predecessor elements. Element 2 takes .4 minutes and can't be started until element 1 is completed. This means that both can be done at the same work station or that element 2 can be performed later. Figure 11–4 shows in schematic form the sequential relationships listed in Figure 11–3.

FIGURE 11–3

Task element	Element time (minutes)	Preceding elements
1.	.2	—
2.	.4	1
3.	.7	1
4.	.3	2,3
5.	.8	4
6.	.6	5
7.	.2	6
Total	3.2	

We will suppose that an output of approximately 65 units per hour is required and the plan is to produce them all on one assembly line. This translates into a maximum work package time, or job cycle, for each job station of .9 minutes per unit. Thus, our objective is to assign task elements to work stations such that the maximum time of every station assignment is close to, yet not more than, .9 minutes.

A simple situation like our example can be solved without the aid of a computer. All one has to do is, through trial and error, to try different combinations until the best combination is developed. This, as is shown

FIGURE 11–4

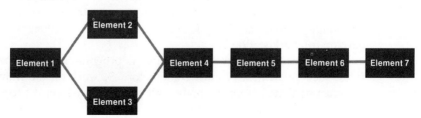

FIGURE 11-5

Work station	Task elements assigned to work stations	Total task time (minutes)	Slack time in work station
1.	1,3	.9	0
2.	2,4	.7	.2
3.	5	.8	.1
4.	6,7	.8	.1
Total.		3.2	.4

in Figure 11-5, proves to be elements 1 and 3 for station 1; 2 and 4 for station 2; 5 for station 3; and 6 and 7 for station 4, A total of 4 work stations is required. In an hour, 65 units, representing 208 minutes of work will be finished by 4 workers putting in 240 minutes of time. So this arrangement is 87 percent efficient.

Using the computer

Although this problem was solved without a computer, it was also run off on a computer. We asked the computer to generate work station assignments for two other production rates, 75 per hour and 46 per hour. The computer run sheet for these two rates and for the original problem, 65 per hour, is shown in Figure 11-6.

At 75 per hour, the computer arrived at 5 work stations, combining elements as follows: 1 and 2, 3, 4, 5, and 6 and 7. This works out to .8 minute work station cycles. In an hour, 5 workers put in 300 minutes and do $75 \times .32 = 240$ minutes of work. So this arrangement is 80 percent efficient.

The 46 per hour rate produced a 3-station solution with a 1.3-minute station cycle time. It combined elements 1, 2, and 3, 4 and 5, and 6 and 7. In an hour, 3 workers put in 180 minutes and do 147 minutes of work, so this arrangement is 82 percent efficient.

With computers it is easy for the analyst to investigate a large number of interrelationships and to compare their costs. It is only necessary to have good estimates of labor times and the costs of operating the work stations, including tools, conveyors, and so on.

Sometimes a given heuristic analysis does not arrange the minor tasks into the very best combinations. Once a minor task is assigned to a work package for job 1, for example, the computer regards this as disposed of and does not consider it in its further searching. It removes all job 1 duties from its list of remaining duties and goes on to search for another set of duties for the next work station.

Unless all of the billions of possible combinations are analyzed (which is impractical) a perfect set of job assignments is not guaranteed. The perfect set might, for example, require withdrawing some of the duties initially put into job assignment 1 and reassigning them elsewhere, where they would fit even better.

FIGURE 11-6

```
PROGRAM IDENTIFICATION
? CALCULATOR
ASSEMBLY LINE BALANCE FOR      CALCULATOR


INPUT PRECEDENCE RESTRICTIONS
INPUT TWO ELEMENT NUMBERS SEPARATED BY A COMMA.
THE FIRST ELEMENT NUMBER ENTERED INDICATES THAT
THAT ELEMENT MUST PRECEDE THE SECOND ELEMENT
NUMBER ENTERED
TERMINATE THIS PORTION OF INPUT BY ENTERING 0,0
? 1,2
? 1,3
? 2,4
? 3,4
? 4,5
? 5,6
? 6,7
? 0,0
 ENTER ELEMENT TIMES IN CONSECUTIVE ORDER
 TERMINATE THIS PART OF THE INPUT BY ENTERING A 0
? .2
? .4
? .7
? .3
? .8
? .6
? .2.
? 0
 TOTAL ELEMENT TIME=  3.2000    NUMBER OF ELEMENTS IS   7
 NUMBER OF PRECEDENCE RESTRICTIONS IS    7
 CYCLE TIME. ENTER A 0 WHEN NO FURTHER RUNS ARE DESIRED
? .9
```

			ASSEMBLY LINE BALANCE														
STATION			CYCLE TIME = .90														SLACK
NUMBER																	TIME
1	1	3	0	0	0	0	0	0	0	0	0	0	0	0	0		.00
2	2	4	0	0	0	0	0	0	0	0	0	0	0	0	0		.20
3	5	0	0	0	0	0	0	0	0	0	0	0	0	0	0		.10
4	6	7	0	0	0	0	0	0	0	0	0	0	0	0	0		.10

```
 CYCLE TIME. ENTER A 0 WHEN NO FURTHER RUNS ARE DESIRED
? .8
```

			ASSEMBLY LINE BALANCE														
STATION			CYCLE TIME = .80														SLACK
NUMBER																	TIME
1	1	2	0	0	0	0	0	0	0	0	0	0	0	0	0		.20
2	3	0	0	0	0	0	0	0	0	0	0	0	0	0	0		.10
3	4	0	0	0	0	0	0	0	0	0	0	0	0	0	0		.50
4	5	0	0	0	0	0	0	0	0	0	0	0	0	0	0		.00
5	6	7	0	0	0	0	0	0	0	0	0	0	0	0	0		.00

```
 CYCLE TIME. ENTER A 0 WHEN NO FURTHER RUNS ARE DESIRED
? 1.3
```

				ASSEMBLY LINE BALANCE													
STATION				CYCLE TIME = 1.3000													SLACK
NUMBER																	TIME
1	1	2	3	0	0	0	0	0	0	0	0	0	0	0	0		.00
2	4	5	0	0	0	0	0	0	0	0	0	0	0	0	0		.20
3	6	7	0	0	0	0	0	0	0	0	0	0	0	0	0		.50

Adapted from Thomas R. Hoffman, *Production Management and Manufacturing Systems*, Wadsworth Publishing Co., 1971.

Heuristic priority choice rules

In order for the computer to do a good job of developing work station assignments, it is necessary to develop a set of rules or policies to guide it as it assigns job elements to work stations. It is unlikely to develop the best sets of assignments if it makes its selections only on how long task elements take as compared to the unfilled work station time (largely the procedure we described above).

Fred Tonge, in an extensive heuristic simulation in which he tested several policies, found that indeed it did not. Tonge tested the following eight policies (as well as others which produced poorer results).[1]

1.   Choose the task with the longest time.
2.   Choose the task with the most immediate following tasks.
3.   Choose tasks randomly.
4.   Choose tasks which first became available for assignment.
5.   Choose tasks which last became available for assignment.
6.   Choose tasks with the most following tasks.
7.   Choose tasks with the greatest work time for following elements.
8.   Choose tasks with the lowest priority number (all tasks having been previously given priority numbers in approximate accord with their required sequence).

Using hypothetical figures and a large number of simulated computer runs (the original data were rearranged randomly after each run), Tonge tested these rules and found that the computer did not always end up with the same number of work stations (because the list of task elements was mixed up differently each time a new simulation was run). As Figure 11–7 shows, repeated reruns of newly randomized sequences of element listings produced job packages which (except in one instance of 21 work stations) assigned the work to 22, 23, and even 24 work stations.

Since each station required one worker, these differences represented differences in the efficiency of the use of labor. Several of these priority choice rules always yielded 24-station assignments whereas others always yielded 22.

Tonge went further in his analysis and gave the computer pairs of priority rules, with the second to be used to break ties. Figure 11–8 shows that this produced a noticeable improvement. Although 22- and 23-station work sets were still the most common, 24-station assignments were fewer. And 21-station assignments were common. In one combination, where policy 1 and policy 8 were used together, 21-station assignments turned up in 60 percent of the simulations.

Tonge's research verifies the seemingly obvious conclusion that the quality of the computer's ability to find minimum station assignments de-

---

[1] This list is adapted from a list in Fred M. Tonge, "Assembly Line Balancing Using Probabilistic Combinations of Heuristics," *Management Science,* vol. 11, no. 7, pp. 727–735.

FIGURE 11–7

Rule: choose task	Number of work stations (percent of time listed)			
	21	22	23	24
1. With largest time..................		100		
2. With most immediate followers.....		44	56	
3. Randomly........................		3	65	32
4. Which became available first.......		100		
5. Which became available last........				100
6. With most followers...............	1	93	6	
7. With largest positional weight......		100		
8. With highest distinct number.......			100	
9. With highest positional number.....			43	57
10. With least time..................				100
11. With fewest immediate followers....		31	48	21
12. With fewest followers..............			100	100
13. With smallest positional weight.....				100
14. With lowest distinct number........			100	
15. With lowest positional number......		17	83	

FIGURE 11–8

Rules	Number of work stations (percent of times listed)			
	21	22	23	24
1 and 7..................	60	40		
6 and 7..................	31	69		
1 and 6..................	24	76		
1 and 11.................	14	40	45	
1 and 9..................	7	43	40	10
1 and 8..................	1	39	55	5
1 and 15.................		69	31	
1 and 14.................		51	49	
1 and 10.................		17	71	12
8 and 9..................		5	56	39
10 and 11................			28	72

pends on the quality of the priority rules given to it. It is a good idea for computer based line balancing programs to allow the analyst to experiment with different priority policy rules. The best policy may produce a solution which saves a station or two and results in less idle time.

INFORMATION NEEDED FOR JOB BALANCING

Before a computer can be used to balance work along an assembly line, it is necessary to gather together quite a bit of information. The kind of information needed is the same for washing machines, television sets, automobiles, or whatever. We will continue to use automobiles as an example.

First, it is necessary to make a list of every minor task required to assemble a car. As was said earlier, "minor" means job elements as short as 5/100 or 10/100 of a minute, not 2- or 3-minute job parts. This list may well run into thousands of minor tasks (which a time study analyst calls "elements"). The list must also show how much time it will take a person to perform each element. All of these things need to be known ahead while work station assignments are being developed and long before any cars have been assembled along the line.

Yet how can an industrial engineer know ahead of time what minor tasks have to be done in order to assemble a washing machine or an automobile? And how can he know before a line is set up just how long each element will take? For the most part the engineers who do this work rely on past experience with similar products to supply this information because much of the work on this year's products is like that on last year's models.

If, however, a company is going into totally new kinds of products, this is a difficult task. In such a case it would be a good idea to assemble a few pilot items in an experimental area so the methods engineers can learn as much as they can from seeing the work done.

In any case, the engineers try to visualize how the work is going to be done along the line and develop the list of minor tasks it takes to do the whole job. Then they try to determine about how long it will take to do each little part of the whole task. (Chapter 14 will show how industrial engineers do this, using catalogs of how long it takes to make basic human movements.)

Elements for line balancing purposes are generally different from those used by time study analysts in setting production standards. For line balancing, elements need to be "transferable work components"—minor activities which can be removed, if need be, from one place and put somewhere else without making extra work. Tightening a bolt is transferable from placing it. But tightening one bolt on a wheel of a car is not transferable from tightening another bolt on the same wheel because the worker has to pick up and put down a bolt tightener, and it is always desirable to hold down tool handling time.

ELEMENT PRECEDENCE

Element precedence matters, as seen in our earlier example, also have to be determined before a computer can go to work. Some elements have to be done before others, whereas in other cases it doesn't matter. A man putting on his clothes in the morning has to put on his shirt before his tie, but it doesn't matter whether he combs his hair and then puts on his shoes or the other way around.

And it is the same with cars and television sets. Sometimes the element sequence matters and sometimes it doesn't. A hole has to be drilled before it can be threaded, and an automobile wheel has to be put on before the bolts that hold it can be put on. But it doesn't matter whether a storage battery is installed before or after the carburetor or whether a front wheel

FIGURE 11–9

Zoning sketch indicating possible zones for assembly operations along a conveyor (conditions for a specific situation will determine "can do" for a given work element in several zones or "must do" in a particular zone)

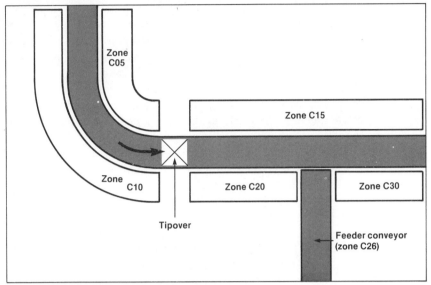

Source: General Electric Co.

goes on before a back wheel. The order of sequence is sometimes "must do" and at other times is "can do" (see Figure 11–9).

"Must do" is both a positive and a negative restraint at the same time. The wheel must be put on the car before its bolts can go on. Similarly, the bolts cannot be put on ("must not do") until the wheel is on.

All "can do" elements finally become "must do." It doesn't matter whether a front wheel goes on before a back wheel or the other way around; they are "can do" with respect to each other. And in the early stages of assembly, it doesn't matter when the steering wheel is put in. But, finally, and well before the car is finished, the steering wheel has to go in. It is "can do" for a long time, but the time will come when it becomes "must do" with respect to the next element.

Often it is a good idea to think of "must do," "must not do," and "can do" elements as they apply to zones or general areas along the line rather than as they relate to particular work stations. An element may well be "must not do" for early zones (a car can't be washed until it is put together); then it may become "can do" for several zones; and, finally, if it has not been assigned earlier, it is "must do" for some particular zone.

Sometimes there are "must not do" constraints because of the nature of the work. Some elements are dirty whereas others are clean, and they should be kept apart. The car should not be greased, for example, adjacent to putting in the upholstery.

General Motors' engineers use a quality or priority index to help the computer slot elements into their most desirable work package. The quality index for each element, which is set by the industrial engineers, reflects their view of its overall priority in the assignments of elements to first jobs along the line.

LABOR CONSIDERATIONS

Normally work station assignments should not be used just as they come from the computer because a good methods engineer can improve upon them here and there. Rearrangements can often be made to avoid having an operator work in an awkward position. The awkward-position duty can be moved to the assignment of some other assembler whose duties have him in a better position.

Also, knowing the person's work assignments lets the methods engineer visualize where an operator will be standing and which direction he will be facing. Instructions for the people loading parts on parts-supply conveyors can be analyzed so that the operator does not have to turn things around. Supply conveyor employees can load suspension springs, axles, differentials, engines, and so on, in the right position and save the assembler's time. Computers cannot see these needs.

Besides the purely physical element-precedence matters, methods analysts need to consider how elements will combine into job packages for the assemblers. The analyst should try to hold down extra "nonproductive" activities, such as picking up wrenches or having a worker move from one side of the car to the other. Nor should a worker have to work first under a car and then on its top.

Nor should assemblers walk while not working, except in a direction opposite to the line's movement. If a worker is to have a one-minute set of tasks to perform while the product takes a minute to move through his work station, he has to work on a moving product. If all the work is done on the product at the same spot, the assembler will have to walk along with it for 25 feet to the end of the station. Then he has to walk back and repeat the cycle. He walks all day long. This often happens in the assembly of automobiles, refrigerators, stoves, and television sets. Sometimes, with floor-level conveyors, the assembler rides along with the product and only walks back.

It might seem that it would be possible to cut out this nonproductive walking back and forth the length of the work station. One way to do this would be to use a stop-and-go conveyor and give each employee a work package of elements which can be performed while remaining in one spot. Yet, if a stop-and-go conveyor is used, everyone is idle during the time the conveyor is moving the product to the next station. And, if anyone is not finished by the time the product moves on, he has to go with it into the next station, and this is likely to interfere with the worker there.

Another possibility is to try to put together minor tasks into assignments so that they go from front to back of the product. On a car the first tasks would be on the front end, then the middle, and finally on the rear end of the car. The assembler can then stand relatively still as he does his work.

Above all, tasks should not be in reverse. Work should not begin at the rear end of a car, followed by work in the middle, and finish with work on the front end.

A methods analyst needs also to pay attention to "closed" and "open" work stations. In a closed station, all the work must be done in the regular area, as, for example, a spray painting booth, nor can other work be done in this area. In an open station, a worker from the previous station can follow the product into the next area if there is any delay. Finishing his work there would not interfere with the next station's workers. Closed-area work assignments need to be shorter than the average for other jobs so that the assembler will almost surely be finished by the time the product moves out of his area. Open-area assignments can be closer to the cycle time since the assembler can follow the product.

Try as one may, however, to foresee everything and to balance the work, there usually will be a good many bugs (unequal work loads, parts can't be fastened as quickly as was expected, quality troubles, and so on) to straighten out when a line starts production, so some rearranging is almost always required.

SUBASSEMBLY LINES

Assembled products are usually made out of subassemblies. Valves, pumps, carburetors, generators, gear sets, wheels, and other components are first put together as components and then assembled into final products.

Figure 11–10 is a diagram of Western Electric's telephone assembly process. It illustrates subassembly and final assembly work being carried on as a single coordinated activity. In such a case, the output rates of subassembly lines have to be geared to the final assembly line's needs.

It often happens, however, that it is uneconomical to operate subassembly lines at rates coordinated with the final assembly line's needs. When this is so, subassembly lines should be decoupled, and each should operate at its own most economical rate. This can be accomplished with different working hours and with between-operations balancing inventories whenever they are needed.

Not only can subassembly lines operate different hours, they can be located in other departments, other plants, or even in other companies. Magnavox assembles television sets using color tubes it buys from RCA. Both the finished sets and the tubes are made on production lines, but the tube lines for Magnavox's TV sets are in RCA's factories. RCA's tube production lines do not produce at the same rates that its finished products lines operate.

FIGURE 11–10

Schematic diagram of subassembly and final assembly of telephones

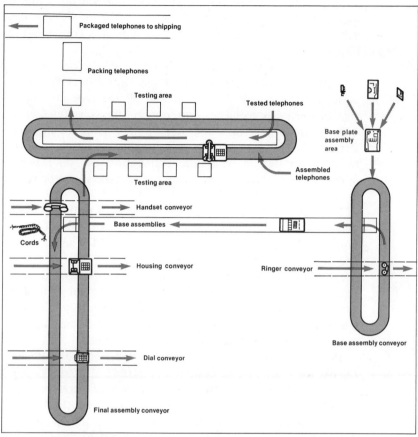

Source: Western Electric Co.

Often, and aside from possibly differing output rates, it is best to do subassembly work in its own area away from final assembly. Subassembled components often need inspection and performance testing, so there is need for a break before final assembly. Furthermore, subassembly lines always have to produce more units than are required for final assembly. Often two or more identical subassemblies are required for a unit (a tricycle requires two rear wheels). Further, almost always there are extra requirements for spare or replacement parts or, as in the case of RCA making tubes for Magnavox, parts for sale to other companies. Finally, within the same company, one plant may produce components for one or more of their other plants, so that—again—the assembly lines' output quantity is very different from its own plant's final-line needs.

PROBLEMS WITH LINES

Lines create numerous problems. One, of course, is the matter of job monotony which has received a great deal of publicity and has been the subject of considerable research. This subject is considered more fully in Chapter 13.

A different kind of personnel problem comes out of line jobs always needing to be filled. As was mentioned in Chapter 8, lines need one or more workers at every work station, all the time. If anyone is absent, someone else has to fill in. Furthermore, the substitutes have to keep up with the line's pace although they be quite unacquainted with the work. Fortunately, job assignments are usually so simple that inexperienced workers can step in with little preparation and do reasonably well. It might, however, be necessary to put in an extra operator at a work station in order to maintain production.

Product variety introduces a second kind of problem. Lines can handle minor but not major variations in products. Some products require operations which are not needed for other products. On an automobile assembly line, four-door cars require people to work on the two rear doors—work which two-door cars do not need. In order to operate economically, a line's output must be confined largely to one main kind of product, with variations being confined to minor differences. It would be quite uneconomical to assemble trucks on the same line with passenger cars; they are too unlike and require too many unlike operations.

In the case of line work on smaller items (radios, kitchen clocks, and the like) a great deal of flexibility in variety of products can be achieved by not fastening them down onto conveyors. Operators can then stay at fixed work stations where they work on the products that come to them. If the products are not fastened to a conveyor, the operators can keep an inventory of two or three products on their work benches. Then, if some kinds of products require an operation which others don't need, those not needing it can go right on to their next operation. But, if two or three products needing one operation come along at one time, the operator just pulls them off the conveyor and lets them wait a few minutes until he catches up.

Product-mix variations can also cause problems. Customer demands force some variety, so lines need to be flexible enough to handle a limited amount of change in product variety. This makes two problems: line balancing and model sequencing.

Variety changes the bits and pieces of work done at the work stations along the line. It subtracts from, or adds to, a worker's assignment and often creates imbalances from unequal work assignments. A nominal amount of variety will not create undue imbalances and can be tolerated. But, if substantial product mix variations seem to be permanent or if they are to last for several weeks, it may be worthwhile to rebalance the work along the line. It is a good idea to have in the file two or three alternative work assignment lists prepared ahead of time so that the supervisors can change to new job assignments whenever the product mix changes, thus avoiding excessive idle time.

Volume variation may also cause problems. Normally, if there is need for less (or more) output from a line, the whole line works fewer (or more) hours. It would seem to be possible, however, to use fewer workers and to send products down the line at a slower rate. Unfortunately this would necessitate rearranging the bits and pieces of work and changing the work packages (into 1½-minute assignments or some other time cycle) for the work stations as shown in our earlier example. Such changing is usually impractical for large items such as automobiles, but it is feasible for small items whose total assembly time is as little as 15 or 20 minutes.

Again, as in the case of product-mix variations, it is possible to pre-compute the worker-package assignments suitable for several production levels. The foreman could use the assignment list which is appropriate to the volume. Changing is a big job, however, and is not often done. It would mean regrouping job elements, rearranging work tools to different work stations, and resetting the line's speed and/or reallocating the line space allocated to work stations.

Another problem is that average job performance times don't always average out in an offsetting way. If, for example, operation B follows operation A, and each average two minutes but has some variation, rarely will it be possible to get one product every two minutes.

Even though each operation averages to take 2 minutes, individual operations in this example might sometimes take as long as 2.25 minutes. So, whenever A takes 2.25 minutes, B has to wait .25 minutes. Then, and only then, can he go ahead with his operation, which then takes 2 minutes. Except in the rare case where B's shortest time dovetails with A's slow time, 4.25 minutes will pass before the 2 operations are completed. The average time the product spends in these 2 operations in this example is 2.125 minutes per operation, not 2 minutes. In practice, the average time would be closer to, but nevertheless more than, 2 minutes.

There would be no trouble if operations A's and B's long and short performance times always dovetailed and so offset each other, but this won't happen very often. The irregularities are bound to cause a certain amount of lost time. It may be possible to take care of such variations, of course, by allowing for a small work-balancing stock of products between operations. This is not, however, a feasible solution to the problem of time variations along a line where the products are large and there are many work stations.

Multiple stations

Sometimes a particular job cannot be economically subdivided into 1-minute assignments and must be treated as a 2- or 3-minute job. If so, then two or three work stations will be needed and the assembler at each station will work on only every second or third product.

In order for this to work well, it is usually desirable for the products coming down the line to split into two or three lines at such stations. Then each person can do their 2- or 3-minute jobs. The product can then move on and resume its place in the regular flow to the following work stations. This is not absolutely necessary, however. The work station can be two or three times as long as usual, and each person can take the second or third product in turn and walk along with it for two or three minutes as they perform their assignment. When they are finished, they can walk back past their one or two fellow workers to the next unit.

FIXED POSITION ASSEMBLY

Large products, such as large factory machines, airplanes, or loco-motives, are not put together along assembly lines in the usual sense. Instead, they are more or less constructed in one spot in the assembly department. They are usually moved only occasionally from one special-ized assembly area to another.

With fixed position assembly, workers come to the work rather than having the work brought to them. Often whole crews work for days or weeks on a product in one location before it is taken to the next general assembly area where the next several crews take over, one after the other.

Job design is very different from what it is along the more usual kind of assembly line. Instead of workers performing a limited collection of minor job elements which may add up to only a minute, they have general overall job-accomplishment assignments. It is like an electrician putting in the electrical wiring in a house. The workers themselves have to determine the bits and pieces of work that need doing and then do them. Usually they work with portable tools because the total number of any one product does not justify extremely specialized equipment, and several successive kinds of work are done at each work station. Specialized equipment, if used, would have to be portable, since—except when it is being used by the one specialized crew today—it would just be in the way of the crews doing other work tomorrow.

REVIEW QUESTIONS

1. What is the fundamental relationship between the number of units per hour a line will turn out and the design of work stations along the line? How should an analyst determine the number of work stations and the length of time each person's work assignment should be?

2. When a computer is used to aid in setting up job packages for workers along assembly lines, the process is often called heuristic. How does a computer do this work when it is doing it heuristically?

3. How are policy decisions concerning job element choices used in setting job assignments for people along assembly lines?

4. What kinds of information are required before a computer (or an analyst) can properly group bits of work into job assignments along a line? How can these job bits be determined?

5. How is element precedence established? How is it made effective in the process of setting up work packages?

6. What kinds of improvements can a good job analyst probably make in improving the collections of work elements as first set up by a computer?

QUESTIONS FOR DISCUSSION

1. How finely should the analyst try to cut up job assignments along an assembly line? If the object is to get 450 units a day and if there are 450 labor-minutes of work to be done on each unit, should there be 1 line with 450 workers each having a 1-minute task? Or would it be better to have 5 lines, each turning out 1 unit every 5 minutes, and each line with 90 workers who have 5-minute job packages? Or would some ·other combination be better? What factors enter into such decisions? Discuss.

2. Bill Parker, a newly hired man for an assembly line job, looked at the forever advancing line bringing him one more product as fast as he could finish the last one. When the foreman came by, Bill said to him: "I'm getting mighty tired of this job; when do we change to something else?" "Next year," said the foreman. "Next year!" said Bill. "Then I quit. I ain't never worked on a job that hasn't got any end." Discuss.

3. When Motorola redesigned a small radio receiver and reduced its number of parts from 210 to 80, it changed (in its Fort Lauderdale factory) from a regular repetitive assembly line back to individual product assembly. Each worker assembles the whole product. The result has been a great improvement in pride of work and quality and a reduction in absenteeism. Is there a "message" here?

4. Tom Manly had been a materials supply man in the stock room, a low-paid job, for six months. When a higher-paying opening occurred along the assembly line, Tom asked for the job, but the personnel department refused to recommend his transfer. The job was to work on the underside of cars passing overhead, which, because Tom was a short man, would mean quite a reach for him. He filed a grievance, claiming that he had been wrongly denied an opportunity to earn more pay. Should the personnel department's desire to put men on jobs for which they are well suited prevail in such a case?

5. Suppose that a company would like to operate an assembly line at different rates of output and use fewer or more people. Wouldn't it have to have different sets of work packages for each change? If so, wouldn't this make problems because the workers would have to learn

other sets of duties? Also, what would happen to work stations and sets of tools? Would the number of stations and the allocation of space along the line need to be changed? And what would happen if the output rate were changed in only a minor way, such as reducing it two or three units an hour? How big a change would it take to justify changing the number of workers?

6. How can absenteeism be handled along assembly lines? Is there any way to avoid having workers not accustomed to the work having to step in and try to keep up with the line?

PROBLEMS

1. It is necessary to set up an assembly line to assemble 3,000 units in a so-called 40-hour week. (Because of start-up and put-away time, as well as rest periods, the workers will lose a half hour each day; so there are only 37.5 productive hours.) There are 6 operations to be done, whose operation times are 1, 1.35, .75, .80, 1.70, and 3 minutes respectively.

a. How many workers will be needed if each job is done at a separate work station? Is it possible to have more than one person at a work station, although, if they are not fully busy, they do not do anything else?

b. How much loss of labor time because of lack of equal work assignments will this program entail?

c. How will this program be affected if it is possible to group operations in various ways, or to shift people around, or have people do two or three operations, and it is not required to use six work stations with everyone tied to one work station? How does this compare to the answers in a and b?

2. General Products Company is planning an assembly line for one of its small products. The plan is for a line which will turn out 75 units an hour, or at the rate of 1 every 48 seconds. Work elements may be grouped in any combination, provided only that the required preceding elements are done, even if in the same work package. They don't need to have been done at an earlier work station. Preceding elements can also be performed several work stations before a following element. The line operates 60 minutes per hour.

Using the work element information below, determine how many assemblers and how many work stations will be needed.

What average percent use of their time does the plan call for?

Work element	Time in seconds	Must follow	Work element	Time in seconds	Must follow
1	5	—	19	16	2
2	13	1	20	24	19
3	31	2	21	12	11,13
4	7	2	22	6	21
5	26	2	23	6	19
6	7	2	24	9	19
7	6	2	25	22	19
8	11	5	26	17	25
9	11	5	27	25	19
10	11	5	28	9	19
11	24	3,5	29	17	20
12	11	5	30	16	8,10,12
13	24	3,5	31	20	27
14	14	8,12	32	19	27
15	12	2	33	18	27
16	14	2	34	15	33
17	13	2	35	10	34
18	34	2	...	...	...

3. In problem 2, could the efficiency of the assembly line be improved by letting banks of work sometimes pile up between jobs? Which jobs? How much improvement in the use of labor could be expected by doing this?

4. Below are given times and precedence restrictions for 37 job elements for part of the work to be done along an assembly line. (Elements may be put into the same work package with other elements which they must precede or follow.)

Arrange these work elements into appropriate job packages in order to turn out 100 finished products per hour. Show which elements go into which work assignments. Show also how much wasted labor time this program's assignments contain because of the failure of job packages to even out perfectly. (Suggestion: Note that 100 units an hour means 1 unit every 36 seconds, or .60 minute. Try to develop work packages of a little less than .60 minute.)

5. Do the same for 150 finished products per hour. How much has the wasted labor time been reduced?

6. Assume that, in problem 5, methods study analysts are able to put in improvements which reduce the time on all elements of 16/100 of a minute and over by one fourth. Now what is the answer?

Element number	Time in hundredths of a minute	Must Precede element number	Follow element number
1	5	3	—
2	80	17,18	—
3	13	7,16,17,18,19,21	1
4	31	12,14	3
5	7	12,14	3
6	26	9,10,11,13	3
7	7	—	2,3
8	6	—	3
9	11	15,32	6
10	11	—	6
11	11	32	6
12	24	23	4,5,6
13	11	15,32	6
14	24	23	4,5,6
15	14	—	9,11,13
16	12	—	2,3
17	14	—	2,3
18	13	—	2,3
19	34	—	2,3
20	29	22,29,30	3
21	16	25,26	3
22	24	31	21
23	12	24	12,14
24	6	34	23
25	6	—	21
26	9	—	21
27	22	21	24
28	17	—	27
29	25	35	21
30	9	—	21
31	17	—	22
32	16	—	9,13
33	20	—	29
34	19	—	24
35	18	36	29
36	15	37	35
37	10	—	36

SUGGESTED SUPPLEMENTARY READINGS

Beck, Ross. "Can the Production Line Be Humanized?" *MSU Business Topics,* Autumn 1974, pp. 27–36.

Chase, R. B. "Strategic Considerations in Assembly-Line Selection." *California Management Review,* Fall 1975, pp. 17–23.

Levitt, Theodore. "Production Line Approach to Service." *Harvard Business Review,* September–October 1972, pp. 41–52.

12

Facilities maintenance and materials handling

Two IMPORTANT service functions to production activities are maintenance and materials handling. Good maintenance insures that the productive facilities will be able to operate effectively. This results from a
combination of preventive maintenance which anticipates machines wearing out and of fixing breakdowns, if any occur, on an immediate emergency
basis.

Good material handling systems also are essential to effective production. Whether materials are moved by simple fork lift trucks or by complex computer controlled conveyor systems, the main job is to move raw
materials, in-process materials, and finished goods throughout the plant
so that the right materials are at the right place at the right time and in
the right quantities.

MAINTENANCE

Because machines and buildings are continually wearing out, they need
repairs and sometimes replacement. On machines, wear on shafts, bearings, gears, belts, and other parts makes repair necessary. Electric motors
must be serviced. Transportation facilities—elevators, conveyors, gasoline-
and electric-powered trucks, hand trucks, hoists, and cranes—all need
continual lubrication and repairs. Plant services—electric power, light,
gas, water, compressed air and steam lines, washrooms, sewers, pumps,
fire protection equipment, and heating systems—all need to be maintained.
So do the buildings themselves—the roofs, windows, walls, floors, and
foundations. In total, keeping everything operable often costs more than
one tenth of all of a company's costs.

THE MAINTENANCE DEPARTMENT AND ITS DUTIES

The responsibility for maintenance is usually assigned to the plant engineer, who is under the general direction of the chief engineer. The plant engineer often has two main departments: a machine shop and a plant maintenance department.

The machine shop keeps the machines and equipment in working order. Its employees include millwrights (general mechanics and people who move machines), machinists, sheet metal workers, welders, oilers, and others who repair machines and keep trucks and conveyors operating.

The plant maintenance group specializes in the building and the building's services. Its employees are electricians, tinsmiths, welders, pipefitters, steamfitters, bricklayers, steeplejacks, painters, glaziers, carpenters, millwrights, window washers, and janitors. Also, the maintenance department usually operates its own spare parts stockroom and orders the materials used on repair jobs.

Besides repairing machines and equipment, the maintenance department in most companies does all minor remodeling and relayout work. It tears down or puts up partitions between departments, builds new concrete foundations for equipment, and makes mountings for machines and motors. Since some of this work requires construction drawings, as well as

FIGURE 12–1

Complex machines require skilled maintenance workers

compliance with laws, the department should include one or more construction engineers who can make the drawings and who are acquainted with building codes and safety regulations.

The maintenance department has to keep all fire prevention equipment in operating order at all times. To do this, the department must periodically inspect the sprinkler systems, valves, fire pumps, elevated tanks, portable extinguishers, fire doors, and sirens. The department also trains the company's inside emergency fire fighting crews in fire fighting methods and in the use of fire suppressing equipment. The maintenance department also takes care of the premises outside the building. It maintains all truck docks, rail sidings, storage yards, parking lots, and fences and landscaping.

THE INHERENT INEFFICIENCY OF MAINTENANCE WORK

A considerable amount of maintenance work must be done to take care of emergency breakdowns. Such demands for services are irregular and impose variable workload demands on the maintenance department. Often, too, the machines being maintained are highly sophisticated, perhaps with electronic controls, and they can be repaired only by highly qualified technicians. To meet such needs the department has to maintain a capability of serving at a high technological level even though high-level service is not often required.

Such irregularities force the maintenance department to operate at less than its peak efficiency. Maintenance workers can give good service only if there are enough of them to answer calls quickly, but they can do this only if they are not very busy. If they are always fully occupied, they cannot give the best service. This need not be a serious problem, however, because there are usually a few necessary but not urgent jobs of relatively low-skill content which they can work at between emergencies. They can work on these jobs when they are not otherwise busy and then drop them to answer more urgent calls.

This is a case where it is necessary to forego optimizing the work of one department in the interest of optimizing the performance of the whole organization.

PREVENTIVE MAINTENANCE

Repairing machines after they fail is often *not* the best maintenance policy because *good* maintenance prevents breakdowns. The biggest cost of maintenance is usually not the cost of repairing, even if it is done at high overtime labor rates. More often the big cost is the "down for repairs" cost. Breakdowns, even when repairs are made quickly, stop production for at least a while. Employees and machines are idle, production is lost, and orders get behind schedule. Finally, getting the delayed orders back on schedule may entail overtime.

Breakdown repair jobs are almost always more costly than preventive repair jobs. It costs something to fix a loose front wheel on a car, but it costs more to fix the car after the wheel comes loose on the road. Then the owner (or his heirs) has to pay for a car wreck.

Preventive maintenance means *preventing* breakdowns. Putting new spark plugs in an automobile before winter comes is preventive maintenance. It anticipates likely difficulties and does the expected needed repairs at a convenient time, *before* the repairs are actually needed. Preventive maintenance depends upon knowledge from the past that certain wearing parts will need replacement after a normal interval of use.

In the case of factory equipment, the maintenance needs are sufficiently irregular that it does not always pay to try to anticipate breakdowns and overhaul equipment which doesn't need it badly. Preventive maintenance should be undertaken only if there seems to be need for it. Machine operators and foremen can pay close attention to their machines and ask for repairs before parts get too worn to do the work. On unusual items, such as air conditioning equipment or elevator motors and cables, the maintenance department inspects them periodically and watches for wear.

Maintainability

Another and quite different kind of preventive maintenance can better be called *maintainability*. Maintainability is concerned with designing machines which will be both trouble free and easily repaired.

Lubricants and hard-to-get-at bearings for today's machines are often designed to operate without attention for years, possibly for the life of the machine. Temperature detectors and gages also reveal trouble spots (they usually get hot) before failures occur. And replacement units are modular so that they are almost as simple to replace as a light bulb. When a part goes bad, the whole unit of which it is a part can be taken out, and a new one can be plugged in. Designing machines with replaceable units is particularly helpful in maintaining their electrical control parts, which are themselves so complex that, in many cases, maintenance people cannot repair them. All they can do is to replace the module.

PREVENTIVE MAINTENANCE ECONOMICS

In general, preventive maintenance wastes the remaining life value of all worn parts which are removed during repairs. The repair mechanic takes out worn but still operating parts and puts in new ones before the old ones wear out completely. This is a little wasteful, as the extra and more frequent repairs can also be. However, repair jobs done on a preventive basis and at a convenient time can be done at low cost, and they do reduce the number of more costly breakdown repair jobs. Considering this important trade-off, the operation of the entire production system may be optimized, albeit at the cost of not maximizing the life of parts and not minimizing the number of repair jobs. In other words, maximizing the life of parts and minimizing the frequency of repairs may be suboptimal.

If a company's maintenance workers spend as little as 25 percent of their time on emergencies and "crash" work, they are probably doing a good job of preventive maintenance. Normally, without preventive maintenance, they will spend a good bit of their time repairing breakdowns. If they spend most of their time on emergency jobs, the company is most likely experiencing costly production hold-ups which may require overtime. If this is the case, preventive maintenance expenditures should probably be increased.

Preventive maintenance, however, need not be carried too far. A machine doesn't need an overhaul every time a simple bearing wears out. If a car owner lets the garage fix everything they say the car needs, the owner will have a big bill—and it will include some repairs which are hardly needed. Worse is the possibility that the repair mechanic, while repairing something that is not critical, unintentionally damages other components or gets something else out of adjustment.

In some cases, a preventive program may not be necessary because a breakdown policy is reasonably satisfactory—when there is little need for immediate repair and little harm will be done by waiting. If an automatic dishwasher gets out of order, the dishes can be washed by hand. This might be a problem in a restaurant but not in a home. A repair would be needed, but it would not have to be rushed at high overtime pay rates.

In a factory a machine may even be used wastefully in the interest of maximizing the whole. Suppose, for example, that a $500 electric motor will be ruined if it is kept running, but an entire production line will be shut down—with a loss of $2,500—if it stops. By all means the motor should be kept running while everything possible is being done to replace the motor before it burns out.

Standby capacity

Preventive maintenance is less important when production is at low levels than when production is high. At low levels there is excess capacity because machines are not being used to their fullest. When there are several machines, it doesn't matter if one machine breaks down. Production can be transferred to another machine with minimal trouble. The machine which needs repairs can be repaired at the convenience of the maintenance department without suffering any penalty cost because of the breakdown. Excess capacity operates, in a sense, in lieu of preventive maintenance.

This same philosophy can be incorporated into a preventive maintenance program when operations are at high levels. Excess standby capacity can be provided for use in case trouble occurs. This excess capacity can be complete machines, or it can be major parts or components which take a long time to get.

The decision to use this strategy is a matter of cost trade-offs. It may be expensive to carry the replacements, but they reduce total costs by minimizing breakdown interruptions. Suppose, for example, that it is necessary to keep a fleet of 20 fork lift trucks in operation and that it costs $40 a day to own a truck, whether it is in use or not. If only 1 or 2 of the 20 trucks are not in operation, then the work can still be done by using hand lift trucks to help out. Doing it this way will, however, cost $50 for each lift truck not operating.

But, if three, four, or more of the trucks are out of order, the hand truckers can't handle the work. There will be production holdups during the day and overtime costs at night as the remaining fork lift trucks catch up on the work. The costs are $100 per day each for the next three fork lift trucks out of order. If more than a total of five are out of order at any one time, production will be held up, and the cost will be $500 per day for each truck over five not in use.

FIGURE 12–2

Number out of order	Cost	Proba- bility	Expected costs (no extras)	Costs with 1 extra	Ex- pected costs	Costs with 2 extras	Ex- pected costs	Costs with 3 extras	Ex- pected costs
0.....	$ 0	.09	$ 0	$ 0	$ 0	$ 0	$ 0	$ 0	$ 0
1.....	50	.30	15	0	0	0	0	0	0
2.....	100	.25	25	50	13	0	0	0	0
3.....	200	.15	30	100	5	50	8	0	0
4.....	300	.10	30	200	20	100	10	50	5
5.....	400	.05	20	300	15	200	10	100	5
6.....	900	.03	27	400	12	300	9	200	6
7.....	1,400	.02	28	900	18	400	8	300	6
8.....	1,900	.01	19	1,400	14	900	9	400	4
		1.00	$194		$ 97		$ 54		$ 26
Add cost of extras........			0		40		80		120
Total...............			$194		$137		$134		$146

Figure 12–2 shows how these various costs would be affected if the company decided to carry one or more extra trucks as standbys. In Figure 12–2, the column of probability figures is based on the record of how frequently various numbers of trucks have been out of order in the past.

In Figure 12–2, the figures in the cost columns were multiplied, in turn, by the probability figure in that column. The vertical summation of each cost column shows the expected cost for trucks being out of operation over a period of time. These costs go down markedly with more and more standby trucks. But, when the cost of the standby trucks is added in, their costs quickly become equal to and then greater than the losses from trucks being out of operation. In this example, as Figure 12–3 shows

FIGURE 12–3

Cost effects of having standby trucks available

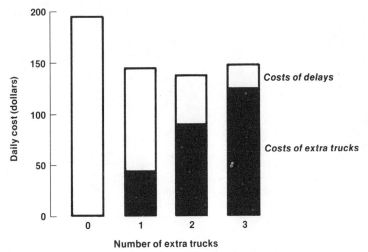

graphically, that the lowest costs are realized by owning a fleet of 22 trucks.

Preventive maintenance repairs

Often preventive maintenance is a matter of overhauling entire groups of machines rather than letting them operate until they break down. Here, too, it is possible to calculate which policy is best to use.

Suppose, for example, that there are 50 machines to keep in service, and they can be overhauled on a preventive basis at a cost of $200 per overhaul. Such a policy, if overhauls were frequent, would prevent nearly all breakdowns (breakdown repairs cost $700). The question would be whether to repair the machines only when they break down or to follow some kind of a regular preventive repair schedule. And, if a preventive schedule should be followed, how often should the machines be overhauled.

Experience shows that breakdowns will occur in the manner shown in Figure 12–4. Figure 12–4 shows a slightly greater probability of a breakdown right away than a little later on. This is because once in a while the overhaul is itself faultily done, thus leading to an almost immediate new breakdown. If a machine gets through the first month without a breakdown, there is little likelihood of its needing repair until it begins to wear out from use.

The first step is to calculate what it would cost to follow a repair-on-breakdown policy. This requires only calculating the average length of time that machines can go without repairs. This proves to be 8.42 months. (The calculation is done by multiplying each figure in column 1 by the corresponding figure in column 2 and adding them up.) A repair-on-

FIGURE 12–4

(1) Months until breakdown after overhaul or repair	(2) Probability of breakdown
1	.05
2	.02
3	.03
4	.04
5	.04
6	.05
7	.08
8	.11
9	.13
10	.14
11	.15
12	.16

breakdown policy would therefore average to cost $4,157 per month. (50 machines × $700 ÷ 8.42 months = $4,157)

Calculating the cost of periodic overhauls is a little more complicated because it costs $10,000 each time to overhaul all 50 machines, and, in spite of this, there will still be a few breakdowns anyway. Besides this, there will be a few cases where a machine recently overhauled will again break down soon.

The formula for calculating this, as well as the work for our example, is given in Appendix D. These calculations produced the figures given in Figure 12–5.

The cost figures for each maintenance policy (preventive overhaul of every machine every month, or every two months, or every three months, and so on) are given in Figure 12–5.

FIGURE 12–5

Preventive maintenance every n months	Total expected breakdowns in n months	Average number of breakdowns per month	Expected cost of breakdowns per month	Cost of preventive maintenance per month	Total cost of PM program, including $10,000 for periodic overhaul
1	2.50	2.50	$1,750	$10,000	$11,750
2	3.63	1.82	1,274	5,000	6,274
3	5.23	1.74	1,218	3,333	4,551
4	7.44	1.86	1,302	2,500	3,802
5	9.68	1.94	1,358	2,000	3,358
6	12.54	2.09	1,463	1,667	3,130
7	17.03	2.43	1,701	1,433	3,134
8	23.28	2.91	2,037	1,250	3,287
9	30.90	3.43	2,401	1,111	3,512
10	39.44	3.94	2,758	1,000	3,758
11	48.93	4.45	3,115	909	4,024
12	59.62	4.97	3,479	833	4,312

FIGURE 12–6

Relative costs of various preventive repair policies

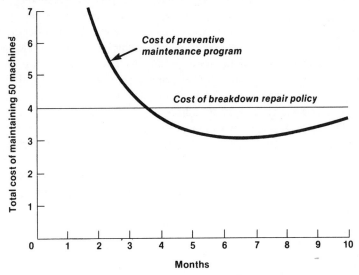

These cost figures, which are plotted in Figure 12–6 show that preventive maintenance should be used. The horizontal line is the expected cost of the repair-on-breakdown policy, calculated earlier as $4,157 per month. The dish-shaped curve is a plot of the costs of the alternatives as presented in Figure 12–5. The best policy would be to do preventive overhauls every six or seven months, the lowest point on the curve. Such a policy would entail monthly costs of $3,130 and would save $1,027 a month as compared to the repair-on-breakdown policy.

WAITING LINE ANALYSIS IN PREVENTIVE MAINTENANCE

Often it is difficult to get good evidence about the merits of preventive maintenance—at least by mathematical formulas—because the process is just too complex. Simulation can often be used in such cases. Various policies and cost relationships can be tested out to see which combination will result in the least cost. Examples of these methods are presented in Chapter 26.

CENTRALIZATION OF MAINTENANCE

Large factories are usually so spread out (they may cover 100 acres or more) that it takes a long time for maintenance workers to get from place to place. The managers of such plants have, therefore, to decide which things to do centrally and which to decentralize.

Area maintenance

In general, the closer that maintenance people are to the place where there will be need for their work, the better service they can give but at a slightly extra cost, because they will not always be fully occupied at their highest skills. The waste in their not being fully utilized is usually less than the time wasted by their getting to jobs from central maintenance departments. Equipment duplication is also wasteful, but this is usually only minor since only small tools are usually involved (most of the specialized costly equipment is kept in the central office).

Decentralized area maintenance people are usually kept busy as members of fixed small crews on routine maintenance. On larger jobs they often receive extra help from the central department.

Area maintenance people feel more sense of responsibility for their own limited areas, and they become more familiar with the equipment and with each other. Costs sometimes are better controlled when they are directly associated with a given area.

Central maintenance

Yet, even with area maintenance there is usually still a central department to provide back-up service of the kind not called for often. And some organizations—if they are not spread out too much over too wide an area—prefer to have the central department do all of the maintenance. Central maintenance makes it easier to adjust crew sizes and craft mixes to task needs. Crews' work assignments can be more specific and can usually better utilize the workers' skills.

In central maintenance the supervisors are craft oriented (an electrician foreman supervises the electricians, and so on), but in area maintenance the individual craftsmen seldom receive any craft supervision. Area maintenance sometimes underutilizes particular craftsmen (there is not enough work requiring their specialized skills to allow them to keep busy just on that work), who are nonetheless kept there rather than released to possibly more productive use in other areas.

The slight advantage which central maintenance seems to have over area maintenance disappears, however, when factories become very large. In these plants the distances and travel times become too great and cause so much waste that they are usually compelled to go to area maintenance —yet with a central maintenance back-up group.

INSIDE VERSUS OUTSIDE MAINTENANCE

Normally an organization staffs its maintenance department with enough employees with the necessary skills to do all of its day-to-day repair work except where a very high level of technical competence is required and where the needs are irregular.

Most companies do not, for example, repair their own elevators or telephones or computers. Nor do they do any but minor construction work, because large projects would impose heavy extra work loads. Often such jobs as window washing and lawn care are contracted out, as is maintenance work on company-owned automobiles.

Complications can arise over matters of inside versus outside maintenance. If a serious breakdown requires extra work, the organization's own maintenance people may object to the company's bringing in outsiders because they could lose considerable overtime (overtime pays 50 percent more per hour than the pay for regular hours). The same thing can happen on not-so-minor construction projects: The inside people can do them, but because so much extra work is involved they can do them only on overtime. Again, they may object to allowing an outside contractor to do the work. Finally, labor problems can arise when the company decides to discontinue certain work that was formerly done by its inside people and to contract it out permanently.

Labor contracts need careful formulation to cover the company's right or lack of right to use outsiders in any of these cases. If the contract is not clear, arbitrators and courts will usually hold that the company cannot make such decisions without bargaining over them with the union. So, this is often a decision which managers are not wholly free to make on their own.

REPAIR OR REPLACE?

Should a maintenance mechanic repair worn machine parts or replace them with new parts? The answer would seem to be whichever is less costly. When a person gets a small dent in his car fender, he wants it straightened out. But, if it is badly dented, it may pay to put on a new fender rather than straighten out the old one. It depends on costs.

But this is only half the story. Old automobiles and old machines that need repairs sometimes keep on needing other repairs. No one ever knows how much added performance life is being bought when one repairs an old automobile or an old machine.

Here, however, our concern is whether a repair mechanic should repair a faulty part, thus making it operable, or discard it and repalce it with a new part. Often the problem is similar to that with automobiles. If the machine is old, the mechanic should probably fix up the part at a minimum cost on a "make-do" basis if this can be done so that the product will operate a little while longer. It won't have to last very long because the machine will be worn out before long whether this part is repaired or replaced with a new part.

Also, the repair or replace decision might depend on how busy the maintenance people are. If they are not busy, they might take the time to repair worn parts. But, if they are very busy, they probably should use replacement parts. Because today's maintenance labor costs are so high, there is a tendency (more so than in the past) to replace worn parts with new parts rather than repair worn parts.

Sometimes the problem is a little different. If a machine has three critical bearings and one fails, should the other two be replaced at the same time so long as the product has been taken apart? Only the first bearing really needs replacing at this time.

It is easy to say that this depends on the likelihood of one of the other bearings failing soon and making another machine overhaul necessary before very long. But it is, in fact, hard to know what to do if the other two bearings, in spite of having been in use for a while, still give the appearance of being in good condition and are costly items. If reasonable life expectancy statistics for these bearings can be generated, then Monte Carlo simulation (as described in Chapter 26) can be used to determine the best alternative policy to follow.

MAINTENANCE IN LINE PRODUCTION AND AUTOMATION

In Chapter 11 we saw that assembly line production in a factory operates like a large machine; everything operates or everything is idle, and even a few minutes delay is expensive. Preventive maintenance therefore becomes very important.

Preventive maintenance should start with the design of machines and equipment which can be easily maintained. Machines should be designed to operate dependably, accurately, and steadily for long periods of time without breaking down. Some of them are designed with removable sections which in emergencies can be replaced quickly with spare sections or parts. Also, in line production, a maintenance mechanic should be close at all times to take care of minor emergencies. Maintenance supervisors need to think in terms of *maintaining production* rather than maintaining machines. Maintenance mechanics, rather than being on call to make repairs, should be on patrol to anticipate them.

Breakdowns are often caused by the tooling, not by the machines themselves. To prevent the tooling from wearing too much and breaking in use, cutting and grinding tools should be inspected frequently. Some companies even attach counters to each tool (to show how many times it has performed its operation) so they can anticipate its wearing out and replace it before it fails.

CONTROL-PANEL MONITORING SYSTEMS

Process industries (oil refineries, cement, chemicals, and the like) are usually highly automated. The processing is done in pressure vessels, vats, tanks, mixers, and so on that may be automatically controlled by computers. Materials are moved in enclosed pipes or ducts—again, all automatically.

In such cases the entire integrated process is frequently controlled from a central monitoring station whose walls are covered with control gages, lights, meters, push buttons, and switches, or are controlled by computer systems which automatically make adjustments in the process and signal the monitors when problems arise. Interruptions to operations, wherever they occur, are flashed immediately to the central control, and maintenance people are dispatched by telephone or radio to the point of interruption.

Similar control consoles are sometimes used in other kinds of automated production, such as steel rolling mills, where 20 or 30 successive mills operate as a unit and are centrally monitored by on-line computer systems.

BUDGETING MAINTENANCE COSTS

Most large organizations—and some small ones as well—try to control maintenance costs by budgets. The expected costs of repairing and keeping production equipment in operation are allocated in separate budgets for each producing department. The foreman of each department is responsible for keeping maintenance costs within the budgeted amount. Capital expenditures and large repair projects also are covered by separate budgets.

Unfortunately, however, budgets do not keep machines from wearing out: *Maintenance costs can't be budgeted out of existence.* And if budgets are set too low, some things may be postponed until heavy and costly repairs become necessary.

Actually, many maintenance costs *can* be postponed and money can be saved thereby—particularly in the case of such cosmetic things as painting. Some maintenance jobs are like car washing: A person doesn't *have* to get one's car washed every month. In many cases, however, the apparent savings may be wiped out when a straw—so to speak—breaks the camel's back and a serious breakdown or accident occurs. For example, a person can wait only so long before he has to get new brakes or tires for his car. Maintenance should be postponed only as a calculated risk, and the risks should be properly evaluated.

MATERIALS HANDLING AND TRANSPORTATION

Every company is, in effect, in the materials transportation or materials handling business, whether it wants to be or not. Materials have to be moved from incoming freight cars or trucks to "receiving inspection" and then on to raw materials storage. From there they go to the first operation, then to other operations, and to and from temporary storage points between operations, and to finished stores, to the shipping room, and, finally, to the outgoing freight car or truck. During their trip through the plant they are picked up, moved, and put down many times. In and of itself, every kind of materials handling or transportation is unproductive in that it does not change the form of the product. Eliminating any part of such movement increases efficiency.

Companies which make materials handling equipment report that few companies spend less than 15 percent of their labor costs for handling materials. Most companies probably spend from 20 to 30 percent of their factory payroll for materials handling—or something well over $3,000 per employee per year! A company with 1,000 employees probably spends more than $3 million every year carrying things around! Large companies spend *hundreds* of millions annually carrying things around.

Few companies know the extent of their materials handling costs because accounting reports rarely show all of these costs. They know the cost of handlers and truckers, but besides this a great deal of materials handling (picking things up and putting them down) is done by machine operators and assemblers incidental to their work. These employees are classified as production workers, and all of their pay is recorded as pay for productive work, ignoring the fact that part of it is for materials handling costs. In addition, although neither stock room employees nor inspectors are classed as materials handlers, they too spend time picking things up and putting them down. Many companies, particularly small companies, do not give handling costs the attention they deserve.

The best way to handle materials is *not* to handle them; but, if this cannot be avoided, then "hands off" handling is next best. Materials handling costs can be cut by (1) eliminating the handling whenever possible, (2) mechanizing—largely by conveyors and power-driven trucks—whatever handling still remains, and (3) making the necessary handling more efficient by reducing movement distances.

Often there is a question of what to move—people, tools, or materials and products. In parts making, it is almost always more economical to move materials and parts to machine operators. But for large items such as airplanes, or ships, or locomotives it is more economical to do assembly work in one or only a few areas. The product remains stationary as workers with portable tools assemble the product's components.

SUPPLYING PARTS TO ASSEMBLY WORKERS

Supplying parts to assembly workers along assembly lines is more than a matter of just moving materials. In all, it is necessary to bring hundreds of different parts to dozens of assembly stations. Each part has to go to the station where it is attached to the product; yet, except for very small items, very few parts can be stored at these stations.

The object is to keep a steady, though small, stream of parts arriving at the assembly stations just before the assemblers need them but to do it so that materials suppliers are not carrying one and two parts around all the time. This can be done economically by using service conveyors with pans or trays which are loaded in behind-the-scenes stock rooms and which pass by the assemblers who take what they need from them. Parts may also be gathered into sets in the stockroom and, by conveyor or truck, taken in pans to the assemblers. The pans can have sections for separate parts so that assemblers do not have to fish around for the part they want next.

Small items (washers, cotter pins, and the like), however, should be stored in ample supply at the assemblers' work stations. This saves expensive stock room handling of many small minor items.

ECONOMICS OF MANUAL HANDLING

When a large volume of products is to be handled, it is usually possible to calculate how best to do it. Suppose, for example, that incoming materials are typically received and stacked near the receiving point. Later they must be moved to another storage point closer to the operations. We will assume that there is a pile of cased products, each case weighing 30 pounds, and that they are to be moved and stacked again.

The various methods for moving them are (a) by hand, with a laborer carrying one case at a time; (b) manually, with a laborer pushing or pulling a two- or four-wheeled truck; (c) manually and mechanically, by putting the cases on a pallet and then using a fork lift truck; (d) mechanically, by using a fork truck with the cases already on pallets; or (e) by using a conveyor.

At the moment, we are calculating only worker costs and are not concerned with equipment costs. The handler costs $4.50 per hour, or $.075 per minute.

If the laborer carries the cases, he will take ⅓ of a minute to get a case off the pile, will walk at the rate of 250 feet per minute, and will take another ⅓ minute to put the case on the new pile. This costs $.025 per case for "unpiling," $.03 per 100 feet per case for carrying, and $.025 per case for piling—or $.05 plus $.03 per 100 feet per case. Using a two-wheeled hand truck requires the following: unpiling, ⅓ minute; piling on truck, ⅓ minute; travel at the rate of 200 feet per minute for a load of 5 cases; unpiling from truck, ⅓ minute; and piling onto stack, ⅓ minute. This comes to 1.33 minutes for handling each case plus .5 minute of travel per 5 cases. The cost is $.10 + $.0375 ÷ 5 = $.10 + $.0075 per 100 feet per case.

The four-wheel truck requires the same handling as the two-wheel truck, but travel is at the rate of 150 feet per minute for loads of 20 cases. The time requirements are 1.33 minutes' handling plus .666 minute per 100 feet per 20 cases. This costs $.10 + $.05 ÷ 20 per 100 feet, or $.10 + $.0025 per 100 feet per case.

Using a fork lift truck requires unpiling the cases (⅓ minute each) and piling them on a pallet for the truck at another ⅓ minute per case. They travel at the rate of 600 feet per minute in a 15-case load. At the depositing end, the fork truck puts a loaded pallet on the stack in ½ minute. Handling at the beginning is ⅔ minute per case; travel is ⅙ of a minute per 100 feet per 15 cases; handling at the end is $\frac{1}{3}$ minute per case. In total, handling comes to $2\frac{1}{30}$, or .7, of a minute. This costs $.053. Travel costs are $.0125 per 15 cases, or $\frac{1}{12}$ of a cent per 100 feet per case.

The stacked cases could, however, already be on pallets. If this is so, getting the cases onto the truck would be reduced to $\frac{1}{2}$ minute per pallet, or $\frac{1}{30}$ minute per case. Handling at both ends would be $\frac{2}{30}$ of a minute, or $.007 per case. Travel would continue to cost $\frac{1}{12}$ of a cent per 100 feet per case.

FIGURE 12–7

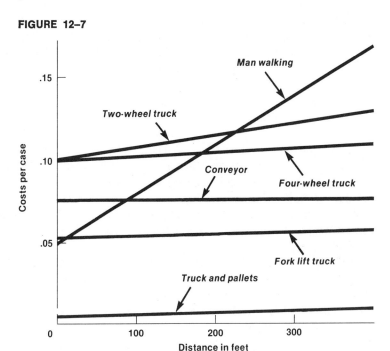

If a conveyor were used instead of a fork lift truck, the travel cost for the employee would be eliminated. Unpiling cases and putting them onto the conveyor would take $\frac{1}{2}$ minute per case. Taking them off at the other end and piling them there would take another $\frac{1}{2}$ minute. Handling time would then total 1 minute per case, at a cost of $.075 per case, with nothing extra added for distance.

Figure 12–7 shows how these alternatives compare. It shows (rather dramatically) the cost savings possible from using palletized loads, which reduces the costly handling of cases one by one. Figure 12–7 also shows that although the distance hauled adds to the cost it is, at least for short distances, only a minor cost. The big cost is for the manual handling at each end.

A summary of the relative costs of these methods shows these costs per case:

	Handling cost	Travel cost per 100 feet	Total cost for	
			100 feet	300 feet
Employee walking..........	$.05	$.03	$.08	$.14
Two-wheel truck...........	.10	.0075	.1075	.1225
Four-wheel truck...........	.10	.0025	.1025	.1075
Fork truck.................	.053	.00083	.0538	.0555
Truck and pallets..........	.007	.00083	.0078	.0095
Conveyor.................	.075	.000	.075	.075

This example deals only with manual costs and assumes that the various kinds of equipment are already available at no extra cost. In a real-life problem the alternative equipment cost would have to be included. The total volume of cases to be handled would also be a factor. For very low volumes it might pay to choose hand trucks rather than fork lift trucks and pallets or conveyors.

FIXED VERSUS VARIED PATH EQUIPMENT

Equipment for moving materials may be divided into "fixed path" and "varied path" equipment. Varied path equipment (fork lift trucks, for example) handles material in separate lots whereas fixed path equipment (such as conveyor belts) usually handles material continuously. Varied path equipment is flexible and fixed path equipment is relatively inflexible. Fixed path equipment is more economical if large quantities of material follow the same path, but it is uneconomical if materials follow diverse paths. Varied path equipment must have portable power units for each piece of equipment, or each piece of equipment must be hauled by a worker. Fixed path equipment is usually driven electrically or, in the case of materials transported downward, by gravity.

Since fixed path equipment fixes the path that materials follow, it reduces the need for identification tags, separate work orders, and records of individual operations. Also, conveyors can be used to pace the worker; in assembly lines, workers must keep up with the work.

Fixed path equipment

Conveyors are the main kind of fixed path equipment for moving materials. Large facilities often use several miles of conveyors.

Conveyors can be put overhead, or at work level, or on the floor. Overhead conveyors generally operate by chain, cable, or connected links suspended from a monorail and have separate pans, hooks, or carrying cradles in which or on which materials are placed. Overhead conveyors are used primarily for horizontal transportation, but they can also go up or down to other floors. Generally, they move continuously rather than stop and go.

Both overhead and work-level conveyors are frequently an integral part of the producing process, and operations are often performed automatically or by a worker as the conveyor moves the material along. Painting, baking, cooling, cleaning, degreasing, electroplating, washing, and many other operations can be done in this way.

Conveyors are also often used in raw materials stock rooms and warehouses, where materials are stored on sloping roller conveyors. As they are wanted, quantities are released automatically by computer and electronic controls—as orders come in. The quantity slides off the storage conveyor onto a collecting conveyor which moves the items to an order makeup area. The savings possibilities are great where large numbers of items are stored and the volumes received and issued are high.

Fixed path conveyors at floor level are often used in assembling large products—for example, automobiles and farm tractors. Depending on the kind of conveyor used, the products may be set on the conveyor, or they may be towed or dragged by cable arranged below the floor. Often wheeled cradles are attached to a tow line and materials are put in them. In still other cases the frame of the product is fastened to the conveyor, and, as it moves down the line, parts are added to the frame.

Automatic transfer machines, like the one depicted in Figure 10–6, page 228, use conveyors. Products are fastened in exact position to the conveyor at one end, which moves a fixed distance to the first machine and stops while the machine does its work. Then it takes the product to the next machine, where it stops again. This goes on until the product is completed. The conveyor is a very important part of this process, even though it is only supporting the automatic machines that do the operations.

Cranes are a second type of fixed path equipment for handling materials. Overhead cranes, operating on tracks running the entire length of a work bay, are common. They can service any point in an area, whether at floor level or above and whether it is accessible from aisles or not. They carry materials by means of hooks, buckets, or magnets. Large overhead cranes are operated by an operator in a suspended cage that is attached to the crane. Operators of smaller overhead cranes control them from the floor by means of suspended controls.

There are many other kinds of fixed path conveying equipment besides conveyors and cranes. Automatic and nonautomatic elevators are commonly used to move materials as well as people in multistory buildings. Chutes can frequently be used to advantage where material is moved downhill, but, if the materials can be easily damaged, the slope must be moderate. Pipes, ducts, and tubes are often used for bulk materials (particularly liquids). Air pressure and vacuum systems are used for dry bulk materials. Often entire material handling systems are designed around the fixed size of the items being moved. For example, the shoe industry has its equipment designed to carry shoe boxes. This homogeniety of size allows for greater efficiencies in handling. In another example, luggage manufacturers have their fixed path in-process inventory handling system designed to carry parts around the plant in tote boxes about the size of a child's wagon.

Varied path equipment

Practically all moving equipment which can follow a varied path is some kind of truck. Manually operated trucks are generally four-wheel platform trucks which also must be loaded and unloaded manually. One variety of hand truck, the lift truck, hoists already loaded skids and so eliminates the truck's being idle at loading and unloading points. Many variations of dolly trucks (a "dolly" is almost any kind of four-wheel carrying rack) and mobile racks are used. Some are especially designed for particular purposes and are generally used for short-distance moves. Even super-market pushcarts are sometimes used. Today, most lift trucks that are used for heavy loads are powered, although they require a trucker to operate the controls and guide them.

Hand trucking is generally confined to short-distance hauls, perhaps from a machine to temporary storage. Trucks that are powered by gaso-line motors or electric storage batteries and driven by truckers are faster and generally more economical for long hauls. Hand trucking is not only slow but, with heavy loads, somewhat unsafe. Truckers may try to pull overloads or may start and stop heavily loaded trucks too quickly and so may injure themselves. There is also more likelihood of damage to ma-terials that are moved on hand trucks. Smooth and level floors are de-sirable for power trucking but are absolutely necessary for hand trucking. If hand trucks are used, elevators must be large enough to hold the trucks so as to move them from floor to floor. If power trucks are used, ramps can connect the floors. Where the path of transportation varies, most plants use powered and driver-operated industrial trucks.

Most industrial trucks have power-driven pickup devices. The metal forks in front of fork lift trucks can be lowered almost to floor level and run under skids or pallets to hoist them and carry them to their destina-tions, then set them down on the floor or stack them on top of each other. This is done mechanically, and fast. Although fork lift trucks are very common, they require 12-foot aisles, which is wider than the aisles in some plants. Walking fork lift trucks (where the trucker walks and guides the truck by a handle), being smaller and more maneuverable, require less room and can be used where aisles are narrower. One-way aisles can also be used.

Tractors and trailers are used by some companies for the transporta-tion of materials. The trailers can be parked and left to be loaded or un-loaded whenever it is convenient. When they are to be moved, a trucker hooks them, one behind the other, to a power-driven truck and hauls them to their destination.

MATERIALS HANDLING DEVICES

The amount of materials handling for production operations is often reduced by mechanical lifting devices, such as jib cranes, chain hoists, compressed air hoists, block and tackles, and winches. Specialized devices at the machines include materials holding fixtures, magazine feeds, automatic product ejectors, welding positioners, elevating sheet-feed tables, and automatic scrap disposers. Robot fingers and arms are used wherever there is excessive heat, exposure to acid, or dangerous emissions of fumes or rays from processes or products.

Many kinds of devices are used to reduce the handling required to get materials on and off trucks and conveyors or transferred from one conveyor to another. They include up-enders, down-enders, turn-overs, rotators, transfer equipment, positioners for materials and platforms, regular and portable elevators, and conveyor unloaders. There are also many devices which permit the handling of loads rather than individual pieces. Tote boxes, skids, and pallets are universally used. Carrying cradles, wire baskets, collapsible wire containers, wire-bound wood slat containers, sacks, and movable racks also are used. Steel strapping is sometimes used to hold loads or packs on their pallets. Tote boxes, skids, pallets, and other types of materials holders should be "tierable" even if special corner posts have to be provided.

REVIEW QUESTIONS

1. Why is it that inefficiency is inherent in maintenance work?
2. Under what conditions is preventive maintenance *not* of considerable importance?
3. Is central or area maintenance better for (*a*) small factories, (*b*) very large factories?
4. What factors should be considered in "make-buy" maintenance decisions?
5. How should materials used by maintenance workers be charged? What ways are available? Discuss.
6. Compare (give good and bad points) of using fixed and varied path materials moving equipment.
7. In general, are costs higher for moving materials over considerable distances or for handling them at both ends of a move?
8. What are the pros and cons of using tractors and trailers to move materials? Where are they most suitable? Where are they poorly suited?
9. How does it happen that a great many companies do not really know what it costs to move products around and to handle them?

QUESTIONS FOR DISCUSSION

1. "When my maintenance people have nothing to do, the plant is running well and we are doing a fine job." Comment on this statement.

2. Does the supervision of maintenance workers differ from the supervision of workers who work on the product? Are maintenance workers of such high caliber that they don't need watching over? What problems arise? How can they be solved?

3. If a plant closes down for two weeks in the summer for vacations, what does this do to or for maintenance work?

4. What trade-offs are important in the "repair or replace" decision?

5. Some years ago when the government made a check, it found that repairing airplanes at Norfolk, Virginia, and Alameda, California, cost just about the same. Looking into the figures, however, disclosed that Alameda's labor costs were much higher but its costs for materials and parts were much less than Norfolk's. Why might this be? Which distribution of expenditure is better? Discuss.

6. How should an analyst go about the task of producing an estimate of the costliness of a company's materials handling?

7. Suppose that the analyst in the question above is also asked to develop a program for reducing the costs of materials handling. How should he go about this assignment?

8. Under what conditions should things be moved to people? People moved to things?

PROBLEMS

1. In trying to reduce maintenance costs, the maintenance inspector has tried inspecting all of the machines frequently and infrequently. Frequent inspection, followed by immediate repair of machines in need of repair, has reduced the number of emergency repairs. Results of the experiment showed:

Number of inspections per week	Number of emergency repairs	Number of preventive repairs
0	37	0
1	20	39
2	14	44
3	8	47
6	2	52

Preventive repairs cost $15 each and emergency repairs cost $50. Inspection costs $1.50 each for the 75 machines in the department. How many inspections per week should be scheduled?

2. Using the text's example of keeping fork lift trucks in operation by having standby extras, suppose that the cost of standby trucks is $75 a day and the cost of out-of-service trucks is $100 per truck. In this case, however, this cost does not increase (per truck) if several trucks break down at the same time. What is the proper number of standby trucks to have and what will this minimum cost come to?

3. The Roe Company has 20 machines to keep in service. Preventive overhauls cost $100 each. Overhauls from breakdowns in service, however, cost $300. These machines are hard to get into adjustment, and often they need repairs again right after being repaired. If, however, they operate without trouble through the initial period, they usually operate a good while before needing repair again. The probability of breakdown since the last overhaul is as follows:

Months after overhaul	Probability of breakdown	Cumulative probability of breakdown
3..................	.10	.10
6..................	.02	.12
9..................	.03	.15
12.................	.04	.19
15.................	.04	.23
18.................	.05	.28
21.................	.08	.36
24.................	.12	.48
27.................	.16	.64
30.................	.22	.86
33.................	.10	.96
36.................	.04	1.00

What preventive maintenance policy should be followed?

4. The Dow Company, to remove cases of bottled detergents from the end of the container line, has to build pallet loads for fork lift trucks. Cases may contain 9, 12, and 24 plastic or glass bottles. Because plastic and glass bottles differ in shape, they take different amounts of handling time. This information is available about the operation:

Container	Time (in hours) per 100 cases		Annual volume (thousand cases)		Cases per load	
	Plastic bottles	Glass bottles	Plastic	Glass	Plastic	Glass
9-bottle cases............	.286	.536	1,125	130	75	45
12-bottle cases............	.286	.386	2,500	550	84	50
24-bottle cases............	.327	.410	2,400	410	70	42

The employees who do this work get $7.40 per hour (plus fringe benefits costs of 25 percent more), and fork life truck time (including pay for the trucker) is calculated as $10 an hour. It takes 0.78 hours per load to haul loads from the conveyor to the point of shipment.

There are two ways to mechanize this load-building work, and either method would eliminate the employees now building truck loads. One is to use 3-lane accumulating unit system capable of handling all kinds of plastic bottles and the 12- and 24-glass bottle cases (9-unit glass bottle cases would be continued as at present). The second alternative uses 4 accumulating lanes and can handle all 6 combinations. The automatic load accumulators would be located closer to the point of shipment and would reduce trucking time to .043 hours per load.

The automatic methods would require one employee's full time (2,000 hours a year at $7.50 per hour) to attend each lane and would cause the following additional costs annually:

	3 lanes	4 lanes
Maintenance	$9,300	$10,200
Extra insurance and taxes	1,080	1,200

The installed cost of the 3-lane arrangement is $312,000 and that of the 4-lane arrangement is $336,000. The equipment life is figured at 15 years with no salvage value. Money costs 12 percent.

Should Dow put in either of the proposed automated load accumulators? What would be their rate of return on the investment?

5. A conveyor costing $3,500 to connect operations A and B would save half an hour a day of $7.30 an hour labor time. It would also boost the productivity of machines A and B by 5 percent. Machine operating time is worth $12 an hour. Will this conveyor pay for itself in one 2,000-hour (250-day) year? What rate of return will it yield on this investment?

6. The Sunbeam Company wants to know how many pallets to buy and whether to leave loads on them in storage, thus tieing them up, or to unload them and keep them in use. For the purpose of this calculation it is not necessary to consider whether the materials are to be kept in stock very long. It is to be assumed that, so far as pallets are concerned, this is a matter of buying more pallets versus unloading them. The relevant figures are:

Cost per pallet	$5
Pallet life	5 years
Pallet maintenance	$.03 per use
Space costs	$.08 per cubic foot per year
Pallet size when loaded	48″ × 40″ × 6″ (a loaded pallet occupies 6.7 cubic ft.)
Cost to unload and load	$.50
Total loads per year	1,000

How many pallets should Sunbeam have? How much floor space will be needed? How long will the pallets stay in storage?

CASE 12–1

The Bow Company (500 employees) has had a maintenance department of 50 employees, but these people have not been very busy. There just is not a great deal of work requiring skilled maintenance work. Upon investigation, Bow has discovered that it can contract its maintenance work and have it done by the Jackson Services Company at a savings of $75,000 a year. The Bow Company accordingly has entered into a contract with Jackson and reduced its own group to a skeleton crew.

The union has filed a grievance with the National Labor Relations

Board accusing the company of engaging in an unfair labor practice. It claims that changing to contracting out the maintenance work is a bargainable issue and that the company should not be allowed to proceed with this action without bargaining about it.

Discuss this case.

SUGGESTED SUPPLEMENTARY READINGS

Hardy, S. T., and Krajewski, L. J.   "A Simulation of Interactive Maintenance Decisions." *Decision Sciences,* January 1975, pp. 92–105.

Hildebrand, J. K.   *Maintenance Turns to the Computer.* Boston: Cahners Books, 1972.

"Materials Handling" (Special section). *Purchasing,* May 20, 1975, pp. 38–47.

section four

DESIGNING AND CONTROLLING HUMAN INPUTS

SOCIETY LOOKS to managers of production to produce goods and services in the most economical way possible. Our competitive system in the United States provides for the survival of effective producers and the ultimate elimination of organizations (at least in the private sector of our economy) which do not produce effectively.

Economical production is partly broadly conceptual and partly a matter of paying careful attention to minor details. Major make-buy decisions would, for example, be broadly conceptual. These are matters of concern to high-level managers.

Chapters 13, 14, and 16 go into the ways to improve individual jobs. Chapter 13 shows how an analyst can go about designing and improving individual jobs. His working tools and how to use them are explained. Chapter 14 discusses how to set production standards and the use of incentives.

Chapter 16 considers a somewhat different approach to the general idea of the conservation of resource inputs. Cost-cutting drives and areas of cost savings opportunities are presented. There are, however, several possible pitfalls to avoid. It is easy to embark on a program to economize on resource inputs and then find that this has been done, but at the cost of unwise actions in other directions. The wanted gains are achieved at unwanted costs in other directions. Chapter 16 analyzes these dangers.

Job design includes the safety and health of workers on the job. The obligations of managers to society for worker safety and health and the methods of carrying out this responsibility are considered in Chapter 15.

13

Job design

How can we provide products and services at less cost? How can we make them with less human effort? How can we simplify work? How can we make work more humane? How can we make products from less costly materials? All organizations are continuously trying to answer these questions. They are always trying to determine how to produce and to serve more economically—and, if they improve their effectiveness today, they try to make further improvements tomorrow.

A person might think that after a while few opportunities would be left to improve operations. And it would get harder as time goes on if products and services themselves did not always keep changing. But they do keep changing. With the coming of new products, new operations become necessary and new processing methods also keep coming on.

A company making push-type lawn mowers, for example, decides to produce power lawn mowers. This means making motors, gears, mounts, and so on, and it means people doing new jobs—jobs never done before. Next, the company decides to manufacture powered rotary mowers. Again, this means performing operations both in making parts and in assembling the finished products, which were not done before. Both parts-making jobs and assembly jobs are new jobs.

Then it is found that some customers want power mowers they can ride, so the company begins to manufacture them too. And again the company must design new parts and new jobs to do the new and different operations. And later on, since first methods are usually not yet well worked out, there are almost always still more opportunities to redesign and to improve jobs even further.

The task of improving jobs never ends. Probably the time never comes when it is not possible to make any more improvements. The payoff from the effort directed at improving jobs can be substantial since a great deal of unnecessary work is often eliminated.

Good job design reduces human effort by determining how to do things more quickly; yet, curiously, many people dislike the thought of saving human effort. To many people, "efficiency" is a bad word. They seem to think that when anyone redesigns a job so that more production results this somehow takes advantage of the worker because—using the new method—he turns out more production.

And the worker on the job often thinks so too. A yard worker who. is provided with a power lawn mower can probably mow twice as much grass as he did before with his old hand-pushed mower and without his working as hard. But he is still likely to think about it as if *he* were doing twice as much work (spending twice as much effort) as he did before. The same thing often occurs in organizations. Workers often oppose job improvements (or even any change) because they are sure that they must be working harder when more output results. They are also opposed because improvements sometimes eliminate jobs. Curiously, the same worker who objects to job improvement in a factory will buy a power saw for his basement workshop at home. He can see there that the power saw saves his energy and lets him get more work done—and often better work done—and without his working any harder.

Negative attitudes toward improvements in jobs can sometimes be turned into positive attitudes through "participatory" programs where people aid in the designing and in the reshaping of their jobs. Workers are encouraged to suggest improvements and are often rewarded for suggestions which can be applied. They may be given money, or a certificate, or have their picture in the company paper. Or they may simply become more motivated because they have made a suggestion and it was approved and put into use.

Industrial engineers often find that they win support for improvements by getting both workers and supervisors involved. Participation and involvement often cause them to become interested in improving the way they do their jobs. Industrial engineers, however, may have to "plant" ideas about improvements in people's minds and wait for the seeds to germinate. Supervisors, who often resent suggestions from the outside, sometimes come to think of the planted idea as their own. From there on they not only accept the idea but put extra effort into implementing "their" ideas.

JOB ENLARGEMENT AND JOB ENRICHMENT

Sometimes jobs can be made a little more interesting by enlarging or enriching them. Job enlargement means expanding horizontally, adding a few more duties to increase the variety and reduce the monotony, but job responsibility is not increased. Job enrichment is vertical job expansion and responsibility expansion and is more on the psychological side. Workers are told more about what is going on, particularly things that relate to their jobs, and they are consulted about changes in their jobs.

Both job enlargement and job enrichment are reported to heighten worker interest, motivation, and satisfaction on the job. But neither one can be developed by the workers themselves. The changes in job design that enlarge or enrich jobs have to come from above. Job design engineers and supervisors have to determine the specific things that workers do while keeping in mind the enlargement and enrichment possibilities.

Job enlargement

In the case of job enlargement, the issue is one of giving up extreme specialization with a probable small loss in efficiency in exchange for a reduction in boredom and monotony, which makes for better satisfied and more effectively motivated workers.

The simplest kind of job enlargement is just giving the workers more duties to perform. Machine operators might, for example, go after their own materials or sharpen their own tools, things formerly done by someone else.

Another fairly common practice is to have workers exchange jobs now and then. This can be done where there are groups of almost identical machines doing much the same kind of work. Drill press operators, for example, sometimes change machines week-by-week or even daily. Each week they move over to the next machine. This introduces a little variety and reduces complaints about favoritism.

Another way to enlarge jobs is to use "work modules." A work module approach breaks a worker's job into several kinds of tasks and lets him do one kind of work for, say, an hour or two, as he sees fit. For example, a supermarket employee's tasks may be stamping prices, stocking shelves, running a checkout cash register, and performing inventory control work. The employee may choose, within limits, which modules he does and when. Some days, he may stamp prices and stock shelves most of the day, whereas on other days he spends less time on these activities and more on inventory control.

In a factory, a stockroom employee may open and check in newly received materials for an hour or two. Then he may switch and trade off with another employee and service the stock issue window for a while. Or he may change and do clerical work, bringing the stock records up to date for an hour or two. Being able to change from one kind of activity to another largely as he wants to improves a job's acceptability.

On factory production lines, the evidence is not clear on just how much less boring a three-minute job is than a two-minute job. Nor is the evidence conclusive that less specialized but more strongly motivated workers turn out more work. Often the benefits claimed to have resulted from job enlargement are phrased in terms other than increased output or lower costs as such. Job enlargement is said to result in more motivated employees, lower labor turnover, and lower absenteeism. Yet even these gains do not always materialize. The Internal Revenue Service redesigned clerical jobs to give them increased autonomy, variety, and wholeness. Error rates did not improve and production went down as a result of the more complicated methods.[1]

Industry in general is giving job enlargement a try although the gains have not been great or else we would see more of it.

Job enrichment

Job enlargement, obviously, offers only limited possibilities for making jobs more interesting and more meaningful, but the horizons are broader with job enrichment.

Job enrichment is advocated by many social scientists as a way for allowing people to fulfill their need for "esteem" and "self-actualization." According to these social scientists, all of us have, deep within us, a desire to be esteemed by others and to work at our highest skills levels and to accomplish something which we can claim as our own accomplishment. If jobs can be designed so that these needs can be fulfilled, the result will be more motivated employees who produce more and better work and who are absent and who quit less often than if these needs are not fulfilled.

In trying to carry out this philosophy, the Eaton Company (maker of door locks and automobile parts) has found that many of its employees want to be involved in deciding the minor details of the make-up of their jobs. They want to be in on the measurement of the quality of their work, and they want to do their own inspection instead of having others do these things. Eaton found, too, that its factory workers wanted to do their own minor machine maintenance. They also wanted to be in on deciding their work schedules and such matters as the use of assembly "teams" of workers instead of production lines.

Another area where job enrichment might be used is in the operation of almost wholly automatic machines. Often these machines are so automatic that all the operator has to do is to load the machine and push a button. While the machine is operating, the operator has nothing to do. His job would surely be more interesting if he were given something to do during the waiting time. Perhaps he could operate several machines or be given the responsibility for inspecting his own work.

Obviously, however, since people differ from each other, not everyone wants an "enriched" job. Some people avoid creative type jobs and favor the security of the familiar so long as the physical work environment, fringe benefits, and pay are satisfactory. To many, the job is *not* of primary interest to them.

---

[1] Reported in Mildred E. Katzell, *Productivity: The Measure and the Myth* (AMACOM, 1975), p. 6.

Assembly teams

In the early 1970s, Sweden's Volvo and Saab-Scania's automobile companies received a great deal of favorable publicity from their innovation of discarding the traditional line assembly method and substituting teams or small groups of workers who collectively assemble such subcomponents as a car's electrical wiring system or its spring suspension system. These teams are free to organize themselves as they see fit and set their own work speed and coffee break times so long as they meet their production goals. Reports were that this method worked better than had the older conventional production lines.

Naturally, these reports interested both American employers and American unions as well as the Ford Foundation. In November 1974, the Ford Foundation sent a group of six Detroit automobile workers to Sweden to work in one of these groups in a Saab-Scania factory for four weeks.[2]

The Detroit workers did not like the experience and felt that the pace was too fast and that the atmosphere was not free and open. Some of the comments were:[3] "If I've got to bust my ass to be meaningful, forget it; I'd rather be monotonous." "Group assembly becomes boring after a while."

"Things are more open at home and you have better counsel from your foreman. The workers associate better too. They're more part of it. Here it is separate." "In the States you have your boredom, but you still have your more outward-going, more happy-go-lucky [attitudes]. We make the workplace happy while we are there."

"Somehow, I have the feeling, you're being had! They knock themselves out to make this place [good] for you to be able to work in and like it, even though it's really—how can I say this—they make it easy for you as possible to swallow a hard pill. In the States, even though it's dirty, and even though it's noisy, there you don't have to swallow anything." "Here you see the foreman, and that's it. You're on a last name basis with him. [At home] I call my general foreman, 'Hey, Jasper.' [Here] I don't even know his name." "It's a family here . . . but it's a type of family where the father will provide for all of the comforts of his children to see that they get everything they need. But they have no freedom, really, to go against his wishes."

Variable work schedules

One approach to making jobs more attractive is to allow for variation in the work hours. Sometimes it is possible to adjust work schedules and to allow employees a certain amount of freedom to work whatever hours they want.

---

[2] Their reactions are reported in *A Work Experiment: Six Americans in a Swedish Plant* (Ford Foundation, 1976).

[3] Ibid., pp. 33–37.

Several arrangements are possible. In its extreme form, workers would be free to work whatever hours they care to. Rarely are operations so flexible that they can be carried on effectively with such irregularities.

Sometimes two part-time employees share a job, one working the first half shift and the other working the second half shift. This has been tried at times in areas where full-time workers are scarce but vacationers and older people are available.

"Flextime"

Another variation, called "flextime," is gaining acceptance. With flextime, workers may come early or late and leave early or late just so they put in 8 hours of work in a day. They may even take time out during the day for shopping.

Flextime, which originated in West Germany in the late 1960s, is a growing practice and is now being tried on a limited basis by a number of organizations in the United States, among them, General Motors, Montgomery Ward, National Cash Register, and others. The federal government has also been using it in some places in the armed forces, in the Social Security Administration, and in certain other civil service jobs. (As yet, however, it is estimated that fewer than ½ of 1 percent of American workers are on flextime.)[4]

As it is used at Hewlett-Packard, flextime allows workers on this system to come to work at any time between 6:30 and 8:30 A.M. and to quit from 3:00 to 5:00 P.M. with as much as 2½ hours out during the day for lunch, shopping, or other personal business. Hewlett-Packard reports only good experience with this program with greater productivity, better morale, and so on. There have also been numerous reports of good results in Europe and Japan from using flexible work hours. It has been particularly helpful to working mothers with school-age children whose time demands often conflict with regular eight-to-five workdays.

In spite of these favorable reports, one needs to discount them a little. Obviously most workers would like the extra freedom it gives them. As against this, tardiness and absenteeism almost always interfere somewhat with effective operations. And it doesn't matter whether the absent worker is out shopping or has gone home early; his not being on the job when others are there interferes with joint work. Nor, in many situations, can a worker who comes in early be very productive working all by himself.

Flextime may make it necessary for white-collar workers to punch time clocks, and most of them do not like this. Administration costs are also higher. Sylvia Porter reports that some labor union leaders regard flextime as a "back-door" attempt to deny workers overtime pay and eliminate the eight-hour day.

---

[4] See Mark R. Tomasch, "Flexible Hours—Coming Factor in Your Job?" *Automation,* June 1975, p. 64. See also "The Flextime Concept Gets a Wider Test," *Business Week,* May 24, 1976, pp. 37–38.

Obviously, too, flexible hours are hard to arrange in organizations which have to provide 24-hour service, such as is needed in some maintenance work, in long-haul truck driving, in hospital emergency service, in many airline services, and the like. It remains to be seen whether flextime will be widely adopted or not.

Four-day workweeks

Another variant from ordinary work schedules, the four-day workweek, is regarded by some people as a method of job enrichment. The four-day workweek is composed of four ten-hour days. This has been tried, and, although it has received a good press, four-day workweeks are uncommon. It has enjoyed its greatest success in small service-type organizations where the days off can usually be arranged to correspond to slow periods in calls for service.

In favor of the four-day workweek is that it saves workers going to work a fifth day and gives them long weekends. Against it is the fact that everyone's children have to go to school five days so there can't be long weekends for the whole family. Also, many workers do not like to leave home shortly after 6 A.M. and get back shortly before 6 P.M. Besides, the man of the house doesn't know what to do with Friday off.

And, from the employer's point of view, having the establishment closed down on Fridays disrupts service. Shipments in and out on Fridays are delayed. Staggering the four days so that some workers work Monday–Thursday and others work Tuesday–Friday may help. This is, however, quite an unsatisfactory arrangement most of the time in the factory because some machines and production lines need to be staffed with full crews if they are to operate at all. Also, productivity per hour will drop from fatigue during the long 10-hour days.

Unions also oppose the four 10-hour day arrangement unless they get time-and-a-half pay for the last two hours each day (11 hours' pay for ten hours of work). This would increase labor costs 10 percent, to say nothing of the slightly lower average hourly output which can be expected during the long 10-hour days. Unions are, however, strongly in favor of four 8-hour days in a week with 40 hours of pay. With this method's 25 percent increase in costs, it is understandable that this arrangement is probably nonexistent, and certainly so in unionized organizations.

Other unusual schedules are occasionally used. Thus, where seven-day-a-week operations are needed, workers might work four 10-hour days, then have four days off. Different workers can have different sets of four days which can be staggered so that out of any seven workers, four are always working and three are off on any given day.

In other cases, and this is a little more common, workers alternate shifts; perhaps one week on the day shift, one on nights, then back to days, and so on.

These various alternating arrangements may enrich jobs in that they spread favorable and unfavorable situations around. Usually this is at least a little uneconomical from a production point of view, and some workers do not like changing.

JOB IMPROVEMENT LIMITATIONS

Jobs are not always improved as much as they could be, partly because there is so much change. There is always a need to start new jobs by performing them at first as best one can and then improving them as time goes along. Also, some jobs are not of much consequence, or they won't be performed very often. It costs less to let them be done inefficiently than to study them carefully and figure out how to improve them when they are done for only 15 minutes a day.

Nor does careful job study pay off unless jobs are standardized. All of the relevant factors—products, processes, materials handling methods, working conditions, workplace arrangements, as well as methods and the worker's motions—need to be standardized. The improvement and standardization of these factors are two of the main objects of all job improvement work, but, if they vary continually and cannot be standardized, the improvement possibilities are limited.

It would seem to be unnecessary to add that top-level backing is needed in order for job improvement to be very successful. Yet such backing is sometimes not provided. When this is so, lower-level people find it easy not to put into effect the job improvement suggestions made by industrial engineers if doing so makes extra work even though the savings may be great.

DESIGNING FUTURE JOBS

Job design aims to improve jobs; yet, it may be wasteful to start doing a job one way and then change it. Also, with so many people opposed to changing, it is better to determine the best way to do an operation before starting to do it at all.

This is where job design and methods study can be useful. Admittedly, it is hard to see ahead of time just how every future operation might be done and then improve it before it is actually done. Nonetheless, this is the approach that mass producers of consumer products take. Before production lines are set up, industrial engineers try to visualize the bits and pieces of work to be done at successive work stations. They sometimes use workplace mock-ups. They try to divide the work evenly among workers, and to arrange the workplaces, and to develop tools—all ahead of time. Then, when operations start, most of the changing has been done. Improvements developed this way avoid the costs of changing later and at the same time avoid much of the opposition to change.

JOB DESIGN OBJECTIVES

Just as product engineers design products, so should industrial engineers and supervisors design jobs. They should study the needs of the operation and the capabilities of people and machines and develop jobs to strike the best possible balance which satisfies all of the relevant factors.

Usually, the main objectives are to save human effort, to minimize labor costs, and to provide some reasonable amount of job satisfaction. Yet, job designers should not strive for ultimates. Frequently, if a person were to ask an industrial engineer what he is trying to do, the time-honored answer will come back: "I try to find the one best way to do every job." This is not really what he should be trying to do, though. He should be trying to find a *better* method. The difference is important. If he always tries to find the *best* way, he will spend all his time seeking ultimates on too few jobs. Job designers usually have to be satisfied with figuring out a *better* way at reasonable expense. It costs too much to be a perfectionist.

In trying to improve jobs and make them easier for workers, the analyst tries to do three things: (1) to get rid of as many human movements as possible, (2) to shorten the movements he can't get rid of, and (3) to make the necessary movements less tiring.

But the job designer should not stick solely to human movements and overlook other improvements. Often he can't simplify a person's move-

FIGURE 13–1

How job study leads to greater production

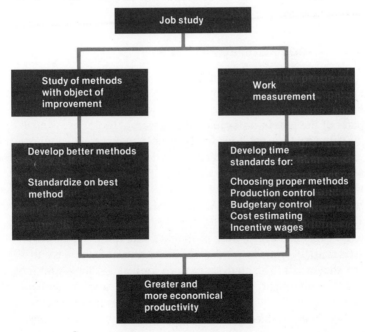

ments unless he rearranges the workplace, or gives the person some special tools, or changes the machine or even the product itself. In fact, the analyst should not study a person's motions at all until he has improved the job as much as he can in other ways.

Suppose, for example, the worker's job is to paint a part. The reason for the operation is to cover a surface—to protect it or to make it look attractive. The analysts should *not* start with the way the worker handles the paint brush; they should start by asking: Does the job have to be done at all? Product engineers should be able to answer that question. Assuming that they say yes, the analysts should ask when, where, and how the paint should be put on? Maybe the paint ought to go on the part at no extra cost when the assembled product is painted. But if the part must be painted by itself, they should ask themselves how the worker should get the paint on. Can it go on with a spray gun or a brush, or by dipping the part in it, or by smearing it on with a sponge. The analysts should pick the best method, and then—not before—get down to considering the worker's movements and *how* they should be made. Job design work should not be confined to a study of the motions of workers.

Often, the first questions about a job must be answered by product design or tool or machine design engineers. If the job is to drill a hole in a steel casting, an early question might be: Why not make the part out of a steel stamping and punch the hole instead of drilling it? Or suppose that a worker is putting pieces of material, one after the other, into a machine. The natural question to ask is: Could the tool engineers design an automatic feed? Again, the study of the worker's movements comes as the last step in methods improvement.

METHODS FOR IMPROVING SPECIFIC JOBS

We have been discussing "macro" or overall job design matters. However, in order to design specific new jobs or redesign old jobs, analysts have to come down to the "micro" level. They have to study the minor parts of the job. In order to do this, several "tools" are available.

The first tool methods study people need is an inquiring mind. They will not get far if they accept such ideas as "We've always done it that way"; "The present method works, doesn't it? So it must be all right." Methods which "just grow" are almost never as good as those which have been analyzed. Instead, analysts should assume that the usual way of doing a job is the wrong way. Or that, if we are still doing a job the same way we did it two years ago, we are probably doing it the wrong way.

If wasted motions carried red flags, it would be easy to improve jobs. But they don't. The analysts have to look at the job—and look at it minor part by minor part, not as a whole—to see what movements the worker makes. Then the analysts must decide where improvements can be made.

The analysts have six working tools (beyond an inquiring mind) to aid in this job design or redesign:

1.   Process charts.
2.   Motion study guidelines.
3.   Thought-provoking questions.
4.   Micromotion study.
5.   Therblig analysis.
6.   Task-force groups.

These tools can be used separately or together. Of the six, numbers one, two, and three are most often used.

PROCESS CHARTS

There are any number of kinds of charts which the analysts can use to aid in visualizing a job and to see ways to improve it. Somewhat like a picture, a chart holds things still—so to speak—so they can be studied. And it lets the analysts see the entire job, not just one little thing at a time. Often things can better be analyzed on a chart than out on the factory floor or service facility. In the case of charts for new jobs, they allow the analysts, within limits, to see ahead of time how the jobs will work. If improvements seem possible, they can be made and a new chart developed —all before the new job is started.

Nonetheless, one cannot expect too much from charts. A chart, by itself, does not design a job nor does it improve a job; it takes a person to make improvements. All a chart can do is to depict arrangements. Nor do charts need to be precisely drawn to be useful. They should, however, contain considerable detail because some of the opportunities for improvement are in the details. The important things, the obvious things, that obviously required improvement in the past, have probably already been taken care of. To improve most jobs any further, it is necessary to get down into the details of the job.

Process charts of all kinds show the details of some action. They describe what is done. Besides this, nearly all charts have a symbol for each detail. The time it takes to do tasks and the distance things are moved are also commonly shown. Summaries of how often each kind of detail occurs are also common.

But, one might ask, why symbols? What good are little squares, circles, flat-sided circles, arrows, triangles, and so on? They are classifications of details. Large circles are usually operations; they show that something is being done to the product or a service is being rendered. Small circles or arrows mean that the product is moved. Triangles or flat-sided circles mean the item is being stored. Squares mean inspections.

Classifying the details with symbols as codes allows the analysts to see how often each kind of activity happens. It also points out where these things are done. This is useful as the analysts try to rearrange details to combine some things and eliminate others.

When making up a chart, the analysts should be sure that it shows what *is* happening—not what *is supposed* to be happening. An exception is in charting future jobs which show how a job will be done.

The purpose of charting is to let the analysts see the job in detail so that they can search for ways to improve it. As part of the process the analysts may need to draw up one or more working charts depicting interim stages of improvement before they get their final method worked out.

It is unfortunate that names for the different kinds of charts are not standardized. However, those we use are fairly common and are listed below:

1. Charts which show the complete processing of a product.
   a. Flow diagrams. A material flow diagram shows, on a floor plan, how a product moves through the plant. Symbols show where

FIGURE 13–2

Flow process chart

	Summary			Analyze present method to
	Present	Proposed	Saved	1. Eliminate
Distance	50 ft.	40 ft.	10 ft.	2. Combine
				3. Improve
◯ Operation	13	11	2(17 min.)	4. Change—
				a. Sequence
▷ Transportation	3	2	1	b. Person
				c. Place
☐ Inspection	1	1	0	
				ASK–Where, When, What,
▽ Storage	0	0	0	Who, Why, How
▷ Delay	1	0	1(10 min.)	

Fill in symbol	Proposed detail description	Time or distance	Reasons
1 ▷	Deliver packed valves to stockroom on caster table	20ft.	Delivers valves without carrying
2 ◯	Clear up table for next order	1/2 min.	
3 ◯	Pick up and arrange packing supplies ordered	1/2 min.	Ordering ahead saves delay time
4 ◯	Requisition supplies for next order	3 min.	Helps stock man plan
5 ▷	Push caster table back to packing room	20 ft.	Saves carrying valves
6 ◯	Pick up tote box of valves	1/4 min.	
7 ◯	Dump tote box on table	1/4 min.	
8 ◯	Put prefolded cartons in jigs (2)		New cartons cost 4¢ more per 100
9 ◯	Place flat instruction sheet over carton		Use instruction sheet as wrapper. Saves paper-9¢ per 100
10 ☐	Inspect 2 valves at a time	Total of	More complete visual inspection
11 ◯	Place valves in cartons (2)	8 sec. per valve;	Use both hands
12 ◯	Close cartons (2)	13 1/3 min. per	Handles 2 at a time
13 ◯	Put on pressure - sensitive labels	100 valves	New labels 3¢ per 100 more
14 ◯	Place cartons in shipping carton		Approval to proceed: *James Carlson*

Action taken and resultant savings–
    Put casters on table, changed sequence, simplified packing, did 2 at a time, smoother motions, eliminated motions, eliminated some packing supplies.
Better labels.
Saved 27 min. per order of 100, and 2¢ per 100 in supplies.

operations are done. This kind of chart is often used with another sheet of paper describing the operations and other details shown on the chart by symbols.

b. Flow process charts (see Figure 13–2). This kind of chart tells the same story as the material flow chart but as a list without a floor plan. It also provides spaces for showing how much time it takes to do things and spaces for showing the distance materials are hauled. Figure 13–2 is actually the "after" chart of a "before-and-after" pair of charts. As a result of a study the analysts, in this case, reduced the number of operations from 13 to 11. The moves were cut from 3 to 2 and delays from 1 to 0. The 1 inspection and zero storages remained unchanged.

c. Operation process charts. These are similar to the first two

FIGURE 13–3

Operation chart

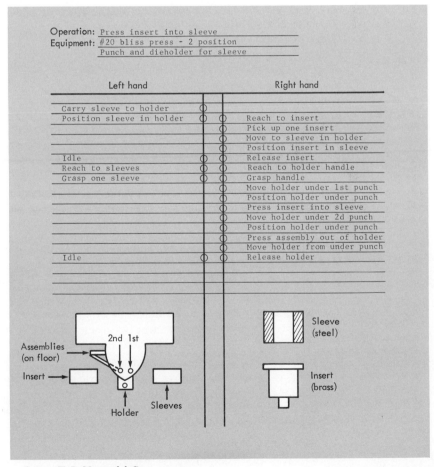

Operation: Press insert into sleeve
Equipment: #20 bliss press - 2 position
Punch and dieholder for sleeve

Left hand			Right hand
Carry sleeve to holder	①		
Position sleeve in holder	①	①	Reach to insert
		①	Pick up one insert
		①	Move to sleeve in holder
		①	Position insert in sleeve
Idle	①	①	Release insert
Reach to sleeves	①	①	Reach to holder handle
Grasp one sleeve	①	①	Grasp handle
		①	Move holder under 1st punch
		①	Position holder under punch
		①	Press insert into sleeve
		①	Move holder under 2d punch
		①	Position holder under punch
		①	Press assembly out of holder
		①	Move holder from under punch
Idle	①	①	Release holder

Source: H. B. Maynard & Co.

charts, but they emphasize how and where parts come together and what happens before and after they are assembled.

2.   Charts showing details of single operations.

    a.   Operator-machine charts.   These charts list the activities of a machine operator (or more than one operator) and the machine operated. The vertical part is a time scale, and activities are listed at exactly the time they have to happen. Doing this makes sure that the operator does not have to be in two places at once. Symbols are not often used in operator-machine charts.

    b.   Operation charts.   Figure 13–3 is a left- and right-hand chart without a time scale. Each hand's activities are listed opposite each other whenever they are done at the same time. Small circles are used for every activity, no matter what kind. (This is for counting and highlighting the lack of balance of work between the two hands.)

    c.   Simo charts.   Simultaneous motion charts are used in rare cases. They are extremely detailed and depict in detail what each hand does or even what each finger does.

3.   Office procedure charts.

Charts of the type described here can be used to analyze office and other service jobs as well as factory jobs. Office procedures, however, introduce a problem not found in factory charts. Office forms are often made in several copies which go to different departments, so the chart maker has to devise charts which follow more than just one copy of a form.

MOTION STUDY GUIDELINES

Motion study guidelines, the second kind of job improvement tool, provide general rules to follow for improving jobs. Some of these are listed below.

1.   Rules for minimizing human movements.   Never do a job the hard way if there is an easier way.

    a.   Don't do jobs by hand if machines can do them. Transfer everything possible to machines when practical. In particular, try to design machines which not only will do the operation, but which will first place the product in position and then eject it after the operation.

    b.   Eliminate handling. Bring materials as close as possible to the point of work and remove them by gravity if possible; if this cannot be done, do it mechanically. If materials must be handled by a person, handle as many as possible at one time. Design machines to do two or more operations once the material has been put in position.

    c.   Use the fewest motions possible. Move as little of the body as is necessary to do the job; in fact, move only the fingers if finger motion will do. Don't reach; put things where little reaching is necessary.

d. Use fixed positions for all materials and tools. Put them close to and in front of the worker to reduce searching as well as reaching for them. Motions then become automatic.

2. Rules for making the best use of people. A whole person produces more than part of a person.

a. Use two hands but avoid using hands purely as holding devices. Idle hands do no work. If both are not busy, redistribute the work between them. On light assembly jobs mechanical holding devices can often make a job into a one-handed job, in which case an identical job can be done with the other hand. The worker will not do twice as much work as with one hand, but he is likely to do half as much more. Working with two hands may take practice, but it is quite possible. Typists do it all the time.

b. Use the feet as well as the hands if they can be used to push a pedal or do some useful movement. Hands and feet can both be used at the same time. Does it sound impossible? Fifty million of us do this every day when we drive our cars.

c. Study and analyze all hesitations and short delays within jobs and eliminate them when possible.

d. Where unavoidable delays occur, give people other work to keep them productive.

e. The time an expert takes is possible for everyone. Try to get all people to do as well.

3. Rules for saving energy. Tiring movements waste energy.

a. Transfer all heavy lifting to mechanical lifting devices.

b. Use momentum where possible, rather than force. A person cannot, for example, push a nail into a board even with a hammer. But, if he swings the hammer, its momentum does the job. Avoid momentum, however, if muscular effort has to be used to stop it.

c. Continuous, curved motions are easier and less tiring than motions involving sharp changes in direction.

d. Assign all work to the body member best suited for it; in typing, for example, don't do it all with the little finger.

e. Use the body to the best advantage mechanically. If force must be exerted, exert it at heights and in positions where the body can employ the most force.

f. Eliminate working conditions which add to fatigue. Use power-driven tools. Improve poor lighting, poor ventilation, fumes, dusty conditions, temperature extremes, and humidity. If possible, provide a comfortable chair, and arrange work so the operator can stand or sit as he wishes.

g. On fatiguing jobs, allow rest periods. The heavier the task, the more necessary are frequent (but short) rest periods. Many short rest periods are better than a few long rest periods.

    h. On monotonous jobs, provide an occasional break; monotony and fatigue are related. Consider job enlargement and job enrichment to lessen monotony.

4. Rules for placing people. Use labor to its best advantage in view of the jobs to be filled and the people available.

    a. Where several workers do the same job day after day, break the job up into small tasks and let each worker specialize but with some rotation allowed. Each will acquire greater proficiency, and the group will produce more.

    b. Put workers on jobs well suited to them, and place only well-suited people on the jobs.

    c. Avoid using high-price labor on low-price work even if this work is but a small part of a high-price workers's job. Divide the job and assign work to the grade of worker required.

THOUGHT-PROVOKING QUESTIONS

Thought-provoking questions are the next job improvement tool. They are much like guidelines, but they are more numerous and detailed. Merely asking some of the following questions about almost any job is likely to make analysts think of one or more ways to improve it.

First, there are general questions which apply to all jobs. They include: By whom, where, why, and how is the job done? Is this movement necessary? What does it do? What would happen if it were eliminated? Can it be shortened? Can it be transferred to a machine? Can it better be done at another time? Can it better be combined with another movement?

These questions would start almost anyone thinking, but they are not really what we mean by thought-provoking questions, which are more specific. Here are a few which apply mostly to metal products:

If the operation is performed to improve appearance, is the added cost justified by added salability?

If the operation is to correct a subsequent difficulty, is the corrective operation less costly than the difficulty?

Is this operation made necessary because of the poor design of tools that are used in a previous or a following operation?

Is the machining of a surface done merely to improve appearance, and, if so, can a suitable appearance be obtained in some less costly way?

If design requires special tooling, can it be altered so that standard cutters, multiple drilling heads, jigs, and the like can be used?

Is the job inspected at the critical point instead of after the job is done?

Are the suppliers furnishing material on which they have performed an operation that is not necessary for its use?

Could molded or cast parts be substituted to eliminate machining or other operations?

Are closer tolerances specified than are necessary?

Both the process of thinking up the questions as well as answering them help bring opportunities for improvement to the analysts' minds.

MICROMOTION STUDY

This way of improving jobs (though rarely used) takes moving pictures of jobs and then runs the film slowly through a projector (even stopping the film to look at each picture separately). Since moving picture cameras take 16 pictures a second, counting the pictures will reveal how long its movements take.

It is possible to cut picture taking and analysis costs by using time-lapse photography. This means taking perhaps 1 picture a second instead of 16 per second. An even lower ratio of pictures may also suffice. (This is what is done in pictures of flowers blooming—a 3-day growth can be condensed into a 1-minute movie segment.)

Or the analysts can go in the reverse direction and get greater detail by using "memomotion" study—taking, say, 50 to 100 picture frames a second. This lets them study the movements in slow motion when the film is run at normal rates.

Taking good indoor movies is not an amateur's job. Usually it is necessary to put up floodlights, string wires around, and generally disrupt a factory department in order to take the movies. It also costs money to do all of this, and most of the people concerned—supervisors and workers on jobs—don't like the idea. Unions nearly always oppose it. It is small wonder that micromotion study is rare in industry.

Moving pictures of jobs, however, can also be useful in other ways. They furnish an enduring record of how a job is done, and they can be used to help train new people. And micromotion study can be used to advantage in large companies for short-cycle jobs that are done millions of times a year.

THERBLIG ANALYSIS

Therblig analysis, like micromotion study, is rarely used. It is just too detailed and costly except for very short-cycle jobs which are done thousands of times. A therblig is a small part of a job—a very small part. It is usually much too short to time with a stopwatch.

When time study analysts set production standards, they analyze jobs part by part, but their parts of a job (they call them "elements") would stop at, say, "tighten bolt." "Tighten bolt," however, is made up of several very short therbligs: Move hand, get ready to pick up wrench, grasp wrench, move hand with wrench, position wrench, and turn wrench. Other therbligs are: Search, select, grasp, move hands empty, move hands holding something, hold, release load, position something, preposition something, inspect, assemble, take apart, use, unavoidable delay, avoidable delay, plan, and rest.

Therblig analysis, when used, can help the analysts because it forces them to look at minor parts of a job. True, sometimes it is possible to cut out big parts of jobs or even whole jobs, but sometimes more time can be saved by looking at the therbligs, one by one. It is often possible to work out job improvements quite effectively with therblig analysis if such analyses are combined with predetermined times for fundamental movements such as methods time measurement provides (see Chapter 14). With this type of analysis the analysts can evaluate alternative methods before production is started and so adopt the best methods.

But let us return to the "tighten bolt" part of a job. The worker reaches for the wrench and for the bolt; then he reaches again in putting the wrench out of the way. If the wrench and the bolt are put closer to him, he will save reaching time. Next, if the wrench and bolts are always put in the same places, he can pick them up more quickly. He won't have to grope around for them or look each time to find them. Putting the wrench in a slot or holder so that it sticks up lets the worker get hold of it more quickly.

And it is the same with every therblig. Each needs to be looked at separately because different things are needed to improve each one.

After the analysts have done all this, the "tighten bolt" element will probably take less time than it did before. But the improvement will be the result of looking at the details, not the overall job.

TASK FORCES

Another way to improve jobs is by using task forces. Usually they are set up as part of a special cost-cutting drive. Two or three industrial engineers, and two or three supervisors, and perhaps some of the people actually doing the work are appointed as a task force to study each supervisor's department to see what improvements they can think of. Often they see opportunities for improvements which were missed before. Also, if changes in the layout, in tools or machines, in materials used, or whatever, are beyond a supervisors' authority to make, the task force can bring greater authority to bear and so help implement the improvement suggestion.

DESIGNING JOB PRICE STRUCTURES

How much is a job worth? Should a factory production line assembler be paid as much as a carpenter? All employers, in public as well as private organizations, have to answer the question: How much shall each job be paid?

This question is usually answered through job evaluation methods. Job evaluation sets up a wage or salary "structure" which slots jobs into pay brackets so that different amounts of pay will reflect overall job difficulty.

JOB EVALUATION

Individual job base rates are usually determined by a "job evaluation" process. By far the most widely used method for determining job prices is "point-type" job evaluation plans. A few organizations use the "factor comparison" method and a very few use "grade descriptions." Grade descriptions are, however, common in federal government organizations.

Job evaluation is intended to develop equitable pay differentials among unlike jobs. It is, however, impossible to develop any one single job evaluation plan which can measure *all* jobs equally. The content of the job of a salesman, a factory supervisor, an office clerk, or a factory machine operator is just too different. Yet all of these jobs exist in every manufacturing company. Other types of organizations probably find just as much diversity in the nature of their jobs.

This is not, however, an unsurmountable difficulty. Rather, two or three different job evaluation plans are used, one for each general category of job. For illustration purposes we will discuss factory work job evaluation, yet recognizing that there are other plans for other groups.

JOB DESCRIPTIONS

The first step in evaluating jobs is to collect information about them and to write up descriptions of each job. These descriptions list the duties, the things the worker does. Such descriptions supply information to the evaluators, and they become permanent records, serving later on as references in hiring, promotion, grievance settlement, and other matters. For evaluation purposes, the specific things done by workers on each job are described, although minute details are unnecessary. Details such as are needed for time study, for example, are not required for evaluation.

POINT PLANS

There are many varieties of point plans, most of which are patterned after the National Metal Trades Association plan. This method regards all factory jobs as being composed of varying amounts of 11 factors.[5] The amount of each factor in a job is determined and assigned a number of points. The total of the points assigned for all factors becomes the rating of the job. After all jobs have been rated in this way, a scale showing the monetary value of the points is set up. Reference to the scale shows how much money should be paid on each job.

---

[5] In the NMTA plan there are 11 factors. They are weighted in order of relative importance on typical factory jobs and are as follows: Skill factors: education, maximum points 70, experience, maximum 110 points, initiative and ingenuity, 70 points. Effort factors: physical demands, 50, mental and visual demands, 25. Responsibility factors: for equipment and process, 25, materials and products, 25, safety of others, 25, work of others, 25. Job conditions: working conditions, 50, and unavoidable hazards, 25 points.

FIGURE 13–4

A job description showing the details of the job

JOB TITLE____ WASHER ASSEMBLY STOCKMAN

DEPARTMENT__ Lock Washer and Nut Assembly_____ JOB CODE NO. 89–262

NO. OF EMPLOYEES ON JOB_____1_____   ☐ DATE_____

STATEMENT OF THE JOB

Under the direction of the WASHER ASSEMBLY SETUP MAN, receives and breaks down mill box loads of incoming stock, sorting according to classification of product, in preparation for distribution in department; services WASHER HAND ASSEMBLERS by lifting mill boxes of work on to assembly tables, weighs completed work on floor scale to measure production, and delivers to Department 96 on hand truck to be packed.

DUTIES OF THE JOB

1. Receives, sorts, and delivers stock; carries mill boxes of washers and bolts from stock to selected locations on floor according to size and type of plating, as directed by WASHER ASSEMBLY SETUP MAN; selects proper boxes by reading travel ticket and lifts onto work tables to be assembled by WASHER HAND ASSEMBLERS or places on hand truck, pulls loaded truck to Washer Assembly machines, and selects proper boxes to place at each machine, as directed, according to type of stock.

2. Weighs completed work in mill boxes; hauls completed work to scales on lift truck to weigh by placing boxes on scale in groups according to shift and work group as shown on production ticket; records weight on production ticket to show amount produced by shift and work group.

3. Delivers all mill boxes of completed work to Department 96 by hand truck to be packed.

4. Does errand work for the department such as hauling mill box loads of work by lift truck from the Plating Department and to the Heat Treat Department.

The manual or plan

When point plans are used, jobs are evaluated by comparing them to several preset definitions of degrees (usually five degrees are set apart) of each of the factors used. The definitions describe, in general terms, situations requiring the factor, graduated from slight amounts up to considerable amounts.[6] The definition which most nearly describes the

---

[6] For the physical demands factor the following are definitions of the 5 degrees: Degree 1 (10 points): light work requiring little physical effort. Degree 2 (20 points): light physical effort in working regularly with lightweight material or oc-

requirements of the job being evaluated is selected and its value (in points) is given to the job.

The job factors, degree definitions, and point equivalents used in the procedure all must be decided before job evaluation takes place. They are agreed upon and put into a small booklet called a manual or plan. Most companies do not develop their own manuals but, instead, use one of the well-known plans.

SPECIFICATIONS AND EVALUATION OF JOBS

When a job is evaluated, it is compared with each factor in the manual. In making the comparison, the evaluators refer to the list of duties which make up the job. Such a list generally does not, however, furnish enough information for evaluation since it omits, for instance, a description of the working conditions which are necessary to make the evaluation. A specification or secondary type of description, therefore, is usually drawn up for each job.

The specification is, in part, a rewrite of the job description, listing the requirements of each of the factors rather than listing the duties. The specification is divided into sections paralleling the factors listed in the manual. In each section appears a statement of the job requirements of the job content of each factor. These are compared, by the evaluation committee, with the manual. The most appropriate degree of each factor is selected for the job; that is, the degree definition which most nearly covers the job content of the factor is determined.

Each degree of each factor carries a point value, so the selection of the appropriate definition automatically gives the job a certain number of points. After the selection of the proper degree has been made for each of the 11 factors, the points are added up to get the total points the job is worth.

MONEY VALUE OF POINTS

When a job evaluation plan is first installed, it is necessary after all the jobs have been evaluated in terms of points to establish the jobs' monetary value. This procedure requires that the analysts know, for every job, its point rating and its existing base rate. The point ratings come from the job evaluation and the base rates come from the personnel department records.

A dot for each job is then plotted on a chart, as in Figure 13–5, cor-

---

casionally with average-weight material; or operating machine tools where machine time exceeds the handling time. Degree 3 (30 points): sustained physical effort requiring continuity of effort and working with light or average-weight material; usually short-cycle work requiring continuous activity, such as the operation of several machines where the handling time is equivalent to the total machine time. Degree 4 (40 points): considerable physical effort working with average- or heavyweight material; or continuous strain of a difficult work position. Degree 5 (50 points): continuous physical exertion working with heavyweight material; hard work with constant physical strain or intermittent severe strain.

FIGURE 13–5

Scatter plot for job wage rates and their job evaluation point totals with labor grades based on the regression line

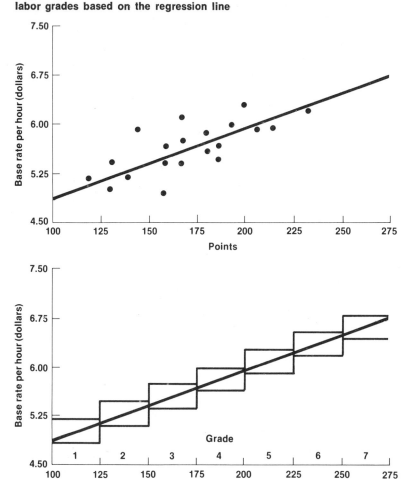

responding to its point total and its base rate. In general, these dots will fall along a line extending from the lower left to the upper right of the chart. The dots will tend to follow a line because it is probable that the old, informal job-base-rate structure was reasonable and, in general, paid small amounts for simple jobs and more money for more difficult jobs.

The next step is to calculate the exact location of the line, technically known as a "regression" line, which reflects the relationship between points and job base rates. Usually this is done by the "least squares" method.[7]

_____

[7] See Problem 7 at the end of this chapter for a description of how the least squares method is used for this purpose.

If the old, informal job evaluation produced base rates reasonably consistent with job content, the points will be close to the regression line, some a little below and some a little above. If not, many points will be farther from it.

LABOR GRADES

The regression line showing the monetary value of all possible job ratings could be used directly for determining the base rate for every job (but probably never is) because there is a dollar-and-cents value for every possible point total. Were the line used to determine base rates, there would be a great many different job rates because only jobs with identical point ratings would have identical pay rates. Every difference in point totals among jobs, even a difference of one point, would produce different base rates. Such a base rate structure, though usable, would be unwieldy and awkward.

Considering jobs in groups is therefore customary. One group might comprise all jobs between 150 and 174 points; another, jobs between 175 and 199 points; and so on. All jobs falling between the group limits are treated alike and are paid the same base rate. The groups are called labor grades. The full range of point values for all jobs in a factory is usually divided into ten or more labor grades. Labor grades may be of identical point ranges or may have wider ranges for jobs of higher point value. Having the same range of points for all grades is common, however.

The base rate for each grade is often treated as a range rather than a fixed rate. For example, instead of paying a $5-per-hour base rate on all jobs within a grade, some companies apply a range of pay, say $4.90 to $5.10 per hour. The limits of pay for the range usually follow closely what the regression line indicates. If, for example, the direct monetary value of a job rated at 150 points is $4.90, this figure will probably be chosen as the minimum wage paid for all jobs rating between 150 and 174 points. If the line shows that 174 points should be paid $5.10, this will probably be the maximum rate. The full range of pay for the labor grade, however, is available for all jobs within the grade, whether they are at the bottom or the top of the point range of the grade.

Within the range of pay, the rate which is paid to individual employees may be based on merit (which is usually determined by the foreman) or on length of service or both. In practice, in many companies almost everyone gets the labor grade's top pay.

USE OF JOB EVALUATION

Since job evaluation has been used for many years in almost all companies, its use is largely for determining equitable base rates of pay for newly set up jobs and for old jobs which have been changed. Friction from differences of opinion about what jobs should pay is reduced to a minimum.

REVIEW QUESTIONS

1. How is job enlargement related to job enrichment?
2. How do assembly teams work and how successful have they been?
3. Compare and contrast different variable work scheduling arrangements. Which seem to be best (or worse) under different circumstances?
4. How widespread is the reluctance to try to improve jobs? How can a job analyst who is supposed to improve jobs win people to a cooperative viewpoint?
5. "I try to find the one best way to do every job," says a method study analyst. Discuss this statement.
6. How can an analyst do motion study work for jobs which have not yet been done? Why would this be necessary?
7. How can a process chart be of any help to a job analyst?
8. Can micromotion study ever be justified? Justify your answer.
9. What is the "manual" or "plan" in a job evaluation plan using points? How can it be used?
10. How are job points made into job base rates in job evaluation procedures which use points? Explain.
11. What is the difference in the wage paid to a worker on a job at the low end of a labor grade and to a worker on a job at the higher end in the same labor grade? Why is this?

QUESTIONS FOR DISCUSSION

1. Are not the possible gains from improving manual jobs really quite limited? Aren't the truly large gains the ones which can come from mechanization? Discuss.
2. The Arc Company makes typewriters which it sells for $72 and which sell at retail for $100. Foreign imports of lower-price, lower-quality typewriters have been cutting into the company's sales, so the president tells his job analyst to "knock $10 out of the cost per typewriter so we can produce a model which will compete." How should the analyst go about doing this?
3. In the purchasing department the introduction of preassembled sets of purchase order forms reduced the order preparation time of the typists by one third. Yet after two months there was no visible evidence of any cost reduction. What problems may be present here?
4. The use of task forces, which are more or less job improvement committees, is supposed to make foremen more receptive to suggestions by "outsiders" about how to improve the work in their departments. Will it really work this way? Discuss.
5. At the Pennsylvania Steel Company the men doing chipping work on castings were told by the foreman to squirt oil on the castings so that they could see better what they were doing. The men said that

squirting oil from a can was not in their list of job duties and they refused to do it. After a three-day layoff as a penalty for their refusal to do the work assigned, the men filed a grievance asking for pay for the time off, claiming that the layoff was improper. What should the arbitrator decide? Why?

6. "I fill in for the boss whenever he isn't around." How should this situation be handled so far as job evaluation is concerned?

7. After a week's search, the personnel department has been unable to fill a request by the line foreman for a skilled boring mill operator. The only apparently qualified applicant wants $7 an hour whereas the company's rate for this work is $6.50. Surveys have indicated that the company's rates are in line with other companies in the area. Should the man be hired and paid $7? What alternatives are there? What are the implications of this problem for personnel, production control, and line management?

PROBLEMS

1. Place five piles of paper before you, then assemble sets of five in order and staple them. Make a chart of the method you used. If you had to do this by the thousands, what improvements in method can you suggest? Develop an improved method and estimate the percent savings.

2. The Champion Company's advertising department sends out thousands of direct mail pieces annually. A big item is a five-page booklet which is hand assembled, stapled, and inserted into a mailing carton. Last year this job took 2,000 hours of clerical time. Next year the volume will be 2½ times as much.

Harry Trolley, the methods man, is asked to see what he can do to improve the job. Here are his times for the present method:

Element	Minutes per 100 booklets
Assemble five sheets	5.46
Stack five sheets	4.92
Inspect assembled sheets	6.67
Staple	7.21
Shape carton	6.04
Insert into carton and aside	4.32
Replenish pages	1.47
Replenish cartons	2.39
Total	38.48

Trolley estimates that by installing a fixture costing $400 he will save .02 minute per booklet of the assembling element and another .02 minute of the stacking element. He also expects to save half of the replenishing time by having a materials handler preposition the pages and cartons in a special rack costing $50. The handler's time is not important in solving this problem since he is on the job anyway. Clerical time costs $5.50 an hour.

Disregarding coffee breaks and other time out, what is the yearly output using the present method? How much will the proposed method save (if it will save anything) during the coming year? If the new method saves money, how long will it take to get back from savings the money spent for fixtures? Does it appear that Trolley has exhausted the savings possibilities?

3. On machine M it takes .32 minute to unload a product from the machine and to load in the next part to be processed and .95 minute to machine the product. On machine N it takes .24 minute to unload and load and .85 minute for the machine to do the same work. Machine operating costs are $5 and $4 per hour respectively. The operators of both machines earn $5.50 an hour.

a. Make up a plan with one operator running both machines. Each machine is automatic, once it is started. But the machines do not stop automatically when they finish their operations; the operator must be there to stop them. A worker can, however, stop and unload a machine and then attend to the other machine before loading the first one. Machine unloading time is one fourth of the unload and load time.

b. As opposed to having two operators, one running each machine, how much will the company save (or lose) by the plan in (a)? How much operator idle time is there under each plan? How much machine idle time?

4. It costs $7.20 an hour to operate a retort to impregnate wood with a fire resistant chemical. The impregnating time (during which the retort is closed) is 38 minutes. It is possible to use 1, 2, 3, or 4 people working as a crew to change loads. The changing time is 33, 22, 17, and 15 minutes respectively, depending on the size of the crew. The workers have other work to do while the retort is closed, so there is no need to be concerned with them except during load changing times.

a. What is the optimum size crew if the workers are paid $7.50 an hour?

b. How much bonus could the company afford to give the workers if they reduced the changing time by 10 percent?

5. The Dix Company is building a parking lot and has to cut away a hill and use the dirt to fill a lower spot. It will be necessary to use a power shovel to scoop up the dirt and dump trucks to haul it. Here are the figures on how long this operation takes:

	Minutes
Load truck	6
Travel to dump area	5
Dump load	1
Return	4

a. This is a big job, and the power shovel costs money, so it is desirable to keep it busy. To do this, how many dump trucks will be needed?

b. What is the most economical combination if the shovel costs $40 an hour and the trucks $22 an hour? Use a chart if it would be helpful.

6. On a large-volume item, the following figures show the time it takes for one of the operations needed to make the item:

	Minutes
Unload machine..................	.2
Load.........................	1.7
Machine time..................	7.0

Several machines are doing this operation, and since the machines are automatic an operator can operate several machines. They are so close together that the time it takes to go from one machine to the other can be neglected. The machines do not, however, stop after they have finished their operations; the operator must be there to take out the finished pieces.

a. How many machines can a person operate? Draw up a worker-machine chart showing how your plan works, or make a tabulation of consecutive times showing what the operator is doing all the time.

b. Suppose that in answer (a) you have to concern yourself with costs and suppose that a worker costs $.12 a minute and machine idle time costs $.15 a minute. The object is to minimize costs. Is the answer still the same? Show your figures.

c. Is the answer any different if the machines stop automatically after completing their operation, thus freeing the worker from having to be there the moment the operation is finished?

d. If there were a large number of machines, is there any way to eliminate the idle time of both machines and workers?

7. The RUR Company has completed the evaluation of its factory jobs and is ready to set up labor grades and pay ranges for each job. From the many job ratings, the following have been selected as typical:

Job	Point rating	Hourly base rates used in the past	Job	Point rating	Hourly base rates used in the past
Automatic screw machine operator.............	275	$6.00	Machine operator (tool room)...........	311	$6.46
Bench lathe operator........	241	5.86	Punch press operator....	271	5.98
Bench work (filing and assembly)...............	164	5.61	Soldering..............	216	5.73
			Stores clerk...........	205	5.73
Casting grinder and polisher..................	209	5.93	Tool crib attendant.....	246	5.86
Drill press operator.........	224	5.81	Tool maker............	381	6.44
Milling machine operator....	311	6.09	Turret lathe operator....	331	6.26

Plot the ratings and base rates on a chart on coordinate paper. Using the least-squares method, compute the line of relationship between points and money. (The formula for the line is $Y = a + bX$. It can be plotted by solving the following two equations simultaneously: $\Sigma Y = na + b\Sigma X$ and $\Sigma XY = a\Sigma X + b\Sigma X^2$. The point ratings are the X values, the base rates are the Y values, n is the number of jobs. Note also that in algebraic notation ΣXY does not mean the sum of the X's multiplied by the sum of the Y's. It means the respective X's and Y's are multiplied by each other and then summed up. Similarly, ΣX^2 means to square the individual X's and then add them up.)

Set up ten labor grades based on the line, and in an accompanying table show the point limits for each grade; and using a $.05 per hour overlap, show the minimum and maximum wages to be paid for each grade.

Which jobs, if any, will have to have their base rates adjusted to bring them within the newly established limits?

CASE 13–1

The time study analyst has had a request to set a production standard on a new job done on milling machines. In line with his usual practice, he observed the operator perform the operation several times before starting to write down the times.

On similar jobs it is normal for the operator to fasten several pieces into the machine together and machine them all at the same time, much as a person might cut several pieces of paper at the same time on a paper cutter.

This was not the way the operator did it, however. He placed one piece carefully and then did the cutting operation on it, and then continued to the next pieces, but one at a time. The analyst asked the operator to put them in six at a time, but the latter refused, saying that this was the way he did the operation and this should be the way to be covered by the standard. The analyst called the supervisor and told him that he could not set the standard unless the job was done as it should be done.

The supervisor smiled and said: "Come on, Stan, give us a real study. You know you should mill six at a time." Whereupon the operator replied rather heatedly: "Look here, who is being time studied? You or me?"

What should be done? Who should decide work methods?

SUGGESTED SUPPLEMENTARY READINGS

Hackman, J. Richard. "Is Job Enrichment Just a Fad?" *Harvard Business Review,* September–October 1975, p. 129–38.

Nadler, Gerald. *Work Design: A Systems Concept.* Homewood, Ill.: Richard D. Irwin, Inc., 1970.

Susman, G. I. "Process Design, Automation, and Worker Alienation." *Industrial Relations,* February 1972.

14

Work measurement: Standards and incentives

STANDARDS are highly desirable for almost every kind of organized work. Managers need to have some idea of how long work will take, how many employees will be needed, and what it will cost. Only with this information can they make intelligent decisions about schedules, facilities, people needed, and costs and selling prices.

Holiday Inns needs to know how long it will take to clean a room and change the bedclothes after a guest leaves. American Airlines needs to know how long it will take to unload the baggage when an airplane lands. Smith-Corona needs to know how long it takes to put together a typewriter, and U.S. Steel needs to know how long it takes to make a steel rail.

In all of these cases, managers need to have some idea of the times it takes to do things. They measure the time that work usually takes and set standards so they can plan. But they don't stop here. After the event, they check to see if the standard was met. If it took longer than the standard called for, then it cost more than it should and used up some of both the time and money needed for other activities.

So the first use of standards is for planning and deciding what to do and what not to do and what things will cost. The second use is to compare what does happen with what is supposed to happen.

This leads to a third, and a very important, part of managerial work. The comparison between actual and expected will usually show a number of discrepencies. Most of the time the plan, the standard expectations, is not accomplished in all respects. Reasons for the discrepencies are then investigated and remedial actions taken, where possible, to help insure that expected accomplishment will occur in the future. Most of the work in this area falls in the realm of budgetary control, which is discussed in Chapter 16.

Here we are interested in the standards themselves and how to set them. Sometimes reasonably good standards can be set just by looking back at what has been done in the past. Holiday Inns, American Airlines, Smith-Corona, and U.S. Steel can look to the past and get rough answers to the questions we posed.

Yet setting standards for work just by looking back is not a very good way to do it. There is no "plus" in it. The time taken to do things in the past includes the method used as well as the casual pace so often found in unorganized work. Unless the job has been studied and a good method worked out, then the time taken in the past is almost surely more than it should be. It includes all of the inefficiencies of poor methods, and it includes all of the waste times that uncontrolled work always includes.

Properly set production standards specify the time it should take to do work when it is done in the best way. Such standards can be set only after the job has been analyzed and the best way determined and timed when performed by a normally proficient worker.

Saying that production standards are needed and that operations will be more effectively controlled if they are used is not to say that they are always used. Managers don't always use all of the managerial tools, including production standards, which are at their disposal. Furthermore, production can be accomplished without standards. Workers working on machines and materials will get something done. They will produce products, but without standards rarely will they produce as much as they would with standards. And, lastly, desirable though it is to have production standards, some kinds of work are not susceptible to measurement, so good standards cannot be set.

The discussion here will be centered on production standards as they are set and used in factory operating situations because these are usually well worked out. Sometimes, too, these same techniques can be adapted and used for determining standards in other settings, such as offices, banks, and services provided by governmental units.

In factories, production standards are most often set by time study methods with a stopwatch being used to time the work. In many companies the end product, the time standard, is used in setting piece rates for pieceworkers.[1]

There are also other important reasons for wanting standards. Consequently, many companies, which do not use piecework incentives, use time study and set up time standards. And conversely, a few companies which use incentives set their time standards without using time study.

---

[1] Production standards and time standards are the same thing. One says that a worker ought to do the job 20 times in an hour, and the other says that the job is a 3-minute job. Occasionally, when a standard is stated as a quota, the quota actually represents the quantity of production needed in a given period of time in order to keep unit costs down to the figure used in setting selling prices.

Aside from piecework, production standards are needed in order to find out what the work ought to cost, to estimate the cost of new jobs, and to determine what it costs to do work in alternative ways. Standards are needed in order to know how much work machines will turn out, and for scheduling work as well as for setting quotas for machine-paced work. They are also needed for work along assembly lines so that assemblers' work may be divided equally. And they are needed, too, for planning the number of machines and workers needed for future production.

CONCEPT OF A PRODUCTION STANDARD

A production standard embodies a concept of normality and reasonableness. Almost all jobs can be done fast, or slow, or in between. The idea of a standard implies choosing a particular rate as being reasonable and expected. Other performance is then regarded as better than standard or poorer than standard. The process of choosing and deciding normal times is implicit in standard setting, as is the fact that choosing means judging. Standards, therefore, always contain a subjective element of judgment. Standard setters cannot escape having to judge normality as they try to set fair and reasonable standards.

To illustrate how important this is, we might consider the simple task of walking a mile. If several men were to walk a mile, some of them would finish before the others. Perhaps the fastest man would finish in 15 minutes, the slowest man would take 30 minutes, and the others would be spread out in between, with most men taking 19 or 20 minutes. (A time of 20 minutes [3 miles per hour] is somewhat leisurely for most people.)

If it were cold weather or if rain were threatening, the average time would probably be less. The men would have an incentive not to dawdle. The same would be true if those who finished the mile in 20 minutes or less were to get a reward; probably almost everyone would make it and be rewarded. But, if only those who finished in less than 16 minutes were to be rewarded, fewer of the men would make it. A person has to hurry to walk a mile in 16 minutes, and to some of the men the incentive might not be enough to cause them to hurry this much.

Several points are involved here which are pertinent to setting production standards. The casual workaday pace of people differs, and their best performance capabilities also differ. So does their response to incentives. Furthermore, performances differ both because of chance variations (some of our walking men might have had to wait for traffic or a traffic light) and the effort a person is willing to exert. A person can go faster or he can slow down, as he wishes. All of these variations exist on production jobs. The time it takes workers to do jobs varies and for similar reasons.

It might seem that the proper way to set production standards would be to see how long a job takes in the overall and use that time as the standard. But this time observed would depend wholly on whom was observed and his performance during the period of observation. Returning to our walking men, the man we happened to pick to observe might be the one who walked a mile in 15 minutes or it might be the one who took 30 minutes. Of course, neither 15 nor 30 minutes would be reasonable to use as a standard. More certainty of reasonableness is needed than just accepting the time observed as standard.

The next step in the way of improvement in standard setting would seem to be to see how long a job takes on the average—over several performances and with several workers. This method is much better than using the time taken on one performance as the standard. Yet it is still not perfect as a standard setting procedure because the workers observed might all be fast (or slow), and, if this is so, their average time would not be a reasonable standard. If the workers observed were all very good, an average of their times would not allow enough time for the standard.

Using the average of the observed times is an imperfect solution also because workers have control over their work pace. If the time a worker takes is to become the standard, he would be working against his own best interest if he performed the task in his minimum time. It would only be human nature for him to slow down and stretch out the time. Furthermore, he would have few friends among his fellow workers if he did not try to get loose, easy to meet, standards. The surprising thing is that workers don't always slow down when standards are being set. There is enough slowing down, however, to make it unwise to accept observed times, even an average of several observed times, as being reliable for standards setting purposes.

It becomes necessary, therefore, not only to gather data on how long it takes to perform jobs but also to "pace rate" (judge the normality) the performances observed. If 10 men were observed walking 1 mile and they all did it between 15 and 17 minutes, their average would be 16 minutes, but this average is better than normal and should be rated as such by the standards setter. The pace rating should indicate that this is, let us say, 125 percent of standard. Thus the standard, when it is set, will allow more time than the 16 minutes actually taken; in this case 1.25 as much time, or 20 minutes in total.

Or, at the other extreme, the men observed could have walked very slowly and averaged, perhaps, 25 minutes. If this were so, the standard setter's pace rating should be below 100. This time, when he calculates the standard time, he should arrive at something less than the average of the times observed. If their performance was rated at 80, then .8 of the time observed will become the standard and .8 × 25 = 20 minutes. Again, a 20-minute mile would be regarded as the standard.

As we said, it is necessary for the standards setter to judge the normalcy of the pace observed, but the concept of normal is somewhat abstract. As applied to factory jobs, it should be the pace, or time, that it would take an ordinary, experienced worker to do a job while applying himself in a normally diligent fashion (but not his pace when he is really pressing himself).

This concept of normality is particularly important where wage incentives are used because the production standard is the basis on which a worker's bonus is calculated. If a job is regarded as a 5-minute job, then the worker is expected to perform the job 12 times in an hour before he starts to earn a bonus. Production of 15 units would earn him a 25-percent bonus. Should 6 minutes be regarded as the standard time, however, the worker would get a bonus for all production in excess of 10 an hour. If he could get up to 15 units, he would get a 50-percent bonus. Thus, the *reasonableness* of the standard is very important.

NUMBER OF CYCLES TO TIME

Production standards are usually set by a standards setter (a time study engineer) who watches the operator doing the work and writes down how long it takes him to do each part of the job. When the operator finishes his job, he repeats it on another unit of product, and this goes on and on. If the analyst watches only a few work cycles, he gets a fairly good idea of how long the job takes, yet his findings are not as reliable as they would be if he watched a larger number of cycles. One question, therefore, is how many cycles are enough to provide reliable figures rather than just happenstance averages which might differ from typical job averages.

For the moment we will overlook the possibility that the worker slows down while being studied. Most companies want the calculated time value to have a 95-percent probability or more—of being within 5 percent of the true average of observed times. So they set up tables for analysts to use, tables which specify how many work cycles to study in order to provide the desired reliability. Westinghouse uses the table shown in Figure 14–1.

It is, of course, very important to observe enough cycles so that enough times are recorded to provide reliable averages. Yet the standards setter should not mislead himself by thinking that many recordings will of necessity give him a more accurate average time to use as the job standard. If the worker slows down, he can slow down almost as easily for many cycles as for a few, in which case the average of his times will be an average of poor performances. Thus, there is little safety in large numbers of observations. The analyst will still have to rely on his pace rating adjustment in order to set a proper standard.

NEED FOR TIMING JOBS BY ELEMENTS

As was suggested, it might seem that the way to time a job would be to look at the clock when the job starts and again when it ends. The

FIGURE 14–1

| Cycle time | Number of cycles per year | | |
	10,000	1,000–10,000	1–1,000
	Number of cycles to study		
8 hours.....................	2	1	1
3..........................	3	2	1
2..........................	4	2	1
1..........................	5	3	2
48 minutes.................	6	3	2
30..........................	8	4	3
20..........................	10	5	4
12..........................	12	6	5
8..........................	15	8	6
5 minutes..................	20	10	8
3..........................	25	12	10
2..........................	30	15	12
1..........................	40	20	15
.7..........................	50	25	20
.5 minutes.................	60	30	25
.3..........................	80	40	30
.2..........................	100	50	40
.1..........................	120	60	50

elapsed time is the time for the job. But even apart from the pace rating problem, this is too simple a method to give accurate results.

In order to get accurate results, it is necessary to consider the separate parts of each job and to time each part and this in spite of the fact that the parts add up to the whole. When the analyst considers the job part by part (he calls these parts "elements") and watches the worker do the whole job several times, he finds two things. First, he finds that the time the worker takes to do parts of the job vary and, second, that the sub-parts of the job, as it is performed, are not always exactly the same every time the worker does the operation.

If the analyst timed the job only on an overall basis, he would never know about either of these things. Or, if he noticed them, he wouldn't know what to do about them. So, in order to figure out a proper rate, he needs to write down a list of the job elements and to time them separately.

Writing down the times for each element's performance helps the analyst get a better idea of how long each regular job element takes. In successive work cycles the amount of time it takes to perform an element varies somewhat. The time study analyst needs to consider these differences when he makes his choice of the time to use as the element's time.

Writing down separate element times also helps him arrive at the appropriate time to allow for irregular elements, those which occur only now and then. He needs to know how long they take when they occur as well as how often they occur. Furthermore, some of these irregular elements will prove to be necessary for the job, but some are likely to be unnecessary. Operators sometimes do extra things that are not part of the regular job in order to add to the job's time. And workers also sometimes perform the occasional but necessary parts of the job more often than is necessary.

Both of these actions by workers make the job take longer than usual during the period of observation. In order to arrive at a proper production standard, the analyst needs to exclude all extraneous elements. Yet, he must be sure to include the time needed to be taken for all necessary but irregular elements according to how often they ought to occur.

TAKING THE STUDY

The first thing the analyst does when he starts to collect data for a production standard is to decide the job's elements, the parts of the job he will time separately. Then he writes the element descriptions in sequence on his recording sheet preparatory to recording their times.

This can be seen in Figure 14–2, which is a time study on an operator assembling roller skates and packing them into cartons. In Figure 14–2

FIGURE 14–2

Element	Time in hundredths of a minute					
Preassemble toe clips..................	08	36	315	55	47	94
	8	*14*	*16*	*13*	*10*	*13*
Toe clips to frame and run on...........	30	55	33	76	72	811
	22	*19*	*18*	*21*	*25*	*17*
Assemble front wheels to frame.........	47	70	47	506†	86	27
	17	*15*	*14*	*(30)*	*13*	*16*
Tighten axle nut and aside.............	56	80	62	16	95	37
	9	*10*	*15*	*10*	*9*	*10*
Assemble rear wheels to frame...........	71	93	88*	29	710	54
	15	*13*	*(26)*	*13*	*15*	*17*
Tighten axle nut and aside.............	82	205	99	42	35‡	63
	11	*12*	*11*	*13*	*(25)*	*9*
Attach frame halves, bolt and nut on.....	100	28	418	64	55	79
	18	*23*	*19*	*22*	*20*	*16*
Tighten nut and skate, aside...........	22	53	42	87	81	900
	22	*25*	*23*	*23*	*26*	*21*
Skates, straps, and ankle cushion pads into carton liner.....................		83		620		31
		30		*33*		*31*
Carton liner into and close carton, aside...........................		99		37		53
		16		*17*		*22*

* Picked up wrong piece.
† Received instructions from foreman.
‡ Dropped nut off axle.
Performance rating for whole job: 110.

the elements are "Preassemble toe clips," "Toe clips to frame and run on," and so on.[2]

From here on the analyst writes in the time it takes to perform the elements. Usually he lets his stopwatch run continuously and records its reading at the end of each element. Later he subtracts the elements' ending times from their starting times to get the net time for each element (hence the two sets of times for each element in Figure 14–2).

In Figure 14–2 the elements succeed each other in vertical sequence. Thus, for the first work cycle, element 1 took $\frac{8}{100}$ of a minute, element 2 was finished at $\frac{30}{100}$, element 3 was finished at $\frac{47}{100}$, and so on. When the operator finished the first roller skate, he went right on to the second one, and again the element times follow in vertical sequence. This time, however, the operator had a pair of skates, so he packed them into a carton, and he continued in this way after every second roller skate.

Before leaving the job, the analyst should also record his pace rating of the operator's performance so that he can later make the appropriate adjustment when he calculates the standard time. In our roller skate assembly study this rating was 110.

SETTING THE STANDARD

The first step in setting the standard from the raw data is to subtract the elements' ending times from their starting times. This was done in Figure 14–2, producing the actual time that each element took. These times are in italics and are the figures used in the calculation from this point on.

There are several readings for each element, and it can be seen in Figure 14–2 that the individual times vary somewhat. In this analysis we used a simple arithmetic average of the element times observed, except that the times in parentheses were omitted as not typical.

These averages appear in Figure 14–3 as the *element time* figures. Next, these times were multiplied by how often the element occurs per unit of output. When our sample study was taken, the analyst timed putting on the skate's front wheels and tightening the axle bolt as different from assembling the back wheels, but these turned out to be identical activities; so, in the write up in Figure 14–3, putting wheels on appears as only one element but is said to occur four times per pair of skates.

After each element's time was multiplied by how often it occurred, the typical cycle time was totaled up as 3.027 minutes. To this was added a 12-percent allowance for fatigue and personal time. Next, the 110 percent performance rating was used, causing the addition of 10 percent more time and a total time standard of 3.729 minutes per pair of skates.

---

[2] This study was done in a college classroom as a demonstration and with only the skate key for a tool. Obviously, this work would go much faster when done in a factory on a repetitive basis and with appropriate tools used at a properly designed work place by an experienced worker.

FIGURE 14–3

			Time in minutes
Element	*Frequency*	*Element time*	*Time per pair of skates*
Preassemble toe clips...................... 2		.123	.246
Toe clips on frame......................... 2		.203	.406
Assemble two wheels....................... 4		.148	.592
Tighten axle nut.......................... 4		.108	.432
Attach frame halves....................... 2		.197	.394
Tighten frame nut and bolt................. 2		.233	.466
Pack two skates into carton liner............ 1		.313	.313
Insert liner into carton and aside............ 1		.183	.183
Total average cycle time observed.................................			3.032
Add 12% for fatigue and personal time..........................			.363
			3.395
Adjust for performance rating of 110%..........................			.339
Time standard in minutes per pair................................			3.734

Standard hourly output: 60 ÷ 3.734 = 16.1 pairs per hour
Piece rate at $4.50 an hour: $4.50 ÷ 16.1 = $.28 per pair

This method, as described here, is typical of how time standards are set. Personal and fatigue allowances are sometimes set a little lower, perhaps at 10 percent.

Many factory jobs, of course, are more complicated than assembling roller skates. If they have quite a few miscellaneous elements that are done irregularly, this makes it difficult to find out how much time to allow for them. One way is to take a much more extended time study and handle such elements on a proportional basis, just as we did with putting the skates into cartons.

This, however, may take a long time to do well because of the infrequency of many such elements. Sometimes, therefore, the analyst turns to "work sampling" (explained later in this chapter). If an operator is observed performing miscellaneous tasks one fifth of his time and main elements four fifths of his time, it is assumed that miscellaneous elements take one fourth as much time as main elements and they are therefore given one fourth the time of main elements.

MACHINE TIME WITHIN WORK CYCLES

Many factory machines are semiautomatic; once they are set up and the material is inserted, the machines perform all the operations. All that the operator does is take out the product just finished and put in the next one. While the machine works, there is nothing for the operator to do, so there is a question of how the element "wait for machine" should be handled in the production standard. If the wait is short or if the machine needs watching, "wait for machine" should be listed along with all of the other elements and incorporated into the standard. If a job takes 2 minutes to unload and load and then a ½ minute wait while the machine runs, this would be a 2½ minute production standard. But if unload and load time is 2 minutes and then the machine runs by itself for 10 minutes, this job probably should be considered a 2-minute, not a 12-minute, job. The operator is given other work to do during his idle 10 minutes—possibly operating other machines.

SETUP AND CHANGE TIME

Machines nearly always have to be "set up" for each job or changed over from the previous job. The tools, tool holders, material holders, and so on all must be put in place and adjusted. But before that starts, the old setup from the last job has to be torn down and its tools and gadgetry put away. Besides this, the operator usually has to make a trip to the tool crib to return his last-used tooling and get the next tooling, and perhaps a drawing. Along the way he rings out on his old-job time card and rings in for his new job.

The work of setting up on many semiautomatic machines is often done by a setup mechanic who does nothing else. He is usually paid by the hour, so there are no production standards for tearing down and setting up.

Many workers on incentive pay plans, however, are on jobs where they set up their own machines and then run them themselves. There are three choices (none of which is perfect) of how to pay for setting up: (1) pay for it by the hour, (2) set standards for setting up and pay for it on an incentive plan, (3) put the setup time in with the running time on a pro rata basis and have one production standard cover both setting up and running the machine.

Number 1, paying for setup at an hourly rate, is a somewhat unsatisfactory choice, particularly if a pieceworker is to be paid his regular job's base rate for it. Since he is earning no bonus doing this work, he feels that his pay is cut while he is setting up. But if he is paid his average earnings, including his usual bonus, while setting up jobs without standards, he will take a rest while doing it. In fact, on his time card he may exaggerate the time the setting up takes and so boost his earnings.

Number 2, having standards for the setup jobs, is a better choice, and the best so far as incentives are concerned. But it is poor in that there must be hundreds of standards for hundreds of kinds of setups. These standards are slow and costly to make up because the same setups don't turn up very often and they take a long time when they do turn up. Weeks may pass before the time study analyst can have an opportunity to watch even two or three setups of a given kind. Also, the operator can sometimes use part of the previous job's tooling, so that complete setups are not always required. (A similar problem arises in processing situations, as, for example, in paint mixing. It takes more time to clean the equipment and go from black to white than from white to black because in the former case the equipment has to be cleaned more thoroughly.)

Number 3, allowing time for setup on a pro rata basis within the regular rate, is chosen sometimes and is a fairly satisfactory method. It does not solve the difficulty of having to do considerable standards setting work, nor of having to set standards for setups based on very few observations, or of partial setups. It *does* avoid having hundreds of standards for setups on the records, but they have to be set anyway before they can be put into the standard for operating a machine on an average basis, so there is no saving of standard setting effort.

Putting setup time into the standard for operating a machine on a pro rata basis usually works reasonably well but not if the average length of run changes a great deal—if, for example, a machine requires a minor new setup for every new job—as for example would occur with a printing press. The main job is running sheets of paper through the press. From past experience the analyst knows about how many sheets are usually run off each time. Assuming an average run is 200 sheets, the operating time for turning out 200 sheets is 4 minutes. If we assume that it takes 2 minutes to change to a new job, these two times can be added together, and we find that it will take 6 minutes to run off 200 sheets of paper, or 3 minutes per 100.

This works fine if the runs average 200. But, if the operator gets numerous orders for 25 sheets, he has to run 8 such orders to turn out 200 sheets. He will spend 4 minutes running the machine and 16 minutes changing to new jobs, a total of 20 minutes. Yet, the standard gives him only 6 minutes' credit and 6 minutes' pay. On the other hand, he might get a run of 1,000. He takes 20 minutes to run them off plus 2 minutes' change time, a total of 22 minutes, but the standard allows 30 minutes.

Including anything—in this case setup time—on a pro rata basis makes standards tight or loose if the frequency of occurrence changes.

PROBLEMS IN SETTING PRODUCTION STANDARDS

Most of the problems in setting production standards center on situations where the analyst has to use judgment. And of these, "pace rating" (also called leveling) is probably the most open to question. It is apparent that some particular pace ought to be thought of as reasonable and that this pace should not be either a worker's best or poorest performance. Yet, it is hard to convince everyone that the end result, the time standard, is exactly right when everyone knows that the times allowed contain an adjustment reflecting the analyst's judgment of normal.

No better way seems to be available than to have the standard setter make such a leveling judgment. Some companies try to refine this by having the analyst make several pace ratings, one for each element, and adjust each element's average time to "normal" before summing up the times to get the whole-job standard. A very few companies even try to have their analysts rate every occurrence of every element. Probably such extra effort on their part produces a better standard; yet, the process is still one of judging.

It might seem that the need to judge pace could be reduced or even eliminated by studying all the members of a group and using their average time as the standard. But we have already noted that this is unfair to groups of good workers who turn out more work than a fair standard should call for. And we also noted that such a standard would be equally wrong if it were an average of slow performers. There is the added difficulty that there are only one or two workers on a good many jobs. And there is the still greater difficulty that workers who are being studied usually slow down somewhat, be they one or ten in number. As was said earlier, there is no safety in numbers.

Judgment must also be exercised in the matter of how often certain things should be done. An operator may have to stop the operation in order to gage the material, or sharpen a tool, or replace a broken or worn tool. But, how often must he stop the operation to sharpen the tool? When has it become dull enough to need sharpening? It is a matter of judging. In occasional cases, there is even a question of whether certain elements are really needed at all as part of the job. Sometimes the work is really someone else's work. Again, judging plays a part in the setting of the standard.

LIMITATIONS TO USE OF TIME STUDY

Production standards can be and are used in many instances where the work itself cannot be timed. Most such production standards, however, are only approximations. Rarely are they as good as time study standards; yet, approximate standards are usually better than none. The weaknesses of time study as a method for setting production standards can be enumerated as follows:

1. An analyst can time only what he can see. This eliminates the timing of the thinking parts of jobs and leaves only manual jobs.

2. If an analyst times a job, it has to be a specific job—with starting and stopping points and separable into units so that it is possible to count how many times it is done. This cannot be done with, say, the work of a janitor, or plant guard, or with most office jobs.

3. It doesn't pay to set standards for some jobs because they are not repetitive enough. The gain from setting standards for a small job that will be done only once or twice in the future won't pay for the analytical work. Standards setting by time study is limited to repetitive jobs.

4. Nor does it pay to time jobs and set standards on them when workers do a great many things. A maintenance department carpenter, for example, does too many things to have standards for all of them (his daily

work report would sometimes be several pages long). Also, it is too costly to verify what he says he did. And when no one checks reports, many workers on piecework will report that they have turned out more work than they did.

5. It usually doesn't pay to have standards for only part of an operator's work. If it isn't possible to put all of their work on standards, some workers will exaggerate the time they report spent on daywork (for which they get paid by the hour) and so keep their earnings up. A worker may have spent four hours on piecework and four on day-work (not in single stretches of time but all mixed up during the day), but he may report that he did the piecework in three hours and the day-work in five hours, and no one can prove that he didn't. It looks as if he did nine hours' work in the day (four hours of piecework [done in three hours] plus five hours of daywork) instead of eight. The foreman is put on the spot of having to give him nine hours of pay or arbitrarily (although perhaps correctly) cutting his claim of five hours of daywork to four.

6. If quality is hard to define (as in polishing a surface), standards and production incentives may cause quality to fall off. The operator may say that he has done the job well enough when he hasn't.

The analyst should think twice before accepting this criticism of production standards, though. If a worker is not on piecework but is on daywork instead, he might, and if he is allowed to, maybe will, shine a polished surface all day and be proud of the fine job he does. Unfortunately, he cannot be allowed to spend so much time on an operation that it makes the cost go way up. Jobs where quality is hard to define are exactly the places where production standards, as well as quality standards, are needed.

7. Unions often oppose time study; and, where a union is opposed and where it is very strong, it may be able to stop or preclude time study work. Standards might be set by other methods but not by time study.

WORK SAMPLING

Work sampling (occasionally called ratio-relay study) means observing, at irregular time intervals, what is going on. An analyst goes past a work place, say 500 times, over a period of weeks and notes what the operator is doing each time. Perhaps an office secretary might be observed typing 250 times, filing 150 times, telephoning 50 times, and doing personal things 50 times. Thus, 50 percent of her time is spent on typing, 30 percent on filing, 10 percent on telephoning, and 10 percent on other things.

This method can be used to find out how often the minor job elements of factory jobs occur and so provide the information needed to incorporate time for them into factory production standards. Work sampling can also be used to set complete standards for factory jobs and not just the time for the miscellaneous parts of jobs. Work sampling is also useful for setting production standards for hard-to-set work, such as most office work.

Work sampling is often thought of as a low-cost way to set standards, and this may be true. Yet this is not always true because the job being observed may require a trip for each observation; also, the observations should be taken at various times of the day and not be concentrated in the hours when the observer may happen to be near the operation. Also, it takes a long time to get 500 observations. If, for example, 500 observations are wanted, it will take 50 a day for 2 weeks.

One advantage of work sampling is that it probably represents true-to-life situations. Operators don't get much chance to dress up their performance to try to mislead the analyst. Against this is the disadvantage that there is no pace rating. In order to set a standard without pace rating, the analyst would have to know how many units were turned out in a day. Both a fast and a slow typist might very well be typing 50 percent of the time, but the fast typist types more pages in a day. Thus, there would be a question of how many pages to expect in a day. Work sampling does not get at this and is therefore of limited value in standards setting.

OTHER WAYS TO SET PRODUCTION STANDARDS

Production standards for semiautomatic machines are sometimes set by starting with a machine's ultimate output possibilities. Something less than this, say 90 percent of perfect output, is then decided to be the best that can be hoped for. Then a decision is made that even 90 percent of perfect is very good and that this much output merits a bonus, perhaps 25 percent. So 90 percent of the best expected production is regarded as being 125 percent of standard, and so the standard is $100 \div 125 \times .90$, or 72 percent of perfect. Thus, if a machine could, theoretically, turn out 500 pieces an hour, 450 units would be regarded as top production and the standard would be 360 units per hour. A pieceworker who turned out 450 would earn a 25-percent bonus.

Production standards for piecework purposes are sometimes set by direct negotiation between a company's industrial engineers and the union's standards committee. In the shoe and textile industries it is common for these people to sit down together, look over the new patterns, compare them to the old patterns and standards, and thereupon agree on the new standards. Such a practice, however, would be unusual in other industries.

Another method for setting standards, which is used commonly enough to merit mention, is simple estimation. The foreman or an experienced estimator looks at a drawing or product design and, based on his past experience, estimates how long the work should take. Contractors in the building trades have to do this all the time when they bid on contracts to build houses. And in factories, too, this may be about the best that can be done when it comes to setting a standard for making such a product as a dust collecting duct system for a construction project.

PRODUCTION STANDARDS FOR OFFICE WORK

Most office work is different in nature from most factory work. Usually it is not possible to set office production standards by using stopwatches and timing jobs. In practice, office standards (except for budgets) are not used very often. They are sometimes used, however, when office jobs can be timed in the same way as factory jobs. In other cases work sampling is used.

STANDARD DATA

New jobs are often similar in many respects to old jobs. Often, certain parts of a new job are identical to parts of old jobs. In such cases, using the time values from old standards for the same activities would save considerable standards setting costs. This situation is common enough that time values for certain activities and sets of movements can be regarded as established data that are available for use in future standards.

Such standard data are of two main kinds. One uses job element times from past studies in what can be called a "macroscopic" method. The other regards all jobs as collections of very short or minute movements, which can be called a "microscopic" method. Once someone makes a catalog of their times, no one ever has to do it again—for any job. All anyone has to do is list every little movement an operator makes, get the time for each movement out of the catalog, and add the times up.

Macroscopic methods are like building a prefab house: The analyst works with the big parts (elements) of a job, just as a prefab house is made from preassembled sections of walls, floors, cabinets, windows, and roofs. Microscopic methods are like building an ordinary house—out of bricks, nails, boards, and glass. Such jobs are made up of little movements: reach, pick up, carry, insert, and so on.

Macroscopic methods are limited to particular operations, such as operating a turret lathe, and they apply to any and all jobs done on that size and kind of lathe. Microscopic methods are universal and can be used for all operations and all jobs.

Macroscopic methods

Macroscopic methods use standard data which are often put into formula form and so can be easily computerized. Sometimes they are put into precomputed tables, and sometimes they are presented in charts.

Macroscopic methods assume that, as between jobs done on the same machine or similar machines, certain elements are constant irrespective of the specific operation. Oiling a machine's bearings takes the same amount of time irrespective of the job the operator is working on. So does blowing or brushing out chips. So does loosening or tightening tool holder jaws.

Certain other elements are variable. The time it takes to drill a hole, for example, or to plane or grind a surface depends on the depth and diameter of the hole or the size of the area to be planed or smoothed and how much metal is to be removed. The times for the job element varies, *but in a predictable way.* Other elements, such as making spot welds, are constant, but their total time depends on how many times they need doing.

In all of these cases the analyst, by looking at a drawing, can predict the time an element will take on a new job. Most elements are either clearly constant or they are variable. And in almost all cases where an element's time varies, the analyst can determine, by formula, how long it will take. He can then list the times for constant elements and the calculated times for variable elements. Adding these figures produces production standards for new jobs without waiting for them to be done.

Microscopic methods

In Chapter 13, therbligs—the basic, minute movements which make up all of a person's physical movements—were discussed. They provide the basis for the microscopic method for setting job standards.

Industrial engineers have developed lists of minute human movements (reach, grasp, move hands, and so on) and have also, by using high-speed moving pictures, studied these movements carefully and set a time value for each. Catalogs of times for these minute movements are available, and part of such a catalog is shown in Figure 14–4.

The time values shown in such a catalog are listed in very short inter-

FIGURE 14–4

Time values for therblig "reach" in TMUs (.0006 minutes)

Distance moved (inches)	Kind of movement					Case and description
	A	B	C	D		
¾ or less	2.0	2.0	2.0	2.0	A.	Reach to object in fixed loca-
1	2.5	2.5	3.6	2.4		tion, or to object in other
2	4.0	4.0	5.9	3.8		hand or on which other hand
3	5.3	5.3	7.3	5.3		rests.
4	6.1	6.4	8.4	6.8	B.	Reach to single object in loca-
5	6.5	7.8	9.4	7.4		tion which may vary slightly
6	7.0	8.6	10.1	8.8		from cycle to cycle.
8	7.9	10.1	11.5	9.3	C.	Reach to object jumbled with
10	8.7	11.5	12.9	10.5		other objects in a group so
15	11.0	15.1	16.3	13.6		that search and select occur.
20	13.1	18.6	19.8	16.7	D.	Reach to a very small object
25	15.4	22.2	23.2	19.8		or where accurate grasp is re-
30	17.5	25.8	26.7	22.9		quired.

Source: MTM Association for Standards and Research.

vals. Perhaps the best known type of these catalogs of times is called methods time measurement (MTM). MTM times are shown in TMUs (time measurement units), which are $\frac{1}{100,000}$ of an hour (30 TMUs = 1 second).

To use microscopic methods, the analyst lists the operator's movements in great detail and then looks at a catalog of times to see how long each movement will take. This work is not for the amateur since an operator sometimes is doing one thing with one hand and another with the other. The analyst has to pay attention to which time to use.

Proponents of microscopic methods say that by using these methods an analyst can get very accurate time standards more quickly than by any other means. They also claim that the thorough investigation needed to write up the bits of a job causes the analyst to see so many places to improve the job that he is always able to make numerous improvements.

MTM standards are usually quite accurate but each one takes a good bit of time to set up, even with the catalog of times available. The time required and the cost entailed are serious handicaps in companies where the labor contract requires standards to be set within three days on all new jobs. And this is a common requirement.

To meet this problem, MSD (master standard data), GPD (general purpose data), and MCD (master clerical data) have been developed— to shorten the standard setting time. These adaptations of MTM combine sets of therblig data into bigger "building blocks," not so big as time study elements but big enough to reduce drastically the MTM standard setting job. Using bigger building blocks reduces the cost of setting standards and thereby allows its use in more places, including offices.

In some companies MSD, GPD, and MCD are kept on computer tapes, which has further lessened the time and cost of setting standards. IBM, not unnaturally, is one of the companies which uses computer files for such basic data. The standards setter just lists the code for each basic data time and a computer calculates the standard.

H. B. Maynard and Company, a consulting organization, and the principal proponent of MTM, has also developed a simplified version of MTM which it calls MOST (Maynard Operation Sequence Technique). MOST eliminates much of the time consuming detail of MTM by working with groups of movements instead of specific individually detailed movements.[3]

IMPLEMENTING STANDARDS

We have been discussing the matter of setting standards as if the job were complete when the standard is set. Yet, in one sense, this is only part of the job. Standard setting should be more than measuring. It

---

[3] This method is described in Kjell B. Zandin, "Better Work Management with MOST," *Management Review,* July 1975, pp. 11–17.

should also be an implementation process. In order for standards to make their fullest contribution, they have to be accepted and used.

Acceptance starts with the start of the standards setting procedure. The operator should be told ahead by his supervisor that a study is going to be made of his job. It should be explained to him that the standards setter is an expert at what he does and that he, the operator, is an expert at running the machine. All of this by way of leading up to an expectation that the two of them are expected to work together to develop a fair and honest standard.

After the data are collected, the standards engineer should go over the figures with the operator to see if anything was omitted, or if anything should be deleted, and if the frequencies are reasonable. This is both to improve the accuracy of the data and to help show the operator that the figures are right.

If there are differences, they should be resolved before the standard is set and preferably by the operator and the engineer themselves. Such differences should be resolved to the satisfaction of the operator, the engineer, and the supervisor. This process is very helpful in producing acceptance of the standard when it is set. Interestingly, doing all of this is reported not to be a seriously time-consuming step.

Only after such decisions and agreement should the standard be set. After it is set, the operator should be told what it is.

The standard should be backed up by the detailed record of the work method which it covers. Variations and changes from this method should be watched for and new standards set when methods change.

Such an approach to standards setting should improve both their quality and their acceptability. Part of the improvement comes from the standards engineer himself having to do his best job all the time since his work is always reviewed by the operator.

METHODS OF PAYING FOR WORK

Most people have to work for a living, and most people do not have enough money laid aside to be wholly free from being interested in the amount of their pay. They have to live on their wage or salary so their pay is very important to them.

At bottom levels most people are paid an hourly rate. Except where the work is paid for by piecework, this means that the pay rate for the job is the one established by job evaluation. A person's pay is the hourly rate multiplied by the number of hours worked. Besides this there may be extras such as for high production or for overtime. (This differs from "take-home" pay because of deductions for income taxes, social security taxes, union dues, and possibly others.)

In a relatively few cases, bottom-level factory workers are paid monthly salaries. This contrasts with office workers who are almost always paid salaries. High-level managers in business firms as well as most salespeople are paid bonuses for good performance. Bonuses are, however, almost never paid to government employees nor to managers of nonprofit service organizations such as hospitals.

PAYING FOR TIME WORKED

Paying workers by the hour (sometimes called "daywork") or by monthly salary has both advantages and disadvantages. In its favor are that it is easy to understand and to calculate and it avoids the troublesome problem of trying to measure people's outputs. Its administrative costs are low.

But it has one serious weakness: It overlooks what workers do. A worker's productivity plays almost no part in his wage. Once a worker gets to the top of the job's pay bracket (and nearly all workers soon get there) the only reward left for the worker is satisfaction from doing his work well, praise from his supervisor, and possibly promotion to a higher-paying job. Payment by the hour, or by salary, has very low incentive value. A good producer gets no more pay than a mediocre producer.

Measured daywork

In factories, "measured daywork" is an attempt to couple high production with high hourly rates, but this is suitable only where productivity can be measured. A high daily quota is set, and the worker is given a high hourly pay rate for meeting it. Both the output expectations and the pay are usually higher than with regular pay by the hour. When a given quantity of output, and no more or less is wanted, measured daywork is often satisfactory. It has an advantage over regular hourly pay in that the company gets more production out of its machines, thus holding costs down and at the same time the workers earn higher pay rates.

INCENTIVE PAY SYSTEMS

Incentive pay systems offer more money for more output. Most workers, if given a chance to earn more by turning out more output, respond by producing more. Good producers earn more money than poor performers.

Consulting industrial engineers generally believe that incentive workers outproduce nonincentive workers by at least one third. Psychologist Edward Lawler says, "Even the most conservative studies seem to suggest that incentive plans can increase productivity from 10 to 20 percent.[4]

Typically, incentive workers earn bonuses amounting to perhaps 20 percent or more over their base pay. The starting points for incentive pay

---

[4] Quoted in Mildred E. Katzell, *Productivity: The Measure and the Myth,* (Amacom, 1975), p. 5.

systems are job base rates and production standards. A worker is paid the job's base hourly rate for standard production or less, with production in excess of standard being rewarded with extra pay. Many years ago there were many kinds of formulas for the calculation of bonuses, most of which paid less than proportional extra pay for extra output. Today, probably almost every incentive plan pays proportionally extra for extra output.

It might seem that there would be little reason for a company to pay proportional extra pay for extra output since the company would not gain anything. The unit cost of the product would stay the same. There is a gain, however, in lower machine and overhead costs per unit. So, since incentives normally result in greater productivity, they reduce total costs.

Incentive plans based on individual worker productivity are perhaps a little less common today than they were many years ago.[5] Curiously, incentives are much more common in Europe than in the United States. Here, it is estimated that perhaps no more than one fourth of all hourly paid workers work on incentive plans, whereas in Europe the figure is over 50 percent.

In the United States, mechanization, automation, and assembly lines have changed jobs both by transferring skill and work to machines and by making workers more into machine tenders and members of work crews or groups rather than independent workers. When they are paced by the speed of the line, they cannot turn out more products than the line allows just by their working harder. And, today, because there are more people doing service type work, there are more jobs which are not satisfactory for regular production incentives.

Nonetheless, individual incentive plans are very much the rule in the textile and clothing industries and in the shoe industry. And by no means have incentive plans disappeared from metal working shops. In the steel industry, incentives of the group kind are the rule. Some 60 percent of the factory workers in these industries work on incentives.

Curiously, some worker groups, such as the United Automobile Workers, are strongly opposed to incentives (only 5 percent of factory workers in Detroit work on incentives), whereas the United Steel Workers and the United Electrical Workers will go on strike rather than give them up.

Over a period of time incentives tend to become negative, and, from a psychological point of view, this is unfortunate. If a worker is offered more money for extra productivity, and, if he works hard and is rewarded with extra pay, this is positive. But time passes. The worker keeps on working hard and earning extra pay until he gets used to it. From then on he no longer thinks of his pay as being made up of two segments:

---

[5] The U.S. Bureau of Labor in its *Monthly Labor Review* publishes, from time to time, results of surveys of the use of incentives.

the main part for doing his job and the extra portion for being very productive.

Once he gets used to thinking of his total pay as the usual thing, the incentive becomes negative. He cannot work harder and earn still greater pay. On the contrary, if he does not keep up his high level of productivity he will earn less. So, since he can do no better, only worse sometimes (then his pay would go down), the incentive system is negative from this point on.

PROBLEMS WITH INCENTIVES

Incentive plans pay extra for output above the standard: A first problem, therefore, concerns the standard itself. Normally, production standards are set by time study procedures and even though this method is reasonably satisfactory, production standards are somewhat dependent on judgment. Workers sometimes object to them claiming that they call for too much output.

Another problem is that standards get out of date. To continue to be accurate, they should be reset every time a job changes, however little. And although industrial engineers should reset all standards when the jobs change, this is not always done right away or even later. (The engineers may not even know about some job changes.) And since most changes reduce the time it takes to do jobs, it is not long before some of the standards do not ask for enough production.

Another problem concerns pay raises. If everyone gets a raise, all piece rates have to be recalculated. Furthermore, if pay raises are incorporated into the piece rates, workers who have been earning large bonuses get a bigger pay raise than those who have been earning small bonuses. The latter don't get the same pay raise that the good workers get. To avoid this problem, general pay raises have to be kept apart and not incorporated into the piece rates. An employee's pay is then made up of his piece rate earnings plus the pay raise, which is added as an extra "override" or "overlay." The override is the same amount for good and poor workers alike.

"Across-the-board" pay raises where everyone gets the same amount of increase (and negotiated pay raises are often of this kind) makes, over the years, a serious problem even if incentives are not used. If high-skilled jobs originally paid twice the rate of low-skilled jobs, successive across-the-board raises wash out the relative differential. If a laborer once got $2.50 an hour and a tool and die maker got $5.00, the difference was 100 percent. But, if, over the years across-the-board pay raises amount to $5.00 an hour, then the laborer gets $7.50 and the tool and die maker gets $10.00, a difference of 33 percent.

"Cola" (cost of living adjustments) has accentuated this problem. When new labor contracts are negotiated (usually every three years), wage increases may be agreed upon to be different for unskilled and skilled groups. But nearly all labor contracts today contain a provision giving everyone automatic pay raises during the period of the contract if the cost of living goes up. These pay raises are usually the same amount of money for everyone and are, in effect, across-the-board increases.

Although not all pay increases are negotiated as across-the-board equal increases, enough of this has gone on to generate a great deal of dissatisfaction among skilled workers.

Other problems with incentives include the following:

1. Piecework brings out the dishonesty in people: Some employees will exaggerate the number of pieces when they report how much work they do.
2. There are problems of quality: Since workers are paid for the *quantity* of work they turn out (that is, the quantity that passes inspection), quality will suffer unless quality standards are fully enforced.
3. Minor yet frequent interferences to an employee's work become a problem. If there are interferences and if they hold a worker back, it seems reasonable to pay him an allowance for the time he has lost. The problem is whether there were indeed such interferences and, if there were, how much allowance to give.
4. Daywork done by a pieceworker becomes a problem. A worker who normally does incentive work and earns a bonus but who is temporarily put on nonincentive work wants to keep getting his regular incentive pay. Daywork pace, however, doesn't merit incentive pay bonuses.
5. Employees who are transferred to other work, which is new to them and on which at first they are not able to earn a bonus, want to be guaranteed their old earnings during their learning period. The problem is how much to guarantee and for how long, when they are not producing at incentive pace.
6. Nonincentive workers constitute a problem. Skilled workers on high-base-rate jobs (but without bonuses) don't like seeing incentive workers on relatively low-skill jobs making as much or more than they do (because of their bonuses). And other workers on low-base-rate jobs (without bonuses) feel that they are denied the incentive workers' chance of working hard and earning higher pay.

EMPLOYEE BENEFITS

For every dollar paid in wages to American workers, an additional 35 cents is spent for extra fringe items. (In Europe, the fringes cost more than 60 percent in addition to the wage.) Fringes are of several kinds: (1) health benefits, (2) payment for time not worked, (3) payment for unusual work hours, (4) payment for job related costs, and (5) company paid life insurance.

Workers usually think of all these extras as above and beyond wages. They don't think that they are costing *them* any money. But to a company, the costs of fringe benefits are all just labor costs made in lieu of wage payments of comparable size. It is a matter of workers' choosing (although not always recognizing that they are making such choices) to take money in the form of fringe benefits instead of wages.

Actually, however, workers gain more from these benefits than they would gain from an equal pay raise. The costs of benefits are not regarded by the government as taxable income whereas the same money, if given to workers as wages, would be taxed. Besides this gain, the costs of such benefits as hospitalization and sickness and accident insurance are less when they are bought in group plans than they would be if bought by workers individually. And lastly, the benefits paid out to workers under the various protection plans are not regarded by the government as taxable income.

REVIEW QUESTIONS

1. Why are production standards necessary even in companies not using piecework? What are they used for?
2. Discuss the need to time a large number of work cycles by way of adding to the reliability of the averages of the work time observed for standards setting purposes.
3. Why is it desirable to time jobs element by element, as against overall timing? How will this produce a better standard?
4. Where is judgment usually exercised in setting production standards? Discuss how judgment can be eliminated, reduced, or improved in standards setting.
5. Explain briefly how a time study analyst makes up a time standard after collecting the raw data.
6. In practice, time study cannot be used everywhere. Why not?
7. Could production standards be set by work sampling without using a stop-watch? How satisfactory is work sampling? Why?
8. Compare macroscopic and microscopic methods for setting production standards by using standard data instead of time study.
9. "Positive incentives are good; negative incentives are bad." Discuss these statements.
10. What are some of the problems encountered in using piecework? How can they be handled?
11. Incentive plans for people who work on products are more common than for indirect workers. Why? What problems are there in putting indirect workers on incentives? What solutions are there to these problems?
12. Is it true that workers are better off because they receive fringe benefits? Or wouldn't they be better off to take the money cost of the fringe benefits as an added wage instead?

QUESTIONS FOR DISCUSSION

1. "Standards cannot be set in service organizations because service is too subjective." Discuss.

2. When a time study analyst sets a time standard and has a choice of operators to study, should he study a good worker? or whom? Why?

3. What should a supervisor do when one of his workers says that the piece rate is too low and that he thinks it should be adjusted upward?

4. A leading industrial consultant reports that management often permits a standard to be bargained instead of measured. Or it permits workers to do the job their own way instead of the best way. This consultant sees both practices as bad. What is wrong with these practices?

5. Both the United Automobile Workers and the International Ladies Garment Workers unions have time study engineers on their payrolls. Wouldn't this be a big help in deciding upon the reasonableness of disputed standards? The union's and the company's time study analysts could, together, study the job and jointly arrive at a standard satisfactory to both. Discuss.

6. In the text, it is said that ratio delay is not a good way to set production standards because it reports only what people do and contains no judgment factor concerning whether the observed performance is good or bad. How might this weakness of the ratio delay method be remedied?

7. The union has fined a company employee for violating the production quantity ceiling the union set on a factory job. The employee seems to have no alternative but to hold his production down and pay the fine or else quit or be fired. Is this reasonable? Is it legal? Discuss.

8. Why not get rid of across-the-board wage increases? How can they be incorporated into existing piece rates?

9. Would you work harder or less hard if you were a member of a group being paid on a group incentive plan? Why?

10. In most places of employment women are allowed six-month maternity leave with pay. After the Civil Rights Act was passed several years ago, quite a few men complained that this discriminated against them. What should be done?

11. Women live longer than men (at least five years more on the average), which makes their pensions cost more. To be fair, shouldn't men get larger monthly pensions so as to make their pension costs the same as those for women?

PROBLEMS

1. An operator took 8 hours to set up a machine and turn out 130 units of product. For this job the standard time for setting up is 50 minutes and 4 minutes per piece for doing the work.

   a. What was the operator's "efficiency" for the day?

   b. If the operator were working on piecework and the job has a base rate of $5 an hour, how much money would he earn?

2. What is the time standard for the following job? Add 15 percent for allowances and show the figures. The times shown are continuous watch readings in minutes.

Element	Cycle							Performance rating
	1	2	3	4	5	6	7	
Get two cases.........	.11		.55		1.05		1.51	1.05
Put part into case.....	.22	.41	.65	.83	1.16	1.34	1.60	1.15
Fasten parts into position............	.29	.48	.73	.97	1.23	1.41	1.82	.95

3. Martin Wilkie and Norman Hutchinson both operate punch presses of the same kind and both work on piecework. Their base rates are $6.00 an hour (this is guaranteed). The production standards for the 4 products which they spend all their time on are: product A, 5 per minute; B, 10 per minute; C, 15 per minute; and D, 20 per minute. In 1 specific week when they worked 8 hours every day, their production records were as follows:

Product	Wilkie					Hutchinson				
	M	T	W	T	F	M	T	W	T	F
A............	1,200		1,500		900	600			1,500	300
B............	3,000	3,000			900		900	1,200	1,800	3,600
C............			900	8,100	900	5,400	5,400	3,600		
D............		5,400	3,600	3,600	2,400	4,800	2,400			2,400

   a. Calculate the wages, day by day, of these two operators.

   b. If both operators work consistently hard, which (if any) of the standards would appear to be out of line? Which are the tight standards and which are the loose standards?

4. A and B do the same operation on 2 similar machines. The machine cost in each case is $8 an hour. A turns out 120 pieces per hour and is paid $7.00 an hour. B turns out 115 pieces per hour.

   a. What is A's cost per piece?

   b. What would B's hourly rate be if his unit cost is equal to that of A?

5. Workers A and B each produce 100 pieces per hour, but A's rejects are 2 percent as against ½ percent for B. Rejects are repairable at $.18 each.

   a. Each worker is paid a straight hourly pay rate of $7.00 an hour. What is the cost per unit of this item for each worker?

b. If you paid each one so that both would have A's cost per unit, what would each one's hourly rate be?

6. For purposes of determining the allowance for miscellaneous elements for setting a job standard, the analyst has collected 500 ratio-delay figures. These show that the operator was performing the operation 392 times. He was away from his machine 32 times, and 76 times his machine was not running while he adjusted it, gaged the work, and did other miscellaneous work associated with making products. From time study data the analyst had previously established that just doing the main parts of the operation takes 4.2 minutes. What should the job standard be?

7. If every stroke were used to turn out products so that a semiautomatic machine could produce 600 units per hour, what would the production standard be if 85 percent of top possibilities were regarded as worth a 20-percent bonus?

8. The company and the union are nearing the close of their negotiations and seem about to agree to a $.09 per hour wage increase. The union proposes that the increase be given as an override so that everyone gets the same amount, $.09. Yet, the union does not seem strongly opposed to having the raise incorporated into the piece rate structure, provided only that everyone gets an increase of $.09 an hour.

You are given the job of working out a method of incorporating the increase into the piece rate structure. Try to do it so that Brown, White, and Black all get a $.09 raise. Brown works on daywork at $7 an hour. White's base rate is $6.80, but he is on an incentive job and earns $7.05. Black is on a $7.10 base rate incentive job, on which he earns $7.75 an hour. Show the figures to support your recommendation.

9. The following data have been collected to provide a basis for setting up standard data for winding coils in a coil winding department. The winding times have been leveled to make them comparable (otherwise they would sometimes reflect either fast or slow performances).

Study no.	Core diameter	Core length	Length of wire wound	Wire gage	Winding time
1.	1½″	5″	3,200′	30	2.10 min.
2.	½	4	1,500	10	1.60
3.	1	4	1,800	20	1.25
4.	1¼	5	2,600	15	2.30
5.	½	3	1,200	40	.55
6.	1	3	1,525	30	.89
7.	¾	4	1,475	15	1.27
8.	1	5	2,000	25	1.30
9.	½	4	1,600	35	.78
10.	1¼	5	2,400	10	2.60
11.	¾	3	1,500	25	.99
12.	½	2	600	40	.42
13.	1	4	2,200	15	1.80
14.	1¼	5	2,800	20	2.10
15.	½	2	1,500	40	.70
16.	¼	1	200	15	.50

a. Set up curves so that time values for new sizes of coils can be read off.

b. Using the curves, read off the time for the element "wind coil" for coils which will have a ⅜-inch core diameter and a core length of 2 inches and will contain 3,800 feet of 37 gage wire.

c. Do the same for a 1-inch core diameter and a core length of 4-inch coils containing 2,200 feet of 12-gage wire.

CASE 14–1

Todd Evers' father Jim had worked for the Heavy Duty Truck Company for 25 years. His job as stockroom clerk was not the highest paid job in the department, but he liked the work, and the department head was glad to have so dependable a man and one who knew the stock so well.

After finishing high school, Todd and his parents thought it would be a good idea for him to work a year before he entered college. With his father's help, he got a job at the Heavy Duty Truck Company operating an external grinding machine. The work was piecework, and young Evers quickly became proficient. In less than three months his paycheck exceeded that of his father.

The father's feelings were a mixture of pride and chagrin. Todd's mother felt very differently, however. When Todd brought home a check larger than his father's for the second consecutive pay period, and it appeared that he would continue to do so, she berated her husband severely. What kind of a husband was he anyway? Through all the years she had lived on his meager earnings. Now she finds that in only three months her 18-year-old boy can make more than his father. Before long, Jim had to move out of his house in order to have any peace. Jim brought his problem to his foreman.

What is the basic problem? Is it job evaluation? Is it piecework? What should be done both in Jim's case and in the company to prevent similar problems in the future?

SUGGESTED SUPPLEMENTARY READINGS

Dearden, John. "How to Make Inventive Plans Work." *Harvard Business Review,* July–August 1972, pp. 117–24.

Muchinsky, P. M. "Utility of Work Samples." *Personnel Journal,* April 1975, pp. 218–20.

Niebel, Benjamin W. *Motion and Time Study.* 5th ed. Homewood, Ill.: Richard D. Irwin, Inc. 1972.

15

Worker safety and health

WE HAVE HAD, for over a hundred years, legislation providing for some kind of financial payment to workers injured on the job. But for most of that time the employer was not liable if the injury came from an accident which was caused by the worker's own carelessness or that of a fellow worker. Now the employer is fully liable, no matter the circumstances, even to the point of being liable if the worker injures himself while violating the company's safety rules.[1]

Not only is the employer financially liable for injuries, but also for job caused impairment to health. Until very recent years, this area of employer liability, health impairment, was very small compared to liability for accident caused injuries. But in the 1970s, health impairment claims became much more common. These will be taken up later in this chapter.

Obviously, almost every manager of every kind of organization wants its workers to work under safe working conditions. Managers want to provide safe working conditions and to have workers use safe methods and not to hurt themselves.

Nonetheless, people still get hurt on the job so the effort to reduce accidents becomes an unending job. Actually, on a relative basis, factories, stores, and most places of employment are quite safe places to work. Statistically speaking, life is safer on the job than off—more people get hurt at home than at work.

Yet, so long as there is even one accident which causes human suffering, it is one too many. Accidents cost in human suffering and in money so worker safety is always high on the list of factors to consider in job design.

---

[1] A very good history of safety legislation over the last hundred years is given in *Safety Standards* magazine for July–August 1973.

THE INJURY HAZARD

The total working population in the United States is a little over 85 million people. Of these 85 million, some 5 to 6 million suffer some kind of injury or work related illness every year.[2] Half of those injured (about 1 in 30 of those working), miss one day or more of work as a consequence of their injury. A third or more of those who miss a day have to spend one day or more in bed.

Injury hazard by industry

Industries vary a great deal in their hazard. The automobile industry has the best record with 3 disabling accidents (where a disabled worker misses 1 day or more of work) per 1,000 workers per year. Others under 10 accidents per 1,000 worker-years are aerospace, electrical equipment, textiles, chemicals, steel, and storage and warehousing. At the other extreme, all with over 50 accidents per 1,000 worker-years are mining, air transport, meat packing, and transportation.

In general, the severity rates of accidents parallel the frequency rates. In the storage and warehousing, electrical equipment, communications, and automobile industries, workers average to lose a little over one third of a day each in a year because of injuries. At the other extreme, workers in the lumber, construction, fertilizer, and surface mining and quarrying industries average to lose the equivalent of 3 days per year per worker. Underground mining is far worse yet, however. Here, employees lose an average of 30 days of work every year because of injuries.

Fatality hazard by industry

Work related deaths come to 14,000 a year (or 1 in every 6,000 people working). This contrasts with 26,000 deaths from accidents in the home. The work related deaths are spread among industrial groups as follows:

Group	Number of deaths	Deaths at rate of 1 per:
Trade	1,300	14,900
Manufacturing	1,700	11,800
Service	1,900	9,900
Government	1,800	7,600
Transportation and public utilities	1,700	2,900
Agriculture	2,200	1,600
Construction	2,900	1,400
Mining and quarrying	700	900

---

[2] The U.S. Department of Labor reports that there are some 6 million work related injuries and illnesses each year. The National Safety Council reports 8 million injuries of which only half require medical attention and the injured worker does not miss as much as one day of work.

The 60 million people who work in trade, manufacturing, and service are working in the safest places. The 13 million people who work in the mining and quarrying, construction, agriculture, transportation, and public utilities industries are in far more hazardous occupations.

Within these figures is one subset which is important. Over one fourth of all of these deaths are auto accident deaths. They are not "on-the-job" deaths in the sense of occurring at a regular work place. Making improvements in job working conditions will not reduce this kind of fatality.

Another important subset in the figures is the low total for manufacturing. To many of us, "work related deaths" generates a mental picture of factory operations. Yet fewer than $\frac{1}{12}$ of worker deaths occur in manufacturing. Making *factory* jobs more safe will have little impact on the 14,000 total. Improvement must come everywhere if much is to be accomplished.

Injury hazard trends

Both accident and death rates have gone down year by year for many years. This has been brought about by the constant efforts of managers to reduce them. Recent legislation, particularly the Occupational Safety and Health Act, which took effect in 1971, with its strong penalties for unsafe working conditions, no doubt stimulated even more the substantial effort which managers had been putting into job safety before that law was passed. Since the passage of the OSHA act, accident rates have continued to come down, but, because of efforts in the past, present reductions are small. Really dangerous hazards are almost nonexistent so further gains are very hard to achieve. (Several manufacturing companies have had records of over 10,000 employee-years of work without an accident.)

THE COSTS OF ACCIDENTS AND HEALTH IMPAIRMENT

The human suffering caused by accidents is itself enough to justify the constant effort of managers to try to reduce it. But besides this the monetary costs are high. How high is impossible to estimate accurately.

First, there is the cost of the working time lost by injured workers. Some 50 million worker-days are lost each year by the 5 or 6 million of our 85 million employed people who are injured. But this is only a small part of the total. There may also be property damage. But much larger are the costs of interruptions to the work of others, the time others spend with injured workers, the cost of first aid facilities, and the cost of doctors, nurses, personnel department employees, and others. And there is all of the record-keeping and investigating and recording and reporting of accidents, filing payment claims, and so on.

Some years ago a *Fortune* article estimated that, if the full costs of injuries could be totaled, the bill would be over $9 billion a year.[3]

---

[3] Reported in Dan Corditz, "Safety on the Job Becomes a Major Job for Management," *Fortune,* November 1972, p. 113.

In the United States, workmen's compensation benefits are paid to workers injured on the job. In case of serious injuries, the total costs of a single case can run into many thousands of dollars. Workmen's compensation laws are state laws and differ a good bit in details. But in nearly all states the payments are made out of taxes paid by employers with those having the highest accident rates paying higher tax rates. (The laws usually specify the payment to be made for each kind of injury and the injured employee may not sue for more.) These costs can easily come to 4 percent of the payroll so there is a considerable cost reduction incentive to managers to provide safe working conditions for employees.

The Occupational Safety and Health Administration is also active in promoting and policing safety. If OSHA inspectors find unsafe conditions, the agency can assess fines. Employees may also file complaints with OSHA charging that conditions are unsafe. It is even possible for the Secretary of Labor to order a factory or service establishment to close down if it has dangerous working conditions which are not remedied. The law even allows, in extreme cases, for managers who knowingly permit a seriously unsafe condition to exist, to be fined or even put in jail. Such laws have been in effect in England and France for some time but they were new in the United States with OSHA.

THE HAZARD IN THE JOB

It usually takes a combination of hazardous conditions and carelessness on the part of human beings to make accidents. An oily floor does no harm in itself. Most people who walk on an oily floor do not fall; but, when many people habitually walk on oily floors, falls are almost certain to occur. Cleaning off the oil would help, but extra care on the part of those who must walk on them would also prevent most of the possible accidents.

Although hazardous conditions cannot always be eliminated, often they can be. The first step in their elimination is the recognition that they exist. Many situations are obviously dangerous—a piece of material projecting into a dimly lighted aisleway, for example. Other situations, just as hazardous, are not obvious but will be revealed by an analysis of accident statistics.

A list of accident hazards in factories, including the less obvious ones, would be lengthy. It would include slippery floors and steps, the use of ladders and scaffolds, protruding materials, unguarded fast-moving machinery, particularly belts, gears, and cutting tools, dies, drill presses, flying particles from grinding wheels, slivers from lathes, chippers, and so on. It would include unguarded balcony edges, stair wells, elevator shafts, low-hanging overhead conveyors or other objects, handling heavy materials, trucks with heavy loads, narrow aisles, blind corners, and employees smoking where there is a fire or explosion hazard. In addition, in many companies, there are dangers from high voltage electricity, molten metals, high temperatures, chemicals, irritating fluids, noxious fumes, various kinds of dust, burns, fires, and explosions.

Many hazards are within the job itself. Metal pieces shaped by forming dies usually have to be placed precisely by hand. Punch presses, too, need to have the part spotted exactly. Welding is another place where workers have to hold pieces while the operation is being done. In all of these cases, operators need first to place the piece in position and then keep their hands out of the way. The danger is that they will not get their hands out of the way before the machine operates.

It is easy to be too negative toward managers who do not eliminate every hazard. People fall down stairs; so stairs are a hazard. Workers using ladders sometimes miss the step and fall and hurt themselves. And on the consumer front, bicycle riders get hurt; so bicycles are hazardous, almost as much so as motorcycles. Housewives burn themselves on hot stoves. And skiers twist their knees and ankles and break their legs.

There is a hazard in every one of these situations; yet, there is little that a manager of a manufacturing or a service organization can do to prevent hazards such as these from causing accidents. Both governmental regulators and the general public sometimes seem not to appreciate the impossibility of eliminating all hazards on jobs, and those related to jobs, and to consumer use of products. The best that managers can do is to take the most effective preventive measures possible.

The problem of safety is not one problem but many. The hazards are so different and so varied that such improvements as can be made have to be of many kinds. There is no one solution to these problems.

MAKING WORKING CONDITIONS SAFE

Safe working conditions are management's responsibility. The degree of safety found in any plant is a matter of machine design, plant layout, lighting, good housekeeping, good maintenance, and the provision and *use* of safety guards and equipment.

Machine designers have for years been putting more and more of the moving parts under cover. This trend seems to have been motivated partly to improve the appearance of the machine by presenting smooth curved surfaces to the eye and partly by the desire to make it safer to operate. Today machinery buyers are often insisting on safety features being built into machines in addition to those required by safety regulations.

Better and better equipment is being made for what used to be dangerous work. Acid burns and lung damage from fumes in electroplating have been materially reduced over the years. Dust explosions in flour mills, food products, and candy companies are almost unknown. In steel mills, burns from molten steel, let loose when ladles or other equipment break, have almost disappeared. The use of better equipment is largely responsible. Portable saws, drills, grinders, brushes, and the like, and their extension cords are now much better protected than formerly.

Plant layout and good lighting are also important to safe working conditions. Narrow aisles with blind intersections cause accidents to industrial truck drivers. Poorly lighted aisles and workplaces sometimes cause accidents. The slope of ramps, if used by industrial trucks, should not exceed 10 percent in grade. Pipes, conduits, drains, valves, heaters, fire apparatus, and so on should be located where they are convenient for repair or access but are out of the way of ordinary traffic.

Floors, stairs, and ramps must be kept free of water, oil, and grease. Spillage should be controlled and, when it occurs, cleaned up. Floors, if subjected to liquids, should be provided with proper drainage. Materials, containers, scrap, trash, and other obstructions should be put in places where workers will not stumble or slip on them and where trucks will not bump into them and knock them over. In the winter, loading docks, receiving platforms, and aisles in outside storage yards should be cleared of ice and snow.

To remain safe, a plant must be well maintained. Worn machinery is not always dangerous, but worn materials handling equipment, crane cables, hoists, elevators, industrial trucks, conveyors, storage racks, or electrical wiring can be very dangerous. Most of these situations are as dangerous to maintenance employees themselves as they are to others, if not more so.

In spite of all that can be done to create safe working conditions, there will still be a few situations which cause some people to have accidents. Aisles cannot always be straight, and it is impossible to remove all posts, overhanging projections, and step downs. Such hazards should be painted a bright color to make them noticeable. Alternate diagonal orange and black stripes are sometimes used. Mirrors suspended from the ceiling at an angle permit truckers to see if anything is coming around blind intersections of aisles. Steps or sloping floors which might cause falls can be coated with an abrasive nonslip covering. All of these practices help reduce accidents.

SAFETY EQUIPMENT

Safety equipment can be of many kinds. Perhaps the best is equipment which is fastened onto or built into machines, thus making an accident difficult. Machine guards are of many types, depending on the machine. Motors, driving belts, gears, and electrical control panels are encased or are in wells surrounded by guard rails. Transparent shields cover grinding wheels. The whole wheel is sometimes encased. Rotary saws, except for the cutting section, are covered. Punch presses are equipped with protection devices such as a sweep arm or an attached glove or arm shackle. With the downstroke of the punch, the sweep arm clears the operator's arm from the punching area. The glove or shackle is fastened to the machine in such a way as to draw the worker's hand back from the machine as the punch descends.

Shears, brakes (bending machines), and other sheet metal equipment are required by law to be provided with guards. Forming presses for shaping metal are equipped with electrical control buttons which the operator must be pushing as the die descends. There is a button for each hand and both must be pushed while the machine operates. They are located clear of the die so as to make certain that the operator's hands are in the clear. Safety push buttons are especially helpful where two or more workers operate a machine, since, without them, one worker might start the machine's stroke before the others are clear. Sometimes forming presses are equipped with barrier "doors" which have to close and interlock, keeping the operator's hands out, before they will operate. Some of these machines are equipped with electronic or even ultrasonic sensors which will stop the machine if the operator's hands get into the danger zone.

Safety devices on machines frequently pose difficult problems for designers. First of all, safety guards must protect the worker. Second, they should not slow down the machine's operations very much because slow operations increase operating costs. Furthermore, if a safety device slows down the work too much, the worker, particularly if he is working on piecework, will try to circumvent it. (He tapes down the push buttons or removes the sweep arm or doesn't wear the glove or shackle.) Third, if serious accidents are possible, even though highly improbable, as in "calendering" in the rubber, linoleum and plastic film industries, the safety device, if tripped, must be made to stop high-speed equipment instantly.[4] It must also be located so that it would probably be tripped almost instantaneously should a worker get caught in the rolls.

Chemical and electroplating processes often give off noxious fumes and vapors. Other operations are extremely dusty. Most of the hazards to employee health can be eliminated by providing hoods, canopies, or ducts over the operation to convey the fumes and dust away by an exhaust fan.

A second type of safety equipment is the kind that is fastened to or worn by the worker. There are safety glasses, goggles, and hoods for welders. Rubber aprons, gloves, and boots are used by electroplaters. Leather gloves are needed for many operations where sharp, rough, hot, or cold materials are handled. Shoes with nonslip soles should be worn where floors are slippery. "Safety" shoes, having a steel toe cap, are a protection for heavy materials handlers. Respirators worn over the nose and mouth to purify the air are used for spray painters and workers in extremely dusty places. Ear plugs or ear muffs protect the hearing of workers where the operations are noisy.

Almost without exception, most workers do not like to wear protective devices. The devices are usually uncomfortable to wear and most workers consider them to be nuisances. The injury hazard is often slight, and, when the protection equipment is uncomfortable to wear, the company usually has to insist, on penalty of discharge, on their use.

A third type of safety equipment is needed in case of a disaster, particularly fire. In the case of wooden buildings, overhead sprinkler systems

---

[4] "Calendering" is a rolling operation in which materials are squeezed between closely set rollers.

are required by law. A water tank to supply water and to keep up water pressure in case of a fire may also be required. Fire extinguishers and fire hoses should be provided at numerous locations in the building. In most factories several types of fires are possible. Fire may be caused by defective electrical wiring, oil, explosive fumes and dusts, or other combustibles. Since fires of different kinds respond to different treatments, different types of fire extinguishers are needed, e.g., burning oil or magnesium cannot be extinguished by water. An appropriate type of extinguisher is needed for each type of fire.

MANAGING SAFETY AND HEALTH

The overall responsibility for carrying out organizational responsibilities for the safety and health of employees rests largely with the production or operations manager of the organization. Usually most of the organization's employees work for him. But this is a specialized area which needs the attention of a specialist. Consequently, nearly all large organizations have safety engineers and medical people who see to the safety of others. All of this work normally comes under the general direction of the industrial relations director.

These specialists are responsible for hunting out hazardous conditions and for working with industrial, maintenance, and machine design engineers to correct unsafe or unhealthful conditions. They are also responsible for keeping up to date on new safety regulations and standards. They develop and manage organizationwide health and safety programs, and they watch over heating, lighting, ventilation and good housekeeping. Typically, these programs are ongoing and include worker safety training programs and the proper orientation of new workers from the safety point of view. They also handle such things as the publication of "accident-free days to date" statistics.

Physical examinations for job applicants help in safety in that already existing disabilities are unearthed, thus helping to place people where these disabilities will not be aggravated. Occasional physical examinations later can also be helpful because everyone grows older. What may have been an appropriate job for a worker may no longer be so because of changes in his health so he ought to be put on other work. Some companies also give periodic physical examinations and suggest individually tailored programs of physician-monitored exercise in company provided recreational facilities. The objective of these health programs is to help upgrade the physical well-being of the organization's employees.

ACCIDENT PREVENTION: THE HUMAN ELEMENT

Most accidents involve both unsafe conditions *and* unsafe human practices. According to the National Safety Council, unsafe acts occur in close to 90 percent of all accidents.[5] (Goodyear Tire reports 92 percent.) The installation of safe machines, safety guards, and so on is not enough to reduce accidents very much. It is hard to keep a 22-year-old fork lift truck driver from driving his truck too fast around the plant. Nonetheless, workers must work safely. It seems to be human nature always to expect accidents to happen to someone else so it is hard to instill a safety attitude in people. Consequently, they continue to take chances and accidents continue to happen.

Years ago smoking during work hours by factory workers used to be forbidden in most factories. Now, it is forbidden, as a rule, only where it creates a fire hazard or in confined spaces where it might annoy non-smokers. In spite of possible fire hazards, however, workers sometimes do smoke in restricted areas. The company *must* try to enforce its no-smoking rules where safety is involved.

Most company managements recognize that carelessness contributes to most accidents, so they try to educate workers in safety. Workers should be told of the hazards and shown how to work safely, but for the most part educating workers in safety is a matter of developing a safety-conscious frame of mind rather than teaching them specific things to do. Safety consciousness can be fostered by the way in which warnings of hazards are phrased. One company found that it was more effective to say, "Even 240 volts can prove fatal—660 volts here!" instead of "Danger, high voltage."

Accidents are depressing, and workers don't like to think about them. Quoting figures and showing pictures of accidents or injured workers don't impress workers with the need for safety because they don't want to listen to, or look at, such material.

The fact is that relatively few workers do get hurt. Naturally, therefore, it is hard to "sell" safety to them. Various schemes are used to get employees to work safely. Shop rules usually require that goggles and other safety devices be worn where conditions warrant caution; sometimes the penalty for failure to do so is discharge.

Some companies have tackled the problem of safety education through union-management safety committees. Sometimes they make any injured worker, upon his return to work, a safety committee of one in his department. He must look over the department for hazardous conditions and practices and report them.

The company paper should give special recognition to accident-free departments. Sometimes a "dunce prize" is given to the department having the last accident. It is retained and has to be displayed at the department entrance until another department has an accident; then that department must display it. Safety competition should never, however, be permitted to become so deep that minor injuries are unreported and untreated just to preserve the record.

Posters and cartoons displayed on bulletin boards and in the company

---

[5] *Accident Facts,* National Safety Council, annual.

FIGURE 15–1

Humor in safety posters attracts attention and conveys a message

paper are effective in safety education (see Figures 15–1 and 15–2). Sometimes they can be made humorous without being grisly. Workers look at "guffaw-with-a-message" posters and laugh, but they do look and, as a result, probably think a little more about working safely. "How-to-do-it" and "how-not-to-do-it" posters are less interesting than humorous posters and, of necessity, have to be quite elementary. "Misery" posters, aiming to make the reader aware of the grief that can come from unsafe acts, tend to stir up fear which many people think does not cause workers to work more safely. Besides, they emphasize the *results* of unsafe acts rather than the acts themselves.

Accident records show that some workers are more accident-prone than others. Putting them on the safest jobs lowers the accident rate. However, it is rarely possible to detect accident-proneness among job applicants. By the time they have worked long enough to establish an accident record, a lot of damage has been done. Reassigning accident-prone workers to safer jobs is not, therefore, a quick way to reduce the accident rate.

THE OCCUPATIONAL SAFETY AND HEALTH ACT

The Occupational Safety and Health Act, which took effect in 1971, imposed much stiffer safety regulations than had applied before. It also

FIGURE 15–2

Cartoons of the type which are guaranteed to get more than one look

AVOID SUDDEN STOPS
...you're liable to spill the
load, suffer injury and damage
the truck.

**KEEP—AND TO KEEP—YOUR ARMS AND
LEGS WHERE THEY BELONG**
...never place them between the uprights
of the most or outside the running lines of
the truck.

KEEP CLEAR OF EDGE OF LOADING DOCK
..."sky hooks" are not standard equipment
on fork trucks.

WATCH REAR-END SWING
...this can be dangerous,
in a fork truck, too.

extended the coverage of existing laws to cover almost everyone working, including those in the construction industry, who had been omitted before.

This law set up the Occupational Safety and Health Administration (OSHA) in the Department of Labor to handle all safety matters. OSHA inspectors have the right to go into plants to see if unsafe practices are going on. And, although the agency has far too few inspectors to do the inspection part of their work very effectively, the very existence of OSHA has improved conditions in many places.

In its early days, OSHA was guilty of issuing quite a few arbitrary and not very logical regulations. Ice in drinking water for employees was banned. So were full round toilet seats, and so were all protective railings which were not exactly 42 inches high. And there were others. Such rulings, collectively, put almost everyone in a violation position and lost a great deal of public support for the good that was supposed to come out of the new law.

After Congress told OSHA to get rid of its nuisance standards, it modified a great many of its seemingly unnecessary regulations. OSHA has also modified some of its early rulings because of economic rulings. Its first regulations covering keeping workers' hands out of dies made it almost impossible for them to do their work and at the same time made almost all of the equipment in the nation in violation. To conform with the regulation, the required modifications would have cost anywhere up to $35,000 per machine. The costs of die-made products would have sky-rocketed, and many small employers would have been forced out of business.

Within OSHA one of its main departments develops standards while another department enforces regulations. Inspectors, if they find a violation, issue citations (like traffic tickets). In flagrant cases there can be fines and court orders closing down the operation. Fines can be as much as $1,000 a day until the condition is corrected.

NOISE

In the 1970s noise reduction became part of the spillover from the new emphasis on both safety and on environmental improvement. Industry had not been unaware of noise as a problem, and factory designers had done much to reduce it, but most factories were still noisy places. The setting of standards for allowable noise levels on the job is one of OSHAs responsibilities.

Interestingly, noise is not always considered disagreeable. Many young men like the loud roar from their motorcycles or automobiles. They like the feeling of power that seems to go with it. And, indeed, rock music concerts have sometimes been measured at 125 decibels.[6]

Although doctors know that long exposure to excessive noise will ultimately impair a person's hearing and that workers exposed to high levels of noise are several times more likely to develop high blood pressure than those in quieter environments, doctors don't know much about the levels of noise that do harm. Noise affects some people more than others. Also, most people's hearing deteriorates as they get older even when they have not been overly exposed to noise. And, unfortunately, the harm which might be caused in younger people working in noisy surroundings usually does not show up until they are older.

OSHA regulations regard exposure to average noise levels of 90 decibels or over for 8 hours or longer as probably injurious to most people. As a rule of thumb, if a work area is too noisy for comfortable face-to-face conversation, it probably is a hazardous noise level. OSHA regulations do not prohibit higher noise intensities but limits a person's exposure to them. Figure 15–3 lists the restrictions and relates them to familiar noise levels. The government's Environmental Protection Administration (EPA) has also set a noise limit for factory operations at 85 decibels. OSHA and EPA are not in agreement on this point.

Companies must limit noise exposure to the levels indicated in Figure

---

[6] Noise is measured on a logrithmic scale in terms of decibels, which are a measure of sound intensity. Thus, a sound of 70 decibels is 10 times as loud as 60 decibels. Eighty decibels is 10 times as loud as 70 decibels, and so on.

FIGURE 15–3

Source of noise	Decibels above the start of hearing	Maximum daily exposure (hours)
Painful noise..........................	130	0
Jet engine at passenger ramp..............	115	¼
Riveting, chipper, planer, circular saw......	110	½
Textile loom, screw machine, subway train passing station........................	105	1
Noisy factory, punch press, blast furnace....	100	2
Jack hammer, grinder.....................	95	4
Lathe, motorcycle, Niagara Falls..........	90	8
Very loud radio in home, spinner, lathes....	80	—
Average street or factory noise............	70	—
Typical office...........................	60	—
Quiet office.............................	50	—
Quiet home.............................	40	—

15–3 or else supply workers with ear plugs or ear muffs or reduce the time exposure. Workers, however, often refuse to wear plugs or muffs. Employees who are continually exposed to an average of 85 decibels must be given hearing tests annually.

Noise control methods

Noise is merely air vibrating at frequencies which the human ear interprets as sound and which is not wanted. So vibration and noise are related. Vibration and noise can't be eliminated altogether, but they can often be "damped," "sponged up," reduced, or confined to limited areas,

FIGURE 15–4

Legally permissible noise limits for employee exposure

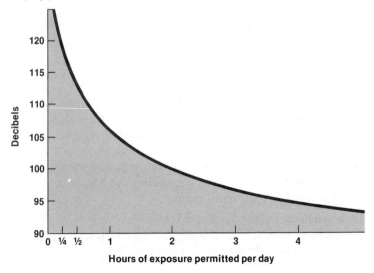

Hours of exposure permitted per day

thus reducing harmful effects. Noise from old and worn equipment can be reduced by putting in new and better fitting bearings and parts. Noise from impacts such as is made by stamping dies is hard to stop, so it is best to set these machines off by themselves. Vibration from heavy equipment can be minimized on the ground floor by mounting heavy machines on separate foundations with small spaces between the foundation and the regular floor.

On upper floors other methods have to be used. Many kinds of vibration isolators are used. Machine mountings are made of springs, rubber, felt, cork, and other elastic materials. Suspension arrangements are also sometimes used. These methods of vibration control are in addition to vibration reducers built into the equipment itself. In the machines, vibration and noise may be reduced by pads, snubbers, bumpers, flexible joints, shaft seals, and other means.

Noise and vibration may be airborne, structurally borne, or may be transmitted by diaphragms. If the source of the noise can't be eliminated, damping methods will have to be directed at the means by which the noise is conveyed. Baffles, curtains, and acoustically covered walls will reduce airborne noise or vibration. Flexible mounts will reduce the amount conveyed by the machine structure. Heavy concrete masses with their high inert inertia reduce vibration. Separate foundations for heavy machines also help. If walls and ceilings tend to act as diaphragms transmitting noise, soundproofing acoustical materials will help.

All of these noise reduction methods cost money, and it has been estimated that meeting OSHA levels by 1978 (the end of the grace period allowed for making changes) would have cost nearly $15 billion. The ultimate cost could double if the Environmental Protective Agency gets its way. The EPA wants the long exposure level reduced to 75 decibels.

Possibly these cost estimates are on the high side. Armstrong Cork reports that it can bring a medium-sized metal working plant's noise level down to 85 decibels for about $20,000. Armstrong sells a "Noise Control Package," which consists of strategically placed hanging wall panels, noise protection screens, wedge-shaped sloped noise absorbers, baffles, and vibration damping tile.[7]

HEALTH IMPAIRMENT

In the past, safety concern was almost wholly directed at reducing accidents with little attention being directed at job-induced health impairment. There were, however, a few exceptions, such as in the case of silicosis which caused lung damage to coal miners, radium burns of workers putting illuminated numbers on clock dials, and lead poisoning in the paint industry.

Now, however, with more years of experience and better detection re-

---

[7] Reported in "Sponging Up Plant Noise," *Factory,* August 1975, pp. 25–27.

search relating cause and effect, health hazards are being found in more places. Many of these had gone unrecognized before because so many situations cause health impairment only over a long time period of exposure.

It is now known that there are health hazards, including a great incidence of cancer, among workers who work with polyvinyl chloride, asbestos, certain insecticides, and in the coke making part of the steel industry. Hazards have also been found in the use of beryllium and certain chemicals.

Since some of the disabilities are so slow developing and since people not associated with these industries also have cancer and other of the job related impairments, it is difficult to evaluate the various hazards. The hazards in the making of polyvinyl chloride seem, however, to be well established, and its manufacturing processes are now closely regulated.[8] Similar close regulations now cover the processing of asbestos and coke.

The OSHA has been trying to find out what levels of exposure are dangerous so that standards can be set to confine exposure to safe hazard limits over a period of time. At the start, since the cumulative effects of long-time exposure to small amounts of the hazard are not known, the initial standards may be overly stringent. These can be relaxed if long experience indicates that they are overly restrictive. By the mid-1970s OSHA had already set some 400 standards related to job induced health hazards. These include regulations covering the manufacture and processing of such items as chloroform, mercury, sulphuric acid, carbon monoxide, silica, and even cotton dust.

The costs of health impairment protection

The costs of health impairments caused by working conditions have, in the past, been much less than the costs of injuries from accidents, but they are going up more rapidly. Impairments are usually uncomfortable and sometimes seriously so, but people don't die from them as a frequent matter among working age people. The costs of individual cases of health impairment sometimes go on for a long time so individual cases can easily cost more than most accident injury cases.

Two other developments have increased their total costs even more. First, workers who develop arthritis, lower back pains, high blood pressure, migraine headaches, alcoholism, and any number of other ailments which are somewhat psychosomatic in nature have been blaming their jobs for this. And it is true that all such conditions can be caused by or made worse by the stresses of life, including working conditions. Requests for extra compensation based on such claims are not always approved, but they are approved often enough to contribute the rapid rise in the costs of health impairment.

---

[8] The health problems in this industry are reported in Paul H. Weaver, "On the Horns of the Vinyl Chloride Dilemma," *Fortune,* October 1974, pp. 150 ff.

Second, former employees, now retired, sometimes claim that their present disabilities—often of the kind associated with growing old—were caused by job conditions years earlier. Such claims like those of present employees are sometimes approved so again the costs of health impairment are boosted.

FINANCIAL LIABILITY

Employers are financially liable for accidents and for many work-induced illnesses. Injured workers are paid compensation. The amounts they get are covered by workmen's compensation laws, which are state laws and differ to some extent in every state. In almost all cases, the law, at the same time, prohibits injured workers from suing in court for greater damages.

The amount of the compensation is spelled out in the law in the form of money awards per week for each kind of injury. More serious injuries call for larger weekly payments and for more weeks, perhaps up to several years, and in some cases, for life.

The erosion of the value of compensation benefits because of inflation has made most of them quite inadequate. There always seems to be a lag in adjusting the amounts of the awards upward fast enough to keep up with inflation. In Massachusetts, the loss of a hand brings compensation of $5,200. In Michigan it is $17,000 (215 weeks at a maximum of $80 a week). Federal employees are covered by a different law: their hands are worth $127,000.

In recent years, the low payments and prohibition against suing the employer have generated a flood of lawsuits directed against the manufacturer of the machine on which the accident occurred. Many of these lawsuits have resulted in very high awards, which in turn has skyrocketed the costs of insurance. Some small companies have gone out of business.

Obviously, under these conditions it is easy to appreciate that employers who manufacture equipment are just as anxious as OSHA to get rid of hazards.

REVIEW QUESTIONS

1. Classify the kinds of safety equipment commonly used in industry.
2. What kinds of safety devices are there to keep people's hands out of the die in stamping machines?
3. Who is commonly responsible for managing safety and health in an organization?
4. Are accident prevention programs generally effective in reducing accidents? What makes good programs work?
5. What are the general powers of OSHA?
6. What is the current noise standard which is being enforced by OSHA?
7. How can noise be controlled in industry?

QUESTIONS FOR DISCUSSION

1. Should producers of consumer products and of machinery be liable for "potential" hazards? Discuss.

2. How far does a company's responsibility extend in the matter of safety for workers? Does it cover the worker's being required to use safe methods? Or does it stop with the company's providing safe working conditions?

3. How can an employer get workers to do their work safely? What problems must be solved?

4. Which cause accidents; hazards or people? Discuss.

5. Does a person who is hurt while disobeying company safety rules get workmen's compensation benefits? What is the logic behind this practice?

6. Can an injured worker covered by workmen's compensation sue anyone? Discuss.

PROBLEMS

1. Visit a local manufacturing organization (or service), and write a brief report on their jobs safety and health program. How do they manage this function and what is their attitude towards OSHA?

2. Brown Manufacturing must decide which kind of safety device to install on a new metal stamping machine which is being installed. These devices are required to assure that the operator's hands are out of the die area during the machine's stamping cycle. They have narrowed their choice to three alternatives: double button system (both hands must push a button to activate the machine); arm shackles which jerk hands out of the die area before the machine cycles; and the ultrasonic system which senses hands if they are in the danger area and stops the machine cycle. The per machine cost of these three devices and the cycle time per part for the three parts made on the machine vary as follows:

Device	Cost/ machine	Cycle time per part by type (minutes)		
		A	B	C
Double button	$200	.1	.3	.05
Arm shackles	$ 75	.15	.4	.1
Ultrasonic sensor	$800	.05	.2	.1
Percent of parts made on these machines		30%	50%	20%

Which device should they install? Are there any "behavioral" problems which should be considered in this problem? If you need more information in order to solve this problem, what information do you need?

CASE 15–1

A sheet metal shear at the Treadway Company had no guard on it and, therefore, was dangerous, making it possible for people to lose their fingers. The state safety inspector ordered Treadway to install a safety shield and control buttons so that the workers could not operate the shear unless they had their hands out of danger.

A year and a half later, Bill Gott, an employee, lost three fingers in the still unprotected shear. The safety inspector had not been back in the interim and in the ordinary course of events wouldn't have been back for at least six months more. Shortly after the safety inspector's visit, Jack Combs, a former machine operator, had been made supervisor of the department. He said he'd never heard of the safety engineer's order.

What allows such things to happen? Suggest a remedy.

CASE 15–2

After a company appointed a safety engineer, accidents went up to a new high, so the personnel department interviewed the supervisor with the worst records to see what was happening. Here are some of the answers. "Safety? That's not my job anymore. Safety's the safety engineer's job. He'll get the credit, so let him work for it." What should be done at this point?

CASE 15–3

"My foreman is a fair guy but pretty slow with a hospital pass. If you cut your finger and yell for relief, he hands you a Band-Aid. You could bleed to death before a relief man arrived. He hopes that you'll let it go and that he won't have to get a relief man or report having an accident. Same thing with a headache or a cold. He'll give you an aspirin pill and tell you that it will make you feel better soon. He doesn't want you going to the hospital. He goes against the labor contract all the time because he isn't supposed to refuse a man a trip to the hospital."

This report comes to you, the safety director. What do you do?

SUGGESTED SUPPLEMENTARY READINGS

Ashford, N. A. "Worker Health and Safety: An Area of Conflict." *Monthly Labor Review,* September 1975, pp. 3–11.

Betz, G. M. "You Make It Safe, Workers Won't Cooperate—Now What?" *Automation,* March 1976, pp. 60–63.

Dunbar, R. L. M. "Manager's Influence on Subordinates' Thinking about Safety." *Academy of Management Journal,* June 1975, pp. 364–69.

16

The management of productivity

THE ONLY WAY a society's standard of living can be increased is to increase its per capita productivity. We can consume more only if we produce more. This, increasing the per capita productivity, is essentially the mission of production and operations managers. In order to increase productivity, managers have to get greater output from each unit of input. They have to get more output from each labor-hour used and from each dollar of investment used.

In the abstract, probably almost everyone would agree that increasing productivity is desirable. But it is quite a different matter when one gets down to the specifics of doing it. Some ways of making investment dollars more productive, such as eliminating small selling items from the product line, or consolidating the advertising of different products and using one single advertising agency, do not normally generate much opposition.

But getting more output from the dollars spent for salaries and wages is another matter. Managers usually meet with opposition when they try to get more output per labor-dollar or per labor-hour. Workers often object to the introduction of new and more effective machines, and they object to improved methods which increase output per labor-hour.

Fortunately, the matter of increasing productivity is many-sided and is by no means confined directly and only to improving worker output. It can have to do, as is suggested above, with product lines and such things as advertising agencies. It can also relate to office procedures and to paper work or to wasteful uses of money spent on purchased materials from paying too much. It can, in fact, relate to every item and every activity for which money is spent or on which labor-hours are expended.

The important thing is that managers need always to be watching costs and trying to control them, otherwise the organization's resources are likely to be used up without their having produced any reverse image of production or income flows.

To combat this, managers need to *reject* the idea that costs are incurred to satisfy some useful function and to *reject* the idea that just because resources are being used they are being well used. Indeed, it would be better if they assumed that some inputs are almost surely being used uneconomically. Also, it is important for managers to keep in mind that nearly everyone in the organization can help to use resources more economically.

Cost *reduction* and cost *control* mean about the same thing; both try to use resources to best advantage. Cost control that doesn't try to keep whittling costs down is mere recordkeeping. Yet, cost reduction drives that go on forever lose their effectiveness. Many companies have found that an occasional special cost reduction drive pays worthwhile dividends, even though what these drives amount to is asking everyone to do a better job at what he or she is (or ought to be) already trying to do well.

LABOR CONTRACTS AND PRODUCTIVITY

Production managers are not wholly free to use the organization's resources as they think best because there are restrictions in the labor contract. They may, for example, in the contract, have given up some of their rights to make methods improvements which would result in the more economical use of resources. Usually such restrictions on management's right to act are not agreed to voluntarily by managers but are concessions resulting from collective bargaining or even from a strike at some time in the past. Such restrictions are unfortunate in that they often stand in the way of using resources to the best advantage.

Worse, however, are situations where managers, by failing to exercise their rights to manage, lose their right to do certain things. Dana Corporation lost an arbitration case when it tried to install a permanent production standard for an assembly line because it had used a temporary (and too loose) standard too long. Because Dana had let this inefficient operation go on for a while, the arbitrator denied it the chance to improve the situation.

Dana also had trouble in another case. First it agreed to show the shop steward new production standards before they became effective. Out of this came the practice of the steward's initialing all standards as evidence that he had seen them. Standards did not go into effect without his initials. From then on the company found it couldn't set a job standard without union approval because of the steward's refusal to initial those he didn't like. The labor board upheld the union and agreed that the right to initial meant the right to approve or disapprove a standard. Later, at the bargaining table, the company had to win back its right to set standards.

Any kind of job control by a union stands in the way of possible job improvement. No company can make the best use of its resources and have low operating costs if its bargainers give away the managers' rights to set standards or to change methods, or if, by their practices, they abdicate their right to make improvements.

THE AFFLUENT LIFE AND COST CONTROL

As top officials get older, they usually "have it made" financially. Their homes are paid for and their children have been educated, so their expenses go down. Yet, their salaries are higher than ever, and they may well have a growing income from investments. There is no need for them to pinch pennies—to drink beer instead of highballs or eat hamburger instead of steak. They can afford to live the affluent life, the comfortable life.

It is small wonder that such managers often run their companies the same way, particularly when the company is affluent too. Suppose, with affluent managing, a company earns $25 million in a year whereas, with penurious managing, the figure could have been $30 million. Why should an affluent manager care?

Often the answer is he doesn't care. The fact that the stockholders pay him well to serve them well and that he should do his best is beside the point. The point is that affluent managing may well happen, and it is dangerous. A company which is not always working at staying efficient becomes flabby. Then the $25 million dwindles and may turn into a loss. Companies which are well off are often that way only because they always try to use resources to best advantage. But, if they let up and condone inefficiencies, their managers soon don't recognize inefficient operations when they see them or don't know what to do about them if they recognize them. The road back is usually difficult. Top managers always need to be vitally interested in cost control and economical operations.

A corollary to this point relates to doing things too well. This can relate to product designs, manufacturing policies, or to the thoroughness with which work, particularly staff work, is done. Too much staff work, and too-well done staff work, is common in well-off companies. Resources are used wastefully. These wastes are held down in cost-conscious companies.

RESOURCE CONSERVATION ATTITUDES

Economizing on the use of resources is essentially cost control, which in turn is as much an attitude of mind as it is an activity. But, unfortunately, it seems not to be a natural state of mind. This makes the process of controlling costs become partly an educational process, which takes time because attitudes change slowly.

The attitudes which need changing might be called laissez-faire attitudes: "Leave well enough alone, we're getting along all right." "You're messing up my operation." "We tried that before and it didn't work." "We are aware of this, and we expect to do something about it (but we never get it done)."

Even more difficult to deal with is the view that, "We can't cut any lower." And it is usually difficult to reduce costs in mature industries which have been combed over for cost saving opportunities many times in the past. Yet it is not quite so futile as trying to find a cheaper post office (and even here there is always United Parcel, which is often a lower-cost alternative). Nor does cost control always mean cost reduction. In these days of inflation, it is more likely to be a rear guard action aimed at circumventing cost increases.

Not unnaturally, the whole matter of economizing on resource use is unpopular. None of us wants to be pushed nor to have to push other people; instead we want to be liked. We would rather relax and choose the lines of least resistance. Cutting costs sometimes has unpleasant aspects, and we do unpleasant things only if we are actually forced to do them. We would rather do other things—almost anything else—first.

We might use the typical foreman's attitude to illustrate the problem. So many costs are incurred at the bottom level (at least in a factory) that the foreman is the key person in controlling resource inputs. Yet how much effort directed at trying to improve operations will you get from a person who says? "All my men are working. What are they hollerin' about? Stock chasers drive me crazy. Every day they want something else. Tools don't cost much and they last a long time. Materials cost is my problem, but I can't do anything about them. Maintenance won't fix 'em, so how can I keep my machines running? Why can't they let us alone? They're always makin' changes. It's only a little change. Why stir up trouble? Engineers can't understand. They never come into the shop. You can't time study indirect. No two jobs are alike. Why bother with budgets? They're just a lot of numbers. Overhead is a mystery to me. We just listen and grin."

This picture of foremen is more typical than rare, but we would do foremen a disservice if we implied that they are the only people with such attitudes, which are actually very prevalent in industry today (and in government and other service organizations as well). Superintendents, engineers, purchasers, accountants and clerks often feel the same way. Their organizational empathy and loyalty do not go so far as to cause them to push hard for effective and economical operations.

All of these people need to be instilled with a desire to conserve resources. Obviously, too, they will have to be provided with some know-how so that they can do it. And it will probably be necessary to keep prodding them.

In all of this, the foreman is the key person since he has most to do with his department's effectiveness. Almost surely, at the start, such a foreman will be opposed to changing his ways in order to operate more economically. If he is won over to where he cooperates reluctantly, this is a gain. Finally, the top manager would hope to get him to be favorable. And certainly it should be made clear to him that controlling costs is part of his job.

He will be won over more readily if he is "brought into the act" and allowed to suggest improvements. He needs to be given a chance to have his say when cost goals are set. And he needs to be allowed to implement changes in his area of responsibility which he thinks are necessary to achieve his goals.

Naturally, too, top managers will be more likely to get support for their improvement programs if they review the foreman's performance against his goals with him. They should also praise good work when they find it and not just be negative about poor performance. This helps build acceptance. If subordinates are negative, they can be quite ingenious with their foot dragging. Top managers should try to avoid having subordinates feel threatened.

COST REDUCTION PROGRAMS

In order to minimize inputs and to keep costs down, most companies find that they need an occasional shot in the arm—a special cost reduction program. Such a program will itself cost a certain amount of time and effort, but here a top manager has to resign himself to the need to spend a little money in order to save more money. Also, a program may not produce substantial results right away (it may take months to get into high gear), but the gains from having trained people to become more cost conscious and to think of saving resources ought to persist for a long time. The program should end up by becoming a new and continuing way of life.

Some companies go at cost cutting by using edicts. The president tells his vice presidents to cut 10 percent off their costs. He may also tell them: "If things don't get better soon, there will be some new faces around here." The vice presidents tell their works managers, the works managers tell the superintendents, and the superintendents tell the general foremen who tell the foremen: "Cut 10 percent" The order goes down the line to every manager at every level. Lower-level managers are told to cut costs and still get their work done as usual. The assumption is that the cuts will be made where they will harm operations the least.

Edict methods are ruthless and they sometimes work out badly. Yet expenses *are* reduced. And probably they do stop a certain amount of wasteful use of resources. Edict methods, however, can be unwise because worthwhile productive activities may also be cut in the process. Some years ago, Beckman Instruments cut 7 percent everywhere, including its sales force. But 7 percent fewer salesmen sold fewer products, so it was a poor economy strategy. Resource saving programs should pay attention to the essentiality of activities before cutting them off.

Some companies carry on cost cutting with more participative type programs. They try to get the whole managerial team to pitch in and work together willingly and enthusiastically at cost cutting. They try to pinpoint weak spots which can be improved. These are not, however, "soft" programs; subordinates are still expected to reduce the costs of getting essential work done.

There are several requirements for successful participative type resource-economizing programs. First, the program needs top management interest —and active interest. Everybody thinks that he has been doing a good job, that he has been working hard, and that he has done all he can. But in spite of this he almost certainly can, and will, do even better if the high brass works with him and if he knows they are watching over his accomplishments. And he will try especially hard if the top managers make it clear that resource economy is part of the basis for judging promotions and pay raises.

Such a program really ought to start with the top managers calling a meeting in the board of directors' meeting room to impress people. The general idea, "We must reduce costs," is put before everybody, and all are asked for their ideas as to how to go about it. If the crisis is serious enough, it helps for the executive to take a salary cut. Then everyone is *really* impressed.

This original high-level committee will probably decide to set up several subcommittees to handle different areas (product design, materials, manufacturing methods, office costs, and so on). One or more of the near-top managers will be on each of these subject or area subcommittees, but some still lower down managers will also be put on these committees. Committee membership will cut across departmental lines. It adds push to the program if some high officials sit in with subordinates who are farther down when committees meet. This adds greatly to the chances of success of a program. Also, it is important not to leave out any area; every department should be included.

One might ask what is expected of such committees. First, higher-level officials need their help in setting resource saving goals. Top managers expect lower managers to look over their areas and to set resource saving goals to try for—short-term goals and long-term goals. The committees can look into all trouble spots and put a dollar value on each cost saving opportunity. The committees might also set up reporting procedures to show the kinds and causes of excess costs. The object of reducing costs is half won when opportunities have been unearthed.

Second, the committee members will, in the end, have to do the things which will result in conserving resources. They will not do this as committee members but as heads of their own departments. As individuals, some of them will hesitate to do anything about costs, some will defend the present practices, and some will want to go ahead but will not know how. Being on the committee lets them see the need for saving resources. This makes everyone more willing to find cost cutting opportunities and to try to make the cuts.

Third, no program keeps going by itself after it is started. After goals are set, and as time goes along, reports are made of what is done and comparisons are made against the goals. The committees make the comparisons. And they pay particular attention to all spots where someone did not reach his goal. Where did he fail? Why? What else can he do to reach it? And so on. The committees go over all of these matters and so help make the cost cutting program work.

Fourth, committee meetings help develop a climate in which people will learn to appreciate that resource inputs either are money or they cost money. They will learn how to reduce costs. The committee meetings should be educational. Department heads who don't know how to go about cutting costs get ideas from their fellow committee members about how to do it. They also come to identify themselves more with the company and to think and work toward overall company goals. Then they are more willing to work out solutions which are best for the company, not just best for their own department.

Fifth, committees work in an ambience of social pressure. No supervisor looks good if he says that he can't cut costs when everyone else has agreed to do his bit. Nor does any supervisor look good if he doesn't cut the costs he told his fellow committee members he thought he could cut. Every supervisor knows that his fellow committee members are watching his results.

A few near-top committees don't do all this by themselves; each committee accepts the responsibility for overseeing a whole resource expenditure area. Each member of these committees gets a job of setting up one or more committees below him with the same kinds of assignments but in a lower, smaller part of the organization. Later he reports his own committees' cost cutting successes back to the higher committee.

Members of these lower committees agree to set goals for cutting expenses under their jurisdictions and to get their subordinates to do the same. The program ends up with everyone including foremen participating: Everyone tries to save resources. Some companies even discuss programs with union officials before they proceed. Union officials often appreciate the problem and are willing to "go along," but they cannot be expected to give any visible support. If they did, they probably would not get re-elected because some of the expected savings in costs are in labor costs.

Having everyone go to committee meetings would seem to be a costly offset to the gains produced by cost reduction programs. Hopefully, however, it would not work out this way. Everyone always finds the time to do the things he wants to do and which he thinks are important. And cost reduction programs are always important. People find the time to work at cost reduction by cutting down on less important things that they have been spending their time on. They, themselves, become more efficient.

MAKING A PROGRAM WORK

Assuming the willingness of department heads to try to operate more economically, they can do so only if they know how to do it. They need the help of committees of the kind just discussed. And they also need the help of industrial engineers in the search for places to make improvements. But, perhaps of even more importance is their need for having accomplishment goals and frequent up-to-the-minute reports showing how they are doing compared to what they should be accomplishing considering the goals.

The reports need to be individualized and to cover only the responsibility areas of single department heads. When a department head gets a report covering *his* operations, he can tell how well *he* is doing. Such reports should be designed so that they highlight unsatisfactory spots so he can direct his attention to the trouble spots. The reports should go to *him* so that he can react and try to improve. But copies should also go to his superior or the committee responsible for his area. The superior or the committee should hold frequent review sessions with him where failures to meet the plan are looked into.

In these review sessions, finger pointing should be avoided, and the sessions should not be turned into punitive sessions. No one is on trial. The object is to find out why the goal was not accomplished so that the cause can be removed. The goal is to be corrective, not punitive, although it is good to keep some pressure on everyone. Reviewing performance makes opportunities to help and also to praise good performance.

ECONOMICAL OPERATION OPPORTUNITIES

Cost savings opportunities are everywhere—in every department and in every expense (see Figure 16–1). Normally, these opportunities, individually, range downward from substantial to minor, rather being opportunities to save large amounts of money. This is because department heads have probably already done a good job of controlling costs where big savings are possible.

The savings, therefore, which can come out of economy drives, are likely to be small and many, rather than few and large. Yet they add up into consequential amounts. One company gave its workers free work gloves whose cost came to over $10,000 a year. Talking economy to the workers did no good but having them pay half the cost did. Usage went down 60 percent. This was only a little item, yet the savings added up to several thousand dollars a year.

Here are some ideas which could be followed up in just the production end. If production costs are high because there are many new employees, the foreman should try to train the new workers well and quickly and also try to cut down on turnover so there won't be so many new people. If excessive absenteeism is making the foreman shift workers around a good bit and do unfamiliar work, he should try to cut down absenteeism. Or it may be that his workers sometimes have to wait for their next jobs, in which case losses can be reduced by better scheduling.

Also, since some workers are always better producers than others, the foreman should study how the good ones do the work and then train the

FIGURE 16–1

Cost saving opportunities

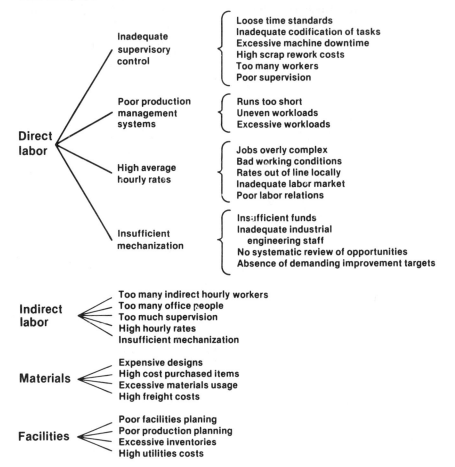

Direct labor

- Inadequate supervisory control
  - Loose time standards
  - Inadequate codification of tasks
  - Excessive machine downtime
  - High scrap rework costs
  - Too many workers
  - Poor supervision
- Poor production management systems
  - Runs too short
  - Uneven workloads
  - Excessive workloads
- High average hourly rates
  - Jobs overly complex
  - Bad working conditions
  - Rates out of line locally
  - Inadequate labor market
  - Poor labor relations
- Insufficient mechanization
  - Insufficient funds
  - Inadequate industrial engineering staff
  - No systematic review of opportunities
  - Absence of demanding improvement targets

Indirect labor

- Too many indirect hourly workers
- Too many office people
- Too much supervision
- High hourly rates
- Insufficient mechanization

Materials

- Expensive designs
- High cost purchased items
- Excessive materials usage
- High freight costs

Facilities

- Poor facilities planing
- Poor production planning
- Excessive inventories
- High utilities costs

others to work the same way. And, if assemblers on the assembly floor have to "fit and file" parts before they fit, the foreman should see that parts are properly made before they get to the assembly floor and thereby save this waste. Or if new and untrained employees are put in groups where they hold things up, the foreman should keep them out of the groups until he has trained them to hold up their end. Also, double work should be avoided: if one department inspects parts as they leave, the next department should not inspect them again when they arrive. Finally, buying from reliable vendors will reduce receiving inspection.

The foreman should not interrupt his workers or keep them waiting for instructions, tools, or orders. Similarly, he should cut the time wasted by employees at starting and quitting times and see that they start promptly and don't quit until closing time. (A Battle Creek, Michigan, company changes the color of coffee cups every 15 minutes to keep coffee breaks from stretching out.) Nor should foremen let workers waste time around the sandwich cart. He should hold down clean-up time, both of the work area and personal clean-up time. Nor should he allow union committee members to roam the shop to "investigate" grievances all the time. Nor should high-priced machine operators have to go to a stock room for materials. Instead, the materials should be brought to them by lower-cost materials handlers or by conveyors.

Other savings opportunities

The above discussion illustrates how lower-level managers can conserve an organization's resources. And even in the production areas there are many more possibilities of cost leaks than the few we have mentioned. There may be wage guarantees to piece workers while they are learning, extra pay as allowances to piece workers who are sometimes delayed, pay to employees for attending grievance meetings, the cost of reworking products that need repairs, and the cost of lost production of machines that are not operating whatever the reason.

Managers should also look into "accepted costs," such as die maintenance and tooling costs. Such costs are necessary but they may be too high. "Getting fat" costs should come in for particular attention. When times are good, everyone has to have "assistants" or "secretaries." Yet sometimes when they are eliminated, no one can figure out just what they did.

There are savings opportunities in the maintenance area, as there are in the big area of materials, purchasing, store room operation, materials in process, finished goods, materials handling, and the like. Other opportunities are related to scheduling, schedule changes, specifications, engineering changes, and supplies and tooling. Accident costs also offer savings opportunities.

Nor are all of the opportunities to conserve resource inputs confined to the production area. There are just as many places to save money in selling, warehousing, traffic, offices, paper work—in every part of the company. Sometimes, also, there are "leaks" in one department which are caused by another department. For example, the sales department causes extra costs in manufacturing when it asks for special products, or that nonstandard (and more costly) items be sold at regular prices, or for "gold plated" or "fur lined" free trimmings, free repairs, too easy a policy on returned goods, orders for one each of many things, rush deliveries, and free estimates for special items.

Office departments also offer opportunities, especially as all office workers are knee deep in paper. No physical activity is performed in our modern age without a piece of paper's going along to guide it. Someone has said that it takes two tons of paper to produce one ton of product, and, although this may be exaggerated, desk work and paper work go hand in hand. There is no escaping a huge flow of paper—so huge that it takes quite a staff of typists, stenographers, and clerks to make out reports and file them. Work directives are put out and reports of work done are received, letters and memorandums are written, and forms are filed in duplicate, triplicate, and quadruplicate.

LIVING WITH HARD TIMES

When sales go down and stay down, resource conservation assumes even greater importance. It is necessary to shrink the organization to the size which today's sales will support. There is neither the need to do all of the things done yesterday when the organization had greater sales, nor is there enough money today to pay for the large organization needed for yesterday's larger sales volumes. Failure to prune may well bankrupt the organization. In a factory, direct labor and material costs will go down almost automatically because they are closely tied in with production, but with other factors it is different.

In one such circumstance, Boeing, among other actions, laid off 5 percent of all its indirect workers, cut inventories, and published the company magazine less often. Lockheed dropped its plans for an electronic computer because it would not pay off for five years. American Motors closed and sold an unused factory in Detroit, saving a half million dollars a year in heating costs alone. Glidden stopped making edible oils and sold its plant on Long Island. Buying the oils saved $300,000 the first year. Besides this, all of Glidden's executives took a 22-percent salary cut. General Motors Frigidaire employees passed up two years of already negotiated pay raises rather than to see operations closed down.

The service sector of our economy is less responsive to marketplace needs, but it too sometimes has to come to grips with limited resources. When New York City could not pay its bills in the mid-1970s, it reduced employment in all departments, closed down its child day-care centers, and the City University of New York began charging tuition.

In general, economizing in hard times is easier than at other times because there is little opposition to it. Even a wage cut does not hurt morale much because, when disaster threatens, it is better to have a lower-paying job rather than no job at all.

PITFALLS IN COST REDUCTION

Cost reports comparing performance with goals are the heart of cost control, and resource inputs can be conserved only with the support of proper reports. But managers need to be very sure that they show what they seem to show and that reported improved conditions really mean improved conditions.

For example, maintenance costs go down (for a while) if everything is let go to rack and ruin. Or scrap is cut to zero if everything is passed as good. Production is grand (for a while) if machines are run as fast as they will go (but it's better not to look at tool costs). Also, rework costs on rejects are low if the rejects are just scrapped (but don't look at the scrap costs). Absenteeism will be low if everyone, whether sick or well, is told to come to work every day. Inventories can also be cut to the bone (and the factory be out of stock half the time). A manager needs to look at *all* the figures, not just one or two, to see if things are better.

Even cutting out idle time can be wrong (but not often). Large expensive machines, or series of machines, ought to be kept operating. Their idleness can cost hundreds of dollars a minute (as in a steel rolling mill). If one or two half-idle employees have to be close all the time to keep big machines going, by all means this is better than having the big machines idle from time to time.

Managers need to be careful, too, about interpreting figures on reports. Is a department's indirect labor ratio up? (This shows that more labor-dollars are being spent for indirect labor per direct labor-dollar than formerly.) Normally this is bad; but it is not always good to have a low overhead ratio. The overhead ratio will go up every time there is a cut in direct labor costs unless indirect labor costs are reduced proportionally. Yet it is good to reduce direct labor costs even if indirect labor costs are not also reduced.

It is the same with overhead. When a department mechanizes, overhead goes up and direct labor cost comes down, so the ratio between them goes way up. Indeed, one General Motors' parts making plant has an overhead ratio of more than 1,500 percent! Overhead charges are $15 for every $1 of direct labor payroll! This sounds much too high, but it is not too high because it has come from extreme mechanization, which, it is true, boosted overhead costs. At the same time, however, the mechanization saved far more direct labor costs than the overhead increase.

Supervisors, inspectors, and service people are all part of overhead costs. A department's indirect-direct ratio will look better if these costs are reduced, but, if the number of supervisors is reduced, the work done by the direct workers may suffer. If inspectors are cut, poor work may get by. And, if service workers are eliminated, the machine operators will have to go after their own materials and tools and sharpen their own tools, meanwhile leaving their machines idle. All of these potential economies need to be evaluated in the light of the concommitant diseconomies.

It is possible, too, to keep the overhead ratio down by buying parts instead of making them. This substitutes material costs for machine and labor costs. It may result in cutting the overhead ratio, but at the expense of the more costly bought parts.

It is even possible to reduce the overhead ratio just by letting direct labor costs go up. Using direct workers inefficiently will make direct labor costs go up and so make the ratio of overhead to direct costs go down! No one would want that; yet, if a manager were to look at just the overhead ratio, his worst foremen would look the best.

Nor should overhead be covered up under the classification direct costs. For example, if an allowance is put into a piece rate to pay for delays, the worker's pay is partly for lost time, but it all shows as direct labor cost. By paying for it within the piece rate rather than as an extra outside allowance, too much is shown for direct labor and too little for wasteful overhead. The calculated overhead ratio gives a false picture. Also, foremen should not give idle workers wasteful make-work jobs just so the costs will seem to be for productive day-work time and not for lost time.

Totals and averages should not be relied on if it is possible to get the details. Suppose that a foreman, in meeting his budget total, spends too much on one item and stays under the budget on another. The total is met but the fact is that there is a weak spot which ought to be rectified.

Also, how are costs figured? On an average basis? Perhaps on a per pound basis? If so, a manager who looks at a department's reduced cost per pound may praise the foreman for reducing costs. But a heat treating department will have low costs per pound when it handles big, chunky items. So will a foundry. Next week, with smaller items, the costs go back up. For a while the record looked good, but it did not reflect more efficient operations.

Top managers should look searchingly, also, at the savings claimed for improvements—particularly savings in overhead. Often they are only illusions, or else they won't stay nailed down. Suppose, for example, that a machine is speeded up so it does its work in 7 hours instead of 8. Its overhead charge is $10 an hour. Has there been a savings of $10 of overhead? Are the taxes less? Is building depreciation less? Are research costs less? They are all overhead items, but there probably will still be $80 worth of overhead a day. It would therefore be better to increase the hourly overhead charge to $11 an hour because the shorter processing time probably did not save $10 in overhead costs.

Floor space is another example. Accountants say that floor space costs so much a square foot—for office space, perhaps up to $10 a foot per year. Cutting down job space by 30 square feet would seem to save $300 a year, but probably there is little or no real savings. Unless this space can be used profitably for something else, there is no savings at all.

Also, improvements in work methods—particularly for indirect people of all kinds including office people—are often not worth making because they won't stay nailed down. Suppose that industrial engineers cut a one-hour clerical task to half an hour. Is there any savings? Probably not. The employee just "soaks up" the time and does no more work. Or as soon as the industrial engineer leaves, the employee goes back to his old hour-long method.

Pointing out pitfalls in interpreting figures (and there are many more than we have listed) warns of dangers but does not tell us how to avoid them. The truth is that there is no good solution. It just isn't possible to devise figures which tell the whole truth and nothing but the truth. Nevertheless, managers should not let their emphasis on a "good figure" cause the subordinates to make a figure look good at the expense of the true situation.

THE NEED FOR COST DATA

The obligation of managers to get as much productivity as possible from using the organization's resources to best advantage becomes largely a matter of choosing the least costly ways for doing things. All resources cost money and, as they are applied to the producing of products or services, their costs are transferred to the products and services.

In order to compare and to determine the most effective means for doing things, managers need cost data. Such basic information should be used by all managers in both production and service organizations. Admittedly, in some government situations such figures are not highly important. A registrar of deeds at a county court house would not have much use for a cost per deed registered figure.

But, in nearly all service organizations and all business organizations, managers need to know the costs of rendering services or of making products. Pricing decisions and budget allocations of money need to rest on good cost information.

CALCULATING COSTS

The costs of individual products or services are neither easy to calculate nor are they very exact figures when they are arrived at. This is because many expenses are incurred for the general advantage of the whole organization or for large segments of it, or for several products and not just one. These general expenses have to be charged to products and services through a series of steps of allocations and reallocations.

The problem is much like figuring out what a meal at home costs. Should part of the house rent be counted? Should part of the cost of owning a car for going to the store for groceries be counted? How about the cost of the silverware used on the dining room table? How about the housewife's time? The cost figure arrived at would depend on how these and other costs are valued and apportioned.

The calculation of costs of individual products and services start with records of expenditures. These need to be kept apart by class of expenditures as well as by department and even the kind of product or service for whose benefit the expense was incurred. These figures can then be used to compare what has been happening, so far as costs are concerned, with what was supposed to happen. Variances from budgets and plans can then be analyzed to see why. If possible, the causes for excess cost variations are removed. Then, having made improvements and armed with this information from the past, similar budgets and plans for the future can be made up.

Job lot costs

In companies which do varied work, every job is given an identification number. Then an account for it is set up in the cost accounting department. (Production control uses this same job number when scheduling the lot's production.)

As a job moves through manufacturing, all of its costs are listed in its account. Materials requisitions supply the value of the materials used. Factory workers' job tickets supply the cost of the labor on the job. Then overhead is allocated. When all of these costs are added up, plus any other costs incurred for the job, the total shows the cost of making the lot. Dividing by the number of units yields the unit cost.

The same thing is done when it is necessary to quote a price on a future job which the sales department wants to bid on. The estimating department lists all of the materials *expected* to be used, the labor it will *probably* take, and overhead assessed at the usual rate. When these are added, a reasonably accurate cost projection is obtained.

Process costs

Continuous production has to use process costs. Process costs are always average costs because it is not possible to separate the cost of making one gallon of gasoline from another, or one television set from another of the same model, or of one bolt of cloth from another bolt of the same cloth. Nearly all products follow the same path through production.

To find the process average cost, it is necessary to keep a record of how much it costs to carry on production for a period of time, perhaps a week. Dividing this total by the number of units produced shows the operation's average cost. Where there are several operations in a process, the cost of each one is added in to get the total cost per unit for the whole process.

DIRECT AND INDIRECT COSTS

Direct costs are those which can be traced directly to a product—the cost of materials used and the cost of labor put into it. All other costs are indirect—costs not incurred for any one product. Indirect costs include the wages of employees who do not work on the product and the cost of supplies, office expenses, insurance, depreciation, taxes, and so on. In total indirect costs often amount to double the direct costs.

Every product should finally (through the allocation process) be charged with a share of the indirect or "overhead" costs. Every item's cost should include its own direct costs plus its share of indirect costs.

Direct costs are sometimes called "variable costs," meaning that the total amount spent for them in a month or year goes up or down along with production. The more a company produces, the more it spends in total for these items. Indirect costs are called "fixed costs," meaning their total is not affected much by volume changes. Neither of these terms should be taken as a hard-and-fast term, however. Not all variable costs would be cut in half if production were cut in half. Nor would every fixed cost stay unchanged if production were halved.

COST ELEMENTS AND COST UNITS

When getting a product's cost, accountants have to deal with (*a*) the items for which money is spent: materials, labor, services, depreciation, insurance, taxes, and (*b*) the things for which cost information is wanted: products, operations, and areas of responsibility. What money is spent for, accountants call "cost elements." What information is wanted about, they call "cost units."

Cost accounting *collects* information about what money is spent for. With that information, it then *computes* the cost of products, operations, programs, and areas of responsibility.

In general, the larger the cost unit, the more cost elements can be charged directly to it. If the cost unit is a manufacturing department, the foreman's salary, as well as depreciation on all equipment in his department, become direct costs of that department. But if the cost unit is a large department occupying a whole building, even depreciation on the building itself becomes a direct charge to that area of responsibility.

The same things should be done with *product* costs. Everything possible should be charged directly to individual products. This means less apportioning later, and it produces better cost data.

Load centers

A load center (or "production" or "machine" center) is just a part of a department. Often it is a very big and expensive machine or group of similar machines. So far as cost accounting is concerned, a load center is one kind of costing unit—it is a distinct part of a plant. Its costs are collected separately just as if it were a department. Collecting costs for load centers helps pinpoint costs of operating the load center so the right amounts can be charged for its use to the products using it.

ALLOCATING COST ELEMENTS TO COST UNITS

The end product of cost accounting is the cost of the cost unit. Departments are one kind of cost unit. Department costs are often end results in themselves, but they are also steps on the way to getting product costs. It is not possible to get good product costs without having previously gotten department costs.

We have said that only people can do anything about costs, and department operating costs are needed so that responsibility can be traced to individuals. The person in charge of every department is supposed to keep his department's costs down. Department operating cost figures, therefore, are useful in themselves.

To get department costs, the accountant starts by keeping, in *each* department's account, all of its own costs. To its costs are added a share of overhead costs incurred outside the department. But allocating the outside costs requires several steps. First, *plantwide* overhead costs are assessed to *all* departments. Then the costs of all *indirect* departments are assessed to the *operating* departments (those that work on the product). This is necessary because costs cannot be allocated to *products* except by charging them with the costs of the departments that worked on them. So it is necessary to charge operating departments with the costs of all nonoperating departments. After this has been done, the department's own overhead, its assessments, and its direct labor and material costs are summed up, producing the cost of running the department.

If only department costs were wanted, the cost accounting job would be done. But since product costs are wanted too, it is necessary to allocate each operating department's costs to the products it turned out. This starts by comparing the direct labor cost in a department to the rest of the department's costs (the department's own overhead plus its overhead assessments). Suppose that last year the direct workers in a department put in 1 million hours of work and were paid $7 million in wages, which comes to an average of $7 per hour. And suppose that the department's overhead costs came to $7 million, which is equal to 100 percent of direct labor costs. (Materials costs are left out of this example because they are usually charged directly to the product and do not have to be allocated.)

Now the record of direct work done in the year comes into play—how many labor-hours or dollars were spent on products A, B, and so on. Suppose the record shows that the workers put in 20,000 hours working on product A and turned out 30,000 units of product A. Direct labor costs for product A came to $90,000. The overhead assessment, at the rate of 100 percent of direct labor, would also be $90,000. Total costs (omitting materials) come to $180,000, or $6 per unit for product A.

Now we have the cost of making product A in this department. But product A also required work in other departments. The costs of working on product A in other departments are figured the same way and then added together to get product A's total cost. Materials costs are also added in. The total is divided by the number of product A made to get its individual unit cost.

Product A's cost in each department needs to be figured separately. This way it is possible to make heavy charges for overhead to products which are made on big, expensive machines. Departments with expensive machines sometimes have overhead charge rates of 400 to 500 percent instead of the 100 percent used in our example.

ABSORPTION OF OVERHEAD

In our product A example we found that overhead amounted to 100 percent of direct labor costs. That was last year's experience figure. Barring changes, this is what should be expected for the year ahead. But, if volume goes up or down (and no one knows whether it will change or not), this ratio will be different for the coming year.

If a company forecasts that there will be no change in volume, it will start out the year saying that the cost of this year's products will include overhead charges figured at 100 percent of direct labor. And if the volume does not change, this will be about right. But if the company has a good year and sells one fifth more products than it expected, direct labor costs will come to $5.4 million instead of the expected $4.5 million.

During the whole year the company will be charging overhead at 100 percent of labor, so it assesses products with $5.4 million of overhead costs. But the overhead might actually stay at last year's $4.5 million since most of it is fixed cost. If it stays the same, the company ends up overcharging its products to the tune of $900,000. If overhead in fact goes up to $4.8 million, the company would end the year assessing $560,-000 too much. It "overabsorbs" its overhead, overstates its costs, and understates its profits.

If business goes down, the reverse happens. The company ends up passing on too little overhead (underabsorbing it), understating costs, and overstating profits.

What can be done about this? It doesn't seem very intelligent for managers to quote wrong costs all year and then, all at once, wake up at the end of the year to find that they have made more or less money than they had thought. This is not exactly how it works. The managers know full well, all year long, what is going on. They don't wake up and discover it at the year's end.

Then why should they quote wrong costs all year? This is not exactly the way they look at it, either. They want to know what their costs are, including a normal overhead assessment, if they can get their usual sales volume. They try to set selling prices to yield some profit at this volume level. They know that greater volume will *reduce* the proper overhead assessment per unit of product. They know full well that they will end up making *more* per unit than their first calculation (for the expected normal volume) showed. And they are just as aware of what happens on the downside.

The real point is that they do not cut prices when business is good in order to hold profits down, nor can they raise prices when business is bad. They let prices pretty well alone, so they may as well let their calculated unit costs alone too and recognize that, because of overhead, high volume results in extra profits while low volume makes losses.

BUDGETS

Budgets are the main elements in planning and control systems. They can be expressed as plans for money expected to come in or money to be spent, or both. In a factory, budgets are always spending plans. Yet one can ask: What good is a spending plan? Will it help cut spending? Viewed just as a plan, a budget will not cut spending, but it is *more* than a plan. Figure 16–2 shows a budgetary information flow system.

A budget should also be a maximum limit spending goal—department heads should have to work hard to get the work done without spending more than the budgeted amount. A budget motivates them. A budget is also a yardstick. Actual costs will be compared to the budget to see where, and by how much, subordinate managers did better or worse. These comparisons then lead on to "why" and to what can be done to keep

FIGURE 16–2

Budgetary information flow system

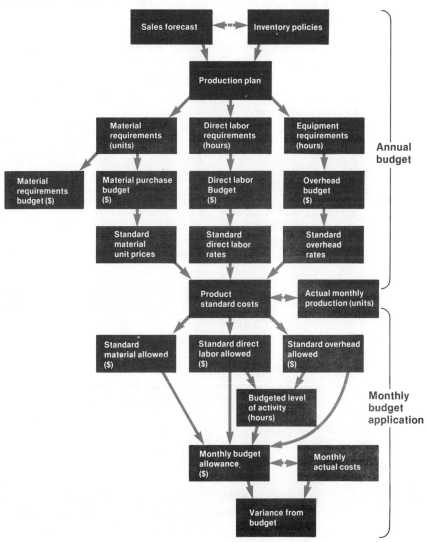

unplanned cost excesses or underachieved goals from happening again in the future. So the higher managers arrive at their real goal; controlled and lower costs or higher achievement per unit of input.

Budgets do not, however, solve all problems. A budget or plan to increase the sales or to cut costs does not, by itself, do either. With or without budgets, managers ought already to be doing their best to increase sales and cut costs. A company can't exactly budget itself into a profit, but budgets help it get there. Most people do a better job with budgets than when they don't have them, so, in a sense, managers can budget their companies into a profit.

Budgets need to be used with discretion because it is possible to save money unwisely as was shown in our section on "pitfalls of cost reduction." Also budget makers tend to tighten up budgets every time a new one is made out. Usually this is reasonable because everyone should always try to do a little better, but it could be harmful in that people might not do their best lest they get too stiff a budget the next time.

A review of the past is an important part of the procedure of using

FIGURE 16–3

Diagram of the responsibility path

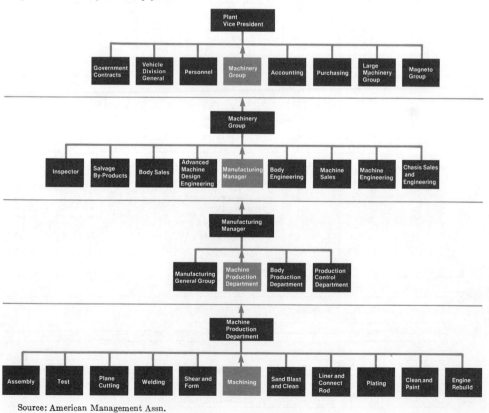

Source: American Management Assn.

budgets. But it is easy to get off the track here. The past is frozen; only the future is fluid. A manager can do nothing about the past, and he should look at it only to help him see how he might improve the future. So budgets should be almost wholly forward looking. They concern things which are to happen in the future.

Furthermore, only *people* can make things happen. If a *product's* costs go over its budget, they will stay there unless some *person* cuts them in the future. If a product's cost goes over its budget, it is necessary to find out why and to trace the cause back to a department. Then the superior can go over the matter with the manager in charge. It is the job of the manager in charge to get the costs back in line. Figure 16–4 shows such a report for one foreman.

FIGURE 16–4

Monthly report of performance compared to budget and showing variances for one supervisor's area of responsibility

RESPONSIBILITY OF MR. FOREMAN OCTOBER AREA 201 MACHINING

CURRENT MONTHS			AREA OR ACCT.	DESCRIPTION	YEAR TO DATE		
BUDGET	ACTUAL	UNDER OR OVER (−) BUDGET			UNDER OR OVER (−) BUDGET	ACTUAL	BUDGET
$ 3,568	$ 4,553	$ 985−	100 MANAGEMENT		$ 2,165−	$ 45,331	$ 43,166
286	285	1	110 CLERICAL		52−	1,750	1,698
3,184	3,709	525−	120 MATL HANDLING		1,691−	33,842	32,151
152	122	30	140 LOST TIME		80	955	1,035
1,943	2,023	80−	150 PROPY ATTEND		411−	19,691	19,280
	603	603−	170 SALABLE LABOR		867−	867	
1,985	2,059	74−	180 SUNDRY LABOR		420−	16,930	16,510
$ 11,118 *	$ 13,354 *	$ 2,236−*	TOTAL INDIRECT LABR		$ 5,526−*	$ 119,366	$ 113,840 *
2,815	3,729	914−	200 VACATION PAY		9,140−	37,290	28,150
2,476	2,004	472	210 HOLIDAY PAY		4,720	20,040	24,760
1,738	2,316	578−	220 FICA		5,780−	23,160	17,380
934	2,222	1,288−	230 UNEMPLOY TAX		12,880−	22,220	9,340
410	473	63−	240 WORK COMP INS		430−	4,530	4,100
1,157	1,661	504−	250 SOCIAL INSUR		4,815−	16,517	11,702
1,661	2,362	701−	260 PENSIONS		7,010−	23,620	16,610
	37	37−	270 OVERTIME PREM		85−	85	
929	1,044	115−	280 SHIFT PREMIUM		1,150−	10,440	9,290
$ 12,120 *	$ 15,848 *	$ 3,728−*	TOTAL PAYROLL COSTS		$ 36,570−*	$ 157,902 *	$ 121,332 *
1,579	805	774	300 DURABLE TOOLS		5,651	6,218	11,869

7,355	5,939	1,416	800 UTILITIES CO		14,160	59,390	73,550
200	434	234−	810 INTRAPLT TRNS		2,340−	4,340	2,000
19,705	18,372	1,333	820 MFG SERVICES		13,330	183,720	197,050
4,241	4,625	384−	830 MANPOWR SERV		3,840−	46,250	42,410
864		864	840 ENG SERVICES		5,650	3,050	8,700
7,544	6,489	1,055	850 SPECIAL SERV		10,550	64,890	75,440
$ 39,909 *	$ 35,859 *	$ 4,050 *	SERVICE CHARGES		$ 37,510 *	$ 361,640 *	$ 399,150 *
$ 9,079 *	$ 7,061 *	$ 2,018 ^	UNCONTROLLABLE EXP		$ 15,175 *	$ 75,615 *	$ 90,790 *

| $ 82,256 * | $ 84,192 * | $ 1,936−* | TOTAL OVERHEAD COST | | $ 17,150−* | $ 835,862 * | $ 818,712 * |

45,405	51,512	6,107−	10 DIRECT LABOR		49,918−	509,819	459,901
$ 127,661 *	$ 135,704 *	$ 8,043−*	TOTAL AREA COSTS		$ 67,068−*	$1,345,681 *	$1,278,613 *
20,920−		20,920−	EARN VARIANCE		171,090−		171,090−

| $ 106,741 * | $ 135,704 * | $ 28,963−* | TOTAL EARNINGS | | $ 238,158−* | $1,345,681 * | $1,107,523 * |

to Exh. 82

to Exh. 82

CURRENT MONTH VARIANCE ANALYSIS

LABOR				OVERHEAD		EARNINGS	
CAUSE	STANDARD	ACTUAL	VARIANCE	CAUSE	VARIANCES	CAUSE	VARIANCE
HOURS	19,321	21,735	2,414−	LABOR EFFICIENCY	$ 5,214−	PRODUCT MIX	$ 13,391−
EFFICIENCY	100 %	88.9 %	$ 5,673−	SPENDING	$ 1,260	VOLUME	$ 7,529−
RATE	$ 2.35	$ 2.37	$ 434−	UNCONTROLLABLE BUDGET	$ 2,018		

Budgets, therefore, need to be plans for things which are to happen with reference to the *people* who will make them happen. This means that budgets need to be coextensive with the responsibilities of individual people. There should be a budget for the works manager, which should cover all items over which he has charge. There should also be a budget for the plant superintendent, and there should be other budgets for each foreman and supervisor. Each one's budget should cover *his* and *only his* area of responsibility. Then the results of *his* work will be apparent when his superior reviews his performance at the end of the budget period.

But all this may still seem to be emphasizing the wrong thing. In a factory, supervisors make *products,* and they run their departments wholly for this purpose. Would it not be better, then, to set up budgets for product costs instead of for department costs? Top managers can and do set up product budgets, and these budgets help subordinate department heads control the costs of products. Yet, they are *not* the real control. The real control is department budgets, not product budgets.

BUDGETS AS SPENDING LIMITS

Budgets are sometimes only plans for spending, but they can also be used as authorizations. A purchase budget for the next six months is both a plan and an authorization. As authorizations, budgets let the department head spend the budgeted amount for each item without asking permission. Actually, if work has to be done, a supervisor can spend more, although he will have to explain it later. But, if he is spending very much more, he should report it right away so the top manager will know what is going on.

Budgets which limit expenditures are commonly used on construction or repair jobs, research projects, and for special nonrecurring expenses. Budgets even for special projects do not, however, provide perfect control over the amount of expenditure because the costs of work, once started, cannot always be held down to the amounts originally planned. When a project uses up its budget before it is completed, it is usually better to go ahead and finish it rather than drop it and lose the money already spent. But with budgets and progress reports, managers get to decide whether or not to continue.

Sometimes managers must choose between meeting their schedule or meeting their budget. Usually, when a factory is very busy, any job that gets behind schedule can be gotten back on schedule only by working overtime. If the delivery date is important to the customer, it is usually better to deliver on time, even if the overtime makes the costs go over the estimate.

Budgets sometimes work in reverse as spending limits. If a department head is near the end of a period and has not used all the money available he spends it lest he get a smaller budget next time. Otherwise, he thinks (and probably correctly) that he will have to fight to get it back. Budgets should not work this way, but sometimes they do.

CONTROLLABLE AND NONCONTROLLABLE COSTS

Some of the costs of running a department are in no way controllable by its supervisor; usually he has no control over his department's assessment of general factory overhead costs, nor is he expected (in his budget) to hold that cost down.

A supervisor's controllable costs are those over which he can exercise *some control*. They include direct and indirect labor in his department, materials and supplies used, repair costs, losses from poor workmanship, accident costs, and so on. Calling these things controllable does not mean that his superior thinks that the supervisor can get rid of them altogether but just that he can, by trying, keep them down.

The savings which are expected from using budgets come altogether from keeping controllable costs down. Budgets usually set the amount for controllable cost elements at low enough figures to require the department head to do a good job if he keeps within the budgeted figures.

FLEXIBLE BUDGETS

Changes in production volume and product mix upset budgets because schedules end up asking for (and getting) different quantities of products than those first planned for. The old budget is not likely to be a fair statement of cost expectations.

Accountants have tried to take care of this by setting up flexible budgets—budgets which vary with volume and product mix changes so that they are always fair statements of cost expectations.

BUDGET VARIANCES

Budget variances should never go unnoticed—particularly the bad ones. Someone spent too much—why? Department heads should always have to explain—because a foreman who knows that he will have to explain variances tries not to let them happen. Variances which are justifiable will, he knows, be accepted. But other variances, such as for labor inefficiency, are often not wholly justifiable. He will have to explain these, too. He has to try to keep within the budget and so keep costs down—which is just what budgets try to get him to do.

Naturally, management's response to budget variances must be judicious. Good reasons for bad variances should be accepted, and help, rather than punitive action, should be offered.

REVIEW QUESTIONS

1. What danger should managers be aware of so far as labor contracts and their relationship to productivity are concerned?

2. How can a manager go about getting a supervisor to cut costs? Why do supervisors need special attention?

3. How should a good cost cutting drive be organized? What requirements must be met if it is to succeed?

4. How can committees help reduce costs? Explain.

5. In which areas are cost savings opportunities the greatest. In each case, what action might be taken?

6. The text warns of certain pitfalls in cost reduction; enumerate some of these and tell how to avoid them.

7. How accurately can the cost of making a product be calculated? What makes it hard to do?

8. Why bother with past costs? Aren't we just wasting our money on something we can't do anything about? Discuss.

9. Contrast job-lot costs and process costs. When should each be used? How are product costs obtained in each case?

10. What are cost elements and cost units? How are they related to each other?

11. Can overhead be overabsorbed? How? Is this good? Discuss.

12. A budget is a plan for spending money and getting work done, but sometimes the money is spent although the work is only partly done. Should this happen with budgets? If it does, how does, or how can, a budget help?

13. Why are budgets for people (as distinguished from budgets for products) so important?

QUESTIONS FOR DISCUSSION

1. "Trying to get people to improve doesn't always get them to do it. There is a low compliance with management's requests for improvement. Foot draggers show considerable ingenuity to defeat the purposes of a cost control system." Discuss the validity of these statements. What can be done about them?

2. Why fight so hard to put in cost saving practices over the opposition of operators and foremen as well? Why not just accumulate improvements and keep them, so to speak, in the desk? Then we would build a new plant somewhere else and incorporate all of the new ideas, meanwhile shrinking operations in the old, inefficient plant. Discuss.

3. After the meeting where the Agriculture Department expert told of new and better farming methods, one farmer said to the other: "It sounded pretty good. I think I'll give it a try. How about you?" "Nope," said his neighbor, "I ain't farmin' now half as good as I know how." How can business leaders get their subordinates to "farm as well as they know how"?

4. "It's the people near the bottom who have to make the cuts anyway, so why not just issue edicts from the top and let these people figure out where and how to make them." Discuss.

5. Should a frequent need (or at least frequent requests for permission to work) for overtime be regarded as evidence that a department is understaffed? Discuss.

6. "Look, boss," said the supervisor, "how can I ever satisfy you? You are always beefing about too much overhead, so I get my overhead ratio down, and now you yell because unit cost went up. I thought you'd be happy to see that lower overhead ratio." Discuss the supervisor's position.

7. The Solvay Company computes each production department's direct labor excess-cost ratio by dividing the actual cost by the standard cost of the work done. Is this a good way? Explain. Suppose that some operators beat their standards and others do not; is the answer the same?

8. If operations can be performed on products on any of several machines, should the cost of each operation be budgeted as if it were always to be performed on the best machine for it? If yes, is the proper answer still yes if the best machine is busy so that the work has to be done on a less well-suited machine? If the work is done in less than standard time on this machine yet still at a higher cost than that of the best machine, how should this be handled?

9. What base for allocating overhead would be appropriate for allocating:
   a. Workmen's compensation taxes?
   b. Building depreciation?
   c. Electricity?
   d. The works manager's salary?
   e. Real estate taxes?
   Give reasons for the choices made.

10. The company accountant thought that it would be simpler to lump all overheads with direct labor so far as maintenance was concerned. This produced a $30-an-hour charge for maintenance work. Soon each department began to acquire all kinds of minor repair equipment. It was cheaper to buy a new stepladder and to do one's own minor maintenance than to call in the maintenance department. Comment on this matter.

11. "Budgets? Cost accounting? We don't need budgets or cost accounting. We just sell products, collect bills, and pay bills. We set prices where we have to meet competition. If we have more money at the end of the year than we started with, we know that we made money." Comment.

12. To what extent might budgets cause supervisors to be too department-minded at the expense of the company as a whole?

13. Why is it thought to be a good idea to let department heads help develop budgets for their departments?

PROBLEMS

1. The purchasing agent wants to go outside to buy a product which costs $10 per unit to make. The $10 is made up of $3 materials, $3 labor, and $4 overhead. The purchasing agent can buy the item outside for $8 and save the company $2. Some 5,000 of these items will be used per year. Can the company afford to pass up these profits?

2. The following figures show certain information about products A, B, and C:

	A	B	C
Sales price per unit.	$120	$100	$75
Raw material cost per unit.	35	30	20
Production hours per unit.	4	3	2

These products are all made on the same production facility and so are, in fact, alternative uses of that facility. Direct labor costs $7 per hour. All overhead, including depreciation, comes to $14,000 per year.

Which product should the sales department push? How much will the best choice gain for the company as against each of the two less profitable choices?

3. Assume that the overhead cost ratio in a department is 150 percent of the labor cost based on last year's costs, when the labor bill in the department came to $1 million. Business this year is much better and labor costs for the higher business volume have come to $1.5 million. Overhead also went up to $1.8 million. Was the overhead overabsorbed or underabsorbed? By how much?

4. Company A applies overhead as 100 percent of direct labor costs; company B applies overhead at 100 percent of material cost; and company C applies overhead at 50 percent of the sum of direct labor and material.

The companies make the same products. In setting its prices, each company adds 50 percent to factory costs to cover selling and administration costs and to provide a profit.

What will the prices of each company be if direct labor costs $2 a unit and material $8 a unit? What will they be if labor is $8 a unit and material $2 a unit?

Would you expect there to be an industry problem here? How can you resolve it?

CASE 16–1

"We can't make any money on that job; it has too much labor in it," says Joe Guzik, the foundry foreman, to Harry Taylor, the cost estimator for the Doe Iron Foundry. The foundry, *like its competition,* always estimated costs (on which prices for jobs were based when quoting prices on prospective orders) on a per pound basis.

Complex castings were regarded as class A castings and were quoted at a higher price per pound than more simple castings. Somewhat complex castings were class B and were quoted at a lower price per pound. Still simpler castings, class C castings, were quoted at the minimum per pound price.

In the case of the order at hand, Guzik felt that the class A price would not be high enough. It would almost surely cover all variable costs but would contribute little to carrying overhead.

Should Doe start quoting higher prices for castings requiring extra labor? What will happen if it quotes prices that fully cover all costs? Should the estimates be based on the cost of the man-hours required plus materials costs?

CASE 16–2

You are the president of the company and you find this clause in the proposed labor contract:

"The company shall have the right to change or eliminate any local working condition if, as the result of action taken by Management under Article Fifteen—Management—of this Agreement, the basis for the existence of the local working condition is changed or eliminated, thereby making it unnecessary to continue such local working condition; provided however, that when such a change or elimination is made by the Company, any adversely affected Employee may process a grievance on the ground that the changed condition did not warrant the change or elimination of such local condition."

How would this clause affect your operations? Would you sign the contract? Give your reasons.

SUGGESTED SUPPLEMENTARY READINGS

Belavic, A. M.   "Productivity: The Manufacturing Engineering View." *Automation,* January 1973, pp. 58–59.

Howes, M. F., and Yates, B. D.   "How to Control Personnel Costs in Overhead Functions." *Personnel,* July–August 1976, pp. 22–29.

Rosenbloom, Richard S.   "The *Real* Productivity Crisis Is in Government." *Harvard Business Review,* September–October 1973, pp. 156–64.

section five

PRODUCTION AND INVENTORY PLANNING AND CONTROL SYSTEMS

THE PRODUCTION process adds value to materials by changing their form into individual items well suited for particular uses. In this new individualized form, the products have far greater value than they had as raw materials.

Within all production systems it is necessary to decide what to make and who should do things in order to bring about production. Materials must be procured, work hours must be set for departments, and allocations of machine time to orders must be made. Many directives must be prepared telling people what to do.

It might seem that buying materials should come first. But, actually, the decision of what to make comes first and even that comes after decisions are made about what will sell.

The making of master schedules for completed complex products and of forecasting the demand for lesser items are discussed in Chapters 20 and 19. The calculation of raw materials needs and basic inventory concepts are in Chapters 20 and 18. Purchasing is considered in Chapter 17.

The management of in-process inventories and the directing of production operations is presented in Chapters 21 and 22. Chapter 23 concludes this section with a consideration of the special problems of mass production.

17

Purchasing

MOST manufacturing companies spend more than half of the money they take in for materials and component parts that are already made. International Harvester spends $1.9 billion a year for materials (59 percent of its sales dollars). General Mills spends $1.3 billion (67 percent of its sales dollars) for bought materials. General Motors spends $18 billion (49 percent).

Purchasing would seem to be an easy job since it is easier to pay out money than to bring it in. And it is easier to buy cleverly than to make things economically. When buying, a company can get the benefit of effective management just by placing orders with the lowest cost yet reliable suppliers. But, when a company makes its own components, its costs depend on its own operating effectiveness. It is easier to *choose* an effective source than to *be* an effective source.

Purchasing is more, though, than just spending money. A person who spends wisely pays less for what he buys. If a company sells $1 billion worth of products (in 1975, 203 manufacturing companies in the United States sold more than $1 billion worth of products, but they had to spend more than half of their sales income for bought items), it is selling products which probably contain purchased materials that cost over $500 million. The difference between a good and a poor job of buying could well be 5 percent or more. At 5 percent, the possible savings would come to over $25 million for such a company. So, even though purchasing is easier than selling, purchasing is still very important.

In some cases the money which can be made (or lost) on inventory can outweigh the earnings-or-loss possibilities from regular operations. The price of cotton and wool varies so much that textile companies can lose heavily by poor buying. Meat packers and flour millers have the same problem.

Purchasing's main job is to get things the organization needs when it needs them and to pay as little as possible considering the quality requirements. But this looks at the job too narrowly. Today many companies say that the purchasing department is responsible for "outside manufacture." This puts a different slant—a managerial slant—on the job. Vendor companies are thought of almost as if they were departments of the customer company.

With this view, purchasing becomes more active and less passive. The purchasing agent views his job as more than just placing orders. He becomes interested in the supplier's costs and his quality control procedures. Should the vendor need it, the buyer even arranges to send his own company's specialists to the vendor's plant to help it become a more effective source of supply.

MATERIALS MANAGERS

Some companies which buy quite large quantities of materials have set up a materials manager job in order to coordinate everything having to do with materials. Purchasing is one of the big activities. And so are the operation of the stores department and inventory control activities. These activities are closely associated with purchasing, but they are usually not under the direction of the purchasing agent. They would, however, become part of the assignment of a materials manager. The traffic department, too, would probably become part of his domain.

On the other hand, the factory's production control department probably should remain outside his jurisdiction even though it has much to do with materials used and with controlling inventories in process. Production control's closest ties are with the factory's producing departments, not with purchasing.

PURCHASING DEPARTMENT ORGANIZATION

The purchasing department is headed by a purchasing agent or director of purchases. He may be a vice president, but more often he is not, in which case he usually reports to the executive vice president, or even to the manager of manufacturing.

No two purchasing departments are alike, but all of them buy thousands of different things and usually from thousands of suppliers. U.S. Steel buys 40,000 items from 50,000 vendors. General Electric buys from 40,000 suppliers. Having to buy so much material and from so many sources means that buyers get a chance to specialize.

Besides buying materials and manufactured parts for the company's products, the purchasing department also buys supplies, containers for products, energy (or coal), equipment, and repair parts. In most companies the purchasing department also operates the salvage department and sells or disposes of scrap and low-value by-products.

Here are the people whom General Electric's apparatus division purchasing agent (he is a vice president) has reporting to him, together with their specialties:

Buyer and assistant buyer—Fabricated copper, brass, bronze, nickel, silver (except ingot), lumber (including poles, ties, and the like), packages and packing materials (wood, cleated, corrugated, bobbins, reels, and so on), woodwork patterns.

Buyer—Refrigerator hardware and accessories, asbestos, rubber and rubber parts, molded parts, glass (including globes and lenses), hose, pipe covering, name plates, nonferrous metals except copper.

Buyer—Mica, mercury, polishing and grinding supplies, textiles, rope and twine, springs, leather and leather products.

Assistant buyer—Paper and paper products, transmission appliances (including bearings, gears, and the like), hardware, refrigerator insulation gaskets, packing, and fiber.

Buyer—Large tools and machinery, automobiles, jewels, coal.

Assistant buyer—Steam, gas, and water supplies (except hose, gaskets, packing, and pipe covering), oilers and lubricators, small tools, brushes and brooms.

Assistant buyer—Oils, greases, and petroleum products, furniture (including typewriters and duplicating machines), roofing materials, steel shelving and racks, partitions.

Assistant buyer—Electrical supplies (including clocks and meters), instruments, carbon brushes, and painters' supplies.

Assistant buyer—Screw machine products, stampings, bolts, nuts, washers, rivets and screws, hospital supplies, stationery and printing, and office supplies.

Buyer—Steel (sheet, strip, and stainless), aluminum (including wire and all forms except ingot), alloys, and nickel.

Buyer—Pig iron, castings, ferro-alloys, chemicals, foundry supplies, factory supplies (except coal, oils, greases, and petroleum products), sand, gravel, and clay.

Buyer—Iron and steel (except sheet, strip, stainless, pig iron, and castings), nails, forgings, railway supplies, iron and steel wire, packages and packing, and tanks.[1]

Purchasing departments are not large, rarely going as high as ½ of 1 percent of the employees. But small numbers only highlight the importance of buyers, who spend perhaps $5 million each in a year—or up to $2,500 an hour! It costs anywhere from one half a cent up to more than one cent to spend $1. And it costs $15 or more to handle even a small order.

Buyers should know and abide by all laws about purchasing and ship-

[1] Stuart F. Heinritz, *Purchasing Principles and Practices,* 2d ed. (Englewood Cliffs, N.J.: Prentice-Hall), pp. 65–66.

ping products. And they should always be on the lookout to see if less costly materials can be used. Naturally, they can't tell whether the less costly materials will do the job (engineering has to decide this), but they ought to tell the others about the prices.

They should listen to suggestions from salesmen, who may have something new to offer. And, if something sounds good, they should not keep salesmen from seeing people in other departments who are qualified to judge new things. Some buyers are reluctant to let a salesman get into the plant.

MAKE OR BUY

Make-or-buy decisions are junior-sized vertical integration decisions. But make or buy is specific: this item, this order—does a company make or buy it? As a rule, the more it buys the less a company's investment in machines, and the smaller the company need be. But it also earns less money because it does a smaller fraction of the total manufacturing job. In general, the pros and cons of making versus buying are the same as they are for large vertical integration matters. And it does not always pay for a company to "do it yourself."

Purchasing departments are always concerned in make-buy decisions because they always have to supply the cost figure for buying. And, if the decision is to buy, they have to do the buying.

Normally every company is in a certain business and not in others, so there is no major make-buy question. For most items this sourcing decision is made by a committee when each product's original bill of materials is made up by design engineers. For most items, a company makes certain parts or components or else it does not make them.

Yet a radio manufacturing company which assembles transistorized radios could make the transistors. It could also make the integrated circuits and plastic cases it uses. Possibly it will make them all, but more likely it will buy them all because companies specializing in these items can make them at less cost than most buying companies can make them. Such make-buy decisions are more or less permanent, and normally a company does not change back and forth from buying to making.

Since a company usually earns more money on what it makes than on what it buys, there is a real question of why it should buy anything which it can make. One reason for buying, in such a case, is that the company is so busy doing its main work that it can't make everything it uses. A second reason is that two sources of supply (making and buying at the same time) provide insurance. On difficult-to-make items that is important. A machine breakdown, stopping a company's internal source, will not close the operation down. Third, outside price competition helps keep inside departments sharp on costs.

Making and buying at the same time has some disadvantages. It cuts the volume both for the inside department and for the outside maker.

Cutting each one's volume may raise unit costs a little. Besides, a company needs two sets of tooling, gages, and so on. And it may be hard to get both sources to make the products exactly alike.

Sometimes a company buys what it could make because the seller does it better and cheaper than it can. Ford Motor once tried making automobile tires but went back to buying. Goodyear and the other tire makers can make tires at less cost than Ford.

Make-buy decisions are influenced by the amount of money involved. Most metalworking companies could make the paper clips they use in their offices, but for $10 to $20 a year making them is not worth the bother. But add a few zeros and the answer is different. Daisy Company, maker of air rifles, over the years changed from wooden gun stocks (which it made) to plastic stocks (which it bought) for almost all of its models of guns. The day came when it was buying $1 million worth of plastic gun stocks a year, and Daisy then went into the plastics business itself. At IBM, making or buying magnetic tape is a top-level decision. Firestone Tire used to buy all its nylon cord for tires; now it makes its own.

Make-buy decisions on specific items sometimes depend on work loads. When a company is very busy, it sends many orders out, but when work is slack, it brings them back. This lets it operate more evenly, and since it already owns the necessary machines, no new machines have to be bought. As a company goes from boom to slack and back again, make-buy decisions become matters of priority. Which work goes out first? Which last? Which comes back first? Which last?

Up to here the discussion about make-buy has been in terms of products, parts, and materials. But it is sometimes a decision about a process instead of a product. Should a company do its own heat treating? Electroplating? Painting? Sometimes it is a matter of services. Should a company buy or do its own research? How about maintenance? And minor construction? The pros and cons are like those for making or buying products.

There is probably a bias in most make-buy calculations that favors a make decision. This is particularly true when the question comes up during slack periods. Various overheads are not put into the calculation because they are already provided. Making would be a matter of using idle capacity and underused staff and therefore would seem to cost only variable costs. This is true so long as the slack continues. But when normal operations resume, the full costs of making will creep up. Before long, making will be causing its full complement of overhead costs, something the calculation did not cover. At full costs, making may be uneconomical.

Make-buy in multiplant companies

In multiplant companies, sister plants sometimes make items which come up as make–buy choices for a particular plant. Somewhat different considerations apply here.

If, for example, one division of a company wants to make an item which it has been buying from a sister plant, it will probably be allowed to do so unless this decision would idle a substantial output capacity in the division which formerly made the item. In such a case the buying plant may have to continue buying or take over the formerly used production facility and operate it itself. (This would be highly improbable.)

Similarly, on items bought outside the plant, sister plants are usually given a preference. Usually items are transferred at a price lower than outside prices. And, again, the buying plant is usually free to buy where it wants to except when large amounts of money are concerned. Then it may be required to buy from a sister plant.

PURCHASING PROCEDURES

No one procedure is satisfactory for buying all of the 50,000 items or so that big companies buy. Some items (like sheet steel for a can maker) are shipped in steadily and, over a period of time, cost millions of dollars. Other items (like the equipment to make automobile motor blocks automatically in a new factory) are one-shot orders that cost millions. Between these extremes—steady, high demand or giant one-shot contracts—there is every combination of volume, repetition, and variety—clear down to 10-cent items bought once a year.

Besides variety in kind and quantity, purchasing deals with bulk items (liquids, powders), packaged items, standard items, special items, items always bought, and items sometimes bought and sometimes made (or both).

Steadily used items used in large volumes

For important items that are used all the time, the purchasing department gets its authority to make purchase commitments directly from purchase budgets which are based on the approved production schedules for the months ahead. It does not need requisitions from either production control or the stores department. Purchasing has, in its files, lists of all the things to buy, and it knows how much to buy in order to make a single unit of each of the company's major products. All it has to do is look at the scheduled quantities and multiply to get the amount of material needed. Today computerized systems do most of these calculations. (This is discussed in Chapter 20.)

Most of these items are bought on "blanket" or "open end" contracts which cover a whole year's supply. Blanket contracts leave quantities and times of delivery (and sometimes price) to be set as the materials are needed. The buying company sends out, several months ahead, estimates of its expected volume requirements but which are not specified in detail. They then follow this up by sending out monthly (or even weekly) release orders telling the vendor how many or how much to deliver and when and where. These releases usually go to the supplier directly from

FIGURE 17–1

Chart of a purchasing system

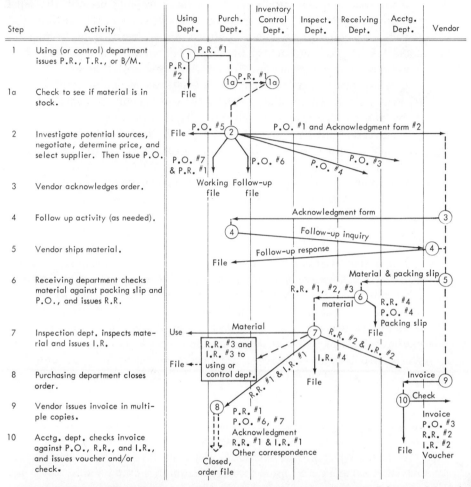

Step	Activity	Using Dept.	Purch. Dept.	Inventory Control Dept.	Inspect. Dept.	Receiving Dept.	Acctg. Dept.	Vendor
1	Using (or control) department issues P.R., T.R., or B/M.							
1a	Check to see if material is in stock.							
2	Investigate potential sources, negotiate, determine price, and select supplier. Then issue P.O.							
3	Vendor acknowledges order.							
4	Follow up activity (as needed).							
5	Vendor ships material.							
6	Receiving department checks material against packing slip and P.O., and issues R.R.							
7	Inspection dept. inspects material and issues I.R.							
8	Purchasing department closes order.							
9	Vendor issues invoice in multiple copies.							
10	Acctg. dept. checks invoice against P.O., R.R., and I.R., and issues voucher and/or check.							

P.R. = purchase requisition; T.R. = traveling requisition; B.M. = bill of materials; P.O. = purchase order; R.R. = receiving report; I.R. = inspection report.

Source: Lamar Lee, Jr., and Donald W. Dobler, *Purchasing and Materials Management* (New York: McGraw-Hill, 1971).

the factory's planning department. Purchasing is not active in this part of the contract's operation.

Contracts for these steady-use, high-volume items are not really open to competition in the wide-open sense, except that a company may buy from *two* sources instead of one just for safety. The buyer-seller relationship is much like that of a company department with a sister department. Supplying companies often keep certain contracts for years. ELTRA, for example, made most of Chrysler's auto ignition systems for 30 years.

Goodyear has never failed to get a good share of General Motors' tire business for over 50 years.

These big contracts usually do not "travel around" because the seller takes as good care (price-, quality-, and servicewise) of the customers as anyone else could. Also, these contracts are so big that no competitor could take one on and deliver overnight. He would have to build whole new factories, then tool up, and line up whole new work forces.

One exception is basic raw materials (materials of nature: cotton, wool, rubber, lumber, wheat, and so on). There are many suppliers of such items, and their prices go up and down. Here buyers do not always stick to one vendor but go where they can get the best deal each time they let a new contract. Buyers should not forget, however, that dependable service is important in such items. It is best not to switch a company's whole volume to unknowns, though an unknown might well be given a trial order now and then.

Large special orders

Large special orders are different. They usually are machinery for a newly built factory, or equipment for an electric-power dam, or some other construction, or even for a warship. On these projects, months go into planning. Discussions are held with several machinery makers. Alternative designs are considered. Sometimes the advance work takes so much engineering work that the customer pays an engineering fee to prospective bidders. Otherwise a prospective vendor may be unwilling to spend $50,000 on engineering work planning for a job he might not get. Vendors have to bid separately for every one of these large jobs.

Middle-sized orders

Here the buyer in the purchasing department is nearly always buying only after someone else inside the organization has asked him to. He gets a purchase requisition from the production control department or from the stores department. Quite a little of the work done in purchasing departments is for such orders. Production control sends in purchase requisitions for items needed for making the products on the factory's production schedule (except for the heavy and steadily used items discussed above).

Middle-size repeat orders are usually placed with the same vendors. But they don't work like releases against blanket orders. Vendors get specific purchase orders from purchasing for every order. Every new order again describes the product and orders a certain quantity to be delivered by a certain date. Figure 17–2 shows a purchase order.

But whether middle-size orders are for old or new items, it is common to ask two or three vendors to bid. Generally the contract goes to the low bidder if he is dependable. Sometimes, if middle-size orders are for standard catalog items (and particularly on rush orders), the buyer may

FIGURE 17–2

A purchase order

| ALUMINUM COMPANY OF AMERICA | | PURCHASE |
| PITTSBURGH 19, PA. | | ORDER |

	REQ'N NO.	P.O. DATE	P.O. NO.
A-B-C Box Company	510444		657508
2345 Main Street	AUTH. NO.	DEL'Y REQ'D	SHIPM'T PROMISE
Pittsburgh 5, Pa.			As Req'd
	SHIP VIA		
	Motor Freight		
	F.O.B.		
Aluminum Company of America	New Kensington, Pa.		
Building 242	TERMS OF PAYMENT		
New Kensington, Pa.	1% 10 days - Net 30 days		

Please ship the following items as instructed above.

ITEM NO.	QUANTITY	DESCRIPTION AND SPECIFICATIONS	PRICE
1	50,000 -	No. 3383-24 Alcoa Wrap Cartons, size 12-3/8 inch x 8-3/8 inch x 12-1/2 inch, 175 lb. test, R.S.C., printed 1C - 4 P.	$183.00 per M
2		Set-Up Charge for Each Release	19.50
NOTES			
A		Cartons must be manufactured with extreme care since they will be filled and sealed by automatic equipment.	
B		Cartons must be palletized 400 per pallet, with protective cover on corners to prevent top layers of cartons from becoming distorted.	
C		Each pallet to be marked with quantity and item number.	

KRG:mrw

NOTE: In accepting this order it is understood the Seller agrees to the terms and conditions shown above and printed on the back hereof. The Buyer hereby objects to any conflicting or additional terms or conditions.

ALUMINUM COMPANY OF AMERICA

BY _____

Source: Aluminum Company of America.

not shop around to try to get the best price but just order the material wherever he can get a good price with an agreement to deliver soon.

Small orders

Small orders are one of the headaches of purchasing. It costs $15 or more in clerical costs to handle a purchase requisition and to place a purchase order, so it would help to be able to cut out all the little orders for one or two items or for fifty cents or $1 worth of materials. Unfortunately, such items are needed and, worse yet, they may be as badly needed as big items. They, too, can be rush orders.

Most companies let these orders go through the regular procedure, cost what they may. Some, however, try to cut the cost down. American Can uses the following policies to reduce small order cost: (1) Don't reorder little things often; order two or three years' supply. It doesn't matter that some day part of the supply of some item may not be needed and may be thrown out. It is still less costly than buying little dribbles all the time. (2) Let departments buy directly all things costing less than $50. Don't bother the purchasing department about them. (3) Place blanket orders with suppliers; then just order by telephone what is wanted now and then, without making out a purchase order every time. Cut out the paper work. Kaiser Aluminum sends a blank check (valid only up to a limited amount) along with its order and lets the vendor fill it in. Modern computer systems monitor the levels of these items and, when new orders are required, automatically print out the purchase order and even the blank checks.

Follow-up

Keeping large supplies of materials on hand is so costly that no one wants to do it. This means things are not bought, or at least not delivered, until shortly before they are needed. But this also means that if anything goes wrong and the vendor doesn't deliver on time, the customer is in trouble. And vendors *do* let customers down more often than either they or their customers would like. So buyers "follow up" orders for things that are on a tight schedule. (The factory production control department should keep the buyer informed about which items it is most anxious to get.)

The buyer might call the vendor on the telephone or write him a letter and ask him whether the order is coming along all right. He might even "hound" and annoy him and repeatedly remind him that he is counting on getting his order on time. All this helps. The vendor will get the order out just to get the buyer off his back. Likewise he should tell the vendor if the order may be delivered later. This gives the buyer more credibility when he asks to receive his order on time or even earlier than scheduled.

Most purchasing departments have a few expediters who do most of the follow-up, even going to vendor plants to see if the vendor needs any help. Not only does follow-up of this sort get more orders delivered on time, but, if an order is going to be delayed, the customer finds out about it sooner. This gives the customer company more time in which to change its plans.

It might seem that it would be cheaper just to carry a few more items in stock and then not every delay would catch the company short. Actually, however, this often does not pay because it takes too much extra inventory to provide very much protection. Besides, even with the bigger inventory, there will still be occasional stockouts. So it would be necessary to do some follow-up anyway, and the customer would still be out of some material now and then.

Receiving inspection

Purchasing is not complete until the material is in hand. Because receiving usually is not under the purchasing department, purchasing has to be told (it gets a copy of the receiving report) when materials come in as ordered so that it can clear the orders out of its file and tell accounting to pay the bill. The bill (or invoice) has by this time come in by mail to the accounting department. So has the freight bill covering shipping costs. If the material is not right in any way, purchasing has to handle all dealings with the vendor concerning what to do about it.

Yet sometimes it is not possible for receiving inspectors to tell if incoming products pass inspection unless they make special tests—chemical, electronic, or other. Normally, for example, a receiving clerk can't tell if a shipment of thermostats for stoves is all right. Or picture tubes for television sets. Sometimes he will need to call on engineering or the laboratory to pass final judgment.

HOW MUCH CENTRALIZATION?

When a company has several (or many) plants scattered around the country, it is possible to have one central office do all of the buying or only part of it. There is no pat answer as to which is better. Nearly all companies end up doing some of it centrally and some of it locally. General Motors decentralizes its buying to 52 divisions, which in turn decentralize the actual buying to more than 100 purchasing offices. To aid prospective vendors, GM puts out a directory booklet listing all of its purchasing offices and something about what each one buys.

Buying centrally means dealing in larger volumes, and this sometimes means better prices, possibly up to 10 percent better. And it means more "clout" in periods of materials scarcity. Future supplies are more assured. The total volume of any item is not, of course, increased by central buying. But the volume dealt with on a single contract will be the whole company's volume, not just one plant's volume, so this will probably mean a better price.

More specialized people will be doing the buying when it is done centrally. Buyers don't have to be so all purpose as buyers in small divisions of a company. Also, central buying cuts out duplication of orders and so saves clerical costs. It gives top management tighter control over the whole company's inventory policies, and it forces more standardization in designs. The American Management Associations report that there is a trend toward more centralization of purchasing in large companies.[2]

Against centralization is that it is often slow and too cumbersome for minor items. The thousands of little things can be bought better by

---

[2] Reported in *Management's Forum,* November 1975.

separate purchasing departments at the plant level. Also, plant inventories cannot be controlled very well from a central office. The controls are quite likely to become too rigid. Central people just cannot know local needs.

Also, even with central buying it is risky to buy *all* of any important item from only one supplier. It is well, just as insurance against strikes and other holdups, to divide the orders for most important items and place orders with at least two suppliers. But, of course, if this is done, part of the possible quantity discount expected from centralized purchasing is lost because each supplier gets smaller orders.

Freight is another item. If high-volume orders are placed with only one or two suppliers, and if they ship to all of the customer's plants, long freight hauls may cancel out any quantity discount obtained from volume buying. This does not apply, however, if the vendor is also a multiplant company and can ship to a customer's Midwest plant from its Midwest plant, to the customer's Pacific Northwest plant from its Pacific Northwest plant, and so on. But if the vendor of any item does not have plants close by, it will probably pay to give up central buying of that item and let each plant order its needs from a nearby plant just to save freight.

Materials which don't pass inspection and "short" shipments also turn up at times. These can be handled much better locally than centrally. Local buying also gives plant managers more responsibility, and it creates community goodwill.

Large companies usually end up centralizing all buying where large amounts of money are involved or where highly technical knowledge is required. They also centralize most capital expenditure buying because of the enduring nature of the commitment. Buying is also centrally done where reciprocity enters the picture. All other things are bought *decentrally* in the separate divisions. Often some dollar limit is set for local purchasing, and all contracts for more money must clear through central purchasing. The central purchasing department also sets up policies and procedures for the decentralized groups to use.

VALUE ANALYSIS

Value analysis tries to reduce the costs of purchased materials by studying the purpose to be served by a part or component being bought and by seeing if there are other less costly ways of accomplishing this purpose. Although the purchasing department is almost always active in this work, value analysis is encompassed in the larger subject of value engineering (which we discussed in connection with product design in Chapter 6).

KNOWN COST

The known-cost idea is very similar to value analysis and usually includes some value analysis work. "Known cost" is a term sometimes used to describe a policy of large retail buyers, such as Sears Roebuck or Kresge.

The customer company's buyer decides, for complete finished products or for parts, what he can afford to pay for an item, considering his resale price. The customer company may want, for example, a man's shirt which it can sell for $6. Then the buyer buys them on a set-price basis. He hopes to get good or even fine quality; yet, the price is often set so low (because of the low end product sale price) that there is strong pressure to reduce the item's production costs. Sometimes the supplier can't get his costs down this low without sacrificing quality. If so, a compromise is reached, and the price is raised or the quality is lowered, or both.

The term "known cost" comes from the idea that the customer company knows the price it will pay before negotiations start. The negotiations are concerned more with the quality it can get for the price than with the price which will be paid for a given quality. If either price or quality has to yield, quality—not price—becomes the variable factor.

Manufacturer buyers as well as retailing company buyers also practice the known-cost idea.

MASS PRODUCTION PURCHASING

General Motors spends over $1.5 billion a month for materials. It takes some 320,000 tons of steel, costing more than $90 million for bumpers and springs alone for Chevrolet cars in one year. But a company does not have to be General Motors to find itself buying many items in million dollar quantities in a year.

These contracts usually are so big that neither buyer nor seller wants to take any chances on price; yet, each wants to be sure of the contract. So the contracts are often written with the price left open, to be settled every now and then during the year. Quantities are also left open, to be set as the customer orders week by week. Or the price, if the item is a manufactured product, is often subject to negotiation if raw materials prices change. If steel prices go up, General Motors pays more for its bumper steel, or the reverse if steel prices go down. That way no one gets hurt much when prices change. Often there are penalty charges if the vendor does not deliver or if the buyer cancels.

Quantities in mass production are so large that neither buyer nor seller wants to carry enough inventory to last more than a few days, so both try to mesh their schedules exactly. Supplier dependability is even more important than price. In busy times Chevrolet cars eat up steel for bumpers and springs at the rate of more than 1,000 tons a day, which, at 50 tons to a freight-car load, means 20 freight car loads a day! Yet the factory rarely carries more than a day or two's supply on hand. In fact, it would want the freight cars of steel to come in at regular intervals all day long rather than all at once. Both the vendor and the railroad know this and try to deliver on this kind of schedule.

On the other hand, lead time is very important. To get steel in July, it needs to be rolled in the steel mills in June. Steel mills plan June's production in May, so General Motors has to place its order in April. But in April, Chevrolet's July car-making schedule has not yet been firmed up. Of course everybody knows that cars will be made in July but not how many or exactly what kinds. Purchasing has to go ahead anyway and place the order and then, in May or even June, ask the vendor to change the quantities to correct for any errors in forecasting. All of this schedule changing makes a great deal of extra work in the purchasing department and in the vendor plant's production control department.

HOW MANY TO BUY AT ONE TIME

Very few purchases are one-shot items. Nearly everything bought is bought again and again, so there is a question of whether to buy few and often or more at a time and less often. For big day-to-day, bread-and-butter items the answer has already been given: use blanket contracts covering perhaps a year's needs and then get frequent shipments as needed. For the bulk of other items—those bought repetitively but not on blanket contracts—the purchasing department, as we said, usually buys things only in response to specific requests from someone else.

Purchasing should not be too passive, though, in following other people's requests because they may ask for small quantities to be bought often. And it is expensive to order small items in little dribbles. Yet buying more at one time increases inventory carrying costs, so someone should try to balance out these costs. Inventory control and purchasing people should work together on problems of how many items to order at a time.

Companies sometimes "speculate" when buying big-volume, regular-use raw materials. If they think prices will go up, they may contract for even a year's supply in order to take advantage of today's price. This would be risky and would be quite uncommon and would need the approval of the board of directors because of the large financial commitment. Contracting for a year or more's needs is generally called speculation, for three months to a year is called forward buying, and for one month to three months ahead is called buying to requirements. Contracting for less than one month is called hand-to-mouth buying and is done only when companies are short of money or when they think prices will go down. Of course, such short-term contracting usually results in higher unit costs for the moment because of the small quantities bought on each order.

Standard quantities

Inventory controllers determine how many of an item they will need in the near future when they ask buyers to buy new supplies. For items which will continue to be used, however, the buyers should have some freedom to increase or decrease the quantity asked for to allow for buying in standard packages, full barrels, and whole bundles. Nearly always, if an order is for part of a standard package, the price per unit is higher. So the quantities actually ordered should be adjusted when necessary to come out to full standard packages.

On small items, it is often possible to set a fixed quantity (which recognizes standard packages) to reorder every time. Supplies are often ordered this way. So are minor "free issue" items, such as nuts and bolts. Ordering fixed quantities saves clerical time and costs.

This type of savings also applies elsewhere. It often applies where freight or truck rates are consequential. Perhaps the full railroad car freight rate for steel applies to orders of 30,000 pounds or more, but the inventory controller wants only 25,000 pounds right now. The shipping rate per pound is higher on all shipments of less than 30,000 pounds. It might even result that the total freight cost on 25,000 pounds at the less-than-carload rate would be *more* than the cost for 30,000 pounds at the full-carload rate.

Unless the company just does not need the extra 5,000 pounds *at all,* or not for a long time, it may be better off to order 30,000 pounds. The freight cost savings will outweigh the costs of carrying the extra 5,000 pounds a little longer than usual.

PRODUCT DESCRIPTIONS

Purchasing is a matter of buying what the organization needs, but, when a vendor is 500 miles away from his customer, he has to figure out from a piece of paper (the customer's purchase order) what the buyer wants. And if the vendor has several things which are almost alike, the customer doesn't get to choose except as he chooses from the vendor's catalog, where the differences are described.

This isn't like a customer going into a paint store for a paint brush, where he can see and feel the brushes. He can ask about them; he can tell the clerk what he wants the brush for and ask for his recommendation; and he can come away with a brush which suits him. Compare buying a brush this way with telling someone else to buy you a brush of the kind you need. Anyone who has tried to help someone else out by buying something for him knows all too well that his friend often doesn't like what is bought.

Actually, describing products is not easy. Sometimes, though, it is unnecessary to write lengthy specifications. Often standards that are generally understood by the trade can be used. Or the customer can specify an item's catalog number, or a trademark name, or maybe he can furnish a drawing or sample.

Written descriptions of materials are called specifications, and they must be used for many items which can't be described any other way (see Figure 17–3). Specifications describe an item in considerable detail and list certain requirements, such as chemical content, surface hardness, tensile strength, moisture content, heat content, and so on. Usually the

FIGURE 17–3

PURCHASING SPECIFICATION 2010996

RADIO CORPORATION OF AMERICA
PRODUCT ENGINEERING CORPORATE STANDARDIZING CAMDEN, N.J.

PAGE - 1 OF 3

DATE - MARCH 15

SUBJECT LAMINATED SHEET, EPOXY, GLASS-CLOTH BASE, FLAME-RETARDANT,
COPPER-CLAD (MILITARY TYPE GF, NEMA GRADE FR-4)

CODE IDENT NO. 49671	REV
COMM CODE	1602	5

1. Scope - This specification applies to flame-retardant, glass-cloth, epoxy-resin laminated sheet with copper foil bonded to one or both sides.

   The material is intended for use in the manufacture of printed circuits with fine etched lines when moisture resistance and high mechanical strength are required.

2. Reference Specifications - The following RCA Purchasing Specifications form part of this specification:

   2010995 Laminate, Glass Epoxy, Flame Retardant (NEMA Grade FR-4)

   2015200 Test for Solderability (Solder Dip Method)

   2015218 Flame Retardance of Plastic Laminates,Test Procedures and Requirements

3. Material - The copper-clad laminate shall meet all the requirements for Type GF in Military Specification MIL-P-13949C and any additional requirements of this specification.

   3.1 Laminate - The glass-cloth base, epoxy laminate shall conform to the requirements of RCA Purchasing Specification 2010995, except that the color, finish, and punching quality shall be as prescribed in this specification.

   3.2 Copper Foil - The copper foil shall be at least 99.5 percent pure and shall be uniform in quality and condition. It shall be clean, sound, smooth and free from internal and external defects detrimental to fabrication and uniform etching.

   Pits and dents shall not exceed those allowed by Class A

The thickness tolerances for sheet material as given in Table 1 are in accordance with Class I tolerances of Military Specification MIL-P-13949C for thicknesses of .031 inch and greater. At least 90 percent of the area of a sheet shall be within the tolerances given, and at no point shall the thickness vary from the nominal by more than 125 percent of the specified tolerance. Cut sheets less than eighteen inches by eighteen inches shall meet the applicable thickness tolerances in 100 percent of the area of the sheet.

The tolerances for thickness of the copper foil shall be as follows:

Nominal Thickness, Inch	Tolerance, Inch
.0014	+.0004, -.0002
.0028	+.0007, -.0003

4. Properties and Methods of Test - The material shall conform to the following requirements:

4.1 Composite Sheet -

   4.1.1 Squareness - The sheets as received from the vendor shall have the edges straight and the corners square within the limits of ninety degrees plus or minus 0.25 degree.

   4.1.2 Warp or Twist - The warp or twist of the sheet as received from the vendor shall be measured within one hour after the shipping package is opened and shall not exceed 0.5 inch on sheets 18.25 inches square to 18.25 inches by 21.25 inches. The measurement shall be made at the highest point on the sheet

Source: RCA Corp.

requirements are stated as test scores which will have to be met when the material is given certain tests.

Sometimes specifications have to describe characteristics that are not easy to describe. A surface may be required to be "reasonably free from surface defects"; a finish may be a "smooth satin finish"; a specially made product may have to be "of good and workmanlike quality." These seem to be rather vague instructions, but sometimes it is hard to do any better.

Sometimes, in purchasing, the customer has a choice of using a brand-name item or of ordering practically its equivalent by specification. Which to do is a moot question. Such choices are available with wire, chemicals, cement, flour, tool steel, cutting oils, grinding wheels, cleaning compounds, paints, and so on. All of these can be bought by using the vendor's trademark or catalog numbers. Or the customer company can ignore these and write his own specifications, stating what he wants in the way of chemical composition, size, performance requirements, and so on.

When a customer company buys all of its large quantities by specification, it will usually save money. It gets exactly what it wants. Trademark items may not be just right for a given job—maybe they are too good, or not good enough. Also, trademarked items are advertised and people who buy those items pay for the advertising.

On small orders, on the other hand, specification buying will probably cost more than buying trademarked materials. If the vendor has to make a special run of materials for an order, the cost of the special item may be more than the price of trademarked items. In general, for small quantities of anything, the customer should buy trademarked items.

CHOOSING VENDORS

The purchasing department nearly always decides which company to buy from. Equipment buying is an exception; so are some trademarked items that engineering or someone else insists on; and so are reciprocity deals, where top management tells the purchasing department whom to buy from.

To choose vendors intelligently, the purchasing department's buyers need to know which things are sold by which companies. This they learn from salesmen who call on them and from advertisements in technical and trade directories and buyers' guides. Also, they have a file of catalogs of vendor companies and their price and discount lists.

When deciding who gets an order, buyers should consider several things. Price, important though it is, is not the only thing. Reliability usually is more important than small price differences. Can and will the vendor company deliver the order on time? Will the materials pass inspection after they arrive? If they don't, will this vendor fix things up right away without argument? Schedule changes may also be a factor. Will this vendor take care of schedule changes and rush orders? How about service if something goes wrong? Or will he extend credit? Any of these matters might be important.

Assuming that all other factors are equal, often it is still not altogether clear which vendor's price is the lowest. In the following case, for example, from which vendor should the company buy? Each of the companies has submitted a bid in which a separate charge is listed for the special tooling which will be required plus an additional charge per unit with or without volume discounts.

Supplier	Tool charge	Price per unit	Discount for volume	
			Price	Volume over
A.............	$220	$.80	$.70	1,000
B.............	320	.72	.60	3,000
C.............	180	.96	.85	500

This problem can be solved by the break-even comparison method described in Chapter 3. The choice is, in all cases, the source with the lower tool cost for all volumes below the equal cost point and the source with the lower unit cost for volumes above the equal cost point.

To compare A and B at regular prices:

$$220 + .80x = 320 + .72x$$
$$x = 1,250$$

FIGURE 17–4

	Break-even Quantity			
	B Reg.	B Disc.	C Reg.	C Disc.
A Regular.............	1,250*	500*	250	800
A Discount............	−5,000*	1,000*	154*	267*
B Regular.......................................			583*	1,077*
B Discount......................................			389*	560*
* Nonapplicable answer.				

For volumes below 1,250 units, the choice is A, above 1,250 units it should be B. Actually, this particular comparison yields an irrelevant answer because at 1,250 units, B's volume discount price would not be in effect.

In our example there are 12 comparisons needing to be made before a decision can be made. Of these 12, only 2 are useful. Figure 17–4 lists the 12 comparisons. The stars indicate nonapplicable answers, nearly all because the answer is a quantity to which the price used in the calculation does not apply.

In summary, only the two comparisons of A regular prices with C regular prices and C discount prices are left. Because of C's low tool charge, purchases should be made at C's regular prices for volumes up to 250 units. Above 250 units, purchases should go to A at regular prices. At 500 units (this does not show in Figure 17–4) C's discount price comes into play and orders should be shifted to C. But at 800 units A's lower unit price again comes into play. A should get all orders for quantities above 800. There is no point where B should get any orders at all.

RECIPROCITY

"Dear Red," wrote FMC Corporation's board chairman to a Ford Motor Company vice president. "This is just a note to express appreciation for the good news we had, that your company had decided to purchase part of your Nashville requirements for soda ash from our company.

"Effective as of now, wherever possible, our people are to purchase Ford products. I believe that our salesmen and service fleet now amounts to 600 to 700 cars. As you know, our two company chauffeured cars are Continentals which we buy new each year, and our family has only Continentals."

It took a court order to unearth this letter in a Federal Trade Commission investigation of reciprocity practices. Thus, reciprocity is industry's version of "You scratch my back and I'll scratch yours"—or you buy from me and I'll buy from you. Back in the old days, when Henry Ford and Harvey Firestone were alive, they were friends; so Henry put Firestone tires on most new Fords, and Harvey used Ford cars and trucks in his tire company.

Buying from each other sounds reasonable, although most people—particularly purchasing agents—condemn it. Most companies even deny they practice it; but, on the other hand, they don't give customers a cold shoulder when they place purchase contracts. That would be a fine way to lose customers. Customers are not at all above asking "If we buy from you, are you going to buy from us?

The FMC board chairman, for example, also sent a "Dear Roger" letter to the head of U.S. Steel in which he pointed out that FMC had bought $3,446,000 worth of U.S. Steel products whereas U.S. Steel had bought only $453,000 worth of products from FMC. Then he wrote: "I wish you would send my letter to whomever is in charge of reciprocity for your company and would see that they are alerted to our relationship with your company. There are a number of chemicals which we are in a position to sell your company." He suggested that an FMC vice president meet with the proper U.S. Steel executive. In many companies the reciprocity person is called the "trade relations representative."

Actually, every company has to buy from someone, so it is not surprising that reciprocity is a common practice. Purchasing agents regard it as a necessary evil. But one might ask what is bad about it? Does it matter what make of steel filing case is used in the office? Or whether salesmen drive Chevrolets or Fords? Why shouldn't purchasing agents face up to the fact that the company has customers?

Purchasing agents don't like reciprocity because they have to buy some items where they are told to and don't get to shop around. They are afraid they might have to take inferior materials or pay higher prices and get poorer service. This would not be particularly important for supply items which are consumed, but it could be quite important for materials and components that go into finished products.

It is true that all of these things *may* occur—and some of them *will* occur once in a while. But purchasing agents look at only one side of the coin. Just as sure as a company sometimes loses a little on buying, it gains on the selling end. Surely a company gets some sales where its products are not the very best or least costly. Probably reciprocity balances out.

If reciprocity hurts anyone, it is small companies. They don't buy enough to command much attention. Big companies have to buy from their *big* customers to keep them. Their big customers demand it. Small customers demanding a share of what a big company buys do not always get far with their threat to buy elsewhere. Actually, though, even small customers often get a share of a big company's purchases. Big companies try to satisfy *all* their customers by dividing their ordering at least a little.

Every now and then the Federal Trade Commission speaks out against reciprocity. But, although its interest in reciprocity started a decade or more ago, the FTC has not pushed very hard—not hard enough to curtail the practice very much.

BIDDING VERSUS NEGOTIATED CONTRACTS

When the government lets contracts, normally it is supposed to ask for bids and take the lowest price, provided the lowest bidder is deemed capable of fulfilling the contract. Private industry has no such required rules. Sometimes private organizations don't even ask for bids but just dicker with their main supplier and agree on a contract, price and all.

At first this does not sound like the best way because the company cannot be sure that it is getting the best possible deal. But, in fact, the purchasing agent usually has a pretty good idea because either his own company makes some of the same things itself and he knows the company's costs or he occasionally asks for bids from other companies. Or possibly he will have his company's engineers go over the vendor's expected cost figures to be sure that he is reasonably efficient and that his price is reasonable. In the end, some of the biggest buying contracts are negotiated and not bid.

On the other hand, most middle-size orders and most large special contracts are bid for. And, if the purchasing agent does not give the contract to the lowest bidder, at least the one who gets it has to be near the low bid. Buyers, supposedly, should always choose the lowest bid from among those from vendors who probably can do the job well.

But thousands of little things that are bought are neither negotiated nor bid. They are just ordered from a catalog at list price less the usual discount. About all the buyer does is look in two or three vendors' catalogs and order from the one who quotes the lowest price. The money involved doesn't justify much effort in trying to save a few pennies.

GOVERNMENT CONTRACTS

More than $20 billion a year of government contracts go to companies making defense products and space products. Most of this goes to airplane, missile, and electronics companies.

Often single contracts total hundreds of millions of dollars, and often, too, each individual product (an airplane, for example) costs many millions of dollars. As a rule the government places a contract for a complete contract with one company, and it becomes the "prime" contractor. Prime contractors then buy whatever components they themselves don't make. In a few cases the government will buy and furnish major components, such as jet engines for airplanes. Boeing, Lockheed, and the others do not make these components, nor do they themselves buy them. The government buys them from General Electric or other firms and supplies them. But for the thousands of other items bought, the prime contractor places the order.

Prime contracts are usually (but not always) let on a competitive basis. Sometimes, when they are essentially continuation contracts, the terms are set by negotiation. Prices are usually set expecting the contractor to earn 7 percent of the sales price as a profit (10 percent of research contracts). The government's pricing policies, however, shift from time to time.

As of 1976, most of the largest contracts were not at fixed prices but were "incentive" contracts. Such contracts specify a price that is based upon expected costs, performance, and delivery schedules. But if costs overrun and go higher, the company and the government share the excess. Or, if there are cost savings, these too are shared. Similarly, bonuses are given for performance above expectations and for delivery ahead of schedule. And, in a parallel way, subspecification performance and late deliveries are penalized.

Government contracts differ from most others in that they rule out assessments of overhead not related to the contract. The government also expects the learning curve (see p. 181) to operate. Prices on large contracts contemplate that final products will cost less to make than initial products.

The prime contractor, if it is an airplane maker, probably has to buy such items as aluminum sheets, landing gear, and radar because it doesn't make these items. It is free to buy these items wherever it wants, except that the government requires it to buy American-made items and that a stated portion of subcontract business be given to small companies.

Besides having to subcontract, the prime contractor is responsible for seeing that the subcontractor is capable of doing the work, that the prices paid to subcontractors meet all regulations, that the sub can finance the contract, and that it does not make too much money on the contract. The prime contractor is responsible for seeing that all subcontractors obey all work-hour, nondiscrimination, and wage regulations, and also that the quality and reliability of their products meet government requirements and that they meet their promised delivery schedule. Sometimes subcontractors are so anxious to get contracts that they promise anything the prime contractor asks and then can't make good. The prime contractor's purchasing department may have to send in various specialists, particularly inspectors and quality control engineers, to help out.

PURCHASE CONTRACTS

Purchase orders, after acceptance by the vendor, become legal contracts which bind both parties. If either one doesn't live up to the contract, the other can sue. Trouble is rare though, because both parties usually do what they agree to. And, if one side violates a small part of the contract (as when delivery of the materials is a few days late), the matter is rarely of enough importance to make much difference. Or if a small part of a shipment is rejected, the customer accepts the balance and pays accordingly. Or if it is all rejected, either the vendor replaces it or the contract is dropped and the order is placed elsewhere. Even if a customer cancels an order or wants to return materials, the vendor is usually willing to do what the customer wants just to keep him satisfied.

It is easy for each side to be agreeable in most minor contract violations because no one is going to lose much. But, if someone has to take a big loss, the contracting parties are not always quite so agreeable. If the prospective loss is great, the two parties sometimes submit their differences to arbitration, or even go to court. In court the *contract as written* is the basis for the decision as to whether an actual breach of contract has occurred. Whichever party is judged to have breached the contract will be liable for damages.

Standard printed contracts are used as the order form when the amount of money is small, but on large orders special contracts are written almost every time. Such things as the possible return of goods, contract cancellation, price adjustments, and provision for the arbitration of disputes between buyer and seller are all written into the contract. If there is any doubt about a contract's wording or interpretation, the purchasing department should consult the legal department before contracts are signed.

DISCOUNTS

In the United States at the retail level, we are used to a one-price system. The seller sets a price, and we either pay it or don't buy. Discount houses flourish, though, in all of our big cities, proving that most of us shop around to get the best buy. We don't argue with a vendor about price, but in effect we bargain on prices by going elsewhere when we think a price is too high.

Company purchasing agents almost never buy at retail prices, nor does the one-price system work very well in industrial buying. As we have seen, purchasing agents ask for bids or negotiate prices on all big and middle-size contracts and on all small contracts for special items. On smaller orders for catalog items, they expect and get discounts from list prices.

Sometimes they get two or three discounts in series (such as 20 percent off, then 10 percent off the balance, and maybe another 5 percent off that) on the same order. Catalog items' list prices are supposed to be retail prices, and they are the prices a manufacturer almost never pays.

Regular discounts are of three kinds: trade, quantity, and cash. Trade discounts are supposed to be a certain percent for retailers and a bigger percent for wholesalers, jobbers, or other manufacturers. Manufacturers of items that are sold finally at retail sometimes get only as little as one third of the retail list price. Trade discounts are supposed (even required by the Robinson-Patman Act, a federal law) to be the same for all buyers in the same class (as, for example, wholesalers). The law is not too effective in the case of manufacturers' buying from other manufacturers because they ask for slightly different items—items not sold to others at all. So there can be no direct comparison between what they pay and what someone else pays.

Quantity discounts, which are generally offered to customers who buy big quantities, are usually quite small compared with trade discounts. Quantity discounts are in addition to trade discounts and are supposed to be equally available to all customers. Large buyers are sometimes able to coax still bigger discounts (for themselves only) out of vendors by threatening them with buying elsewhere. Under present laws, vendors are allowed to pass on, in the form of lower prices, the savings in cost that large orders make possible, but *no more* than that. The difficulty of figuring the exact savings keeps this law from being very effective.

Cash discounts are often offered as inducements to pay fast. Most bills are due in 30 days, but vendors don't want to wait that long for their money. Cash discounts of 2 percent if the bill is paid in 10 days (instead of 30) bring in most of the money sooner. Besides, they also cut bad-debt losses. Two percent off for paying sooner is a fine windfall for the customer; it is equivalent to a 36 percent return a year on his money. Most customers will pay up fast even if they have to borrow money from a bank to do so. Yet why would a vendor rather have 98¢ in 10 days than $1 in 30 days? He would probably rather wait and get more, but he has to meet industry customs.

Competition has brought other kinds of concessions that amount to discounts. Freight equalization is common when competing vendors are not located the same distance from the customer. A faraway vendor offers to pay the difference between the freight cost from his plant to the customer's plant and the freight cost from a competitor's plant that is nearer to the company's plant. Other practices, amounting in effect to discounts, include postdating the bill, thus extending credit for longer times; offering to pay part of the customer's advertising costs on the assumption that he will advertise the vendor's product; and offering free engineering or other help.

PURCHASING PROBLEMS

How much price pressure?

Although the same prices are supposed to be quoted to all customers in each class (manufacturer, jobber, wholesaler, retailer), it doesn't always work that way. A large customer in any class can chisel down the price he pays until it is not far above an item's cost to manufacture. All he has to do is threaten to place his order somewhere else or to make his own items. Little customers can play at this game, too, although not quite so effectively.

Gifts

Should an appreciative vendor show his appreciation for getting a contract? That is, should he show it by giving the person who sent him the order (another company's buyer) a gift? It is so easy to answer no that we seem to have disposed of the problem. Any other answer opens the door to kickbacks, rebates, and outright bribery—to the detriment of the buying company—because bribed buyers will place orders where *they* get the most out of it, not where the company benefits the most.

But the problem can't be put down so easily. Vendors are appreciative, and most of us like to be appreciated. We corrupt easily on the receiving end when we receive gifts. Spending money just seems to breed graft, at least small-scale graft. Most companies have hard and fast rules against their buyers' accepting expensive gifts, but most of them don't object to, say, free meals, a box of cigars, a cigarette lighter, or a few bottles of liquor at Christmas time. But a TV set or an automobile—no. Mink coats and lavish entertainment during big-city visits also are out.

Curiously, the ethics of gifts seems to be all one-sided—we always hear about the person who *receives* a gift and whether this is proper. But someone has to *give* gifts. Can a company logically forbid its buyer to receive a gift and at the same time pay the bills for the gifts given by its own sales department?

The very embarrassing disclosures in the mid 1970s that several American companies had paid bribes to officials in countries around the world in connection with selling airplanes or to win contracts to construct power plants, steel mills, and so on shows what the practice of giving gifts can come to. There are some countries in the world where this is the accepted way of doing business, but it is not according to the code of ethics in most Western countries. And particularly since the bribery disclosures, surely managers will try even harder to see that none of this goes on so far as their organization is concerned.

MISCELLANEOUS FUNCTIONS OF THE PURCHASING DEPARTMENT

The purchasing department should always be on the lookout for less costly materials. Sometimes this means that they need to try out new materials. This means sample runs in the factory and performance tests to see how the new materials work. Purchasing should follow all such trials, noting their success or failure. Purchasing should also keep informed about the quality of what it buys. Whenever the factory has trouble with bought items, purchasing should take it up with the vendor and try to eliminate the problem.

Another duty of purchasing is to handle all matters relating to rejected purchased materials—whether they are rejected when received or later in processing. All correspondence having to do with disposing, reworking, or returning anything is handled by the purchasing department. Purchasing also sells all of a company's salvage and waste materials. It gets this job, rather than the sales department, because these are materials, not finished products. The purchasing department knows materials markets better than does the sales department.

REVIEW QUESTIONS

1. How important is purchasing? If wages make up 20 percent of a company's total costs, how important is it to get greater productivity from workers as against doing a more effective job of purchasing?

2. Suppose that purchasing is regarded as "outside manufacture." In what way does this viewpoint affect purchasing?

3. What part should the purchasing department play in make-buy decisions? When, if ever, should the purchasing department instigate a change from one policy to the other? How would the purchasing department come to realize that such a change should be made?

4. The text says that big, steady-use items are often bought on a more or less continuing basis for years from the same supplier and that contracts for such items are not really open to competition. Is this wise? Discuss.

5. What is the "known-cost" concept? This concept brings purchasing closer to quality determination problems. Should this be? After all, the purchasing department is not highly qualified in the quality area. Or is it? Discuss.

6. Most large companies buy their big items by specification rather than by brand name or trademark. How far down the volume scale should this practice be carried? Why?

7. The Federal Trade Commission does not like reciprocity. Why, then, does it not order it stopped? Discuss.

8. Purchasing agents usually object to reciprocity as a practice. Why? What might the company president's views be? Why?

9. How does the typical American one-price system operate so far as industrial buying is concerned? What part do discounts play in actual pricing?

QUESTIONS FOR DISCUSSION

1. The president wants to know if his purchasing department is doing a good job, so he calls in a consultant and asks him to investigate and tell him. How should the consultant go about his work?

2. Purchasing and sales are two sides of the same coin. Is there any occasion for having men with different training in these two departments?

3. A large company with government contracts finds from its past experience that small suppliers are so often unreliable that it would be better off in every way to cut way down on subcontracting. Should it do so? Why?

4. When a company buys instead of making parts, it would seem that it would incur extra transportation and packing costs and that it would have to carry more inventory and be out of stock more often than if it made the items itself. How, therefore, can it ever be wise to buy instead of make?

5. Should one division of a company be allowed to buy from the outside when the same items are made by a sister division of the same company? (The buying division thinks it can save a little money by doing this.) Discuss.

6. A San Francisco plant manager wants to buy his printed forms locally and not have them printed by the central print shop in the Chicago office. Should he be allowed to do this? Discuss.

7. When a company buys by specifications, it writes its own specifications. Isn't there a danger that these may not be rewritten and updated enough to incorporate new developments? How can a company protect itself against obsolescence in the design of purchased parts?

8. Assume that you are the buyer who places orders for all of the blackboard erasers in your school. How do you decide what kind to buy? How do you decide when to buy them? Would you buy them by specification? Write out the item description you would use.

9. In order to convince the vendor of the urgency of the company's need, the expediter wants to go to the vendor plants involved. Should the company send him? What can he do? To whom will he talk? When should outside-of-the-plant expediters be used?

10. The expediter is happy. He got the order through even though it took air express to get some of the parts. Should this please the president? Why?

11. What should the president tell the purchasing agent about how much price pressure to put on vendors?

12. It is found that the purchasing agent owns 100 shares of Du Pont stock, a company with which he places orders for paint for the company. What should be done about this situation?

PROBLEMS

1. Should the company buy or make steel stampings in the following example? They can be bought for $44,000. The company figures that it will cost $50,000 to make these same stampings, with its costs being as follows: materials, $15,000; direct and indirect labor, $7,500; machine costs, supervising, tool design, handling, labor fringe benefits, and so on, $20,000. These total $42,500. General overhead of $7,500 brings the inside costs up to $50,000. The plant is not operating at capacity and could make these stampings if this were the decision. Discuss.

2. Should the company make or buy the following three items?

	Product		
	A	B	C
Quantity needed.	40,000	15,000	24,000
Material costs/unit.	$ .046	$.0185	$.0275
Direct labor hours required.	360	300	100
Purchase price/unit.	$ .141	$ .172	$ .090

The direct labor cost rate is $6.40 per hour. There are also variable overheads, which go up and down with labor, which cost $6 per labor-hour. Fixed overhead is $4.20 per direct labor-hour (based on 2,000 hours a year).

If the decision is to buy these items, would the fact that the plant is heavily loaded or is working far below capacity change the decision in any way?

3. The steel supplier quotes the following prices for rolls of strip steel:

Number of rolls ordered at a time	Price per roll
0–24	$24.00
25–74	23.85
75–199	23.75
199 and over	23.70

The company uses 400 rolls of this steel a year. It costs $50 to place an order and 20 percent to carry inventory. How many rolls should be bought at a time? Note: The economic lot size idea explained in Chapter 21 would help here, but it is not necessary for getting an approximate answer.

4. Two suppliers have sent in bids for supplying component part X. These parts will be needed at the rate of 1,000 a month for a year but not thereafter.

Supplier A is 1,000 miles away and has been known not to deliver on time every time. His quality control is also a little less than perfect, and once in a while a shipment will have to be rejected. His proposal:

Cost of tooling (to be paid by you)	$1,000
Up to 1,000 units	.28 ea.
1,000 to 5,000	.27 ea.
5,000 and over	.26 ea.

Supplier A will ship as many or as few as are wanted, according to the customer's delivery schedule, but he needs 10 weeks' lead time.

Supplier B is 100 miles away and is very dependable. His proposal:

Cost of tooling (to be paid by you)	$1,000
Up to 1,000 units	.32 ea.
1,000 to 2,000	.31 ea.
2,000 to 4,000	.30 ea.
4,000 and over	.29 ea.

B will also ship according to the customer's delivery schedule and needs 2 weeks' lead time. Buying from B saves $.01 per unit in freight costs.

It costs ¼ cent a week to carry product X in stock.

What purchasing and stocking policy should the company follow if it expects B never to let it down but A to let it down four times in a year, each time costing $200 for the delay?

5. The company is considering making versus buying a heavily used part. This part goes into a new finished product whose total volume is very much a question. The market forecasters estimate that there is a 90-percent probability of selling at least 5,000 units. They estimate that there is a 75-percent chance of selling at least 15,000 and a 40-percent chance of selling as many as 30,000.

To make the items, it would be possible to choose between two alternative methods. The first would require an investment of $5,000 in tooling and $1.30 per unit in variable costs. The second would require $15,000 for tooling and $.50 per unit in variable costs.

These items can be bought in quantities up to 5,000 for $3 per unit. For orders of more than 5,000, the price is $2 each. For orders of over 10,000 units, $1.50, and for orders above 15,000, $1.25.

What should the company do? Show the figures.

CASE 17–1

The plant manager is on the telephone calling you, the purchasing agent, about production holdups. He says that several jobs are being held up in the factory from the failure of purchased parts to arrive. He has just called the supplier, who has told him that there is no reason for the delay. The supplier could easily have got the parts delivered if he had only known that you wanted them.

What happened was that, because of production trouble with materials, an unusual number of items were spoiled in process and more were needed. The factory's production control department, being forbidden to call suppliers direct, had called the buyer in the purchasing department asking for a rush shipment. But the buyer was out sick with a cold for two days and didn't get the call and missed learning about it when he came back.

Should the factory's production control department ever call suppliers direct? What reasons are there for and against their doing this?

CASE 17–2

The Mississippi Company found that it could buy the wiring systems used in the machines it made for considerably less than its past cost for making them. Since the savings came to $25,000 a year, the company decided to buy instead of make, even though this meant laying off ten workers and putting others in the wiring department on short hours.

The union said that the company had no right to do this and asked for an arbitrator to decide. The company refused but the union carried it to court; it lost in the district court but was upheld by the appeals court, which ordered the company to arbitrate. The labor contract said nothing about making or buying.

You are the arbitrator. You decide. Does the company have the right to subcontract work outside in this case?

CASE 17–3

   The manager of the Lux textile mill looked forward glumly to the next three months. They were the low months of the year, months when there would be only four days of work a week for only one quarter of the usual work force.

   Then his phone rang. It was a buyer from a large chain store with a proposition. He offered to buy enough material from Lux to keep the mill operating normally through the whole slow period. Furthermore, he hinted at repeating the offer next year if this year's arrangement worked out well.

   There was a catch in the deal, however. The chain store buyer quoted a price which was not very much over the cost of materials and labor. If Lux accepted the order it would get back only a small amount of the overhead costs it stood to lose if it refused the order. So if Lux accepted, it would be selling below total costs.

   The offer was not easy to refuse, however. If it were accepted, the work force would be kept busy and Lux would be less worse off than if it turned the offer down. In the short run, Lux would be better off to accept the offer. But in the long run the low-price items offered for sale by the chain store would cut the throats of Lux's regular customers. To make the choice even more difficult, Lux's manager couldn't prevent his customers' getting hurt just by holding his head high and turning the offer down. There were too many other textile mills. Someone, somewhere, would accept the offer.

   What should be done in this case?

SUGGESTED SUPPLEMENTARY READINGS

Ammer, Dean S. "Is Your Purchasing Department a Good Buy?" *Harvard Business Review,* March–April 1974.

Dowst, Somersby. "Supplier Rating: Vendor Evaluation Turns Predictive." *Purchasing,* November 18, 1975.

LaLonde, B. J., and Cambert, D. M. "Management of Purchasing in an Uncertain Economy." *Journal of Purchasing and Materials Management,* Winter 1975, pp. 3–8.

18

Basic inventory concepts and generalized control systems

During 1975 General Electric sold $13.4 billion worth of products and at the end of the year owned $2.1 billion worth of inventories—stocks of materials and products. General Foods sold $3.7 billion worth of products and ended the year owning $580 million worth of inventories. RCA sold $4.6 billion worth of products and services and finished the year owning an inventory of $600 million. In these three companies (and they are typical) inventories tied up more than one fourth of all the companies' invested capital.

Some inventories are in the form of *raw materials and purchased items* to be used in making products. Some inventories are *supplies* to be used up. Some are *half-manufactured items* in production departments. Some are *finished parts* ready to be put into assembled products. Some are *finished products* in shipping rooms and warehouses.

Inventory is *money* that is temporarily in the form of a bar of brass, a sheet of steel, an iron casting, a bag of chemicals, a bolt of cloth, or a spare grinding wheel. But it isn't at all like money in the bank. It is money on which the company *pays* interest rather than earns interest. After a year, $100 in the bank may be worth $107. After a year on the shelf, $100 of inventory is worth nearer $80, because it has cost $20 in expenses to carry it.

Most companies estimate that it costs 20 or more percent of the value of inventories to carry them for a year. This is because inventories cost money in several ways. They take up space and space costs money; they have to be put into and taken out of storage; they tie up money and cause an "opportunity cost." Usually inventories are insured, resulting in insurance premiums; and there are property taxes on inventories. They need

424

to be managed (they even have to be counted now and then), so it is necessary to keep records. They need to be protected from the weather and from pilferage, but, even so, some things will deteriorate or disappear. Some items (rubber products, for example) have only a limited shelf life, and some obsolescence occurs all the time. All of these costs, added together, may easily exceed 20 percent.

Inventory control people monitor inventories, but there is more to the job than mere recordkeeping. They have to try to reach several objectives which are actually in conflict with each other. They try: (1) never to run out of anything while (2) never having much of anything on hand and (3) never to pay high prices because of buying in small quantities. Inventory managers try to determine what the proper inventory level should be while trying to give good service to manufacturing departments and to outside customers yet while holding down the costs.

It is not easy to produce and sell large volumes of products while owning almost nothing in transit and at the same time never run out of anything or pay high prices because of hand-to-mouth buying or production. Yet huge sums of money are involved. If GE, through poor control, let its inventories go up 10 percent, it would have to put $210 million more into the inventories it owns. But if proper control were able to cut 10 percent off its present investment, it would have $210 million it could invest elsewhere. Besides that, GE would save some more millions from not having to store all the extra inventory. Ten percent means $58 million to General Foods and $60 million to RCA. Ten percent of its inventory investment means a whopping $570 million to General Motors.

An uncontrolled inventory is usually *too much* inventory. It is particularly pernicious because it is painless—even pleasant. No harm is done if new supplies do not come in on time. The production department never runs out of anything. Nor does a customer ever have to wait for a finished product. Everyone is happy; but the money tied up in inventory can be enormous, as are all the other costs that large inventories entail.

It would not be quite so serious if everything finally was used up. But uncontrolled inventories always seem to contain a substantial number of "buggy whip" items which eventually have to be thrown away. (Think of the once "useful" things in your garage which are now "junk.") Their investment is lost, as are the expenses of carrying them for several years before they are thrown away. (See Figure 18–1.)

Now we need to back up a little. Inventory control which looks *only* at holding down the level of inventory could easily be suboptimal and be poor control. Managers need to consider the impact of inventory policy on the entire organization. As was said in Chapter 8, it is sometimes desirable to build up inventories during low demand periods in order to allow the factory to operate economically. While our attention here may seem to be directed wholly towards holding down inventory costs, this should *not* be done when it runs counter to the interest of overall effective operations.

FIGURE 18–1

Why do we have so much of it?

RAW MATERIALS

Heavily used raw materials are usually bought on blanket contracts with deliveries scheduled to match the organization's needs. Almost no reserve supply is carried—incoming shipments are scheduled to arrive daily or even at specific times during the day. This usually works well if the items are made locally. But for shipped-in items it is usually necessary to allow more lead time. Rarely is it safe to carry less than two or three days' supply as a safety stock. Release orders to suppliers, telling them exactly how much and when to ship, are usually given directly to the vendors by the production control department. This amounts to the production control department (not the materials control department) controlling the small safety inventories of heavily used raw materials.

Less heavily used raw materials are usually controlled by dollar limits, time limits, or other methods to be discussed later.

One minor problem in raw materials control is material shrinkage. Shrinkage comes from buying in one unit and issuing in another. For example, sheet steel is bought by the ton and issued by the sheet. If the sheets are a little thicker than usual, there are not as many sheets in a ton as would be expected, and the sheet inventory will run out sooner than if they were thinner.

Also, some things are measured out as they are issued: wire (bought by the pound, issued by length), liquids, pipe, lumber, and so on. Issuers nearly always give liberal measure, so the supply ends up short. Or, as in sheet metal, pipe, lumber, or glass, the lengths or sizes bought are standard, but there is wastage in cutting to size. Experience will reveal what shrinkage to expect, and inventory controllers can factor this into their material requirements planning.

IN-PROCESS INVENTORIES

Materials moving through production account for a large portion of total inventories in all companies which have manufacturing cycles (the time it takes to make products) in weeks or months. (At Westinghouse they account for 80 percent of the investment in inventories.) Controlling work in process is largely a matter of moving products through production as fast as possible, but it is also concerned with getting orders out in their proper priority order.

This is a scheduling problem and is production control's responsibility. But even companies which count their manufacturing cycle in days instead of weeks can have substantial amounts of money tied up in inventory in process.

SUPPLIES

Supplies are supporting materials that are used up in running the plant or in making the company's products but which do not themselves go into the product. (Sometimes these are called MRO items—for maintenance, repair, and operating supplies.) While the cost of MRO items over a year is low compared to that of materials going into products, their control should not be neglected. In many companies, unfortunately, particularly small ones, supplies are often handled carelessly and wastefully. They are handed out without requisitions, and no check is made on their use. Since most supplies are expendable, except perhaps complicated tooling, it is difficult to check on their proper issuance and use.

To control supplies, it is often necessary to have several separate supplies stockrooms: one for maintenance department supplies and materials, another for tools and tooling, another for cutting oils and lubricants, another for stationery supplies, and so on. Materials (except for very little things) should be issued from them only upon presentation of written requisitions, properly authorized and showing the account to be charged, unless, of course, the cost of this paperwork is high compared to the value of the supplies. Budgets can be established limiting departments in their use of supplies in order to discourage numerous little "private inventories" besides those of the stockrooms.

ENCLOSED STOCKROOMS

Most materials, particularly infrequently used items, are kept in enclosed stockrooms, from which they are issued only when a person presents a requisition. Materials in enclosed stockrooms are generally better cared for than things left out in the open. Also, enclosed stockrooms are essential to accurate records of the stock that comes in and goes out (see Figure 18–3). This is especially important for computerized inventory control systems.

Separate stockrooms are often needed for raw materials, semifinished items, finished parts (including finished subassemblies), finished products,

FIGURE 18–2

Order picking with narrow aisles and high rack storage

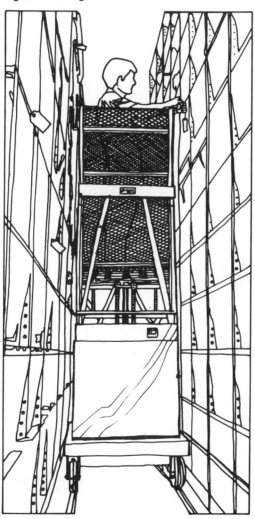

and supplies. Often, more than one stockroom is needed for each kind of material so each will be near its point of use.

Having small substockrooms is, however, a mixed blessing. Even if one-day replenishment service is given from central stores, substores tend to accumulate supplies as if they were the sole source. Each substockroom manager remembers that "Central stores was out of stock last time"; or he says, "It's too much trouble to reorder so often."

Timken Roller Bearing found that 3 substores were each using 20 U belts a month, and each one averaged 50 on hand. Besides this, central stores used 40 a month and carried 200. In total, a stock of 350 belts was carried to support a usage of 100 a month. Timken then changed its procedure and saved over half of the inventory by not allowing the substores to reorder until they ran out and then confining their reorders to only one month's requirements.

Individual stockrooms often stock several thousand items so often there are some real problems with receiving materials, identifying them, knowing where they are kept, and putting them away. Besides this, there are record-keeping problems as well as problems of stockroom arrangements and indexes to where things are stored. Computer controlled systems, however, are improving these problems. See Figure 18–3 for the characteristics of a good stockroom operation.

OPEN STOCKROOMS

A great deal of paper work and handling of materials can be saved by point-of-use storage (storing materials right next to the operation where they are needed). This can be done where the same kinds of material are used day after day and where the materials are not likely to be stolen or otherwise misappropriated. It can also be done with parts along assembly lines. As parts are made or as bought parts arrive (particularly if they arrive in small quantities in frequent repeat shipments), they are checked in and taken directly to their point of use and left there rather than in stockrooms. The operators just help themselves to whatever they need. In the accounts of the company, the value of the materials used is charged to the products made on a standard cost basis. Neither reports of materials used nor requisitions are necessary.

Even when open stores are used, however, the supply (or "bank") of materials stored at the operation is usually relatively small because there is very little storage space next to operations. Rarely (for large items) is the open supply sufficient to carry on for more than an hour. New supplies must be continually added from larger "backup" storerooms, where the conditions described in Figure 18–3 should prevail.

When parts are made in lots instead of continuously, they go first into finished parts stores because a lot is likely to be a month's supply or more of an item. Assemblers work from open bins which are replenished continually from the enclosed finished parts stockroom.

FIGURE 18–3

Characteristics of a good stockroom operation

1. The inventory is stored inside a stockroom that has preassigned bins and an overflow area that is clearly identified.
2. The stockroom has a fence.
3. The fence has a door.
4. The door has a lock on it, and there are very few keys, which are distributed only to authorized people.
5. No unauthorized people ever wander in and out of the stockroom.
6. Service is prompt, and the stockroom hours are known in advance.
7. Every receipt is accompanied by a proper document.
8. Every issue has a corresponding document identified with it.
9. The stockroom people are well trained; a job description is available, and there is a break-in period for new people.
10. The objective of zero defects is clearly well understood.
11. Time is allowed every day to reconcile transactions with inventories.
12. Audits are taken periodically, and discrepancies are totally unacceptable.
13. The users have complete confidence in the stockroom's integrity, and that is most important.

The inventory in a company is cash, and the stockroom is the local bank, a company from which we can learn a lot. Is it not remarkable that the average manufacturing company with several million dollars' worth of parts in inventory—more than your local bank would ever have in cash—does not insist on similarly stringent procedures? Even though it is our money in the bank, we do not walk in and help ourselves but follow definite procedures. A stockroom storing parts must be operated in the same way.

Source: George W. Plossl, *Materials Requirements Planning and Inventory Records Accuracy*, International Business Machines, 1973, p. 3.

Open stores do not work as well, however, when *assembly* is by lot. Before even one finished product can be assembled, it is necessary to accumulate *all* the different parts needed and in the right quantity for the lot. Then the total supply of all the parts could be issued, and the products put together one after another. But, although it is best to keep such lots in enclosed stores until all component parts have arrived, it is also better to take only a day or two's parts needs to the assembly area at any one time, lest they take up too much room, become damaged, or disappear.

There is also a second, very different kind of open stores. Here, "open stores" refers to the arrangement of the stockroom itself, and it really means random stacking of large tote boxes or metal storage containers mounted on pallets. Sometimes a stockroom stores several hundred such portable storage containers of component parts. The stock of one single kind of part may fill up one or several of these storage containers. Usually, these containers have rigid corner posts some three feet high, thus permitting loads to be stacked and tiered a half dozen or more tiers high. Often, too, the materials will be stacked three or four rows deep. In any case, many kinds of parts will be stored in a given stores section, and the loads will be put into and taken out of storage in a somewhat random arrangement.

All that is required for such a system is to keep records of the locations of loads in the storeroom. This can be done with a simple card file system or by using a computer to keep the record.

Permanent spaces are not assigned to any products. When new supplies arrive they are put wherever there is room. Then the trucker reports the location where he puts each load to the stock controller. It doesn't matter if supplies of a single item are stored in several locations, nor does it matter if the trucker has to move several loads to get the one he wants. With tiering fork lift trucks, he can put in or take out loads quickly and be on his way.

Random storage areas need not, however, be totally random. Often, the items which are moved into and out of storage more frequently than others are stored close to the production floor to minimize material handling time.

Such storage areas are usually "open" in the sense that they are not in an enclosed area. Loads usually don't disappear since each one can consist of a half ton of largely unsalable parts (unsalable to a thief) which cannot be reached without a tiering lift fork truck or some other material handling device.

PHYSICAL INVENTORIES

Inventory records can never stay wholly accurate, so an actual count needs to be made (a "physical inventory") of what there is on hand from time to time. Companies used to close down for a week at the end of the year to count everything. This is still done sometimes, but now it is more common to count all the time. The stores clerk counts what is on hand in the bins in one section this week, another section next week, and so on. This periodic checking, called "cycle counting," is usually scheduled into the regular duties of stockroom clerks so they can check the entire inventory two or three times a year.

Counting at least once a year is usually desirable. The government insists that a company's inventory records be accurate because income taxes depend on profits. And profits are the difference between sales income and the cost of sales. And the cost of sales equals the January 1 inventory value plus the cost of things bought and made in the year, minus the December 31 inventory. It is kind of a long way around, but the amount a company claims its inventory is worth affects its profits and that affects the government's taxes, and the income tax collector says: Be sure it's right —count.

Besides federal taxes, local property taxes on inventories have to be paid. So local authorities, too, are interested in the counts of inventories being accurate so that the value put on inventories will be right.

Actually, it is not legally required to count everything at the end of the fiscal year or even during the year. A company's auditors are allowed to certify the accuracy of the counts shown on the records if their (the auditors') own small sample counts verify the card records or the computer records for the items they sample. Samsonite (luggage maker) reports that its computerized inventory control system keeps its inventory records accurate to within less than 3 percent of their physical inventory. This is accurate enough to have allowed it to dispense with almost all physical cycle counting.

IDENTIFICATION SYSTEMS

It is hard to imagine a supermarket where the cans are without labels. No one would ever know what they were getting. Factory stores items are more varied in looks than tin cans, but without identification they are just about as hard to identify. Figure 18–4 is a picture of gears, but they are all different. A person cannot tell what they are for just by looking at them. An assembler asking a stock clerk for a certain kind of gear might have difficulty describing it correctly.

An identification system is mandatory. First, word descriptions of each item are needed—descriptions which tell what every item is and descrip-

FIGURE 18–4

**Gears need
separate
identification
numbers**

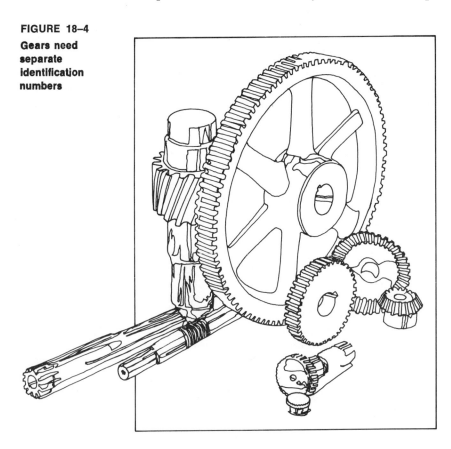

tions which set every item apart from other items. But word descriptions which clearly set every item apart from every other item are too long and cumbersome for most uses, so, second, a number system is needed. Numbers are shorter and they are unique. Coded number systems (or number-and-letter systems) are used to give similar numbers to similar items. This helps people who have to work with the records to recognize the items more readily.

For raw materials, the code usually shows the kind of material. Groups of numbers are reserved for sheet steel, steel bars, tool steel, steel wire, steel castings, malleable iron castings, and so on. Other groups of numbers stand for brass items. Paints and varnishes have a totally different number set.

The coded part of coded numbers is usually on the left. If an item's entire identification number has six or eight digits, the first two or three show its general class. The next one or two show its subclass. Only the last three digits are probably uncoded. An index is then used to find out exactly what the item is. The index would also provide the full word description. Many computer systems keep a dictionary of verbal descriptions of each item which may be called out by keying in the number. If the number isn't known, the user can enter "key" words describing the item until the computer finds the exact item.

The base used for coding raw materials (the *kind* of material) cannot be used with finished parts and components because finished items are often whole assembled products. They might be pumps, electric motors, compressors, or such items. None of these can be classified according to what they are made of. Besides, trying to classify finished parts by what they are made of doesn't help people tie the product and its number together in their minds.

Using kinds of materials would give different numbers to steel, brass, nylon, and fiber gears. But since all are gears and serve the same purposes, it would seem better to have groups of similar numbers for the kinds of items. Then gears of all kinds would have similar numbers. Some companies do this. But this is not a perfect arrangement, either, because it can give the parts of a finished product unlike numbers.

For finished parts, it seems best to class things on a basis of use. Separate groups of numbers are set aside for parts for each finished product or each kind of finished product. This is the way most number codes for finished parts are set up, although there will always be many exceptions.

Using related use, electric motors, pumps, roller bearings, and oil cups would be numbered in the number system of the product they go in. But that would cause unlike numbers for electric motors. Pumps, bearings, and oil cups, too, would bear unlike numbers.

Common parts also upset all orderly numbering schemes. Such parts are used in several products, and so their number is always out of series in all lists for a product's parts except one. Some companies give common parts a separate series of numbers; but then, of course, the number tells nothing about the item except that it has several uses.

There are also problems in all numbering systems because design changes cancel some old parts and their numbers and add others. Old part numbers should not be reassigned to new parts (at least not for years), or there will be confusion.

Airplane companies use a double numbering system. Every part on an airplane has a regular number, but—besides—it has an "indent" number. The indent number tells at what point the part enters the airplane. This information is needed to schedule its manufacture at the right time. A part may, for example, go into the left wing flap, which goes into the left wing, which goes into the airplane. Some items go into one subassembly, which goes into another subassembly, which goes into another, and so on for seven or eight "generations." These relationships result in an "indented" bill of materials and is sometimes referred to as a product tree. (These are discussed in Chapter 20.)

The indent number system gets to be quite complex, but there is no other way to get the quarter of a million parts of a big airplane together at the right time and in the right order. Indented bill of material numbering systems help get the parts and subassemblies ready at the right time.

The government may also upset a company's numbering system. Companies selling products to the government may be required to use the government's parts numbers. Sometimes the government furnishes some parts which are identical to parts the contracting company uses regularly in other products but with the government numbers attached. Thus, two numbering systems must be maintained.

Engineering drawings both help and confuse identification problems. Most parts for assembled products have drawings showing their size, dimensions, and other information. In the engineering department, the drawings must be numbered. So many companies just use the drawing number as all or part of a part's identification number. But some parts, such as pieces of wire in a radio set, and such materials as welding rods and paint need identification numbers but have no drawing numbers. Their numbers are usually part of the raw material series.

IDENTIFYING MATERIALS

In addition to an identification system designed for recordkeeping, it is also necessary to identify the items themselves. There are two easy ways to do this so far as items in stock are concerned. For packaged items, the items' descriptions can go on the package. And for all items, packaged and unpackaged, a tag on the storage bin can identify its contents. For materials in process, the material or its container can be tagged. This is important because the material is changed in form a little after every operation, often making it difficult to tell what an item is by looking at it.

Tags and labels take care of most of the problem. These tags may be manually marked, or they may be computer generated punched cards on special labels which can be read by computer-based electronic scanning devices which automatically keeps track of items as they move throughout the production process and into and out of inventories. But tags get lost and separated from materials. Tags can't be run through heat treating furnaces or degreasing tanks. They have to be removed from the containers and later be reattached. Or five tote boxes of an item go through an operation, but the operator puts them into six boxes afterwards; yet, he has only five tags. Errors can easily occur.

Also, some items—steel sheets, castings, and others—are not suitable for tagging, nor are they kept in bins. In these cases it is better to stamp, mold, paint, or etch some kind of identification on every item. Castings nearly always have their numbers molded into them. Bars and sheets of metal are stacked and are usually painted with coded colors on the end.

A few companies have a curious identification problem. To prevent employees stealing parts they can sell, the companies intentionally put wrong numbers on them. TV and radio manufacturers sometimes put false numbers on popular kinds of parts to discourage pilferage.

MATERIALS REQUISITIONS

A materials requisition is a request to the stockroom to issue materials. It shows the kind and quantity of materials wanted, the use to be made of them (or the account number to be charged), and often the signature of the authorizing person. In a manual system, when the stock clerk hands out the material, he writes down the material identification number on the requisition and sends it to the stock record clerk. The record clerk subtracts the quantity issued from the record card, writes in the amount remaining, puts the price per unit on the requisition, and sends it to the accounting department. There the unit price is multiplied by the quantity to get the value of the material issued. The record clerk subtracts that amount of money from the materials account and adds it to the account for which the material was withdrawn. All of this detailed work is, of course, almost always done today by computers rather than by hand. The inventory controller keys in the part number, quantity, and other information, and the computer takes it from there.

Requisitions for *materials* to make into products may be made out by the supervisor of the department doing the first operation. More often this is done earlier by production control, using a computer. The requisitions are either given to the supervisor of the first department to use when the materials are required or they are held in the production control dispatch office until shortly before the first operation is to start. Then they are sent to the stockrooms, from which the materials are delivered to the first operation just before they are needed.

Requisitions for *parts* for assembled products are often copies of the assembly manufacturing order which has been "released" to the factory.

This document lists the parts and quantities of each part needed. A copy goes to the subassembly goods stockroom and serves as the stockroom clerk's authority to issue all the parts listed.

Materials requisitions are just so much extra paper work, and sometimes they can be eliminated. The use of regular day-to-day items is easy to determine because every product takes its required items and amounts of material. If 1,000 electric irons are to be made, the stock clerk knows that 1,000 handles, 1,000 heating units, and so on will be used. Assemblers don't need to use requisitions or get heating elements out of enclosed stockrooms. They pick handles and heating units out of bins at their workplaces without paper records of every part issued.

Occasionally, however, things disappear and the inventory records become inaccurate. Occasionally, too, because of faulty recording, the record shows less than there is, which results in too much inventory being carried.

Except for the possibility of theft or when gross errors can creep into the inventory records, requisitionless issuing of materials is usually the best for low- and medium-valued regular use items.

PRICING THE MATERIALS ISSUED

When materials are made into products, their money value is taken out of the raw materials account and added into the account showing the value of work in process. Later, their investment is taken out of the work in process account and added into the finished products account.

This sounds simple, but there is a troublesome problem. Suppose there is a bin full of an item—say 125 in all. Suppose that they were acquired (whether purchased or were manufactured internally is immaterial) as follows: 25 units at $5 each, 50 units at $6 each, and 50 units at $7 each. These differences are extreme, but they will illustrate the point. The actual investment is $775 (although buying them all at today's price would cost $875). Now suppose that 100 pieces are issued. What price should be put on the requisition—$5, $6, $7, or some combination thereof?

There are four choices or methods for answering this question: Fifo, Lifo, weighted average cost, and standard cost. It is not unknown for this to be called "transfer pricing," but this is not at all what transfer pricing usually means. In its usual meaning, transfer pricing means the price that one division of a large company charges another division for its products. When GM's A-C sparkplug division sells sparkplugs to GM's assembly division, the price is a transfer price but this price includes a profit for A-C.

Fifo

Fifo means, "first in, first out." Using Fifo, the first 25 items issued would be priced at $5, then 50 items at $6, and the last 25 items at $7, giving a total of 100 items issued and reported as costing $600. The 25 items left in stock would be shown to be worth $175. In our example, Fifo understates the cost of materials, and this in turn decreases the calculated costs of goods sold, increases apparent profits, and increases taxes.

Lifo

Lifo means "last in, first out." Using Lifo, the first 50 items issued would be priced at $7, the next 50 items at $6 for a total of 100 items costing $650. The 25 items left would be shown to be worth $125. Lifo has the opposite effect on profits and taxes from Fifo. During times of increase of raw material prices profits are held down as are taxes.

Weighted average cost

The 125 items cost $775, or an average of $6.20 each. So, using this method, the 100 items issued would be priced at $6.20 each, or a total of $620. The 25 items left would be shown to be worth $155.

Standard cost

Here, some standard figure that items *should* cost is determined. This method is commonly used for items a company makes itself because no two lots ever cost exactly the same. Suppose the standard cost in our example is $5.75. All items going into inventory would be priced in at $5.75 each, with all actual cost differences being carried to a variance account. If 100 items were issued, they would all be charged out at $5.75—a total of $575. The remaining 25 items left in the bin would also be valued at $5.75 each, or a total of $143.75.

Discussing these several methods of pricing may all sound picayunish—just a play on numbers because the actual costs are the same and so are the selling prices, no matter how the matter is handled. Actually, it is not picayunish, because the problem goes on forever (prices and manufacturing costs are always changing), and it affects nearly every item used in making products.

Each method produces somewhat different product cost figures. This means the calculated profits are different, and this affects the company's income taxes. Also, if prices of finished products are set based on manufacturing costs, the method of charging for material used affects selling prices and probably the sales volume too.

Fifo gives lower cost figures during periods of raw material price increases. In such a case, Fifo would show more apparent profit and would result in higher income taxes. Also, remaining inventories will be valued at a higher amount, which can increase inventory taxes.

Lifo is the reverse. As raw material prices go up, the calculations say that the last purchased, and most costly materials, are used first. Lifo boosts apparent costs and holds down profits and taxes, but it values remaining inventories lower, resulting in lower inventory taxes. (In the mid-1970s when raw materials and bought component prices went up substantially, many companies changed their accounting procedures to Lifo.)

INVENTORY LEVELS AND BUYING TO MARKET PRICES

As we saw at the beginning of Chapter 17 on purchasing, the cost of materials is a very large item in most manufacturing companies. It is also very important in many public and service organizations. And, as we shall see later in this chapter, the greater part of materials costs is usually for a relatively small portion of all of the items bought. Automobiles, for example, use millions of tons of sheet steel every year. Shoe companies use millions of cowhides. Chocolate companies use millions of pounds of chocolate, and bakeries use enormous quantities of flour. In the public sector, a large city's public works department uses millions of gallons of gasoline and thousands of tons of asphalt.

The usual inventory control techniques, as described in our chapters on inventory control, often do not really apply to the inventories of these big items. Raw materials, when they are the products of nature, are often bought on organized commodity exchanges where prices fluctuate daily. The prices fluctuate in response to worldwide conditions of supply and demand. And the amount used in large companies is so great that these fluctuations and the reasons for them need careful watching. Any consequential changes in prices should cause the organization to review its purchasing and its inventory policies. If prices appear to be going up— then bigger inventories will be laid in. Conversely, prospective lower prices lead to hand-to-mouth buying with very small inventories being carried.

As a consequence, inventory levels are much more the result of a company's forecast of future materials market conditions than they are of any inventory control policy as such. Inventory levels of these materials are results of raw material price expectations rather than being based on what is needed to support near future product sales expectations.

In the case of heavily used manufactured raw materials, the item is frequently bought on large blanket contracts with materials suppliers. And, again, the usual "inventory control" methods do not apply.

INVENTORY ABC ANALYSIS

Many large organizations have to stock and keep track of 10,000 or more different items which are outside of the MRP (Materials Requirements Planning) system which is described in Chapter 20 and which covers most of the materials used in making products. (In the case of the Armed Forces of the United States, the numbers are enormously greater.) In most companies the items outside of the MRP system are minor end products, or they are parts or components of end products which are not included in MRP calculations. Some are service parts for products no longer made, or they are supplies, or raw materials for general use, or maintenance items, and items for various other purposes. The investments in such items is substantial, and the recordkeeping is costly.

They may even be MRP items in that they go into end products covered by the MRP calculation process. But, if they are relatively minor and if they are used in quite a few different end products, it may be more economical *not* to calculate their needs as part of the MRP process but rather to calculate the needs for each end product and then add all of the demands together. It may be more economical just to replenish these items on a maximum-minimum basis (described in the next few pages).

One purpose of inventory control is to control inventories at the least cost. Some items like paper clips and rubber bands aren't worth keeping detailed records for. It is better just to keep a supply of such items on hand and let people help themselves. It doesn't matter if these little things are used somewhat wastefully because it usually costs less to absorb the waste than to keep the records.

Obviously, loose controls should be limited to unimportant items. This means that a decision has to be made as to which items are little things and which need more careful control. Pareto's "vital few" and "trivial many" concept, the "20–80 principle" mentioned in Chapter 10, applies here. The inventory controller should look over the stock records, item by item, and classify them into A, B, and C groups.

Back in Chapter 10 we constructed a Pareto curve. Such a curve would show clearly which items are A, B, and C. Figure 18–5 is actually the same chart as the one in Chapter 10, as are its numbers and calculations. Here, however, we are assuming that the numbers are for the usage of materials and parts. And again the conclusion is the same: A few of the items are responsible for most of the cost of all materials and parts used.

"A" items are the large investment items: the vital few. Ten percent of the items commonly account for 70 percent of the amounts spent on materials. A items should be carefully controlled. Their needs should be calculated ahead of time according to the period of use, and their manufacture or purchase should be scheduled so that they arrive just before they are needed. These are the items most suitable for using the computerized MRP methods which are described in Chapter 20. In most cases these items should be ordered a few at a time and frequently, in order to hold down inventories. The inventory levels of A items should be watched very carefully.

At the same time, there are occasions when the inventory of particular A items should *not* be controlled (in the usual sense) at all. This will be true for basic raw materials bought in enormous quantities (as in the case of cotton, rubber, coffee, and the like) when buying to world market prices is so important as to make their inventories subordinate to forward buying policies based on future price expectations. (These problems were discussed in Chapter 17.)

FIGURE 18–5

Typical ABC inventory distribution

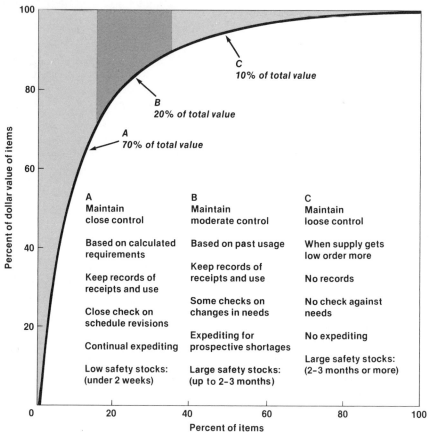

"B" items are the 15 to 20 percent of the items which account for some 15 percent of the investment. While they are less important than A items, they are costly enough to make it desirable to keep careful records of their use. Here "maximum-minimum" controls can be used, and past usage, rather than future schedule requirements, can be the basis for reordering. For the most part, MRP methods (which calculate the exact future needs of each item) need not be used for B items. In many cases B items qualify for MRP treatment in that their needs for end products can be calculated, but it costs more to do this than it is worth.

Minimum stock limits and standard reorder quantities can be set and used. Replenishment reorders can be made out automatically whenever the stock of an item gets down to its reorder point. "Economic order quantities" (see Chapter 22) can be used to advantage here.

"C" items are the "trivial many." It is not uncommon for 75 percent of the items to account for only 10 percent of the cost of materials. C items

FIGURE 18–6

Computer printout for ABC inventory classification

				A B C INVENTORY CLASSIFICATION			
PART NO.	RANK OF ITEM	USAGE PER YEAR	UNIT COST	ANNUAL USAGE (DOLLARS)	CUMULATIVE USAGE (DOLLARS)	CUMULATIVE PERCENT OF USAGE	ABC GROUP
360467	1	141,500	.620	87,730.00	87,730.00	2.58	A
528445	2	340,000	.201	68,340.00	156,070.00	4.59	A
351708	3	24,625	1.200	29,550.00	185,620.00	5.46	A
362401	4	22,823	.350	7,958.05	193,608.05	5.69	A
351748	5	14,725	.400	5,890.00	199,498.05	5.86	A
140868	1250	858	.020	17.16	3,400,000.00	100.00	C

Source: Univac, Sperry-Rand Corp.

should get short shift on planning and records. It is only necessary to order plenty of paper clips, cotter pins, washers, solder, and so on. C items can be put at the operatives' workplaces, where they can help themselves without using requisitions. Future needs of C items usually do not need to be calculated. Nor should they be priced to products individually; they can be charged to an overhead account.

Loose controls of C items will increase their investment and their costs from shelf wear, obsolescence, and wasteful use but not nearly so much as to offset the savings in recordkeeping costs. The organization will usually end up ahead with loose controls on C items if they keep a large enough quantity on hand. They should be sure, however, *not to run out of a low cost but critical item*. For example, an inexpensive washer used in the manufacture of lawn mowers might be classified as a "C" item. But, if the lack of such a washer might hold up final assembly of lawn mowers, the down time costs could be substantial. So, while C items need not be watched too closely, they should not be allowed to run out unless replacement lead time is virtually instantaneous or unless an allowable substitute can be used. In the final analysis, C items, too, are often essential.

MAXIMUM-MINIMUM CONTROLS

People sometimes say that they use "maximum-minimum" inventory control methods in their companies. There is no specific method that goes by the name "maximum-minimum." A person saying this is usually using a system whereby a warning low point is set for each item carried in stock and this warning point serves as a reorder point. When the supply gets down to this danger point (reorder points are discussed in the next few pages), it triggers a reorder.

Paired with this danger point warning is a reorder *quantity* for each item. This is the amount reordered. The term, "maximum-minimum," actually really ought to be reversed, because the system is really a minimum-maximum method. There is a set minimum stock which serves as the reordering point, but there is no formally set maximum quantity for each item. The maximum depends on how much old stock is left over when a new order comes in.

B items whose use is not keyed directly with demand devolving from end product demand and perhaps some A items should get maximum-minimum control. Normally, however, B items whose demand derives from scheduled end products should be controlled by MRP methods and not maximum-minimum methods.

INVESTMENT LIMITATION CONTROL METHODS

Inventory turnover

Inventory turnover is the cycle of using and replacing materials. It is a ratio—the number of "turns" to the investment in a year. If a company sells $100,000 worth of products a year and has an average inventory valued at $50,000, it has two turnovers a year. But, if this company could get by with an inventory worth $25,000, it would have four turns a year. More turns reduce the investment and save carrying costs as well.

Some companies use the turnover ratio as an inventory control method. They insist on a certain number of turns a year. This idea should not be carried very far, however. A high turnover rate means very low inventories, but very low inventories means being out of stock more often. High turnover and low inventories at the same time also force frequent and often uneconomical small reorders which can result in higher unit costs.

Sales volume and reasonable inventory turnover ratios are also related. It is not difficult to obtain more turns when sales volume is high. But, if volume decreases to half and if inventories are also cut in half in order to keep the turnover ratio up, there will be more cases of running out of stock. This could lead to many costly, frequent, and small-quantity reorders.

Dollar limits

Most companies set dollar limits or budgets on the amount which they will allow to be invested in each class of materials. Each class has an account in the accounting department showing its investments. The inventory control manager is responsible for seeing that the amounts stay within the allowed budgets.

This approach is usually applied only to classes of materials and not to individual items except possibly A items. Otherwise it is just too costly to set dollar limits for each item separately. Dollar limits do not tell inventory controllers when or how much to reorder; all they do is to tell them not to exceed an upper investment limit. They have to determine how much of each individual item to provide, while keeping the investment for the item class within the limit.

Dollar limits should be used with discretion when prices or business levels change; otherwise, they automatically tighten or loosen the amount allowed to be carried. If, for example, prices go up and the dollar limits are not changed, the inventory control manager has to cut the quantities carried. Similarly, if business improves, dollar limits, if unchanged, hold down the inventories when some increase is really needed to support the added sales. There is need to recognize what the method does to inventory control policies.

Time limits

Time limits are a common way to put dollar limits into effect. To translate dollar limits into time limits, it is only necessary to divide the dollar limit by the dollar usage per month. A $20,000 limit is a two-month limit for an item used at a rate of $10,000 per month.

While dollar limits can best be used directly to control only A items, time limits can easily be applied to every item. In fact, one single time limit can apply to any number of items at the same time.

Time limits do not directly determine when or how much to order. They merely say, for example, do not have more than 30 days' supply on hand. Indirectly, this sets upper limits on how much can be ordered at one time. To hold the average investment for a class of items down to a month's usage, the inventory controller can never order more than a month's supply of any item on a single order.

For long lead time items, time limits control when reorders go out as well as how much is ordered. If it takes three months to get an item and inventories are limited to one month's supply at one time, it will be necessary to place a new order every month for one month's needs, but each order will always be for the third month ahead. There will always be several orders out at the same time. (Items on order do not count in the inventory so far as investment is concerned.)

The inventory "coverage" (the quantity on hand plus the amount on order) is the true available inventory. Assuming reliable lead times, the coverage, in our example, is adequate even though much of it is, for the moment, in the form of open orders rather than stock on hand. The short time limit permitted for stock on hand does not mean that we have to run out of stock of long lead time items.

Time limits are easy to set, easy to change, and easy to operate. And they can be different for different items. If an item's use changes, the time limit can remain unchanged because the reordering quantity can change to reflect the new requirements.

A disadvantage of time limits is that they are not often the very best for entire groups of products, although they are usually applied to entire groups. A 30-day limit is probably too much for some items in a group and too little for others. For this reason, both dollar limits and time limits, while commonly used, are not always appropriate.

FIXED ORDERING TIMES

Many, perhaps most, organizations do not order any and every kind of material every day, whenever the need becomes known. Instead, in some cases, they order only once a month (see Figure 18–7). Warehouses commonly order stock this way. The first week of the month they order all the steel items, the second week all nonferrous items, and the third week, all purchased components, and so on. Ordering entire classes of products together saves clerical work because the order can be just one long listing of requirements.

This method has a disadvantage in that it probably will result in inventories being slightly higher than they need to be. When orders have to be placed, the inventory controller has to look ahead to see if the stock level might get down to a danger point at any time before the next ordering period. If it might run short, he must place his order right now because (except for emergencies) he cannot order more until the next ordering period. So he places the order now, and the new supply will probably come in before it is really needed. This does not have to happen, however, since an order can be placed now and the vendor told when to deliver it.

FIGURE 18–7

Reordering on a periodic basis results in reorders occurring regardless of the exact quantity on hand at the date for reordering

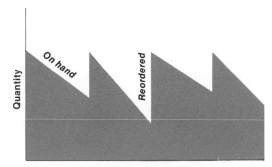

Reordering every month

REVIEW QUESTIONS

1. The text says that holding inventories down may be unwise sub-optimization. How is it that this might be unwise?

2. Compare enclosed and open stockrooms. When should each be used?

3. How often should actual physical counts of inventories be made? Why?

4. What kind of an identification system seems best for raw materials? Why? What kind is best for finished parts? Why?

5. Why are materials requisitions used? Can they ever be done without? When?

6. Should actual purchase costs or actual production costs be used for pricing requisitions? Why or why not? What problems are involved? If neither of these cost figures should be used, what price should be used?

7. What methods for pricing materials out of stock are available? Which is best? Why?

8. Should each separate subinventory of items stocked at several points in the same large factory be controlled separately? What problems are involved?

9. Inventory turnover is commonly used as part of the method for controlling inventories. What dangers might appear if this idea is pursued too far?

10. How do inventory ABCs work? How does a company, which recognizes this concept, benefit as compared to one which does not? Discuss.

11. Describe the differences in inventory control techniques which should be used for A, B, and C items in inventory.

12. If a company uses dollar-limit control and the limits stay fixed, what happens to the inventories when business volume increases? When prices decrease?

13. What kinds of items should be controlled by fixed quantities? Dollar limits? Time limits? Economic lot sizes (discussed in Chapter 21)?

QUESTIONS FOR DISCUSSION

1. Who should the inventory controller listen to as he tries to do his job? The purchasing agent does not want to have to expedite orders. The treasurer wants him to hold down the average inventory investment. The sales manager wants him never to run out of anything. The plant manager doesn't want to have production held up by not having materials, and he also wants long runs on production jobs. Try to reconcile these conflicting desires.

2. A question from the inventory controller: "How can I get the information I need to analyze and to prove that I am doing a good job?" How can this question be answered?

3. If a company is to end up with a certain number of obsolete items in stock, where is it worst for this to occur? In raw materials? In in-process materials? In finished parts? Or in finished products? Why?

4. Do inventories contribute to reducing overall company costs, or do they increase total costs? Discuss.

5. Do large inventories have any effect on worker productivity? If so, what effect?

6. Should a company ever engage in speculation? Discuss.

7. Isn't it more or less fruitless to try to hold inventories to the barest minimums when railroad companies sometimes hold freight cars for several days in order to make up long trains? Discuss.

8. How hard should a company try to keep inventories down on parts it makes itself when the machine setup costs in some departments run as high as 25 percent of all labor costs? Is this bad? Discuss.

9. How can a company count heavy material, such as bins partly full of 100-pound castings?

10. In the 1970s many companies changed from Fifo to Lifo inventory charging practices. Why?

11. Will fixed reorder cycles result in higher inventories than fixed reorder systems? How would this work?

PROBLEMS

1. Item 294's record shows the following:

Received January 24.......	300 @ $.42 each
Received February 15......	200 @ .46 each
Received March 27........	400 @ .51 each
Received April 15........	200 @ .47 each
Received May 25..........	350 @ .54 each

Issues were as follows:

From January 24 to February 14.......................	176
From February 15 to March 26........................	145
From March 27 to April 14...........................	502
From April 15 to May 25.............................	120
From May 25 to June 1...............................	47

If the company uses Fifo, what price was put on the withdrawal requisitions for the stock withdrawn in each period? What would the prices have been if the company had used Lifo? What would be the calculated remaining inventory value each time a new stock came in?

2. Suppose that the following 15 items are representative of the 40,000 items kept in stock. Construct a maldistribution curve and find out what proportion of the items are A, B, and C items. What fraction of all items probably is responsible for the greatest 80 percent of the value of all items used?

Thousands of dollars of value use in one year:

Item	Dollars	Item	Dollars
1	6	9	40
2	45	10	9
3	17	11	12
4	4	12	5
5	13	13	60
6	32	14	3
7	2	15	26
8	1		

CASE 18–1

The Elk Company has analyzed its stockroom investment turnover and found it to be considerably below what the management thinks it should be. A quick review of the stock cards showed that a six-months' supply of many items was on hand. Very few items had less than two months' supply on hand. The purchasing agent of the company bought the major materials used in the company's products. They were bought on the basis of price forecasts, and it was felt that that practice should be continued. The stocks of items ordered from the cards by the stock card clerk were regarded as excessive. The record clerk ordered replenishment supplies of these items as he saw fit, although he was supposed to order no more than three months' supply on any one reorder. He could, however, use his own judgment as to when to reorder, and, if he thought that the demand might increase, he ordered a new supply sooner than he normally would, even when the current stock was ample for the time being. Before he took the job, the shop had been held up frequently for lack of stock. He was quite proud of having solved that difficulty.

Is there a problem here? Since it will all be used in due time, is there any harm in having plenty of stock on hand? Set up a procedure to reduce the inventory without running out of stock.

SUGGESTED SUPPLEMENTARY READINGS

Davis, Edward. "A Look at the Use of Production-Inventory Techniques: Past and Present." *Production and Inventory Management,* 4th quarter 1975, pp. 1–19.

Edwards, J. D., and Barrack, J. B. "Last-In, First-Out Inventory Valuation as a Way to Control Illusory Profits." *MSU Business Topics,* Winter 1975, pp. 19–27.

Edwards, J. D., and Roemmich, R. A. "Scientific Inventory Management." *MSU Business Topics,* Autumn 1975, pp. 41–45.

19

Forecasting demand for products and services

THE FORECASTING of future sales of products and the usage on components is very important in production planning and control. Good forecasting is essential to efficient production operations.

Forecasting is sometimes done by a "top-down" method. In other cases, the reverse, a "bottom-up" method, is used. And in still other cases, past experience is projected forward and extrapolated into the future by using mathematical procedures.

Top-down forecasting

The top-down method starts by using forecasts of general business conditions made by economists in the government and in large companies and universities. Such forecasts appear frequently in newspapers and magazines. The experts may say, for example, that next year's gross national product will be $1,700 billion. In a company making kitchen stoves, refrigerators, disposals, dishwashers, and the like, the question then becomes: How will this affect us? The forecaster in the company must first translate general forecasts into terms of his industry's future business. Then he has to estimate his company's share, and, finally, how many of each product the company will be able to sell each month.

Often, as they try to develop specific forecasts for major individual products or for important groups or classes of products, the forecasters use mathematical procedures. These have sometimes been referred to as "extrinsic" forecasting. Extrinsic forecasting methods are usually used for forecasting groups of products, such as lawnmowers, men's shoes, or electric motors. These forecasts are usually developed by the marketing staff of the organization.

Extrinsic forecasting assumes that, in the past, there has been some relationship between the sales of an item or group of items and one or more external factors, such as population growth, personal incomes, number of people employed, or the number of new houses being built. It also assumes that since changes in these external factors have had a strong relationship with the product's sales in the past, this relationship will continue in the future.

The most common statistical method used to find these relationships is regression analysis, which calculates an equation which, for example, might be:

$$\text{Expected demand} = 100 + .001P + .02E + .30H$$

Where:

$$P = \text{personal income}$$
$$E = \text{number of people employed}$$
$$H = \text{number of new houses}$$

If the estimates for next year's personal income, employment and housing starts in the company's market area are \$10,000,000, 20,000 and 500, respectively, this company's forecast of sales for next year would be:

$$\text{Expected demand} = 100 + .001(10,000,000) + .02(20,000) + .30(500)$$
$$= 100 + 10,000 + 400 + 150$$
$$= 10,650 \text{ units}$$

In order to use this method, analysts need historical data from which to develop the equations, and they also need to be able to get estimates of the predictor factors (as we did above) in order to make a forecast. Obviously, if the estimates of the predictor factors prove to be wrong, as sometimes happens, then the company's estimate of its future sales will also be wrong.

Fortunately sometimes one or more of the predictor series "leads" other series. It moves first and then is followed by other series. If employment and personal income go up, then a little later the sales of automobiles and other durable consumer products will go up. When one or more such leading sets of data can be found, then their today's performance reveals what will happen to the following series tomorrow.

The method for determining regression equations which can be used in forecasting will not be explored here since they are covered in detail in statistics textbooks. However, a word of caution is in order. These methods, which can be calculated easily on computers, require skill and judgment in determining the proper predicting factors and their importance in predicting sales.

Bottom-up forecasting

The bottom-up method starts with individual end product sales expectations. How many of each end product does it appear that the company will sell next year? In this method the forecaster gets estimates from sales people and from dealers and customers. He also looks at past sales patterns. Finally, he adds up the different product forecasts and gets a total, which is the aggregate forecast.

Actually, most companies use both the top-down and the bottom-up method at the same time and combine the resulting projections into a single forecast. But before settling on a final forecast, they probably also use the "jury of executive opinion" (sometimes called the "Delphi" method) approach to adjust judgementally the more technically determined forecasts. The numbers are adjusted up or down according to what the organization's top people think about the future.

Neither the top-down and bottom-up methods are, however, very useful for forecasting how many of each of the thousands of individually relatively unimportant products to make. Here, the most common method is to extrapolate past trends into the future by mathematical procedures. At first this does not sound very practical because such mechanistic forecasts do not pay any attention to known outside factors and so are not always very good forecasts. At the same time, however, the other methods of forecasting described above are much too complex to be used for each individual item of the thousands of items in normal inventories. Extrapolations and calculations of future needs by computers, using mechanistic methods, are perhaps the best that one can do for the large bulk of items.

DEMAND INTERPRETATION

Unfortunately, forecasting operates in a dynamic economy and therefore can never be perfectly done. As weeks and months pass and actual sales figures become available, it is almost always found that forecasts did not anticipate sales perfectly. This introduces a new complication: How should the departures of sales from forecasts be interpreted? The first thing that happens when sales differ from forecasts is that inventories become different from those planned. This immediately raises the question: Should such differences be continued? Or should production levels be changed instead? And if so, how much and how soon? A new forecast is needed, and this new forecast will probably require the development of new inventory plans and new production schedules.

To illustrate the problem, suppose that the forecast and sales of product A for the first four months of the year are as shown in Figure 19–1. It is now May 1. The figures are in thousands.

The sales forecasters now have the problem of determining what to do next. How should they interpret the April sales running way over the forecast? Was there a strike at a competitor's plant? Did customers just buy earlier this year? If there is no evidence that extraneous factors such as

FIGURE 19–1

Month	Sales		Inventory (end of month)	
	Forecast	Actual	Forecast	Actual
January	30	10	30	50
February	30	25	60	85
March	40	55	100	110
April	120	160	60	30
Total	220	250		

these caused the sales upsurge, then customers have either bought ahead (in which case lower sales probably lie ahead), or else the forecaster has underguessed the market. If the latter is the case, production schedules should be revised upward right away. The inventory is already down 30,000 below the plan.

This is a capacity problem, a scheduling problem, and an inventory control problem. Up to now (through April) the schedulers have not changed the master production schedule and instead have let the inventory level go down. Now, though, with sales catching fire and if the best months are still ahead, the production rate should probably be increased immediately and substantially. Otherwise product A may soon be out of stock.

We won't decide here what to do in this case, but this is one of the problems of controlling capacities, schedules, and inventories. To appreciate the importance of the problem, it should be remembered that it exists with every one of a company's many finished products. Also, its effects reach all the way back to raw materials stores. If production schedules are increased or are cut back, this upsets all the raw materials inventory plans, and even purchase order delivery schedules and supplier plant production schedules. It is important to emphasize the point that, because wholly accurate forecasting is not possible, production planning and control systems should be designed so that schedules can be changed quickly and at low cost when necessary. Forecasts can never be wholly accurate, no matter how sophisticated the forecasting methods utilized nor how stable the demand normally is.

SPECIFIC ITEM FORECASTING

As we said, neither top-down nor bottom-up forecasting helps much in forecasting the demand for the thousands of small items that some companies make. Consider, for example, the sales prospects at Singer for 6-inch scissors, or at Black and Decker for ¼-inch portable electric drills, or at Eli Lilly for aspirin sold in 5-grain pills in 100-pill bottles. Neither top-down nor bottom-up forecasting tells the sales forecasters how many of these individual items are likely to be sold during the next several months. And, because there are thousands of such items, it is not practicable to spend much time or money having specialists make forecasts for each item. Yet, these companies have to manufacture these items and so have to decide how many of each to make and when to make them.

This is an area where computers have taken over a large part of the work. It is an important function because in many companies it covers tens of thousands of items which constitute a substantial part of the company's sales.

The simplest forecast of next month's demand is this month's usage, but rarely is this very reliable because the usage of most items varies too much. Furthermore, the inventory controller does not even know what this month's usage of an item has been until after the end of the month, which by this time the order for next month's supply has already been placed. Yet, in practice, these two objections are not of overriding importance. When the inventory controller does not know what the future will be like, he can usually do no better than look to the recent past and decide that the future will be similar. And this is true even if past usage has varied considerably; and it is true even if it is necessary for the forecaster to forecast before the most recent data have been compiled.

Using an item's record of use in the past to forecast future demand is called "intrinsic" forecasting. The record of past sales or past usage is a "time series" which shows the items' historical demand by week, month, or year. A historical time series may contain several subpatterns. These subpatterns may be caused by *trend, seasonal, cyclic,* and *random* forces at work. Figure 19–2 shows an example of these components of a time series for a hypothetical item.

In Figure 19–2, the broad dip, which bottoms out in year two and has risen in the years since, appears to be part of a five-to-six year cycle. Yet this may not be so, and it might be an economic recession and recovery which will not recur. Secondly, in years two to four, there is an upward trend which may not last. This upward trend may be caused just by the recovery of the economy, or it may reflect new markets opening up, less competition, or obtaining a larger share of an existing market. Third, demand seems, in Figure 19–2, to vary "seasonally." Sales are greatest each year around January and July with low points in February and September. Such seasonal patterns are quite common in the demand for products and services, and they can usually be isolated and planned for in forecasting. As examples, the sales of soft drinks are usually highest in the summer and lowest in the winter, and college textbooks have sales peaks at the beginning of each school term.

Finally, there may be "blips" in any time series. Often these are caused by a known abnormal condition, such as the Olympic games, a baseball World Series, a sales campaign, or some other explainable and nonrepetitive reason. In other cases the blips are "random effects" whose causes are either unknown or cannot be easily explained as cyclic, trend, or seasonal effects.

FIGURE 19–2

Time series showing effects of seasonal, cyclical, trend, and random factors operating together

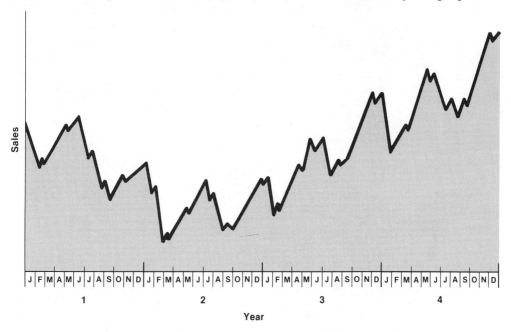

INTRINSIC FORECASTING METHODS

There are many different methods used for forecasting mathematically, using statistical methods.[1] We will present a few of these methods which are the most widely used.

Figure 19–3 shows a four-year sales record for a finished item we will call a NEEDEM. These figures are plotted later in Figure 19–6. There it is apparent that there are trend, seasonal and some random effects in operation. The overall trend is upward; seasonal peaks usually occur in March and August, with valleys usually occurring in May and December; and there seems to be some randomness in the series.

To illustrate statistical forecasting methods, we are going to use only the first three years (36 months) of NEEDEM sales figures in our analysis. Then we will forecast the monthly sales for the 12 months of the fourth year. Actually we already know the monthly sales for the fourth year so this will allow us to review the accuracy of our forecasts to see if the methods we used are satisfactory.

Trend calculation

A common method for calculating the trend is to draw or "fit" a straight line through the plot of sales figures so that the points above and below

---

[1] A good review of different forecasting methods is given in John C. Chambers, Satinder K. Mullick, and Donald D. Smith, "How to Choose the Right Forecasting Technique," *Harvard Business Review*, July–August, 1971.

FIGURE 19–3

	Month	Period number	Sales		Month	Period number	Sales
Year 1	January....	1	100	Year 3	January....	25	146
	February...	2	128		February...	26	175
	March.....	3	138		March.....	27	173
	April.......	4	127		April......	28	161
	May.......	5	112		May......	29	150
	June.......	6	115		June......	30	162
	July.......	7	128		July.......	31	171
	August.....	8	134		August.....	32	173
	September..	9	130		September..	33	168
	October....	10	116		October....	34	157
	November..	11	100		November..	35	130
	December..	12	95		December..	36	125
Year 2	January....	13	125	Year 4	January....	37	161
	February...	14	148		February...	38	178
	March.....	15	155		March.....	39	183
	April.......	16	138		April......	40	178
	May.......	17	128		May......	41	158
	June.......	18	142		June......	42	178
	July.......	19	152		July.......	43	190
	August.....	20	156		August.....	44	188
	September..	21	140		September..	45	176
	October....	22	122		October....	46	165
	November..	23	108		November..	47	158
	December..	24	100		December..	48	135

the line are more or less equal in number and distance from the line. Such a line can be calculated mathematically, using the "least squares" method, or it can be drawn in by inspection.[2] When calculated mathematically, this line is called a "regression" line and is expressed by the following equation:

$$Y_c = a + bx$$

Where:

Y_c = trend value at time period x
a — trend value when $x = 0$
x = time period where $x = 1, 2, 3, \ldots, n$ time periods

For our NEEDEM example, we used a computer to calculate the regression line (or trend line) for the first three years of our NEEDEM data. The computer found that the equation for the trend was:

$$Y_c = 114.35 + 1.22\,x$$

Regression analysis of this sort produces a "Y_c" (or Y computed), value for every month. When these are extrapolated ahead, they become

---

[2] For an explanation of how to calculate this line by the least squares method, see David W. Huntsberger, Patrick Billingsley, and D. James Croft, *Statistical Inference for Management and Economics* (Allyn and Bacon, 1975).

FIGURE 19-4

Forecast for future months	Y computed	Seasonal index	Y forecast
37 January......................	159.4	0.94	149.9
38 February....................	160.7	1.14	183.2
39 March.......................	161.9	1.17	189.6
40 April........................	163.1	1.06	172.9
41 May.........................	164.3	0.96	157.7
42 June........................	165.5	1.02	168.9
43 July.........................	166.7	1.09	181.8
44 August......................	168.0	1.11	186.6
45 September..................	169.2	1.04	176.2
46 October.....................	170.4	0.93	158.4
47 November...................	171.6	0.79	135.5
48 December...................	172.8	0.74	128.1

(before adjustments for seasonal variations) the forecasts for the months ahead. These extrapolations for year four are shown in Figure 19–4.

Seasonal calculation

In our analysis of the sales figures for NEEDEMs, the computer program we used calculated both the trend and the seasonal variations. Seasonals were calculated by averaging ratios of actual monthly sales to the trend figure for each month. The calculation of the seasonal index for March, for example, was as follows:

	Actual sales	Trend line value	Ratio of actual to trend
March, year 1.................	138	118	1.16
March, year 2.................	155	133	1.16
March, year 3.................	173	147	1.18
			3.50

Average = 3.50 ÷ 3 = 1.17

This index of 1.17 means that March sales are typically 17 percent above the trend value in any year. If instead the index were .85, this would mean that March is typically a poor month and normally is 15 percent below the year's trend calculation.

Forecast for year 4

Our computer program, after computing the trend line and the seasonal indices, then extended the trend ahead for year four (months 37 to 48). It also applied the seasonal indices to each month's Y_c to get the forecast for year four after adjustment for expected seasonal variations. These are shown in Figure 19–4.

In Figure 19–4, the calculation for January requires first getting the Y_c value:

$$Y_c = 114.35 + 1.22\,(37) = 114.35 + 45.09 = 159.44$$

Then the January seasonal is applied:

$$159.44 \times .94 = 149.87$$

(The computer printout sheet showed the calculations carried out to four places to the right of the decimal although in fact the last places have no meaningful accuracy. In Figure 19–4, we have shown only four-place numbers.)

The least squares trend line and the monthly forecasts for year four are plotted in Figure 19–5, as are the actual monthly sales figures for year four (which we kept out of our calculations for comparative purposes.) The "EXSM" forecast, also shown in Figure 19–5, will be explained in the next few pages.

As can be seen, this method, using regression analysis plus a seasonal adjustment, forecasts year four quite well for this particular time series. It should be strongly emphasized, however, that this approach may provide poor forecasts for other time series if, for example, there are cycles or changes in trends. Then other forecasting methods would need to be used.

FIGURE 19–5

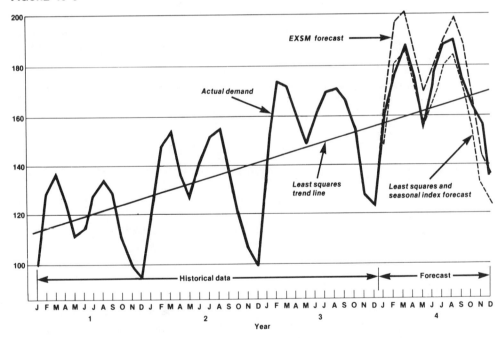

EXPONENTIAL SMOOTHING (EXSM)

The extrapolated trend plus seasonal method of forecasting which we have just discussed gave no direct consideration to trend changes, nor to cyclical movements, nor to possible changes in seasonals or random effects as time unfolds and more historical data are known.

Another method, "exponential smoothing," handles these matters much better. The EXSM method "washes out" random fluctuations; it allows for trends, and it takes seasonal influences into account in determining a forecast. And, as time unfolds, it updates the influence which each of these time series components has on forecast values. While the EXSM method does not directly calculate long-term cyclic patterns, it does, by its very nature, help reveal major turning points in the cycle by showing a lessening or increasing of trends. We will continue to use our NEEDEM time series to illustrate how this method works.

EXSM is a moving average of a time series. If we wish to develop a forecast which smooths out random effects in a time series, we might compute the average demand for January through May. This average might then be used as our forecast for June's demand. When June's actual use becomes known, we then would drop out January's actual use and compute a new average demand for February through June and get a figure to use as our forecast for July, and so on. This would be called a five-month moving average.

If we wished to have an even "smoother" forecast (one which does not respond or "react" up or down so much to the most recent actual figures) we might increase the number of months in our moving average. Conversely, if we wanted to give more weight in our forecast to the more recent actual demands, we could decrease the number of months in our moving average.

Usually, a moving average ought to be based on 12 months. This eliminates the effects of seasonalities, since it always includes all of a year's peaks and valleys in the sales or use of an item. From a practical point of view the EXSM essentially does this (it does not wash out seasonals, rather it incorporates them in diluted form) and, once started, is just as easy to calculate as a 12-month moving average.

EXSM is a weighted moving average, but it needs only two numbers to produce a forecast—the current period's *actual* use of the item, and the *forecast* made earlier for this same month. A new weighted moving average is calculated every month by adding together some fraction (say 90%) of the last weighted moving average and the complement (100% − 90% or 10 percent) of the current month's actual usage. The 10-percent weight given to the current month's usage (sometimes called the "smoothing constant") is represented by α, the Greek letter alpha. Although many users of this method use an α of 10 percent, this is not necessary. A higher or lower percent could be used if it gives better forecasts.

We will present examples of three different EXSM models. Model 1 is the simplest model, and essentially it does the same thing that a moving average does; it smooths out the random effects in a time series. Model 2 is designed to be used where both random effects and trend effects are apparent in the time series, but no seasonal pattern is evident. Finally,

FIGURE 19–6

EXPONENTIAL SMOOTHING MODELS

MODEL 1 = SIMPLE EXPONENTIAL SMOOTHING MODEL
MODEL 2 = EXPONENTIAL SMOOTHING WITH TREND COMPONENT
MODEL 3 = EXPONENTIAL SMOOTHING WITH TREND AND SEASONAL COMPONENTS

EXPONENTIAL SMOOTHING CONSTANTS
AVERAGE   .10
TREND   .10
SEASONAL .40
MAD   .40

NUMBER OF PERIODS IN A YEAR   12

SEASONAL INDICES FOR EACH PERIOD IN A YEAR

1	2	3	4	5	6	7	8	9	10	11	12
.94	1.14	1.17	1.06	.96	1.02	1.09	1.11	1.04	.93	.79	.74

		MODEL 1		MODEL 2				MODEL 3				
T	D(T)	F(T)	MAD	F(T)	T(T)	E(T+1)	MAD	F(T)	T(T)	I(T)	E(T+1)	MAD
0	-n*	100.00*	-0.0*	100.00*	1.22*	112.18*	-0.0*	100.00*	1.22*	.74*	95.15*	-0.0*
1	100*	100.00*	0.0*	100.00*	1.10*	110.97*	4.9*	101.73*	1.27*	.96*	117.43*	1.9*
2	128*	102.80*	11.2*	102.80*	1.27*	115.47*	9.7*	103.93*	1.36*	1.18*	123.20*	5.4*
3	130*	106.32*	20.8*	106.37*	1.49*	121.24*	14.9*	106.56*	1.49*	1.22*	114.53*	9.2*
4	127*	108.39*	20.8*	108.39*	1.55*	123.89*	11.2*	109.23*	1.61*	1.10*	115.34*	8.5*
5	112*	108.75*	13.9*	108.75*	1.43*	123.06*	11.5*	111.42*	1.67*	.98*	125.03*	5.3*
6	115*	109.37*	10.8*	109.37*	1.35*	122.88*	10.1*	113.05*	1.66*	1.02*	125.03*	5.3*
7	128*	111.24*	14.0*	111.24*	1.40*	125.25*	8.1*	114.98*	1.69*	1.10*	129.51*	4.3*
8	134*	113.51*	17.5*	113.51*	1.49*	128.40*	8.4*	117.08*	1.73*	1.06*	123.56*	4.4*
9	130*	115.16*	17.1*	115.16*	1.51*	130.21*	5.7*	119.43*	1.79*	1.06*	112.73*	5.2*
10	116*	115.25*	10.6*	115.25*	1.36*	128.87*	9.1*	121.57*	1.83*	.94*	97.48*	4.4*
11	100*	113.72*	12.4*	113.72*	1.07*	124.46*	17.0*	123.71*	1.86*	.80*	92.92*	3.7*
12	95*	111.85*	15.0*	111.85*	.78*	119.64*	22.0*	125.85*	1.89*	.75*	122.27*	3.0*
13	125*	113.16*	14.2*	113.16*	.93*	121.50*	15.3*	128.03*	1.92*	.96*	152.89*	2.9*
14	148*	116.65*	22.5*	116.65*	1.10*	127.63*	19.8*	129.52*	1.87*	1.16*	160.31*	3.7*
15	155*	120.48*	28.8*	120.48*	1.37*	134.20*	22.8*	130.96*	1.83*	1.21*	146.22*	4.3*
16	138*	122.23*	24.3*	122.23*	1.41*	136.33*	15.2*	132.05*	1.76*	1.08*	130.87*	5.9*
17	128*	122.81*	16.9*	122.81*	1.33*	136.08*	12.5*	133.51*	1.73*	.97*	137.79*	4.7*
18	142*	124.73*	17.8*	124.73*	1.39*	138.59*	9.8*	135.65*	1.77*	1.03*	151.06*	4.5*
19	152*	127.46*	21.6*	127.46*	1.52*	142.66*	11.3*	137.50*	1.78*	1.10*	156.52*	3.1*
20	156*	130.31*	24.4*	130.31*	1.65*	146.84*	12.1*	139.23*	1.77*	1.12*	149.38*	2.1*
21	140*	131.28*	18.5*	131.28*	1.58*	147.13*	10.0*	140.12*	1.68*	1.04*	133.25*	5.0*
22	122*	130.35*	14.8*	130.35*	1.33*	143.69*	16.1*	140.60*	1.56*	.91*	113.35*	7.5*
23	108*	128.12*	17.8*	128.12*	.98*	137.88*	23.9*	141.49*	1.50*	.78*	106.66*	6.6*
24	100*	125.31*	21.9*	125.31*	.60*	131.28*	29.5*	142.10*	1.41*	.73*	138.46*	6.6*
25	146*	127.37*	21.4*	127.37*	.75*	134.82*	23.6*	144.29*	1.48*	.98*	169.54*	7.0*
26	175*	132.14*	31.9*	132.14*	1.15*	143.61*	30.2*	146.24*	1.53*	1.18*	178.13*	6.4*
27	173*	136.22*	35.5*	136.22*	1.44*	150.63*	29.9*	147.35*	1.49*	1.19*	160.55*	5.9*
28	161*	138.70*	31.2*	138.70*	1.54*	154.15*	22.1*	148.88*	1.49*	1.08*	145.91*	3.7*
29	150*	139.83*	23.2*	139.83*	1.50*	154.86*	14.9*	150.79*	1.54*	.98*	156.91*	3.9*
30	162*	142.05*	22.8*	142.05*	1.57*	157.79*	11.8*	152.82*	1.59*	1.04*	170.12*	4.4*
31	171*	144.94*	25.3*	144.94*	1.71*	162.01*	12.4*	154.49*	1.59*	1.10*	175.20*	3.0*
32	173*	147.75*	26.4*	147.75*	1.82*	165.91*	11.8*	155.88*	1.57*	1.12*	163.02*	2.7*
33	168*	149.77*	23.9*	149.77*	1.84*	168.15*	7.9*	157.94*	1.62*	1.05*	145.34*	3.6*
34	157*	150.50*	17.2*	150.50*	1.73*	167.75*	9.2*	160.84*	1.75*	.94*	127.42*	6.8*
35	130*	148.45*	18.5*	148.45*	1.35*	161.93*	20.6*	162.92*	1.78*	.79*	120.08*	5.1*
36	125*	146.10*	20.5*	146.10*	.98*	155.89*	27.2*	165.38*	1.85*	.74*	164.50*	5.0*

Program provided courtesy George A. Johnson, Idaho State University.

Model 3 is designed to account for all three; random, trend, and seasonal effects. In addition, we will also discuss a measure of the errors in forecasts, called the "mean absolute deviation," or MAD.

Again we ran our NEEDEM 36-month time series on a computer, this time using a program designed to do all the calculations for Models 1, 2, and 3. The computer outputs are presented in Figures 19–6 and 19–7. Then we had the computer forecast the monthly sales for the 12 months of year four. This forecast is then compared, in Figure 19–8, with the actual usage in all four years.

Model 1

The equation for Model 1 is:

$$F_t = \alpha(D_t) + (1 - \alpha)F_{t-1}$$

Where:

F_t = the smoothed average for the present period, t, and the best estimate for the next period, $t + 1$

α = the smoothing constant

D_t = current actual usage

F_{t-1} = last period's smoothed average

As we said, F_t is actually a weighted moving average which is calculated in our example by adding 10 percent of the current month's actual usage or sales of an item to 90 percent of its last previous moving average. The new weighted moving average becomes the forecast for the immediately coming up month or, if commitments have to be made farther ahead, as the forecast for the several months whose demand must be forecast.

FIGURE 19–7

```
SEASONAL INDICES
   1       2       3       4       5       6
  .98    1.18    1.19    1.08     .98    1.04


   7       8       9      10      11      12
 1.10    1.12    1.05     .94     .79     .74


FORECAST
**********************************************
 PERIOD * MODEL 1 * MODEL 2 * MODEL 3
**********************************************
   37 *   146.10 *   155.89 *   164.50
   38 *   146.10 *   156.87 *   198.92
   39 *   146.10 *   157.85 *   203.90
   40 *   146.10 *   158.83 *   186.56
   41 *   146.10 *   159.81 *   171.15
   42 *   146.10 *   160.79 *   183.90
   43 *   146.10 *   161.77 *   196.84
   44 *   146.10 *   162.74 *   201.33
   45 *   146.10 *   163.72 *   190.52
   46 *   146.10 *   164.70 *   172.29
   47 *   146.10 *   165.68 *   146.61
   48 *   146.10 *   166.66 *   138.76
```

In order to begin the smoothing process, there has to be an assumed starting weighted moving average. We will start by assuming a previous period's average (F_{t-1}) of 100. If an analyst is starting today and has no old figures to look at, he can just use today's actual figure to start with. If he has older figures and is going to calculate moving averages for them all, he might start with the first number he has or an average of the first two or three numbers. It doesn't matter very much how he starts because the effects of the starting number will soon wash out as the smoothing process carries on.

Using our series of NEEDEM sales, calculations for the weighted mov-

FIGURE 19–8

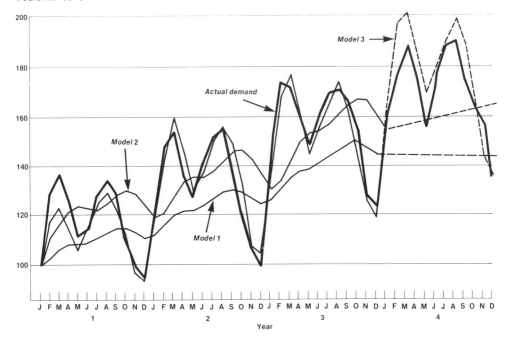

ing averages for the first four periods (as shown in Figure 19–6, Model 1, in the column headed "$F(T)$") are:

Period

1	$F_t = .1(100) + .9(100) = 100.00$
2	$F_t = .1(128) + .9(100) = 102.80$
3	$F_t = .1(138) + .9(102.8) = 106.32$
4	$F_t = .1(127) + .9(106.32) = 108.39$

Similar calculations were made for all 36 months of the first three years and the EXSM figures were plotted in Figure 19–8. Although, as can be seen in Figure 19–8, this method smooths out the irregularities in our time series, it consistently underestimates the actual demand. This is because this particular series contains an upward trend, and a moving average always lags behind whenever there is a trend. If there were a downward trend, the lagging effect would cause the weighted moving average to be too high.

Model 2

The equations for Model 2, which accounts for trend effects in addition to random effects, are:

$$(1) \quad F_t = \alpha(D_t) + (1 - \alpha)F_{t-1}$$

$$(2) \quad T_t = \alpha(F_t - F_{t-1}) + (1 - \alpha)T_{t-1}$$

$$(3) \quad E_{t+1} = F_t + \frac{1 - \alpha}{\alpha}(T_t) + T_t$$

Where: Equation (1) is the same as Model 1

T_t = average trend in the present period
T_{t-1} = average trend in previous period
E_{t+1} = forecast average for next period,
     considering random and trend effects.

As in Model 1, we have also arbitrarily chosen $\alpha = .10$ for the trend effects and have determined an "initial" average trend for the previous period to be 1.22 which is the "b" coefficient from our earlier least squares analysis. Alternatively, we could have estimated it from a freehand plot or simply set it at zero initially. Calculations using this model are also shown in Figure 19–6. The first two period's calculations are:

Period

1
$$F_t = .1(100) + .9(100) = 100$$
$$T_t = .1(100 - 100) + .9(1.22) = 1.10$$
$$E_{t+1} = 100 + \frac{1 - .1}{.1}(1.10) + 1.10 = 110.97$$

2
$$F_t = .1(128) + .9(100) = 102.80$$
$$T_t = .1(102.80 - 100) + .9(1.10) = 1.27$$
$$E_{t+1} = 102.8 + \frac{1 - .1}{.1}(1.27) + 1.27 = 115.47$$

Similarly, each E_{t+1} for Model 2 has been plotted in Figure 19–8. The figures for years one, two, and three are forecasts in the same way that the year four figures will be forecasted. When plotted, these forecasts for past periods can easily be compared to what actually happened. It will be seen in Figure 19–8 that the Model 2 forecasts are quite smooth and they follow the general upward trend of the actual demand. Model 2 forecasts do not, however, effectively "track" seasonal fluctuations.

Model 3

Model 3's equations, which are designed to account for random, trend, and seasonal components in a time series, are more complex. In addition to choosing a smoothing constant for smoothing the seasonal indexes (we chose .40), we must also develop initial seasonal indices for each month. We used the indices from our previous least squares seasonal analysis procedure here. They are also listed in Figure 19–6. The equations are:

$$F_t = \alpha \left(\frac{D_t}{I_{t-L}}\right) + (1 - \alpha)(F_{t-1} + T_{t-1})$$
$$T_t = \alpha\,(F_t - F_{t-1}) + (1 - \alpha)T_{t-1}$$
$$I_t = \alpha \left(\frac{D_t}{F_t}\right) + (1 - \alpha)(I_{t-L})$$
$$E_{t+k} = [F_t + (k \times T_t)] \times I_{t-L+k}$$

Where:

L = number of periods in a year
k = number of periods to project the forecast
I_t = current average seasonal index for period t
I_{t-L} = old average seasonal index for period $t - L$
E_{t+k} = forecast for the $t + k^{\text{th}}$ period

The model 3 calculations are also shown in Figure 19–6 and plotted in Figure 19–8. The computation for the first two periods are:

Period

1    $F_t = .1 \left(\dfrac{100}{.94}\right) + .9(100 + 1.22) = 101.73$

$T_t = .1(101.73 - 100) + .9(1.22) = 1.27$

$I_t = .4 \left(\dfrac{100}{101.73}\right) + .6(.94) = .96$

$E_{t+k} = (101.73 + 1 \times 1.27) \times 1.14 = 117.43$

2    $F_t = .1 \left(\dfrac{128}{1.14}\right) + .9(101.73 + 1.27) = 103.93$

$T_t = .1(103.93 - 101.73) + .9(1.27) = 1.36$

$I_t = .4 \left(\dfrac{128}{103.93}\right) + .6(1.14) = 1.18$

$E_{t+k} = (103.93 + 1 \times 1.36) \times 1.17 = 123.2$

Finally, we have plotted the forecast values for all three models on Figure 19–8 and back on Figure 19–5 for comparative purposes. Model 3 tracks actual demand reasonably well; however, the monthly forecast for year four overshoots actual demand for all but November and December.

At this point in the process the analyst might try some other smoothing constants and rerun the program to see if improvements can be made in the forecast. While the constants we used (.10, .10, and .40 for F, T and I) are commonly used in practice, others may be more appropriate for other time series.

MEASURING FORECAST ERRORS

The easiest way to measure forecast errors is simply to compare the forecast against the demand which actually occurs. However, when thousands of items are being forecasted each month, it is usually more practical to use some calculated measure of forecast error which can be monitored by the same computer system which is generating the forecasts. It is common to program the computer to notice when actual demand seems to be varying substantially from forecasted demand and to bring this to the attention of inventory management people. These reports of "exceptions" allow managers to review all such situations and revise the forecasts if market conditions seem to warrant it.

A common measure of forecast error is the "mean absolute deviation," (MAD). This is simply the difference between the forecast and the actual demand. In formula form the forecast error for a single period is:

$$\text{Forecast error} = |D_t - \text{Forecast}|$$

In this formula, the vertical bars mean absolute value, paying no attention to whether differences are positive or negative.

We can calculate a simple moving average of errors in forecasts or we can use exponential smoothing just as we did for the forecasts themselves. The equation for this model is:

$$MAD_t = \alpha|D_t - \text{Forecast}| + (1 - \alpha)MAD_{t-1}$$

As before, we must choose an initial value for MAD_{t-1}. In our example $\alpha = .40$ and $MAD_{t-1} = 0$, which are commonly used. MAD calculations are shown for Models 1, 2, and 3 in Figure 19–6 and the computations for the first three months in Model 1 are:

Period

1	$MAD_t = .4|100 - 100| + .6(0)$	$= 0$
2	$MAD_t = .4|128 - 100| + .6(0)$	$= 11.2$
3	$MAD_t = .4|138 - 102.8| + .6(11.2)$	$= 20.8$

The mean absolute deviation can be used two ways. First, the analyst can evaluate the MADs generated to determine which model and which smoothing constants seem to produce the best forecasts. For example, the MADs in Figure 19–6 for Model 3 are generally smaller (the forecasts are, therefore, better) than those in Models 1 and 2 which can be seen in the plots in Figure 19–8.

Tracking signals

The second use of MADs is for forecast monitoring; to check the performance of the forecasting model being used as actual demand unfolds over time. Here another error measure, called a "tracking signal," can be used. Tracking signals are used to call attention to management when forecasts differ substantially from actual demand experience.

A tracking signal is simply a warning given by the computer that the forecast errors have become unduly large. But, in order to give this warning, the computer has to be given rules telling it how to tell if the error is unduly large. The method used here is first to calculate a running total of the net forecast errors, with minuses offsetting pluses. Thus, unless the forecasts are very poor and are also consistently too high or too low, the cumulative total should not get very far above or below zero.

The next step is to evaluate the magnitude of the cumulative errors so that the computer will send out the danger signal if this number gets too large. The danger signal is obtained by dividing the cumulative error by the exponentially smoothed MAD figure. If the signal is ±3 or more, something is probably very wrong with the forecasts.

We will use an example to illustrate the method. Our hypothetical numbers used in Figure 19–9 are no longer the NEEDEM figures but are chosen to illustrate the tracking signal procedure. They are also obviously ·quite extreme. No good forecasting system would continue to forecast demand going up in the face of sales going down month after month as occurs in Figure 19–9.

FIGURE 19–9

Period	Forecast of demand (1)	Actual demand (2)	Difference (3)	Running sum of forecast errors (4)	Exponentially smoothed MAD* (5)	Tracking signal (6)
1.............	100	102	+2	2	0.8	2.50
2.............	105	104	−1	1	0.88	1.13
3.............	110	112	+2	3	1.33	2.25
4.............	115	108	−7	−4	3.6	−1.11
5.............	120	105	−15	−19	8.16	−2.32
6.............	125	100	−25	−44	15.16	−2.90
7.............	130	95	−35	−79	23.1	−3.42
8.............	135	100	−35	−114	27.86	−4.09
9.............	140	90	−50	−164	36.71	−4.46
10.............	145	85	−60	−224	46.02	−4.87

* $\alpha = .4$; $MAD_{t-1} = 0$.

In Figure 19–9, column 1 shows the forecast, column 2 the actual sales, and column 3 the error in each month's forecast. Column 4 is the cumulative net error. Column 5 is the exponentially smoothed MAD, and column 6 is column 4 divided by column 5, or the cumulative error expressed as the number of MADs. This column provides the tracking signals.

Figure 19–9 is presented here only to illustrate how the tracking signal is calculated. The use of this signal rests on statistical relationships which are explained in statistical inventory control books.[3] These relationships tell us that the numbers in column 6 should, by chance, exceed ±3 only 2 percent of the time and ±2 only 11 percent of the time.

Obviously, our example given in Figure 19–9, where the tracking signal is almost −5, is far above these limits so the forecasting method being used is very unsatisfactory. The computer can be programmed to watch these tracking signals for the thousands of relatively minor items, and it

[3] See, for example, Oliver W. Wight, *Production and Inventory Management in the Computer Age* (Boston: Cahners Books, 1974), p. 154.

can be programmed to print out lists of all cases where the signal is ± 2 or more (or whatever ratio is regarded as signaling danger), thus bringing these items to management's attention.

Adaptive response systems

Calling managers' attention to the need to adjust the forecasting procedure does not in itself make any improvement. Usually if the forecasting procedure has become unreliable it will be because of abrupt changes in levels of demand or in seasonal patterns. To take care of these, the managers would probably temporarily increase the value of α as used in the calculations. Later, when the system has adjusted to the new conditions, it can be changed back.

Even this part of the work, too, can be computerized. IBM has a forecasting "package" in their Communication Oriented Production Information and Control System (COPICS) which will cause the computer to adapt its calculations and to improve its forecasts.

THE BOX-JENKINS METHOD

The Box-Jenkins method of forecasting time series has, in recent years, become popular and so needs mentioning here although it is too complex to explain here.[4] Basically, this method is related to the family of "autoregressive-moving average" time series analysis methods. These methods relate future demand to past demand by determining the weights which should be placed on current actual demand, last period's demand, demand two periods ago, three periods ago, and so on. These weights are updated as the time series unfolds.

REVIEW QUESTIONS

1. Compare top-down and bottom-up methods of forecasting. Which should a manager use and why?
2. Should sales forecasts be expressed in terms of money or of physical units? Why? If money, who translates them into units, and when? Is this more important in continuous production or in job-lot work? Why?
3. Differentiate between "extrinsic" and "intrinsic" forecasting.
4. What are the subpatterns in a typical time series? What causes each?
5. How can regression analysis be used to calculate trend?
6. What is a seasonal index? How is it calculated?
7. What is a moving average? What component of a time series is it designed to "wash out"?

---

[4] See George E. P. Box and Gwilyn M. Jenkins, *Time Series Analysis: Forecasting and Control* (San Francisco: Holden-Day, 1970).

8. How is the length of a moving average related to the "smoothness" of a forecast?

9. Why use EWMA instead of a moving average?

10. What are the three EWMA models designed to account for in a time series?

11. Generally how does the size of the smoothing constant relate to the weight given to the most recent actual demand?

12. How does the analyst know which smoothing constants are best for a particular time series?

13. What is a "mean absolute deviation"? How is it used?

14. What is a tracking signal and how do managers use them?

15. How do adaptive response systems differ from tracking signals?

PROBLEMS

1. The sales department expects the sales of model A record players to go up this year (from last year's total of 10,000) to 15,000. Past experience shows the following probable seasonal sales pattern and next year's calendar shows the number of work days:

Month	Percent of average month	Number of possible regular work days
January...................	60	23
February.................	50	20
March...................	60	23
April....................	120	20
May.....................	200	22
June....................	180	22
July....................	90	11*
August..................	70	23
September...............	90	20
October.................	120	22
November...............	100	21
December...............	60	19

* Plant closed first half of July.

Make up a schedule of expected sales, month by month, for model A record players for the year. Be sure to pay attention to the fact that sales are trending upward. This means that the trend is upward within the years and not just between the years.

To solve this problem, first calculate the monthly average for each year. Then find the difference between the two averages and divide this difference by 12 to get the increment by which the trend increases each month.

The average for the first year is regarded as the trend figure for the middle 30 days of the year, or June 15 to July 15. Adding one monthly increment gives the trend value for the next 30 days, July 15 to August 15. Next, these two months' trend figures are averaged together to get the trend for the calendar month of July, the 30-day period centered on

July 15. (The different number of days in months is neglected in calculations of trend values.)

After the figure for July is arrived at, trend values for other months can be obtained by adding the appropriate number of monthly increments until the trend is extrapolated for each month in the year ahead.

Finally, each month's sales estimate is obtained by multiplying each month's trend value by the month's seasonal percent. The January trend would be multiplied by .60, February's by .50, and so on. Once the sales estimates are calculated for each month, production and inventory planning can proceed.

If these products are all made in the month of sale, what will be the daily average rate of production each month? If production is leveled out, what will be the daily rate each month? Show, month by month, what the month-end inventory will be. If it costs $2 a month to carry a finished record player in stock, what will the inventory carrying cost come to?

2. The forecast of sales during the first four months of the year for product A was 22,000, 18,000, 35,000, and 50,000. Actual sales have been 16,000, 19,000, 41,000, and 61,000. This leaves the April month-end inventory 12,000 under the expected figure, although there are still 30,000 units in inventory.

Production has been at the rate of 40,000 per month for several months and can go as high as 60,000. The earlier sales forecasts anticipated sales of 70,000 per month for May through September.

What schedule changes should be made right now, if any. Why? Make a forecast of sales, production, and inventories at each month-end for the next five months.

3. The following demand data represents a trend situation without seasonal effects. Initial value for trend should be ten.

Quarter	Demand
0	90
1	100
2	110
3	120
4	130
5	140
6	150
7	160
8	170
9	180
10	190
11	200
12	210

Examine the behavior of the three EXSM forecasting models using the following smoothing constants.

Condition	Average	Trend	Seasonal
1	.1	.1	.4
2	.3	.3	.3
3	.01	.3	.3

Smoothing constants

Examining the response of the forecasting systems can be accomplished by a plotting of the actual demand versus the forecast and by examining the unsmoothed MAD values for each model over time.

4. The following time series represents an extreme random observation. Examine the behavior of the three EXSM forecasting models to this situation. Again use the smoothing constants specified in problem 3.

Quarter	Demand
0......	100
1......	100
2......	100
3......	100
4......	200
5......	100
6......	100
7......	100
8......	100
9......	100
10.....	100
11.....	100
12.....	100

5. The following time series represents a model with a strong seasonal component. In year 3 there is also a trend component. Using initial seasonal indexes of 1, calculate E_{t+k} using model 3. Next recalculate using as the initial seasonal indices the final seasonal indices from the first set of calculations. Use the smoothing constants of condition 1 in problem 3.

	Demand		
Month	Year 1	Year 2	Year 3
1......	259	259	269
2......	500	500	500
3......	707	707	737
4......	866	866	906
5......	966	966	1016
6......	1000	1000	1000
7......	1000	1000	1070
8......	966	966	1046
9......	866	866	956
10.....	707	707	807
11.....	500	500	610
12.....	259	259	379

6. The following figures are the record of the demand for a finished product of the Scientific Products Company. Experiment with the data, using different smoothing constants until you find a good model.

Quarter	Demand
0......	100
1......	102
2......	98
3......	110
4......	114
5......	99
6......	105
7......	101
8......	92
9......	109
10.....	99
11.....	105
12.....	88

7. The Rex Company produces air conditioners. Three years of past sales data are given below. Experiment with the data to find a good forecasting model and smoothing constants.

Month	Demand		
	Year 1	Year 2	Year 3
1.....	274	283	263
2.....	510	431	462
3.....	656	680	695
4.....	915	909	931
5.....	1221	1081	1121
6.....	943	941	895
7.....	1097	918	1070
8.....	909	971	1036
9.....	866	880	1050
10....	661	748	830
11....	531	506	621
12....	275	275	425

8. The actual demand for an item is not behaving as was forecasted as can be seen below. Using an $\alpha = .4$ and an initial MAD value of 0, when would the tracking signal exceed limits of ± 3?

Actual demand	Forecast
80......	100
100.....	100
110.....	100
100.....	110
90......	110
80......	120
70......	120
60......	130
50......	130

SUGGESTED SUPPLEMENTARY READINGS

Adam, Everett, E., Jr. "Individual Item Forecasting Model Evaluation." *Decision Sciences,* October 1973, pp. 458–70.

Chambers, John C.; Mullick, Satinder K.; and Smith, Donald D. "How to Choose the Right Forecasting Technique." *Harvard Business Review,* July–August 1971, pp. 45–74.

Gerstenfeld, A. "Technological Forecasting." *Journal of Business,* January 1971, pp. 10–18.

20

Master scheduling and material requirements planning

MASTER PRODUCTION SCHEDULES: MANUFACTURE TO ORDER

A MASTER schedule is a list showing how many of each item to make in each period of time in the future. Ideally, once made up, it remains fixed for the immediate future so that production can progress. In fact, however, master schedules are usually changed as time moves along in response to changed conditions. This textbook was, at one time, on the master schedule of the Richard D. Irwin Company and was to be produced in November and December. But extensive revisions by the authors delayed it so its place in the schedule was reassigned to another book. This book was finally actually produced in March and April.

When products are made to customers' orders, the job of master schedule making is largely one of looking at the future work load of orders already on hand and seeing when the customers want their orders and when new order deliveries can be promised. This means that the schedulers must know approximately how many labor-hours, or tons, or some other overall measure of workloads the orders already accepted will amount to in each major department. This reveals how soon there will be some open capacity in each department. Then, for the orders that the sales department is bidding on, estimates need to be made concerning how much capacity they will require, department by department.

It is necessary also to pay attention to the sequence of work loads in different departments. If an item needs to be designed, the engineering work load will have to come early. Capacity will be needed in the foundry or forge or sheet metal shop later on, and still later in the machine shop, and so on. Unless the work loads needed in the early-stage departments

471

can be handled on time, work in later-stage departments will be delayed even if they have open time earlier. When an order is accepted, its work load is added to the loads of the appropriate departments and their uncommitted capacities are reduced accordingly.

The master schedule is, when manufacture is to sales orders, only a summation made out new at the end of each month of the booked but unfinished jobs for future months. It extends as far ahead as the last delivery date on the last order already on hand. And it shows, month by month, the orders which will be finished and shipped.

In this kind of master production schedule development, the production control department takes an active part because production control knows how large the existing back logs of work are in terms of capacity commitments.

Manufacturing to sales orders is not without its problems so far as schedules are concerned. Sometimes, when bidding for jobs, tentative promise dates are made on several possible contracts, although only one contract is expected. All of these promise dates are predicated on using the same open time, but this causes problems if two or more of the orders are obtained and if capacity cannot easily be expanded. Another problem arises when a promise date is offered and the customer places the order but wants delivery sooner. Also, there are cancellations, or the factory may not get things done on time, or customers may delay signing the contract during which time the open capacity is assigned to other orders and then still want the factory to meet the originally promised delivery date. This often occurs on large government contracts.

When sales are tied directly to customers' orders, usually a copy of the sales order (or an abstract of it) is production control's authority to prepare the factory directives and see that the products are made. This is the way Otis Elevator goes about making elevators when it gets a contract for the elevators in a new building.

A different situation occurs where the sales order is a blanket order (usually from another manufacturer or a chain store or mail order company) for a large quantity of a product to be delivered in frequent small shipments as directed by the customer's production control department. Such orders constitute a large part of many manufacturers' business. In this situation, new releases of authority to make more products come directly to production control from the various customers and not from anyone inside the company. In these cases, the production control department receives many authorizations from many sources and at different times instead of receiving its authorization from a master schedule itself.

Similarly, when manufacturing is directly to sales orders for large individual products, the orders usually are sent to production control from the sales department whenever they are received rather than all at one time. At any one time the master schedule is merely the summation of orders passed on to production control in the past.

WORKLOADS AND PRODUCTION CAPACITIES

Master production schedules and production programs try to level out sales peaks and valleys; yet, in practice this is not carried very far because it costs so much to carry inventories. Production controllers end up having to do a great deal of schedule changing as they go along. Many of these changes are carried into effect by changing work hours up or down in response to sales changes. Yet steady operations are important so the first response to sales changes is probably not a change in work hours.

Rather, if order backlogs begin to build up a little, the sales department gives new customers more distant promise dates. But, if backlogs build up very much, most companies would try to expand capacity by increasing work hours because they don't want to lose customers. And, conversely, if the backlog shrinks, capacity is not cut as the first move. Instead, new customers get earlier promise dates on their orders. If orders continue to shrink, operations may be curtailed or else a new sales promotion campaign to stimulate new orders is undertaken.

MASTER SCHEDULES: MANUFACTURING TO STOCK

Manufacturers of almost all consumers' products—the things you and I buy—manufacture "to stock." Products are made and assigned to sales orders as they are finished, or they are put into finished goods inventory in anticipation of their sale. Many such products are assigned to large continuing contracts with large selling companies such as Sears Roebuck and K-Mart. At the same time a good many of the "to stock" items have not been sold at the time they are being made and no one knows exactly who will buy them. Companies manufacturing to stock forecast what and how many of everything that they think their customers will buy and then try to make these items in those quantities. This kind of forecasting was discussed in Chapter 19.

The development of a master production schedule for manufacture to stock begins with a sales forecast. As a rule this forecast will have too many extreme ups and downs to allow its direct use as a production schedule. The peaks and valleys usually need some leveling out which can be done by building up inventories during low periods. The amount of leveling which can be done depends on the relative costs of carrying inventories versus the costs of changing production levels up and down.

Changing production levels may involve overtime or layoffs, the purchase of new machines or letting certain machines set idle, and other similar costs. There is also need, as in the case of automobile tires, to forecast the product mix because some of the factory's equipment is specially designed for certain tire sizes.

Production control participates in the adjustments made as the tentative schedule congeals into the approved master schedule since it has to say whether the factory can handle the tentative schedule. Will there be enough machines? Will more employees be needed, or will some have to be laid off? These and other questions have to be answered by production control.

One of the major functions of master schedules when manufacturing to stock is to smooth out the differences as much as possible between irregular sales and steady production, largely by using inventories to cushion the differences. This has the effect of "decoupling" production and sales.

As a typical example of this in operation, we might consider the Jones Company. The Jones Company makes toys—mostly music box toys which have rubber belts with molded-on bumps to play the tunes. The music boxes are put into all kinds of toys and play tunes when a handle is cranked. It is a highly seasonal business, with Christmas being the big selling peak. For the Jones Company, this means an August and September production peak, since retail stores do most of their Christmas buying at this time.

FIGURE 20–1

Expected sales of model A toy banjos (in thousands)

Month	Unit sales forecast	Accumulated sales
January	30	30
February	30	60
March	40	100
April	120	220
May	80	300
June	60	360
July	140	500
August	300	800
September	250	1,050
October	80	1,130
November	40	1,170
December	30	1,200

Jones's problem is not to lose sales in its peak period, yet to level out production as much as it can without carrying large inventories. Also, it doesn't want to get caught with Mickey Mouse products after Mickey has had his day. (Most toys have only a one-year life cycle; then they are finished.)

Jones first makes a sales forecast for an item month by month for 12 months—for example, a toy banjo (model A) with a crank-operated music box inside. Figure 20–1 shows its expected monthly sales and cumulative sales for a year.

In working out a production schedule, Jones's schedulers have to contend with a cost of changing production levels of $100 per 1,000 units of change each time the production level is changed up or down. It also costs $60 per 1,000 units carried over each month end. And, if the banjos run out of stock at any time, it is estimated that although little of the unfilled demand will be lost, there is nonetheless a loss in goodwill of $10 per 1,000 units of orders that have to be backordered.

The schedulers' problem is to develop a schedule which will minimize the combined cost of production level changes, inventory carrying costs, and losses from stockouts and backorders.

If the schedulers opt for no carrying costs, they would have to produce to match sales demands and would have to change production levels almost every month with consequent high change costs. If they choose to avoid changes, they can do this by producing steadily and building up inventories. With this choice, inventory carrying charges would be high.

The schedulers might, as we did, try first to see how steady production throughout the year would work out. We tried 100,000 a month and found that this did not work out very well. The build-up of inventory in the first half of the year was insufficient to prevent the banjo production from being behind orders all through the fall. Although this program incurred no production level change charges, the inventory carrying costs and the costs of backorders came to $77,210.

Next, we tested a schedule of producing exactly to sales expectations. This program eliminated both inventory carrying charges and backorder costs but entailed costs from changing production levels of $66,000.

One might suspect that a compromise strategy somewhere between these two extremes ought to produce a lower total cost. Figure 20–2 (depicted graphically in Figure 20–3) shows a first attempt to develop such a compromise strategy.

FIGURE 20–2

Compromise strategy

Month	Sales fore-cast	Produc-tion schedule	Change in production rate	Capacity change cost	Inventory at end of month	Inventory holding costs	Stock-out costs
January.........	30	50	0	$ 0	20	$ 1,200	
February.......	30	50	0	0	40	2,400	
March.........	40	60	10	1,000	60	3,600	
April..........	120	100	40	4,000	40	2,400	
May...........	80	100	0	0	60	3,600	
June..........	60	160	60	6,000	160	9,600	
July..........	140	160	0	0	180	10,800	
August.........	300	160	0	0	40	2,400	
September......	250	160	0	0	−50	0	$500
October........	80	130	30	3,000	0	0	
November......	40	40	90	9,000	0	0	
December......	30	30	10	1,000	0	0	
				$24,000		$36,000	$500

Total costs:
Capacity change costs..................	$24,000
Inventory holding costs.................	36,000
Stockout costs........................	500
Total costs.......................	$60,500

FIGURE 20–3

Compromise production schedule which allows sales needs to be met economically

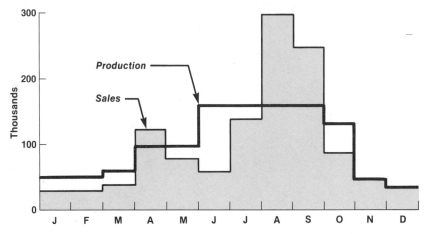

This proposed schedule (the heavy line in Figure 20–3) is much flatter than the sales forecast line. The top production of 160,000 banjos per month from June through September is down almost to half of the August sales peak. From the factory's point of view, this is a great improvement over the extremely fluctuating sales line shown by the thin line in Figure 20–3. This schedule is also less costly at $60,500 than either of the first two alternatives.

This schedule is not perfect, however, from the production point of view because peak production is still more than double normal off-season production. And even this much production leveling can be accomplished only by building up inventories during the slack season. The scheduler could test other proposed schedules and might find that some other strategy may produce even lower total costs.[1]

Figure 20–4 shows Jones's forecasted inventories of the toy banjo. It is a plot of the figures in Figure 20–2 where it was found that the inventory will reach a peak of 180,000 banjos at the end of July. Yet the average inventory for the whole year is only 50,000 or about two weeks' average monthly sales.

Figure 20–4 shows a negative inventory at the end of September—although there can't really be a negative inventory. The minus figure just means that for a week or so at the end of September Jones will not be able to fill all of the expected orders out of stock or out of current production. Jones's managers hope it won't lose any sales if it gets those orders filled early in October. By then they will be caught up.

---

[1] This problem can be formulated as a linear programming problem to determine the optimal (least cost) production rate over a planning horizon. See Frederick C. Weston, Jr., "Mathematical Programming and Aggregate Production Planning," *Production and Inventory Management*, vol. 15, no. 1, 1974, pp. 37–48.

FIGURE 20–4

Planned inventory levels needed to take care of sales needs while allowing the factory to produce somewhat evenly

Our example uses only one item: model A banjos. But Jones has to do the same thing for all its main items, one by one. For lesser items, Jones will probably forecast for groups at a time—perhaps using only sales dollars figures. After making forecasts, production schedules, and inventory projections for the items separately, Jones will combine them into overall figures—probably just in dollars since we can't add Mickey Mouse water pistols to model A banjos. Here we are concerned with the factory's overall or "aggregate" capacity and how this capacity can be adjusted to respond to total sales needs, taking capacity change costs, inventory holding costs and stockout costs into account.

PRODUCTION PROGRAMS

Many companies make end products which can be completed in a very short time (hours or days), but these are usually made out of materials or parts which require longer lead times to buy or manufacture. Some companies work from production "programs," or lists of general classes of products to make. And because of the high volume (as in automobile upholstery fabrics and automobile tires), they use so much raw material that they have to plan for and to order materials months ahead of time.

Production programs differ from other master schedules in that an approved program does *not* give production control authority to produce anything. Rather, these programs authorize the materials control department to procure raw materials with long lead times, and they give suppliers with blanket contracts a preview of the probable near future delivery needs.

The production control department gets its authority to go ahead and schedule products to be made in the form of weekly "releases" against the program. The releases are decided by the finished products inventory control group, which is closely associated with the sales department.

FIGURE 20–5

Tentative allocation of factory capacity to varying quantities of several main products

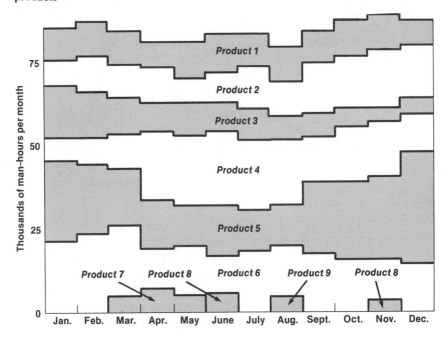

These releases come to production control only two or three weeks before the products are required. This method, therefore, can work only where the manufacturing cycle is short. Nonetheless, it gives the factory considerable flexibility to shift from one product to another (as from one automobile tire size to another or, in a shoe factory, from one size or style of shoe to another) and to follow market trends. It requires only that the total volume forecast be flexible enough to handle normal variations in the product mix. The total volume forecast has, however, to be reasonably accurate because raw materials come in on a schedule to meet this volume.

MASTER SCHEDULES: CLASSES OF PRODUCTS

Some companies make thousands of products, very few of which considered individually, amount to much in dollars. Companies making plumbing fittings, pipe connections, tees, ells, and so on, or nuts and bolts, or even medicines of hundreds of kinds and in many sizes of packages are like this.

Some companies that make thousands of items use master schedules for only whole classes or groups of products. Their quantities are shown in dollars, tons, pounds, gallons, or some other unit common to all items in the class. Their planned inventories are also shown only for classes of products.

It is up to production control to decide how many to make of each individual item and when to make them. Production control has to meet the planned overall inventory size and keep the factory working as planned and yet try not to run out of any item very often. In cases like this, production control usually sets its own finished product inventory levels, and it keeps records of past production and sales.

MASTER SCHEDULES: THE TIME PERIOD

Master schedules may cover production for as much as a year ahead in companies where it takes a long time to make products as, for example, airplanes or oil drilling rigs to drill for oil in the ocean. Not many things, though, need a year's lead time in manufacturing.

But *forecasts,* on which master schedules for complex products are based, need to extend a year or more ahead most of the time—particularly where a company makes annual models. Forecasting a long way ahead is necessary so that decisions can be made about how much mechanization (the "depth" of tooling) is necessary and to plan for other required capacities such as labor and plant size. Large volumes usually allow high payoffs from heavy mechanization because they spread the investment over so many items that production costs per unit are very low. But these new machine requirements have to be determined, and they have to be ordered so they can be installed by the start of the model year.

Although companies making annual models do forecast sales for an entire year ahead in order to help them decide on the degree of mechanization, they usually do not make master production schedules nearly so far ahead. During the course of the year, they use production programs with releases authorizing production for only short periods ahead.

Some companies (makers of machinery, locomotives, and so on) make long lead time products which require months to complete so they need to have master schedules that actually authorize production several months ahead. They need to be far ahead, not only because the products take a long time to make, but because raw materials control is likely, in these cases, to be production control's job too. The production control department has to know what end products are going to be made at least six months ahead in order to determine what materials or parts to make or buy. Then it has to order the materials and, when they arrive, begin making the parts.

There are two different kinds of long-term master schedules. One kind covers the next five or six months, often broken down into weekly requirements. When one month ends, the sixth month ahead is added. This is how General Motors' electro-motive division (which makes diesel electric locomotives) plans.

The other way, six months at a time are added. For example, in February a schedule is set up through the following December, but it is not extended any farther in March or April. Then, in August, a schedule is issued for another six months, January to June, of the next year. Then nothing more until February, and so on. The Cincinnati Milicron Company plans this way, and so do many other machinery makers.

The reason for the difference is largely a matter of volume and the degree of product standardization. The first method (where one future month is added every month) is usually used wherever there are not many different kinds of products and where at least a few of them are included in every schedule. Most products are being made most of the time, but their quantities vary. But when the products are less standardized, the second method (six months at a time) is more frequently used.

The second method is better in this situation because it is sometimes desirable to make complex end products in lots. We might suppose that one kind of machine sells 12 units a year. Making them at a rate of one per month sounds good until we think of making the parts. It would be possible to make enough parts in January for all 12 units and keep them in bins, some until December. It is also possible to set up the parts making machinery to make just enough parts for one product in January, and then to do it again in February, and so on every month, or 12 times.

It would almost certainly be wasteful to make parts for one machine at a time. Surely it would be less costly to make parts for, say, six machines at a time, and then one lot of six could be assembled in March and another lot of six in September. This would allow for manufacturing at a reasonable cost and would allow customers to be given better service. A customer who orders in January or February can be told to wait until March, but a March customer gets a machine right away; so do the April, May, and June customers. Their machines come out of stock. Then July customers have to wait until September, and so on.

But, one may ask, why can't this be done just by adding one month at a time to the schedule? Why is it better to move the schedule forward several months at a time? It is because some products will be made (assembled) over a two- or three-month period rather than over one month.

The problem is this: Suppose that at the end of February the schedulers "firm up" July's assembly schedule and add it to March–June. In July, let us say, ten units of product X appear on the schedule (having been off the schedule for several months), and, because of long lead times for certain parts, it is necessary to order the material right away and to start making these long lead time parts.

At the end of March, August is added. August's schedule has ten more product X's on it. And later, when September is added, ten more product X's turn up on that schedule. The difficulty with this kind of schedule is that the factory's production controllers find out about the parts requirements a little at a time. In March, on the long lead time items, they ordered the right number of parts to complete July's assembly requirements. Had they known about August and September, they could have made some of the parts orders in large enough quantities to take care of them all—and, most likely, at much lower costs. In April and May it is probably too late to increase the lot sizes of the parts orders for July's products because they are already halfway through production.

Sometimes, of course, parts can be made in a short time. In such a case what has just been said does not apply. For short lead time items, July's parts probably won't be started until June anyway. By that time, the schedulers have firm schedules for August and September and can set lot quantities to cover them all if it is economical to do so.

MASTER SCHEDULES: BASIC COMPONENTS

Complex products are often made in considerable variety. For example, factory machines such as lathes, grinders, and drill presses are often built in different sizes and different designs. But many of their component parts, such as roller bearings and electric motors, may be the same for several kinds of finished products.

These standardized components are sometimes called "basics," and, since they have a demand from several sources, they can be made on a schedule of their own which is not directly tied in with the schedule of any single kind of finished product. Storage batteries and automobile headlights are examples of basics. Also, eight-cylinder engines for automobiles can be made without regard for the product mix between station wagons and two- or four-door cars. As basics are finished, they can be assigned to specific finished products, or they can go into finished parts stock temporarily. Using the basics approach uncouples the strict timing of their manufacture from assembly schedules and allows for more economical production.

PARTS

Production control's authority to make end products almost always comes as orders or schedules for *whole products*. This grant of authority and responsibility includes seeing that all parts manufactured internally are made in the required quantities and on time. Authority to make parts derives from the authorization to make finished products. Production control has to determine what parts have to be made, how many, and when. Usually this is all done on computers using "material requirements planning" procedures, which are described later in this chapter.

ASSEMBLY ORDERS

The master schedule shows the kinds and quantities of end products to be assembled in each time period. The production control department usually issues to the assembly department specific assembly orders covering each kind of product to be made in each period.

This assembly order is actually a listing of the parts and components which have to be put together to make the product. It is made by combining the scheduled quantity of the product and the product's "master bill of materials" (a parts list,. sometimes referred to as a "B/M"). An assembly order differs from a master bill in that it shows how many end products are to be assembled *this time* and how many of each part and component will be needed. It also shows the assembly period and has an order number for identification purposes and for cost collection in the accounting department.

One copy of this assembly order goes to the supervisor of the assembly department to tell him what the assemblers are to make. Another copy goes to the finished parts stockroom supervisor to tell him to deliver the parts to the assembly floor by the specified date. Today computers make up almost all of these orders.

MATERIAL REQUIREMENTS PLANNING

When manufacturing products such as factory machines, computers, and suitcases, it is always a problem to get the right number of parts made and purchased and ready at the right time to assemble into final products. For complicated end products, the complexity of the planning and of the paper work needed is almost beyond belief.

Today this work can be simplified with a computer using "Material Requirements Planning" (MRP) methods. MRP (sometimes called "time phased requirements planning") is actually a refinement and extention of earlier methods which integrates piece-meal methods into a single system. This is now feasible because today's computers handle large volumes of data and make calculations fast and accurately at reasonable costs.

Much of the developmental work on MRP was done by Joseph Orlicky, Oliver Wight, and George Plossl.[2] Today these methods are widely used in computer based production and inventory planning and control systems.

The MRP concept is easy to grasp; yet, because the products for whose production it is used are complex, MRP operation becomes somewhat complicated. Figure 20–7 illustrates the concept. Figure 20–7 is an assembly diagram (or a "product structure tree") for a very simple product, product A, which is made from only two kinds of parts and two kinds of subassemblies. The last operation, indicated at the top is to make end product A by putting together one B assembly with two C assemblies and two D parts. Product A, the end product, is, by convention, called a "level 0" item.

---

[2] See Joseph Orlicky, *Materials Requirements Planning* (New York: McGraw-Hill, 1975); George W. Plossl and Oliver W. Wight, *Production and Inventory Control* (Englewood Cliffs, N.J.: Prentice-Hall, 1967); and Oliver W. Wight, *Production and Inventory Management in the Computer Age* (Boston: Cahners Books, 1975).

FIGURE 20–6

Elements of a materials requirements planning system

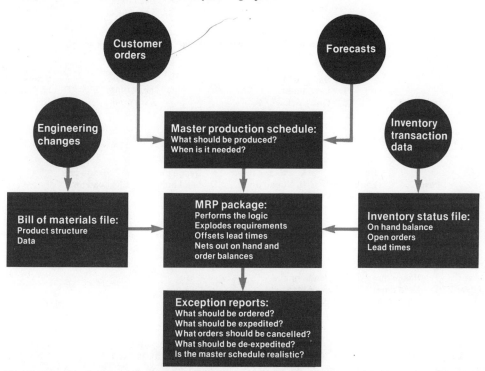

Source: Jeffrey G. Miller and Linda G. Sprague, "Behind the growth in Materials Requirements Planning," *Harvard Business Review*, September–October, 1975, p. 84.

But product A cannot be put together until its components are available. So whatever number of A's are wanted must be supported by there being a sufficient number of its components available. If 10 A's are wanted, there must be 20 C assemblies available. Thus, it is necessary to "explode" the number of level 0 items needed and find out how many "level 1" components will be needed. (Level 1 items are subassemblies, components, and piece parts which go directly into the end product.)

These requirements are then combined with any other requirements for the same items from other end products to get a "gross requirements" figure for each level 1 item. Next, these gross requirements are checked against any stocks of these items which are on hand or on order and a net (remaining required) figure arrived at.

If there are still more levels—lesser subassemblies going into higher-level assemblies (there are two more levels in product A's structure tree) a similar explosion process is carried on for each level until finally the number of each kind of item entering the product at its inception stages is established.

Along with the quantity determinations we have been talking about,

FIGURE 20–7

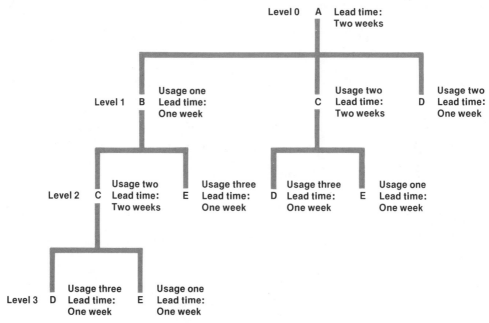

This example is adapted from IBM training materials, with permission.

MRP also pays attention to lead times. If it takes two weeks to assemble an order of A products, then its components have to be finished two weeks before A's assembly starts. And since these components also require time to make, *their* processing must start earlier yet.

Thus, MRP establishes the quantities of parts and subassemblies which will be needed and also sets the times when they will have to be ready in order to allow the end products to be assembled on schedule.

MRP can even help managers anticipate the wearing out of tooling. All that is needed is to list the tooling on the bill of materials on a ratio basis. If the molds for making a fiberglass insert are likely to wear out after producing 250 inserts, the bill of materials could show that 1/250 of a mold is needed for each insert. Thus, four of these molds would be required in order to make 1,000 inserts.

MRP is regarded primarily as a method for calculating materials and parts requirements. But MRP also allows for the calculating of labor and machine time needs. Once what will be made and when is known, it is easy for the computer, using master parts making "route sheets," to calculate labor and machine times. This is called "capacity requirements planning."

Dependent versus independent demand

An important concept in MRP is "independent" versus "dependent" demand. Independent demand comes from the outside. It is the demand from customers for the company's finished products or for spare parts for repair purposes. If a company manufactures vacuum cleaners, the finished cleaners and replacement parts for repairs are, for example, "independently" derived from actual customer orders and forecasts of future demand from customers. At any particular time the independent demand for end-products (when production is not to order) is not yet truly "demand" at all but is merely a forecast of what sales will be. For MRP purposes, however, such forecasts are treated much as if the products were actually sold. Such products are put on the schedule and their production is started.

The demand for the *parts* needed to make independent demand products is "dependent" demand. A forecast that 1,000 vacuum cleaners will be sold during a given period of time in the near future generates a dependent demand for 4,000 wheels, 1,000 tanks, 1,000 plastic molded end pieces for the front end, and 1,000 similarly molded but different plastic covers for the back end and for a sufficient number of nuts, bolts, washers and other items to assemble the 1,000 finished vacuum cleaners.

The point to distinguishing between independent and dependent demands is that independent demand is not wholly calculable. In planning, the quantities of independent demand items needed come from orders, if there are such orders. Or, if manufacture is to stock, the independent demand comes from forecasts even though these are recognized to be somewhat unreliable. For planning purposes, once a quantity of an independent demand item has been accepted as part of the master schedule, the quantities of dependent demand items (usually parts) generated are determinable, and it is possible to *calculate* their demand with considerable accuracy.

An additional point is that some components are sold for repair purposes as well as their being used in newly assembled end products. Their total demand is therefore a sum of the dependent demand generated by the end products into which they go, plus their own independent demand.

Moving back one step farther in our vacuum cleaner example, if we make the tanks for the cleaners ourselves out of sheet metal, then we can calculate the amount of sheet metal needed since we know how much each cleaner requires. Similarly, if we make the plastic end covers, then a dependent demand for a certain amount of plastic raw material is generated.

Lead times

Lead times are the times it takes to get things done. For items we make, lead times are the times it takes to prepare the necessary papers, plus the time to perform operations, plus the dead time between operations. For purchased items and raw materials, lead times are the times it takes to get orders filled.

The total lead times for items we buy is actually, however, much greater than our own internal lead times because it extends back to suppliers and includes *their* "make times," or "through-put" times, and shipping times, and possibly the make times and shipping times of *their* suppliers. Long chains of sequential lead times must sometimes be allowed for. Not only that, but each successive earlier vendor's through-put time includes not only his make time, but his present work backlog.

Common use items

In most manufacturing situations, some component parts and a good many kinds of raw materials are used in two or more end products. Thus, their total requirements are sums of requirements being generated from two or more sources. These several requirements for common use items ought almost always to be combined into single orders or manufacturing lots in order to save on ordering and setup costs. MRP procedures do combine these needs as they determine each item's net requirements.

Data files for material requirements planning

The requirements coming from independent demands and those generated by dependent demand for each of the thousands of components and parts which can exist in a typical fabrication oriented job-shop are usually stored in five computer files. First, materials records, tool requirements, and lead times are typically stored in a bill of materials file processor. Second, machine times, routing, and labor requirements are stored in a manufacturing routing and engineering data file. Third is an inventory transaction file which maintains running balances of parts and subassemblies. Fourth is an "open order" file listing orders placed but not yet received or completed. And, fifth is the master production schedule file.

Product structure trees

Figure 20–7, on page 484, is a graphic representation of a bill of materials, or a "product structure tree." Normal procurement lead times are also shown in Figure 20–7. Such a tree is only to help conceptualize the idea of assembled products being the end results of sequential series of levels of assemblies as small assemblies go into larger assemblies which finally go into end products. It would obviously be impossible to make up such a tree for any but the simplest products.

Figure 20–8 is a similar product tree for a second very simple product, product F. We are going to use product F along with product A to carry through an MRP calculation. As in the case of Figure 20–7, Figure 20–8 shows the make-up of the end product and the necessary manufacturing lead times. Products A and F bear no relationship to each other except that they use the same components but in different quantities and in different combinations, a common situation in many lines.

FIGURE 20–8

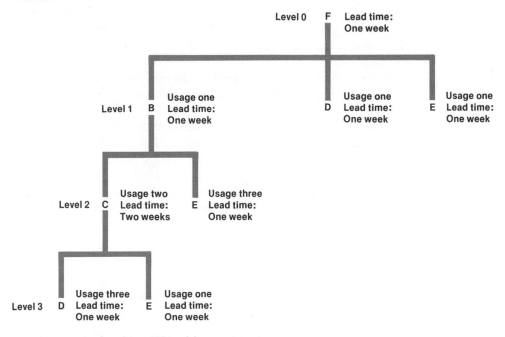

This example is adapted from IBM training materials, with permission.

"Level" codes

The knob on the end of the platen roller of a typewriter is a piece part. It goes on the end of the platen roller and will later be used to turn the roller. The platen roller assembly goes into the typewriter's movable carriage. Still later the whole carriage assembly is assembled onto a typewriter.

Computerized material requirements planning first identifies the "level" at which every item enters the product. An end product, such as a typewriter, or as in our examples, an A, or an F item, is an "0" level item. Its assembly occurs in the schedule period shown on the master schedule as the period when the product should be completed.

Anything which goes directly into an end product in the form of an assembled component or as a piece part is a level "1" item. A typewriter carriage assembly is a level 1 item. Level 1 items are made in an earlier period before the final assembly period, how much earlier depends on the end product's lead time.

Components of level 1 items, both assemblies and piece parts are level 2. A typewriter platen assembly is a level 2 item. Level 2 items are made up of level 3 items, and so on. The knobs on the end of a typewriter platen roller assembly are level 3 items. They have to be made considerably earlier than the period when the typewriter is to be finished.

Figures 20–7 and 20–8 illustrate the "levels" concept. The computer must know the level number of every part and subassembly so that proper backwards extensions of lead times from end product completion dates to parts manufacture start dates can be made for scheduling the making of the components.

In Figures 20–7 and 20–8 we see that items B and D are level 1 items in the case of both A and F. C is also needed at level 1 for product A and also at level 2 for both A and F.

In Figures 20–7 and 20–8 we see the need for the different components, some of which appear at two or more levels. For computer calculations of when items will be needed, it is necessary first to identify each item with one and only one level and *that is its lowest level.* "Lowest level" here means the farthest down in the structure tree. Thus, a level 3 item is a lower-level item than a level 1 item. Our low-level codes for the items in our example are:

| | Level of item | | Low level |
Item	Product A	Product F	code
A....................	0		0
B....................	1	1	1
C....................	1, 2	2	2
D....................	1, 2, 3	1, 3	3
E....................	2, 2, 3	1, 2, 3	3
F....................	0	0	0

Time "buckets"

Before explaining how the computer proceeds with MRP calculations, we need to discuss certain other matters. The first of these is time periods. In computer language these are time "buckets" or standard time increments.

Schedules for making parts and products usually do not specify the exact expected starting and finishing times for operations. Often they do not even indicate the day, although the operations needed for making piece parts are frequently assigned "wanted completion dates" where the date used is a given day, not a week.

As a usual thing, however, assembly work is scheduled instead as so many units to be put together within a specified week. In such cases and where parts to support these assembly schedules are made in quantities related to assembly needs only, the lead times between parts making and assembly are usually also stated in weeks. So are the parts manufacturing lead times.

Often these time increments are in weeks up to the next six months, then months for the rest of the year, and quarters thereafter. For complex products with long manufacturing cycles, such as commercial jet aircraft engines, a time horizon of weekly buckets may extend ahead for more than a year.

In our example, we are going to develop in the next few pages requirements for the parts needed to make 25 units of product A and 25 of F, using time buckets of one week. The master schedule calls for 10 units of product A to be completed in week 5 and 15 units in week 8; 13 units of product F are required in week 4 and 12 in week 7.

On-hand stocks

Our example assumes that products A and F are regular products which have been made before and which will continue to be made in the future. We may, therefore, already have on hand or on order a few of the necessary components carried over from the past. It is customary to carry at least a few of many items more or less permanently as safety protection against running out of stock. MRP methods can, however, reduce the needs for safety stock by calculating exactly what quantities of parts will be needed and when.

As MRP develops the requirements quantities for future production, it considers any quantities already on hand, reducing the quantities needed wherever a supply exists or will become available from past orders not yet received. Actually, the real stock available is the sum of the "on-hand" stock plus the safety stock and the stock on order. MRP, however, recognizes the intent of safety stocks to be for safety protection and does not consider safety stocks to be available for regular use.

"Netting" and "exploding" orders for end products

The problem we are going to work through starts with the following data: The master schedule specifies that 10 units of product A be completed in week 5 and 15 units in week 8. Product F's requirements are for 13 units in week 4 and 12 units in week 7. Item C, a component part of both end products A and F, also has an independent demand for repair purposes of 1 unit every week.

Thirteen units of item B were ordered some time ago and are scheduled to arrive in week 2, and 100 units of C are to arrive in week 1. There are 15 units of B in stock of which 10 are regarded as safety stock. There are 2 units of C in stock, which is far below its intended safety stock of 30. Item D has 25 in stock, of which 5 are safety stock. There are 5 of E in stock with no safety stock needed.

All of these starting figures have been recorded on the computation sheet, Figure 20–9, where they are circled. All noncircled figures are developed as the MRP process unfolds. The process is one of finding, first, the "gross" requirements of all end products (level 0 items) for each time period and then noting any stocks already on hand or on order to determine their "net" requirements.

In our cases with products A and F, there are no stocks on hand or on

FIGURE 20–9

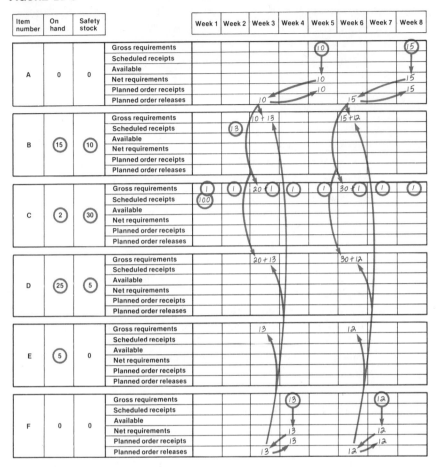

order for either of these end products so their gross requirements become their net requirements. Net requirements must be procured so, paying attention to the lead times indicated in Figures 20–7 and 20–8, "planned order releases" orders for the appropriate quantities are placed *in the proper weeks.* The placing of orders carries with it the expectation that receipts will come in in the weeks when they are needed, so these expected receipts are posted as "planned order receipts." These steps are carried out in Figure 20–9 in the sections for items A and F.

The next step is to "explode" the net requirements of all level 0 items (in our case A and F). Exploding the requirements for A and F only means multiplying their needs by the number of each part or component going directly into them, to get preliminary gross requirements figures for all level 1 items.

This step is shown in Figure 20–9 as the preliminary gross requirements for items B, C, D, and E are generated. For example, the 10 units of A ordered in week 3 generates a demand for 10 units of B in week 3 (the requirement here is that all components which are used to make A items must be ready during the same week that the assembly orders for making A items are released). In addition to this, the planned order releases for 13 units of F in week 3 generates a demand for 13 of B in week 3. Similarly, a gross requirement for B is generated in week 6 from the planned orders placed there for A and F.

Next, the explosion process moves to item C. Two C's go into each A as direct components so the 10 A's needed in weeks 3 and the 15 A's needed in week 6 will produce gross requirements of 20 and 30 C units respectively. Two D items go directly into A products so a similar gross requirement for D (20 and 30) is generated.

Product F also needs 1 unit of D so F requires 13 D units in week 3 and 12 units in week 6. And, finally, F needs 1 unit of E so it results in a demand for E of 13 and 12 units in weeks 3 and 6 respectively.

At this point we have established both gross and net requirements for items A and F and have developed preliminary gross requirements for B, C, D and E.

The next step is to develop *net* requirements for all items whose *low level* is 1. Only B has level 1 as its lowest level (it is not used at any deeper level in products A or F). The development of B's net requirements and its following explosion into gross requirements for level 2 items, offset to their proper time period, are depicted in Figure 20–10. (The requirements for C, D, and E cannot yet be netted. Their gross requirements will be modified through subsequent explosions for lower level items.)

In Figure 20–10, all of the numbers arrived at in Figure 20–9 are carried over in their proper blocks. The changes indicated in Figure 20–10 all stem from our analysis of the gross and net requirements for B. Week 3's gross requirements for B come to 23 units. There are 15 B's on hand, and 13 are due to be received, making 28. But, of these, 10 are safety stock, so only 18 are available. Since we need 23, this leaves us with a net requirement of 5 B's in week 3.

As before, the net requirement of 5 is offset to week 2 because of lead time, so 5 are to be ordered in week 2. And again, the planned receipt of the order is posted in the column for week 3. Then, the order for 5 B units is exploded into gross requirements for C and E of 10 and 15 respectively. Similar calculations for the 27 B units to be ordered in week 5 generates gross requirements of C and E of 54 and 81 respectively.

At this point we have netted B's requirements and have exploded B's needs for its components, C and E. Doing this completes our use of Figure 20–10.

The calculation now moves on to Figure 20–11, where the gross requirements of all the items whose low level is 2 (only C) are netted, then offset

FIGURE 20–10

Item number	On hand	Safety stock		Week 1	Week 2	Week 3	Week 4	Week 5	Week 6	Week 7	Week 8
A	0	0	Gross requirements					10			15
			Scheduled receipts								
			Available								
			Net requirements					10			15
			Planned order receipts					10			15
			Planned order releases		10				15		
B	15	10	Gross requirements			23			27		
			Scheduled receipts		13						
			Available	5	18	18					
			Net requirements			5			27		
			Planned order receipts			5			27		
			Planned order releases	5				27			
C	2	30	Gross requirements	1	10+1	21	1	54+1	31	1	1
			Scheduled receipts	100							
			Available								
			Net requirements								
			Planned order receipts								
			Planned order releases								
D	25	5	Gross requirements			33			42		
			Scheduled receipts								
			Available								
			Net requirements								
			Planned order receipts								
			Planned order releases								
E	5	0	Gross requirements		15	13		81	12		
			Scheduled receipts								
			Available								
			Net requirements								
			Planned order receipts								
			Planned order releases								
F	0	0	Gross requirements				13			12	
			Scheduled receipts								
			Available								
			Net requirements				13			12	
			Planned order receipts				13			12	
			Planned order releases			13			12		

for lead times. C's net requirements are then exploded to determine additional gross requirements for items D and E.

Finally, we come to low level 3 and net items D and E. As before, we offset for their lead times and post their planned order releases and planned order receipt quantities in the proper buckets.

This completes stage 1 of our example showing how material requirements planning works. We now know how many of everything to order and when. Had there been more levels, it would have been necessary to have carried through more iterations of the kind we have just been through. It is hard to believe that our simple little problem could have produced such a complicated calculation just to get the right quantities of parts and subassemblies ordered at the right time. It is obvious from looking at what our problem required that real-life complicated products would require a computerized MRP system to handle all of the necessary calculations and updating as time unfolds.

FIGURE 20–11

Item number	On hand	Safety stock		Week 1	Week 2	Week 3	Week 4	Week 5	Week 6	Week 7	Week 8
A	0	0	Gross requirements					10			15
			Scheduled receipts								
			Available								
			Net requirements					10			15
			Planned order receipts					10			15
			Planned order releases		10				15		
B	15	10	Gross requirements			23			27		
			Scheduled receipts		13						
			Available	5	18	18					
			Net requirements			5			27		
			Planned order receipts			5			27		
			Planned order releases		5			27			
C	2	30	Gross requirements	1	11	21	1	55	31	1	1
			Scheduled receipts	100							
			Available	72	71	60	39	38			
			Net requirements					17	31	1	1
			Planned order receipts					17	31	1	1
			Planned order releases			17	31	1	1		
D	25	5	Gross requirements			51 + 33	93	3	3 + 42		
			Scheduled receipts								
			Available	20	20	20					
			Net requirements			64	93	3	45		
			Planned order receipts			64	93	3	45		
			Planned order releases		64	93	3	45			
E	5	0	Gross requirements		15	17 + 13	31	1 + 81	12 + 1		
			Scheduled receipts								
			Available		5						
			Net requirements		10	30	31	82	13		
			Planned order receipts		10	30	31	82	13		
			Planned order releases	10	30	31	82	13			
F	0	0	Gross requirements				13			12	
			Scheduled receipts								
			Available								
			Net requirements				13			12	
			Planned order receipts				13			12	
			Planned order releases			13			12		

RAW MATERIALS REQUIREMENTS

Once reorders for parts have been placed, they generate a whole new secondary MRP process. Sometimes this is incorporated into the overall MRP process and is not separated as a secondary process. This secondary process concerns raw materials. Factory orders for parts are exploded back to their materials requirements; again gross requirements are first arrived at. And again, supplies on hand and on order are considered and net requirements are established.

This secondary explosion process cannot always be tied directly into the first part of the MRP process because the timing of raw materials needs are dependent on the way parts requirements are grouped into actual parts orders. The grouping of parts requirements into orders for their manufacture or purchase will be discussed in Chapter 21.

Raw materials procurement lead times also come into the process since they determine when the materials will need to be ordered so that they will arrive on time. Furthermore, the "planned order release" quantities really represent minimum ordering quantities which may need to be adjusted upward in the interest of buying economies.

EXTRANEOUS DEMAND FOR PARTS AND COMPONENTS

We have just said that MRP at the conclusion of stage 1 tells us how many of everything we need to order and when. But this is not altogether so, as we have explained it up to this point. Instead, we have a good, solid base statement of minimum needs, but many of the quantities are too low.

Our discussion of MRP has not considered production attrition nor the need for repair service parts (except for factoring in an expected demand for one C component every week for customer repair parts orders). But both of these needs are facts of life so the quantities shown in Figure 20–11 as the planned order releases all need to be increased.

Production attrition is the loss from items being spoiled or rejected at one or more stages of manufacture. Some of this will always occur and needs to be allowed for. More pieces will have to be started through production than are needed for end use purposes. Expected attrition rates can be found by looking at past records of losses and an extra quantity must be factored into the calculations of needs to take care of this.

Similarly, customers often need repair parts. For wearing parts, such as bearings or cutting tools, the sales of extra parts for replacement purposes is often a substantial business. Even nonwearing parts (automobile fenders) also become damaged and need replacement.

As in the case of attrition, the need for repair service parts means that more parts will have to be made than will be needed just for the end products being assembled. Past experience will show how many extra parts of each kind to make. As some companies use MRP, these needs are factored in as added quantities although we did not show this in our example. In some other companies where production of end products is more or less steady, such needs are not factored in but are allowed to cause temporary reductions in the safety stocks. These are made up by increasing future order quantities.

It is also necessary to continue making some old parts long after the main product is out of production. (Automobile manufacturers are required by law to supply repair parts for ten years.) Someone, somewhere, is still using a 50-year old product and now and then wants a repair part. Because old tooling and old machines are probably gone, it may be necessary to make replacement parts for discontinued products on a custom basis. Ordinarily the need for these items is outside the mainstream MRP system.

PRIORITY PLANNING AND RESCHEDULING

At the start of this chapter we reported that master schedules were often changed, thus upsetting all of the MRP calculations. Such changes are caused by customers wanting to change the quantities on their orders or to change the delivery schedules; or there may be changes caused by delays in the arrival of raw materials or changes in the bill of materials; or changes may be made for other reasons.

One of the nice things about a computerized MRP system is that the computer will recalculate everything quickly and usually at reasonable cost. This is especially helpful when changes cause changes in the priorities among orders. Priority planning is discussed in more detail in Chapter 22.

LOT SIZES AND THE TIMING OF ORDERS

The planned orders for parts and components generated by MRP are, as part of the procedure, posted to the proper time periods. But, so far, our discussion has given no consideration to whether these planned order releases should or should not be combined into larger orders. Obviously, the quantity actually ordered should be large enough to cover near future needs, but this is a minimum. It may be more economical to order considerably more than near future requirements in order to save reordering small quantities so often. If this is done, then it means combining the needs of more distant future periods with immediate needs. Such combining is called "lot sizing." Several MRP-oriented lot sizing methods exist to help determine the "best" number of later time buckets' orders to combine with earlier time buckets' orders. Lot sizing is discussed in Chapter 21.

REVIEW QUESTIONS

1. When the company manufactures to sales orders, how does the production control department get authority to make parts?
2. When using production programs, how does the production control department get its authority to issue orders to the factory to go ahead and produce?
3. Contrast the use of master schedules in production control work when manufacture is to order and the use of master schedules when manufacture is to stock.
4. Why are some master schedules extended another month ahead continually as months go by whereas in other companies future schedules are pushed ahead six months at a time?
5. When should master schedules be stated in terms of classes of products instead of in terms of specific products?
6. How does the idea of using "basics" and scheduling their production independently from final assembly help in schedule making?
7. How do assembly orders differ from master production schedules?
8. Distinguish between independent and dependent demand.
9. How are lead times used in materials requirements planning?

10. How does a "product structure tree" relate to a bill of materials?
11. Why are level codes important in MRP systems?
12. Define gross and net requirements in MRP.
13. Trace the steps involved in the "explosion" process from the list of finished products needed back to the parts and raw materials required.

QUESTIONS FOR DISCUSSION

1. Where does the production control department get all of the information it needs, and what kinds of information does it need? To what departments does production control issue orders, and how does it go about getting goods produced? How does it get everything to come out on time at the shipping dock?
2. Discuss the logic of MRP netting, exploding, and offsetting for lead times to determine planned order releases.
3. How can allowances for scrap, tools, and spare parts be incorporated into an MRP system?

PROBLEMS

1. The Home Appliance Company has been developing a new line of washing machines and expects to have them on the market by November. The company has installed enough capacity to make 4,500 units per month. First-year sales are expected to be:

January	4,000	July	5,500
February	3,500	August	7,500
March	2,500	September	6,000
April	2,000	October	4,500
May	3,500	November	5,000
June	4,500	December	5,500
			54,000

a. The personnel director wants level and stable production throughout the year. If the plant were to produce steadily, what would the inventory level be at the end of each month? And what would inventory carrying charges be at $3 per machine on the quantity in inventory at the end of each month?

b. The treasurer is worried about inventory carrying costs and suggests considering an increase of capacity at a cost of $60 per unit of added capacity. If the personnel manager's viewpoint can be neglected and if production can be raised or lowered, should any new capacity be added? How much capacity? Show the new production schedule and the inventories in prospect at the end of each month. (For purposes of this calculation, any costs incurred because of changing production levels can be neglected.)

2. Fishburn Fabricators has a backlog of orders for product A (which is made up of 2 units of part B and 1 unit of part C). B is a purchased item and has a lead time of 2 weeks. C is manufactured internally and has a lead time of 1 week. Once parts B and C are available, end item A has a 1 week lead time for final assembly. There are 100 B's and 200 C's now on hand, and an order for 100 B's is due in week 3. Given the following requirements for product A by weeks, what size orders for B's and C's should be released for purchase and production and when should these orders be released? (Do not combine orders but release them as their needs indicate.)

Week number	Number of A's needed
1	0
2	0
3	0
4	400
5	300
6	200
7	400
8	200

3. Given the following product structure trees and master production schedule for items A and F, determine the size and timing of planned order releases for items A, B, C, D, E, and F. All lead times are one week and, unless otherwise indicated, one unit is required for the parent item.

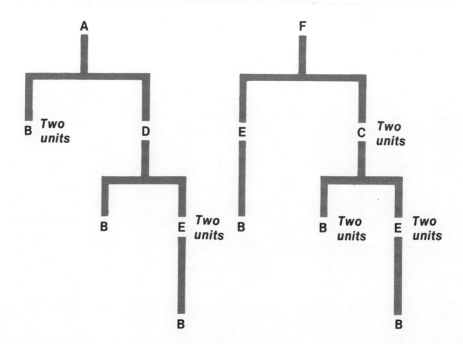

	Item					
	A	B	C	D	E	F
Independent demand (week)						
1					10	
2					10	
3					10	
4					10	
5	30				10	50
6	100				10	100
7			20		10	
8	50				10	75
Currently on hand	0	50	0	10	10	0
Scheduled receipts (week)						
1		10				
2			200			
3				200		
4	20					
5						
6						20
7						
8						

SUGGESTED SUPPLEMENTARY READINGS

Miller, Jeffrey G., and Sprague, Linda G.   "Behind the Growth in Material Requirement Planning." *Harvard Business Review,* September–October, 1975, pp. 83–91.

Orlicky, Joseph A.   *Material Requirements Planning, The New Way of Life in Production and Inventory Management.* New York: McGraw-Hill, 1975.

Wight, Oliver A.   *Production and Inventory Management in the Computer Age.* Boston: Cahners Books, 1974.

21

Inventory management: Order points and order quantities

REORDERING POINTS (ROP)

WHEN and how many items to reorder are the perennial inventory control questions. Reordering points are the "when." The ROP operates as a "trigger" point which triggers the reorder. When the supply of an item diminishes to the reorder point quantity, a new order is placed for more of the item.

In Chapter 20, in the discussion of materials requirements planning, we found that the needs of assembled products for subassemblies, parts, and raw materials, have to be calculated both as to how many and when they will be needed. We also saw that by working backwards from end product master production schedules we could determine when subassemblies, parts, and raw materials needed to be ready.

By working backwards and allowing for procurement lead time, we also found the time period when subassemblies and parts themselves had to be started. And we noted that essentially this becomes the reordering point. In this instance the reordering point is a point in time and not a quantity. The reordering quantity is the quantity needed for the end products on the schedule, and the time for reordering is set by the cumulated lead times needed.

In a great many, probably most, large companies today, the needs for parts and components are calculated by the MRP process using computers. Yet this is less true of small companies. Hoover Ball and Bearing company, a large automobile parts supplier, for example, reports that over one half of its small competitor auto supplier companies do not use computer systems.

Furthermore, in almost all companies, the items needed to repair and maintain the companies' facilities number in the thousands and they are outside of the MRP system, as are supplies consumed in operations that do not become part of end products. The annual cost of such items is, however, much less than the cost of parts and materials going into a company's end products.

But, no matter how a company calculates its expected needs, whether it generates them by a computerized MRP explosion process or manually, it arrives at a list of parts and components that will be needed and it knows when they will be needed. This applies not only to A items but to B and C items as well. When these needs are compared to supplies on hand plus any others already ordered, the additional quantities needed to take care of the demand are established.

For the biggest and most heavily used items, these needs become the basis for order "releases" to suppliers, such releases being issued week by week during the year. There is no "ordering" in the usual sense since the vendor has a contract to supply the company's whole year's needs. The vendor gets releases specifying exactly the quantity wanted in each period. Such quantities are based almost altogether on the needs of the end products called for by the master schedule.

For parts made inside, the process is much the same. Parts and components are being made either all the time or in frequent large lots whose exact quantities reflect the assembly needs.

But, by no means all items are made in this continuous or near-continuous fashion. A great many items, B items in particular, and even C items, are made in less frequent lots. Even though their demand is generated through an MRP process, they are not reordered in quantities exactly in accord with the specific needs of near future assembly needs.

It is often more economical, at this point, to use maximum-minimum inventory controls, with reorder points serving as the basis for reordering. Often this is combined with using economic lot sizes (discussed later in this chapter) to determine the reorder quantities. Burroughs, the nation's second largest computer manufacturer, for example, uses reorder points and economic lot sizes (which are factored into its computer calculations) for determining reorders for nearly all B and C items used in the computers it makes.

Whenever the reorder point is used in this fashion, it is a number and not a time period. The reorder point is the sum of the quantity of an item expected to be used during the reorder cycle time plus a small additional "safety" quantity which serves as protection against variations in use or in replenishment lead times. Each item has to have its own reorder quantity. The inventory level fluctuates as is shown in Figure 21–1.

When reorder points are used in this fashion, there is really no need to *calculate* the future need for each item. Everyone knows that items used in end products will continue to be used but the exact quantities do not have to be known. They can be replaced on a usual use basis. Many com-

FIGURE 21–1

Relationships between reorder points and usage when usage is regular and procurement lead times are constant

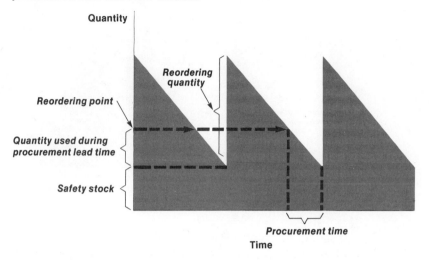

panies, particularly small ones, in fact, do not calculate the needs of all B and C items. Instead, and particularly in the case of multiple use items, these companies just estimate future needs, largely by looking at the recent past. If, for a certain item, the recent use has been 50 per month, then 50 per month will be the estimate for the near future (unless there is some good reason to think that it will be different).

It is the same with how long it takes to get more. How long did it take in the past? Usually six weeks? Then this is the lead time to use. And how much variation has there been in usage and in lead times? After looking over recent experience the inventory controller can decide upon a safety quantity. Actually looking at the past will often show a picture of usage and procurement times like that shown in Figure 21–2 rather than that in Figure 21–1.

In real life it is not possible for the inventory controller to spend the necessary time to give each item much consideration. There are just too many items—thousands or even tens of thousands of items. It is necessary, therefore, to develop policies, rules, and computational procedures for computers so that they can do a reasonable job in this matter.

We will use an example to show how the job of determining reorder points can be performed by a computer. In Figure 21–3 column 2 is the actual history of the use of a B type item whose demand has not been calculated by MRP methods. This item is not important enough to justify its future demand being forecasted using careful economic analysis done by people so we have to rely on a projection of expected demand which can be made by a computer using past data.

FIGURE 21–2

Inventory of an item whose usage and procurement lead times are both variable

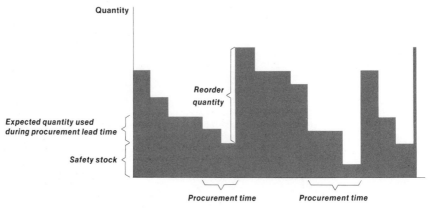

It should be pointed out that a table such as Figure 21–3 is unreal in that it is a static picture of a dynamic situation. It depicts the generation of data as time passes. In real life, this table would never exist as a working tool because, month by month, a new line is added at the bottom and all preceding figures recede into relatively immaterial history.

The purpose of Figure 21–3 is to establish the reorder point for one item. We will end up with a reorder point, which is really made up of two parts: first, the expected usage in the normal replenishment lead time; and, second, a safety stock whose size will be set to provide us with a 95 percent service level. (Service levels will be discussed shortly.)

FIGURE 21–3

Date	Use in month	Moving average	Change in column 3	Trend	Expected use	Forecast of use in lead time	Actual use in lead time	Error in predicted use in lead time	Average of deviations squared	Standard deviation in units
1	2	3	4	5	6	7	8	9	10	11
Start........		201.0		0				31	901	30.0
January....	194	200.3	−0.7	−0.07	199.7	399	373	26	879	29.7
February ...	211	201.4	+1.1	+0.05	201.9	404	393	11	803	28.3
March......	162	197.5	−3.9	−0.34	194.4	389	428	39	875	29.6
April.......	231	200.9	+3.4	+0.03	201.2	402	371	31	884	29.7
May.......	197	200.5	−0.5	−0.02	200.3	401	393	8	802	28.3
June.......	174	197.9	−2.6	−0.28	195.4	391	466	75	1285	35.9
July........	219	200.0	+2.1	−0.04	199.6	399	492	93	2021	45.0
August.....	247	204.7	+4.7	+0.43	208.6	417	468	51	2079	45.6
September..	245	208.7	+4.0	+0.79	215.8	432	432	0	1871	43.2
October.....	223	210.1	+1.4	+0.85	217.8	436	398	38	1828	42.7
November..	209	210.0	−0.1	+0.76	216.8	434				
December...	187	207.7	−2.3	+0.45	211.8	424				

We have said that a new horizontal line of figures is generated every month in Figure 21–3 and that it should be regarded as an ongoing data set. Consequently, we are not much interested in old starting data (the method soon washes out the effects of starting data). To explain Figure 21–3: Column 2 represents actual data, the demand for an item month by month. Column 3 is the exponentially smoothed demand arrived at just as was explained in Chapter 19. (Last month's exponentially smoothed demand × .9 + the current month's actual demand × .1).

Columns 4 and 5 are adjustments for trend and bring us to column 6. (The calculations are the same as those used in Chapter 19.) The January figure in column 6 is 199.7, which we use as our best estimate of the demand for near future months. If we could get replenishment stocks in one month, then this 199.7 would be our estimate of February's usage. In our example, however, we will use a replenishment lead time of two months so we will use the 199.7 as the estimate of usage for February and March as well. This produces the 399 in column 7 which, all the way down in Figure 21–3, is double the numbers in column 6.

To see how this works, let us move down toward the bottom of Figure 21–3. At the end of October, our best estimate of the use of our item for November and December is 217.8 units each month or 436, in column 7, for the two-month lead time. By the end of November and having the actual usage for November before us, we recalculated December's expected usage and arrived at 216.8, making the expected usage during December and January become 434. The demand for this item continued to fall off in December, so that the revised expectation for January became 211.8, and the projection for January–February made at the end of December became 424.

ERRORS IN EXPECTATIONS OF USE DURING LEAD TIMES

Column 8 shows the actual use in the lead time and is, of course, determined after the lead time has gone by. Our item's actual use in February and March was 373 units. This contrasts with the forecast expectation (made at the end of January) of 399 units, so the forecast proved to be off by 26 units. March and April's actual use totaled 393 units as compared to the 404 expected in the forecast made at the end of February, so here the forecast was off 11 units.

Column 9 compares the forecasted use with actual demand. It shows the amount of the forecast error (disregarding whether the estimate was too high or too low) during the procurement lead times.

Column 10 values are further steps on the way to column 11, the one we want. They are based on column 9, and are "exponentially smoothed values" of column 9's forecast errors squared.

To start the smoothing of squared forecast errors, we assumed that the column 9 values for the three months before our table started were 29, 30, 31. Thus, the sum of the squared forecast errors for these previous three months is $29^2 + 30^2 + 31^2 = 2,702$ and the average for these three months is $2702 \div 3 = 901$, the starting figure in column 10. We then calculate the next values in column 10 by simple exponential smoothing. For example, January's value is: $.1(26^2) + .9(901) = 879$; February's is $.1(11^2) + .9(879) = 803$, and so on.

The column 11 numbers are the square root of the column 10 numbers and are actually *smoothed standard deviations*. This is the measure of forecast error we have been working toward for use in setting safety stock levels for specified service levels.

The big advantage from using this method is that everything has been reduced to rules which a computer can follow. A computer can apply such rules to 50,000 items; yet, if need be, it can individualize the procedure and use different smoothing models and or weighting factors if certain items need individual treatment.

SERVICE LEVELS

"Service levels" in inventory control refers to the probability of not running out of anything. It is important in inventory control because, if inventories are large enough never to run out of anything, then they are too high. It takes very large inventories to have enough never to run out of anything before new supplies arrive. Usually it is less costly to have smaller inventories on hand even though this will cause occasional stockouts.

Managers may wish therefore to set a service level objective such as; to have enough stock on hand so that in 95 percent of the cases new replenishment stocks will arrive before the old stock runs out. If usage were wholly predictable and if lead times were wholly reliable, there would be no need for considering the service level concept. Reorders would be placed at the proper time so that new supplies would arrive just as the last of the old supply is used up.

But usage and lead times both vary so it is necessary to *estimate* how many of an item will be used up during the *typical* lead time. The reorder point then becomes the sum of two numbers: first, the expected usage during the lead time, and, second, a safety stock for protection if usage is heavier than anticipated or if the lead time is longer, or both. A service level of 95 percent anticipates setting a reorder point so that in spite of irregularities in usage and lead times new stocks will arrive in time to prevent stockouts about 95 percent of the time.

Such a service level objective can be translated into a reorder point quantity by using the column 11 number in Figure 21–3. This number is the standard deviation of the smoothed forecast errors for the two-month lead time required to replenish the supply of our item. It is always two months behind the current period since it is calculated only after the two months have passed. Meanwhile two more months have passed, and estimates have already been made of the item's use during those months.

FIGURE 21–4

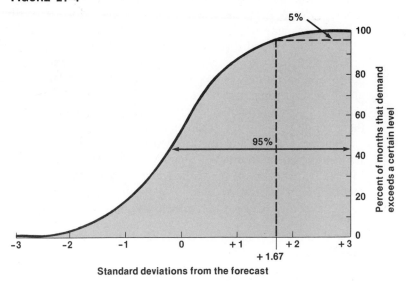

Standard deviations from the forecast

Thus, at the end of December, the expected use during the January–February, 60-day procurement lead time is 424 units. Also, at the end of December, the latest standard deviation of forecast errors is for October when it proved to be 42.7 units. This 42.7 is the standard deviation we will use to calculate the number of units to carry to provide a 95 percent service level for this item.

Figure 21–4 shows a cumulated normal curve with the horizontal scale being marked off in standard deviations from the mean or, in our case, from the expected use of our item. We draw a horizontal line across from the 95-percent level to where it intercepts the curve and then go down vertically to the bottom scale and find that the intercept is at +1.67 standard deviations. (We don't have to do this graphically; instead, we could have referred to the figures for the area under the cumulated normal curve as given in Appendix E, page 729. It tells us that 95 percent of the cases are included in the mean +1.67 standard deviations.)

The required safety stock to give 95 percent protection is then 42.7 × 1.67 = 71 units. When this is added to the prospective usage of 424, it gives us a reordering point of 495 units. Thus, when the inventory level for this item gets down to 495, another order is placed.

Limitations to reorder points based on service levels

Reorder points based on service levels ("statistically determined" reorder points) are most useful where the future demand for an item has to be *forecast* rather than *calculated* and when the usage rates are fairly stable. In other words, reorder points based on service levels is best for independent demand items, not dependent demand items.

In some cases statistically determined order points are not wholly appropriate for A items because they always allow for safety stocks which, for A items, may not be needed. Some companies, when they installed MRP systems, found that by *calculating* when new supplies will have to arrive and hence when to place orders, they were able to eliminate a large portion of their safety stock. Also, by automatically tracking actual demand against forecasts (as described in Chapter 19), they can spot possible stockout conditions before they occur and do something about them before they disrupt production or lose sales.

Sometimes parts and materials are withdrawn from stockrooms infrequently, yet in substantial quantities when they are withdrawn. While this is often convenient for the assembly department and for parts manufacturing departments, it creates a record of "lumpy" demand on the storeroom's records. Because the withdrawals are for large quantities, lumpy

FIGURE 21–5

Probabilities of simultaneous availability

Number of component items	Service level (percent)	
	90	95
1	0.90	0.95
2	0.81	0.90
3	0.73	0.86
4	0.66	0.81
5	0.59	0.77
6	0.53	0.74
8	0.43	0.66
10	0.35	0.60
15	0.21	0.46
20	0.12	0.36
25	0.07	0.26

demand situations have the effect of increasing the size of the safety stocks and consequently increasing average inventory levels. In the case of dependent demand items, MRP methods eliminate the need for large safety stocks in spite of the lumpy nature of the withdrawals from stock and at the same time reduce average inventories.

Another argument against the use of statistically determined order point methods (particularly against the 95-percent service level idea) for dependent demand items is demonstrated in Figure 21–5. If, for example, the service level on *each* dependent demand component part is 95 percent, and there are ten component parts which are made into an end item, the joint probability that all ten items will be simultaneously available is only .599 or 59.9 percent (this is simply 0.95^{10}). For 25 items, it is only 26 percent! For 100 components (not too uncommon for complex products) it is only 0.6 percent!

These are rather bad odds. These poor chances of having all components available to complete end items are what causes some firms which use the 95-percent service level idea to be continually in a *reactive* state of having to expedite a large share of their component parts. Excessive expediting is costly. It upsets schedules, sometimes requires machine setups to be torn down and set up for behind-time jobs and generally results in more expediting and longer lead times. This is why the MRP approach is generally more appropriate than ROP methods for dependent demand items.

OTHER PROBLEMS

Space does not permit us to pursue the matter of statistically determined reorder points further, but there are many more facets to it. Some of them are quite complex.

We have not, for example, pursued the possibility of lead times varying just as usage does. If lead times vary by much, then the safety stock will need to be increased a little. Just how much to raise it to allow for variable lead times, as well as variable usage, gets into complicated calculations.

Nor have we gone into the overall service level, considering that 95 percent protection against reorders' not arriving on time is only part of the story. Sometimes, for example, the stockroom is out of stock but the factory is not. The 50 items the factory just withdrew depleted the stockroom's stock, but they will keep the factory going for a week. The *factory* is not out of stock.

How long an out-of-stock situation continues also is often very important, but this is not in the calculations. So, also, is the question of how many items is the stock short, which is not in the calculations. Nor did we really get into how costly it is to run out. Sometimes, too, a little money spent on expediting would bring the new supply in quickly, thus holding down the out-of-stock costs.

Nor did we say anything about substitutions. If there is need for a 75-watt light bulb and it is out of stock, sometimes a 100-watt bulb will do very well instead. But this upsets the statistics for both items. Sometimes, too, people wait for an out-of-stock item, and when it comes in its use is unnaturally high. This distorts the usage figures for the month when the new supply arrives. We also mentioned seasonal patterns in demand but did not go into what to do about them. Also, sometimes it is better to forego low inventories and build up stocks in order to give the factory reasonable operating schedules. Or, if money is short, it may pay to cut not only reorder quantities but safety stocks as well.

Some of these complicating conditions can be handled well by computers, but some of them remain problems that baffle even computers. Monte Carlo simulation (see Chapter 26) can help in such cases. In general, however, computers can do most of the work we discussed in this chapter and do it economically.

DETERMINING REORDER POINTS WITH STOCKOUT COSTS
AND VARIABLE LEAD TIMES

If the cost of stocking out and of carrying inventory can be estimated and the demand during lead times is known, we can evaluate alternative reorder points and determine the one which promises the least expected cost even though procurement lead times are variable.

An example will show how this can be done:

Use: 50 per week
Cost of running out: $200
Cost to carry 1 unit in stock for 1 week: $.75
Past reorder experience:

Weeks elapsing between ordering and receiving new supply	3	4	5	6	7
Number of instances in last 25 reorders	2	6	10	4	3
Percent of instances	8	24	40	16	12

The problem is to find the reorder point with the least expected cost.

If orders are placed three weeks ahead, the reorder point will have to be for at least 150 units because 150 units will be used during the three weeks. At the end of three weeks the inventory will be down to zero: then it will jump up to 150 and begin to work down again. The average inventory will be half of 150 or 75. The cost to carry 75 units for one week is $75 \times \$.75 = \$56.25$.

But, because of the variability in lead time, most orders will not be received in three weeks, and this item will almost always be out of stock (in 92 percent of the cases) before the new lot comes in (100 percent − 8 percent = 92 percent). Thus, the expected out-of-stock cost will be .92 × $200 = $184 every three weeks, or $61.33 per week. The total cost per week of this alternative is $117.58.

Next, the same calculation can be made using a reorder point of 200 units, the normal four-week usage. Other calculations can be made for the other possibilities, with the results being those shown in Figure 21–6. In this example the reorder point which minimizes total expected weekly costs is about five weeks usage, or about 250 units.

Calculating reorder points this way does not indicate what fraction of

FIGURE 21–6

Lead time (weeks)	Number of instances	Percent of instances	Usage during lead time	Weekly average inventory during lead time	Weekly cost of carrying average inventory	Percent of time out of stock	Cost per order of outage	Cost per week of outage	Total cost per week
3	2	8	150	75	$ 56.25	92	$184	$61.33	$117.58
4	6	24	200	100	75.00	68	136	34.00	109.00
5	10	40	250	125	93.75	28	56	11.20	104.95
6	4	16	300	150	112.50	12	24	4.00	116.50
7	3	12	350	175	131.25	0	0	0	131.25

the inventory is regarded as the safety stock. The safety stock quantity, however, is implicit in the calculation. If 250 units are ordered each time, they will be received in three weeks 8 percent of the time. One hundred units would still be on hand after the 150 were issued during the three-week lead time.

The new 250 units will arrive in four weeks 24 percent of the time, so 50 units would still be on hand. The new order of 250 will arrive in five weeks, just as the old stock is used up 40 percent of the time. The rest of the time the stock will have run out before the new supply comes in, so there would be no stock on hand. Having 100 units 8 percent of the time and 50 units 24 percent of the time translates into an expected average on hand balance of 20 units ($100 \times .08 + 50 \times .24 = 20$). In this instance a safety stock of 20 units is implicit in the reorder calculation.

REORDER POINTS USING MRP

When MRP methods are used, reorder points are not quantity triggers but time period triggers. This is one reason why MRP is sometimes called "time phased requirements planning." MRP systems can probably reduce the size of the safety stocks for most dependent demand items in the MRP system. The reason is that there is less need to provide for variations in demand and lead times are assumed to be quite fixed and not variable.

Where safety stocks still seem to be appropriate, it helps to express them in terms of added lead times instead of quantities. Safety stocks in MRP would be expressed as "so many days' or weeks' worth of stock." Safety stocks would become components of the total lead time.

Figure 21–7 shows how reorder points can be calculated when safety stocks are expressed in terms of time. We have purposely made the requirements quite irregular (or "lumpy") throughout the ten-week planning horizon. Our problem assumes that normal lead time is one week, safety time is two weeks, and the order quantity is 500 units. (Admittedly, it would be unusual to need a two-week safety stock when new supplies can be had in one week, but doing this in our example helps to show how the system works.)

FIGURE 21–7

Lead time: 1 week
Order quantity: 500 units
Safety time: 2 weeks' unit requirements

						Weeks					
	0	*1*	*2*	*3*	*4*	*5*	*6*	*7*	*8*	*9*	*10–13*
Requirements...........		100	110	90	80	0	150	175	100	35	200
Scheduled receipts.......		—	—	—	500	—	—	—	500		500
On hand................	400	300	190	100	520	520	370	195	595	560	860
DDNLT + DDST.......		280	170	230	325	425	310	335	435	600	—
Order releases..........		—	—	500	—	—	—	500		500	—

This means that every week when we consider reorders, we will look ahead three weeks beyond the current time period and add up the requirements for the various items. These requirements are then compared to the amount on hand and any new supplies due to be received during the three weeks. If these requirements ("demand during normal lead time" (DDNLT) plus the "demand during safety time" (DDST)) exceed the amount that will be available, then there will be a prospective negative balance so a replenishment order is placed. A negative number serves as a reorder point.

In Figure 21–7 we begin with 400 units "on hand." This amount is reduced to 300 after deducting week 1's requirements of 100 units. The sum of the requirements for weeks 2, 3, and 4 is 280, but there are 300 available so no more need to be ordered yet. After week 2 has passed, the available stock is down to 190 units, but this time only 170 units are needed for weeks 3, 4 and 5 so there is still ample stock.

After week 3, the supply is down to 100 units which will not take care of the 230 needed for weeks 4, 5 and 6. This triggers an order for 500 (this is our standard reorder quantity in this example), placed in week 3 and expected to be received in week 4.

In Figure 21–7 it is easy to see how safety time (and the resulting safety stocks) can be reduced or even eliminated by using the calculated order point method if requirements and lead times are reasonably accurate. Note that the "on-hand" quantities are always well above the requirements for the next week, the normal lead time. The average inventory proves to be 392 units.

The program illustrated in Figure 21–7 is not nearly as economical as it could be. As we said earlier, a two-week safety stock for a one-week lead time item must of necessity be most uneconomical. We have changed this in Figure 21–8 by eliminating the two-week safety stock altogether. As one would expect, the new calculation reduces the average inventory substantially (to 192 units).

The feasibility of eliminating the safety stock, of course, depends on the accuracy of the requirements figures and of the one-week lead times.

FIGURE 21–8

Lead time: 1 week
Order quantity: 500 units
Safety time: 0

		Weeks									
	0	*1*	*2*	*3*	*4*	*5*	*6*	*7*	*8*	*9*	*10–13*
Requirements..........		100	110	90	80	0	150	175	100	35	200
Scheduled receipts......		—	—	—	—	—	500	—	—	—	500
On hand..............	400	300	190	100	20	20	370	195	95	60	360
DDNLT..............		110	90	80	0	150	175	100	35	200	300
Order releases.........						500				500	

However, as mentioned in Chapter 20, the ability of computerized MRP systems to update requirements weekly, daily, or even in real time, allows safety time and safety stocks to be reduced materially by highlighting those items which need attention and possibly expediting them.

LOT SIZING

Lot sizing has to do with how many to order at one time—which is a question that is not answered in calculations and estimates of future needs even when the needs are relatively known for each near future period of time.

The problem is one of minimizing the sum of the "costs of acquisition" and the "costs of owning" stock. It costs money (whether the item is made inside or bought outside) to do the paperwork associated with ordering, and it costs more yet to set up equipment to produce the item. These are acquisition costs and are one-time costs for every order whose total is unaffected by the quantity ordered. Obviously, the acquisition costs *per unit* go down as the quantity ordered in a single order goes up.

But the larger the order quantities, the greater the inventory when the new supply arrives, and the longer it takes to use it up. And, as we have seen before, it costs money to carry inventories. The larger the quantity ordered, the greater the cost of carrying the ensuing inventory.

There are several methods for determining how large the individual orders should be. Orlicky lists nine of them in his book, but none of these nine is clearly superior in all situations, and all of them have weaknesses.[1]

One method is always to order in fixed amounts, say 100. This method allows for paying attention to such things as machine batch capacity, die life, and standard packages. A second method is to order in "economic lots" (discussed in the next few pages).

A third method is "lot-for-lot" ordering. This means ordering just what you need, neither more nor less, as late as possible considering lead times. This is sometimes done with MRP if the calculated needs are more or less regular. Another method is to order whatever is needed for a certain number of weeks. This method, too, is often used in MRP. It is much like lot-for-lot ordering except it considers the needs for two or three near future time periods rather than just one. Another method, the "least unit cost method," is somewhat similar to the calculation we worked out in Figure 21–6. The least unit cost method calculates the combined ordering and carrying cost per unit when ordering for each period separately, for two periods combined, for three periods, and so on, and selects whichever method produces the lowest unit costs.

Orlicky describes still other less commonly used methods. Whatever

---

[1] See Joseph Orlicky, *Material Requirements Planning* (New York: McGraw-Hill, 1975), Chap. 6.

method is chosen should, however, be flexible, at least upward, when ordering a few more the first time will save making out another order again in the near future for only a few items.[2]

Looking back at the MRP we see generated planned order releases for item C (as shown in Figure 20–11 as "planned order releases") of 17, 31, 1 and 1 for a 4-week period. Surely lot-for-lot reordering would be uneconomical here. Ordering 17, then 31, then 1 and 1 again would be wasteful. So would 2 weeks' ordering. This method would order 48 and then 1 week later, none, and then in the third week, would order 2. Obviously, the standard practice of ordering no more than 2 weeks' needs is not appropriate, and the original order should probably be 50 units.

ECONOMIC ORDER QUANTITIES (EOQ) OR ECONOMIC LOT SIZES (ELS)

The best known lot sizing methods are the family of "Economic Order Quantity" or "Economic Lot Size" models. This idea works for both purchased and manufactured items. In theory this idea is simple. The best lot size is the quantity which yields the lowest cost per unit, cost being made up of acquisition costs and costs of possession. The optimum quantity, where the total cost will be the least, is the quantity where the cost of orders plus the cost of carrying inventories are at a minimum. Larger lots run up the costs of possession more than the decline in the cost of acquisition. Smaller lots require more orders which increases acquisition costs.

Figure 21–9 shows these relationships in graphic form. It is interesting to see that the total cost curve is almost flat for some distance. This means that it is not necessary to hit the economic lot exactly in order to get low costs. In fact, costs are usually almost as low for reorders up to 25 percent more (or less) than they are for exactly the economic lot.

Since it is unnecessary to hit the EOQ exactly in order to get low costs, most companies that calculate economic lots use simple formulas which leave out such minor factors as the likelihood of obsolescence. Here is the most commonly used formula:

$$\text{EOQ, in units} = \sqrt{\frac{2 \times \text{the expected annual usage} \times \text{the setup or ordering cost}}{\text{Labor, material, and overhead cost per piece} \times \text{annual carrying cost } \%}}$$

Working this out for an expected annual usage of 2,000 units (used more or less steadily throughout the year), an ordering cost of $10 per order, a $2 per unit value, and an inventory carrying cost of 25 percent, we get:

$$\text{EOQ} = \sqrt{\frac{2 \times 2{,}000 \times \$10}{\$2 \times 25\%}} = \sqrt{\frac{40{,}000}{.5}} = 283 \text{ units}$$

[2] For a good discussion of lot sizing methods for MRP systems, see, Theisen, E. C., Jr., "New Game in Town—The MRP Lot Size," *Production and Inventory Management,* 2nd quarter, 1974, page 1–13.

FIGURE 21–9

Although the economic lot can be computed as a specific quantity, total cost is relatively flat over a range of 25 percent above and below the EOQ.

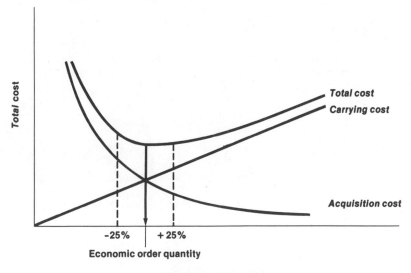

Economic order quantities can also be expressed in terms of months' supply. The formula is just expressed differently:

$$\text{EOQ, in months' supply} = \sqrt{\frac{24 \times \text{the cost to place an order}}{\substack{\text{Monthly usage in dollars} \times \\ \text{annual carrying cost } \%}}}$$

Economic lots with delivery over a period of time

Sometimes ordered items do not all arrive at once. This is particularly true with high-volume steadily used items which flow rather regularly and continuously into inventory as well as flowing out at a fairly constant rate. When this condition exists, the formulas previously given will produce too small an answer. They assume that the peak inventory w   include a complete new lot. But actually, since some of the items they are delivered, the peak inventory will never be t carrying charges are overstated because average invent

When a new supply comes in over several days ar up before the last of the order comes in, the saw-too 21–1 becomes slanted, as in Figure 21–10.

To correct for this in the calculation of the E(

FIGURE 21–10

Delivery of an order over a period of time allows it to be used to hold down maximum inventories

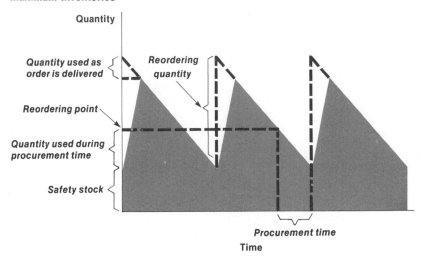

adjust the denominator under the square root sign in the EOQ formula **by** multiplying it by:

$$1 - \frac{\text{the use rate}}{\text{the production rate}}$$

Here is how this works:

Use per year.....................................	100,000 (400 per workday)
Setup cost per order................................	$30
Labor, material, and overhead cost per piece..........	$15
Carrying charge rate...............................	20%
Maximum production rate per year..................	300,000 (1,200 per workday)

First we will solve this problem with the whole lot arriving at one time:

$$\text{EOQ} = \sqrt{\frac{2 \times 100,000 \times \$30}{\$15 \times .20}}$$

$$= \sqrt{\frac{6,000,000}{3}}$$

$$= \sqrt{2,000,000}$$
$$= 1,414, \text{ which is about } 3\tfrac{1}{2} \text{ days' usage}$$

Now, allowing for usage during the delivery of each order:

$$\text{EOQ} = \sqrt{\frac{2 \times 100,000 \times 30}{15 \times .20 \times (1 - 100,000 \div 300,000)}}$$

$$= \sqrt{\frac{6,000,000}{3 \times \tfrac{2}{3}}}$$

$$= \sqrt{\frac{6,000,000}{2}}$$
$$= \sqrt{3,000,000}$$
$$= 1,732, \text{ or about } 4\frac{1}{3} \text{ days' usage}$$

It is also possible to express all economic lots on a daily use, a daily supply, and a carrying cost per day basis. Doing this does not, however, affect the answer.

EOQS IN MANAGERIAL DECISION MAKING

So far we have discussed EOQs only with respect to setting the size of manufactured or purchased lots. They can, however, be used to help managers choose the best course of action when there are alternatives.

Purchasing decisions

Whenever the purchasing department can get quantity discounts, this makes a different EOQ for each price offered. But sometimes the economic lot cannot be bought at the price quoted because the vendor does not offer his lower price unless more than the economic quantity is bought. Yet his price cut for larger quantities may save enough to justify buying more than an economic lot.

Suppose, for example, that it costs $10 to place a purchase order and 25 percent a year for carrying costs and that 2,000 units a year are needed. The vendor quotes a price of $2 per unit for all orders under 500 units and $1.95 for 500 or more. How many should be ordered?

To answer this question, it is first necessary to calculate the EOQ for each offer. So far as the buyer's needs are concerned, at $2 the EOQ is 283 units and at $1.95 it is 286 units. The price difference is so small that it doesn't change the EOQ much. But, actually, the buyer does not get to choose between these two EOQ quantities because he cannot get the $1.95 price unless he buys 500. Will it pay to go up to 500 to get the benefit of the $1.95 price?

If the customer buys 283 units at a time, he will spend, in a year, $71 for 7.1 orders and another $71 to carry an average inventory of 142 pieces valued at $2 each. The total annual cost of this practice will be $142.

The alternative is to buy 500 units at a time for $1.95. With this policy the costs will be $40 for 4 orders and $122 to carry the average inventory of 250 units valued at $1.95 each. This policy will cost $162 a year, or $20 more than ordering the economic lot quantity. But at the $1.95 price there will also be a savings of $100 in price. This reduces the $162 to $62 as the annual net cost for buying in lots of 500. This saves $80 as compared to buying in the economic lot at the $2 price. The manager's decision should therefore be to buy 500 at a time. If more than one price break is offered, the same procedure as outlined above can be used.

FIGURE 21–11

Quantity discounts for purchased items complicate reorder problems because the price reduction often makes it economical to reorder considerably more than the economic lot

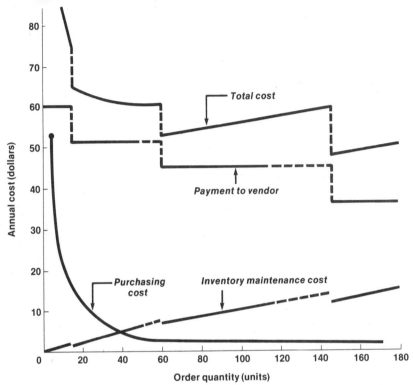

Source: International Business Machines.

Releasing capital

The EOQ can also be helpful if, for example, money is tight and management would like to reduce inventories in order to release capital. This could be done if order quantities were reduced and reorders placed more often. The managers know that placing extra orders for smalled quantities is somewhat uneconomical, but this is the price they will have to pay in order to reduce the inventory investment.

The question is: How much will it cost to release the capital? We will use our earlier problem as an example. It cost $10 to place an order, 25 percent a year for carrying costs, and $2 per unit for the 2,000 units needed in a year. The EOQ was 283 units. If we omit the safety stock, the average inventory would be 283 ÷ 2 = 141.5 units, which would have a value of $283.

Management asks: How much will it cost to cut the inventory investment by one fourth, thus releasing $71 in capital? The new ordering quantity would be 212 units (75 percent of 283). The average inventory would be 106 units, valued at $212. Ordering 212 units will necessitate 9.43 reorders a year (2,000 ÷ 212 = 9.43), which will cost $94.30. The carrying charge will be .25 × $212 = $53. So the total costs are $147.30, which is $5.30 more than the total of ordering and carrying costs of $142 if the order quantity were the EOQ of 283. Therefore, an inventory reduction of $71 can be realized at a cost of $5.30, the equivalent of a 7.5-percent cost of the capital. This rate seems reasonable, so management should order the inventory reductions.

Actually, order quantities perhaps should often be set at something less, possibly as much as 25 percent less, than the EOQ. This is because the curve is relatively flat in the area near the EOQ. Quantities below the EOQ do cost a little more but they release capital.

A manager should be careful, however, when using this kind of analysis. The approach we have just used may be incorrect if the unit price varies for different order quantities. Suppose, for example, that the vendor charges $2.05 per unit for orders as small as 212 units (as against $2 when ordering in lots of 283). The extra unit cost would increase total costs by $100. This would entail a total cost of $105.30 to release $71 of capital from inventory investment, a 148-percent cost! *All* of the ramifications of changing an order quantity policy should be considered in this type of analysis.

Enlarging reorder quantities during slack periods

Another instance where EOQ analysis can help may arise during slack periods. The question in this case is whether to make more parts or products than are needed in the immediate future in order to keep the work force busy. We will continue to use the same example, except that the $10 ordering cost is the cost of placing a factory shop order and the $2 is the cost for direct labor and materials.

Again the EOQ is 283 units and the average inventory is 141.5 units. But, in order to keep the work force busy, management wants to know what it will cost to double the order quantity. This means making lots of 566, or 3.5 orders, a year, costing $35. The average inventory would be $566, which would cost $141.50 to carry. Total costs would be $176.50, or $34.50 more than the total cost using EOQs. Actually, management would not, of course, plan to do this all year long but perhaps only over a short period of one to three months. The actual cost, therefore, for the part year involved would probably be less than one quarter of $34.50, or $8 more or less. Knowing this cost, managers can decide what to do more intelligently than without this analysis.

EOQs as tests of rule-of-thumb practices

Managers can also use EOQs to test rule-of-thumb practices. One company, for example, which does not use EOQs, uses the following practices in determining reorder quantities for the parts it makes. If setup costs are less than $10, it orders 4 months' supply. For setup costs up to $25, it orders 6 months' supply. Above $25 it orders 8 months' supply.

This policy may be more costly than using EOQs. To test it, examples can be worked out. One example might assume a usage of 7,500 units a year, setup costs of $20, and inventory carrying charges of 25 percent, with material and direct labor costs being $3 per unit.

In line with company policy, the inventory controller orders six months' supply of this item each time. Thus, he reorders 3,750 units twice a year. The average inventory is 1,875 units, having a value of $5,625. Inventory carrying costs are $5,625 × .25, or $1,406.25. Ordering costs are 2 × $20 = $40. So the total annual cost for this inventory policy is $1,446.25. Next, the EOQ is calculated:

$$EOQ = \sqrt{\frac{2 \times 7,500 \times \$20}{\$3 \times .25}}$$

$$= \sqrt{\frac{300,000}{.75}}$$

$$= \sqrt{400,000}$$

$$= 632$$

If 632 units are ordered each time, the ordering cost per year is 7,500 ÷ 632 = 11.9 orders per year × $20 = $238. Carrying costs would be 632 ÷ 2 = 316 units average inventory × $3 = $948 average investment × .25 percent = $237. The total cost would be $475.

The company's rule-of-thumb policy is, therefore, in this example, costing an extra $971 to handle the inventory of this one item in a year ($1,446 − $475 = $971). Similar tests could be made for other examples. If other items are anywhere near comparable to this example, the failure of the company to use EOQs are costing it a great deal of money.

Imputed carrying cost rates

The EOQ approach can be reversed to compute the imputed carrying cost rate for a given inventory order size policy. In the example above, the calculation would be:

$$\text{Imputed rate} = \frac{2 \times \text{annual usage} \times \text{cost to prepare 1 order}}{\text{Cost per unit} \times (\text{ordering quantity})^2}$$

$$= \frac{2 \times 7,500 \times \$20}{\$3 \times 3,750^2}$$

$$= \frac{300,000}{3 \times 14,062,500}$$

$$= \frac{300,000}{42,187,500}$$

$$= .0071$$

The company's reorder policy would produce an EOQ of 3,750 units only if the annual carrying charge rate were 0.7 of 1 percent. But for any higher rate, the EOQ is less than 3,750.

Sensitivity analysis

Managers can also use EOQ calculations to see how sensitive the solution is to changes in any of the factors that go into its calculation. They can change the carrying charges, for example, to see how sensitive the answer is to the size of this factor. (It will usually be found that the formula is not very sensitive to minor changes in any single factor but is quite sensitive to large changes because the change in the EOQ varies according to the square root of changes in individual factors.)

Curiously, using EOQs to aid in decision making seems to be rare. All of the several possible applications given here seem to have greater merit than is recognized.

REASONS FOR NOT USING EOQS

Many companies do not use EOQs, probably because of both practical and technical reasons.

Among the practical reasons is the need to use data that are often not available unless money is spent to collect figures. These figures include the cost of reordering and factory setup costs. Besides, both rates of use and material costs keep changing, and this makes the EOQ keep changing. To stay accurate, EOQs should be recalculated from time to time.

Among the technical reasons is the fact that EOQs are best suited for only B items in any case. Technicians also object to the implicit assumption in the formula of steady use. The formula considers an item's average inventory to be half of the reordering quantity plus the safety stock. But the patterns of use of some items are not like that. Instead, withdrawals from stock are infrequent but large, thus probably invalidating this basic assumption. Obviously, EOQs should not be used for such items if their investment is of consequential proportions.

The EOQ assumption of steady use is also invalid when there are strong seasonal variations in demand. EOQ formulas can be adapted to handle seasonal variations but the mathematics are more complicated.[3]

Another reason for not using EOQs is that they suboptimize, which is not always advantageous to the whole company's operations. This is particularly true in their overuse of capital. Ordering a little less than the EOQ will usually release a certain amount of capital at the equivalent of a very low interest rate.

EOQ methods (and statistical reorder point methods) are generally not

---

[3] For a method for handling seasonal variations see Edward A. Silver and Harlan C. Meal, "A Simple Modification of the EOQ for the Case of a Varying Demand Rate," *Production and Inventory Management*, 4th quarter 1969, pp. 52–65.

applicable to the largest A items nor to most C items. The A items need more careful attention than EOQs and the usual associated ROPs can provide, while C items need less attention than EOQs provide.

Further, the common use of dollar limits, time limits, and the increasing practice of making parts against known future requirements using MRP methods leaves a smaller area for EOQ use.

Orlicky thinks that the MRP approach will continue to reduce the area of EOQ applications.[4] The EOQ is but one of many ways of determining the lot sizes to be ordered. As mentioned earlier, there are several other lot sizing methods that are designed to be used with MRP systems. Each trades off the higher ordering costs of separately ordering each "planned order" quantity against the cost of combining later planned orders with earlier planned orders—thus reducing acquisition costs—but incurring higher inventory carrying costs. However, Burroughs, the computer manufacturer, uses EOQs as the basis for lot sizing when it makes up orders for computer parts, so EOQs are not yet outmoded.

REVIEW QUESTIONS

1. Why shouldn't order point methods be used for most dependent demand items?

2. Explain how to calculate the size of the safety stock by the method which uses a dollar penalty figure for being out of stock.

3. How are order points defined in MRP systems?

4. How are maximum-minimum controls related to (a) reorder points, and (b) economic ordering quantities?

5. What are the relationships between the reorder quantity, the average inventory, and order frequency? Would ABC analysis help in analyzing policy alternatives arising from these relationships?

6. Is it true that in all EOQ diagrams, such as that shown in Figure 21–9, the EOQ is the point where the declining and sloping curved line crosses the rising straight line? Explain.

7. Would it ever be true that the EOQ curve is not relatively flat for volumes of, say, 25 percent above and below the EOQ? If yes, explain how it could be.

8. Is the economic order quantity ever a part of the safety stock? When?

9. Explain the procedure which could be used to find out how much it would cost to release capital from investment in inventory by ordering less than economic lot quantities.

10. The company is considering using mathematical decision rules to set the size of safety stocks. The analyst is told to gather the necessary data. What data does he need and why?

---

[4] Orlicky, *Material Requirements Planning*, Chap. 6.

11. In computerized inventory control, why does the computer calculate the expected error in a product's usage during the reorder lead time?

12. On page 508, in the calculation table, the following figures appear on the first line: 8, 150, 75, $56.25, 92, and $184. How were these calculated?

13. If a company aims for a 95-percent service level in reordering, does this mean that 95 percent of the time when stock is needed it will be on hand but that it will be out of stock 5 percent of the time? Explain.

14. How does the constant usage rate assumption of EOQ sometimes make EOQ inappropriate for dependent demand items?

QUESTIONS FOR DISCUSSION

1. "We don't use reorder points because our turnover is so high that we are often out of stock before the replenishment order arrives." Is this a reasonable statement? Discuss.

2. "Most mathematical treatments of stockouts exaggerate the problem a little because when the stockroom issues 50 units to the factory, thereby running out of stock, no one is yet being held up. The 50 just issued will take care of the factory's needs for several days. There is stock on the assembly floor even if there is none in the stockroom." Discuss this statement.

3. Is it possible to put a figure for being out of stock into EOQ formulas? How? Should a company want to do this? Why?

4. In a company using direct costing, will its calculations of economic order quantities be like everyone else's? Why? If no, whose kind of calculations gives the right answer?

5. If the new labor contract gives everyone a pay raise, is it necessary to recalculate all EOQs? Discuss.

6. The company's stock of storage batteries has a loss of life of 3 percent a month from shelf wear. How can this be handled in EOQ calculations?

7. "One reason why it appears to cost little to reduce ordering quantities is that the cost of greater exposure to running out of stock (from ordering more often) is not included in the calculations. EOQ formulas put no penalty charges into the formula for this. Consequently, the gain from releasing capital at minimal costs is slightly specious because it overlooks these occasional costs." Comment on this situation.

8. In EOQ formulas, a carrying charge of 20 percent or more is common. Yet, the calculations in the text claimed that, by ordering less than the EOQ, capital could be released at an implicit interest charge

of a much lower rate, perhaps 7 percent. If this is so, isn't there something wrong in the calculation which bases the EOQ on a claimed cost of 20 percent? Discuss.

9. "As a forecasting technique, exponential smoothing is nothing more than a form of weighted average, and it suffers from the same deficiency as all other weighting techniques. It cannot distinguish between random variations and significant changes; therefore it responds equally to both. Forecasting requires forward-looking information as well as past history. Without adequate forward-looking data, exponential smoothing could prove to be an exercise in futility." Comment on this view. Is there any way to take care of the difficulty posed?

PROBLEMS

1. The inventory record card for item G–2357 reads as follows:

Date	Quantity ordered	Received	Used	On hand
1–15	—	300	—	300
1–16	—	—	75	225
2–16	—	—	75	150
3–16	—	—	75	75
3–17	300	—	—	—
4–16	—	—	75	0
7–19	—	300	—	300
8–25	—	—	75	225

These items are worth $7 each and cost $.10 a month to carry in stock. Assuming that standard package limitations can be neglected, set up a reordering policy. When should they be reordered and how many?

2. Calculate the reorder point for the following item:

Use	2,000 per week
Cost of running out	$1,200
Value of one unit	$20.80
Carrying cost	25%

The past record of time elapsed between ordering and getting new supplies is:

Weeks	Number of instances
3	1
4	2
5	6
6	6
7	7
8	3

3. Vendor A is located 500 miles away from the Davis Company. Shipment of part M–62, an item bought in quantity by Davis, is by rail. From ½ to 1 week must be allowed for shipment. Vendor A's plant needs another 2 weeks to process orders.

The smallest quantity of M–62s which can be produced economically is 5,000 or ½ week's usage of the Davis Company. Davis's usage, however, fluctuates between 8,000 and 12,000 per week.

How far ahead should Davis release orders? How big an inventory of item M–62 should Davis carry? If more data are necessary in order to answer, what data? With such data, how should one go about calculating the answers to these questions?

4. Given: an item whose value is $3 per unit, reordering cost $25, and inventory carrying cost 20 percent. This item's stock record card shows the following:

Withdrawal quantity	Days until next withdrawal	Reorder lead times (days)
69	12	20
58	19	30
93	8	15
76	12	20
81	17	20
59	10	10
64	7	30
51	7	20
49	19	25
60	14	30
Total 660	125	Average 22

Find:
a. The reorder quantity.
b. The reorder point.

5. Given the following:
   A safety level of 75 units.
   Replenishment lead time of 15 days.
   Maximum inventory of 810 units.
   Usage of EOQ in 35 days.
Calculate the reorder point in units and days.

6. Calculate the economic lot quantity for the following products:

Product	Cost per unit (excluding setup)	Cost of one setup	Carrying charge	Annual usage
A.....................	$ .50	$ 100	20%	10,000
B.....................	.20	60	15	25,000
C.....................	2.00	300	25	100,000
D.....................	.75	1,000	25	500,000
E.....................	5.00	1,000	20	40,000

7. In problem 6, what change occurs in the EOQ if product A's carrying costs are 10 percent instead of 20 percent? 30 percent? From these

answers, what should be concluded about the sensitivity of EOQs to variations in the carrying charge rate?

8. In problem 6, what change occurs in the EOQ if usage of product A is cut in half? If it doubles? From these answers, what should be concluded about the sensitivity of EOQ to variations in the usage rate?

9. In problem 6, how much capital will be released from inventory by an edict to cut the overall investment by 25 percent? What will be the cost effects of such an edict? What will be the effective interest cost rate to the company for the released capital?

10. After the cut required in problem 9, what will be the implicit interest rate if the new ordering quantities are regarded as the EOQs but at a higher rate?

11. The Equipment Manufacturing Company has decided to purchase a certain type of rheostat required in the operation of a machine which it manufactures. The company uses 2,000 rheostats per year; the average use is 8 per working day; the minimum use is 5 per working day and the maximum is 10 per working day. It takes 30 working days to receive delivery on the rheostats after the ordering point is reached. The cost of putting through each order is $10. The inventory carrying charges are 20 percent of the average inventory investment. The purchase prices are as follows:

$4.60 each on orders of 200 or less
  4.50 each on orders of 201 to 400
  4.40 each on orders of 401 to 600
  4.35 each on orders of 601 to 800
  4.30 each on orders of 801 to 2,000

Determine the safety reserve, the ordering point, the ordering quantity, and the normal maximum inventory.

12. In the past a company has followed this general rule and has not calculated economic quantities:

Setup cost	Order
Under $10	4 months' supply
$10–25	6 months' supply
Over $25	8 months' supply

Following this policy, item 319, with a setup cost of $20 and an annual usage of 6,800 units, was ordered in lots of 3,400. Labor and material for item 319 cost $.75.

If it costs 25 percent to carry inventory, how good is the company's general rule? How much does following the rule on item 319 cost the company in a year? If item 319 constitutes 2 percent of all inventories, and, if this finding applies to all other items proportionally, what is the approximate cost to the company of following these general rules?

13. A company uses 500 units in a year and pays $3.10 each for them. They have been ordered 100 at a time and ordering costs are $25. What is the implicit interest rate?

14. An item's use record has been, month by month, 57, 43, 62, 51, 63, 72, 77, 69, 62, 43, 67, and 70. Using the method described in the text, what is this item's expected use in the reorder period of three months following the last month of those given here in this example? Also, what is the standard deviation of the errors in reorder quantities?

If the policy is to reorder so that new supplies arrive before present stocks run out in at least 90 percent of the cases, what is the reordering point?

15. Hanson Industries has an MRP system and utilizes safety time in their reorder points. Given the following requirements for an item, when will orders be released?

	Weeks										
	0	*1*	*2*	*3*	*4*	*5*	*6*	*7*	*8*	*9*	*10*
Requirements......		200	0	100	200	200	100	0	0	400	100
On hand..........	200										

Lead time: 1 week
Order quantity: 300
Safety time: 1 week's units requirements

SUGGESTED SUPPLEMENTARY READINGS

Hoyt, J. "Order Points Tailored to Suit Your Business." *Production and Inventory Management,* 4th quarter 1973, p. 42.

Moore, S. M. "MRP and the Least Total Cost Method of Lot Sizing." *Production and Inventory Management,* 2d quarter 1974, pp. 47–55.

Pursche, S. "Putting Service Level into Proper Perspective." *Production and Inventory Management,* 3d quarter 1975, pp. 69–75.

22

Scheduling and control systems for job-lot production

PRODUCTION control is the organization's nervous system. In a very real sense, very little of an organization's work is making *products* because most products are made of *parts* and most of a factory's activities have to do with making *parts*. Until the parts are assembled there is no product, just parts. Production control tells the factory what kinds of parts to make, how many to make, and when to make them. And it tells the factory what assembled products to make, and when, and out of what parts.

But parts are often not completed in a single operation. To make a chair leg, for example, it is necessary to saw, plane, sandpaper, drill holes, and do other things to a piece of wood. It ends up the right size, shape, and finish to be a chair leg, but these changes are not accomplished all at once. They are accomplished bit by bit, operation by operation. So it is in a factory. Production control does not just tell the factory to make chair legs. It gives the factory detailed directions telling the workers to do certain operations to certain lots of materials. Making parts is a directed process with the production control department giving the directions.

Manufacturing is just as varied as the products we buy—only more so because many products are made and used that we consumers never see. (They are component parts which are hidden away, like the inside of a television set. Or else they are equipment or supply items used up in manufacturing processes.)

Production control is also varied among different companies and different industries. It takes different kinds of directions to tell people what to make (or do) in a shoe factory, a nut and bolt factory, and an airplane factory or in the service industries, in a hotel, an insurance company, a police department, or the post office.

One of the most difficult production control jobs is in factories making assembled products out of metal parts, and perhaps the most difficult production control of all is in the aerospace industry. In no other industry is it necessary to make a quarter of a million parts, all on schedule, so that they can be put together into one product, an airplane or a spacecraft.

Production control is difficult, though, even with products simpler than airplanes. An automobile has 16,000 parts. Even a typewriter has 2,000 parts. A metal part which can be made in as few as 10 operations is a simple part. When making assembled products from metal parts, production control may have to direct thousands and thousands of operations.

In talking about production control we will spend most of our time on assembled metal products because of their complexity. While other "production" activities in manufacturing and service organizations can be complex, their production is usually simpler to control than this widespread class of manufacturing activities.

PRODUCTION CONTROL FUNCTIONS

Although production control work is different in every situation, there are nevertheless certain activities that are common in all production control work. These include the following:

1. Participate in developing master production schedules. Report to the sales department what promise dates are feasible for prospective customers' orders.
2. Participate in planning labor requirements needed to meet schedules.
3. Receive orders to manufacture products.
4. "Explode" the orders for assembled products, thus determining the quantities of parts and operations needed. Issue purchase requisitions for parts to be bought.
5. Determine raw materials requirements for manufactured parts.
6. Determine the tools necessary for production. Issue purchase requisitions for tools to be bought.
7. Operate the raw materials stockroom and maintain the stocks. Issue purchase requisitions for the necessary materials.
8. Do original routing (determine, the first time a product is made, the operations and machines required to make products and parts).
9. Make out production orders directing the performance of the operations necessary to make parts and products.
10. Make schedules for the performance of operations and the use of machines.
11. Insure that everything needed for production will be ready when orders are "released" to the factory.
12. Decide and assign jobs to particular people and machines.
13. Direct the transportation of materials in process.
14. Receive reports of work done and compare them with that scheduled. Keep up-to-date records of progress of jobs through the plant.

15. Help solve problems which cause delays in production.
16. Revise plans when original plans are not carried out and when there are changes in the size of an order or its required completion date.
17. Operate the finished parts stockroom and control the stock of parts.
18. Operate the finished products stockroom and control the stock of finished products.
19. Answer inquiries concerning the progress of orders in process.
20. Aid in developing cost estimates for prospective new orders.

These basic functions are usually assigned to the production control department in most companies, but sometimes a few of them are assigned to other departments. Also, one or more nonproduction control duties, such as operating the plant's mail service or the tool storeroom, or setting time standards for incentive purposes, are often assigned to the production control department.

There might appear to be one important omission in this list: Only numbers 2 and 12 mention people. Production control has very little to do with staffing the factory. In some companies production control determines how many people the factory will need. The production control department may be assigned the responsibility for translating future work schedules into future labor needs (as was described in Chapter 8) so that the personnel department can work out staffing plans. But it is usually the supervisors' and the personnel department's job to provide the necessary workers. Except during extremely high levels of production, production control does most of its work assuming that the necessary workers will be there.

Production control also usually has little to do with providing the facilities required for production. In some companies, everything having to do with getting production started the first time a new product is made is turned over to a product engineer who has final authority over how things are made. He may even have to choose the machines, order their purchase, decide the layout, supervise machine installation, and stay with operations until production is going smoothly. The product engineer will also have to decide on all of the tools needed and order them and to decide on which materials to use. But production control usually places the orders for materials.

TERMS

If industries would settle on words and definitions, it would be easier to talk about production control. But industry is not very consistent in its use of terms, so it is difficult to set exact definitions.

For example, the name of the main department doing most of the production control work may be the "production department," "production control department," "production planning department," "production planning and control department," or some similar title. In metal working industries, more companies probably use "production department" than any other term. This means that the "production" department is *not* a factory department working on the product. It is the department which makes and issues directives to the factory and controls production.

Various parts of production control activities also have different names in different companies. A list of parts for an assembled product may be called a "bill of materials," a "materials list," a "parts list," or a "requirements list." A list of operations for making a part may be a "route sheet," a "process sheet," a "layout," or an "operation list." "Scheduling" may mean: (1) setting dates for the completion of *orders*, (2) setting dates for the completion of individual *operations*, (3) setting specific *starting* and *stopping* times for operation performances, or (4) making up lists of jobs needing certain machines. There are few areas in production control where terms have standard definitions; however, this is being improved by APICS (American Production and Inventory Control Society), the professional organization for people who work in this field.

THE PRODUCTION CONTROL DEPARTMENT ORGANIZATION AND FUNCTIONS

Production control is usually headed by a production control manager who reports to the plant manager.

In middle-size companies the production control department may have the responsibility to do all the things in our list of functions (above). In small companies some jobs, such as forecasting labor needs, are not done at all. At the other extreme, giant companies separate some of the work, particularly raw materials control, from production control. Original routing, or deciding how things are to be made, also is often done by production engineering, not production control.

Also, production control's activities in continuous production differ from their work in job-lot manufacturing. In continuous manufacture, production control's responsibilities are simply to keep production inside the plant flowing and to see that the *rates* of *making* and *using* parts match up. Their work is still very important, but there is only a fraction as much paperwork and plant directives as in job-lot manufacturing.

The point is that *how* the department is set up depends on the work it is given to do. And, although the things given to a production control department to administer depend in part on the kind of manufacture, they also depend on the managers' views. Some companies say: "Engineering *designs* the products; production control (with the help of the factory) decides how to make them." Others say: "The engineers design the product and also specify how to make it."

Also, there is the matter of who tells the people in the shop what job to work on next. Production control does this in some companies, but in others it simply sets the dates by which jobs are to be done, and the supervisors assign jobs to their people.

FIGURE 22-1

**Relationship of planning and scheduling subdepartments of the
production control department**

Production control department	
Planning department	*Scheduling department*
Capacity calculations	Shop order making
Overall labor requirements	Shop loads
Distant-future schedule	Order release to factory
construction	departments
Procurement of tooling	Other priorities
Procurement of long lead	Progress reports
time raw materials	Expediting
Drawings, specifications and	Shortages and delays
inspection instructions,	Rework and makeup orders
and equipment	Internal transportation
	Order closing

Inside the production control department there are usually two main divisions (see Figure 22–1). One, often called the planning department, handles the longer-range details. It takes future product demand requirements for weeks and months ahead and determines the parts, materials, and tools requirements. Then it checks to see what is already on hand or on order and determines orders for what will be needed and when it will be needed.

The other main division of production control deals with the near future and the present. Often called the scheduling department, it makes up specific factory orders to do work, and it sets the time by which things are to be done. It also monitors what is done, and, whenever things do not go according to schedule, it tries to eliminate the problems.

ORIGINAL AUTHORITY TO MAKE PRODUCTS

Among the objectives of production control is never to have the factory make anything which can't be sold in the near future, yet to make as many of everything as can be sold soon. This means that all production ought to be authorized specifically so that just the right number of products will be made and so that the proper materials can be procured.

While production control gives the factory its authorizations, rarely does production control itself decide what the factory should make. Production control, in turn, receives authorizations to make products. Someone, somewhere, has to start things. Generally, production control gets this essential information and authority from master schedules covering the demand for each product for the next several months. Master schedules were discussed in Chapter 20.

PRODUCING AUTHORITY

The factory gets its authority to make products from the production control department. Nearly always production control tells the factory four things: (1) what to make, (2) how many, (3) when, and (4) how. The first three give the factory "producing" authority to go ahead and make products. The fourth gives the factory "processing" authority.

Producing authority tells the factory (1) to assemble parts into finished products, (2) to make single piece finished products (such as a casting sold to customers), (3) to make individual component parts, or (4) to process bulk materials (liquids, powders) and pack them into various sized packages.

Assembly orders tell the factory's assembly department what and how many finished products to make and provide lists of the subassemblies and parts needed for each assembly order. The manufacture of parts and individual-piece finished products, however, often requires more detailed producing directives. In most companies *every operation* done on parts and integral products must be separately planned for and *individually authorized.*

Producing authority is one-time authority. When the factory finishes what it has been authorized to do, it needs more directions. New producing authorizations must be issued continuously. And, although we call it "authority," the factory has no discretion. Production control's directions are also *orders.* This "authority," then, tells the factory to make the quantity of products the master production schedule calls for, and it must try to get things done on schedule.

PROCESSING AUTHORITY

Processing authority deals with the specifications for making products, which smaller companies leave to experienced supervisors. They let the engineers determine the product's shape, size, and material requirements but let the supervisor determine how to make it.

But, in larger companies, leaving it up to the supervisor leaves too many things to chance. Engineers design parts and products; then other engineers decide how to make them. Some of these people are called product engineers, and sometimes they work in the production control department. Industrial engineers and methods people also help decide how workers are to perform operations—not only in parts manufacturing, but also in assembly.

Master bills of material (B/M)

Engineering develops a "master bill of materials" for each kind of assembled product. It is primarily a listing of the subassemblies and parts needed to assemble one unit of the end product. It also shows how many of each component and part will be needed. The master B/M lists all parts names, identification numbers, drawing numbers, and the source of the item, whether it is made inside or bought outside.

A master bill for an end product lists subassemblies as if they were individual parts. Each subassembly in turn has its own master bill of materials. If the subassembly is composed in part of lesser subassemblies, each of them has its own master bill. And, each component for these lesser subassemblies may have its own "mini" bill.

The list of parts is arranged in such a way as to indicate the order in which the parts are to be assembled so, in effect, the master B/M is also a form of processing instruction. For some purposes, the list is rerun in other orders, such as in order of part number, or in order of the arrangement of the finished parts stockroom.

The master bill shows the sequence in which items go together into subassemblies rather than directly into the product as piece parts. Engineering usually decides this, but in some companies production control can switch things around based on practical considerations. It is not always possible to tell, on an engineer's drawing board, which sequence is best. Should, for example, an automobile door lock be assembled first and then put into the car door, after which the door goes on the body, and finally the body be put on the chassis? Or should the door be put on the body and then the lock assembled to the door? Sometimes such questions can be decided better after people see how things go out in the shop.

Master bills are usually confined to listing the items that make up the end product. But some companies have extended the idea to include expendable tools. If, for example, a tool is likely to last for the production of 1,000 units before it will wear out, the bill of materials will list a requirement of 1/1,000 of a tool per unit of product. When the quantity of output nears 1,000, a second tool is provided just as if it were any other raw material or part.

Master bills of material, which are of course updated continually to keep up with design changes, confer continuing processing authority on production control. Production control may use this authority over and over again for repeat orders for the same product.

Master route sheets

Engineering also puts out for each part a "master route sheet" showing the operations and their sequence needed to make the part.

Master route sheets list the operations necessary to make the part, the machines needed for each operation, the special tooling required, the machine time needed to set up for the operation, the machine time needed to perform the operation on one part, the normal between operation dead time, and the kind and amount of raw materials needed to make one unit. In some companies, the route sheet also shows the classification of the worker who will perform each operation or the piece rate if the company uses incentives.

As in the case of master bills of materials, master route sheets confer continuing processing authority on production control. Repeat orders can be made out without new processing instructions from engineering.

In some companies, usually small ones, engineering does not make out master route sheets. Instead, the shop supervisor decides how to make things. In this case, the record of how it is done the first time serves as a master route sheet for future reorders.

In many large companies, too, the manufacturing department's production engineers may redesign parts in minimum ways to suit manufacturing needs. In such cases, the route sheet as first issued by engineering is really only a preliminary draft which becomes final after any such minor adjustments.

Processing instructions

The master route sheet lists the required operations; yet, these descriptions of operations are so brief (the words "clean," "paint," "broach" and so on in Figure 22–2 are operations) that operators sometimes need more specific instructions covering what is to be done. Usually both an engineering drawing and a "specification" go along with orders to the shop to provide these more complete instructions.

Manufacturing instructions are incomplete without instructions concerning the inspection tests that items need to pass to be acceptable. Engineering must develop instructions about how tests are to be carried out and how inspectors can tell acceptable parts from unacceptable. Often special testing equipment has to be bought or developed for particular tests, and inspectors need to be trained in their use. Also, procedures need to be set

FIGURE 22–2

A shop order (all the information, except the order number, quantity, processing times, and start dates, comes from the master route sheet)

PART NAME								
DATE 10/20	DATE DUE 1/20		PART NO. 8638P ORDER NO. 1624		NO. OF SHEETS 1 ORDER QUANTITY 200			
OPER.	OPERATION DESCRIPTION	MACH. CENTER	TOOL NUMBER	LEGEND	PROCESSING TIME	START DATE	DEPT.	
	CR STEEL SAFE 1020							
10	CLEAN	1		1	320	572	25	
20	PAINT	2		3	100	581	25	
30	FACE SHORT HUB SWEEP 1 IN DIA FORM HAND GRIP	30	3687	2	334	584	34	
40	FACE FIN TURN AND RAD HUB FORM RAD ON GRIP CTR DR AND REAM	30	6211	7	306	594	34	
50	DR AND REAM	21		5	85	587	31	
80	BROACH	53	6329	8	180	603	33	
90	BURR	3		9	160	608	33	
110	POLISH	47		4	60	610	33	
120	INSPECT	4					44	

up for reporting test results back to engineering so that it can keep informed about the quality of work done by manufacturing in case a product or part needs redesigning to overcome some problem.

Most factory workers do about the same thing every day. So once they are trained to do their job, there are few problems with shop instructions, and drawings usually provide sufficient directions. Sometimes, though, particularly on difficult assembly jobs and jobs with many wires to fasten, more instructions are needed. Sometimes a person's assignment covers a half hour or more of work per item and includes a hundred or more little things that need to be done.

Here very careful instructions on the whole set of things to be done are required. And the worker may need occasional instruction later, too, if he forgets or if something goes wrong. Tape recordings, televised instructions, and colored slides help in such cases. Hughes Aircraft has used such an arrangement for a long time. Hughes reports production gains of more than 50 percent, and inspection and supervision costs were reduced 75 percent when this kind of instruction was first put in.

The assembler can also be supplied with a tape recording explaining what to do step by step. He can turn it on any time he forgets. Collins Radio has developed a sound-track moving picture projector with a six-inch screen to serve this same purpose. The operator can turn it on and see and hear how to do the job. General Electric uses closed-circuit TV to flash pictures or drawings to the drafting, assembly planning, and assembly areas. Users can even control a zoom lens from their viewing station if they want a close-up.

All of these methods for passing out instructions are big improvements over less thorough methods used in the past, but they are costly and would not pay off everywhere.

ORDER BILLS AND SHOP ORDERS

When production control receives an order to make a certain number of products, it makes out individual assembly orders and, for the parts, individual shop orders. Both tell the factory what to make and so constitute producing authority. We call the orders to assemble "order bills" and the orders to make parts "shop orders." When these documents are completed and a check has been made to see if enough materials are available, these orders are ready to be "released" to the shop.

Order bills differ from master bills in that they show what is wanted *this time*. If the order is for 50 units, the quantities of all the items on the master bill are multiplied by 50 (the master shows how many of every part are needed for 1 product). Also, an identification number is assigned to the order as is a schedule (dates by which the products are to be made). Cost records are usually kept for every lot. Copies of order bills go to the assembly department, the finished parts stockroom, and wherever else they are needed.

Shop orders to cover the making of parts provide specific processing authority. Figure 22–2, a shop order, lists the required operations, and how much time each operation will take in order to turn out the full order of 200 items. Cleaning will take 32 hours, painting 10 hours, and so on.

The *start date* column may be confusing because this company is using a "1,000-day calendar" and cleaning is to start on day 581. With 1,000-day shop calendars, every scheduled workday for four years ahead is given a consecutive number. These numbers are used on all work schedules instead of regular dates. Everyone in the company also has a regular calendar with the equivalent day-number printed in. Outside purchase orders, however, use regular calendar dates. The advantages to such calendars is to avoid ambiguity on very long lead time items and to facilitate computation of the timing of orders in computerized systems.

ORDER SCHEDULING

Assembled product schedules show certain quantities to be made (assembled) in a month or week. Some are actually assembled early in the month, others late. In job-lot manufacturing, normally *all* the parts and subassemblies are finished and complete *before* the first finished product in the lot is assembled. This makes for some big piles of parts on the first day of a month. To keep the piles within reason, parts lots are sometimes cut up into several smaller lots which are scheduled to be finished one after the other during the month as they are needed.

But whether a month's needs of a part is processed as one lot or not, schedule setting for subassemblies and parts starts with the end product assembly schedule. The scheduler then works back from the final-assembly completion dates and to final-assembly start dates, then to subassembly completion dates and to subassembly start dates. This is essentially what MRP (described in Chapter 20) does.

This provides the dates by which parts need to be finished. And again the scheduler works back from the finishing date for the last operation to its necessary starting time. Then he allows for a between-operations time allowance back to the end of the preceding operation; then he goes on back to its starting time, and so on. Finally he gets back to establishing times to start first operations. All of this, of course, has to be done separately for each different part, and usually it is all done on a computer.

This process produces a desired date for releasing the order to the factory for each parts order and is the date that goes on the shop order. Sometimes the desired completion date for every operation is put on the order. This serves as a priority system and tells supervisors which jobs to do first and whether jobs are on time or are behind schedule.

What we have just described is "backward" scheduling. It starts with the wanted completion date and works back to necessary start dates. Sometimes, however, the process is reversed and starts with a specified order starting date and lets the processing cycle determine the completion date.

Safety lead times

If an order falls behind, it is usually not too hard to get it back on schedule if the cause for its delay is taken care of quickly. This can usually be done because the normal lead time allowed to make the order usually has some "safety lead time" built into it. More lead time is actually allowed between operations than is really needed.

Much of this safety lead time factor is not apparent but is inherent in the way computerized methods operate. Back in Chapter 20, in our example explaining how MRP operates, we used a lead time of two weeks for final end product assembly and another two weeks for making one of the main subassemblies. Thus, end products wanted by the end of period 5 were said to need to have their main subassemblies ready at the end of week 3. And the subassemblies in turn were to be made from parts, which were to be ready at the end of week 1.

But these lead times are very arbitrary. They were not set with any particular quantity in mind (an order for 10 and an order for 100 would have the same lead time), and they do not give specific consideration to the true time needed—witness there being no lead times stated as fractions of a week. If there is a true "make-span" of three days, it would become one week.

Our discussion here has used the word "date" as if it meant a specific calendar day. And it is true that computers can calculate lead times down to exact days, and undoubtedly this is done in some companies. But statistical inventory books rarely talk in these terms. MRP "time buckets" are usually weeks and not days. We might infer from this that scheduling to the nearest week is the most common practice. And this seems to be the case. If it is so, then such lead times are all somewhat loose. A few behind time orders or a few high priority orders, if they are only few, can easily be expedited successfully without causing much disruption to the schedules.

Overlapping operations

Perhaps the ultimate in condensing lead times in job-lot work is to "overlap" operations (meaning that operation 2 starts on the first items through operation 1 *before* the whole order has gone through operation 1). In job shops, operations are almost never overlapped because this would increase materials handling costs and would put work on such a tight schedule that any delay becomes serious.

Although operations are almost never overlapped, jobs behind schedule often are pushed along (often by expeditors) by "squeezing out" some of the between-operation time allowed for in the normal scheduling procedure. This between-operation time, which has sometimes been called

FIGURE 22–3

Order schedule report

07/15– –   Page 1

ORD. NO.	PART NO.	ORDER QTY.	LEAD TIME	EARL. START DATE	LATEST START DATE	GIVEN END DATE	CALC. END DATE	RED. % MAX.	RED. % USED	OPRTN NUMBER	WORK CENTER NUMBER	CALC. SPLIT NUMBER	START DATE	END DATE
32470	204–162	23	12	019	023	065	065	20		150	20262		026	028
										160	30272	2	029	031
										200	30274		031	036
										250	30401		037	040
										300	30405		040	045
										310	30409	2	046	048
										320	25880		049	054
										350	25890		055	056
										400	22402	2	057	059
										450	30401		060	062
										500	30405		063	065
37460	304–206	120	27	026	026	053	053	15	15	50	20264		026	030
										100	25880		031	033
										150	25890		034	040
										180	30273		041	045
										200	30276	4	046	053
31620	134–908	6	47	026	026	071	073	40	40	50	20265		026	029
										60	22665		030	030
										70	22675		031	033
										100	22685		034	043
										120	28120		044	045
										150	30401		045	047
										200	30405	3	048	057
										250	25880		058	060
										300	25890		061	065
										310	26120		066	068
										350	26220		069	073
32380	919–734	14	90	026	026		106	30		200	20260		026	030
										250	30272		031	040
										300	30274		041	053
										320	30276	1	054	059
										350	30402		060	065
										400	30408	2		
										450	25880			
										500				

Source: Univac, Sperry-Rand Corp.

"queue" time or "waiting" time, often accounts for most of the total time it takes a job to be completed. The elements of operation lead time are shown in Figures 22–3, 22–4, and 22–5.

Overloads at work centers

The one problem which is almost impossible to solve well is when a job shop has too many orders. Overall schedules do not purposely try to overload work centers, but variations in the product mix sometimes cause some departments to end up with unplanned overloads which may require overtime, subcontracting, or simply late orders.

Overloads are also sometimes caused by customers who send in their orders today and want them tomorrow. So sales pushes the factory to add a few more orders, in addition to the regular schedule. These extra orders can easily be added if the original schedule was a little light. They can also be handled easily if the department is working on some orders for stock as well as other direct orders for customers. Stock item orders can usually be pushed aside and finished later as long as they are finished before their stock runs out. And, if the special rush orders are highly

FIGURE 22–4

Processing cycle of a shop order

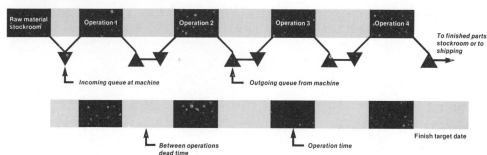

profitable, it may even pay to let the stock items run out of stock for a short time.

It would seem that the factory should not always be in a jam when rush orders come in. The original master schedules can allow for a little slack in the schedule. Master schedules are, in fact, sometimes made with this

FIGURE 22–5

Time compression possibilities for shortening processing time by overlapping operations

A.

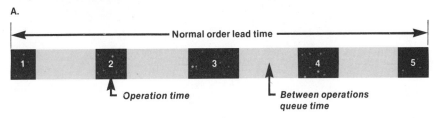

B.

in mind. When they are made up and when commitments for delivery dates are made to customers, only about 90 to 95 percent of the available capacity is allocated or "loaded" for these jobs. If there are more orders, they are pushed off into future periods rather than into these near-full close by periods. The other 5 to 10 percent of the capacity is thus available for last-minute rush jobs. Often this works out reasonably well.

LOADS

The factory's load is the amount of total capacity that has been allocated to orders from customers or to the production of items for stock. It can be expressed in tons, dollar value, time, or in other ways. Mostly, for production control use, it is expressed in time. A plant, department, or machine is said to have so many hours', days', or weeks', or months' work ahead.

Master schedules should not be approved until their load requirements are compared to the factory's capacity. Generally this is done only in the overall terms mentioned above or, if the company makes only a few kinds of products, in product units. If, however, the organization has a sophisticated computer based MRP system, rather detailed comparisons can be made between master schedule requirements and specific machine center capacities.

If a company manufactures to order, the load is the summation of the capacity needs of the orders already in hand for as far into the future as there are orders for. New orders, as they come in, are added to the present load, not as increases to today's load, but as extensions of the assigned capacity in future months. These orders get more distant promise dates according to when the work can be done.

A plant with a load which matches its overall capacity usually has all departments loaded about equally. Product-mix variations, however, sometimes throw unequal loads onto departments as is shown in Figure 22–6. Similarly, within departments, individual machine loads vary. Thus, when it appears that the approved schedule will provide for a smooth, balanced operation, it does not always work out quite so smoothly at the machine. The point is that orders can be scheduled which will apparently not overload the plant, and then it is found that some machines are overscheduled while others are underscheduled. MRP methods often include checking the work loads that parts orders generate at different work centers against the loads the centers already have.

"Infinite" versus "finite" loading

Some companies do not, at least at first, check loads being generated by new orders against the loads already in existence for work centers. Instead they just go ahead and calculate the new added loads without regard for the amount of uncommitted capacity of work centers. This is called "in-

FIGURE 22-6

Work center load report

07/15/—

WORK CENTER: 20516

PER-IOD	TIME UNIT FROM-TO	AVAIL. CAP.	REQ'D. CAP.	REQUIRED CAPACITY IN PERCENT 0 100 200 300	AVAIL. CAP. (SUM)	REQ'D. CAP. (SUM)	REQUIRED CAPACITY IN PERCENT (SUM) 0 100 200 300
06	026-030	36.0	40.0	111.1	36.0	40.0	111.1 ....
07	031-035	40.0	30.0	100.0	76.0	90.0	105.2 ....
08	036-040	40.0	56.0	140.0	116.0	136.0	117.0 ....
09	041-045	45.0	60.0	133.3	161.0	196.0	121.8 ....
10	046-050	45.0	72.0	160.0	206.0	268.0	130.1 ....
11	051-055	45.0	34.0	75.5	251.0	302.0	119.9 ....
12	056-060	40.0	16.0	40.0	291.0	318.0	109.3 ....
13	061-065	40.0	20.0	50.0	331.0	338.0	102.1 ....
14	066-070	40.0	12.0	30.0	371.0	350.0	94.3 ....
15	071-075	32.0	8.0	25.0 ...	403.0	358.0	68.8 ....
16	076-080	64.0	80.0	125.0	467.0	447.0	95.7 ....
17	081-085	80.0	96.0	120.0	547.0	543.0	99.2 ....
18	086-090	80.0	115.0	133.7	627.0	658.0	105.0 ....

FUTURE CAPACITY: 139.5

WORK CENTER: 23363

PER-IOD	TIME UNIT FROM-TO	AVAIL. CAP.	REQ'D. CAP.	REQUIRED CAPACITY IN PERCENT 0 100 200 300	AVAIL. CAP. (SUM)	REQ'D. CAP. (SUM)	REQUIRED CAPACITY IN PERCENT (SUM) 0 100 200 300
06	026-030	40.0	60.0	150.0	30.0	60.0	150.0 ....
07	031-035	0.0	60.0		30.0	120.0	300.0 ....
08	036-040	24.0	60.0	250.0	63.0	180.0	281.0 ....
09	041-045	80.0	60.0	75.0	133.0	290.0	186.0 ....
10	046-050	80.0	48.0	60.0	223.0	288.0	128.6 ....
11	051-055	90.0	42.5	53.1	303.0	330.0	108.8 ....
12	056-060	90.0	42.5	53.1	363.0	373.0	97.1 ....
13	061-065	80.0	40.0	50.0	464.0	413.0	89.0 ....
14	066-070	80.0	45.0	56.3	533.0	368.0	86.2 ....
15	071-075	32.0	48.0	150.0	576.0	516.0	89.6 ....
16	076-080	32.0	48.0	150.0	608.0	564.0	92.7 ....
17	081-085	40.0	48.0	120.0	648.0	612.0	94.4 ....
18		40.0	54.0	135.0	688.0	676.0	98.3 ......

FUTURE CAPACITY: 56.3

Source: Univac, Sperry-Rand Corp.

finite" loading. Infinite loading shows how much work we would like to load in each work center in each work period. If an overload results, then work centers may have to go on overtime or some orders may have to be shifted around to balance needs with capacities.

In contrast to infinite loading, "finite" loading systems try to fit planned order releases into future uncommitted work center capacities, recognizing the prior allocations of capacity to other orders. Finite loading systems often fall short of their promise and do not do a perfect job of loading because of the complexity of the problems and the dynamic nature of most master production schedules.

Actually, infinite loading is not such a haphazard matter as it might sound. Normally the overall capacity requirements, stated in general terms, of new orders are considered before these orders are accepted and promise dates set. The company's managers know just about how much load the present schedules are calling for. Rarely would they accept new orders and make promise dates beyond what can be handled. Top managers would accept a known overcommitment only if they were willing to approve overtime or the delaying of other orders. Generally a load that is feasible for the whole factory is also feasible for its internal departments individually.

One minor point: Work center load records, if they are expressed in labor-hours, probably should be kept in terms of *standard* hours of work backlog. When a job is done, its standard hour time—not the actual time it took—should be subtracted from the load balance. Doing this keeps the total from becoming inaccurate from being affected by how fast a person works. On the other hand, if people work at 125 percent efficiency, they will do 10 hours' work in 8. A work load of 200 standard hours for a machine would, in fact, be about 160 hours.

Actually, computers make it unnecessary to keep load records and adjust them up when new loads are added and adjust them down when jobs are finished. Instead it is easy for the computer just to run off a new report every week or even every day. There is no great need to keep a running balance of work loads.

MACHINE SCHEDULING

Schedules for the use of individual machines are usually made out only for large key machines or for bottleneck machines. These can be prepared by the computer for each day's runs if this is helpful. Reports of the outputs from such machines are likely to be "on-line" reports to the computer so it is easy to get new up-to-the-moment reports of the remaining orders ahead of these machines and of how much time each order is likely to take.

In job-lot work where successive jobs are different, different tooling is usually required for every job. Whenever new jobs require new tooling, it is well for production control to check to see if this new tooling is available before the operation is scheduled. The tooling is sometimes not ready when it should be. Checking up on its availability results in production orders not being released until the tooling is ready. Hold-ups in process are thereby reduced.

GRAPHIC LOADING AND SCHEDULING

Almost all of our discussion relating to production and inventory control assumes the use of computers, but there are a great many smaller companies where the problems are relatively simple and where computers are not needed for shop loading and scheduling purposes.

Graphic planning boards, once used widely, are still often used to show plans and the progress of production against the plans. Productrol boards, Schedugraphs, and Boardmasters have been used for years. All of these use a time scale across the top. Along the left side are lists of machines, orders, or inventories, whichever are being pictured. Bars extend from the left to the right according to the activity being depicted. Control boards are most often kept in the central production control office and not out in the shop.

There are other commercial devices, such as magnetic boards and roll charts. With magnetic boards it is only necessary to place metal bars on the board, and they will stay wherever they are put. With roll charts, the chart is rolled from right to left, one day's space each day, and the bars are extended on the chart to the right.

Control charts are helpful in that they are relatively simple, and they highlight possible trouble spots usually before trouble occurs. A certain amount of work is required to keep them up to date, and they replace no other records; this work is all extra. Unless they are posted right up to the minute, they may actually be misleading because here and there they show wrong information. Also, as days pass, they run off the right side of the board, and it is necessary to keep redoing them and moving them back to the left. But they are useful for small-scale operations. The Richard D. Irwin Company, for example, used such a board in the planning of the production of this book.

REDUCING PAPERWORK

One of the gains years ago from letting foremen pass out work orders and control the progress of orders through their department was the savings in paperwork. It reduced the need for written move orders for truckers and written reports of completed work that central office people used to hand-post to records of job progress. Today, with computers and remote terminal reporting on a real-time basis of work done, the paperwork has been largely cut out.

Actually, even before computers, there was not necessarily much loss in control if some of this paperwork was eliminated. Unless a factory is swamped with work, most jobs will go through production on time. They *have* to go through because the factory is working and turning out jobs hour by hour and day by day. Workers and machines need jobs to do, and this need "pulls" work through the plant. So long as the factory is not given more orders than it can handle and so long as the supervisors pass out first jobs first, most orders will be completed on time. It is not necessary to "push" jobs through.

The problem is, and computer systems cannot altogether handle this either, that troubles, large and small, interfere. Workers are absent, a machine is out of order for a day or two, more materials are spoiled halfway through than was expected, an order is lost, and so on. Usually none of these things happens to impede the progress of any particular order, and most orders go through on time. But some of these delays are always occurring and some orders do get held up.

If the reporting system did not exist, the production control department would not find out about delays until the finished item was wanted. By then the item would be needed badly. Advanced on-line computer systems have made a double contribution here. They have gotten rid of most of the paperwork; yet, by being on-line, they keep the status of jobs right up to the minute. They periodically call attention to orders that fall behind.

SCRAP, SHORTAGES, AND LOST ORDERS

Whatever system is used also needs to keep production control supplied with a physical count of items as individual operations are finished because it needs to know the "attrition" rate (how many items are spoiled or rejected and thrown out after each operation). The remaining number of items in a lot diminishes a little after most operations. A report only of jobs on time or behind schedule does not show what the attrition rate is. If an order ends up with too few pieces, it may be necessary to send through a rush order for enough pieces to bring the lot up to size—and such orders are very expensive. A materials shortage list is shown in Figure 22–7).

False counts and "disappearing" orders also cause problems. Piece workers sometimes report that they turned out more than they did. Or sometimes workers spoil items and, in order to avoid criticism, throw them away without reporting them. If the controllers believe the job card reports, sometimes they will not know about a shortage until several operations later. It helps here to have inspectors count production when they inspect the products, if not always, perhaps on a random basis.

Orders are lost, too. There are so many trays, racks, or tote pans of materials for jobs ahead, jobs done, or jobs held up and lying around that jobs just are lost now and then. Sometimes traveler copies of the shop order are lost, so no one knows what the half-made parts are. Or a lot is held up until some of its rejects are reworked, or because it is rejected, or because the next operation's tools aren't ready.

FIGURE 22–7

Materials shortage list

07/15/—											PAGE 1
ITEM NO. 40000100 LIGHTING MECHANISM START 277 DUE 292 QTY. 200											
						OPEN		ORDERS			
COMPONENT NO.	REQ. DATE	QTY. REQ.	ON HAND	RSRV. QTY.	DUE DATE	QTY.	DUE DATE	QTY.	DUE DATE	QTY.	NOTE
40200000	277	1200	200	1200	267	400	277	400	289	400	200, SHORT
30200100	277	200	0	200	277	1000					
40300000	277	400	400	400							
10101000	277	400	200	400	277	100	282	100	287	100	100, SHORT
40300002	277	200	50	200	272	400					
30410000	277	200	400	200							

Source: Univac, Sperry-Rand Corp.

Every company and department has its nooks and corners where such things pile up with no one interested in them until some day when a wild-eyed expediter comes desperately looking for them. Meanwhile top management have been wondering why in-process inventory values are so high.

EXPEDITING

Expediters ("stock chasers") are the "informal" system for moving production through the shop (as contrasted with records and reports as the "formal" system). They are a necessary evil in order control. They move troublesome or rush jobs through the plant, find lost orders, circumvent reasons for holdups, and push orders through in a hurry. They work from a "hot list" or a "short list" of orders behind schedule. They are necessary because things go wrong, and they help to get them straightened out. They are an evil because often the only way they can rush things through is to get supervisors to disregard regular schedules and even to tear down machine setups to do the rush job. This is unfortunate because it wastes machine production time, reduces total output, and may cause *more expediting* because it upsets the rest of the production schedule.

Hopefully only a small fraction of jobs should ever need expediting. There is less expediting today than there used to be since the formal computerized production control systems allow managers to keep better track of things.

"De-expediting"

There is a common tendency to forget to "de-expedite" an order if the need to hurry disappears. It is frustrating as well as costly to expedite something through several operations and to get it back on schedule only to find that there is no longer any hurry because the end product schedule had been changed. (The same holds for purchased parts which are often expedited and then sit around for weeks until they are finally used.)

One job shop, which fell into this "expedite but don't de-expedite" trap had so many *red* expedite tags on the orders in their shop that they outnumbered the other orders. Their solution was to place *green* tags on the items that "really" needed expediting and, when this didn't work, to place *orange* tags on the ones that "really-really" needed expediting. They had serious problems, and of course all of this was very costly until they did a thorough job of de-expediting orders. Again, computer based systems reduce these problems by keeping track of those items which should be de-expedited as well as those which should be expedited.

DISPATCHING

Dispatching means actually releasing work orders to employees (see Figure 22–8). Normally, dispatching creates no problems, but sometimes

FIGURE 22–8

Daily dispatch list

07/15/—			WORK CENTER: 224				PAGE 1
SHOP DATE: 172			MACHINE CENTER: 224–50				

ORDER NUMBER	PART NUMBER	OPERATION NUMBER	OPERATION DESCRIPTION	SETUP HOURS	RUN HOURS	LOT SIZE	REMARKS
30824	8024X	030	GRIND	.2	2.5	100	
48299	1937A	070	ROUGH GRIND	.1	1.2	50	SPECIAL FEED
87541	2888B	040	ROUGH GRIND	.1	1.5	75	SPECIAL FEED
52204	4155A	070	GRIND	.2	.7	25	
63714	7629X	050	FINISH GRIND	.4	1.1	30	COMMERCIAL TOLERANCE

Source: Univac, Sperry-Rand Corp.

there are more orders than the work center can handle; then problems arise.

Earlier in this chapter we said that departmental work loads sometimes exceed their capacity. When this is so, some kind of order priority system has to be developed, and the due dates on the orders won't fill this need because the department is overloaded. Too many jobs are supposed to be done soon. So it becomes necessary to neglect order due dates, at least to some extent, and set up some other rule to decide which orders should be worked on first and which are to be delayed. Such a rule or rules should be quite mechanistic so that a computer can make the choices. It is just not possible to use rules which depend on human judgment when the choices have to be made from among hundreds and thousands of orders.

We have noted earlier that, theoretically, departments should not be overloaded. But we have also noted that product mix variations sometimes throw unequal work loads on particular work centers when the total plant load approach contains no overload.

Overloads, at least in spots, are common. They come from accepting too many orders for a time period, from changes in master schedules, from product mix variations, from too much unexpected demand from minor independent demand items, from the factory having difficulties and not getting as much work done as usual.

We should also note that priorities among orders is sometimes a problem even when there is no actual overload. It might seem that whenever there is no overload, all orders will be finished and on time because the factory will have to do the work in order not to run out of work. This is largely true; yet, workers don't always look at dates, and they take the easy jobs and the long runs first. Or maybe the tools are not ready and a job is laid aside (and there it stays). Or rejects run too high so the whole order is laid aside until the rejects are reworked or until a replacement order catches up. In any case, orders sometimes fall behind at work centers even when there is no overload.

Rescheduling

Rescheduling also creates problems because it changes priorities among jobs; yet, the traveling copy of the job order that goes along with the products is unchanged until someone comes out in the shop and changes it or replaces it. Changes occur frequently in master schedules because customers change the quantities they want, or they change their desired delivery date, or they cancel their order. Changes also occur in schedules of items made to stock as sales prove to be greater than or less than anticipated. The whole MRP process is, in some companies, redone every week to reflect new quantities, new time schedules, and other things which have changed during the week.

Rescheduling may cause priority conflicts among orders because if one order moves up another may have to move back. If these orders are on tight schedules, then some sort of priority system will have to be developed so that rescheduling causes as few as possible disruptions of the more important orders.

By no means is all rescheduling caused by changes in end product demand. Many internal slippages also occur which affect individual orders. Individual orders should always be planned and scheduled as if nothing ever goes wrong, because things do not go wrong on most orders. Everyone knows the kinds of things that happen that delay production here and there—but no one knows where they will strike next. Tools sometimes will not be on hand and workers will be absent. Sometimes an inspector throws out more (or fewer) than the usual number of rejects. Consequently, there are not enough pieces in the lot (or there are more than was expected). Or some pieces just disappear. Or a whole order is lost. Or engineering (or the customer or the Consumer Product Safety Commission) requires a change in the product design so that some operations have to be done over or new operations must be added, others deleted. Or the customer wants to raise the quantity—or cut it. Or he decides that he has to have his order now instead of next month. Or OSHA orders a machine to be shut down and requires that it be safety-shielded.

Occasionally there are even mistakes in the order. It may not list every operation, or it may list a wrong operation, or ask for the wrong quantity. Neither master bills of materials nor master route sheets nor standard times are always perfect. And occasionally there are errors in the calculations of quantities needed.

All of these changes upset production control's plans and schedules. But none of them can be anticipated as probably delaying *specific orders*. Because of this, individual orders must all be planned and scheduled *as if no delay would occur* to them. Then, when delays occur, the orders have to be replanned. People doing production control work probably spend more of their time remaking plans and schedules than they spend making them the first time. Fortunately, computers can update everything and re-schedule orders so fast that they have made a big problem into a little one.

PRIORITY RULES

Operation wanted completion dates are inadequate as priority guides in so many cases that it is necessary to have other rules to go by to tell machine operators which jobs, of those ready for their next operation, to work on first. (Also shop orders, for parts whose orders were triggered by order points, have no due dates or wanted completion dates specified on them.) Large departments doing machining work often have hundreds of jobs in the department at the same time. This makes it impractical to have *people* investigate the needs of different orders and make decisions. There need to be rules for choosing, and they need to be rules which a computer can follow if a computerized system is in use.

Operations researchers have studied the problem of how best to decide priorities and have used simulation to see which dispatching policy is best. Among the rules they have tested are: first come, first worked on; first come, first worked on but with dollar value classes; choose the one to work on next which has the shortest time for the present operation; or the longest processing time for the present operation; least slack time in the department (due out the quickest); least slack time in all remaining departments; least total slack time between remaining operations; greatest cost penalty if due date is missed; most remaining operations; fewest remaining operations; later passage through overloaded work centers; later passage through presently idle work centers; importance of the customer; and profitability of the item.[1]

Unfortunately, computer simulation has shown that no one policy will solve all the problems. No one policy will get all of the most needed jobs out first. Doing short jobs first causes the fewest holdups, but delaying a few large jobs can be more serious. Hughes Tool Company dispatches "hot jobs first." The decision as to which are hot jobs is made by managers and not by the computer. Then, after the hot jobs, priority goes to jobs with the least average slack time between remaining operations. Hughes reports that by following these rules it has been able to let computers set schedules for factory departments. At the same time it has reduced the number and seriousness of behind-time orders and has reduced expediting costs. New schedules for each department are run off every few days.

Some of the most logical sounding rules relate priority to the order

---

[1] This process is similar to the one we discussed in Chapter 11 where the question was how best to combine job elements into work station assignments along as-sembly lines.

completion due date. One such rule, that used by Hughes, establishes a priority index based on the average slack time (between operation dead time) per remaining operation. Orders with the smallest average slack time get a high priority rating.[2]

Such a priority index is very helpful for MRP generated orders where wanted completion dates are specified. But they would not take care of item replenishment orders which are triggered by reordered points and which do not automatically have due dates. This is not, however, a serious weakness. At the time of the order release, the normal lead time could be projected forward to establish a wanted completion date.

Probably each company should do a little internal research and try to develop priority rules which best suit its needs. The object is to develop rules a computer can follow so that it can handle in a logical way all of the time-consuming work related to setting priorities originally and to updating them all when changes occur. The alternative is to have experienced dispatchers handle priorities—but often, experience will not be enough because of the complexity of the problems.

REGENERATIVE VERSUS NET CHANGE REPLANNING AND RESCHEDULING

In Chapter 20 we explained how orders for end products are exploded down to requirements of parts and subassemblies. Our discussion there more or less assumed that once end product schedules were set up they would be carried through.

Unfortunately, this never happens without at least a few changes taking place. End product schedules are changed, and this makes necessary the changing of all of the supporting parts and components schedules. In addition to these are the many smaller changes that are caused by production irregularities.

It does not always pay to try to follow every change individually as it occurs. Instead, some companies "regenerate" the whole schedule—run it all through the computer—but updated, of course, every week. Hewlett Packard, for example, does this. Everything is recalculated, whether or not there have been changes. Changes are not made during the week except where sizable loss could occur; all changes are usually held and incorporated into the Saturday rerun.

A different way to handle changes is to carry them through on a net change basis as they occur, with recalculations only for the items affected. In on-line systems, changes can be made as soon as they are known. This

---

[2] For a simulation of this rule and certain other rules, see William L. Berry, *Priority Scheduling and Inventory Control in Job-Lot Manufacturing Systems,* Institute for Research in the Behavioral, Economic, and Management Sciences, reprint series no. 471 (Lafayette, Ind.: Purdue University, 1972).

allows manufacturers with short production cycles to remedy problems quickly. Net change systems need not, however, be on-line. They can be made at the end of each day or week. Usually they require less computer time to run than regenerating systems. Since perhaps 80 percent or more of the items will not be affected by changes in any one week, complete regenerated plans may be required infrequently, if ever.

LARGE ON-LINE MANUFACTURING SYSTEMS—IBM'S COPICS

COPICS is IBM's "Communications Oriented Production Information and Control System." It is an on-line version of IBM's batch oriented production and inventory control system (A "batch oriented" system does not update all of its records on an on-line basis. Instead it stores all new information and updates the records only periodically, perhaps weekly.)

COPICS is more than a production and inventory control system. It is an advanced system which not only ties together production and inventory management information, but it also plans and monitors such things as customer order servicing, plant maintenance, certain inspection and quality control activities, as well as certain cost accounting and related financial planning and control records.

On-line information processing

COPICS uses terminals scattered throughout the factory to enter information as things happen or as questions arise. For example, when an employee reports the completion of an operation, the information (employee number, shop order number, and quantity produced) is entered into a terminal in the employee's department and the data are reported on-line to the central computer's memory where the data files are immediately updated.

Net change data processing

COPICS is a net change system rather than a regenerative system. Records are kept up to date through keeping up with all of the changes, rather than just letting change data accumulate and then regenerating complete new data records every week. The system, being on-line, can provide up to the minute answers to questions at any time.

Disadvantages of on-line systems

The primary disadvantages of any on-line system, such as COPICS, are its cost and complexity and the problems which occur if the system "goes down." Normally the computer's data storage devices and terminals need to be restricted to the COPICS system and cannot also be used for other data processing work such as payroll, accounting, and design engineering. (However, the computer itself can usually still perform these other functions along with COPICS functions.)

Also, and even though it is usually a rare event, when the computer systems malfunctions, users often don't have a printout to read to tell them what is going on as they can have with a batch computer system. Even rare malfunctions require production control, supervisors, and operators to be able to get along without the computer until the system is functioning again.

LINE OF BALANCE (LOB)

"Line of Balance" (LOB) is used to plan and control production and delivery schedules for finished products, their major component parts, and for items made in quantity. LOB is more a tool for control than for planning. It is most useful in the transition stage where one-time activities change to the production of limited quantities and is essentially a manual substitute for what computer based MRP systems do.

A program, for example, may call for the delivery of end products on the following schedule:

Month	Each month	Cumulation
April	0	0
May	0	0
June	0	0
July	0	0
August	4	4
September	7	11
October	12	23
November	22	45
December	40	85
January	60	145
February	100	245
March	100	345

Subassemblies and parts to support this end product delivery schedule will obviously have to be started into production considerably in advance of the end product need dates. How far ahead will depend on each item's cumulative lead time.

Suppose that the following lead times are required: subassembly A, 1 month; parts 1 and 2 for subassembly A, 2 months; subassembly B, 2 months; parts 3 and 4 for B, 2 and 3 months respectively; subsubassembly C (a part of B), 1 month; and parts 5 and 6 for C, 1 and 3 months respectively.

The lead times ahead of final assembly, in this case, are:

Item	Months	Total
Subassembly A	1	1
Part 1	1 + 2	3
Part 2	1 + 2	3
Subassembly B	2	2
Part 3	2 + 2	4
Part 4	2 + 3	5
Subsubassembly C	2 + 1	3
Part 5	2 + 1 + 1	4
Part 6	2 + 1 + 3	6

This tabulation of lead times prepares the way for the next step, which is calculating the number of parts which should be in the pipeline and how far along they should be at any given date. Here is a listing of the quantities which will be needed at the end of each month in order to support the final assembly schedule:

Month	Item A	1	2	B	3	4	C	5	6
April	0	0	0	0	4	11	0	4	23
May	0	4	4	0	11	23	4	11	45
June	0	11	11	4	23	45	11	23	85
July	4	23	23	11	45	85	23	45	145
August	11	45	45	23	85	145	45	85	245
September	23	85	85	45	145	245	85	145	345
October	45	145	145	85	245	345	145	245	
November	85	245	245	145	345		245	345	
December	145	345	345	245			345		
January	245			345					
February	345								
March									

An LOB chart is a picture, at some given point of time, of the plan versus accomplishment. Suppose that it is the end of July; at this point we find the following:

Item	Quantities scheduled to be finished	Quantities actually finished
6	145	160
4	85	75
3	45	50
5	45	35
1	23	28
2	23	24
C	23	20
B	11	10
A	4	5

Figure 22–9 is a chart that shows these figures. The line of balance is the solid line which shows the quantities of each item which should already be finished if future end product schedules are to be met. The vertical bars are the actual production. These show that items *6, 3, 1, 2,*

FIGURE 22–9

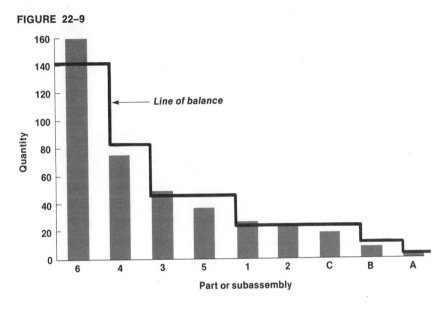

and *A* are ahead of schedule. But *4, 5, C,* and *B* are behind. Extra effort will have to go into getting them up to schedule or the end product schedule cannot be met.

ELECTRONIC PRODUCTION REPORTING

Electronic reporting of production is now common and is replacing older methods. Large, costly operating machines can be hooked in, electronically, directly to the central computer so that their output is reported as it occurs. Closed circuit TV is also commonly used where there is need for production control to monitor operations closely. More often, however, electronic reporting is less directly on-line. When a worker finishes a job, he puts the job ticket (a prepunched tabulating card) into a nearby "transactor" reporting box, which transmits a report of the job's completion to the computer.

Sometimes, though, it is too expensive to have a computer even this much on-line. Many companies do the electronic *reporting* as work is done, but the computer updates its records only once a day or even once a week. It holds all reports until the end of the day or week. Then it updates all records and puts out a report of how things stand for managers' use the first thing the next morning or the following week.

In other systems, the worker places a personal plastic identification card into the terminal. The computer than allows this worker to get from the computer whatever information he needs, either printed out or shown on a viewing scope. Figure 22–10 shows the variety of files that are updated by a "job completion" entry in a sophisticated communications oriented computer system.

FIGURE 22–10

Activities occurring at the end of the job completion

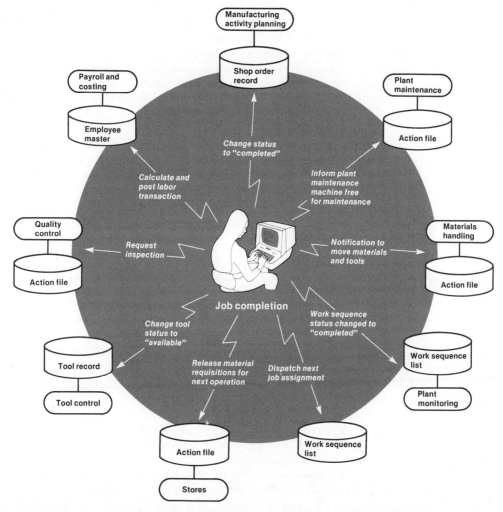

Source: *COPICS, Plant Monitoring and Control*, IBM, 1972, p. 47.

REVIEW QUESTIONS

1. Is a shop order for a certain lot of parts an example of producing authority or processing authority? Where does it come from? Explain.

2. What is processing authority? Where does it come from?

3. If master schedules are in line with the factory's capacity, how does it happen that individual machine centers sometimes end up with more work than they can take care of?

4. What is the difference between order scheduling and machine scheduling? Is either one necessary? Both? When could either one be done without?

5. Are machine loads and schedules the same thing? If they are different, where should each be used?

6. It would seem to be unnecessary to keep records of work loads ahead of any machines at all since work loads for machine centers are reasonably in balance and the operations' wanted start and stop dates are on shop orders, thus establishing job priorities. Why might work center work load records be needed?

7. When manufacturing to order and when business is good, the master schedule allocates the plant's capacity to existing orders for some time ahead. Under what circumstances would still more orders be added to current loads rather than as further extensions of capacity allocations into the more distant future?

8. Differentiate between infinite and finite loading.

9. What is the difference between regenerative and net change replanning in an MRP system?

QUESTIONS FOR DISCUSSION

1. The factory needs to keep operating in order to keep costs down. Is it therefore so bad for it sometimes to go ahead and produce unauthorized production? Presumably this excess production would be for products known to be reordered frequently. Discuss.

2. What is the "pull" of the factory? What has it to do with production control?

3. In the women's clothing industry dress manufacturers cut cloth for exactly the number of dresses ordered. Then any faulty dresses which can't be repaired become shortages on the order to the customer (and are not replaced).

   Isn't this a good practice for all companies to use? What problems would it make in the dress industry? In other industries?

4. Is production control or time study a better place for a person to learn how a factory operates? Why?

5. The lead times for special orders are one month. Yet, under pressure, the factory has from time to time gotten "hot" jobs out in a week. Why not let the sales department really treat its customers well by using one-week lead times for all jobs?

6. "Engineers design products, but they should let the factory decide how to make them." Discuss.

7. A member of the American Production and Inventory Control Society asked for ideas about how to set up a short-cut method for estimating labor for the machine shop, mechanical assembly, and electric assembly work. His company is seeking "ball park" figures and a nomograph, chart, or slide-rule type method. What suggestions might be given him?

8. What might the production control department do to help solve the "contractor's dilemma"? (When the workers see the end of a contract or job approaching with no other job in sight, they slow down to perpetuate their jobs, or even create overtime possibilities in order to get the contract out on time.)

9. It is nearly always possible to push one more order of parts through the plant quickly if the individual operations are "lap phased" instead of "gap phased." Lap phasing means to overlap operations and to start operation 2 on the first units finished by operation 1 before operation 1 is finished with all items in a lot. Lap phasing is not used very often in job-lot production. Why not?

10. Why not simplify the matter of dispatching and just adopt a policy of "do the shortest job first"? Would this result in the fewest number of delayed orders? What would happen to long-production-time orders? Is this a good policy to adopt?

11. Discuss the pros and cons of permitting changes to be made after production has been started in a schedule period.

12. An air rifle company, after its Christmas sales peak, has to repair thousands of misused and out-of-order rifles in the early months of each new year. What problems does this make for production planning and control?

13. The customer has just sent a design change notice. The company is already halfway through making the parts affected so it doesn't want to change. The manager of production control calls the customer and then hands you the telephone so that you, the production scheduler, can explain your problems to him. What do you tell him?

PROBLEMS

1. The customer has, in the last 6 months, ordered a total of 30,000 closure covers at $10 per unit and has just now sent in an order for 10,000 more. He has always ordered 10,000 at a time, each time saying that he does not know whether he will want any more of this design.

It costs $4,000 to set up for a run of these covers and $4 per unit for labor and materials. The production control manager points out that the company could save money by making 20,000 or 30,000 and storing the excess until the next order. It costs $.10 a month to store these covers. And, if it should turn out that the cuostomer no longer wants this design and the inventory has to be scrapped, they have a salvage value of $1 each.

How many, if any, should the company make ahead if there is a 90-percent chance that the customer will take them? Seventy-five percent? Fifty percent?

2. The new scheduler has found that the production operators, being on piecework, turn out work in less than standard time. Here are last month's records of five workers:

Worker	Hours spent on jobs without standards	Hours spent on jobs with standards	Standard hours of work turned out
A	23	145	172
B	5	163	203
C	16	152	169
D	8	120	152
E	11	149	167

a. How much work should the scheduler expect week by week from these operators in the future?

b. What problems will he have to contend with?

3. Part number 127B requires the following operations and has, from past experience, produced the following information:

Operation	Setup time (hours)	Standard operation time per piece (minutes)	Piecework operator efficiency	Scrap percentage
1	.5	4	133	25
2	1.3	9	120	none
3	.6	2	100	30
4	.3	4	115	10

For an order of 200:

a. How many pieces should be started in each operation?

b. Using overlapped scheduling (where the following operation starts on the first units before the whole order is finished in the preceding operation), how many hours after you start to set up operation 1 should you start to set up operations 2, 3, and 4? (Do not start fast operations until a big enough bank has been built up to let them complete the order in one uninterrupted run.)

c. When will the order be finished?

4. An order for an item which requires three operations is to be scheduled. The setup times for the 3 operations are 25, 45, and 15 minutes respectively. Machine operation times are 10, 12, and 6 minutes respectively. Scrap losses on each operation are 1, 4, and 2 percent respectively. For a lot of 200 pieces:

a. How many items should be started into production?

b. What is the least time (using gapped scheduling) to finish the order? (Allow one hour between operations for moving materials to the next operation.)

c. In order to start operations 2 and 3 as soon as the order arrives, how many minutes after the setup on operation 1 is started will it be necessary to start setting up for operations 2 and 3?

d. Using overlapped scheduling, what is the answer to question *b*? (Do not, however, start operation 3 until it can operate steadily; do not have it wait 6 minutes each for items from operation 2.) The transportation delay can also be cut by 20 minutes when overlapped scheduling is used.

e. At $.50 per trip for carrying products from machine to machine, how much extra in transportation costs will overlapping cost as against gapped operations (where only two trips are required)?

5. The Kip Company has an order to make 50 units of a large part. Its costs are $100 per unit plus $1,000 setup costs. Extras over 50 units are all loss; yet, shortages under 50 have to be made up. The rejects which cannot be repaired normally come to 10 percent. (In this calculation, for simplicity's sake, it is possible to neglect the possibility that a replacement unit would itself be a reject.) Losses follow a Poisson distribution and not a normal curve. (The fewest possible number of rejects, if 55 were started through production, would be zero, or 5 less than the average. Yet, in the other direction, the number of rejects could be more than 5.) Here are the Poisson probabilities of defectives if the starting quantity were 55, 56, 57, 58, 59, or 60.

| Number of rejects | Number started | | | | | |
| | 55 | 56 | 57 | 58 | 59 | 60 |
	Probability					
0	.0041	.0037	.0033	.0030	.0027	.0025
1	.0225	.0207	.0191	.0176	.0161	.0149
2	.0618	.0580	.0543	.0509	.0477	.0446
3	.1133	.1082	.1033	.0985	.0938	.0892
4	.1558	.1515	.1472	.1428	.1383	.1339
5	.1714	.1697	.1678	.1656	.1632	.1606
6	.1571	.1584	.1594	.1601	.1605	.1606
7	.1234	.1267	.1298	.1326	.1353	.1377
8	.0849	.0887	.0925	.0962	.0998	.1033
9	.0519	.0552	.0586	.0620	.0654	.0688
10	.0285	.0309	.0334	.0359	.0386	.0413
11	.0143	.0157	.0173	.0190	.0207	.0225
12	.0065	.0073	.0082	.0092	.0102	.0113
13	.0028	.0032	.0036	.0041	.0046	.0052
14	.0011	.0013	.0015	.0017	.0019	.0022
15	.0004	.0005	.0006	.0007	.0008	.0009

How many products should be started into production? What will be the most probable cost of starting this quantity? Show the figures.

6. The order is for 100 aerial rotaters, a product requiring several parts which are different from anything the company has ever made before. The customer makes it clear that he wants 100, no more and no less.

How many of part A, which goes into the rotaters, should be started into production? The finished product requires 4 units of part A for each rotater, and extras are waste.

On somewhat similar items made in the past, the following has been the rate of spoiled parts.

Spoilage percent	Number of jobs
0...........................	0
1...........................	0
2...........................	1
3...........................	1
4...........................	4
5...........................	7
6...........................	12
7...........................	4
8...........................	1
9 and over..................	0

The setup cost is $100 and the material and processing cost per unit is $30. Rejected parts have zero value. Keeping in mind that if there is a shortage it is always possible to set the machines up again and produce enough items to meet the requirements, how many parts should be started into production?

7. There is an order for 2,000 units of product X, which requires the following sequence of 4 operations. Their operating data are:

Operation	Machine service time daily (minutes)	Percent loss after operation	Operation time/unit (minutes)	Operator lost time/8-hour day (hours)
1...............	40	1	2.41	.5
2...............	28	2.5	6.20	.5
3...............	17	1.5	0.76	.6
4...............	44	3	1.37	.4

How many clock hours will it take to process this order if four hours are allowed between operations? How many parts will have to be started into production?

8. Here are figures for a new part which will take five operations:

Operation number	Setup time (minutes)	Standard operation time per unit (minutes)	Operator efficiency	Percentage of time operator works on standard work	Scrap percentage
1....................	10	6	110	100	10
2....................	20	12	140	90	none
3....................	50	20	130	100	15
4....................	40	15	115	80	5
5....................	20	10	105	90	none

The time between operations is 40 minutes after an operation is completed until the next one starts, but setup can start before the lot arrives. How many hours will it take to get out a lot of 1,000 pieces?

CASE 22-1

The Dee Company has had trouble with parts not arriving at the assembly floor. The difficulty has not often been serious but has caused minor delays. Parts intended for particular assembly orders have been made up and put into the finished parts stock instead of being taken to an accumulation bin in the assembly department. When assembly starts, their absence causes delays because they must be brought from finished stores.

Parts are manufactured on individual manufacturing orders and show the part identification and the identification number of the product they go into. The fact that some or all of the parts on the parts order are to be used for a particular assembly order is not shown on the parts order.

Should the assembly order number be put on all manufacturing orders for parts to be used for that assembly order? What if more parts are called for on the order than this particular assembly order requires? Would it be a good idea to deliver all parts directly to an accumulation bin at the assembly floor? How will the accounting department find out about parts orders finished and delivered to the assembly floor instead of to finished stock first? Will it matter if the parts are for two or more different assembly orders? Or will it matter if some of the parts being made are for stock whereas the others are for a particular assembly order?

CASE 22-2

In a situation similar to that of the Dee Company, the Elk Company delivers parts directly to accumulation stalls in the assembly area. The assemblers help themselves to parts from these accumulation stalls as they need them. Parts which don't fit are tossed aside or back into the supply bin and other parts are used. By the time the assemblers near the end of an order, they are short of parts or have only parts which don't fit. How can production control handle this situation?

This problem has also extended into the finished parts stockroom. The assemblers, needing more of a part, go to the stockroom and help themselves. How should this be handled?

CASE 22-3

In order not to run out of stock, the Headington Engine Company tries to have all parts in parts stock one month before starting final assembly. Headington makes large diesel engines requiring several thousand parts, some of which are first subassembled into components which later go into engines as units. Assembly goes on more or less steadily from month to month, but there is some change in the product mix between sizes and types, and most engines sold are special in minor ways.

Assembly orders are passed out to the production control department five months before assembly is to start (assembly usually takes two months). The production controller calculates the parts required and orders them all four months before the month assembly is to start. The parts are all expected to arrive in finished parts stock during the next 90 days. This gives the production control department 30 days for expediting any items not on hand a month before assembly starts.

As a consultant, you are asked for suggestions. What do you say?

CASE 22–4

Every order for special items is assigned to an expediter who sees it through production. The expediters are somewhat demanding at times. If orders ahead of a special order would tie up all the available machines for several days, they insist on their specials being put ahead of the other orders, even rush orders for regular items temporarily out of stock. They also insist, at times, that machine setups be torn down and production halted on other orders to get the specials out faster. The plant superintendent has finally told his foremen never to tear down a setup to put a special order on the machines and to let the specials wait their turn after regular stock rush orders.

What lines of authority should be set up to cover production situations like the above? Who should decide priority among orders? What authority should expediters have? Or should there *be* any expediters? What kind of procedure would take care of the company's problem?

SUGGESTED SUPPLEMENTARY READINGS

Deane, R. H., and Moodie, C. L.   "Job Dispatching for Workload Balancing." *Production and Inventory Management,* 1st quarter 1973, pp. 75–86.

Hutchings, H. V.   "Shop Scheduling and Control." *Production and Inventory Management,* 1st quarter 1976, pp. 64–93.

Wixom, T.   "Plant Scheduling with the Computer." *Production and Inventory Management,* 2d quarter 1975, pp. 66–80.

23

Other production planning and control systems

Almost all companies use order control systems for their job shop operations, but very few companies use *only* order control in all of their operations. Whenever a company begins to receive repeat orders for items or when demand becomes larger and longer production runs are required, management should begin to think of using production control procedures designed for product oriented manufacturing. Product oriented manufacturing control systems have no one universal name; however, one common system is called "flow control." Other less common systems include "load" and "block" control.

LINE-ASSEMBLED PRODUCTS

Standardized products which are made in large volumes—stoves, washing machines, automobiles, farm tractors, television sets, and many more —are made on production lines, using "flow control" production control methods.

A product is put together one or two parts at a time as it moves down a line. People perform their work at separate work stations which are, perhaps, only five or six feet from each other. As soon as a worker puts on his part, the product moves on and another product arrives for its part.

Products *flow* down the line, past work stations and off the end of the line minute by minute. *Parts and subassemblies* have to *flow* into work stations along the line at a rate equal to their use. Thus, a main objective of flow production control is to match up the rates of flow of parts, subassemblies, and final assemblies.

Yet within this flow there is need to control a certain amount of variety in both parts and finished products. Autos, for example, come in different models, colors, number of cylinders, with (or without) power brakes and power steering, and with all kinds of different trims and accessories. Ford and Chevrolet each have so many possible combinations of different things that they could run all year and never make two cars exactly alike. Yet cars continue to flow off the assembly lines. Within this flow there is need to be sure that red cars get red wheels and that four-door cars end up with four doors, not two. Also, if 50 cars are to have 8-cylinder engines, not only are 50 8-cylinder engines needed, but 50 6-cylinder engines are *not* needed. Not every manufacturer has as much variety as auto makers, but most line production companies have some variety.

Balancing the flow of parts to match their use is not an easy task. Automobile wheels may be used at the rate of five per car, and each assembly line makes one car about every minute. Forgetting for the moment that there may be several lines, wheels are needed at the rate of about 1 every 12 seconds. However, producing one wheel every 12 seconds may not be the most economical rate for making wheels. Perhaps the wheel production line works most effectively when it produces 1 wheel every 4 seconds, or 15 a minute, instead of the 5 a minute that the final assembly line needs. This creates a problem. One solution would be to slow down the wheel line, but this would probably be uneconomical since we have just said that the wheel line operates best when it produces 15 wheels a minute.

It would probably be more economical to produce 15 wheels a minute and let wheel inventories accumulate hour by hour. Before noon each day there would be enough extra wheels to keep the final assembly line busy for the rest of the day. If there were only one final assembly line, the wheel line could be closed down and the people could be assigned other work. Often, however, there are two or more assembly lines in the company's several factories, so the extra wheels can be shipped to them.

Sometimes, however, it is the other way around. The wheel assembly line can produce only two wheels a minute whereas five are needed. Then it would be necessary to work two or three shifts on the wheel line for each final assembly shift. Or, as an alternative, a second wheel assembly line could be set up or some wheels could be purchased from outside.

Lack of perfect balance between production rates of parts and subassemblies and final assembly use is the rule, not the exception; *yet, production per day or per week must balance* and without carrying large inventories. Flow production control must cope with this.

The problem of matching parts production and use rates without carrying costly inventories and without running out of anything (if anything runs out, this stops the assembly line, which in turn stops everything else) is even greater for most individual piece parts than it is for lines producing subassemblies.

Many parts are made in lots (if they were made continuously, a year's supply would pile up in a week or two). These parts are usually made in an unending series of successive lots produced perhaps a month or more apart, depending on how their own production rate matches up with the master production schedule's requirements. Fortunately, it is usually unnecessary to use complex order control systems for such repetitive lots because new lots are made so often that everyone knows what the items are and what operations to perform. This saves money because there is no need to make new operation lists each time, nor to collect the costs of making each lot, nor to tell truckers where to haul materials, and so on.

Items bought outside also come in as successive lots. Kelsey-Hayes makes auto wheels, but Kelsey-Hayes can't deliver one wheel every 12 seconds to General Motors or Ford. The best it can do is to send truckloads or freight carloads at the rate of so many a day or a week.

To sum up: Flow control has to keep products flowing off the assembly line; it has to keep subassemblies and parts flowing to the assembly line; it has to control variety; it has to cope with lack of balance in production rates of parts and their use; and it has to deal with parts coming in in lots instead of in a steady stream.

FINISHED ASSEMBLY LINE CONTROL

Controlling finished assembly is almost altogether a matter of controlling the *variety*—seeing that each separate product gets the combination of parts and accessories which is specified by each item's individual bill of materials. Once line production gets under way, the workers soon learn their tasks, and this eliminates the need to tell them what to do thereafter. Similarly, except at first, line assembly eliminates the need for instructing truckers about where to move materials.

Instructions do need to be given, however, to cover variations in the product and in attachments, trim, and so on. In the case of automobiles these instructions are quite detailed. For auto assembly, an "order of run" or a "building sequence" list is needed for the assembly line. It lists every car to be made in a day, and its sequence in the line, and all other details.

Copies of this list go to several points along the line to tell assemblers what items to put on and to tell parts suppliers what parts to "stage" and to line up for cars that will be coming along. Some companies use on-line computers to perform this task. They simply print out parts requirements at terminals located at key points just before the cars come along the line. Also, as a cross-check, every car carries a tag listing the parts and accessories it is to have. This is not very helpful however, in controlling the parts because people along the line don't get to see the list until the car arrives. Often this is too late for them to get the required parts from stock.

Most line-assembled products are easier to schedule than automobiles. Much of the work in making clothing, shoes, radios, television sets, typewriters, cash registers, and telephones is bench work. Except in the cases

FIGURE 23–1

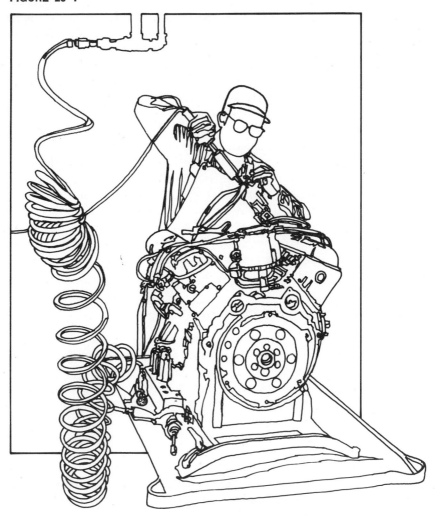

of clothing and shoes, all that is needed are simple tools—bolt tighteners, soldering irons, and so on. Most of the people along the line do almost the same kind of work (see Figure 23–2). They put parts in place, or sew them together, or screw them down, or bolt, rivet, or solder them.

This often gives production control freedom to raise or lower schedules without changing shift hours, provided there are a few extra people available. This applies when it is possible to put in a few more people at extra work spaces along the line. Normally production control does not have to concern itself with the effects of minor changes in production rate on labor capacity. The burden of getting more people (or cutting some off) falls on the supervisor and so does the job of redividing the bits and pieces of the total work so everyone will be busy.

FIGURE 23–2

Assembly of electrical products along a horseshoe-shaped line. Operators push the units by hand between work stations. Each assembly is mounted on a carriage which can be rotated. Parts are brought in next to operators on mobile carts.

CENTRAL PRODUCTION CONTROL

Most companies which are large enough to use flow control are also multiplant companies. Some production control is done in the company's central production control department, and some is decentralized. The company's central production control department begins with sales forecasts and customer orders for specific products. Next, it determines weekly and daily final assembly schedules for each factory. It also determines the part and subassembly requirements for each factory. And, it also sets up schedules for subassemblies and parts production or purchase.

However, it would seem unwise to try to formulate production schedules in Chicago for Atlanta, Dallas, Seattle, and elsewhere. It would seem more reasonable to let each factory's production control department determine its own requirements for subassemblies and parts. And, of course, it might be better to let each plant make up its own schedules wherever there is little interdependency for parts among them. But it is different where components come in from outside, whether from other plants of the company or outside suppliers.

Since supplier plants often have to ship to a large number of customers, the suppliers have to know the customers' *total* requirements so they can plan their production. A producer of fabric for automobile seats, for example, has to plan runs of each fabric. The production and shipping schedule can be determined more easily if they get one list from a central production control department rather than separate releases from a dozen of a customer's factories.

Central production control departments usually make all of these schedules and lists every week or month. And there are thousands of them. For example, every month the Ford division of Ford Motor sends out schedules to 800 suppliers, giving them quantity and timing requirements for sending 10,000 parts to 16 plants. Most of these requirements schedules are generated by computers using MRP systems.

These "order releases" from the central production control department always show delivery schedules day by day or week by week, and they also show cumulative figures—how many in total have been released (ordered) since the start of the year (see Figure 23–3). That lets everyone see how the order stands. If *total deliveries* are below *total releases,* the supplier has to catch up. Underruns in any period have to be made up in the next. When deliveries have not kept up with releases, this means that the customer's supply banks are running low. Or, still worse, it means that they are running completely out of an item now and then so they lose production in final assembly.

Also, all of these schedules have to be redone when there are changes. The company's forecasters can never guess the future market perfectly, so there are often changes in the quantities required. Sometimes it becomes necessary to make an urgent design change, and again schedules have to be changed. Such changes mean that all of the released orders already out in various plants and supplier companies have to be adjusted and new

FIGURE 23–3

Release against purchase order, economy motor division, Standard Motors Corporation

				Release No.: 16	
				Date: 3–14	
Source:			Purchase Order No.: 112579		
XASCO PRODUCTS CO.			Description:		Cigar Lighter
1500 Roag Road			Part No.:		1318534
Detroit, Mich. 48140					

Date to ship	Ship to				All-plant total
	Flint	South Gate	Linden	Kansas City	
Prev. Cum.	109137	34878	38805	39923	222743
Week 3–14	5321	2631	2600	2573	13125
Cum.	114458	37509	41405	42496	235868
Week 3–21	5322	2631	2600	2573	13126
Cum.	119780	40140	44005	45069	248994
Week 3–28	5321	2630	2600	2573	13124
Cum.	125101	42770	46605	47642	262118
Week 4–4	5321	2567	2599	2572	13059
Cum.	130422	45337	49204	50214	275177

FIGURE 23–4

Economy Motor Division
Status of assembly plant parts shipped

Page: 17
Date: 3–14

Part number	Part name	Assembly plant	Shortage 2d. prev. week	Shortage prev. wk.	Required to ship cur. wk.	Shipped	Schedule through current week
1167494	Pointer	FL	1286	3692	6981	39758	46739
1167494	Pointer	SG	1126	3720	6795	45787	52582
1167494	Pointer	LI	704	3129	6144	47042	53186
1167494	Pointer	KC	402	1888	4515	29540	34055
1167497	Pad	FL				52496	52148
1167497	Pad	SG				51437	51052
1167497	Pad	LI				52221	51844
1167494	Pad	KC				35996	35743
1167516	Ring Horn	FL			5499	42322	47821
1167516	Ring Horn	SG				48525	48091
1167516	Ring Horn	LI			4691	29317	34008
1167516	Ring Horn	KC			4027	19503	21598

lists given to them. Suppliers need to know about changes as quickly as possible so they can rebalance their own master production schedules. Everyone's schedules have to be made and remade all the time. Computerized MRP systems are essential in keeping track of all these changes when increases or decreases in demand change the master production schedule.

INDIVIDUAL PLANT PRODUCTION CONTROL

Each plant usually has its own production control department. It takes the weekly schedules sent from central production control and develops order-of-run lists for final assembly. It also makes specific "loading sheets" to tell material handlers what to put on the supply conveyors which bring subassemblies and parts to the assemblers along the line. A loading sheet might instruct a supply person to load a blue dashboard onto the supply conveyor for car number 20, a red one for car 21, and so on.

Back in the supply area, the plant's production control staff monitors parts inventories continuously. Materials suppliers tell production control when these banks of parts begin to build up or shrink. To production control, either one indicates there is trouble somewhere. If a bank goes up, final assembly is probably behind schedule. If it goes down, something is probably wrong in subassembly production. Production control usually gets hourly reports, or even computer-monitored on-line, up-to-the-minute reports of final assembly's production so it knows the final line's use. But with the thousands of things it must watch, watching the parts banks (instead of relying wholly on production reports) is a quick way to detect problems.

SUBASSEMBLIES

Final products should be made out of subassemblies rather than directly from piece parts. It would be hard to imagine, for example, putting, one by one, the separate pieces of an automobile speedometer onto a car going down the assembly line. The assembly line is no place to handle ⅛-inch parts. The speedometer should be put together as a unit and be fastened onto the assembly as a unit. In fact, and better yet, the speedometer should be put into the dashboard first, and then the whole dashboard should be fastened onto the body of the car.

Most subassemblies are made continuously along assembly lines of their own at rates which, in the overall, match the final assembly line's needs. Production control's work with subassembly lines is like controlling final assembly. There is often some variety, and it is still necessary to match the rates of parts production and their use. But controlling any one sub-assembly line is usually simpler than controlling the final assembly line because there are fewer parts and less variety.

Three things about subassemblies are different. First, the quantities made are always greater than the final line uses because allowances have

FIGURE 23–5

Use of Lazy Susan turntables for making subassemblies. The simple assembling fixtures are quickly changeable for many models. A setup operator prepares empty tables for the next job.

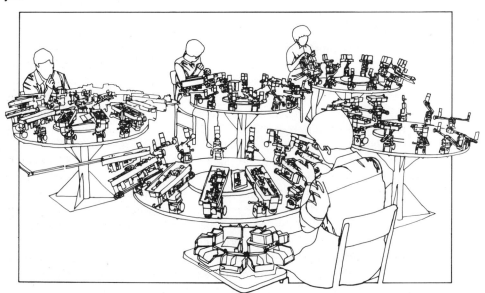

to be made for a few rejects as well as for spare parts for repairs. Second, the main user is final assembly. If the subassembly production rate per hour does not match final assembly's needs (as well as take care of the extras), the subassembly line will have to operate longer hours if its rate is slower or shorter hours if its rate is faster. Third, the main factory makes some subassemblies for all of the company's other plants. In these cases the subassembly quantities are related to the company's total needs and not at all to the main factory's assembly needs.

Because of different production rates between final assembly and subassemblies, and because of the extra requirements for service parts, as well as because of the needs of other plants, managers have to reconcile themselves to having inventories. Subassembly production and final assembly needs usually cannot be matched perfectly. Subassembly lines usually feed their output into temporary storage areas, from which final assembly is supplied. The proper size of these supply banks depends, of course, on the value of the items, how bulky they are, and how critical they are to keeping the final assembly line running. At the same time, should final assembly stop, subassembling will also have to stop from lack of space to store its output.

Purchased items or items shipped in from other plants are a little different. If they come from nearby, perhaps the assembling plant can get by with only a few hours' supply in the bank. But, if they come from farther away, it becomes necessary to try to schedule freight cars on the days when the new supplies will be needed. However, rail service from distant points is not too dependable. The using plant cannot count on getting its items exactly when it wants them, so it will have to carry more on hand to be sure of not running out if a freight car is delayed. On the other hand, large companies have to watch their freight car schedules very closely. General Motors receives more than 2,000 freight cars of materials every day. It is necessary to try to schedule these arrivals to suit the plant's needs.

PARTS CONTROL

Assembly lines are the "showy" parts of manufacturing, where the product takes form. All of the parts are ready—they are the right shape, size, color—and they are ready on time. But behind all the smooth flow of final assembly lines lies the still bigger job: making subassemblies and making parts for subassemblies. All of their production schedules must mesh with assembly line use.

Most parts differ from subassemblies in that they are made in lots and not continuously. Yet, as was said earlier, making parts in lots does not mean using the same order control systems as those used for job shops. These lots are repetitive lots and the process is sometimes called "cycling." With cycled lots, the lot quantities are usually set to suit the lines' immediate needs and sent through, say, a new lot every three or four weeks.

Repetitive lots have no lot numbers and use no move orders, route sheets, or drawings. Individual job tickets and job-lot costing are also eliminated since standard costs are used.

If it takes a week to process a "lot" of a part, a lot perhaps large enough to sustain final assembly's needs for three weeks, is started into production on, say, Monday. By some time Tuesday the whole lot will be past operation 1 and some of the items will be past operation 2. Some may be even past operation 3. By the second Monday the first of the lot will be coming off the last operation, and the whole lot of that part will be finished by, say, the second Tuesday evening.

After finishing this lot, no more of this item is made until a new lot is started through production on the fourth Monday. Then every operation will be repeated. By the fifth Tuesday there will be a new supply on hand. Production control decides how large the lots are to be (two weeks' supply, four weeks' supply, or whatever). And it determines in advance when it will be necessary to have new lots finished and when they must start into production. They also watch the banks of parts being used up as new supplies near completion to make sure that the supply does not run out.

Production control has to watch, too, to see that machines are not overloaded. The machines are used all the time but for successive lots of different parts. If a lot of one part is planned to start on a machine on Monday morning, that machine needs to be free on Monday morning. It cannot still be working, at least not for very long, on some other part that should have been finished last Friday. If the new lot is delayed very long, it may not be finished in time to prevent the item from running out.

Cycling allows most of the shop papers that go with order control to be eliminated. Directions are unnecessary because everyone knows what operations to perform, what tools to use, where to move products, and so on.

Cycling, however, causes many machine setups, and these will be costly unless the engineers design tooling so that it can be put on and taken off machines quickly. Cycling allows machines to be used for several parts and so keeps the machines busy.[1]

Some companies still use shop documents in cycle orders, however. Identification tags may still be needed, for example, when different parts look a great deal alike.

GM's electro-motive division (maker of diesel-electric railroad engines) assigns a sequence number to each repetitive cycled lot. First, a raw materials requisition for enough materials for the lot is produced. This requisition goes to the supervisor whose department will do the first operation. The supervisor withdraws the necessary material from the stock room. Sequence numbers are similar to job order numbers in order control in

---

[1] An analytic method for determining the length of a cycle run for products which share a machine is presented by Elwood Buffa, *Operations Management,* 3d ed. (New York: John Wiley and Sons, 1972), pp. 242–47.

that they identify the job. But they are also job priority numbers. Supervisors must process low numbers first.

There is no regular shop order, however, so the supervisor has to be otherwise told what operations to perform. This is usually unnecessary because he has made many lots of the same item before. Further, he has an operation list covering the operations to be done in his department. He can turn to his book of operation lists if he is in doubt. If an item is not a regular item, he will get a regular shop order, as in order control, which will tell him what to do.

Electro-motive's method also tells the factory's central production control office how the lot is moving through production—but only as it moves from one department to the next, not as it moves within a department. Products going out of a department pass a final inspector who not only inspects what goes out, but reports to production control which lots and how many units have gone on to the next department. Supervisors always tell production control, though, when any lots are held up in their departments. In some companies, completions of each operations are reported to the computer on an on-line basis.

SERVICE CONVEYORS

Except for small parts, only a few items can be stored at work stations along the assembly line because of lack of space. Usually it is necessary to use conveyors to supply a steady stream of parts from stock supply areas to the assembly line. These service conveyors are usually closed-circuit loops which move continuously. People in the supply areas load parts in the pans or trays or on hooks from which the assemblers help themselves.

Loop-service conveyors should have many pans, and they should all (or nearly all) be filled as they leave the stock supply area so assemblers ready for parts will not have to wait. Whenever they need a part, they should be able to reach out and get it from the pan moving by. When there are several assemblers doing the same work, say, assembling electric motors, they all use the same parts. But, even if the pans are all full to start with, the last person served by the conveyor may have to wait while several empties go by before a part arrives.

To keep this from happening often, there should be more pans per minute going past the assemblers than they will ever empty at one pass. Whatever they do not use just stays on the conveyor and goes around again. Since service conveyors often come from distant points and move slowly for ease of unloading and loading, it may take an hour for them to move from the supply point to the assemblers. And since many parts may go around more than once, there may be several hours' supply of parts on the service conveyor all the time. Some conveyor systems travel a rather serpentine path several feet above the factory floor and utilize this space for "in-process" storage.

In the automobile industry, all of the inventories on service conveyors and also on assembly lines are called "float." But the parts brought to the assembly line by conveyors in the automobile industry never go around twice. Instead they come, one after the other, in the exact sequence and at exactly the right place and the right time and quantity to take care of the line's needs.

LEAD TIME

As we said in earlier chapters, lead time is the time between ordering an item and receiving it. Production control has to know the usual lead times on all items and particularly on all items made in lots or items shipped in. Irregular lead times can cause problems, especially for the shipped-in items.

Production control determines "planned order releases" for making parts and assemblies and for purchased items with the usual lead times in mind.

It is so easy to say "allow for the usual lead times" that it makes it sound simple. General Motors assembly division's production control department has to make up several thousand schedules every month just for assembly work alone. GMAD has never counted the huge number of schedules its separate factory production control departments make for piece parts!

For a typical GMAD plant, lead times vary from zero to ten days. This variability depends on where items come from, but part of the time allowed is to take care of irregularities in shipping time. It takes from zero to 30 days to make parts and subassemblies. It takes five to eight days to ship home-plant-supplied parts to the other plants. Then it takes from zero to ten days to produce subassemblies in the other plants. These lead times accumulate in a chain-like fashion. First, it is necessary to allow lead time to receive purchased materials or parts; then, time is required to make parts and subassemblies, to ship to other plants, and for final assembly. This results in total lead time which adds up to anywhere from 5 to 58 days. Production control must continually update lead times for every item.

In addition to these logistical complexities, there are such matters as scheduling things to arrive on different days of the week so entire freight trains will not be waiting to be unloaded on Monday morning and then have nothing coming in on Thursday. Furthermore, every time the forecasters misread the market demand, all of these schedules have to be changed hurriedly in order to try to bring production back into line with sales. There are also strikes in supplier plants or a snowstorm or a flood along a railroad. These also upset production schedules and make it necessary to do them all over again.

Computer based MRP systems can, however, allow much flexibility in responding to these changes by quickly updating lead times, calculating new requirements, and recalculating priorities among orders. Small changes are sometimes held up and then all made weekly. But larger changes might better be made daily or even on a real-time basis.

LOAD CONTROL

Earlier we considered how a job-lot factory determined schedules and paid attention to the load of work ahead. If, however, a company uses "load control," this is a little different from what we talked about earlier. Load control usually refers to developing schedules for one or more large important machines.

A large or key machine may be used for many sizes and varieties of products, and load control procedures apportion its time to jobs. Usually the key machine is a fast producer, such as a printing press that prints magazines, telephone books, Sears Roebuck catalogs, books, and so on. Some of these printing presses produce as many as 10,000 magazines an hour.

But, in one sense, a fast machine is a bottleneck compared with the minor operations before it and after it. The point is that the minor operations which support the key machine usually require little scheduling. Since there is usually plenty of capacity to handle everything that the key machine produces, its schedule is the focal point of production control.

Load control requires order identification so that quantities can be controlled. It is necessary, for example, to get the right pages into the right magazines or books.

The rubber industry has a different situation with its calenders (large machines for rolling rubber mixtures into sheets of exact thicknesses). Calenders are usually assigned to producing a certain material. The only schedule they need is the amount of each size of the product to run each day. Small increases or decreases in the quantity requirements can be handled by varying the number of hours worked daily. And, if they run a little over or under in one day, they even it out the next. (This cannot be done, however, in printing. Extra pages for one book do not compensate for a shortage of pages of another book.)

PROCESS MANUFACTURING

Processing industries change the physical or chemical form of large quantities of materials. Included are companies producing gasoline, chemicals, paint, flour, glass, rayon, nylon, cement, asphalt tile, plaster and paper. "Production" takes place inside tanks, retorts, vessels, and furnaces as materials are mixed or heated to produce the required changes. Equipment is connected by pipes, ducts, and conveyors which move the material from stage to stage.

Normally this equipment runs at full capacity or not at all. Changing quantities means changing work hours. Usually, however, large companies have several processing lines, so they can vary production by changing either work hours or the number of lines in operation.

Production is usually to stock or to large sales orders. However, if it is to stock, not much inventory is carried. Volume is so great that a few days' production would fill all the storage tanks or warehouses.

Process companies use flow production control, but it varies somewhat from that used in parts-fabrication-assembly industries. The factory receives weekly schedules or lists specifying products, quantities, and production sequences. These requirements lists are sent to operators in charge at key points in the operation where the equipment has to be reset to make different products.

Production control usually gives no processing instructions to the factory on *how* to make products because processing instructions are in the supervisor's specification books. Nor are there usually any move orders or cost collection reports since standard costs are used. Production control, however, does receive reports, perhaps hourly, of production, and at the end of each day they receive reports of the exact production quantities. And they receive reports instantly if anything goes wrong during the day. On-line monitoring and reporting by minicomputers is common.

As in automobile flow control, production control in processing companies releases orders to vendors. And the tremendous volume (one or more whole freight trains a day) of materials coming in daily, necessitates careful scheduling and monitoring of the flow of incoming materials.

This is also true of the outgoing shipping schedules. It takes just as many freight cars to haul products away as it does to get raw materials in. Production control, however, is usually not responsible for outgoing shipments. This is the responsibility of the traffic manager or the manager of physical distribution. Production control is responsible, however, for having the materials ready to go out.

There are two production control problems in process industries that differ from other flow control. One occurs early in production, the other late in production.

Processing industries usually start with natural resource materials which are never quite consistent. Sulphur, iron, sand for glass, wood for pulp, and crude oil from different sources are not homogeneous. The laboratory continually has to inspect incoming materials for chemical and physical variations. Nearly always there is some variation which must be compensated for. Sometimes all that is necessary is to mix and blend together materials from different shipments. This eliminates much of the variation in the material which goes into processing. Or it may be possible to adjust mixing formulas, processing temperatures, processing times, or other factors to compensate for nature's variations.[2] The production control department is concerned here because changes in mixing formulas consume

---

[2] Linear programming methods are sometimes used to determine the "recipe" which will compensate for nature's variations. This topic is discussed in Chapter 25.

materials in unplanned ways while changes in processing times affect rates of output.

Production control in processing industries also often has extra work to do in the last stages of production, particularly with packaging and labeling. They have to issue specific directions for the packaging operations so that the right number of each size or package or brand name or the right cuts to size are made.

BATCH MANUFACTURING

In early stages of manufacture it is often necessary to mix and process batches of materials. Batch processing occurs in many branches of the food processing and canning industry where materials are mixed and then cooked. In the paint industry, paints and coloring materials are also made in batches, as are rubber, and pharmaceuticals. Glass is often made by periodically melting fixed quantities of sand. Iron, steel, and other metals are usually made in "heats."

The size of the batch is usually dependent on the size of the equipment. Several hundred pounds of ingredients are brought together into batches and put into masticators or mixers. Sometimes, as in extracting metal from ore, the process is heating rather than mixing. Frequently, chemical reactions are involved.

In batch manufacturing the production control department has to load the mixing or heating equipment to match the time cycle for each batch as specified by the laboratory. They also must set finished product quantities so that entire batches are used up. Since batch sizes are usually fixed and only full batches are made, the entire batch usually is made into finished products. Often, as in the case of foods and rubber, this must be done because mixed but unfinished material is perishable. If it is mixed, it has to be made into finished products immediately. Thus, the exact lot size of finished products made at a given time is more dependent on batch sizes than it is on the demand for finished products. This results in a minimum of in-process inventory, but at times it results in larger inventories of finished products.

The control system most often used in batch manufacturing is load control. Order numbers, operation job tickets, and move orders are usually not needed.

BLOCK CONTROL

Block control, a variation of order control, is used in the clothing industry. For example, in the men's suit industry before suits are manufactured, styles and cloth patterns are decided upon, and pictures and samples of the year's "line" are sent out to the retailers. Retailers make their selections and order the suits they want, distributed as they see fit among sizes, styles, and patterns.

The factory's capacity to produce suits is relatively fixed at so many suits per day. Production control groups the orders by cloth pattern and by style and adds groups together into "blocks." A block is the number of suits the factory can produce in, say, half a day.

All orders in the block will be released to the plant at once. A new block is released each half day. Within a block, *every suit has its own individual suit number* so that the sleeves, pockets, and so on for the suit will be "assembled" together into the right coat. All suits belonging to the same order also carry the order number, and all suits in the block carry the block number.

Each suit is inspected several times during its manufacture, and individual suit numbers are checked off as they pass the inspection station. Any suit in process can be located readily from the records at the inspection stations. Departments are required to finish a whole block before "clearing" the block. If any suit's production progress is delayed, production control knows it right away, and corrective action is taken, or that suit is replaced in the block by one from the next block.

Block control is both a method of releasing identical amounts of work to the factory at some interval (such as twice a day) and a method of controlling throughput. It does not cause any more items to be produced, but it assures that no item gets pushed aside and forgotten.

The women's shoe industry uses a method quite similar to block control except that no block numbers are used and individual pairs of shoes are not given individual numbers.

Women's shoes are not as standard as men's suits, so it is not as reasonable to assume that the plant can produce the same number of pairs of shoes every day or half day. Instead, production control determines the piecework cost of cutting the leather upper part of the shoes on each order. Records show how much money the cutters in the cutting department earn every day, and this is a relatively fixed amount. So, in order to release orders to the factory in an even flow, it is simply a matter of accumulating order by order the cutting cost for each pair of shoes until the total equals what the cutters earn in a day. This many orders, and no more, are then released to the factory for the day.

After production begins, the shoes go through check points where the progress of each order is recorded. Reports are available to the production control department showing the progress of all orders. Often these control systems are computerized, and order progress is captured "online."

In both men's clothing and the women's shoe industries, shop orders are made out showing the number and kind of products to make. Operations are so standard, however, that printed operation lists are used. The list is printed on lightweight cardboard, on which each operation is represented by a detachable stub. When an operation is performed, the piece worker (nearly all work in both of these industries is done on piecework) detaches the stub for the operation just completed, puts it with the others which he has accumulated, and turns them in as a report of the work done. These stubs are usually readable by a computer system through pre-printed characters or punched holes.

Block control uses no schedules in the usual sense of the term. What begins at one end of the factory has to come out the other end and in about the usual time. If it slows down, this will show up when it fails to pass the checking stations.

Bottlenecks are rare because the size of successive departments is in balance. The sewing department is just the right size to handle all that the cutting department turns out, and so on with other departments. Fortunately, normal differences in product mix have little effect on the work loads of different departments.

SCHEDULING AND CONTROL OF SERVICES

The scheduling and control of the "production" of services can be as complex and, in some cases, more complex than manufacturing activities. Scheduling the repair and maintenance of airplanes in order to keep them flying is most complex. Certain components, engines, for example, need periodic overhaul at certain mileage totals, and, when overhaul time comes, they need to be close to the repair base and not 10,000 miles away. Similarly, spare parts may need to be stocked in Tokyo and Paris as well as in San Francisco.

Airlines also have difficult scheduling problems with crews who might have to change going west in San Francisco and then to wait over for a return assignment east on a later flight. Railroads have the same problems with train crews.

One major difference between production planning and control in manufacturing and services is that services cannot be stockpiled. Empty seats on yesterday's airplane flight are not usable today. And yesterday's empty motel rooms don't help with today's crowd. Nor can a city inventory the idle time of firemen who had no fire yesterday but several today.

If a service facility is waiting to serve and there is no demand, the product is instantly perishable. Thus, for service industries, the productive capacity must either be large enough to handle peak demand, or service capacity must be increased or decreased in line with service demands (summer resorts put on many extra people in the summer), or else peak demands are just not met and customers have to wait or go somewhere else. Having customers wait or be turned away has a cost to it, just as a factory has when it runs out of stock.

We will discuss several approaches to solving service problems in our discussion of waiting line models and simulation in Chapter 26.

REVIEW QUESTIONS

1. How can the production control department reconcile the steady use of parts with their being produced or received in lots without carrying large inventories?

2. What problems are there in scheduling work along an assembly line? Explain.

3. What problems differ in controlling subassembly and parts production lines and final assembly lines? How does this affect production control?

4. In a multiplant company, what work should the company's central production control staff do and which work should be left to be done by each plant's own production control staff?

5. How does cycling operate in the manufacture of parts for assembly lines? How is cycling like, and how is it different from, order control?

6. What is the difference between load control and the subject of machine loads as discussed in Chapter 22?

7. How are block and load control alike? How are they different? Under what conditions would each be best to use?

8. How do the variations in raw materials as nature provides them affect the work of controlling production in mass production industries?

9. In companies using block control little attention is paid to the capacities of departments other than the key department whose load is used as the control. How do such companies keep from sometimes ending up with substantially unequal work loads in other departments?

10. How does manufacture by batches affect production control? Explain.

QUESTIONS FOR DISCUSSION

1. Suppose that a product has several generations of subassemblies (a part goes into a minor subassembly, which goes into a bigger assembly, which goes into a major assembly, which goes into the final product). And suppose that final assembly is continuous. What are the pros and cons of making the earlier generations of subassemblies continuously as against making them in lots? What happens to inventories? To production costs?

2. Are lead times more important in flow control than in order control? Explain.

3. When changing models, is it better to close down the plant during the changeover or to phase new models in gradually? Discuss the problems involved.

4. How does parts manufacture for volume production differ from final assembly so far as production is concerned? What problems are peculiar to parts production? What should be done about them?

5. Assembled product manufacturers using assembly lines often go ahead and assemble a product discovered early along the line to be defective in some way. At first this does not sound very smart. Under what conditions might it be smart? What should be done at the end

of the line with the faulty product? What should be done with the parts if they are not attached?

6. At the close of its model year, one of Detroit's big three car companies had 160,000 door handles left over. How can very large-scale production "balance out" and finish with just the right number of parts to complete the final products coming off the line, yet not have, say, 160,000 door handles left over? In discussing this problem one should keep in mind the lead times listed in the text as applying at GMAD.

7. In batch or semicontinuous processing operations, how do the materials handling operations differ from those where order control is used? Would one be more likely to find centralized or decentralized materials handling control procedures? Would highly automated handling systems likely be found in these operations?

8. In terms of the required information flow, how do block and load control compare with order control? For operations of comparable size, would the work load on the production control staff be less or greater with block or load control as opposed to order control?

CASE 23–1

The Reo Company wanted to make the most effective possible use of its machines used in making parts. Accordingly it adopted a "cycling" arrangement whereby certain equipment was used on several jobs during the course of each two days. A set sequence of jobs and regular quantities of parts were turned out each two days. In all, the machines in the cycled group were each used for seven operations.

The objectives of the management (getting a steady flow of parts and full machine utilization) were realized. The management's satisfaction in this accomplishment was somewhat deflated, however, when the records showed that one quarter of the pay of the men on the cycled machines was paid to them for changing machine setups and that the machines were idle one quarter of the time while being set up.

What are the values of short cycles? Are the benefits great enough to justify higher setup costs and machine idle time? Is there any way to work on short cycles and not lose considerable money and capacity because of setups?

CASE 23–2

The S-P Spark Plug Company was somewhat chagrined to learn that its spark plugs were being marketed in the city where the factory was located at a retail price below its factory selling price. A check of dealer records disclosed that Joe's Handy Shop, where the spark plugs were being sold, was not listed as a purchaser. The spark plugs were genuine S-P plugs and were of first quality. It appeared certain that they were being stolen by workers in the factory. A careful watch was kept of all finished stock, but the leak was not discovered.

Production records disclosed no disappearance of materials in process; yet, Joe's Handy Shop continued to sell S-P plugs at prices under factory costs. All the checking was done without fanfare and was carried on for a whole year. One day an unannounced inspection of empty lunch boxes of workers leaving at the end of the first shift was made. One lunch box was found to contain a substantial number of porcelain parts for spark plugs. Upon being confronted with this evidence, the employee explained the leak. Three employees were involved. Each took home an occasional handful of the completed parts made in his department. The spark plugs were assembled at their homes and sold to Joe's Handy Shop. Spark plug parts were made in very large numbers, and no exact counts were made during processing. Production records were all kept in terms of pounds instead of pieces, and tote boxes of parts were filled reasonably full and then sent on to the next operation. The few scrap pieces produced were thrown into scrap cans at the site of the operation. Generally no check was made on the volume of scrap except for an occasional check to see that it remained within the limits permitted. It was easy for workers to remove a few pieces at a time at any point in the operations without detection.

How might a system be devised to control such a situation? Is petty thievery a problem in very many companies? Should a company institute regular lunch box inspection?

CASE 23–3

Richard Hamer, newly appointed head of the production control department of the Rigney Foundry and Machine Company, was 28 years old. He came to the company after two years of college and had been with the Rigney company ever since. In a factory management magazine he read an article describing the operation of "block" control in the textile industry. It pointed out how scheduling was greatly simplified by assigning orders to "blocks" which moved through successive departments more or less as units. The idea seemed good, and Hamer decided to try it out.

He decided that the logical way of grouping orders was to use the molding department as the basis. A block was set as an amount of work which would keep the molding department busy for a half day. Various jobs were to be assigned to each block. Their total molding time requirements would equal that available in a half day. Individual orders would show the block number in addition to the order number. The foremen of all departments were to be required to complete all orders in a block before another block would be cleared out of their departments.

What difficulties would probably arise in using this system in the foundry? What would happen in the machine shop (still assuming that block numbers were set to equate molding requirements of orders)? Can any part of the block idea be used in the case above? A requirement of block control is that the production capacities of successive departments be equal. How can that be accomplished in the above case?

SUGGESTED SUPPLEMENTARY READINGS

Sass, C. J. "Cost Control on the Production Lines." *Business Automation,* July 1971.

Schirier, Elliot. "Production Planning in a Multiplant System." *California Management Review,* Summer 1969.

Walker, W. R. "Batch Scheduling Techniques." *Journal of Systems Management,* February 1974, pp. 42–44.

section six

NETWORK analyses using such system as PERT have proved to be of great value in the production of extremely complex products and of large projects whose production takes many months. The whole production activity is viewed as many subsystems of component activities, all of which must, in the end, tie in together as the final product is made or as the project is finished. PERT and its several uses is presented in Chapter 24.

Operations research techniques are helpful in making many production and operating managerial decisions. Several of these techniques were considered in earlier chapters. Linear programming and, in particular, the simplex method of linear programming can be used as an aid in production planning and control. Chapter 25 shows how linear programming analysis is performed and how it can be used in production and operations management.

Chapter 26 is devoted to waiting lines and simulation and considers their use in the planning of production and service facilities.

24

Project planning and control with PERT

SPECIAL projects are continually being planned and produced in all kinds of organizations. For example, the development of new instant cameras in the 1970s was a multimillion dollar special design project both at Polaroid and at Kodak. Other examples of special projects are: building a space shuttle or opening up a new shopping center.

The management of special projects requires different planning and control techniques than those used for managing repetitive production and service activities.

PERT

The best known and most widely used project planning and control method is called PERT, or Program Evaluation and Review Technique. PERT is an analytical method which is designed to aid in the planning and control of complex projects which require that certain activities be performed in sequence while others may be performed independently of others.[1]

PERT has been used for many kinds of construction activities, for building bridges and unusual buildings such as stadiums, and for coordinating maintenance and installation projects such as refitting ships and installing new computer systems. PERT was used extensively to plan and control the thousands of activities needed in the construction of the Alaskan pipeline for oil. Generally, it is most applicable to rather complex, nonrepetitive projects.

---

[1] PERT and a very similar variant CPM (Critical Path Method) methods are essentially the same. Since the terms are used almost interchangeably we will use the more common term PERT.

PERT CHARACTERISTICS AND DEFINITIONS

PERTs methodology and components have fairly standard definitions, which are as follows:

Activity   An *activity* is a part of the total work to be done; it consumes time and resources and has starting and ending points. Figure 24–1 depicts a network of activities showing the sequence in which activities (the arrows) must be performed.

Event.   An *event* is a "milestone"; it marks the beginning or the end of an activity. In drawing a PERT network, events are symbolized as circles or "nodes." Events are also numbered, with those having to be done early in the project having lower numbers than events coming later in the project.

In a PERT network, each activity connects two events and so lies between a pair of events whose identification numbers indicate the beginning event and the ending event. No two activities are allowed to have both the same beginning and ending events because there would be no way to distinguish between the two activities. (Computerized PERT systems usually identify activities only by their beginning and ending event numbers.)

Activity time   PERT uses three estimates of the amount of time an activity might take to complete. These estimates are obtained from people who have some knowledge about the work and how long it will probably take.[2] They are:

a.   *Optimistic time:* The time the activity will take if everything goes well and no delays are encountered.
b.   *Realistic time:* The time the activity will most likely take under normal conditions, allowing for usual delays.
c.   *Pessimistic time:* The time the activity may take if more than the usual delays are encountered.

PERT weights these three estimates to obtain an "expected time" for an activity by:

$$\text{Expected activity time} = \frac{\overset{\text{Optimistic}}{\text{time}} + \left(4 \times \overset{\text{Realistic}}{\text{time}}\right) + \overset{\text{Pessimistic}}{\text{time}}}{6}$$

Thus, if an activity in a PERT network for building a building were "pour the concrete foundation" and it had estimates of 2, 4 and 12 days, its expected duration would be:

$$\text{Expected activity time} = \frac{2 + (4 \times 4) + 12}{6} = 5 \text{ days.}$$

Precedence requirements   Since some activities cannot begin until others are completed (we cannot pour the concrete foundation until we

---

[2] Most users of PERT do not actually use three time estimates in this fashion. Rather, they simply use the "realistic" time as the expected time for the activity. We will use three times in our example in order to illustrate their use in anticipating finishing dates.

FIGURE 24–1

PERT network diagram

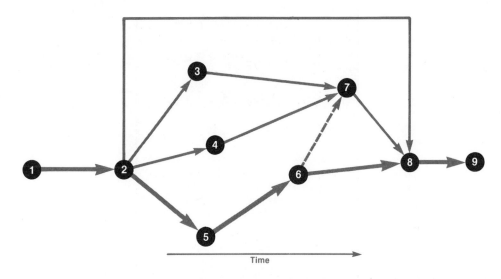

have excavated and built the forms) and others may be performed in-dependently and/or simultaneously, (we may simultaneously pour the foundation and order lumber), we must develop the *immediate precedence requirements* of the activities in the project. The easiest way to do this is ask this question of *each* activity: "Which *other* activities must be completed immediately before we can begin *this* activity?"

Start and finish times   The earliest time an activity can begin, considering the expected activity times and the precedence requirements of all prior activities, is called the *earliest start* (ES) time. The latest time an activity can start without delaying the whole project is called the *latest start* (LS) time. The earliest time that an activity can finish is called the *earliest finish* (EF), and so is equal to the activity's ES + its expected time. The latest time an activity can be completed without delaying the completion of the entire project is called the latest finish (LF) time. This is equal to the activity's LS + its expected time.

PERT EXAMPLE

To illustrate how PERT works, let us consider the example whose figures are shown in Figure 24–2 and which are depicted in the PERT network in Figure 24–3. We will suppose that our project has 12 activities (11 real activities and 1 dummy),[3] designated A, B, . . . L; a set of immediate precedence requirements; and the three times estimates for each activity.

---

[3] A "dummy" actvity is not really an activity. It is indicated on a PERT network diagram by a broken arrow line and is there to preserve proper sequences when one activity does not depend directly on another.

FIGURE 24–2
PERT data

(1) Activity	(2) Immediate precedence requirements	(3) Events Begin	End	(4) Optim. time	(5) Real. time	(6) Pess. time	(7) Expect. time	(8) Starts ES	LS	(9) Finish EF	LF	(10) Total slack
A........	None	1	2	3	4	5	4	0	0	4	4	0
B........	A	2	3	4	7	10	7	4	16	11	23	12
C........	B	3	7	2	7	12	7	11	23	18	30	12
D........	A	2	4	3	5	13	6	4	19	10	25	15
E........	D	4	7	1	5	9	5	10	25	15	30	15
F........	A	2	5	7	8	21	10	4	4	14	14	0
G........	F	5	6	1	7	7	6	14	14	20	20	0
H*.......	G	6	7	—	—	—	—	20	30	20	30	10
I........	C,E,G	7	8	10	10	10	10	20	30	30	40	10
J........	G	6	8	15	23	25	20	20	20	40	40	0
K........	L,I,J	8	9	2	7	12	7	40	40	47	47	0
L........	A	2	8	10	15	20	15	4	25	19	40	21

* Dummy Activity.

FIGURE 24–3

PERT network with data added

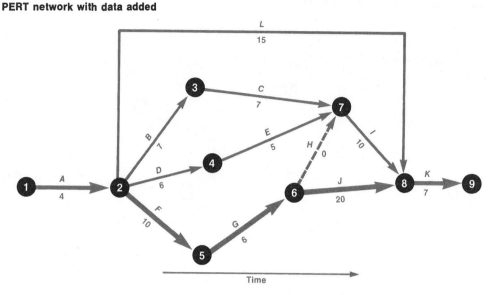

Looking just at columns 1, 2 and 3 in Figure 24–2, we can see that activity A is the first activity. It precedes everything else and must be completed before activities B, D, F, and L can begin. This is shown in Figure 24–3 by the "burst" of activities B, D, F, and L not being able to start until after A is completed at node ②.

At the other end of the project, activity K is the last activity, and it cannot begin until activities L, I, and J have been completed. This is shown in Figure 24–3 by a merge of these three activities before K can begin. Using only columns 1, 2, and 3 in Figure 24–2 and looking at the graphic representation in Figure 24–3, one can see that all of the immediate precedence requirements have been met.

Next, columns 4, 5, and 6 in Figure 24–2 are the three time estimates for each activity. These have been used to calculate column 7's expected times using the formula given above. These expected times have been entered on the network in Figure 24–3.

We are now ready to calculate the early and late starts shown in columns 8 and 9 of Figure 24–2. To do this, we turn to the network shown in Figure 24–4. This is the same network as before but with more information on it. On this network we first draw a ✝ ("tee") at each node or event. Next, beginning at event ① and moving to the right in the network, we put the ES for all activities which burst out of each event on the left side of the tee. (Here we will begin with zero at event ①; later we will see that computer systems use actual dates). For example, the earliest possible starting time (ES) at event ② is simply the ES at event ① plus the expected time (of 4 days) for activity A. It is important to

FIGURE 24–4

PERT network with more information

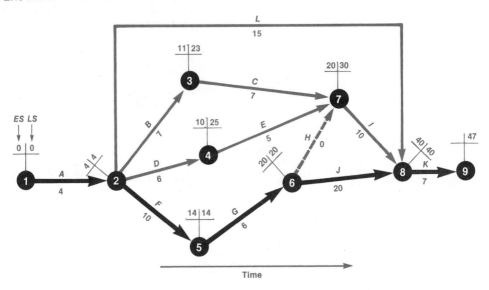

note that these ES's are for all activities bursting from an event. Later we will determine the ES for each activity.

The ES for activity I is the 20th day because it cannot begin until activities C, E, and G (G is dummied through H) are completed. The path through H is longer (20 days) than the paths through C (18 days) or E (15 days), so activity I must wait until G is completed before it can begin. A similar situation occurs at event ⑧. The cumulative time through activity L is only 19 days; through I is 30 days. But through J, it is 40 days, so 40 is the ES for activity K. Since event ⑨ is at the end of the project, it does not have an ES.

The critical path

The *critical path* is the longest path through the network and its time becomes the minimum expected completion time for the entire project. In our example, the alternative paths and their expected completion times are:

Alternate event paths	Total expected completion time	
1 – 2 – 8 – 9	4 + 15 + 7	= 26
1 – 2 – 3 – 7 – 8 – 9	4 + 7 + 7 + 10 + 7	= 35
1 – 2 – 4 – 7 – 8 – 9	4 + 6 + 5 + 10 + 7	= 32
1 – 2 – 5 – 6 – 7 – 8 – 9	4 + 10 + 6 + 0 + 10 + 7	= 37
1 – 2 – 5 – 6 – 8 – 9	4 + 10 + 6 + 20 + 7	= 47

The longest path, that of 1, 2, 5, 6, 8, and 9, takes 47 days. This is the critical path and is indicated by heavy lines in Figures 24–3 and 24–4.

The project can therefore be scheduled to be completed in 47 days.

This becomes the goal and the number 47 is placed on the right side of the tee at node ⑨ . From here we begin to work backwards through the network, from right to left, placing the latest possible start day number (LS) on the right side of each tee. Again there are LS's for all activities which burst from the event, and we will determine each activity's LS later. The LS at event ⑧ of 40 is simply $47 - 7$, the expected time for activity K. Similarly, the LS for activity I is $40 - 10 = 30$. This tells us that activity I could start as late as the 30th day and not cause the overall project to be late. Similarly, C could start as late as the 23rd day; E the 25th day; and B and D could also delay their starting.

However, the correct LS for events ⑥ and ② require some further analysis. Since the LS at event ⑥ is for all activities which burst from it, we must choose the most limiting. The LS coming back through H is $30 - 0 = 30$; through J it is $40 - 20 = 20$. Since the LS through J is smaller, this becomes the LS for event ⑥ . The LS for event ② is similarly constrained by the path back through activity F and is $14 - 10 = 4$. It can be seen in Figure 24–4 that for all events in the critical path, the ES and LS dates are the same. This is always so since activities can't be started any sooner because earlier activities are not completed nor can following activities be started later because then the project will not finish in time.

Slack

Slack is the amount of "play" in the system. When one activity can be finished before the next activity has to start, there is a slack period during which the next activity could be started, but it doesn't have to be started so soon. Slack is thus the time that an activity can be delayed in starting without delaying the completion of the entire project provided that the activities which precede the activity have not been delayed beyond their earliest finish, EF, date. The total slack for each activity is computed as follows: (LS of ending event) − (expected completion time) − (ES of beginning event) = total slack. The slack for each activity in our example is:

Activity	LS at ending event		Expected time		ES at beginning event		Total slack
A	4	−	4	−	0	=	0
B	23	−	7	−	4	=	12
C	30	−	7	−	11	=	12
D	25	−	6	−	4	=	15
E	30	−	5	−	10	=	15
F	14	−	10	−	4	=	0
G	20	−	6	−	14	=	0
H	30	−	0	−	20	=	10
I	40	−	10	−	20	=	10
J	40	−	20	−	20	=	0
K	47	−	7	−	40	=	0
L	40	−	15	−	4	=	21

The total slack for all activities on the critical path is always zero if the desired completion time of the project is the same as the earliest expected completion time. In our example, if the desired completion time for the project were 50 days, instead of 47 days, all activities on the critical path would share 3 days of total slack.

Total slack does not often belong solely to one single activity. It is more often shared among adjacent activities along a path. For example, both B and C have slack of 12 days; however, if B is delayed in starting by 4 days or if it goes slowly and takes 4 days extra, then it takes 11 days instead of 7. This uses up 4 days of the 12 days slack and leaves only 8 days of slack for activity C. This also affects I's slack, reducing it to 6 days. If B's finishing were delayed 4 days and C were delayed by 7 days more, this would reduce I's slack to −1, and the whole project would fall 1 day behind schedule.

Determining the ES and LS for each activity

The early start, ES, for each activity is simply the ES on the left side of the tee at its beginning event. The latest start, LS, for each activity is simply the ES at its beginning event (the right side of the tee) plus the activity's slack. These are shown in column 8 in Figure 24–2.

Determining EF and LF for each activity

Now that we have ES's and LS's for each activity, EF is simply the activity's ES plus its expected time. Similarly, LF is the activity's LS plus its expected time. These are shown in Column 9 in Figure 24–2.

Free slack

Free slack may also exist in a PERT network. It is the amount of time an activity can be delayed without delaying any succeeding activity's ES. For example, activity C could be delayed until the 13th day without violating activity I's ES at the 20th day. On the other hand, if activity D is delayed even one day, then the ES of activity E is also delayed one day. Thus, there is no free slack in D even though it shares 5 days of total slack with E. Free slack for an activity is calculated by subtracting its EF from the ES of all activities to which it is an immediate predecessor.

Probability of meeting PERT schedules

One of PERT's interesting features is that it allows the calculation of the probability that the schedule will be met.[4] Only the critical path is

---

[4] This can be true only if three time values are used for each activity. Many companies use only one time value for each activity and so cannot carry forward this kind of calculation.

FIGURE 24–5

Critical path activities	Pessimistic time	Optimistic time	Difference	Activity's standard deviation	Variance (σ²)	Cumulated variance	Path's standard deviation
A..........	5	3	2	0.33	0.11	0.11	0.33
F..........	21	7	14	2.33	5.43	5.54	2.35
G..........	7	1	6	1.00	1.00	6.54	2.55
J..........	25	15	10	1.67	2.79	9.33	3.05
K..........	12	2	10	1.67	2.79	12.12	3.48

concerned here. For each activity on the critical path, the procedure uses *one sixth* of the difference between the pessimistic time and the optimistic time as an estimate of the standard deviation of the expected activity time (a range of six standard deviations encompasses virtually all the area in a normal distribution).

Since we are concerned only with the likelihood of the whole project finishing on time, we have to compute the probabilities of all of the activities in the critical path, taken together, taking more time or less time than the expected time. To do this, we first (in Figure 24–5) square the standard deviation for each activity to get the "variance" and add these variances cumulatively. Then, we take the square root of these cumulated variances and arrive at the standard deviation of the probable variations in the total time for the project. We can also take the square root of the cumulated variance at any intermediate event in the critical path and get the standard deviation of the expected times up to this event. These standard deviations are shown in Figure 24–5.

It is now possible to see how likely it is that the scheduled completion dates for the whole project or for the successive stages in the critical path will be met. The entire project is expected to take 47 days, and the calculation we just finished tells us that the standard deviation is 3.48 days.

This standard deviation shows that there is a 68-percent probability that the actual time for the project will be between 47 ± 3.48 days, or between 43.52 and 50.48 days. And there is a 95-percent probability that it will be completed in 47 ± 6.96 days. And it is almost certain that the project will be finished in 47 ± 10.44 days.[5]

Suppose that a manager asks the likelihood that the project will be completed in 44 days, or three days ahead of schedule. We can determine the number of standard deviations this is by:

$$\text{Number of standard deviations} = \frac{44 - 47}{3.48} = -.86$$

Going to Appendix E, we find that −.86 of a standard deviation represents about a 20-percent probability. Thus, there is only a 20-percent

---

[5] Based on the characteristics of the "normal" curve where the mean ± 1 standard deviation gives measures which include 68 percent of the cases; ± 2 standard deviation will include 95 percent and ± 3, 99¾ percent.

chance that the project will be completed in 44 days, unless extra resources are made available to speed things up.

If the manager asks about the chances of the project being completed within 55 days, it would be:

$$\frac{55 - 47}{3.48} = +2.29 \text{ standard deviation.}$$

From Appendix E, we find that this results in a likelihood of about 99 percent of the project finishing within 55 days.

The purpose in determining these probabilities is that managers may want to increase the chances of finishing early and so to decide to allocate more resources to activities on the critical path. Conversely, if the project is likely to finish earlier than is needed, resources can be diverted to other work without putting the finishing date for this project in jeopardy. Of course, the validity of these probabilities is based on the assumption that the time estimates are realistic and not under- or overstated. For this (the possibility that the estimates will be somewhat unrealistic) and other reasons, this aspect of PERT has fallen out of favor and is not used much in practice.

PERT/COST

Although PERT is usually thought of as a means for scheduling the timing of activities required by complex projects, it also provides a framework for cost planning and cost control. Every activity that is carried on costs money; so PERT/time and PERT/cost go hand in hand. When a company plans for and schedules an activity, it also estimates its cost so it has cost estimates for each part of the work.

PERT/cost has become increasingly important over the years as people become more aware of its value. Actually, in many cases managers are more interested in the *cost* of a project than in exactly *when* it will be finished. And, as in the case of PERT/time, PERT/cost provides a good control mechanism while projects are under way. Reports of completed activities tell managers when they reach each event point. This gives them frequent opportunities to compare the costs incurred with the expected costs for the work done to date. If the project is running behind on the time schedule or if it is running over the cost estimates, managers learn about it early, perhaps in time to do something to bring the project back on schedule or within the budget.

TIME AND RESOURCE TRADE-OFFS

PERT activities are actually work load assignments and are not directly calendar time assignments. Yet, they are usually shown as work which will take a certain amount of calendar time. These times are based on the expected commitment of normally used resources to the activity.

FIGURE 24–6

Event milestones with activities shaded to show the kind of resources needed

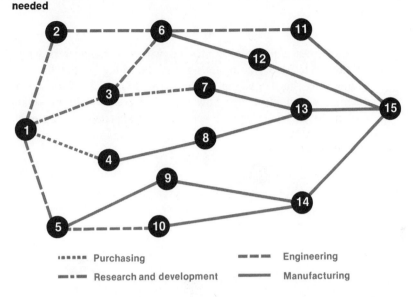

```
•••••• Purchasing              ▬ ▬ ▬ Engineering
▬ • ▬ Research and development  ▬▬▬▬ Manufacturing
```

There is a problem here, however. One hundred labor-hours of work will take 100 hours of clock time if one person is assigned to do the work. But, if 100 people are assigned, this same activity would become a one-clock-hour job. There is usually, therefore, a possibility of a trade-off between resources committed to an activity and the calendar time it will take (see Figure 24–6). Workers on noncritical path work, for example, might be transferred to critical path activities and thus shorten the calendar time required and possibly at no additional total resource cost. Slowing down the noncritical activity is possible because of the slack in the noncritical paths.

In many cases, unfortunately, resources are not wholly transferable because they are not interchangeable in use. If an activity could use more machines and machine operators, neither of the kind needed may be available.

Another problem is that sometimes both the expected time has elapsed and the money set aside for an activity is spent; yet, the activity is not complete. The work is taking longer and is costing more than was planned. Time slippages can usually be made up if more resources are assigned to the late activity. Ordinarily, almost any activity can be speeded up by assigning more people to it, by working overtime, by using air express to get needed parts or otherwise using more resources. And almost every activity can be speeded up by relaxing some of the technical specifications. And, occasionally, work which was planned to be done in sequence can, in part, be done concurrently.

Cost slippages, on the other hand, usually can be made up only at the cost of a sacrifice in quality in other activities.

"CRASHING"

Sometimes a problem comes up where a manager is willing to trade off the costs of extra inputs against the value of the time saved. Some people call this "crashing" a network. Figure 24–7 is a simple PERT diagram which illustrates how time and costs might be related. All but one of the activities can be "crashed" or speeded up, although at a cost.

FIGURE 24–7

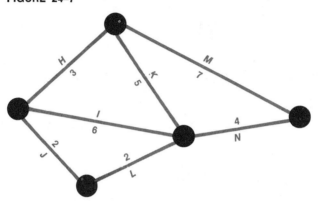

Activity sequence H–K–N is the critical path and requires $3 + 5 + 4 =$ 12 days. The analyst estimates that K's time can be reduced (as is shown in Figure 24–8) as much as two days at a cost of $40 for each day saved. Reducing K by 1 day will allow the whole project to be finished in 11 days at an extra of $40. Still another day can be cut off K for another $40 in cost. This would reduce the critical path to ten days.

But at ten days, I–N and H–M also take ten days, as well as H–K–N. All three paths are now critical to any further time reduction. To get

FIGURE 24–8

Activity	Normal		Crash basis		Cost per day to save days
	Days	Dollars	Days	Dollars	
H...................	3	$ 50	2	$ 100	$50
I....................	6	140	4	260	60
J....................	2	25	1	50	25
K....................	5	100	3	180	40
L....................	2	80	2	80	—
M....................	7	115	5	175	30
N....................	4	100	2	240	70
Total.............		$610		$1,085	

down to nine days, it will be necessary to reduce both H and N because K can't be reduced any farther.

Cutting both H and N one day would cost $120, but K would then need to be cut only one day, so there would be an offsetting savings of $40, making the net added cost become $80. To get down to eight days, it would be necessary to cut M and N another day, each at a cost of $100. To get to seven days, it would be necessary to cut I, K, and M at a cost of $350.

Should the managers make the time cuts proposed for these crash costs? This would depend on the value of the time saved. If we were talking about repairing a machine which is out of production and costing $60 a day every day it does not operate, then the trade-offs are as follows:

FIGURE 24–9

	Days					
	7	8	9	10	11	12
Cost of repairs...............	$1,000	$ 870	$ 770	$ 690	$ 650	$ 610
Cost of production loss........	420	480	540	600	660	720
Total....................	$1,420	$1,350	$1,310	$1,290	$1,310	$1,330

This analysis shows that activity K should be put on a crash program aiming for a ten-day completion. This will hold costs down to $1,290, less than the cost of any other program.

COMPUTERIZED PERT SYSTEMS

As mentioned earlier, most users of PERT use computer programs to aid both in the development of the initial activities network (which is almost never developed graphically because it would be too complex) and to monitor the progress of the project as it is carried forward. Most computer manufacturers have PERT "packages" available for their customers to use. PERT, in use, takes the form of lengthy computer printouts, part of one of which is shown in Figure 24–10.

For large project management, "batch" type packages are normally used. "Batch" here means that all of the required information is first developed and put into punched cards. The initial PERT networks are developed and analyzed by means of batch runs of these cards through the computer.

Further refinements, updates, and changes are then usually made in subsequent weekly batch reruns as the project unfolds. On critical activities, the computer can, of course, print up-to-the-minute reports at any time. Figure 24–10 shows a sample printed sheet of PERT data. It also shows a simple bar time chart as developed by the computer.

FIGURE 24–10

Computer generated PERT report

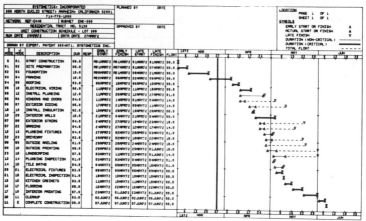

Source: Systonetics, Inc.

On-line PERT systems—MINIPERT

Occasionally the few days' delay in receiving timely information from weekly update runs of PERT data are costly, in which case an on-line PERT system might better be used so that the project can be monitored in "real time." This allows problems to be spotted quickly and corrective action taken quickly. But an on-line PERT system is costly.

To handle this difficulty, IBM has developed an on-line package, which it calls MINIPERT, which is designed to plan and control in detail small projects or subparts of large projects of up to some 200 activities. All inputs and reports go through a terminal so the project's status is in real time and the computer's data file is always kept up to date. The program also pays attention to the kind and amount of resources needed for each activity and thus calls attention to places where more resources of a given kind would speed up the activity if that kind of resource is available. The program essentially regards an activity as a "resource load" which can translate into a short or a long calendar time, depending on the resources committed.

PERT ADVANTAGES

More than any other technique, PERT gives project managers some degree of control over difficult-to-estimate projects and over projects which are surrounded by technological uncertainty. By forcing them to think of the parts of the whole and how they link together, PERT forces managers into making time and cost estimates for individual parts of the whole. Doing this seems to produce greater overall accuracy.

PERT also helps minimize the "crash everything" attitude. It answers questions such as: If there is a delay in an activity, will the whole project be delayed? And if so, how much? PERT also avoids the frequent and lengthy meetings needed for coordination. And it cuts down on cross-checking unrelated activities.

PERT helps detect problems while things are still in the planning stage. It shows, ahead of time, which activities need the most attention so they will not hold up other activities. It also points to bottleneck activities which may have to be speeded up even on a crash basis. PERT also reveals the existence of near-critical paths. They too need watching because a minor holdup in one of their activities will make *them* become the critical path instead of the original critical path. And in the case of holdups in noncritical path activities, PERT shows whether the slack in those paths is enough to absorb the delay or whether costly speeding-up action needs to be taken.

Critical path analyses sometimes surprise managers. On one construction project, Du Pont's engineers thought that labor and overtime would be the factors critical to its completion date. However, the analysis showed that these factors were unimportant and that the tight factors were the electrical design time and the delivery dates of certain equipment. As a result, they readjusted the sequence of electrical equipment installation and saved 21 days, enabling them to begin production three weeks sooner.

Aerojet-General found, when developing one of the early Polaris missiles, that its new fiberglass motor casing was taking longer to develop than was planned. PERT showed that this would probably delay the project for three months. The warning came early enough to give time to switch back to an earlier type of steel casing and avert the delay.

PERT also sets up progress checkpoints. As reports of completed work are made, they are entered into the computer, which compares the progress of each activity with its planned progress. If any chain of activities is falling behind (if there is any "slippage"), PERT reports it. Managers find out about slippages right away before very much harm to the program has been done.

Still another advantage of PERT is that it can be used to simulate certain conditions so that a manager can see how a whole network will be affected if less or more time is spent on certain activities.

PERT has the peculiar characteristic (which can be bad as well as good) of being self-validating to some extent. Because it provides dates for subsidiary events, everybody works toward them and so meets them. The bad part is the failure to move as rapidly as they should in case the expected times are too loose.

PERT can often be abandoned in the last stages of a project. By then, there are only a few things left to do, and they can be watched without the aid of PERT. PERT is most useful in the early stages when hundreds or thousands of activities have to be coordinated.

PERT DISADVANTAGES

By no means is everyone "sold" on PERT. Most building contractors do not seem to like it because they say it doesn't help them. They know how long it takes to build a building. They say that PERT only requires duplicate planning.

There are also critics at the other end of the line, out where projects are near technical frontiers—where PERT is supposed to be at its best. Yet Joseph Freitag of Hughes Aircraft says that it is not possible to use PERT to control or coordinate changes in the configuration of complex electronic projects because this work "is just not networkable." Nor do time estimates for uncertain activities become any more certain from statistical manipulation.

Some managers resist PERT because they see it as taking away part of their jobs. Construction superintendents like to be fountainheads of all knowledge about how long work will take and how the delay of one activity might affect the whole project. And it is true that when a project is made the subject of a PERT analysis and put in a computer this takes away part of a superintendent's need to judge. When PERT is first introduced, the resistance it sometimes meets (which may almost amount to sabotage) may make it almost useless. Most companies report that such opposition soon disappears, but there may be trouble at first.

Some people find fault with PERTs use of three time values. An International Telephone & Telegraph official says that asking people for pessimistic estimates only gives them a built-in excuse for failure. IT&T built a post office building in Providence, Rhode Island, and, when part of the work fell behind, the people responsible said: "I told you that it might take that long."

Another objection to PERT is that almost always pessimistic times vary more from the most likely times than do the optimistic times. The weighted average, therefore, is always biased toward a longer time than the most likely time, and this puts unintended and unwanted slack into all calculations.

Some critics of PERT don't like it because it forces people to estimate times for activities. They say that when a manager presses people to make estimates, they will put in a "fudge" factor and that time estimates will be too liberal. If this happens, none of the ensuing calculations rectify the inaccuracies. Worse yet, liberal estimates may make people work toward minimum performance (since that is all the program calls for) and no more. Perhaps this objection has more validity for PERT/time than for PERT/cost because overliberal cost estimates boost bid prices and lose contracts.

Still another objection to PERT is the cost of reviewing all the reports every week or so to see where things stand. PERT can help only when it is up to date, and this means frequent computer reviews of the data at considerable cost.

There are still other objections to PERT, but most of them are simply complaints that it is not a perfect tool. PERT does not, for example, show if the company *has* the resources the project will need. Nor does it reveal whether the project will need the same resources for different activities at the same time. Nor does PERT reveal if resources are interchangeable.

PERT also makes it look like things have to be done in sequence when, in fact, they can often be overlapped or done in parallel. It is not always necessary to complete one activity before starting the next one. And after projects get under way, PERT reports delays but doesn't reveal very much about causes. Nor does it show up delays until after the activities are supposed to have been started or completed.

PERT does not in itself provide a level work schedule because it pays no attention to the work load it creates in relationship to departmental capacities and work loads caused by other jobs. PERT doesn't work well if the priorities of different projects are changed very much. Nor does it solve the problem of low-priority jobs getting pushed back forever.

PERT is limited in the detail it is practical to report. Rarely should minor details, which take only hours or days, be charted. So PERT does not show everything. Nor are charts updated all the time. It is often too costly to produce new charts frequently, even with computer systems.

Yet, in spite of the list of objections just given, PERT has "arrived" and is widely used. The Department of Defense used to require all of its major contractors to use it on all new projects (this is no longer required of companies which plan well). Industry in general has also taken to PERT. Merck, Sharp, and Dohme uses it for new project planning. Ford Motor uses it when tooling up for new models. Chrysler uses it at every stage in the planning and building of all new plants. PERT has also been used by builders of apartment buildings, bridges, and roads. Small contractors as well as large are among today's PERT users.

RENEWED INTEREST IN PERT

After being developed in the late 1950s, PERT applications grew in popularity through the 1960s, but then interest in it seemed to wane through the first half of the 1970s, primarily for the reasons mentioned above. However, a rediscovery of PERT seems to have taken place in recent years. Much of the credit for this renewed interest comes from the development and availability of improved PERT systems which simplify the initial development of the PERT network and provide more efficient ways to use this information to manage projects.

Modularized PERT

Further, new applications are being developed. Fluor Engineering, for example, uses "modularized" PERT to help them prepare bids for projects such as nuclear power plants. While a power plant may require about 5,000 activities, these can be summarized into perhaps 200–300 "modules" or major components to be built. For example, a power project may need a certain class of pump but with special features required for this particular project.

At Fluor, a catalog of modular or subnetworks has been developed which shows the activities, estimated times, and costs for a number of these generalized major components. The design engineer can look up the modular network for the "generalized pump" in question, see what is involved, and adjust the times and activities for the changes which may be needed for the *specific* pump required. Further, the catalog of modular networks shows "linkages" to other modules. This approach allows design engineers to develop more precise project bids (which include time tables for completion) in a matter of days instead of months.

DART

DART means daily automatic rescheduling technique.[6] It is a variation of PERT which has been developed by the Air Force for use in airplane repair work. It can also be used for scheduling work on other complex yet somewhat individually unique products.

For repair purposes, each airplane is considered to be unique. The work to be done on each airplane depends on the hours it has flown, the number of engineering changes to be made, unpredictable damage, and the modifications necessary to remodel the airplane to adapt it for specific missions.

The purpose of DART is to control the allocation of the three kinds of resources to be used: (1) time-consumed resources (job sequence, labor, and work areas), (2) use-consumed resources (parts, supplies, and kit materials), and (3) nonconsumed resources (facilities, tools, and data).

The DART system starts with a PERT type master network which covers all of the work which an aircraft could possibly require. This master network is then remade. Parts of it are cut out, and it is tailored for each airplane so that it becomes that particular airplane's individual and unique PERT network.

The DART plan also embodies a summation of the resource requirements of the several or many individual PERT networks for the several airplanes being repaired. Whenever too much of any resource is called for, the individual airplane's PERT networks are redone and stretched out over more time so that they reflect the time when the master resource allocation schedule will allow the work to be done.

Such rescheduling is done in accord with a priority list which assigns critical work early priority code numbers. Reports of work done are made daily to the central scheduling office. There each aircraft's progress record is updated daily. If any are falling behind, the reasons are promptly investigated and the causes removed as soon as possible.

Both the individual networks and the overall DART work load summary are updated daily. This allows for a constant review and for

6 A good description of the DART procedure appears in Bob Gessner, "DART— Description and Implementation Consideration," *Production & Inventory Management,* 1st quarter 1969, pp. 51–56.

changing priorities according to current situations. Thus, DART is a working tool which continually monitors the use of resources and redirects them wherever they are needed the most.

REVIEW QUESTIONS

1. Differentiate between planning for projects and planning for repetitive activities.
2. How is PERT similar to assembly line balancing methods discussed in Chapter 11? How is it different?
3. Network planning methods such as PERT work best on what kinds of activities? Give a few examples.
4. How far down into detail and subdetails should PERT analyses be carried?
5. Can an analyst calculate the probable time for completing a project covered by a PERT plan if the plan is used only one time for activities? Can the analyst tell how probable it will be that the project might be finished one week earlier even if no effort to speed up is made? Or does the analyst need three time estimates for each activity in order to answer either of these questions?
6. If PERT activities are truly *work load* assignments, why are they so universally spoken of in terms of the calendar time they will take? Isn't the time a direct function of the resource inputs? Discuss.
7. If PERT reports show that cost slippages are occurring, how can managers pick up this slippage and so end up doing the whole project within the planned cost limits?
8. It is sometimes possible to shorten a project's completion time but at a cost trade-off for the time gained. Explain how this works and show how far it can be carried.
9. Why do many people not like PERT?
10. Why is there a renewed interest in using PERT?
11. Differentiate between batch and on-line PERT systems. When is each most appropriately used?

QUESTIONS FOR DISCUSSION

1. How can a system like PERT help in setting time schedules for hard-to-plan activities, such as designing? It is just not possible to tell how long such things will take? Or is this possible?
2. PERT does not unearth the critical resources needed to accomplish the work along the critical path (or does it?). So it really cannot help to get the work done on time. Is this so? Discuss.
3. How can a manager tell, during the *assembly* part of the work on big projects, whether the work is up to schedule or not? Also, how can he tell whether it is running ahead or behind the cost budget? Fur-

thermore, if it is behind either timewise or costwise, what can he do about it?

4. Valuable though PERT is on giant projects, it is still costly to rerun it on the computer every few days. Yet it would have to be rerun often if it were to be a very helpful managerial tool.

   a. How can a manager judge the cost value of reruns of PERT?

   b. Suppose that the manager is not concerned with the costliness of rerunning PERT; in this case how often should it be rerun? Why?

5. Conceivably every path could become the critical path. And near-critical paths may need just about as much attention as the critical path. How does PERT handle the possibility of other paths becoming critical paths?

PROBLEMS

1. The following information covers part of a large PERT diagram:

Starting event	Following event	Expected time (weeks)	Starting event	Following event	Expected time (weeks)
A	C	11	D	H	12
A	D	6	E	F	2
B	D	5	F	H	8
C	E	7	F	I	12
C	F	5	G	H	4
D	F	9	H	I	8
D	G	10			

What is the critical path and how many weeks will it take to complete this work?

2. What is the critical path in the following set of related jobs? How long will it take to get the work done? If we could cut three days off the longest job in the critical path, how would this affect the solution? If there is a new critical path, what is it?

Event sequence	Time in days	Event sequence	Time in days
1–2	6	5–8	7
1–3	4	5–10	8
1–4	5	6–7	7
2–5	7	6–9	3
2–7	6	7–10	9
3–5	8	7–8	3
3–7	10	8–11	8
4–6	4	9–10	6
		10–11	5

3. Suppose that in problem 1 there were the following variances:

Activity	Variance (weeks)	Activity	Variance (weeks)
A–C	4	D–H	5
A–D	3	E–F	1
B–D	3	F–H	3
C–E	2	F–I	6
C–F	1	G–H	1
D–F	3	H–I	1
D–G	4		

What are the time limits within which there is a 95-percent chance of the work being completed? What are the extreme times that might possibly occur according to the figures in our problem?

4. Suppose, in problem 1, that it would be possible to shorten A–C to 6, C–E to 5, D–F to 6, D–H to 10, and G–H to 3. Which of these changes, if any, would affect the critical path? How long will the new critical path take?

5. Suppose, in problem 1, that it would be possible by putting on extra workers to shorten the times for the activities at the following extra costs:

Activity	Possible time reduction	Cost per week gained	Activity	Possible time reduction	Cost per week gained
A–C	2	$100	D–H	2	$500
A–D	2	400	E–F	0	—
B–D	1	300	F–H	1	200
C–E	3	200	F–I	3	100
C–F	1	100	G–H	0	—
D–F	1	300	H–I	1	300
D–G	3	300			

a. If it were highly important to save all the time possible, regardless of cost, which activities should be shortened? What would the new critical path be? How long would it take? How much would it cost to make the necessary reductions?

b. If there were a $1,000 limit on the amount that could be spent to move things along faster, what would the answers be to the questions in (a)?

6. The following data are from a large PERT diagram:

Immediately preceding	Event	Immediately following
—......................	0	1, 2
0........................	1	3
0........................	2	3
1, 2.....................	3	4, 5, 6
3, 5, 6..................	4	8, 9, 10
3........................	5	4
3........................	6	4, 7
6........................	7	9
4, 12....................	8	13
4, 7.....................	9	11, 12
4.........................	10	11, 12
9, 10....................	11	15
9, 10....................	12	8, 13
8, 12....................	13	14
13.......................	14	15
11, 14...................	15	—

Here are the expected times (in weeks) to complete each activity and the expected times.

Event sequence	Time	Event sequence	Time	Event sequence	Time
0–1...........	4–6–8	4–9...........	1–3–4	9–12..........	1–2–3
0–2...........	6–7–10	4–10..........	2–2–3	10–11.........	4–6–9
1–3...........	1–1–2	5–4...........	1–1–2	10–12.........	1–2–4
2–3...........	1–2–3	6–4...........	1–1–1	11–15.........	2–3–4
3–4...........	3–4–6	6–7...........	1–3–6	12–8..........	5–7–10
3–5...........	1–3–5	7–9...........	3–4–6	12–13.........	1–3–5
3–6...........	2–3–5	8–13..........	1–2–3	13–14.........	1–2–3
4–8...........	5–6–8	9–11..........	3–4–5	14–15.........	4–6–9

Draw up a PERT diagram showing these relationships.

What is the critical path? How many weeks will it take? What are the maximum and minimum probable limits? If this path could be shortened by four weeks, what path would then become critical? How long should it take and what is its probable maximum?

What are the chances that the project will finish two weeks early without any extra effort having been put forth?

7. Visit a local building contractor and gather the necessary information to PERT a typical construction project, analyze it, and write a non-technical report for the contractor explaining your results and how he should proceed in implementing the technique and what costs and benefits are expected.

8. For the following situation, draw a PERT network, and determine the following (add dummy activities where required):
 a. Critical path.
 b. Early start, late start, early finish, late finish.
 c. Total slack.
 d. Free slack.

    e. What would happen if the following time and precedence changes were revised as more information became available:

    (1) Activity A's pessimistic time increased to 8?

    (2) Activities A, D, G, and F's realistic and pessimistic time each increased 20 percent?

    (3) The total time allowed to complete the project was extended four days longer than the duration of the critical path(s)?

    f. Given the answers obtained in Parts a.–d., suppose the project had had fixed costs per day of $1,000. Also, suppose you could reduce the length of the project's duration by expediting (shortening) certain activity's expected times at a given cost per day down to some minimum number of days.

Given the information provided in the last two columns, what would you recommend? *Hint:* Expedite only those activities which are critical and will produce a net savings in fixed costs. When expediting, other activities may become critical as their slack is eaten away. When this occurs, you may have to reduce two or more activities simultaneously in order to reduce the project's duration and reduce fixed costs.

Activity	Immediate precedence requirements	Optimistic time	Realistic time	Pessimistic time	Expedite cost* per day	Minimum expected* completion time
A.	—	1	1	1	$ 900	1
B.	A	3	6	8	400	2
C.	A	4	5	6	700	3
D.	A	2	3	4	800	3
E.	A	9	9	15	—	—
F.	B	7	8	8	300	5
G.	B	4	7	9	500	3
H.	C	1	3	9	700	3
I.	D	5	6	7	—	—
J.	H, F, G	3	4	8	1,100	2
K.	H, I	2	3	7	650	3
L.	H, I	7	7	8	300	4
M.	D	8	9	15	—	—
N.	M	10	15	17	1,400	7
O.	M	3	6	9	600	4
P.	D	6	12	13	550	7
Q.	M	8	9	12	980	4
R.	P, Q	3	6	7	—	—
S.	O, R	7	8	12	—	—
T.	J, K, L, N	6	7	12	520	5
U.	J, K	4	5	5	—	—
V.	J, K	2	2	2	100	1
W.	E, S, T, U, V	5	6	9	—	—
X.	E, S, T, U, V	9	10	10	650	3
Y.	W	3	4	6	50	2
Z.	X, Y	7	8	9	250	4

*These columns are to be used to answer part *f.* of this problem.

9. Develop a PERT network for planning a play which will be produced in your community or college.

SUGGESTED SUPPLEMENTARY READINGS

Bobrowski, Thomas M. "A Basic Philosophy of Project Management." *Journal of Systems Management,* May 1974, pp. 30–32.

Bures, J. P. "Time-Framing a PERT Chart." *Management Accounting,* October 1974, pp. 24–26.

Khtaian, G. A. "Computer Project Management—Proposal, Design, and Programming Phases." *Journal of Systems Management,* August 1976, pp. 12–21.

25

Linear programming

LINEAR programming is a widely used operations research method which is a member of a family of techniques called mathematical programming. In general, mathematical programming methods are designed to allocate limited resources among competing alternative uses for these resources so that some predetermined objective—usually maximizing profit or minimizing costs—is satisfied or optimized.

The term "linear" in linear programming means that the relationships between factors are approximately linearly related or constant. Linear relationships means that when one factor changes so does another and by a constant amount. An hourly paid employee's working hours and wages are linear: the more hours, the more total wages. Linearity can also be negative; the more there is of one thing, the less there is of another. If a person starts with $20, the more he spends on something, the less he has left.

AUTOMOBILE MANUFACTURE: A GRAPHIC SOLUTION

We will illustrate linear programming by using an example of an automobile assembly factory. To keep the problem simple, we will assume that this factory makes only two models: a two-door six-cylinder car and an eight-cylinder station wagon. We will deal with three manufacturing departments: metal stamping, engine assembly, and final assembly. In the final assembly department there are two assembly lines: one for two-door cars and one for station wagons. Both can operate at the same time.

The stamping department can, in a week, turn out enough parts for 7,000 two-door cars or 12,000 station wagons. But it can't do both at the same time. It is possible to do one *or* the other or to make parts for *some* two-door cars and *some* station wagons. It is the same with engines. It is possible to produce 9,000 six-cylinder engines which are used only in the two-door cars, or 6,000 eight-cylinder engines which are used only in station wagons, or to have some six's and some eight's.

The two-door car assembly line can turn out 6,000 cars as a maximum. And the station wagon line's maximum capacity is 4,000. Here, however, both lines can operate at the same time. Increasing the output of one line does not require reducing the other.

These limitations impose several "constraints" to the possible choices in production quantities. In summary, these are:

Departments	*Maximum number for two-door cars*		*Maximum number for station wagons*
Metal stamping................	7,000	or	12,000
Engine assembly..............	9,000	or	6,000
Final assembly................	6,000	and	4,000

No one limitation sets limits for all possible combinations. It is possible, at one extreme, to make 9,000 six-cylinder engines, the kind used in the two-door cars, but there is no need to make this many six-cylinder engines since only 6,000 two-door cars can be assembled. Assembly limitations would rule here.

It is also possible, so far as assembly is concerned, to assemble 4,000 station wagons as well as the 6,000 two-door cars. But actually this can't be done because it is not possible to make enough stamped parts or engines. The stamping capacity will allow making parts for 6,000 two-door cars, but, if this is done, then there is not enough stamping capacity left to make parts for 4,000 station wagons. Nor could enough engines be made to permit making the maximum assembly quantities of each kind of car at the same time.

All of the possible maximum quantity mixes can be defined by using the "linear rate of substitution" between two-door cars and station wagons. For stampings, this rate of substitution is 7,000/12,000, or .5833. For every one station wagon that we stamp parts for, we could instead stamp parts for .5833 two-door cars. Thus, if we stamp enough parts for 6,000 two-door cars, or 1,000 under the maximum of 7,000, we could also stamp enough parts for 1,715 station wagons (1,000/.5833).

Similarly, for engines, for every eight-cylinder engine, we could make instead 9,000/6,000, or 1.5 six-cylinder engines. So, if we made 6,000 six-cylinder engines, this would leave enough additional capacity to make 3,000 more six-cylinder engines, or 2,000 eight-cylinder engines (3,000/1.5).

These relationships can be stated in the form of constraint equations.

If we let T equal the number of two-door cars we can make, and W the number of station wagons, then the stampings department constraint is:

$$T + .5833W \le 7,000$$

For the engine department, the constraint equation is:

$$T + 1.5W \le 9,000$$

Figure 25–1 shows the area of feasible solutions for stamping production. The enclosed area encompasses all possible combinations of two-door cars and station wagons which can be stamped. The diagonal sloping line is the constraint and defines the "linear rate of substitution" between the two models. Any combination of numbers of two-doors and station wagons which falls on the diagonal line will keep the stamping department fully occupied. Combinations within the enclosed area are also possible but will not keep the department busy.

Figure 25–2 shows the solution feasibilities for the engine department. Again, the diagonal line sets off the maximum production combinations. And again, lesser combinations are feasible even though they would not keep the engine department busy, so slack would occur.

The two other constraints, the assembly capacity for each kind of car, are shown in Figure 25–3. These constraint lines are not mutually dependent on each other, and one cannot be substituted for the other so there is no rate of substitution. Again, the enclosed area encompasses the feasible combinations so far as these two constraints are concerned. The constraint equations for the two assembly lines are:

$$T \le 6,000$$
$$W \le 4,000$$

Now that we have determined the maximum capacity of each department, we are ready to determine how many of each model we should

FIGURE 25–1

Stamping department feasibility area

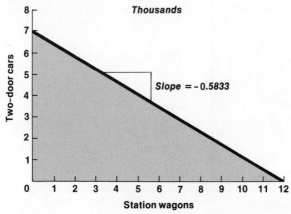

FIGURE 25–2

Engine making feasibility area

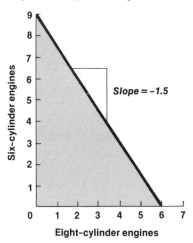

Eight-cylinder engines

schedule for production. We will assume that we can sell all that we can produce and so want to choose the product mix which will yield the largest total contribution. The contribution per unit, it will be recalled from Chapter 2, is the selling price per unit minus the variable cost per unit. In our example, the contribution is $300 for each two-door car and $400 for every station wagon. This means that the contribution from selling 1 station wagon is the same as it is for 1.33 two-doors.

FIGURE 25–3

**Assembly department
feasibility area**

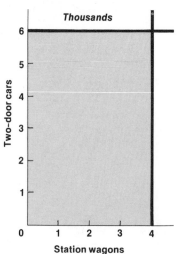

Station wagons

FIGURE 25–4

"Iso-contribution" lines

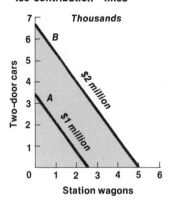

So we have a linear rate of substitution for contribution between the two models of −1.33. This can be depicted graphically by drawing in "iso-contribution" lines one for each contribution total. There could be any number of such lines each for different amounts of money. Two of them, one which shows the sales volume relationships which would produce a total contribution of $1 million and the other $2 million, are shown in Figure 25–4. For example, selling 3,333 two-doors and no wagons produces $1 million as does the other extreme of selling 2,500 wagons and no two-doors. Similarly, $2 million in total contribution would occur at any combination of two-doors and station wagons along the B line in Figure 25–4. If, for example, we sold 5,000 two-doors this would bring in $1.5 million leaving $500 thousand to come from station wagons. At $400 each, sales of wagons would have to be 1,250 to produce the $2 million.

There is a whole family of "iso-contribution" lines for this problem, all having the same slope. The lines closer to the origin produce less total contribution; those farther out, more. Since we wish to maximize the contribution, we want to find how far out (how far to the right) we can draw the iso-contribution line, yet still have it touch one point in the feasibility area. The equation for the iso-contribution line for our problem (which is also called the "objective function") is:

$$\text{Maximize } F = \$300T + \$400W$$

This says find a combination of quantities of T and W which, when multiplied by their respective per unit contributions, will result in a greater total contribution than that produced by any other combination of T and W. The four equations needed to solve this problem are those shown above.

Figure 25–5 combines the first four charts into one. The enclosed area A–B–C–D–E encompasses all possible feasible solutions to the prob-

FIGURE 25–5

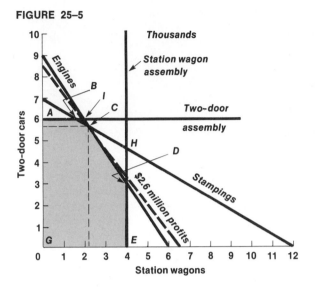

lem. Note that some of our earlier feasible solution areas have been
eliminated because some constraints allow fewer units than others. This
final solution area, which is shaded, is called the "feasible region." The
iso-profit line for $2.591 million touches the feasible solution area at its
maximum point, C.

It is feasible to make two-door cars and station wagons in any of the
infinite number of combinations in the shaded area. We can make 6,000
two-door cars and no station wagons (point A), or 6,000 two-door cars
and anywhere up to 1,715 station wagons (point B). But from there on,
in order to get any more station wagons, it will be necessary to reduce
two-door cars because the stamping department is up to its capacity.
The rate of this substitution as defined earlier is the slope of the line. For
each .5833 two-doors we give up, we can stamp parts for 1 more station
wagon. By the time we get down to 5,727 two-door cars and up to 2,183
station wagons (point C), we run into engine department limitations.
From this point on, as two-doors are cut in order to increase station wagons, engines limit us until we reduce station wagons to 4,000 (point D).
By this time we are down to 3,000 two-door cars. From here on station
wagons can be increased no more because 4,000 is the maximum limit for
assembling station wagons. Even if we cut two-door cars below 3,000, we
could not make any more station wagons.

So far, we have seen how the constraints determine the trade-off between two-doors and station wagons. The plant is operating at its full
capacity in at *least one* department at any point on the line connecting the
corner points A, B, C, D, and E. At points B, C, and D, the plant is
operating at full capacity in the *two* departments defined by this corner
and has excess capacity, or slack, in the other two.

The real goal, however, is not just to keep departments busy but to maximize contributions.

Determining the optimal solution

To determine the optimal solution, we have to find the value of point C in Figure 25–5. This is the point where the stamping department and the engine department lines cross and where both are working at capacity. They are the constraining factors since neither of the assembly lines is working up to capacity. As we already know, the equation for the engines line on Figure 25–5 is: $T + 1.5W = 9,000$ and the equation for stampings is: $T + .5833W = 7,000$. To find the value of point C, we have to solve these two equations simultaneously. This we do by multiplying equation (2) by -1 and adding it to equation (1), thus eliminating the T factor from the equations.

$$
\begin{array}{llrr}
(1) & T + 1.5000W = & 9,000 \\
(2) & -T - 0.5833W = & -7,000 \\
\hline
 & .9167W = & 2,000 \\
\text{At point C:} & W = & 2,180
\end{array}
$$

Substituting 2,180 into equation (1):

$$
\begin{array}{ll}
 & T + 1.5(2,180) = 9,000 \\
\text{At point C:} & T = 5,730
\end{array}
$$

The solution at point C is therefore to make 5,730 two-door cars and 2,180 station wagons. The total contribution realized from this program will be:

$$\$300(5,730) + \$400(2,180) = \$2,591,000$$

Actually this answer should not be accepted as being the best without checking the total contribution of other corners. Figure 25–6 shows the contributions from all of the corner points in our problem.

Slack

While the solution defined by point C uses all of the capacity of the engine and stamping departments, slack capacity remains in the two assembly areas. To calculate this slack, we simply subtract the number of each kind of product in the solution from its assembly capacity. At point C, the two-door assembly department is producing 270 cars less than its capacity, and the station wagon assembly department is 1,820 wagons under its capacity. There is, however, no slack in either the engine or in the assembly departments.

This kind of analysis can be used to aid in managerial decision making. Suppose that it is possible to sell more station wagons if the engine making capacity could be expanded. We could then move to point H in Figure 25–5 and would be assembling 4,000 station wagons.

FIGURE 25–6

	Number of		Total contribution		
				Station	
		Station	Two-doors	wagons	
Point	Two-doors	wagons	($300 each)	($400 each)	Both
A...........	6,000	0	$1,800,000	0	$1,800,000
B...........	6,000	1,715	1,800,000	$ 686,000	2,486,000
C...........	5,730	2,180	1,719,000	872,000	2,591,000
D...........	3,000	4,000	900,000	1,600,000	2,500,000
E...........	0	4,000	0	1,600,000	1,600,000

At point H, the limitations of the stamping department come into play and limit the two-door cars to 4,670. Thus, we would need 1,060 fewer six-cylinder engines than at point C. In total the new engine capacity would have to be capable of making 4,000 eight-cylinder engines plus 4,670 six-cylinder engines, or the equivalent of 10,670 six's or 7,110 eight's. This would require an increase in engine making capacity of 11.9 percent.

Suppose that the company's managers were considering making this expansion, and they find that if they do the charges against the first year's operations would be $350,000. Should they go ahead? The new sum of the contributions would be 4,000 × $400 + 4,670 × $300 = $3,028,000. The present sum is $2,591,000, which shows that this move would increase the contributions by $437,000. This is more than the cost of the expansion, so it should be made.

Sensitivity analysis

Often the most important uses of linear programming are not to find single individual problem solutions, but to use the model to analyze a number of trade-offs by asking "what if" questions. This is called "sensitivity" analysis. It reveals how sensitive the solution is to changes in constraints or values. We might ask, for example, what would happen if we had to cut two-door car prices. Or what would happen if we could reduce the costs of making station wagons. Or we might want to know what the effects would be if we could change the method of producing eight-cylinder engines so that so far as capacity is concerned an eight-cylinder engine would equal 1.25 six-cylinder engines instead of 1.5 six-cylinder engines.

This would mean that eight-cylinder engines would require only 25 percent more resources per unit than six-cylinders instead of the present 50 percent extra. The capacity of the engine department would then remain at 9,000 six-cylinder engines, but the eight-cylinder engine capacity would go up to 7,200. And, again, various product mixes would be possible. It would be possible to calculate how much a change might be worth in terms of added contributions and to compare this against its cost to see if this new process should be installed.

Any time that sales volume is being restricted by a capacity limitation of some constraint, it is possible to make comparisons of the cost of relaxing the constraint and the worth of expanding the capacity of the restraining factor.

Cost minimization

In our automobile example, we found solutions which maximized contributions. Another common use of linear programming is to minimize total costs. The procedure for finding the point of minimum costs is essentially the same as for maximizing income. In the case of cost minimization, however, it is very important not to forget the effects on income. The point of least cost, for example, could easily be the point of no production and no income. A cost minimization problem and its solution using the simplex method is presented in Appendix H.

THE SIMPLEX METHOD

In most problems which can appropriately use linear programming, there may be dozens, hundreds, or, in rare cases, thousands of variables. These require a solution method which can handle these larger number of variables and one which can be programmed for computer solution.

The best known of these methods is the simplex method. It is designed to solve simultaneously a system of linear equations where there are more unknowns than there are equations.

In our automobile production example, where we maximized the monetary contribution, we had six unknowns, or variables. Two of these unknowns were the quantities of the two products; two-door cars and station wagons. These are sometimes called "decision variables" because their amounts are the major things we want to determine.

The other four unknowns, sometimes called "slack variables," were the capacities of the four departments (stamping, engine, two-door assembly, and station wagon assembly). Our procedure in the graphic solution was first to solve for the best mix between the two products by determining the number of each kind of car which could be made out of available resources as defined by each corner of the feasible region. So it was possible for us to solve these equations (at the corners) simultaneously and arrive at the number of each kind of car to produce. And this, in turn, allowed us to calculate the total contribution at each corner and so find the one which maximized contributions.

In algebra, there is a rule which requires that the number of equations must at least equal the number of unknowns in order to obtain answers. Yet, in our automobile example, even though we had six unknowns and only four constraint equations, we were able to solve this problem by choosing which *two* equations to solve at each corner to find solution values for the *two* products. Then, after we had found the optimal solution, we determined each department's slack capacity. Essentially, at each step we were ignoring the other two constraint equations and solving for them later in order to obtain the optimal total solution.

The simplex method solves for all unknowns by choosing at the start of the procedure which two out of the six variables *will* be set at zero and which four variables it will solve for and which four *may* be zero or a positive number. In this way, we have four equations and only four variables or unknowns (the algebraic requirement mentioned earlier) because two of the variables are, for the moment, set at zero. This allows us to get solution values for the other four.

The simplex procedure almost always requires the successive solution of a number of different combinations of four of the six variables (the two originally set at zero may come back into play, one at a time) in order to find the optimal solution. At each step, the method chooses which four out of the six variables it will solve for and which two are set at zero. Essentially, the simplex method searches through combinations of solutions until the best solution is found.

Redefining constraints as equations

It will be recalled that the four constraints were not really equations, except as defined by the limit lines in the graphic solutions. Rather, they were "less than or equal to" constraints since extra or slack capacity was allowed to occur in one or more departments.

We return now to our original example where 1 eight-cylinder engine was equal to 1.5 six-cylinder engines. For engines, our constraint expression was $T + 1.5W \leq 9,000$. To change this "inequality" constant into an equation, we have to add a "slack variable" to it. The equation for the engine department then becomes:

$$T + 1.5W + E = 9,000$$

In this equation, E is the amount of slack capacity (in terms of T's) that exists in the engine department for any solution. If, for example, $T = 1,000$ and $W = 2,000$, then:

$$1,000 + 1.5(2,000) + E = 9,000$$
$$E = 5,000$$

Adding slack variables to the other three constraints in a similar fashion gives us:[1]

Maximize:

$$F = \$300\,T + \$400W$$

Subject to:

---

[1] One other constraint is implied in all linear programming problems: All variables must be greater than or equal to zero.

Engine department	$T +$	$1.5W + E$		$= 9,000$
Stamping department	$T +$	$.5833W$	$+ S$	$= 7,000$
Two-door assembly	T		$+ A_T$	$= 6,000$
Wagon assembly		W	$+ A_W$	$= 4,000$

"F" is the function to be maximized, in this case, the contribution toward profit. E, S, A_T and A_W are the slack variables for each department.

Initial simplex tableau

The next step in the simplex method is to set up an initial simplex tableau or matrix. This is shown in Figure 25–7, which is a computer

FIGURE 25–7

Program provided courtesy Professor George A. Johnson, Idaho State University.

printout of the initial tableau, or "iteration" 0. In Figure 25–7, the computer redefines the factors in our problem into its generalized program language as follows:

1. The variables (T, W, E, S, A_T and A_W) are now called $X(1)$, $X(2)$, $X(3)$, $X(4)$, $X(5)$, and $X(6)$, respectively, where the numbers in the parenthesis are subscripts (e.g., $X(1)$ is the first variable, $X(2)$ is the second, and so on).

2. Only the *coefficients* associated with each variable are shown under the appropriate X column heading. The zeros in a column simply mean that X variable has a zero value for that constraint equation.

3. The contributions ($\$300$ and $\$400$) are called $C(J)$'s, where J is the column number subscript. The zeros over $X(3)$ to $X(6)$ means there is no contribution (or cost) associated with these slack variables.

4. The constant numbers to the right of the equal signs in our equations are under the heading called $B(I)$ on the left where I is the constraint row number subscript.

Initial feasible solution

The simplex method is a step-by-step procedure which moves progressively from a poor solution to a better and then to a still better solution until the best one is found. But the method requires that it start with a "feasible" solution. And, since at the start it is not known what is feasible, the method always starts from zero. In our case, our starting solution will be to make no two-doors and no station wagons. (We are essentially at the origin, point G, in Figure 25–5.) This program will require no capacity in any department and will produce no contribution. *But* this *is* a feasible solution, and the simplex method can use it as a starting point in its step-by-step development of the optimal solution.

In order to use this zero program as its starting point, the simplex method requires being told which variables are to start at exactly zero and which can be more than zero. This is because, if no capacity is required, then the capacity available is slack and has a magnitude. The slack variables will therefore not be zero, but something more than zero. In our initial program, the number of cars and station wagons, the two decision variables, are the two variables which are set at zero. This allows the four slack variables to be more than zero.

Figure 25–7 is a computer run of the first iteration which uses this zero program. Toward the left, the column "BASIS" shows that the initial solution includes the four slack variables, which are now referred to as $X(3)$, $X(4)$, $X(5)$, and $X(6)$. This means, and it is shown by their absence from the BASIS column, that $X(1)$ and $X(2)$ are set at zero.

To the right of the BASIS column is the $B(I)$ column with the values for each of the slack variables. Our starting feasible solution is:

$$X(1) = 0$$
$$X(2) = 0$$
$$X(3) = 9{,}000$$
$$X(4) = 7{,}000$$
$$X(5) = 6{,}000$$
$$X(6) = 4{,}000$$

To the left of the BASIS column in Figure 25–7 is the $C(I)$ column, which is the per unit contribution of the variables in the BASIS. Since there is no contribution from having slack capacity, these $C(I)$ values are all zero. (In more complex problems, slacks may have costs, which can be factored into the problem by including them as negative values in the $C(J)$ row.)

The total contribution of our initial program will, of course, be zero and is shown to be zero in Figure 25–7 by the line at the bottom which says, "Objective function value 0.000." This number is the sum of the per unit contributions in the $C(I)$ column multiplied by the quantities in the $B(I)$ column. We need to know what the process is because this total will not be zero in later iterations.

$$
\begin{array}{cl}
C(I) & B(I) \\
0 \times 9{,}000 = 0 \\
0 \times 7{,}000 = 0 \\
0 \times 6{,}000 = 0 \\
0 \times 4{,}000 = 0 \\
\end{array}
$$

Objective function value $= \overline{0}$

Improving upon the starting solution

The simplex method carries on its step-by-step improvements to the starting solution by removing one variable at a time from the BASIS column and replacing it with a new one. Then it resolves the whole problem and computes the new objective function total. This is all done in a new iteration. In large problems there may be hundreds of iterations. In our problem, iteration 1, as well as iterations 2 and 3, is shown at the top of Figure 25–8.

This process is repeated one or more additional times until there is no further improvement in the objective function total. At that point, the solution is complete. The variables listed in the BASIS column are the ones which will be used; in our case they will tell us the quantity of each kind of automobiles to make. The quantities in the $C(I)$ column will be the per unit contributions of the variables in the BASIS. The quantities in the $B(I)$ column will be the quantities to make.

If $X(3)$, $X(4)$, $X(5)$ or $X(6)$ appear in the BASIS column, this tells us that there is slack in these departments and the quantity in the $B(I)$ column tells us how much.

The decision as to which variable to remove from the BASIS and which one to bring into the BASIS is determined by a specific set of rules which guarantee, under most conditions, to lead to the optimal solution.

Rule for choosing the variable to enter the BASIS

The rule for choosing which variable to put into the BASIS is to look at the next to the last line of Figure 25–7 (which is iteration 0), the line denoted SIMPLEX CRITERION $C(J) - Z(J)$, and select the *largest positive number*. (If all the numbers in this row are *zero* or are *negative,* we have arrived at the optimal solution. The BASIS column becomes the best program to follow.)

In our example, the largest positive number proves to be 400 and is in the $X(2)$ column. This tells us that we are losing more money per unit

FIGURE 25–8

X(2) enters the basis and X(6) leaves   Identity Matrix

PROBLEM   1   ITERATION   1

OBJECTIVE FUNCTION	C(J) =	300.0000	400.0000	0.0000	0.0000	0.0000	0.0000
C(I) BASIS	B(I)	X(1)	X(2)	X(3)	X(4)	X(5)	X(6)
0.0000 X(3)	3000.0000	1.0000	0.0000	1.0000	0.0000	0.0000	-1.5000
0.0000 X(4)	4666.8000	1.0000	0.0000	0.0000	1.0000	0.0000	-.5833
0.0000 X(5)	6000.0000	1.0000	0.0000	0.0000	0.0000	1.0000	0.0000
400.0000 X(2)	4000.0000	0.0000	1.0000	0.0000	0.0000	0.0000	1.0000
Z(J) =		0.0000	400.0000	0.0000	0.0000	0.0000	400.0000
SIMPLEX CRITERIA C(J)-Z(J) =		300.0000	0.0000	0.0000	0.0000	0.0000	-400.0000
OBJECTIVE FUNCTION VALUE	1600000.0000						

X(1) enters and X(3) leaves the basis   Identity Matrix

PROBLEM   1   ITERATION   2

OBJECTIVE FUNCTION	C(J) =	300.0000	400.0000	0.0000	0.0000	0.0000	0.0000
C(I) BASIS	B(I)	X(1)	X(2)	X(3)	X(4)	X(5)	X(6)
300.0000 X(1)	3000.0000	1.0000	0.0000	1.0000	0.0000	0.0000	-1.5000
0.0000 X(4)	1666.8000	0.0000	0.0000	-1.0000	1.0000	0.0000	.9167
0.0000 X(5)	3000.0000	0.0000	0.0000	-1.0000	0.0000	1.0000	1.5000
400.0000 X(2)	4000.0000	0.0000	1.0000	0.0000	0.0000	0.0000	1.0000
Z(J) =		300.0000	400.0000	300.0000	0.0000	0.0000	-50.0000
SIMPLEX CRITERIA C(J)-Z(J) =		0.0000	0.0000	-300.0000	0.0000	0.0000	50.0000
OBJECTIVE FUNCTION VALUE	2500000.0000						

X(6) returns to the basis and X(4) leaves   Identity Matrix

PROBLEM   1   ITERATION   3

OBJECTIVE FUNCTION	C(J) =	300.0000	400.0000	0.0000	0.0000	0.0000	0.0000
C(I) BASIS	B(I)	X(1)	X(2)	X(3)	X(4)	X(5)	X(6)
300.0000 X(1)	5727.3917	1.0000	0.0000	-.6363	1.6363	0.0000	0.0000
0.0000 X(6)	1818.2612	0.0000	0.0000	-1.0909	1.0909	0.0000	1.0000
0.0000 X(5)	272.6083	0.0000	0.0000	.6363	-1.6363	1.0000	0.0000
400.0000 X(2)	2181.7388	0.0000	1.0000	1.0909	-1.0909	0.0000	0.0000
Z(J) =		300.0000	400.0000	245.4565	54.5435	0.0000	0.0000
SIMPLEX CRITERIA C(J)-Z(J) =		0.0000	0.0000	-245.4565	-54.5435	0.0000	0.0000
OBJECTIVE FUNCTION VALUE	2590913.0577						

OPTIMAL SOLUTION

SOLUTION VARIABLE	VALUE
VAR 1	5727.3917
VAR 2	2191.7388
SLK 3	0.0000
SLK 4	0.0000
SLK 5	272.6083
SLK 6	1818.2612

OBJECTIVE FUNCTION VALUE =   2590913.0577

by not making $X(2)$ items than any other item so we should put $X(2)$ into the BASIS.

Before going on, however, we should explain how the 400 is arrived at. In later iterations, the numbers in the SIMPLEX CRITERION line will not be nice round and easily understood numbers.

The $Z(J)$ column totals are sums of the products of the numbers in the $C(I)$ column and the corresponding number in the columns for each variable. Thus, the $X(1)$ figure of 0.000 in the $Z(J)$ row was obtained as follows:

$$C(I) \quad X(1)$$
$$0 \times 1 = 0$$
$$0 \times 1 = 0$$
$$0 \times 1 = 0$$
$$0 \times 0 = 0$$
$$\text{Total } Z(1) \quad \overline{0}$$

Obviously, all other $Z(J)$ totals are also zero in our starting solution.

Now we go to the OBJECTIVE FUNCTION line at the top of iteration 0, and, column by column, we subtract the $Z(J)$ figure from the objective function figure. The answer is the SIMPLEX CRITERION figure we need. For $X(1)$ the calculation is $300 - 0 = 300$, for $X(2)$, it is $400 - 0 = 400$, for $X(3)$, $0 - 0 = 0$, and so on.

Rule for choosing the variable to remove from the BASIS

If $X(2)$, station wagons, is to be put into the BASIS in iteration 1, something already there will have to be removed. The procedure for determining which variable currently in the BASIS must leave is to determine how large $X(2)$ can get before a capacity constraint is met. (Essentially we are moving to the right along the horizontal [wagon] axis in Figure 25–5.)

The question is, which department's capacity do we reach first? It is the wagon assembly's capacity of 4,000 that stops us. This says, at this point in the analysis, that we can make 4,000 wagons but that in doing so the slack in wagon assembly is used up and will become equal to zero. Since wagon assembly slack is variable $X(6)$, $X(6)$ will leave the BASIS (and will be set at zero by its absence from the BASIS in iteration (1)). $X(2)$ will enter the BASIS and will have a $B(I)$ value of 4,000 units.

The rule, then, to follow for determining which of the current BASIS variables is to leave the BASIS and be set at zero is: Divide each entering variable column coefficient that is *positive and greater than zero* into its corresponding row $B(I)$ value. Of the resulting quotients, the leaving variable is the one which has the *smallest positive value*. For our example this calculation is:

BASIS	B(I)		X(2)		Resulting quotient
$X(3)$	9,000	÷	1.5	=	6,000
$X(4)$	7,000	÷	.5833	=	12,000
$X(5)$	6,000	÷	0	=	Ignore
$X(6)$	4,000	÷	1	=	4,000

The 4,000 for $X(6)$ is the smallest positive quotient so $X(6)$ will leave the BASIS and be replaced by $X(2)$. The necessary calculations were carried through by the computer and the resulting figures are shown in iteration 1. $X(2)$ is now in the BASIS, and column $C(I)$ shows 400

($400) for $X(2)$. The objective function, calculated as described earlier, is now $1,600,000, as is shown in iteration 1 in Figure 25–8, a great improvement over iteration 0's total of $0. (Note that this checks with the solution at point E in Figure 25–6.)

Iteration 1 is different from iteration 0 in several ways. There are secondary effects caused by putting $X(2)$ into and taking $X(6)$ out of the BASIS. In particular, putting $X(2)$ into the BASIS, and in a quantity of 4,000, required using up not only all of $B(6)$'s wagon assembly slack, but it also required using up some of the slack in the engine and in the stamping departments. This reduced the remaining slack of $X(3)$, engine making, and $X(4)$, stamping. One could say that $X(2)$'s requirements were "substituted" for iteration 0's assignments of capacity to the production of 4,000 wagons.

Calculating new rates of substitution and B(I)'s

The coefficient values in the body of each iteration's tableau are really rates of substitution between all six variables and the four which are in the BASIS of an iteration. For example, in iteration 0, the coefficient of 1.5 at the intersection of column $X(2)$ and row $X(3)$ indicates that we can substitute 1.5 units of $X(3)$ capacity (engine department) for 1 $X(2)$ or for 1 eight-cylinder engine. And, where column $X(3)$ and row $X(3)$ intersect, the coefficient of 1 simply means that an $X(3)$ is an $X(3)$.

In iteration 0, there is a unique property to columns $X(3)$, $X(4)$, $X(5)$ and $X(6)$. Each column has a single 1 and all other values in the column are zero, and the 1 appears in a unique row. This portion of our tableau is called the "identity matrix," and it always has this structure of 1's and zeros. It identifies for us, or for the computer, exactly which four of the six variables are currently in the BASIS and which two are equal to zero. The four in the identity matrix are the same as the four in the BASIS.

In iteration 1, the identity matrix has changed. Now it consists of columns $X(2)$, $X(3)$, $X(4)$ and $X(5)$.

We need, at this point, to consider how the new coefficients and the new $B(I)$'s in iteration 1 were calculated. These coefficients are really updated rates of substitution.

First, we know what the new identity matrix looks like in iteration 1. Figure 25–9 shows the coefficient and $B(I)$ portion of iteration 1:

FIGURE 25–9

BASIS	B(I)	X(1)	X(2)	X(3)	X(4)	X(5)	X(6)
X(3)	?	?	0	1	0	0	?
X(4)	?	?	0	0	1	0	?
X(5)	?	?	0	0	0	1	?
X(2)	?	?	1	0	0	0	?
			Identity matrix				

The question marks (?) indicate the new rates of substitution and the new BASIS values, which must be recalculated now that $X(2)$ has replaced $X(6)$ in the BASIS. We do this by the simultaneous solution of equations such that the identity matrix ends up being the one in Figure 25–9. First, the new equation which redefines the wagon assembly capacity and the quantity of $X(2)$'s in the BASIS is revised so that $X(2)$ is equal to 1, as required by our revised identity matrix.

The old wagon assembly constraint was:

$$X(2) + X(6) = 4,000$$

Since the coefficient of $X(2)$ is already 1, we do not need to revise it. We simply enter the same coefficients into the $X(2)$ row in iteration 1.

At this point our example does not illustrate the procedure fully. Let us suppose, for the moment, that neither $X(2)$ nor $X(6)$ had coefficients of 1. Suppose that, instead, the constraint was: $4X(2) + 2X(6) = 4,000$. With this constraint, we have to turn to the next procedural rule: Divide through each term in the leaving variable's old equation by the coefficient of the new entering variable. Thus:

$$\frac{④X(2)}{→4} + \frac{2X(6)}{4} = \frac{4,000}{4}$$

This yields:

$$X(2) + \tfrac{1}{2}X(6) = 1,000$$

These new coefficients of $B(I)$ of 1, $\tfrac{1}{2}$, and 1,000 would be entered in iteration 1's tableau. Of course, all other variables' coefficients would be zero.

Returning now to our actual problem. We next solve each of the other old equations simultaneously with this new equation such that the resulting value of the entering variable, $X(2)$, equals zero. Again, this zero requirement is specified by our new identity matrix as shown in Figure 25–9.

First, we will solve the new equation simultaneously with the old engine department equation such that $X(2)$ is zero:

$$X(2) + X(6) = 4,000 \text{ (new equation)}$$
$$X(1) + 1.5X(2) + X(3) = 9,000 \text{ (old equation)}$$

Multiplying the first equation by -1.5 and adding the two equations give us:

$$X(1) + 0X(2) + X(3) - 1.5X(6) = 3,000$$

$X(2)$'s coefficient is now zero. These new coefficients and $B(I)$ values are shown in iteration 1's tableau. The $B(I)$ of 3,000 means that making the 4,000 eight-cylinder engines required for the 4,000 station wagons leaves the engine department with enough slack capacity to make 3,000 six-cylinder engines for two-door cars or 2,000 8's (3,000/1.5).

For the stamping department, the calculation is:

$$X(2) + X(6) = 4{,}000 \text{ (new equation)}$$
$$X(1) + .5833X(2) + X(4) = 7{,}000 \text{ (old equation)}$$

Multiplying the first equation by $-.5833$ and adding the two equations gives us:[1]

$$X(1) + 0X(2) + X(4) - .5833X(6) = 4{,}666$$

As in the case of the engine department, this $B(I)$ of 4,666 tells us that stamping the parts for 4,000 wagons leaves the stamping department with enough slack to stamp enough parts for 4,666 two-door cars or 2,000 8-cylinders $(3{,}000 \div 1.5)$ for wagons.

Finally, the formulas for the two-door assembly department are:

$$X(2) + \quad\ \ X(6) = 4{,}000 \text{ (new equation)}$$
$$X(1) + \qquad X(5) \quad\ = 6{,}000 \text{ (old equation)}$$

Since the two assembly departments are independent, the use of wagon assembly capacity does not affect the two-door assembly department, and its coefficients and $B(I)$ do not change. Thus, these values may be entered directly from iteration 0 to iteration 1's tableau.

The next steps are to recalculate the objective function value and to complete the $Z(J)$ and $C(J) - Z(J)$ rows as before. Notice, that in iteration 1's tableau, the objective function is now $1,600,000 ($400 × 4,000 wagons).

In iteration 1, the largest positive simplex criteria is 300 and is in the $X(1)$ column. This means that $300 will be gained for each $X(1)$ which enters the BASIS (up to some other constraint's limits). In contrast, $X(6)$'s simplex criteria value is -400, meaning that for every unit of $X(6)$ we allow to be put back in the BASIS, there will be a reduction in the objective function value of $400.

Iteration 2

It would seem that no reduction should be made in $X(2)$, wagons, because for every one, up to 4,000 *not* made, foregoes a $400 contribution. Yet, if foregoing 1 wagon would allow us to make more than $1\frac{1}{3}$ two-door cars, then we should give up some of the wagons in favor of two-doors. The simplex method investigates this possibility in iteration 2, which is also shown in Figure 25–8.

Since the simplex criteria value for $X(1)$ has the largest positive value (300), it will enter the BASIS in iteration 2. The leaving variable is determined exactly as before and is $X(3)$, the engine department's capacity. This is analogous to moving to point D in Figure 25–5, where we make 4,000 wagons and 3,000 two-doors, utilizing *all* of the capacity of the engine and wagon assembly departments and part of the capacities in the other two departments. These quantities are shown in the $B(I)$ column of

---

[1] If a $B(I)$ value becomes negative from simultaneous solution, simply multiply each term in the resulting equation by -1 to make the $B(I)$ become positive. This is a requirement in the simplex procedure.

iteration 2, as are the revised unused capacities of $X(4)$ and $X(5)$. Iteration 2 also contains the new rate of substitution coefficients and the new identity matrix. These revised $B(I)$ and coefficient values are solved simultaneously as before such that the coefficients in $X(1)$'s column, the variable which replaced $X(3)$, are 1, 0, 0, and 0, as reflected in the revised identity matrix.

Iteration 2 produces an improved objective function value of $2,500,-000. But there is now a positive value in the simplex criteria row of $50 for $X(6)$, wagon assembly capacity. This means that for every slack unit of this department's capacity we put back into the basis (up to some other department's capacity limit) we will increase the objective function by $50. At this point, we are moving to point C in Figure 25–5, where we make 5,727 two-doors and 2,182 wagons. While the $50 is mechanically calculated following the rules described earlier, an intuitive explanation is in order.

As we move along line segment D–C in Figure 25–5 towards point C, we are *increasing* the number of two-doors and decreasing the number of wagons in the solution. The rate of this substitution as described earlier is 1.5. For each wagon we decrease, we can increase 1.5 two-doors (actually for each eight-cylinder decreased, we can produce 1.5 more six-cylinders which directly affects the quantities of two-doors and wagons). This rate of substitution is shown in iteration 2's tableau at the intersection of column $X(6)$ and row $X(1)$ as -1.5. Here we have a "negative" rate of substitution. This means that for a 1-unit *increase* in $X(6)$ (slack capacity in wagon assembly) we can also *increase* $X(1)$ by 1.5 units. Thus, if we increase the value of $X(6)$ (allow slack capacity to occur) in wagon assembly, this means a reduction in the objective function of $400 for each wagon not produced, but there will be an *increase* of $450 for each 1.5 two-doors that are produced ($300 \times 1.5 = $450). These gains and losses net at plus $50 per unit, which is "opportunity cost" of *not* trading some slack wagon assembly capacity to allow more six-cylinder engines to be built, which indirectly allows more two-doors to be stamped and assembled.

Iteration 3

Iteration 3, also shown in Figure 25–8, shows the optimal solution for our problem. This is indicated by there being no positive numbers in the simplex criteria row. $X(6)$ returns to the basis and $X(4)$, which is stamping department capacity, leaves because its capacity is used up. We are at point C on Figure 25–5.

The computer printout shows the optimal program in the BASIS column and the $B(I)$ column and it is printed separately below. It shows that we should make 5,727 two-door cars and 2,182 station wagons. The objective functional value of this program of $2,590,913 is greater than for any other program.

OTHER USES OF SIMPLEX METHOD ANALYSES

Probably, in most cases, the users of the simplex method are after answers such as those we have just calculated. The answer to our problem is to manufacture 5,727 two-door cars and 2,182 station wagons.

The simplex method can, however, be helpful to managers in several other ways. The final tableau in iteration 3, Figure 25–8, in fact, shows a number of relationships which managers can use in further decision making. Every number in Figure 25–8 has some meaning with respect to the relations of the problem's elements, one to another.

Some, for example, are "shadow prices" and reflect other possible relationships which exist if, for reasons not covered by the problem as stated, the optimum solution is not used. Using the data provided in Figure 25–8 allows managers to calculate the worth of expanding capacities which set limits to the problem as stated. Such calculations include a process called "ranging."

These data can also show managers how sensitive the problem is to changes in factors and how changes in factors will affect solutions. This is called "parametric sensitivity analysis."

Sometimes, too, managers want to know how to minimize costs rather than to maximize contributions. A modified version of the simplex method can be used here.

These and several other attributes of the simplex method go beyond what is needed here in our chapter on linear programming. However, for readers who are interested in these procedures, they are presented in Appendix H.

INTEGER LINEAR PROGRAMMING

The simplest kind of linear programming is "noninteger" linear programming. This is the kind we used in our automobile making example. This means that answers are almost always carried out several decimal places and usually are not whole numbers. For example, a solution might say, that in order to maximize profits and at the same time to meet certain nutritional requirements, we should make hot dogs out of 24.019 percent of meat, 68.207 percent of cereal, and 7.674 percent of other additives.

In order to make 100 pounds of hot dogs, we could just round off the numbers to 24, 68, and 8. This would be all right for hot dogs, and it was all right in our automobile example where we just rounded off the answers to units. The rounded fractions did not represent very much money.

There are times, however, when just rounding off the answers might not give the best answer. Suppose, for example, that an airline company wanted to find an optimal assignment—or schedule—of its jet aircraft to its numerous routes. The goal is to arrive at an assignment which would maximize its profits, yet would meet customer demand for airline service, allow enough time for maintenance, and other constraints.

Using noninteger linear programming, the solution might say to allocate 2.3 planes to the Seattle-Denver route, 1.4 planes to the Chicago-St. Louis route, and so on. Of course, it is impossible to fly .3 or .4 of an airplane. The Seattle-Denver allocation must be either 2 or 3 airplanes. But why not just round off the answers? This cannot be safely done when the problem deals with capital equipment such as airplanes which cost millions of dollars or other cases which require solutions to be integers.

Another kind of linear programming, "integer programming," can be used in such cases. There are several varieties of integer programming methods available, such as "branch and bound," "zero-one," and network methods. These methods are quite complex and are beyond the scope of this book but are covered in books on mathematical programming.

COMPUTER PROGRAMS FOR LARGE LINEAR PROGRAMMING PROBLEMS

All large linear programming problems are solved with special purpose computer programs. Such programs can solve problems with thousands of variables and constraints—their limits being only the size of the computer and the cost of computer time. Such programs are often "mixed integer" programs, meaning that they can solve problems where some variables are required to be integers and some may contain decimal fractions. These programs automatically set up slack, surplus, and artificial variables after the "less than," "greater than," and "equal to" relationships have been defined. They also perform "ranging" and "sensitivity analysis" and allow for "piecewise" approximations on nonlinear relationships.

CAUTIONS IN THE USE OF LINEAR PROGRAMMING

While linear programming is a powerful aid to decision making with a wide range of applications, it is at the same time one of the most difficult of operations research methods to implement and use whether on a one-time basis or on day-to-day repetitive problems.

The problem of determining the structure of the problem (the objective function and the constraints) and the values of the coefficients can be a major task. (Often, there are hundreds or thousands of variables.) Sometimes, by the time the necessary data have been gathered and a linear programming solution found, either the problem has changed, or the data gathered or assumed are out of date.

As we said at the start of this chapter, linear programming assumes that the relationships in the problem are linear (the more of A, the more of B, or the less of one, the less of the other and always at the same ratio of relationship).

But not everything is linear. Machine set up time is not, for example, linear with unit production costs. The setup costs *per unit* depend on how many units are produced in the order. Rates of substitution among things may also vary, depending on the quantities involved.

Often it is possible to work around this difficulty and to use linear programming anyway. One can say the setup costs per unit are $.50 per unit for all orders of from 1 to 10 units; $.20 per unit for all orders of 11 to 50 units; $.07 per unit for all orders for from 51 to 100 units, and so on. Most large-scale computer programs which are designed to solve linear programs are programmed to set up such step-by-step constants when they are needed.

Still one other warning is that linear program solutions are solutions to the problem as posed. If variables or the relations between them change, the old solution may no longer be valid.

REVIEW QUESTIONS

1. What is meant when it is said that linear programming requires linear relationships between factors? What other kinds of relationships are there? Give examples and show how it may be possible to use linear programming in spite of this difficulty.
2. What are linear rates of substitution?
3. Distinguish between an objective function and a constraint.
4. What is a feasible solution? Feasible region?
5. How is "contribution" defined in an objective function?
6. What is an iso-contribution function? Why is there a "family" of them for a given problem, and why is their slope identical?
7. Outline the procedure for graphing a set of constraints to obtain the area of feasible solution or feasible region.
8. What is an optimal solution and how is it determined using the graphic method?
9. How is slack determined and what does it mean? Surplus?
10. What does the simplex method do for us that the graphic method cannot do?
11. How does the simplex method handle problems where there are more variables than equations?
12. How are inequality constraints translated into equations?
13. What guides are there for choosing the variables to enter the BASIS? For leaving the BASIS? Do these guides change when we are minimizing costs rather than maximizing contributions?
14. How do we use the identity matrix to produce a new tableau?
15. How do we know when we have reached an optimal solution in the simplex method?
16. What cautions should be heeded in using linear programming?

PROBLEMS

1. Suppose, in the text's first example of making automobiles, that any one of the three departments could be expanded by 20 percent. Which

one should it be? Assuming that all the cars made can be sold, what would be the new production program? How much better would this choice be than the next best choice?

2. Present production is 800 of product A, and it is proposed to produce 1,100 of product B. The two products each require operations on the same three machines, whose capacities for operation 1 are: A, 1,200, and B, 0; or B, 2,400, and A, 0; or proportional combinations of A and B. For operation 2 the capacities are: A, 1,500, and B, 0; or B, 1,000, and A, 0; or combinations. For operation 3 the capacities are: A, 2,400, and B, 0; or B, 1,200, and A, 0.

Can the present equipment continue to produce the 800 units of A and also 1,100 of product B? If not, which operation's capacity will need to be increased and by how much? (Solve this problem graphically.)

3. A company making typewriters and adding machines has three major departments: stamped parts, machined parts, and assembly. The capacity of each department depends on what they make. The departmental capacities are given below:

	Typewriters	Adding machines
Stamped parts	2,000	6,500
Machined parts	1,500	10,000
Assembly	2,500	5,500

Assuming that the typewriters contribute $50 each and adding machines $40, what is the optimal combination of output? (Solve graphically.)

4. Solve problem 3 with the simplex method and assume that the quantities in problem 3 are the output capacities for a 40-hour week. This makes the time requirements for each product become:

	Hours per 100 units	
	Typewriters	Adding machines
Stamped parts	2.00	.62
Machined parts	2.67	.40
Assembly	1.60	.73

5. A company makes four products, A, B, C, and D, which go through four departments: drill, mill, lathe, and assembly. The hours of department time required by each product per unit are:

	Drill	Mill	Lathe	Assembly	Amount saved by making instead of buying
A	4	0	2	3	$ 9
B	8	3	5	5	18
C	5	7	1	6	14
D	1	8	6	3	11
Hours available	6,000	9,000	8,000	11,000	

How many of each product should be made?

6.* There are two factories and two warehouses in the Core Laboratories production-distribution system. The per period capacities, demands, and the per unit shipping costs for one of their major products from each factory to each warehouse are as follows:

| | Warehouse | | Capacity (units, |
Factory	A	B	regular time)
R....................	$1	$2	600
S....................	5	3	1,100
Demand (units).....	700	1,200	

Since the demand exceeds regular time capacities, extra capacity can be added as follows:

Factory	Capacity (regular time)	Extra capacity from overtime (in units)	Premium cost per unit on overtime
R....................	600	150	$2.50
S....................	1,100	160	2.00

If this item sells for $15 each in both markets, but has variable manufacturing costs (on regular time) of $5 at Factory R and $4 at Factory S, what production-distribution plan, utilizing regular and/or overtime capacities should they use to maximize contribution? Set up as a simplex problem, but do not solve.

7. Formulate Problem 1, Chapter 7, as a simplex problem. Hint: The variables are the 12 possible shipping routes; we wish to minimize shipping costs subject to demand and production capacity constraints.

SUGGESTED SUPPLEMENTARY READINGS

Barchi, R. H., et al. "Production, Inventory and Capacity Expansion Scheduling with Integer Variables." *Management Science,* March 1975, pp. 783–92.

Fuller, J. A. "A Linear Programming Approach to Aggregate Scheduling." *Academy of Management Journal,* March 1975, pp. 129–36.

Koch, J. V. "A Linear Programming Model of Resource Allocations in a University." *Decision Sciences,* October 1973, pp. 494–504.

---

* Appendix H should probably be read before attempting this problem.

26

Waiting lines and simulation

In Chapter 3 it was said that one of the important considerations in the design of services concerns decisions involving trade-offs between the cost of the time customers spend waiting and being served against the costs of providing more service capacity to reduce the waits but at a cost of more idle service capacity during lulls in demand. The general methodology used in such analyses is called "waiting line analysis."

There are two quite different approaches to solving this kind of cost balancing problem. One, which might be called "classical" waiting line analysis, uses "queuing models." This approach uses mathematical calculations which often become quite complex. The second method is to use Monte Carlo simulation.

QUEUING MODELS

Queuing models were first developed by A. K. Erlang, a Danish telephone engineer, in the early 1900s to study the capacity requirements and the performance of early automatic telephone switching systems. There were, however, only a few other industrial applications of queuing until the 1950s when operations researchers began to apply their skills to analyzing industrial problems.

Queuing models are based on mathematical probability assumptions about how many customers will need to be served and how and when they will arrive to be served at a service facility. They are designed to estimate how long customers wait in line, the length of waiting lines, how busy servers are, and what would happen if service times or the calls for service change.

Queuing line models always need three kinds of data: (*a*) the average rate of calls for service, (*b*) the average rate that customers can be served, and (*c*) the number of servers. Other information is also needed in some cases. The spread or variability of arrival times and of service times is usually not necessary because the basic queuing formulas include an assumption that these will follow a "Poisson" probability distribution pattern.

Using this information, queuing formulas will provide answers to such questions as: What will the average waiting time for customers be? How many people (or machines, or airplanes, and so on) on the average will be waiting? How much idle time will the service people (mechanics, airplane landing strips, and so on) have?

Mathematical probability formulas for waiting line situations with several variables can become quite complex. Here we will deal with a few simplified examples to show how queuing models can be used in waiting line situations.[1] In real life, queuing problems are almost always much more complicated than they are in any of our simplified examples.

GASOLINE FILLING STATION EXAMPLE (MODEL 1)

The simplest queuing model, which we will call model 1, can be illustrated by the example of a gasoline filling station, located in an isolated area, which is staffed by one attendant. On the average, customers arrive at the rate of four per hour although sometimes there are more and sometimes fewer. This arrival rate's symbol is λ (the Greek letter lambda).

Service times average six minutes (ten per hour), but this, too, varies. If the attendant is busy serving one customer, then our queuing model assumes that other arriving customers will form a line and wait to be served on a "first come–first served" basis. Our model also assumes that the arrival of customers is "independent" meaning that they don't "decide" whether to arrive or not based on whether they see a line. And it is assumed that once they have arrived, even if there is a line of cars waiting, they, too, will get into line and will not defect.

Given these assumptions, it is possible to calculate the probability that any specific number of customers, $P(x)$, will arrive during a certain time period, T. The formula for the calculation, which uses the Poisson probability distribution, is given in Appendix F, where, for our problem, the following probabilities were arrived at:[2]

---

[1] There are many good books on queuing theory. See Plane, D. R. and Kockenberger, G. A., *Operations Research for Managerial Decisions* (Homewood, Ill.: Richard D. Irwin, Inc., 1972 c.).

[2] Waiting line problems often concern situations, such as the arrival rate of customers, where most rates are small but where some can be quite large. In such cases, no individual arrival rate can be very much smaller than the average rate because they can't be less than zero. But, on the upper side, they can be several times the average. The Poisson probability distribution is well suited to depicting this situation.

Arrivals in one hour	Probability $P(x)$	Cumulative probability
0	0.018	0.018
1	0.073	0.091
2	0.147	0.238
3	0.195	0.433
4	0.195	0.628
5	0.156	0.784
6	0.104	0.888
7	0.060	0.948
8	0.030	0.978
9	0.013	0.991
10	0.005	0.996
Over 10	0.004	1.000

The next assumption in our problem is that the average service time is six minutes. On the average, the attendant can service ten cars per hour. This, ten, is called the service rate and is designated μ (the Greek letter mu). As before, the queuing formula assumes that the variations in the service rate will follow a Poisson pattern.[3] The Greek letter μ simply replaces λ in the Poisson formula.

Other assumptions inherent in the formulas are that the possible number of customers is large, that the line can get to be very long, and that on the average the attendant can service more cars than will arrive in an hour —that the average service rate (μ) is greater than the average arrival rate (λ).

Using these assumptions, the following equations will provide several useful answers about this service system.

Given:

$$\lambda = 4 \text{ and } \mu = 10$$

The average number of cars waiting in line (called L_q) will be:

$$L_q = \frac{\lambda^2}{\mu(\mu - \lambda)} = \frac{4^2}{10(10 - 4)} = 0.267 \text{ cars}$$

The average number of cars waiting in line and being served (called L) will be:

$$L = \frac{\lambda}{\mu - \lambda} = \frac{4}{10 - 4} = 0.667 \text{ cars}$$

The average time a car spends waiting in line (called W_q) will be:

$$W_q = \frac{\lambda}{\mu(\mu - \lambda)} = \frac{4}{10(10 - 4)} = 0.0667 \text{ hours or about 4 minutes.}$$

The average time a car spends waiting in line and being served (called W) will be:

---

[3] Service *times* are assumed to be explained by the negative exponential distribution, which is the mathematical equivalent of service *rates* (average cars being served per time period) being explained by the Poisson distribution. Since the queuing equations presented require only λ and μ, this relationship will not be explained here.

$$W = \frac{1}{\mu - \lambda} = \frac{1}{10 - 4} = 0.167 \text{ hours or 10 minutes.}$$

The average proportion of time the attendant spends serving cars (called ρ, the Greek letter rho) will be:

$$\rho = \frac{\lambda}{\mu} = \frac{4}{10} = 0.4 \text{ hours or 24 minutes per hour.}$$

The average proportion of idle time of the attendant then becomes: $1 - \rho = 0.60$ hours, or 36 minutes per hour.

It will be noticed that the last two of our answers did not need to be calculated by a formula. An attendant serving an average of four cars per hour at an average of 6 minutes per car must be busy 24 minutes and idle 36 minutes. The formulas given here only illustrate that these ratios could be calculated for other combinations of more cars and more attendants, in which case the answers would not be obvious.

Figures such as these would be very helpful in providing an insight into what would happen if arrivals were to double, as for example, on a Fourth of July weekend. The managers will know whether customers might have to face lengthy waits. Other queuing models could tell them whether or not a second attendant ought to be added for a busy weekend.

Possibly, too, the managers might try to alter the arrival pattern. In a retail store, there can be a sale on Wednesday and Thursday, normally slow days, but not on Saturday, the busy day. The customers are influenced to alter their arrival pattern, thus reducing the idle time of the servers, the clerks, and shortening the line lengths and waiting time.

AUTOMOBILE REPAIR SHOP EXAMPLE (MODEL 1, CONTINUED)

Still other problems come up in some situations. In an automobile repair shop, the mechanics coming to the repair parts issue window have to wait while the service employee looks up the part number in the catalog and its storage location. And the mechanics continue to wait while the attendant gets the part from stock. If the mechanics have to wait while one server does everything, including recording the issue of the part, it might help to have two servers, one to look things up and to handle the paper work and another to get the item and bring it to the mechanics.

Suppose that mechanics cost $10 per hour and an extra server (the stock chaser) costs $3 per hour. If arrivals averaged 4 per hour and could be served by one attendant at a rate of 10 per hour, would it pay to add the stock chaser if his help would increase the average service rate to 12 per hour? This time we have also worked out answers using a queuing model but have put the calculations all in Appendix F.

They tell us that the cost of the mechanics' idle time while waiting for parts is $53.44 a day. The stock chaser, should he be added at a cost of $24 a day, would reduce the mechanics' idle time costs to $40. So his addition would save $13.44 but would cost $24, so he should not be added.

But, if a new labor contract increased the mechanics' rate to $13 an hour, and at the same time because of more business, the arrival rate increased 5 percent to 4.2 per hour, then the mechanics' waiting time cost would go up to $104. Under these circumstances, an added stock chaser would cut this to $74.36, a saving of $29.64 per day. This saving is more than his cost of $24, so he should be added.

BANK DRIVE-UP BANKING WINDOW EXAMPLE (MODEL 2)

Our examples so far have assumed that customers needing service, once they have arrived, will always wait in line if need be until they are served.

But people don't always do this. The automobile repair shop mechanics, coming to the parts issue window and seeing a line, will probably wait because they are being paid for their time. But many prospective customers of a gasoline filling station won't wait. They drive on to another filling station. So also it is with bank drive-up banking windows. Sometimes there is space for only a few cars so there is a physical limitation to the size of the line. But, even if there is room, some prospective customers will not get into line nor will they park and go into the bank on foot. They just go away.

Our next queuing line example is that of a bank drive-up banking window. There is only one window and room for only four cars, including the one being served. This limitation imposes restrictions and makes it necessary to use different queuing models from those we have used before.

The question posed is, should the bank provide spaces for more cars? Since there is an ample lawn, it is possible, at a cost, to make more spaces available by reducing the lawn's size a little. As it is now, when a customer arrives and finds four cars in the line, he has to go away, even if he is willing to wait. This is inconvenient for him and if this happens very often, the bank loses business.

The bank's managers estimate that it loses $1 every time a customer can't get in line and so drives away. More parking spaces can be made available at these costs: one space, $600; two spaces, $900; and $200 each for additional spaces.

As we said, the limitation of the number of parking spaces requires the use of somewhat more complicated formulas. These and the necessary calculations are given in Appendix F.

These calculations indicate that nearly 19,000 arrivals may be expected in a year and that roughly one eighth of them will turn away. Their cost, at $1 each, comes to $2,174. Assuming that everyone who arrives will get into line if there is room, then: Providing one more space at a cost of $600 would save $507 in reduction of defectors; two more spaces cost $900 and would save $919; three spaces cost $1,100 and would save $1,221; four cost $1,300 and would save $1,444.

FIGURE 26–1

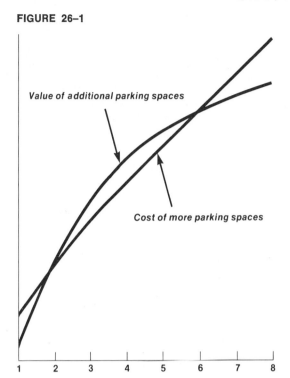

Additional spaces beyond the original four

From here on additional spaces cost more than they add to the savings so the maximum savings will come from adding four more spaces which will produce a net gain of $144 in the first year. Figure 26–1 shows how the costs and savings are related in this example. The future costs of the added spaces would be only their maintenance costs so, after the first year, the savings would be greater.

FIRE EQUIPMENT DISPATCHING EXAMPLE (MODEL 3)

Queuing is also useful in analyzing service levels in such places as a city fire department. We will use an example where the alarm headquarters is staffed around the clock by a single dispatcher who takes all calls and dispatches fire engines in answer to calls.

The questions are, how likely is it that a caller reporting a fire will find the line busy, and, if he gets a busy signal, how long is he likely to have to wait for an open line? Calls come in at the rate of ten per hour, and it takes from one to three minutes to record where the fire is and to relay the call to the appropriate fire station.

Here we assume that the Poisson distribution of service rates does not apply, so different formulas are required. These are explained in Appendix F, where the answers to the two questions are also worked out. They show that there is about one chance in ten ($Lq = .095$) that a caller reporting a fire will get a busy signal and that, if he does get a busy signal, the average wait until the line is free will be .6 minutes, or 36 seconds. This would seem to be an acceptable level of service.

But, if the calls coming in doubled to 20 per hour, he would get a busy signal 76 percent of the time. And, if he had to wait, the average wait would be 2.28 minutes. This would be an intolerable average wait when reporting a fire. Extra dispatching capacity would be needed.

MULTIPLE CHANNEL—SINGLE PHASE (MODEL 4)

The examples given so far have been with one server doing all of the serving. But, in a great many actual situations, there are two or more servers, and often there are whole sequences of service activities.

Figure 26–2 depicts several of these different arrangements in schematic form. Our examples have been of the 26–2a type, with a single server and a single activity, or "single channel, single phase" model.

If there are two or more servers, each taking customers from a single line and serving them independently, this is a "multiple channel, single phase" case, as is shown in Figure 26–2b. A third case, "single channel,

FIGURE 26–2

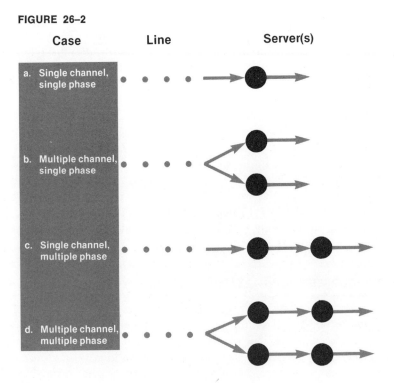

Case	Line	Server(s)
a. Single channel, single phase		
b. Multiple channel, single phase		
c. Single channel, multiple phase		
d. Multiple channel, multiple phase		

multiple phase" (Figure 26–2c) has customers passing by two or more servers. Examples are factory assembly lines with their many servers or cafeteria lines in restaurants.

Finally, (Figure 26–2d) is the "multiple channel, multiple phase" case. Here examples would be factory lines where they split for, say, two operations and four assemblers with two on each side of the line working on every other unit. Another example would be college registration systems where the original line splits up into two or more lines for later processes.

In Figure 26–2b, the multiple channel, single phase case, the situation is similar to the examples we have given except that the customer at the head of the line is served by the server who is next available. Common examples of this system exist at banks and post offices. Customers wait in a single line and are served by the first available bank teller or postal clerk. (We call this Model 4.)

To illustrate the use of queuing in a multiple channel serving situation, we will use the Farquhar Company. Farquhar has two Xerox copiers, located in separate office areas where each one sometimes has its own waiting line. There is no common line for the two.

Each machine can handle an average of 15 jobs per hour (although there is a great deal of variation in job sizes). Clerks arrive with jobs for the copiers at the rate of 8 per hour for each machine, or 16 per hour for the two combined. Clerks run their own jobs off on the copiers and are thus idle only if there is a line and they have to wait their turn.

With the present system, one machine may be swamped with work while the other is idle. It has been suggested that the two machines be moved to a central area where the clerks could wait in a single line for the first machine available. The proposed location is, however, less conveniently located and would require extra walking time by the clerks which would cost 15¢ per order, or $2.40 per hour.

The question is, would the saving in the cost of clerk waiting time be more than enough to offset the costs of the extra walking? Clerks cost $4.00 per hour.

The calculations in Appendix F show that with the present system the average cost of clerks waiting is $4.86 per hour. After putting the two copiers together, this would be reduced to $1.73 per hour, but this would be at the cost of $2.40 in extra walking. The new total would be $4.13 per hour. The saving of $.73 per hour would be $1,518 per year so the change should be made.

MACHINE GROUP SERVICING EXAMPLE (MODEL 5)

A somewhat different type of problem occurs where a group of machines require occasional setting up for new jobs as well as occasional repairs. There is enough of this so that one service mechanic can be assigned permanently to keeping these machines in operation.

In our problem, we will assume that one mechanic has been assigned to keep five machines in operation. The major difference in this model is that there are a limited number of customers—the five machines in this example. (This is called a "finite calling population.") Each machine requires service on the average of once every four hours. When service is needed, it averages a half an hour.

The problem here is to answer several questions: What will be the average number of machines out of production because they are being serviced or waiting to be serviced? What will be the average number of machines waiting to be serviced? What is the average amount of time each machine will spend out of production while being serviced or waiting to be serviced? What will be the average amount of time each machine waits for service?

These answers are explained in Appendix F. Figure 26–3 shows a computer printout of the answers. Most complex queuing problems are solved on computers or with special purpose queuing tables and charts.

This information could serve as a starting point to an investigation of whether the mechanic should serve more (or fewer) machines and whether he should have a helper or not. Costs of machine idle time could be balanced off against the costs of a different number of mechanics or helpers.

FIGURE 26–3

Computer solution to machine maintenance example (using finite calling population model)

```
IDENTIFICATION
? MACHINE MAINTENANCE
 MODEL NUMBER
? 5
 ARRIVAL RATE
? .25
 SERVICE RATE
? 2
 SPECIAL CONDITIONS
? 5
     MACHINE MAINTENANCE

     SINGLE-SERVER QUEUING SYSTEM WITH POISSON
     ARRIVALS  AND EXPONENTIAL SERVICE TIMES.

     THIS MODEL USES A FINITE CALLING POPULATION WITH     5  MEMBERS.
      THE ARRIVAL RATE IS FOR EACH MEMBER NOT IN THE QUEUE OR IN SERVICE

     THE ARRIVAL RATE PER UNIT OF TIME IS              .250

     THE SERVICE RATE PER UNIT OF TIME IS             2.000

     THE AVERAGE(EXPECTED) NUMBER OF CUSTOMERS IN THE
     SYSTEM(QUEUE PLUS SERVICE FACILITY) IS            .832

     THE AVERAGE(EXPECTED) NUMBER OF CUSTOMERS IN THE
     LINE IS                                           .311

     THE AVERAGE(EXPECTED) TIME A CUSTOMER SPENDS IN THE
     SYSTEM(QUEUE PLUS SERVICE FACILITY) IS            .799

     THE AVERAGE(EXPECTED) TIME A CUSTOMER SPENDS
     IN THE LINE IS                                    .299
```

Program provided courtesy Professor Donald R. Plane, University of Colorado.

SPECIAL PURPOSE QUEUING TABLES AND CHARTS

In situations where the conditions of classical queuing models can be met, special purpose tables and charts have been developed to provide pre-computed answers.

TRW Company found, for example, that queuing type problems came up from time to time but that its employees did not calculate answers because the formulas looked too forbidding. TRW solved this problem by developing charts based on the formulas from which they could read off answers to most questions.

Figure 26–4 is a chart used by TRW to give answers to various waiting line questions merely by reading them from the chart.[4] Suppose, for example, that there is a group of machines needing occasional service and

FIGURE 26–4

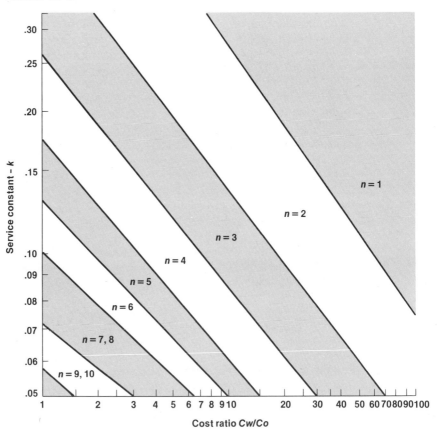

Cw—Cost of an activity waiting per unit time
Co—Cost of a service facility per unit time

$$k = \frac{\text{Servicing time}}{\text{Running time}}$$

---

[4] This chart is one of several presented in *Waiting Line Pamphlet* (Cleveland, O.: TRW, Inc.), pp. 11–20.

there is a question of how many service employees are needed. Figure 26–4 will provide the answer. On Figure 26–4, the horizontal scale is a scale of ratios. To find the ratio to use in our example, the cost per hour for an idle machine is divided by the cost per hour of an idle service employee. Suppose that we say that this is $22.50 divided by $6, or a ratio of 3.75.

The vertical scale is another scale of ratios, the average service time divided by the time the machine runs. If service time averages half an hour per day per machine and if the machines' average operating time is seven hours a day (including the service time), the ratio is .5 divided by 7, or .071. (During the other hour of the day the machines are not operating because the next job is not ready, or the operator is away from his machine, or for other reasons not related to this calculation.)

Reading from Figure 26–4, we find that the two ratios intersect in zone 6. This means that the solution is to have each service employee service six machines. If the company has 24 machines of this kind, it needs four service employees.

This chart does not, however, provide answers to all waiting line questions. To get answers to other questions, such as how many jobs will normally have to wait if there is one server, two servers, and so on, the analyst will have to develop other similar charts, use queuing formulas, or computer programs designed for this purpose.

TRW has a second such chart to use for such things as tool crib waiting line problems. Assume that factory operators arrive and are served at the tool cribs according to the Poisson distribution described earlier. Figure 26–5 shows us how many crib attendants will be needed. Again, the horizontal scale is a ratio scale. This time it is the cost per hour of the machinists who may have to wait divided by the hourly cost of tool room attendants who, at other times, may have to wait.

Suppose that machine operators' idleness while waiting costs $8 an hour and that tool room attendants cost $4 an hour. Eight dollars divided by $4 equals 2, which is the ratio to use on the horizontal scale.

The number to use when reading the vertical scale is the answer obtained by multiplying the average arrival rate by the average service time. If an average of 12 mechanics per hour arrive and ask for tools, and, if, on the average, it takes a tool crib attendant five minutes (or .08 hours) to get and issue tools, then the average calls for service in an hour total .96 hours. This, .96, is the number to use on the vertical scale.

Since the intersection of the horizontal and the vertical ratios, 2 and .96, falls in zone 2, the total idle time costs of mechanics and crib attendants is minimized by having two attendants on duty.

It is often possible, however, to give tool crib attendants other work to do (grinding tools, cleaning up and repairing returned tools, putting a protective covering of oil on them, and the like) when they are not busy serving factory operators. Such odd jobs will salvage a good bit of their idle time, so that the loss when they are "idle" may really be $2 an hour. In this case, the horizontal ratio would be 4. The vertical ratio remains

FIGURE 26–5

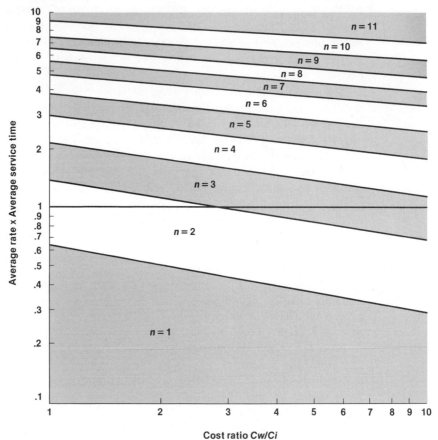

Cost ratio C_w/C_i

C_w—Cost of an activity waiting per unit time
C_i—Cost of an idle service facility per unit time

.96. These two ratios intersect just barely in the 3 zone so there probably should be three attendants although two attendants could almost handle the work.

SUMMARY OF BASIC QUEUING MODELS

The characteristics of the several illustrative queuing models which have been discussed are presented in Appendix F, in Figure F–2. Their formulas are presented in Figure F–3 in Appendix F. And, although these examples do not cover every possible situation, they do cover a great many situations. Other queuing models, some more complex than these, allow for other conditions and cover other situations.

However, sometimes waiting line type problems become so complex that they are impractical to solve mathematically. This would happen, for example, if a company has, say, three enamel-baking ovens whose heating elements sometimes burn out and cause extensive and costly downtime. The question might be, should the company put in all new heating elements every time one of them burns out? Or should it replace only the burned-out element? Or should it replace the others at the same time if they have been in use six months? Or should some other policy be followed? Such a problem is too complex for reasonable mathematical solution. It can, however, be handled quite satisfactorily by Monte Carlo simulation.

MONTE CARLO SIMULATION

Monte Carlo simulation is an alternative to mathematical queuing models. Often it is the only practical way to solve complex problems of the queuing type.

Monte Carlo simulation is a logically organized attempt to imitate a real life situation so managers can test and evaluate various policies. It is a technique whereby a system and its associated possible sequences of events are produced on a make-believe basis. This is usually done by a computer which is programmed to act like the system being studied. Simulation allows managers to investigate changes in systems and results without incurring the costs of manipulating real systems. It also helps decision makers develop an understanding of how systems react to certain stimuli.

The name Monte Carlo comes from the city on the Mediterranean famous for gambling and, as a method, is based on the same kind of probability laws that govern gambling games. (Monte Carlo simulation has actually been used to test the merits of particular betting systems supposed to be sure winners.)

Our interest in Monte Carlo, however, comes from its usefulness in helping managers to analyze a broad range of problems. It has proven to be a helpful tool in the analysis of problems in manufacturing, in service companies, transportation organizations, urban planning, health care, education, agriculture, and in any number of other situations.

The major differences between simulation and queuing models are:

1. Queuing models generally presume that the system is operating at a "steady state," meaning that there are no peaks and valleys, no 5 o'clock rush. Queuing models can calculate the average line length, the average waiting time, and so on but only for steady state conditions. In contrast, simulation models can be developed to estimate line lengths, waiting times, and the like for peak and valley situations as well as for steady state conditions.[5]

2. Queuing models have, of necessity, to be based on a number of

---

[5] Dynamic queuing models are available—but they are extremely complex to use.

FIGURE 26–6

Ways in which simulation can be used

Air traffic control queuing	Industry models
Aircraft maintenance scheduling	Textile
Airport design	Petroleum (financial aspects)
Ambulance location and dispatching	Information system design
Assembly line scheduling	Intergroup communication (sociological
Bank teller scheduling	studies)
Bus (city) scheduling	Inventory reorder rule design
Circuit design	Aerospace
Clerical processing system design	Manufacturing
Communication system design	Military logistics
Computer time sharing	Hospitals
Telephone traffic routing	Job shop scheduling
Message system	Aircraft parts
Mobile communications	Metals forming
Computer memory-fabrication test-	Work-in-process control
facility design	Shipyard
Consumer behavior prediction	Library operations design
Brand selection	Maintenance scheduling
Promotion decisions	Airlines
Advertising allocation	Glass furnaces
Court system resource allocation	Steel furnaces
Distribution system design	Computer field service
Warehouse location	National manpower adjustment system
Mail (post office)	Natural resource (mine) scheduling
Soft drink bottling	Iron ore
Bank courier	Strip mining
Intrahospital material flow	Parking facility design
Enterprise models	Numerically controlled production facility
Steel production	design
Hospital	Personnel scheduling
Shipping line	Inspection department
Railroad operations	Spacecraft trips
School district	Petrochemical process design
Equipment scheduling	Solvent recovery
Aircraft	Police response system design
Facility layout	Political voting prediction
Pharmaceutical center	Rail freight car dispatching
Financial forecasting	Railroad traffic scheduling
Insurance	Steel mill scheduling
Schools	Taxi dispatching
Computer leasing	Traffic light timing
Insurance manpower hiring decisions	Truck dispatching and loading
Grain terminal operation	University financial and operational
Harbor design	forecasting
	Urban traffic system design
	Water resources development

Source: Reprinted with permission of MacMillan Publishing Co., Inc. from *Design and Use of Computer Simulation Models* by James R. Emshoff and Roger L. Sisson.

assumptions about arrival intervals and service patterns, and so on. These limit their use and keep them from being used in more complex situations. Simulation allows much more flexibility in the determination of assumptions.

3. Simulation can be used for other applications in addition to waiting

line analysis. Figure 26–6 lists examples of the many ways in which simulation can be used.

We will illustrate how simulation works by using several examples of its use in different situations.

TRUCK REPLACEMENT EXAMPLE

Advance Air Freight is considering discontinuing its leasing of 12 pickup and delivery trucks. If it does this, Advance will have to buy 12 trucks right away and then buy replacement trucks in the future, one by one, as the old ones wear out. The question AAFs managers want to answer is how many trucks they may have to buy during the next five years (including the initial 12 trucks) in order to keep 12 trucks in operation all the time. At the moment, AAF's managers are not concerned with the fact that at the end of five years they will have 12 trucks on hand, some of which will be relatively new and some of which will be old. The only question is how many will have to be purchased so they can plan their cash requirements accordingly.

Without using a computer, it is possible to perform this simulation by using a random number table. Before using random numbers, however, it is necessary to know how long the trucks are expected to last. Figure 26–7 shows a history of truck life:

FIGURE 26–7

Truck life (months)	Percentage of trucks which have worn out
12	5
15	10
18	20
21	25
24	30
27	5
30	5
Total	100

Next, a method must be developed to simulate the wearing out and replacement of trucks over the next 5 years, or 60 months. This is done by using "random numbers" from the random number table provided in Appendix G. If we pick a number any place in a table of 1,000 random numbers and go across a row or up or down a column in any direction, the probabilities of any of the thousand three digit numbers, say the number 684, being the next number, is 1/1,000. The odds are the same if the numbers are chosen randomly instead of one after the other as they appear in a table of random numbers.

In order to simulate the wearing out of trucks, we assign blocks of numbers between 000 and 999 according to the frequency distribution

FIGURE 26–8

Truck life	Percent which last this long	Random numbers assigned to this event
12..............	5	000–049
15..............	10	050–149
18..............	20	150–349
21..............	25	350–599
24..............	30	600–899
27..............	5	900–949
30..............	5	950–999

shown in Figure 26–7. Since 5 percent of the trucks have had in the past (and we think that this will continue into the future) a life of only 12 months, we assign the first 5 percent of these numbers, 000 through 049, to trucks which will wear out in 12 months. Then we assign the next 10 percent of the numbers, 050 through 149, to the trucks which will last only 15 months. Figure 26–8 shows the complete allocation of numbers to the various truck lives.

Next, we read off random numbers successively from the random number table. We started at the top of column 6 of Appendix G. The first number is 027. The number 027 falls in the range 000–049, which corresponds to a truck life of 12 months.

The next random number is 539, which falls in the 350–599 interval, indicating that the truck which replaced the first one has a life of 21 months and that it will need to be replaced at the end of the 33rd month. The next number is 623, which indicates a life of 24 months. The cumulative months until the failure of this third truck is 57. So these three trucks, considered together, will last less than five years, so a fourth truck will have to be bought. Its random number, 485, indicates a 21-month life so it will be useful considerably beyond the five-year mark.

Since AAF is interested only in the next 60 months, we go on to the second truck sequence. This time only three trucks will suffice and will cover the 60-month period. But the sequences for trucks number 4, 5, 6, and 9 will, as in the case of the first truck, require four trucks each in order to carry on for 60 months.

Figure 26–9 shows how this process works. It shows that 41 trucks will have to be bought within the next 60 months or 5 years (12 initially, plus 29 replacements). At the beginning of the sixth year, the 12 trucks then on hand will have, in total, an expected remaining truck life of 114 months.

AAF can now answer the question first posed, how many trucks will it probably have to buy each year for the next five years. It will have first to buy 12 trucks right away. All of them will last through the first year, but 10 will have to be replaced before the end of the second year. Numbers from 12 to 21 in the cumulation month listing below indicates that the original truck wears out and has to be replaced during the second year. During the third year, 6 more will need replacing (indicated by cumula-

FIGURE 26–9

Truck	Random number				Month (cumulative) when truck wears out and is replaced				Excess truck life beyond 60 months
1........	027	539	623	485	12	33	57	78	18
2........	272	273	852		18	36	60		0
3........	850	840	973		24	48	78		18
4........	198	523	071	532	18	39	54	75	15
5........	025	285	626	890	12	30	54	78	18
6........	283	114	116	453	18	33	48	69	9
7........	406	539	496		21	42	63		3
8........	875	332	963		24	42	72		12
9........	032	298	658	308	12	30	54	72	12
10........	364	587	310		21	42	60		0
11........	123	957	951		15	42	69		0
12........	397	687	057		21	45	60		0
								Total	114

tive numbers from 24 to 33). In the fourth year, it will be 7 and in the fifth year, 6. AAF will have to buy 41 trucks all told before the end of the fifth year. With the knowledge provided by the simulation, it can plan its truck purchases, having some feel for the necessary monetary needs.

How reliable are these results? It is difficult to say exactly how reliable any simulation solution is since no one can know exactly what sequence of events (in our case, the lives of specific trucks) will occur in real life. But, if the distribution of truck lives in Figure 26–7 continues to be valid, then extended simulations provide a good picture of what will happen in real life.

If we were to simulate this situation again, starting at another place in the random number table, we would generate a different set of sequences of truck replacements, but the total replacements would probably be very close to 29. One might ask why we cannot simply use the average life of trucks (which is 21 months) to estimate the needed number of replacement trucks. It would seem that if three trucks have an average total life of 63 months, then in 60 months two replacements for each original truck ought to be enough. It would seem that only 24 replacements would have to be bought instead of 29. The reason that using the average approach fails is that it does not take into account the irregularities of short- and long-lived trucks which do not dovetail in such a way as to average out in the short run. Nor does it recognize that at the end of five years some recently bought trucks will still have many months of life in them.

MACHINE SETUP MECHANIC EXAMPLE

This example deals with a waiting line problem similar to one presented in our discussion of queuing models on page 640. It illustrates the interactions of service calls whose time between arrivals varies as does the time it takes a server to take care of the calls.

The Sunray Solar Heating Company has four machines which are used in a variety of operations in producing parts for solar panels. These machines are set up by a mechanic, and then each is run by a machine operator until the job is completed, after which the machine is out of production until the mechanic sets it up for its next job. Whenever no machine is being set up, the mechanic waits. (He does not actually wait but keeps busy on relatively low-value minor jobs.)

The question is: How many mechanics should Sunray have if they cost $10 per hour and idle machines cost $20 per hour in lost production?

From past records, Sunray has determined that setup and job times have varied as follows:

FIGURE 26–10

Length of job		Setup time	
Hours	Instances	Hours	Instances
4	20%	2	50%
8	30	4	20
16	20	8	15
24	20	12	10
40	10	20	5

First, just as in the truck replacement problem, it is necessary to assign groups of random numbers so that we can generate simulated job length times and setup times.

FIGURE 26–11

Length of job		Setup time	
Hours	Random numbers	Hours	Random numbers
4	000–199	2	000–499
8	200–499	4	500–699
16	500–699	8	700–849
24	700–899	12	850–949
40	900–999	20	950–999

Again we refer to the random number table and generate a simulated list of successive job and setup times. These are:

FIGURE 26–12

Machine	Time (hours)										
	J	S	J	S	J	S	J	S	J	S	J
1	4	2	8	4	24	8	24	8			
2	8	2	16	4	40	2	16				
3	16	12	4	2	4	12	40				
4	16	4	4	12	24	2	8	2	4	2	8

In Figure 26–12, the "*J*" and "*S*" letters refer to job times and setup times. For each machine, they were carried out to simulate the continuing sequence of job time, setup time, job time, setup time, and so on until an 80-hour time period (two weeks) had passed. In our example, we assumed that all four machines were set up and ready to begin their first jobs at the start of our simulation. (This assumption puts a small artificial error into the cost comparisons which follow since the mechanic obviously starts off being idle.)

The next step is to see how it would work to have just one mechanic doing all of the setup work. In allocating his time, we followed the priority rule that in case there are two machines needing him he will first take care of the machine which has been waiting the longest.

In Figure 26–13, the lines and arrows follow the mechanic as he goes about his work. We see that at the start he is idle until time 4 (hours).

FIGURE 26–13

Idle mechanic hours	Idle machine hours	4	3	2	1	1 mechanic
		4	3	2	1	Machine
		0	0	0	0	Machine begins
		16	16	8	4	Machine stops
6	16	30	18	8	4	Setup begins
		34	30	10	6	Setup ends, machine begins
		38	34	26	14	Machine stops
4	14	40	38	34	14	Setup begins
		52	40	38	18	Setup ends, machine begins
		76	44	78	42	Machine stops
4	26	76	60	78	52	Setup begins
		78	72	80	60	Setup ends, machine begins
		86	112	96	84	Machine stops
					84	Setup begins
4	0					
18	56	Total				

FIGURE 26-14

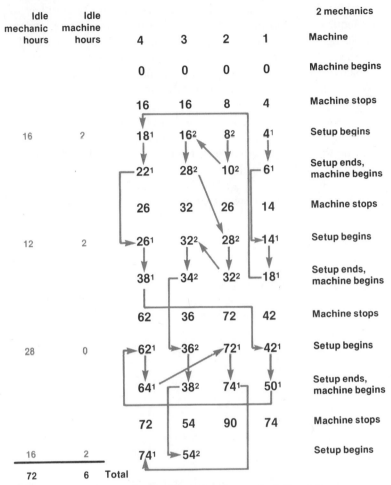

Note: The Superscripts on the times (e.g. 4¹,8²) refer to mechanic #1 and #2.

Then he begins setting up the second job on machine 1, completing it two hours later at time 6. Machine 1 then goes to work on its second job which will keep it tied up for the next eight hours, or until time 14.

Meanwhile the mechanic has to wait two hours from time 6 to time 8, at which time machine 2 finishes its first job. The mechanic then sets it up in two hours, finishing at time 10. Machine 2's new job keeps it busy until hour 26.

Machines 3 and 4 are still busy so again the mechanic has to wait, this time for four hours. Then he goes back to machine 1 which has finished its second job and starts setting it up for its third job. The mechanic's further work and wait periods are shown in Figure 26–13, as are the several instances where the machines have to wait for him.

As the summary at the bottom of Figure 26–13 shows, the mechanic waits a total of 18 hours which, at a cost of $10 an hour, is $180. But with only one mechanic, the machines wait 56 hours, which at $20 an hour cost $1,120, bringing the total cost of idleness to $1,300 during these 80 hours, or two weeks.

Next we turned to the question of whether hiring a second mechanic would pay. Figure 26–14 shows how these two mechanics would shuttle back and forth trying to meet the machines' needs. This time the summary tells us that one mechanic will have 40 idle hours and the other one 32 hours. At $10 an hour, this comes to $720. But idle machine time, at six hours, has almost been eliminated. This cost is only $120, which brings the total for the two-mechanic arrangement to $840. It will pay very well to add a second mechanic.

There is no need to look into the question of whether it would pay to add a third mechanic. The most that he could save would be to eliminate all of the $120 cost of machine idle time, but this would be far less than the cost of the added mechanic.

CAR WASH EXAMPLE

The Quick Car Wash Company is concerned about the amount of business it is losing on Saturdays because so many potential customers, seeing long lines, don't wait but go away. Observations show that rarely will the line of waiting cars grow beyond five cars. When potential customers see that many cars ahead of them, they drive away. But, if there are four or fewer, they nearly always get in line and wait. Since many car wash customers also buy gasoline and some of the defectors may also be lost future customers, Quick Car Wash's manager estimates that he loses $2 every time a car refuses to wait.

It is possible to change the car wash line speed controls so that the line can be speeded up on Saturdays. Modifying the controls would cost $600 and would make it possible for the line to operate at either a medium speed (as contrasted with the present slow speed) or a high speed. At medium speed, one extra attendant would be required, and one more yet for high speed operation. Attendants cost $3 an hour each.

The question is: Should QCW modify the controls so that the line can be speeded up on Saturdays, and, if so, should it operate at medium or high speed? This case is similar to the bank drive-up window example on page 637, except that this time we are using simulation instead of queuing formulas.

Past experience with the slow line speed shows the following distribution in service times (the times vary somewhat depending on the kind and size of car as well as how dirty it is in the interior).

FIGURE 26–15

Service time (minutes)	Percent of cars
6	10
7	40
8	40
9	10

It is estimated that the speeded-up line will be able to reduce the service times to the following:

FIGURE 26–16

Medium speed—One extra attendant	
Service time (minutes)	Percent of cars
5	10
6	40
7	40
8	10
High speed—Two extra attendants	
4	10
5	40
6	40
7	10

Past experience shows the following distribution of time intervals between the arrival of cars when the long lines might occur on Saturdays:

FIGURE 26–17

Elapsed time between arrivals (minutes)	Percent of arrivals
3	10
4	20
5	50
6	20

The next step, as before, is to allocate random numbers in proportion to the percent distribution given in our tables. Although we simulated two hours of Saturday operations in order to get the figures needed for comparing the alternatives, in order to save space, we will reproduce here only the first half dozen sets of figures.

Our first half dozen random numbers for service times were 590, 359, 895, 668, 051, and 482. Those for arrivals were 735, 273, 372, 206, 047, and 252. Translated into equivalent times, these numbers provided service times (for the present slow method) of 7, 6, 7, 7, 5, and 6 minutes. Arrivals were 5, 4, 5, 4, 3, and 4 minutes.

FIGURE 26–18

Time	Cars in line	Time of next arrival	Defect
0– 7.	5	5	yes
7– 9.	4	9	no
9–13.	5	none	—
13–14.	4	14	no
14–20.	5	18	yes
20–21.	4	21	no
21–27.	5	25	yes

Both sets of times were cumulated so that comparisons could be made. We assumed that there were already five cars in the line when our simulation started. The washing of the first of these cars was completed in 7 minutes, the second at 13 minutes, the third at 20 minutes, and so on. The cumulations of arrival times showed the first car arriving at 5 minutes, the second at 9 minutes, the third at 14, and so on.

Now the comparisons can be made. From 0 to 7 the line was full so the car arriving in five minutes defected. Then the first car being washed was finished and moved out at 7 so the line was no longer full. When, at nine minutes, another car arrived, its driver got into line and the line was back up to five. It stayed this way until 13 when the second car in the original line was finished, thus leaving only four cars in line. But, at 14 minutes, another arrival took the empty space at the end of the line, bringing it back up to five cars. This closed the line until 20 minutes. At 18 minutes, another car arrived but, seeing five cars already in line, it did not stay. Then the next car finished at 20, and the line was down to 4 until the 21-minute arrival took the space, and so on as is shown in Figure 26–18. In our little example there were three defections in 27 minutes.

We carried through this kind of analysis to simulate all three line speeds for two hours of operations. The existing method showed five defectors per hour. Their total cost in lost revenues came to $10 per hour. The medium speed plus one extra attendant showed four defectors so this change would not have saved enough ($2) to pay for the added attendant ($3), to say nothing of paying off the cost of the control modification.

Operating at high speed with two extra attendants reduced defectors to two per hour (a saving of three and a saving of $6, but at a cost of two extra attendants at $6). In this case, Quick Car Wash would break even on the savings versus the labor costs, but there would be no contribution toward the $600 cost of making the change. The company should not make the change.

DENVER FIRE DEPARTMENT EXAMPLE

This example presents a description of an actual simulation which was used to aid the city of Denver and the Denver Fire Department in determining how many fire stations it should have, where they should be located, and what type of equipment should be placed in each fire station.[6]

In 1972, Denver's mayor and fire chief recognized the need to consider the application of modern management analysis for the Denver fire department. A multidisciplinary team was set up, consisting of members of the Denver fire department, Denver's Office of Budget and Management, and operations researchers from the University of Colorado. In addition the team was guided by a specially formed Policy Review Committee, which consisted of the fire chief, several city officials, and a university dean. The research study was funded by HUD's Office of Policy Development and Research in early 1973 by a grant of $117,000.

The major assignment given to the research team by Denver officials was rather straightforward: Can the Denver Fire Department provide approximately the same level of fire protection service but at a lower cost?

Fire suppression accounts for about 90 percent of the activities of the Denver Fire Department's $13 million budget. (The Department also answers calls to help people in trouble, heart attack victims, people suffocating, as well as getting cats out of trees, and helping apartment dwellers who have locked themselves out to get into their apartments, and so on.) Nearly all of the money is for the wages and salaries of firefighters.

At the time of this study, it was costing Denver $250,000 *a year* to staff each fire engine or ladder truck with firefighters around the clock. Labor was the big cost, since the vehicle itself cost only some $60,000 and a firehouse, a one-time cost, cost about $400,000. The critical factor, therefore, was simply how many fire "companies" (vehicles with firefighters on board) the city should have and where they should be located.

Static analysis of station location alternatives

When a city like Denver has a large number of fire companies compared to its fire alarm rate and all vehicles are typically available to respond to an alarm, then a so-called static analysis can be performed. This was done in Denver by having the members of the Denver Fire Department develop a comprehensive inventory of fire hazards which exist throughout the city. Further, they developed a large number of potential new location sites for fire stations. Next, each of the hazards was graded as to its severity and translated into maximum allowable response time standards for the first arriving vehicle.

The last data requirement for this static analysis was the prediction of the response time from each of the existing fire stations and potential fire station sites to each of the hazards. This was accomplished through a detailed time-distance study of nearly 1,600 actual runs by Denver fire department vehicles.

---

[6] Reported in Thomas E. Hendrick and Donald R. Plane, *et al., An Analysis of the Deployment of Fire-Fighting Resources in Denver, Colorado,* Santa Monica, The Rand Corporation, R–1566/3–HUD, May 1975.

FIGURE 26-19

Static travel time statistics

Hazard class	Average first arriving pumper travel time (minutes)		Average first arriving ladder travel time (minutes)	
	Existing configuration	Proposed configuration	Existing configuration	Proposed configuration
Very high.........	1.8	1.7	1.9	2.1
High..............	2.3	2.3	2.7	2.7
Medium..........	2.2	2.2	2.9	3.0
Low..............	2.5	2.5	3.4	3.6
Overall average....	2.3	2.2	2.8	2.9

The team then had four kinds of data; hazard location, severity of hazards translated into maximum allowable response time requirements for the first arriving vehicle, the location of existing and of potential fire station sites, and an ability to predict the response time from any firehouse location to any hazard. With these data, the team was able to analyze a large number of alternative station location patterns. This was done by using linear programming and the "Station Configuration Information Model" (SCIM), a specialized computer model developed by the Denver team to show response time statistics of a given station location pattern.

Several alternative location patterns were analyzed in depth. Each pattern specified where pumper trucks and where ladder trucks were to be located. One configuration stood out as being much less costly than all others. Not only was it less costly, it even showed a small improvement in the average response travel time by pumper trucks and only a slight increase in travel time of the first arriving ladder trucks. The specific statistics of this configuration are shown in Figure 26–19.

The important characteristic of this configuration was that it provided approximately the same level of service but *with five fewer companies.* This configuration required the closing of some stations, the building of certain new ones, and other adjustments in the locations of pumper and ladder trucks at various locations throughout the city. This redesigned system with five fewer companies was expected to save Denver more than $2.3 million over a seven-year planning horizon and over $1 million annually thereafter.

Dynamic analysis of location analysis using Monte Carlo simulation

The static analysis described here presumes that each piece of equipment is available to respond to an emergency from its firehouse and is never busy at some other fire when a new alarm comes in. This static assumption may be valid most of the time even though it may not be quite true all of the time. There are times when equipment has to come from farther away stations because the near one is already out on a call.

After selecting what appeared to be the most satisfactory new location pattern, it and several other possible configurations were tested against the existing arrangement by means of Monte Carlo simulation. This "dynamic analysis" allowed the investigating team to systematically study alternative fire station location patterns when fires are simulated to occur in the pattern of occurrence of Denver's actual fire incident experience.

This dynamic analysis showed how well a given station configuration would perform under various alarm rates; it specifically allowed for a fire truck being busy and already at one fire and so unavailable to go to another fire. The simulation considered, for example, how much the travel time would deteriorate (increase) to various places throughout the city if the alarm rate were to increase from say an average of five calls per hour to an average of ten per hour? The Denver study utilized a revised version of the New York City-Rand Institute fire department computer simulation model to perform this dynamic analysis.

This model kept track of "arriving" fires and, in the computer, dispatched the closest available companies to them and kept track of travel time, the time it took to put out the fire, and when these companies would be available to go to the next fire, and so on.

To feed this complex model with data that reflected the Denver situation, a comprehensive analysis of over 17,000 actual fires and other emergencies was performed by the research team to determine the location of various emergencies and when they occurred. A sample of these 17,000 incidents was also analyzed to determine how many vehicles were required to put out the fires and how long each was likely to be busy before it was free to be available to service another emergency.

Using this simulation model, the research team, using various alarm arrival rates, studied the results of several alternative station location patterns. The alarm rates used varied from 2.5 per hour, the 1973 average, to 9.65 alarms per hour, the projected 1978 rate during the busiest hours of the day (4:00 P.M. to 10:00 P.M.) during the busiest month of the year (July).

The results proved surprising. Even at the highest average alarm rate, 9.65 per hour, there was no substantial deterioration in response times between the existing pattern of 44 companies versus the recommended pattern of 39 companies. As Figure 26–20 shows, the extra time in even the busiest periods, with five fewer companies, was about ten seconds.

Other analyses performed with the use of the simulation model corroborated the ability of the 39-company pattern to provide approximately the same level of fire suppression protection as the existing configuration of 44 companies.

In summary, using travel time as the measure of the level of fire suppression service, the project team produced a redesign location pattern of pumpers and ladder trucks which left the level of service essentially unchanged with a proposed reduction of five companies. This reduction of five companies is being accomplished over a seven-year period by closing

FIGURE 26–20

Average travel time for first arrival vehicle (pumper or ladder) needed to do work (based on simulations)

Alarm rate per hour	Travel time (minutes)		Difference (seconds)
	Existing	Proposed	
2.50 (1973 average)................	1.93	2.07	8
3.22.............................	1.95	2.09	8
4.71.............................	2.03	2.16	7
5.12.............................	2.04	2.19	9
6.60.............................	2.06	2.24	11
9.65 (projected 1978 rate)..........	2.14	2.33	11

some stations with obsolete locations and building a few new ones at better locations which were determined by the study.

It is important to note that this seven-year plan is being implemented carefully. It is to be reviewed periodically to see if the recommendations are still appropriate in terms of the alarm rate experience, annexations, and other changes in Denver's character.

VALIDATION OF SIMULATION RESULTS

Once a simulation has been used and a managerial decision made, the die is cast. One hopes that one has made a good decision, but good or not, money and the use of other resources have been committed, often irreversibly.

It is much like buying machines or building buildings. In order to test the wisdom of their decisions, companies sometimes make postconstruction audits. They try to see whether or not the decision was a good one. The purpose is not really so much to see if the action was well advised as it is to evaluate the technique to see if it should continue to be used in the future. Actually not very many companies make postconstruction audits because they cost money, and it is often almost impossible to judge what might have been had a particular decision not have been made.

Post decision validation checks of the validity of simulations may themselves actually be poor indicators of the reliability of the simulation. The sample of actual conditions used for checking purposes may itself not be typical. If this were so, it would differ from the expectations shown by the simulation and would seem to show poor reliability of the simulation when in fact the simulation was a very good predictor of long-run average expectations.

Obviously, too, a postdecision test of a simulation model to check its validity is useful only if the model is to be used again. In the case of the Denver Fire Department study, several checks were made to validate the process. These were not, however, of the post-construction or post-decision type but were carried on along with the analysis itself. In this case the purpose was more to establish the reliability of the procedure as it unfolded than it was as after-the-fact review. Should these checks have revealed that the procedure did not provide reasonable results, changes would have been made.

Several checks were made as the work proceeded to see if the model was providing reliable predictions. For example, the model predicted that the response time using the recommended configuration would be 116 seconds. A check of actual response times showed the average to be 121 seconds. The model made a good showing here.

A second test, this time of the actual work time spent on call, again proved that the times expected from the simulation proved to be very close to what happened. This was true for the system as a whole and for most of the individual companies as well. Three-quarters of the companies were busy almost exactly as much as the simulation predicted (they were less than one tenth off).

A third test investigated the question of the distribution of pumper runs to emergencies actually made by selected pumper companies against that shown to be expected by the simulation. Again the predicted rate of use of individual companies was very close to what actually happened.

In the Denver fire department case, simulation proved to be a very worthwhile tool in the analysis of a difficult problem.

USE OF COMPUTERS IN SIMULATION

Since simulation is usually done on computers, special computer languages have been developed which allow analysts to write simulation programs. While excellent simulation models can be written in such general purpose computer languages as Fortran and BASIC, many analysts prefer to use special purpose languages such as GPSS (General Purpose Simulation System) or GASP IV (Generalized Activity Simulation Program), or SIMSCRIPT, the language used for the Denver fire department study.

Most computer languages have built-in random number generators which can be used in simulating the random arrival of customers, service times, and so on. Many also have "built-in" Poisson probability distributions as well as a number of other distributions of various shapes to match the users' needs. In many simulations, the analyst may combine the use of mathematical distributions such as the Poisson (perhaps for arrival rates) with distributions obtained from observation, such as the car wash time distributions used in the Quick Car Wash example. This is what was done in the fire department study. Arrivals of emergencies were generated through a Poisson process, while work time at the emergencies were determined by analyzing and classifying work times of about 1,100 actual fires and other emergencies.

Computers are thus helpful not only in performing simulations of experiences, but, in the absence of complete data, they can generate approximate data which allows simulation to be used even where more detailed actual data are not available.

REVIEW QUESTIONS

1. What are the two general approaches to analyzing waiting line problems?
2. What kinds of questions do queuing formulas answer?
3. What differences are assumed between the gasoline station, repair shop, bank, fire dispatching, xerox, and machine setup examples given in the text?
4. Why are special purpose queuing tables and charts used? Why not just use the queuing formulas?
5. How does Monte Carlo simulation differ from classical queuing analysis?
6. What would happen to the results of a simulation if we used a different set of random numbers? Under what circumstances would the results be about the same? Different?
7. Explain the way to use random number tables to help develop simulated results in Monte Carlo simulation problems.
8. Is it necessary to have actual experience figures upon which to base Monte Carlo simulations? Explain.

QUESTIONS FOR DISCUSSION

1. If a service operator's calls for service average five calls per hour and ten minutes each, would there ever be times when a facility that needs service would have to wait? Why is this?
2. "Although Monte Carlo methods are useful to help managers see what average conditions will be like, they are of little help to a manager who is interested in extremes." Discuss this statement.
3. Waiting line analysis deals with trade-offs. Discuss.
4. Waiting line problems pervade our everyday life. Discuss.
5. What is queue discipline?
6. Is validation of simulation applications important? How can it be done?

PROBLEMS

1. Customers arrive at a small bank's teller window at an average rate of 20 per hour and can be served at an average rate of 30 per hour. Both arrival and service rates are approximately Poisson distributed. What is the expected length of the waiting line? The average waiting line? The

average time waiting and being served? How busy is the teller? What other things should be considered in analyzing this situation?

2. Given the information in Problem 1, suppose that the bank's managers were considering adding a second teller's window but requiring arriving customers to wait in a single line until a teller becomes available. Additionally, they wish to add some new services to be handled by the tellers. These new services would reduce the service rate to 25 per hour per teller, but would increase the arrival rate to 25 per hour. If adding the second teller will cost $5 per hour and the managers value waiting times of customers at $5 per hour, should they add the second teller?

3. An automatic screw machine department has 8 machines. The service needs of these machines are Poisson in pattern as is the service rate by mechanics. On the average, each machine needs service every 3 hours, and service times average 25 minutes when done by a single mechanic.

a. How many machines would be running if there were 1, 2, 3, or 4 mechanics? Assume service rates double with 2 mechanics; triple with 3, etc. (Use Appendix F.)

b. If machine idle time (waiting and being serviced) costs $30 per hour, how many mechanics should be assigned to these 8 machines?

4. Using the information given in problem 3, and using the TRW diagram (Figure 26–4), determine the most economical number of service men to have. Service men cost $8 an hour. Assume that, except for service time, the machines are in operation.

5. A battery of 16 machines is serviced by 4 mechanics who do both setup and repair work. These mechanics are able to give good service and keep the machines running almost all of the time, but the mechanics themselves are not always busy. Machine time is worth $10 an hour and the mechanics cost $6 an hour. If they are not busy there is standby work for them, so that half of their wage loss is salvaged. A work-sampling study showed that the machines typically were in operation 80 percent of the time, were being serviced 10 percent of the time, and were idle from lack of orders 10 percent of the time.

How many mechanics should be on this assignment in order to hold costs to a minimum?

6. How many service workers should there be at a tool crib which serves machinists who arrive at a rate of 20 an hour and whose service times average 10 minutes. Both arrival times and service times are irregular. The machinists cost $12 an hour (including the cost of their idle machines while they are at the tool crib) whereas tool crib attendants cost $5 an hour. When tool crib attendants are not serving the machinists at the issue window, they spend their time cleaning tooling that has previously been returned. This work is regarded as saving two-thirds of the cost of what would otherwise be idle time.

What would be the answer to this problem if the people who came to the window were $4.50 an hour machinist helpers whose time at the tool crib did not cause any machines to be idle?

7. Records of 100 truck loads of finished jobs arriving in a department's checkout area show the following: Checking out time takes five minutes and the checker takes care of only one truck at a time.

Minutes between arrivals	Number of cases
1	1
2	4
3	7
4	17
5	31
6	23
7	7
8	5
9	3
10	2
	100

As soon as the jobs are checked out, the truck drivers take them to the next departments. Using Monte Carlo simulation, determine (a) what percent of the time there is no load at all at the checkout station, (b) what is the average waiting time, and (c) what is likely to be the longest wait.

8. A study of 100 unemployed people were found to arrive at a one-person state employment office to obtain their unemployment compensation check according to the following frequency distribution.

Time between arrivals (minutes)	Frequency
2.0	10
2.5	20
3.0	40
3.5	20
4.0	10

A time study of the time required to disburse checks yielded the following service time frequency distribution:

Service time	Frequency
1.5	10
2.0	20
2.5	40
3.0	20
3.5	10

Will people have to wait? How many and how long?

9. The Standard Automobile Company's home plant can, when everything goes perfectly, turn out 1,000 cars a day. But, even when sales are high and the schedule calls for 1,000 a day, production varies because of

interruptions. Here is the record during past peak seasons when 1,000 cars were actually scheduled (the problem concerns only the 100-day peak period; there's no problem during the rest of the year):

Production	Percent of the time
750.........................	3
800.........................	7
850.........................	15
875.........................	25
900.........................	23
925.........................	14
950.........................	9
975.........................	3
1,000.........................	1
	100

Standard has a contract with the Truckaway Company to haul out up to 900 cars a day. (This is all that Truckaway's equipment can handle from March through May, the company's peak period.) If there are fewer than 875 cars to be hauled away in any one day, Standard pays a penalty charge of $1 per car short of this amount. If there are more than 900 to be removed, the excess go into a parking lot (storage cost $.50 per car per day) until they can be taken away.

a. What will be Standard's combined cost for penalties and parking charges for 100 days of operation? What will be the largest number of cars in the parking lot at any one time? (In order to reduce the problem-solving time, carry through a simulation for 25 days only and then multiply the costs by 4 in order to get a reasonable approximation of the costs for 100 days.)

b. Will it pay Standard to buy a parking lot which will hold 50 cars if the cost of operating the lot will be $300 a year? (The 100 days in our problem is the only time that the lot would be used.)

c. Truckaway has proposed a new contract covering this peak period. This contract would reduce the trucking cost $.10 per car for all cars hauled away but would call for 925 cars a day to be hauled away with a penalty charge of $1 for every empty space below 925. Should Standard accept this proposal? Use the Monte Carlo method to solve this problem.

SUGGESTED SUPPLEMENTARY READINGS

Godin, V. B. "A Dollar and Sense of Simulation." *Decision Sciences,* April 1976, pp. 331–42.

Keller, T. F., and Laughton, D. J. "An Application of Queuing Theory to a Congestion Problem in an Out-Patient Clinic." *Decision Sciences,* July 1973, pp. 379–93.

Maxwell, T. "Queuing Theory, What It Is and How It Works." *Administrative Management,* December 1971.

section seven

QUALITY MANAGEMENT SYSTEMS

QUALITY permeates most of production and operations management systems. The position of a company in the economy and its image is closely related to the quality decisions its managers have made in the past and to the way in which these decisions have been carried into effect.

The need to design products and services to reach and appeal to certain segments of the market has been discussed in earlier chapters. So has the relationship of quality to costs and the need for designing products and services which are safe for consumers to use. Here, too, managers have to relate their quality desires to the organization's ability to produce the desired quality at a cost which can be supported in the market place by appropriate prices.

Whatever the quality-cost relationship goals may be, they become—once decided—limitations for the organization. The established standards are then put into effect by the quality control system.

Chapter 27 considers quality control from a conceptual viewpoint and as a totality. It gives an overview of the whole problem of product quality enforcement as it is carried on in a manufacturing environment. Chapter 28 presents statistical quality control. Each of the common uses of statistical quality control is considered, both from a technical viewpoint and as they operate in organizations.

27

Quality management systems

"QUALITY," to most people, seems to mean "high quality." It is a little like mother, God, Queen, and country—everyone is for it, and the more quality the better. Yet, one can ask, do people really want the highest possible quality of everything? The answer has to be no, because costs are always a part of customer decisions.

Supermarkets sell millions of pounds of candy, millions of water glasses and dishes, and millions of other things—practically all of which are admittedly of medium or low quality. Not all people buy their candy and glassware and dishes from supermarkets, but obviously many do.

Most people do not want the very best of very many things—at least not to the extent of being willing to pay the cost of high quality. What we want is the best quality we can get for the money we are willing to spend. Our quality-cost calculus is sometimes more cost sensitive than it is quality sensitive. All we want is for the product or service to be good enough.

This is why Sears Roebuck is the world's biggest merchandiser, even though it rarely carries the best of anything. And this is what quality means to a manufacturer. He tries to make the best product he can for the price that most of his potential customers are willing to pay. Hormel doesn't put top grade pork loin meat into Spam because Spam users wouldn't pay the price.

The price that a prospective customer is willing to pay is related both to what he wants and what he can afford to spend for an item. Marketing experts tell us that what people want, their desired "bundle of utilities," includes durability, dependability, workmanship, exclusivity (few other people have one), eye appeal (shape, color, and so on), and price.

Curiously, sometimes consumers are impressed by a high price and seem to think that a higher-priced product must be better and that a very high-priced product must be very much better. Chanel #5 perfume gets part of its reputation from being expensive.

Figure 27–1 shows relationships between quality, costs, and what people might be willing to pay. Note that the cost usually rises at an increasing rate as the level of quality increases. Also, note that the "value" or worth of higher quality increases at a decreasing rate. People usually want something better than the very cheapest and are willing to pay more for higher-quality items or services. But, for most items, not very much more. Before long the worth to them of further extra quality diminishes. An economist would say that this is an illustration of the concept of "diminishing marginal utility."

Conceptually, the optimal level of quality for an organization to build into its products or services is where the gap between the "cost to provide" line and the "value of the bundle of utilities" line is the widest (Point A.)

While Figure 27–1 is nice to look at as depicting relationships, in reality it is hard to draw as reflecting actual relationships because of the difficulty in estimating the shapes of the two curves. The cost curve, for example, depends among other things on the volume of demand. Similarly, the utility value curve is influenced by the availability of substitute products or services, the general health of the economy, and such unpredictable things as "fashion."

Because this is so, product designers need to work closely with marketing people so that the level of quality chosen is within the range between points B and C in Figure 27–1. The quality level which satisfies this requirement is usually determined by market surveys and by test marketing a product in one or two small geographical areas before offering products on a nationwide basis.

FIGURE 27–1

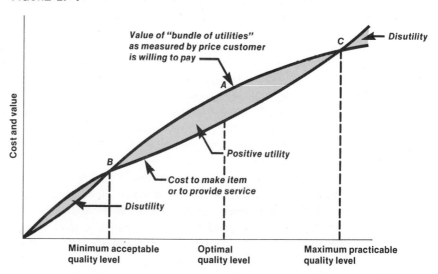

Year by year the quality of most products improves. An automobile or a television set which was a best seller in 1965 was no longer acceptable in 1975. It wasn't good enough. And 1975 cars and TV sets will not be acceptable in 1985. *They* won't be good enough. Quality improves because of technological advances and because both customers and competitors force almost everyone to incorporate these advances into their products.

Sometimes, however, customers do not see quality improvements directly because they take their gain in lower prices rather than in more quality for the old prices. Today's color television sets, for example, are both better and cheaper than they were at first. But they could be even better yet today if customers were willing to pay more. TV manufacturers have found from experience, however, that most customers will not pay much more for still higher quality.

Quality control people usually wince at the idea that most manufacturers try only to make the best for the money instead of simply the best. Many production managers also disagree with this view because they like to think that they are making the best. Yet neither quality control people nor production managers can afford to forget costs. People making Toyotas or Volkswagens are not making Cadillacs, nor are they going to sell them for Cadillac prices.

Quality control people are likely, too, to wince at the notion that dimension and performance standards for parts and components are sometimes too tight. They like to feel that the standards they so zealously enforce rest on solid ground and not on some draftsman's "protect-himself-safe" overly tight specification. It is also true, of course, that no one can ever really know that an item 3/1,000 of an inch away from an exact dimension is acceptable whereas 4/1,000 of an inch is not acceptable.

Designers of military products are said sometimes to put in a "military fear factor" (they make parts three times as strong and as exact fitting as seems necessary). Designers of consumer products also sometimes over-design products. When they do this, the quality standards really ask for too much, and this usually causes unnecessarily higher costs. The parts of a pair of pliers or of a monkey wrench do not have to be made to dimension tolerances (allowable deviations) of thousandths of an inch.

The factory is often accused of being quantity—not quality—minded. Foremen cannot see why the engineers ask for such exact measurements. Their objections may be a lack of understanding of the need for exactly fitting parts. But they may also be based on the knowledge (knowledge that engineers share) that every specification is of necessity a little arbitrary, just as every speed limit on the highway is a little arbitrary.

Most products with slight imperfections are acceptable for most purposes. A Lenox china dish with a speck of ingrained dirt on the underside is not up to standard, but the dinner guest will probably never know. And if the electric cord on an electric typewriter is six inches short, its performance will in no way be impaired.

Neither of these products meets specifications, and both would probably be rejected by the inspectors. But these items are perfectly all right for practically every use. Admittedly, however, it is necessary to draw the line somewhere and to say *this* is acceptable but *that* isn't. It is impossible to escape some arbitrariness when setting standards.

Even more important, products differ and have different advantages and disadvantages. Is, for example, appearance quality? Or is performance quality? Furthermore, competing products are frequently all very good products, but they embody slightly different features. One automobile saves gasoline, another starts more easily in cold weather, another costs more. Is a Ford, Plymouth, or a Chevrolet, the best car? Is a Black & Decker drill better than a Craftsman (Sears Roebuck) drill? Also, which is the better buy when price is considered?

Quality is a hard concept to pin down or even detect. Consumers often can't even tell if there is a quality difference—as, for example, in the case of gasoline, bread, milk, roofing material, and many others. The customer can't tell which is best. Mixing in product characteristic differences as well as price differences complicated comparing even more.

In the service area, customers don't have quite so much trouble defining good service, but the managers of service organizations do. A Holiday Inn manager wants his customers to get good service, but good service is made up of quick service, attentive and sympathetic clerks, clean rooms and bed sheets; plumbing, lighting, television, and air conditioning and heating that work; and quiet, as well as good meals and easy check in and out—and all at a reasonable price.

Very few of these services are rendered under the direct supervisory eye of the manager so he has to define quality standards for all of these things for his staff and to train them in what good quality is and to try to see that his staff gives good quality service.

Service at a Hilton hotel or a Ritz hotel is different, however, from service at a Day's $8 motel. At the Hilton or Ritz, customers want more personal attention and pay more to get it. Usually, at such hotels, one expects to pay more, to wait longer for a meal, and to take longer eating, but to get a better meal. At the other end of the eating spectrum, McDonald's tries to provide a meal of the customer's choosing but from a limited list of offerings and with no frills—no table cloths (not even paper), no waitresses serving meals, no silver (in fact, no knives or forks, not even plastic), and no plates, only a plastic dish.

Perhaps more than in the case of products, people's "bundles of utilities" (what they want) in the way of services differs a great deal. "Good service" is a matter of matching up the quality of the services offered with what certain segments of the market want.

IMPLEMENTING PRODUCT DESIGN POLICIES

We have said that today's managers try to comply with the wishes of society so far as safety and consumer protection are concerned. In order to do this, they may have to set up implementation programs which are in addition to their quality management systems.

The additions are largely in designing products with safety and user protection in mind. Some companies are enlarging the job of the "product engineer" and assigning him this general responsibility. In the past, a product engineer usually had the responsibility for the general overseeing of putting a product into production. He determined the equipment needs, saw that it was ordered and installed and oversaw the initial production runs. He did not, however, design the product, nor control its quality.

His added responsibility today concerning product safety is one of co-ordination, communication, and education throughout the entire organization, so far as product safety is concerned. Whirlpool Corporation uses product engineers for just such purposes.[1] The product engineer gets this part of his authority and general directions from the company's "product safety audit program."

As part of this program, each major product periodically undergoes a formal review by an audit group. This group is led by someone from the engineering laboratory. Its meetings are also attended by the director of engineering for the product being audited and by the director of engineering for a totally unrelated product. Other areas represented are design, test, manufacturing and quality control. All audits for major products are also attended by the director of product safety for all products. In addition, representatives of the reliability group and customer assurance and service are present.

At Whirlpool Corporation, the typical product safety audit covers such subjects as:

1. Performance characteristics during normal use, during misuse, and during foreseeable abuse.
2. Nonperformance aspects: construction, clearances, edges, burrs, and so on, electrical, chemical, certifications, codes, standard tests and procedures.
3. Human engineering: man/machine considerations, instructions, cautions, labels, customer exposure to product.
4. Producibility, reliability, life.
5. Serviceability, removal and replacement of components, accessibility.
6. Product identification on packing cartons.
7. Provisions for handling packed products, shipping containers and shipping performance, unpacking procedures and instructions.

If a product is judged by the review group as being not acceptable in any way, suggested improvements are made and a time table is prepared for corrective action. This action is followed up on to determine compliance.

Whirlpool reports that this approach allows everyone in the company to know their products better and to know what they will do, what they will not do, and how the company will respond to situations involving use,

---

[1] The practice of Whirlpool Corporation on this matter is described in H. E. Brehm, "How to Establish a Product Safety Program," *Quality Progress,* February, 1975, pp. 28, 29.

misuse, and even abuse by the users. They find out if their products will tolerate operator errors without causing damage or causing injuries. With this knowledge, the company can lay out programs for improvement.

SPECIFYING QUALITY

A product's or a service's quality is embodied in its characteristics. The organization's managers decide these characteristics and then they have their designers try to develop products and services which incorporate these characteristics.

The end product of managerial thinking on quality may take the form of quality policy statements. In this form, these statements cannot be used by the factory because they do not contain instructions telling it what to do. They are goal statements. Some samples are:

1. We wish to provide dry cell batteries of such a quality that no more than 2 percent are defective (defective being defined as batteries whose average life in a typical transistor radio is less than 20 hours of playing time or those which leak). Manufacturing cost should be less than 12¢ per unit.
2. The failure rate of our calculators should average 130 percent per year (meaning that they will fail on the average of once every nine months). But we will develop a service repair organization and carry spare parts inventories which can provide "same day service" to 95 percent of our customers.
3. In our city we wish to provide a level of fire protection such that the average waiting time of a fire (once the alarm has been turned in) for the first arriving fire engine will be two minutes, with a maximum waiting time of six minutes under normal traffic and weather conditions.
4. We wish to produce a machine part whose diameter is one centimeter ± 1 millimeter.
5. We wish to produce soap that is 99.44 percent pure.
6. We will make our bread from ingredients which are organically grown and without using artificial preservatives.

Most of these quality goals as stated above are not "operationized." The factory cannot make products using only these instructions. Rather these policy statements are in the nature of the delegation or "mission charges" to designers. After receiving such a delegation, the designers, in conjunction with process engineers and industrial engineers, develop the specific instructions which the factory will have to have when it performs the operations which, taken together, implement these policies.

The instructions to the factory take the form of specifications, drawings showing dimensions and tolerances, or they are formulas, processing instructions, and the like. They also cover inspection and testing methods and specify acceptable levels.

All of these instructions are really, however, statements of goals, of desired quality. The factory then tries to accomplish them. But sometimes the factory falls short and fails to turn out products of the desired quality or turns out too many products which fail to pass inspection.

Quality problems are sometimes beyond the control of the production supervisor. For example, perhaps rejects could be reduced by using better materials. If so, top managers will have to decide whether to buy better (and more costly) materials. Or, perhaps the machines are too old and worn to do the precision work required. Managers would then have to choose between high scrap ratios or rebuilding the present machines, or buying new machines, or relaxing the standards. The responsibility for quality does not rest wholly on factory operators and their supervisors.

Similarly, the quality of the service rendered by service people is not wholly dependent on the attitudes of the service people. Plumbing systems in old hotels are likely to get out of order now and then. And, in the case of an airline, the quality of the service rendered may be almost as much a result of how well the maintenance work is done as it is dependent on the quality of service provided by ticket clerks and stewardesses.

INSPECTION

The primary quality implementation activity that goes on on a day-to-day basis is inspection. Obviously, products and services should be inspected in order to weed out inferior units. Inspecting products while they are being made also avoids further work on already defective units. But, if these savings are all that the inspector accomplishes, then larger gains are being overlooked.

The primary objective of inspection should be prevention—not remedy. The object is to stop making defective items (or stop inferior service). This requires that inspectors tell management not only that a product is being rejected, but also why, so managers can concentrate on improving the situation. Statistical quality control is helpful here because it is performed right at the operation and helps to prevent the continued production of defective units.

TESTING AND INSPECTION

Testing is a specific kind of inspection. "Inspection," a broader term than "testing," includes all activities, among them testing, to see if the products are up to standard. If, to inspect an item, a person has to do more than just look at it or measure it, it is usually called "testing" rather than "inspecting."

Tests may be performance or operating tests, as is depicted in Figure 27–2, or they may be "destructive" tests which end up ruining the particular product being tested. The question may be: How much will products stand before breaking? or how long will it be before they wear out? In

FIGURE 27–2

Performance testing of two meshing gears. The inspection job duplicates operating conditions and shows whether the gears actually mesh.

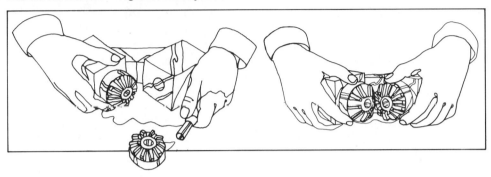

tensile strength testing, for example, the products are broken in the test. A test may also be a chemical analysis of a sample of the product. It too destroys the sample. Not all tests, however, destroy the product. X-ray methods, for example, are nondestructive. Hardness tests, too, are usually nondestructive, since they only make a slight dent on the surface of the product. Performance and operating tests (such as driving automobiles on a test track) of finished products are also typically nondestructive.

INSPECTING PURCHASED ITEMS

As a rule, all purchased items should be inspected to see that they are of the right kind and quantity and so that damaged or unsatisfactory items can be returned to the supplier and new ones obtained quickly.

Most materials and purchased parts create few problems so far as inspection is concerned; yet, this is not true for all purchased *components*. Such things as a specially designed instrument, a hydraulic pump, or an electrical control item are difficult to inspect or test. Receiving inspectors usually cannot tell whether they are good or not, so they need special checking instructions from engineering. Engineers themselves may need to inspect highly technical items.

The receiving department is usually under the direction of the stores department, although it may be administered by the purchasing department. Historically, the receiving inspection department has had little or no direct connection with the factory inspection department, but today receiving departments often use statistical sampling inspection techniques in its inspection of incoming materials. Thus, it may be necessary for the quality control department to develop the proper methods.

Above we have just said that "as a rule" everything purchased should be inspected, but this rule can be relaxed for materials coming from vendors whose final inspection has proved to be reliable. A company can usually bypass incoming inspection where materials have already passed a rigid inspection in the vendor's plant. Automobile's "big three" have been able to eliminate receiving inspection on many incoming items because they put one of their own inspectors in the vendor's plant to oversee the vendor's inspection of these items before they are shipped. IBM even provides special inspection equipment to its vendors. These "source inspection" or "surveillance at the source" or "certified vendor" programs improve the certainty that only good lots are shipped. And it saves double inspection and the wasted transportation costs of faulty lots being shipped out and then returned.

INSPECTING MATERIALS IN PROCESS

Inspectors actually do very little of all the inspecting that goes on. Each worker inspects his own work enough to see if he is doing the job correctly. (At Hewlett Packard's Loveland, Colorado, plant, for example, only three inspectors are required to monitor the work of its 900 highly trained electronics workers.) If things go wrong, the supervisor will try to correct the situation. Workers also catch bad work that comes their way from earlier jobs and put it aside for the inspector to look over. Easily seen defects are usually caught this way.

Regular inspection is usually not directed by the foremen of manufacturing departments. The inspectors in a production department usually report to a chief inspector, who reports to the plant manager or a director of quality control. This separate chain of command exists because, as a general rule, it is a good idea to separate inspection from production. As a rule, managers should not let anyone pass final judgment on the quality of his own work lest this person begins to put quantity above quality. In a sense, a foreman would be passing judgment on his own work if both operators and inspectors worked for him.

A few companies (International Business Machines is one) believe that it is possible to make a supervisor responsible for both quantity and quality, so inspectors report to them. Also, in many companies, the inspectors who are located along assembly lines report to the supervisors of the lines.

Regardless of the method used to inspect work in process, the *final inspection* of the product should be done by an independent inspection department which does *not* report to production supervisors. Final inspection, unlike most in process inspection, often includes a performance test. (Performance testing can rarely be used to test partly fabricated products.)

The engineering department sometimes eliminates large amounts of inspection of products during their manufacture by building automatic inspection devices into the machines. Automatic scanning devices and automatic measuring devices are now built into many machines. The machine (or its tool) may even be automatically reset to correct any deviation from standard. The engineering department also designs special devices to allow workers on the job and inspectors to inspect well and quickly.

HOW OFTEN TO INSPECT

Because of its cost, it is best to inspect as little as possible, while still insuring that the product's quality will be maintained.

But since some inspection is usually wise, the question is: When and how often should we inspect? Like most issues, it is a matter of cost trade-offs. What does it cost to inspect? However, this is a philosophical question rather than a practical question because in many cases one can never know the costs of not inspecting. The cost of not inspecting may be the loss of a customer. In actual practice, companies usually spend 5 percent (or a little more) of their labor cost for inspection. Here are several general rules about when to inspect:

1. Inspect *after* operations which are likely to produce faulty items so that no more work will be done on bad items.
2. Inspect *before* costly operations so that these operations will not be performed on items which are already defective.
3. Inspect before operations where faulty products might break or jam the machines.
4. Inspect before operations which cover up defects (such as electro-plating, painting or assembly).
5. Inspect before assembly operations which can't be undone (such as welding parts or mixing paint).
6. On automatic and semiautomatic machines, inspect first and last pieces, but only occasional in-between pieces.
7. Inspect finished parts.
8. Inspect before storage (including purchased items).
9. Inspect and test finished products. Be sure that nothing is shipped out without inspection of at least a sample of everything. From here on the customer is the "inspector." If the product fails, he goes else-where. Worse yet, he tells everybody that this company's products are no good.

Product safety can also determine the "depth" of inspection. Gates Rubber, for example, inspects automobile power steering belts more thoroughly than water pump fan belts. If a steering belt fails, an accident can occur. If a fan belt fails, the car just gets hot.

HOW MANY TO INSPECT

Should some, most, or all of the products be inspected? Ideally, the products should be made so well as not to need inspection at all. Practically, however, it is necessary to inspect some. One of General Electric's plants inspects 5 percent of production during runs of machined parts but goes up to 10 percent for hand-produced items. For extrusions and stamp-ings, it cuts inspection down to 2 percent.

How many to inspect is again a matter of trading off the cost of inspecting against the costs of not inspecting. But here the element of probability is more important than it is in deciding *when* to inspect.

Probability is important because in most cases inspection can and should be done only by sampling. One hundred percent inspection—looking at every item—is too costly, and, in any case it can't be used in tests which destroy the items tested.

Bulk materials must also be inspected by sampling. It isn't possible to test a coal pile or burn up a tank car of gasoline to find out their heat content or to look at every grain of wheat in a freight car to see if it is moldy. Because of inspection costs, samples are nearly always used for many items which otherwise could be 100 percent inspected. The determination of these sampling procedures will be discussed in Chapter 28.

WHERE TO INSPECT

Inspection can take place either at the job or in a central inspection crib. If it is done at the job, it is called "floor" inspection. Both floor inspection and central inspection have advantages and disadvantages. Floor inspectors, sometimes called "patrolling," "roving," or "first piece" inspectors, move from machine to machine to approve setups before production starts and to catch defective work before a large quantity has been produced. They also check the products of semiautomatic machines from time to time and record the measurements on quality control charts. Defective operations are caught and remedied before serious loss has occurred.

As a rule, floor inspectors have authority to stop an operation if it is out of adjustment. On the other hand, if the item is badly needed by assembly or the customer, or if the defect can be remedied by rework, engineering may let the operation continue temporarily, even though unusual numbers of defective items are being produced. In some companies, though, only the supervisor can stop an operation. The inspector can require 100 percent inspection, but he is not allowed to order the operation stopped.

Floor inspection saves extra handling of materials and allows materials to move faster through the plant by eliminating their need to be hauled to and from central inspection. Nor do they lie around waiting their turn to be inspected, thus reducing lead time. And, of course, floor inspection is the only possible way to inspect large, unwieldy items such as a 50-ton casting or an airplane.

One disadvantage of floor inspection is that workers and machines sometimes have to wait for the inspector. He may be busy somewhere else when a machine operator finishes setting up a machine, but the operator cannot begin to run the job until the inspector approves the setup.

Another disadvantage of floor inspection is that the inspector has to carry around his inspection tools. Yet it is impossible for him to carry around delicate testing or measuring equipment, so inspection that requires this has to be central—if not in a central department at least at the inspector's work bench. Most roving inspectors have a "home" inspection work bench somewhere in the area where they check things that take special gages or are too difficult to check right at the job.

With central inspection, materials to be inspected are trucked to a central inspection crib, where they are left to be inspected. Central inspection has several advantages. First, it saves inspectors' time because they never have to wait for jobs to inspect. Second, the work can be done by less costly inspectors, who work under close supervision and are away from the pressure of the people whose work they inspect. (Actually, central inspectors often do highly skilled inspecting and testing work, while using sophisticated equipment and are high-paid workers.) Third, special equipment can be used to good advantage at a central inspection location.

But there are some bad features to central inspection. Materials handling and transportation costs are higher because of all the trips materials make to and from central inspection cribs. And there are more delays, so materials move more slowly through the plant. Scrap and rework losses are higher because of the time lag between production and inspection. If anything is found to be defective, a large number of defective units have probably already been turned out before the discovery.

Assembly line inspection of mass produced products is really another type of floor inspection in which inspection becomes just another operation along the line. The inspector, instead of going from job to job, inspects each unit as it comes along. Occasionally, inspection on a sample basis is done. This method is a form of central inspection and is used, for example, for inspecting automobile body tops made of single sheets of steel stamped into the proper form. The contour of the stamped sheet of metal can be checked only by taking a body top from the line occasionally and inspecting it at a center, where it can be carefully checked against a master.

The final inspection of a product is usually done centrally. If the product is an operating mechanism, it is usually put through a performance test.

INSPECTION SHORTCOMINGS

Judgment is involved in almost all inspection, even when mechanical devices such as micrometers, gages or comparators are used, because there are always borderline cases. Often an inspector has to judge whether a product passes or not. In the case of micrometers, for example, a tight fit—as against a loose fit—probably changes the measurement indicated by at least .0005 of an inch. Plug gages and thread gages can fit snugly or loosely. An inspector discovering a slight blemish on a surface must decide whether it is bad enough to justify rejection.

The inspector must decide whether the item passes or not, and the decision is important because he enforces standards. If he passes products which should be rejected or rejects products which should pass, he is really making a new and unofficial set of standards for the company.

Care should be taken to be sure that inspectors do not substitute their own standards for those set by engineering.

Inspectors are human beings; all of them make errors once in a while. In central inspection, the work is often repetitious and monotonous. Fatigue may cause the inspector to miss some of the bad products. And, even if he is not tired, he will, at best, surely miss *some* of the bad ones.

In one study of the amount of bad work missed by inspectors, 100 defective items were mixed in with a large lot of good ones. The inspectors were not told about the experiment. Then the entire lot was 100 percent inspected by regular inspectors, who found only 68 of the defectives. Still without telling the inspectors, the lot (with the remaining 32 bad ones still mixed in) was sent through inspection again as if it were another lot. This time the inspectors found most, but not all, of the defective items. The process was repeated a third and a fourth time, after which 98 bad ones had been found; but 2 of them were still in with the good products.

The results of this little experiment may be surprising. What kind of inspectors do such poor work? Well, they *are* just human; they *do* miss things now and then. Also, they do have to pass judgment. Maybe they saw the two defectives but decided that they were not bad enough to reject. Suppose a person has to look at 100 pieces of toast in a restaurant and decide which are too burned to serve to customers. Or a professor has to "inspect" the examinations of 100 students and decide who passes and who fails and must repeat the course. Factory inspectors don't pass judgment on toast or students, but some of their deciding is just as difficult. We must recognize that inspection is partly subjective.

Managers should be careful about letting inspectors think they are using their own judgment. The inspection procedure should eliminate as much of the judging as possible. Still, inspectors like to judge and to think that they have superior judgment. They prefer the kind of judging which allows them to pass things not in accord with the drawings. If the specifications say "Cadmium plate .003 inch thick" and the plating is .0025 inch, the inspector would like to "judge" that it should pass. (After all, the engineers have sometimes accepted such items before.) Managers should be careful that inspectors do not set and follow their own standards.

REDUCING INSPECTION WORK

Most inspection requires handling the product being inspected; the piece is picked up, turned over, and put down. This is repeated every time a product is inspected during its manufacture. It all adds up to quite a few inspectors doing a great deal of manual work. Repetitive manual jobs, including inspection, can often be mechanized. Even the visual part of inspection can sometimes be transferred to the machine. In the automobile industry, for example, mechanical selectors sort oversize valves from undersize valves and put each in with other valves of the same size. In the bearing industry, ball bearings are sorted mechanically to size.

A different approach to the problem of mechanizing inspection is to build machines which check their own work. Some of today's machines do this; some will stop the machine if it is out of adjustment. Others will even correct their settings so they are put back into adjustment. For example, thickness gages on calenders in the paper, rubber, plastic film, and linoleum industries give continuous readings of the thickness of the material being produced, although usually they don't automatically reset the machine if it gets out of adjustment. Martin Marietta, for example, runs test tapes on their numerically controlled machines to check tolerances before they begin working on parts. The inspection of the work turned out by these machines now is sometimes done by minicomputers which analyze hundreds of performance checks every minute and then adjust the machine if it needs it.

Still another approach to the problem of cutting inspection costs is to improve the machine so that it does not get out of adjustment. Such machines (for example, the presses and dies that make automobile fenders) can turn out only good pieces when they are set properly. All that is necessary is to inspect the first few pieces, and then another piece occasionally to assure that the machine is still in adjustment.

Sometimes it is unnecessary to know a part's exact size but only that it is between two limits and not beyond. This lets inspection time be reduced by using go/no-go gages which incorporate the two dimensions but show no measurements. They have two slots, one for the product's smallest and one for its largest acceptable dimension. A part which can slide into the small slot is too small; a part which will not slide into the large slot is too large. If an item does not fit the first slot but does fit the second, it is within limits. Go/no-go gages are so simple that inspection can be done by unskilled people.

SELECTIVE INSPECTION

Selective inspection is sorting inspected parts by size so that over- and under-size parts can be matched. This is important where parts have to fit together and work as mating parts. Selective inspection cuts the losses which would otherwise be suffered where close fits of mating parts are necessary. Instead of rejecting or reworking parts just over or just under the tolerance limits, they are put into piles by size for use with mating parts having offsetting discrepancies in size.

Automobile motor blocks are an example—they have holes for the pistons. If inspection shows that one or more of the holes is either too large or too small, the block does not need to be reworked or thrown away. Instead, each hole is matched with a piston that fits. This is not hard to do because some of the pistons come out a little too large and some a little too small. Similar matching up of slightly varied parts is done in many situations, even in ski manufacture, for example. Since each ski is a little different, they are sorted and matched into pairs so they will perform equally on the slopes.

Obviously, this process should not be carried too far. Products which vary too much from the standard should be reworked or scrapped. Also, assembly work is a little more complicated with selective inspection because the parts are not completely interchangeable. But, properly operated, selective inspection is not only economical but actually makes a good product since, in spite of the fact that the parts are imperfect individually, they are matched to compensate so that the assembled product operates with well-fitting parts. This will not matter for future repairs because, after the product has been used long enough to need repairs, the repair parts are not going to fit perfectly—no matter whether the original block and pistons fitted perfectly or not.

INSPECTION AND TESTING EQUIPMENT

Quality standards are often so high that the inspector cannot, by looking at a product, tell whether or not it is acceptable. Here, special gages and instruments are required. These special gages and instruments, themselves, need periodic checking and resetting, otherwise they too get out of adjustment. IBM's Boulder, Colorado, plant, for example, does this kind of work in a "metrology laboratory" which checks delicate instruments and resets and recalibrates them. In order to insure extreme accuracy, the work is done in humidity and temperature controlled rooms.

A factory inspector may have to check many characteristics, such as dimensions, smoothness of surface, contours, hardness, strength, ductility, resistance to abrasion, ability to withstand flexing, resistance to rust or wear, internal strain, shrinkage, chemical analysis, plasticity, viscosity, color, fastness of color, solubility, life of the product in use, efficiency and speed of operation, electrical connections, and other things.

Sometimes the test simulates the product's use (or even abuse) to see how long it lasts before giving out. In other cases the item is used in its normal way until it wears out. Light bulbs are burned until they burn out. Auto tires are put on cars and driven day and night till they wear out. Paints are put on trial pieces and put out on the roof to see if they will fade in the sunlight and how they weather. Most tests give answers about a product's acceptability right away; but with "wearout" tests it is necessary to wait for answers.

For close measuring (such as detecting variations of less than 1/1,000 of an inch), inspectors need some kind of magnifier or electronic inspection gage. There are also magnifiers which throw an enlarged shadow of the product's outline on a screen, where its proper contour or size can be compared with the specified contour already marked on the screen. And today there are surface smoothness gages which are accurate to a millionth of an inch. There are even devices to gage the thickness of a coat of paint.

FIGURE 27–3

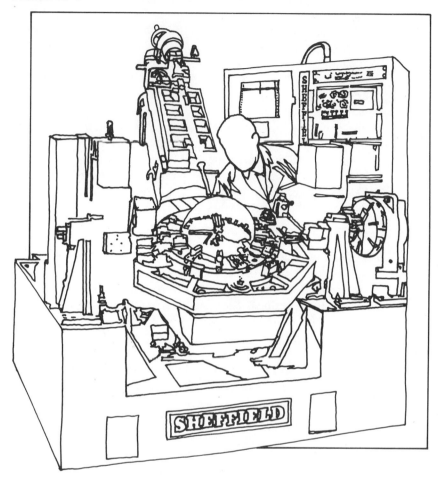

Automatic electronic sorters, which sort items by size, have already been mentioned in connection with selective inspection.

In inspection, infra-red rays can detect minute separations in bonded or laminated materials. X-rays (beta rays) are used to take pictures through opaque materials, just as a dentist takes pictures of teeth. Internal flaws show up as dark spots, or as being different from the surrounding material. X-rays are not very powerful, however. To take a picture of a casting, or forging, or a welded joint by directing rays through it, it is necessary to go to gamma rays, which are many times more powerful.

Both beta and gamma rays are also useful for measuring the thickness of paper, steel, plastic sheet, and the like, or even an electroplated coating. The accuracy of the measurements can range down to millionths of an inch. Radioactive materials are also sometimes mixed in in minute quantities with other materials (perhaps metal for making into castings) or into fluids. Later, by detecting the strength of the emissions in various spots, it is possible to study the flow of the metal or fluid.

In another application of science to inspection, the steel industry uses pictures of the spectrum of light to show the chemical makeup of steel in the making. A photograph is taken of the spectrum of light coming from a "heat" of molten steel. The lines that appear in the spectrum show the chemical elements present, and their width shows the amount of each element. The pictures can be taken and developed quickly, thus permitting corrections to be made in the chemical composition of the heat before it is poured. TV cameras also are used to show operations which are otherwise impossible to watch—as inside a furnace or vat or machine. TV tapes are sometimes used, so the scene can be played over again and studied if anything went wrong.

In the semiconductor industry (microprocessors, computers on a "chip," and so on) tiny chips are 100 percent inspected by special computer systems which have probes which successively "hook up" to each of the hundreds of chips at a time which are printed on small pieces of silicone. These systems test the circuitry of each chip in an instant, and, if one is faulty, it marks it with a felt-tip-like pen so it can be discarded when the silicone disk is cut into the hundreds of chips which are on each one.

DISPOSITION OF REJECTED MATERIAL

Rejected parts and material are rarely thrown out. Often they can be salvaged by rework operations. If this can't be done or if it is too expensive, they can often be made into other items, perhaps smaller-sized ones. Or often the rejected material can be sold as "seconds," as is done with dishes, tires, day-old bread, and the thousands of other things sold through "damaged merchandise" discount stores.

Illogical though it may seem to be, there is still another way to eliminate rejected parts and material: to use them up just as if they had passed to start with! And do it with the engineering department's approval! Some companies have material review boards to pass on rejected material. These boards include everyone who will be affected by the fact that the items may be rejected: the superintendent, the chief engineer, and, in the case of airplanes, the customer (often the government). This often happens where parts are not quite as perfect as they should be, but where the product's operation will be affected little if at all.

This sounds as if standards are set up and then disregarded. But, actually, the standards are not disregarded. The point is that sometimes no harm is done if a borderline lot is passed. Yet passing borderline products should not be a regular practice. If an automobile tire tread is supposed to be a half-inch thick and it comes out nearer to five eighths, this does not hurt the tire if it is still in balance; the customer just gets more rubber than he is paying for. Or if the gasoline gage in an automobile is supposed to be 3 inches from the speedometer but the hole for it in the dashboard is 2⅞ inches away, it can be passed. Or if electroplating is supposed to be a certain thickness and it is more, this does no harm. There are cases where the specification can be relaxed without harm being done. Yet such "relaxations" should be individual decisions, not the general practice.

Another important reason for relaxing standards temporarily comes from the common practice of carrying practically no inventory of parts. This gets a company into a jam every time there is any holdup in parts supply. If many parts are held up, the assembly department will soon have to close down (and then all other parts departments). This is a case where one of top management's policies (to hold inventories down) has an effect (loosening up on quality) that they probably do not want and in fact is rarely recognized as a consequence of their inventory policy.

If a lot is rejected which would close down the final assembly department, engineering—rather than close down the plant—may give in and approve passing the lot "just this once, but don't let it happen again." The same thing can happen with purchased parts. If an assembly department is almost out of the parts which the inspector wants to reject (and for purchased items it may take weeks to get a new supply), the question becomes: Are the defectives bad enough to justify closing down operations, or can they be passed? Again, there is a strong temptation to say OK—pass them this time, but don't let it happen again. But of course it *does* happen again. Actually, these temporary relaxations rarely seem to cause many problems—the products still work, and work well. It makes one wonder if the standards were not too high in the first place.

Of course, vendors were not born yesterday, and they know all about hand-to-mouth inventories. So when a customer rejects a lot and returns it, the returned goods inspector in the vendor's plant may just put the lot to one side. Sooner or later the customer will be very anxious for an extra shipment, which he can get only if he accepts the previously rejected lot. They are the only ones available. The vendor gets rid of the substandard lot and helps the customer out of his tight spot. Customers will eat burned toast when they are hungry and there is nothing else to eat.

Quality standards are, therefore, in fact, somewhat flexible. If a factory is to operate effectively, quality standards must yield at times to pressures which conflict with their strict enforcement.

Reworking rejects

Generally, rejects are either clearly scrap or reworkable. To rework them, additional—and often different—operations are needed, depending on the nature of the defects. Defective items are sorted according to the kind of defect, and the rework operations for each group are decided upon.

All rework is an extra cost which should be charged to the department responsible for it. But this is not always easy to determine. Suppose that a coat of paint tends to flake off. Is it the purchasing department's fault for buying the wrong kind of paint for the job? Or did engineering fail to specify the right kind of paint? Or is the material under the paint the right kind? Or did the shop fail to get the right surface finish on the piece? Or did the cleaning department fail to get every bit of oil off the surface?

"Work away"

In some industries it is possible to "work away" unacceptable materials by mixing them, a little at a time, into future mixtures. Off-color material, for example, can be put into mixtures of dark materials in the rubber, glass, and paint industries, thus saving the full value of the raw materials. If chemical mixtures contain too much of certain chemicals, they can be mixed into new batches that are intentionally made up with too little of these chemicals. This is what Martin Marietta Cement does. By law, they cannot ship defective cement, but they can "recycle" it into future mixtures.

"Work away," as a way of salvaging rejects, is sometimes used by vendors in a somewhat questionable manner. A customer rejects a certain lot of materials—say nuts and bolts—because they find it contains 3 percent defectives whereas the contract said no more than 2 percent. The customer sends the lot back, and the vendor merely mixes it with the next lot, and back they all come as part of the next shipment. This is not always as bad as it sounds. If the next lot started with only 1 percent bad, the new mixture will be 2 percent bad, which is the quality specified.

REVIEW QUESTIONS

1. The text says that "quality" is a hard concept to pin down. Yet a factory has to make products of specified quality. Why not always try to make the best?

2. Students were visiting a factory which makes ready-made dresses for sale by Sears, K-Mart, and other chain stores. A student asked how they determined the quality of the cloth, belts, zippers, and so on. The answer was: "We start with the price, subtract a profit and cost for making, and use the best materials that we can afford to buy with what is left." Comment on this practice. Is this a good way to set selling prices? How would the buyer know what he was going to get? (How could a piece of cloth be defined?)

3. "Quality control starts when the product is still on the drawing boards." Discuss this statement. Shouldn't it both start and finish there?

4. How can product designers resolve the cost/value problem when customers want different things? How can a designer ever settle on a design?

5. Why do foremen often think that engineering sets tolerances too tightly? Is there any merit to their position?

6. Discuss the matter of foremen being responsible both for turning out work and also being in charge of the inspectors.

7. "You can be sure if it's Westinghouse"; so why should a company buying parts from Westinghouse spend money to inspect incoming products which are almost always perfect? After all, Westinghouse gave them a thorough check before shipping them.

8. How should a company go about deciding how often and how many items to inspect? What kinds of rules or guidelines should be issued to the factory?

9. If maintaining quality is so important, why not always use 100 percent inspection?

10. Compare floor inspection and central inspection, giving the advantages and disadvantages of each.

11. How reliable are inspectors? If they carry out 100 percent inspection, how sure is it that the outgoing quality is all that it should be? Discuss.

12. What happens to rejected materials? Is this bad? Discuss.

13. "Selective inspection represents a compromise and weakens the enforcement of quality standards." Comment on this statement.

QUESTIONS FOR DISCUSSION

1. There is always someone who can make it cheaper—but weaker or poorer. And there is always a customer who wants it that way. What should be done about this?

2. Which is the better buy, a deck of Bicycle playing cards bought at a variety store for $.75 or a deck of Congress playing cards bought at a gift shop for $2.50? What makes your choice the better buy?

3. The Firstline Company makes the "best electric iron you can buy." But one of its competitors makes the cheapest. Which is the right policy? Why?

4. What does a high-quality bicycle look like? Does it have small wheels and a "banana seat" set high over the rear-wheel axle? How can a manufacturer of high-quality bicycles maintain leadership in the bicycle market?

5. Pick some commonplace minor item, such as a pair of scissors, a paper stapler, or a ball-point pen. Decide on and define its quality. What are the critical characteristics which you think should be inspected for?

6. In the text it is suggested that customers might have trouble deciding whether a Ford, Plymouth, or Chevrolet is the best car. Which is actually the best? What makes it so?

7. Assume that you have been appointed general manager of the division making the car you put at the bottom of the list in question 6.

You are told to make it the best of the three, but you must still operate at a profit. What will you do?

8. A college student got a summer job in an automobile factory loading seat cushions onto the supply conveyor which took them to the men on the final assembly line. He came to a cushion with a badly frayed spot, which obviously made it defective, so he reported it to his foreman and asked what to do. "Load it on," said the foreman, "maybe no one will complain." Discuss.

9. The text says that "how often to inspect" depends on the cost of inspecting versus the cost of not inspecting. How can a company find out what it costs *not* to inspect?

10. In an airplane factory it is necessary to test the fuel lines and develop a test which will insure that the lines which pass will operate 150,000 hours without a failure.
    a. How can 75 years of use be simulated?
    b. Suppose that after a simulation of 60,000 hours, the line being tested fails. What has the company learned? What should be done?
    c. Suppose that the sample unit does not fail. What does this tell the company? (The question is how much a sample of one can reveal about the other items not tested.)

11. Free service during guarantee periods on new cars costs over $50 a car. Why not spend more on inspection at the factory and cut down on this expense? Discuss.

12. A company has decided to use incentive pay for its inspectors who look for defects in instrument "clusters" that go on the dashboard of the automobiles it makes. What should be done about defects? Should an inspector be paid less for clusters found with defects? Or should he be paid more? And if the decision is to pay more, may it not cause the inspector to pull a wire loose once in a while in order to raise his pay? Discuss.

PROBLEMS

1. A machine is starting on a run of 500 parts. This will keep the machine busy for 4 hours at a cost of $15 per hour. The machine has been set up by its operator, a relatively unskilled worker, at a $6 cost; so it may not be set up just right. Rejects may therefore be 5 percent—decidedly more than the probable 1 percent rejects if a regular setup mechanic had prepared the machine.

The concern here is not with making up the lost quantities but with whether or not a regular setup mechanic should check the setup before starting the job. If he does check, the total cost of added machine dead time, plus the idle operator, plus the setup mechanic's own cost comes to $9. Forty percent of all rejected products have to be scrapped, at a loss of $.58 each. The other 60 percent of rejects can be repaired at $.30 each.
    a. Should the setup mechanic check the setup?
    b. Will it pay to check the setup if defects would otherwise be 4 per-

cent? What is the break-even ratio, where it doesn't matter whether the setup is checked or not?

2. If a part A is not inspected carefully, the 3 percent defectives which are produced will all go through. If they are inspected carefully, one third of the rejects would be caught, thus raising the quality of the parts passed along to the customer to only 2 percent bad. Should careful inspection be done if the cost of inspecting is $.01 per unit and the cost of each defective is $4? What would the answer be if inspection cost $.05 per unit? At what point would it be a toss-up?

3. Supplier A charges $15 per 100 and sends products which are 3 percent defective. It costs $2 to inspect 100 units and to catch 90 percent of the defectives, which are scrapped. Defectives which get through and into assembled products have a 50-percent chance of causing a $25 damage. Supplier B charges $14.50 per 100 and sends 5 percent defectives. From which vendor should these items be bought?

4. In problem 3, vendor A suggests a sliding price scale, depending on how high a quality is desired. He proposes this scale:

Price per 100	Percent defective
$14.00	10.0
14.25	7.5
14.50	4.0
14.75	3.0
15.00	2.5

Using the other figures from problem 3, which price-quality offer should be accepted?

5. A machine has been developed to produce a special product. It costs $9,000 and will probably have a 5-year life and no salvage value. Interest is at 15 percent. This machine produces 5 units an hour and can easily produce the 8,000 units needed in a year. The total cost of operating this machine (excluding depreciation but including the operator's wage) is $8.80 per hour.

The machine produces 6 percent scrap. Scrap products lose all of the $7.30 per unit cost of the materials used.

a. What is the cost of each nondefective unit?

b. How much could the company afford to spend to rebuild the machine so that it would produce only 2 percent defectives?

6. The normal scrap loss for 4 successive operations is 2, 6, 10, and 20 percent respectively. How many units should be started through in order to finish with 1,000 pieces? How much machine time will be needed if the operation times are 4, 2, 7, and 4 minutes respectively?

7. If the normal scrap loss on the milling operation is 5 percent, on the following slotting operation it is 6 percent, and on the following drilling operation it is 4 percent, how many pieces should be started into production in order to get 180 finished pieces? Suppose that the operator

actually spoils 11 percent on the milling operation; how many pieces short is the order likely to be after the last operation? If the order needs 180 pieces and it is held up until a replacement lot can be brought up through milling, how many pieces should the replacement lot contain?

8. A product can be made from grade B material, which costs $1 a pound (each unit requires 1 pound of material) and takes $2 in labor to make 1 unit. The supplier suggests to the customer company that it buy grade A material, which costs $1.25 a pound but probably would save 5 percent of the labor.

Products made from grade B material are 4 percent defective, but half of them can be repaired at a cost of $.75 each. The other half are scrapped, resulting in the loss of both the original material cost and the labor cost. Grade A material is claimed to reduce rejects from 4 percent to 2.5 percent, half of which can be repaired, also at $.75 each.

The customer company thinks that there is perhaps a 50–50 chance if it changes to material A the supplier will be proven correct in his claims. But there is a 50–50 chance that nothing will improve at all, even if it changes. Since certain processing adjustments will have to be made if material A is used, the company wants to feel fairly sure that changing is the better thing to do. Should the company change to material A?

CASE 27–1

Consider that in the following paragraph all letter f's are defects. Inspect the whole paragraph once and count the defects. Mark down your count. (You can check the count later for accuracy.)

"Effective quality control in manufacturing enterprises, in office operations, in service functions, and in job shops has undergone many innovations of late. From early times it has been presumed that if you had few inspectors and they were on the ball, your quality of product would be okay. If your firm still adheres to this outmoded concept, you may be missing an immense potential for quality improvement and defect elimination for your operation. If this test demonstrates anything, it should show the difficulty of finding all defects, even if you have 100 percent inspection. Far better to never build defects into the product in the first place. How can this be done? Many firms have found the total approach to quality control called *zero defects* is the only systematic way to achieve perfection in quality, but it does mean that from first to last you'll have covered most of the possible loopholes in purchasing, receiving, material control, process design, and shipping and packing, at which key points in final product quality are checked out. Above all, ZD is a team effort, which should energize the entire organization toward a common goal. If you'd like to discover how this method has worked and test its possible application to your quality problems, why not enroll one or more of your supervisory management team in the seminar offered by the University of Michigan's Bureau of Industrial Relations. The time will be well spent."

How many f's did you find? Have three other people count the f's.

What do the results of this experiment tell you about the reliability of 100 percent inspection?

CASE 27–2

Many years ago Japanese-made products were always the cheapest and the flimsiest of all. Now their reputation in such areas as cameras is very high.

One of the reasons for this change is the development in Japan of the "QC circle" concept. A QC circle is a small group of workers, sometimes led by the foreman, who volunteer to find ways and means for improving the quality and reducing the costs of the products on which they work. There are many thousands of such groups in Japan. These groups meet, often on their own time, and try to make improvements.

Like the American "zero defects" idea, QC circles try to find causes of defects and remove the causes. These programs, however, are unlike zero defects programs in that they are initiated from the bottom by the workers themselves instead of being instigated by executive decree. QC circles are, in fact, only loosely connected with management. Management does, however, cooperate by furnishing statistics, charts, and help on control charts, sampling, and testing.

Wouldn't this be a good idea for American industry to adopt?

SUGGESTED SUPPLEMENTARY READINGS

Hostage, G. M. "Quality Control in a Service Business." *Harvard Business Review,* July–August 1975, pp. 98–106.

Peterson, Cecil. "Selecting a Product Quality Level." *Industrial Engineering,* August 1970.

Smith, Martin R. "10-Point Guide to Making Quality Control Management Effective." *Management Review,* April 1975, pp. 52–54.

28

Statistical quality
control systems

Statistical quality control (SQC) applies the theory of probability to sample testing, or inspection. A great deal of inspection work has always been done by sampling; a small part of a certain lot of products is inspected and its quality is assumed to be the quality of the lot. This is called statistical inference. The characteristics of the whole lot or "population" are inferred to be like the sample. Sampling, however, is risky because it is always possible that a sample will not have exactly the same characteristics as the lot.

Years ago, before statistical quality control methods were developed, no one knew how much risk was involved. Often larger samples than necessary were inspected. These entailed wasted inspection costs. For other items, higher risks than realized were taken, resulting in, at times, more defects than desired being passed by inspectors. This allowed costs for defects to be too high. With statistical quality control, inspection is more reliable, and it allows for balancing off of these costs at their least costly combination.

Statistical quality control deals with *samples* and their reliability as indicators of lot characteristics. Sampling inspection, where it can be used satisfactorily, eliminates most of the cost of 100 percent inspection, and it is the only possible method for products which must be tested until they fail or break (as in tests of length of life or tensile strength). Sampling is also the only way to test the chemical or physical characteristics of liquids and powdered or granulated material, or the thickness gage of sheet metal, paper, and cloth. Sampling is therefore desirable in many cases because it saves money. And in other cases there is no other way to inspect.

Statistical quality control does not create risks, nor does it eliminate risks. With or without statistical quality control, there is always some

691

FIGURE 28–1

The quality production interaction system

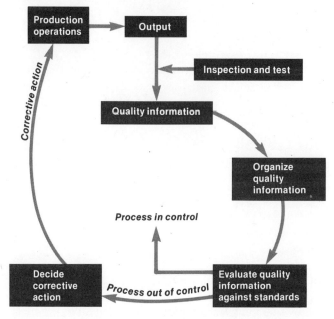

chance that any sample from a lot will not be exactly like the rest of a lot. The objectives of statistical quality control are to show how reliable the sample is and how to control the risks. It lets managers decide the risks they are willing to take (that bad products will slip by or that good products will be rejected). They can then decide whether it will cost more to catch the possible bad products or to let them go and save inspection costs. They can make a conscious decision about how much risk they want to assume. SQC also helps control processing by warning managers if machines are getting out of adjustment so that they can be reset before many defective products are made.

SQC procedures which check products already completed is called "acceptance" sampling. This is where most of the "risk controlling" applies. But SQC (still using samples and still dealing in risks) can also be used to *control* processes *while things are being made*. Not only does SQC indicate when a process is out of adjustment and turning out bad work, but it warns the operator if the machine is getting out of adjustment. It monitors operations and indicates drifts toward defectives. This helps prevent defectives and cuts losses due to scrap.

AREAS OF USE

Statistical quality control has three general uses: (1) to control the quality of work done on individual operations while the work is being done, (2) to decide whether to accept or reject lots of products already produced (whether purchased or made within the company), and (3) to furnish management with a quality audit of the company's products. A fourth result—checking the reasonableness of the quality standards and setup specifications—is generally accomplished, more or less, as a by-product of SQC in operation.

When statistical quality control is used to control operations, samples of products are checked from time to time, and their *measurements* are plotted on "control charts." Since it is impossible to make two absolutely identical products, some minor variations in measurement always occur, even when the machines are in adjustment. A machine will occasionally produce an unacceptable item, even when it is in adjustment. Control charts show when operations are producing too many unacceptable products and indicate to operators when they need to reset their machines.

Statistical quality control for accepting or rejecting entire lots of products ("acceptance" sampling) usually deals with the *proportion* of rejects found in a sample. When a lot contains considerably more or considerably less than the allowable proportion of rejects, this will almost surely be revealed by even a small sample. Additional samples need be taken only when the small initial sample provides borderline (or near borderline) results.

Statistical quality control for quality auditing also operates on a sample basis. Faults in samples of completed products are classified according to their seriousness, and demerits are assigned (see Figure 28–2). Major defects—those which will interfere with the product's salability or its operation or which might be dangerous—may be assigned, say, 25 to 50 demerits, depending on the seriousness of the defects. Minor defects, which might shorten the life of the product or increase its maintenance costs, may be assigned 10 demerits. Incidental defects, such as appearance blemishes, may be given 5 (or even only 1) demerits, depending on their seriousness. Ratios of the numbers of demerits found, per unit of product inspected, can be compared for products made at different periods of time. Ratios can also be combined to get department—or even plant-wide—averages to use in further comparisons.

Quality audits are not just limited to defects detected *before* they are sold. Hewlett-Packard, for example, maintains a worldwide product defect surveillance system which classifies product failures in the field. This information is fed back so SQC, engineering design, and manufacturing can take corrective action.

An SQC by-product is the evaluation of the reasonableness of tolerances and specifications. SQC may reveal that the standards cannot be met satisfactorily with the company's existing labor skill levels and machines. If so, the labor force may need to be trained or upgraded, or the company may have to invest in better machines. Or, finally, if the rejects are still high, the managers may have to relax the standards or simply "live with" high reject rates.

FIGURE 28–2

Portion of a demerit list for quality defects

		DEMERIT LIST—STEP-BY-STEP SWITCH MECHANISMS			
Item	*Dem.*	*Defect description*	*Item*	*Dem.*	*Defect description*
		1. *ELECTRICAL*			Rotary pawl springs:
101B	50	Breakdown between (*parts*) on (*specified*) voltage	2010C	10	opening in loop exceeds specified limit
		Cross or ground between (*parts*):	2011C	10	Rotary pawl play: rotary pawl binds
102A	100	affecting circuit, not readily corrected			Vertical position of rotary armature:
102B	50	affecting circuit, readily corrected	2012B	50	no overlap
			2012C	10	overlap not as specified
102C	10	may affect circuit	2013C	10	Rotary pawl position not as specified
103C	10	Clearance between insulated parts insufficient			Rotary magnet position:
		Open circuit:	2014C	10	rotary dog and ratchet tooth clearance not as specified
104A	100	not readily corrected			
104B	50	readily corrected	2015C	10	armature does not strike both magnet cores
		Current flow; release magnet coil:			
105B	50	more than 10% outside of specified value			Rotary pawl front stop position:
105C	10	10% or less outside of specified value	2016C	10	clearance between rotary pawl and front stop not as specified
106C	10	armature does not release after operation on specified current			Rotary pawl guide position:
			2017C	10	rotary pawl tip does not strike tooth as specified
107B	50	Contacts dirty; breaking continuity			Normal pin position:
		2. *MECHANICAL*	2018C	10	rotary pawl does not strike first tooth in same relative position as other teeth
2001C	10	Bank or wiper contacts not cleaned or treated			

Source: *Western Electric Co.*

SQC may also show that the design itself is faulty. If individual parts meet all the quality standards but the finished product still does not perform well, then the fault is in the design and not in the manufacturing processes.

ATTRIBUTES AND VARIABLES

When inspectors look at a product and say "It passes" or "It is a reject," they are dealing with "attributes." But if they measure "how much," "how thick," "how round," and so on, they are dealing with "variables."

A distinction needs to be made between attributes and variables because they require different statistical procedures. Attributes deal with *percentages* (or proportions) of products rejected. Variables deal with *averages* of measurements and the *extent of the deviations*. Attribute inspection is most important in acceptance sampling—inspecting products away from the operation and after considerable quantities have been made

—as in the case of purchased items. Variable inspection is more important in controlling operations as they are being performed because most of it is done at the job.

Attribute inspection is used (1) when items are obviously good or bad (an alarm clock rings or it doesn't); or (2) when the characteristics cannot be easily measured, thus forcing an inspector to judge them (as in the degree of shine on a polished surface or deciding whether a soldered connection is good enough); or (3) when a characteristic can be measured but the exact amount is not needed (as when go/no-go gages are used to inspect for size). Most inspection of metal, glass, cloth, or painted surfaces for cracks, scratches, or surface irregularities, and most inspection of color finish are attribute inspections.

Most measurements of dimensions, however, as well as all types of length-of-life tests, are inspection of variables. The tested items always differ somewhat, and it is necessary to tabulate and analyze the frequency of each measurement.

REPRESENTATIVE SAMPLES

As mentioned earlier, the entire lot from which a sample is taken is called the "inspection lot," the "total population," the "parent population," or the "universe."

If statistical quality control is to operate successfully, samples *must* be "representative," meaning they *must* have about the same characteristics as the lots from which they are taken. In SQC, the word "sample" always refers to a representative sample. It does *not* mean a nonrepresentative, nontypical, or poor sample. When samples are referred to as "random" samples, the intent has been to obtain a *representative* sample. A random sample from a barrel of material would include materials taken from the top, middle, bottom, outside and inside of the barrel. A random sample of automatically machined products should include items taken at the start of the run, a few periodically during the run, and a few at the end.

Products being sampled should be, and usually are, homogeneous (the same throughout). If they are not—if some tote boxes of parts have more bad items in them than other boxes—the inspector must be very careful to see that he gets a representative sample. He should, for example, draw part of the sample from every tote box or at least allow each box to have an equal chance of being included in the sample. In fact, the inspector should always do this, whether he suspects that the various boxfuls are of unequal quality or not.

In factory inspection, ordinarily only one universe, such as a shipment of products received from one vendor or one run of products from an automatic machine, needs to be considered at a time. It is desirable, however, to consider each day's output from automatic machines as a separate lot. A random sample of each day's, or each hour's, output should be inspected separately in order to catch gradual changes in the products which might be caused by tool wear or by the machine's gradually getting out of adustment.

SIZE OF SAMPLE

It seems logical that large samples should be more reliable than small samples. One might even suspect that if one sample is twice as large as another it would be twice as reliable. Large samples are more representative of the population but not at all proportionally better. We can't say exactly *how much* better a large sample is because, whereas a sample of 20 is considerably more reliable than 10, there is almost no gain in reliability if a sample of 1,000 is increased to 2,000—yet, in each case the sample size is doubled. In fact, in the inspection of variables, the gain in reliability from inspecting a sample of 300 instead of 200 is rarely worth the added inspection costs. Sample sizes in the hundreds are all quite reliable, depending, of course, on how *much* variability there is in the population being sampled and how tightly the item is to be controlled. From there on, little reliability is added by inspecting more pieces. For attribute inspection, typical sample sizes need to be a little higher, but they too become quite reliable at the 300 or 400 level.

Even small samples are almost completely reliable for lots which are quite good or quite bad. When inspecting variables, a sample size of 25 will produce virtually conclusive results if it is found to be *much better* or *much worse* than the limit of acceptability because it is very unlikely that a sample will be very good or very bad when the entire lot is not correspondingly good or bad. A sample of 100 pieces, in such a case, would add little to the reliability of the results found in the smaller sample. But, if a 25-piece sample turns out to be of borderline quality, it is not so certain whether the whole lot should pass. Inspecting a 100-piece sample adds a great deal of certainty that the lot is borderline good or borderline bad.

Another matter is the size of the sample as it relates to the universe. The reliability of a sample *does not depend* on its *proportion* of the universe; its reliability is almost entirely dependent on its own *numerical* size. The size of the whole *lot* has little effect on the *sample's* reliability. A sample of 200 taken from a lot of 5,000 is almost as reliable an indicator of the whole 5,000 as a sample of 200 taken from a lot of 1,000. Yet, in the first case it is a 4-percent sample as against 20 percent in the second case. This fact, used in sampling inspection, permits considerable inspection cost savings by confining the sample to the smallest practicable quantity. Only very small samples, proportionately, need to be inspected from large lots.

Eastman Kodak sets the sample size for much of its inspection by using the following formula (in which n is the sample size and N is the whole lot):

$$n = \sqrt{2N}$$

Using this formula, a sample of 200 would suffice for a lot of 20,000. Eastman inspects larger samples for products it thinks might be of uneven quality. But the largest samples, even if Eastman suspects that a lot is of uneven quality, are limited to 2.5 times the usual sample size, or 500 in the case of a 20,000 lot.

Sometimes, no matter how large a sample is taken and how sophisticated the quality control system is, enough "bad" items slip through which can be disastrous. For example, the Wall Street Journal reported that in 1975 H. J. Heinz shut down its production process for instant dry baby cereal because of the *fourth* complaint over metal particles found in the food. Heinz "recalled" about 600,000 boxes from the market. The total cost of the recall was $250,000.

THE NORMAL CURVE AND THE STANDARD DEVIATION

Statistical quality control is based on the concept that no two things are exactly alike. And that when either people or nature try to make identical products, their actual sizes will vary from small to large with most items being close to the middle size. The most frequent size will be the middle size with less frequent items being at the larger and smaller extremes.

The count of items by size, when plotted on a chart, nearly always approximates a "normal" or "bell-shaped" curve. Occasionally the curve is pulled off to one side ("skewed"), showing that there are more extreme deviations above the norm or more extreme deviations smaller than the norm. If there is an extremely pronounced variation from the normal distribution, different statistical procedures need to be used to analyze the data and the usual kind of statistical quality control methods should not be used.

In a normal distribution there is a progressive tapering off of the number of items above and below the point of greatest frequency, which itself is the highest point on the curve and is in the middle of the curve. This highest point is the average measurement (the "arithmetic mean") of the series. Expected variations in measurements of individual items from the mean can be determined on the basis of the way the data vary when the overall pattern follows the normal curve.

SQC deals with samples, not entire lots. Each item of a sample is measured. Then a tabulation of the frequency of each measurement can be made up, tabulated, and plotted on a chart. Almost always this chart will turn out to be a bell-shaped curve but based on perhaps 50 to 100 measurements rather than 10,000 measurements for an entire lot. The distribution of measurements between large and small in the sample will be about the same as in the parent population. If the sample is of reasonable size and is random, it will be representative of the whole population.

In statistical quality control it is first necessary to calculate the "standard

FIGURE 28–3

The normal curve distribution pattern which lies behind statistical quality control

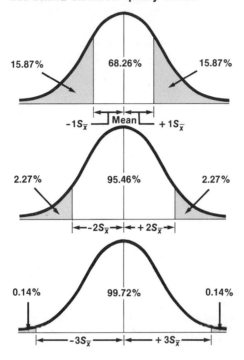

deviation."[1] The standard deviation for a sample is usually indicated by the Greek letter sigma, "σ." The letter sigma refers to the standard deviation for the whole population, which is actually never known when samples are used. When a sample is used, the standard deviation of the measurements of the items in the sample is denoted "S." When subsamples are used, then each subsample has its own arithmetic mean and the measure of variability of these several subsample means is $S_{\bar{x}}$. It is called the "standard error of the mean of the sampling distribution." Its calculation formula is:

$$S_{\bar{x}} = \frac{S}{\sqrt{n}}$$

where n is the sample size.

In a normal distribution, as shown in Figure 28–3, the mean ± 1 $S_{\bar{x}}$ sets limits between 68.3 percent of the measures of the sampled products fall.

---

[1] To compute the standard deviation, it is necessary to find the amount of difference (or deviation) between the measure of each item and the arithmetic mean of the measurements of all of the items. These deviations are expressed as numerical quantities. The procedure is as follows: square each deviation, add the squared numbers, divide this sum by the number of items, and take the square root of the quotient. This square root is the standard deviation. It is expressed in the same measure as is used for the individual items and for the mean. If these measurements are in inches, so is the standard deviation.

The mean $\pm 2\ S_{\bar{x}}$ set limits which include 95.5 percent of the cases, while $\pm 3\ S_{\bar{x}}$ sets limits which include 99.7 percent of the cases.

An example will show how this works. If a part 4 inches long is being manufactured, close measurement will show that the parts vary in size, most of them being close to but not *exactly* 4 inches long. The arithmetic mean of the pieces in our sample, however, ought to be almost exactly 4 inches. We will say that the mean length of the parts in our sample is exactly 4 inches and $S_{\bar{x}}$ is .002 inches. Therefore 4 inches $+$ and $-1\ S_{\bar{x}}$ is 4.002 and 3.998 inches respectively; so 68.3 percent of the sample measurements (or very close to it) are between these limits. Measuring out 2 $S_{\bar{x}}$'s produces measurements of 4.004 and 3.996 inches. These measurements will include 95.5 percent of the cases. Three $S_{\bar{x}}$'s out each way, or 4.006 and 3.994 inches, will include 99.7 percent of the cases.

Statisticians have developed short-cut methods for doing the calculations. An example demonstrating a short-cut for setting control limits for control charts is shown in Figure 28–5.

SQC is also helpful in the cases where extremes are important, as for example, with the weakest link in a chain. It is all very good for the average strength of each link in a chain to be well above the minimum, but, if even if *one* link is too weak, the chain breaks. Charts can be set up so that attention is focused on such extremes.

In other cases consistency is more important. Suppose a company buys two lots of ⅛-inch (.1250 inches) diameter ball bearings. And suppose lot A's mean is .1248 inches but lot B's mean is exactly .1250 inches. But *within* lot A the individual balls range between .1247 and .1251 inches, while in lot B, with the perfect mean, the individual size range from .1240 to .1260 inches. Which lot would probably work out best? Probably lot A, because no ball bearing varies more than 3/10,000 of an inch from the specified ⅛-inch size, while in lot B some vary as much as 10/10,000 of an inch. Many SQC applications deal with this matter of consistency.

Whether the interest is in means, extremes, standard errors, or percentages, statistical quality control is directed (1) towards obtaining measurements, test scores, or percent defectives of items in the sample; (2) to computing the combined measures for the sample; (3) to comparing the combined sample measures to preset scales showing the limits of acceptability; and (4) if the measures exceed the limits of acceptability, some action must be taken to remedy the situation.

CONTROL CHARTS FOR OPERATIONS

Books on statistical quality control do not furnish precomputed control charts for general use. Instead, they explain how to set up and use control charts. This is because every control chart has to be unique for the operation it serves.

Figure 28–4 shows the steps to go through for setting up control charts —the end product of a process that starts with collecting and analyzing

FIGURE 28–4

Steps in setting up a control chart

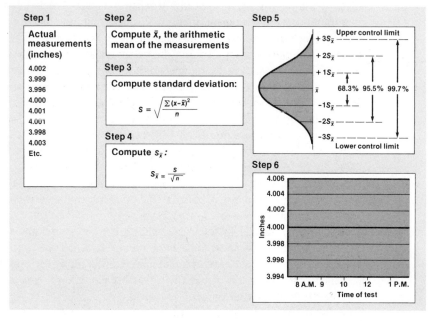

certain figures about an operation. This has to be done separately for *every* job where control charts are to be used.

To make a control chart, it is first necessary to measure each item of a random sample of items made by an operation. Suppose that 40 such measurements are made of parts intended to be 4 inches long. The mean of the 40 proves to be 4 inches exactly and $S_{\bar{x}}$ is .002 inches, as in our earlier example. The 3 $S_{\bar{x}}$ control limits (3.994 and 4.006 inches respectively) are then plotted in along a vertical measurement scale, as is done in Figure 28–4. Horizontal lines are drawn across to the right to "fence in" the area of acceptable measurements. The horizontal scale is a time scale for plotting the measurements taken periodically throughout the day.

Before using a control chart, however, it should be checked against the job's specified tolerance limits. The 3 $S_{\bar{x}}$ limits are 4.006 and 3.994 inches respectively. If the specification says 4 inches ±.010, then the operation can proceed because all of the production is well within the 4.010 and 3.990 limits. But if the specification says 4 inches ±.004, then only 95 percent of the products will pass. The operation will probably have to be improved.

Now that the control chart is set up, it is used by having the inspector in the factory measure a very small sample of products (as few as three to five every half hour or so) and plot the mean of these measurements on the chart, as is done in Figure 28–6. If one of these means falls outside the control limits, something is almost certainly wrong with the production process. This is called *assignable variation* because almost always the variation can be said to be caused by the machine being out of adjustment.

If the mean fluctuates *within* the control limits, these fluctuations are called *chance variations* and are regarded just as normal variability representing the best that the machine can do.

The point is that when the point being plotted falls outside the control limits, this serves as a signal, and the inspector and the operator are warned to stop the machine and get it back into adjustment. Some companies also show lines on the chart for ±2 standard errors. When the means being plotted get beyond these limits, this serves as a warning that the machine is getting out of adjustment, and although it is not yet off far enough as to be producing rejects, it is moving that way.

FIGURE 28–5

Number in each small sample	Factor
2	1.88
3	1.02
4	.73
5	.58
6	.48
7	.42
8	.37
9	.34
10	.31

As we said, however, statisticians have developed a short-cut method for determining control limits for control charts. Suppose we plan to inspect a sample of four every half hour after the chart is set up. First it is necessary to take a random sample of items, say as many as 40. These measurements should *not* be sorted into any order (as from large to small). They should be used just as they come.

For *each* set of four, its mean measurement is calculated, as is its range (the difference between the largest and smallest item in the set of four). This produces ten means and ten ranges. Next, the mean should be calculated (by adding the ten subsample means together and dividing by ten). The grand mean range is calculated the same way (by adding the ten subsample ranges together and dividing by ten).

Reference can now be made to Figure 28–5. Reading down to four, the number in our subsample, we find the factor: .73.

The upper control limit is obtained by multiplying the mean range by .73 and adding the result to the grand mean. The same amount is subtracted from the grand mean to get the lower control limit. Let us assume that the pieces are supposed to be 4 inches long and we find that the grand mean is exactly 4 inches and the mean range of the 10 samples is .009 inches. Multiplying .009 by .73 gives .006. Adding this to—and subtracting it from—4 inches establishes control limits of 4.006 and 3.994 inches. We can now plot these lines as the control limits on the control chart.

We have been talking about controlling the means of subsamples, but there is usually a need to control variability as well. Two pieces, one 3 inches long and one 5 inches long, average 4 inches long. But this is not much comfort to an assembler who wants two pieces each 4 inches long.

Variability is controlled by paying attention to the *range* (the difference between the largest and smallest items in the samples). Control charts to monitor the range are developed in almost exactly the same way as charts to control means. Short-cut methods are also available to allow these charts to be set up in a matter of minutes.

CONTROL CHARTS FOR VARIABLES

The example we just used to illustrate the development of a control chart dealt with a dimension. It required *measuring* the subsample items, so it dealt with a *variable*. It also dealt with the average size and variations from the average.

Control charts of this type are called "$\bar{x}$-charts" (*x*-bar charts). Sometimes the interest is in the *range* between the largest and the smallest. Sometimes there is more concern about the product's *consistency*—the usual variations between sizes. Charts can be developed to control any or all of these. These are called "*R* charts" (for range).

Sometimes there is a need to watch two or more variables at once. If so, it helps to combine their charts and put one directly below the other, as in Figure 28–6. Here we have combined an $\bar{x}$ and R chart. This makes charting simpler and it ties together the results from each sample because they are all charted on the same vertical line. In Figure 28–6, for example, the 10:30 A.M. sample of five items averaged 0.877 inches in diameter, and the largest item in that lot was 0.004 inches larger than the smallest, as shown on the R chart.

Control charts are usually kept near the machine they are controlling. A worker or an inspector checks a small sample of the product periodically and plots its average size on the chart. If any of these averages are beyond the permissible control limit, the products are unacceptable and the operation should be stopped and corrective action undertaken.

CONTROL CHARTS FOR ATTRIBUTES

Attributes are "yes or no" characteristics; products pass or they don't pass. These items are not often measured, and, if they are measured, it is not to determine their exact size, but only to determine if they are acceptable or not. Sometimes it is either impossible or very difficult to measure the quality characteristic (as the shininess of a polished surface or the excess solder on an electrical connection), so the inspector just decides. Sometimes there is no need to measure anything (a glass tumbler has a crack in it or it doesn't), so there is little problem deciding. Instead of measuring every item in a sample, the inspector just looks at each one and decides.

FIGURE 28–6

A combined $\bar{X}$ and R chart in use. Samples are taken periodically during the day and the sample means and ranges plotted

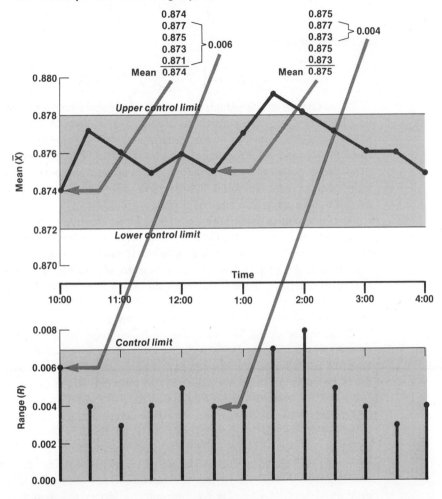

P-Charts

Control charts for attribute inspection (sometimes called *P* charts) are based on the *proportions* (or percentages) of products rejected by the inspector. Constructing control charts for attributes is usually less time-consuming than charts for variables because the inspection itself is generally less expensive (the items don't have to be measured).

To construct a control chart for attributes a random sample of items is first drawn (the sample size for attributes is usually much larger than for variables). The sample is 100 percent inspected and the proportion of rejects in the sample is determined. For example, if a sample of 200 items yields 10 rejects, the rejects would amount to 5 percent. The next step is to calculate the "standard error of a sample reject proportion" (this is similar to $S_{\bar{x}}$, except it is for reject *proportions* instead of arithmetic means of measures). This is calculated by the formula:

$$S_{P_s} = \sqrt{\frac{P\,(1-P)}{n}}$$

In our example:

$$S_{P_s} = \sqrt{\frac{.05\,(1-.05)}{200}} = .0154$$

Next, control limits similar to those for variables control charts are set up. In this case, the control limits of $\pm 3\ S_{P_s}$ would be .05 + (3 × .0154) = .0962; and .05 − (3 × .0154) = .0038. Rounded off, the control limits would be 9.6 percent and 0.4 percent. If the process normally produces 5 percent rejects and this is considered acceptable, then future individual samples between 9.6 percent and 0.4 percent would be acceptable as being within normal process variability.

Attribute charts show both upper and lower control limits. If 5 percent rejects are normal for an operation and the control limits are 0.4 percent and 9.6 percent, why have a lower limit? It would seem to be a good performance to get rejects down to as near zero as possible. This is of course true, but, if rejects actually go below the lower limit as set from past data, the job is not being run the way it used to be. Going below the lower limit reveals that there has been some kind of change.

If managers could be sure that such a good performance (on the record) resulted from improved and cost-effective practices, they would look no further into the matter and would set up new control limits to cover the new performance. But, if the record is going below the lower control limit, this justifies investigation because the "improvement" may be coming from wrong reasons. Possibly inspectors are passing too many items which should be rejected. Or possibly the workers are producing better but fewer products. If the workers are working more slowly and carefully, this increases unit costs. If either of these things is happening, management should weigh the cost trade-off of having fewer rejects. It may prove to be less costly to continue the higher proportion of defects.

C-Charts

Not all attribute control charts deal with proportions. Some deal with *ratios*—often the number of defects per 100 feet of the surface or length of a product. These are called "C-charts." Defect ratio charts are set up the same way as other attribute control charts. Defect ratio control charts are helpful in controlling surface defects in metal, wood, or paper, insulation defects on wire, air bubbles in glass, and imperfections in a bolt of cloth, in rolls of film, and on painted surfaces. In most of these cases the defects are not repaired; they are just accepted as facts. But, as before, the control chart sets limits which are considered acceptable.

Ratio charts may also be developed for defects-per-item situations. For example, one kind of "black box" part of a radar set made by Lear Siegler has 1,800 possible problem points. An inspector has a difficult job checking an assembly of transistors, diodes, resistors, printed circuits, integrated circuits, wires, and so on for possible defects. Lear's inspectors look for defects in the following areas when testing this particular black box:

Improper solder.	Riveting.
Burnt wires.	Missing part.
Wrong component.	Defective part.
Improper installation.	Improperly sleeved.
Probable shorts.	Broken wires or strands.

Other examples of where a number of defects can exist in each unit is an automobile dashboard, with all of its gages and meters.

Ratio charts are constructed much as are charts for variables and proportions. The only difference is in the way the standard error is calculated. Suppose, for example, that we wish to develop a ratio chart for controlling the number of blemishes on the surface of steel coming out of a continuous steel rolling mill. Here we have a situation where the number of possible blemishes is extremely large—virtually all over the steel's surface. Suppose that our inspection procedure here is to count the number of blemishes in, say, each ten feet of steel and, if there are "too many," the rolling process is adjusted or possibly shut down. (This counting is usually done automatically by computer connected scanning devices, but analysts must set the control limits which signal problems.)

For situations like this, the calculation of the standard error is usually based on a probability distribution different than the normal distribution. This is the Poisson distribution. Suppose we randomly sample 100 ten-foot sections of steel coming out of the rolling mill and count the number of blemishes. The result is a total of 2,000 blemishes, so the arithmetic mean per ten feet is $2,000/100 = 20$ blemishes. The standard error is very simply calculated as $\sqrt{20}$, which equals 4.47. The upper control limit would be $20 + (3 \times 4.47) = 33$ blemishes; and the lower limit would be $20 - (3 \times 4.47) = 7$ blemishes. The inspector (or the monitoring computer) would count the blemishes in ten-foot sections, and, if they exceeded 33, corrective action would be undertaken.

ON-LINE AND ON-LINE REAL TIME QUALITY CONTROL

More than ever before, quality control today is being directed toward the quick detection of faulty work so that its cause can be eliminated. Often computers are used, and often they are "on line," and "on-line real time."

Being "on-line real time" means that operation is connected at all times to a central computer or has "satellite" minicomputers located at several key operations which are tied to central controlling computer. The machine's or the process's output is constantly monitored and defects are reported in "real time," or *now*. The computer keeps track of the defects as well as of the good units turned out. Should the *ratio* of defectives go up, the computer reports this to the person whose job it is to fix the trouble, or, in some applications, the computer automatically adjusts the process.

Some companies have "on-line" systems which are not "real time" because operations are not directly connected to the computer. Instead, there are a number of remote terminals in operating departments into which inspectors put frequent reports. Each reporting station serves as a report center for several operations. They are often at "buy off" points, where the products go from one department to another, such as weld, paint, electrical and final assembly line.

It might seem that such a system would not be of much help since the only new thing about it seems to be the quick reporting. But in large factories quick reporting and the quick recognition by the computer that the ratio of defects is going up can be very helpful.

Picture, for example, how helpful it must be in Chrysler's Mound Road plant in Detroit, where they use the method we have just described. This automobile assembly line is 2 miles long and has 1,200 people spread along it. Some 1,500 cars are in the system at any time. Each car has 6,400 parts and 4,500 welds. There are some 4,000 points where defects can occur. Even when things go well, there will be some 30 defects per car, or 15,000 defects in an 8-hour day. Most of these details are minor, and almost all of them are discovered and remedied.

The point to "on-line" reporting is, however, that the computer watches *trends*. Inspectors are busy watching for defects as such, and they are not likely to notice *trends* in defects. The computer keeps track of every kind of defect reported and calls immediate attention whenever the ratio of defects is going up. Chrysler reports that its on-line quality control has paid big dividends.

At Ford Motor, computer systems are used to enable quality control technicians to read, process, analyze, and plot up to 200 separate measurements on their cars undergoing performance tests on their test track proving grounds.

At Martin Marietta Cement on-line real time computers monitor the chemical characteristics of the raw materials in six different storage "silos" as they feed material into the central mixer. Every ten minutes a sample of materials from each silo is drawn and tested in a "spectographic analyzer," which measures the composition of the minerals in the sample. The computer then uses these measurements and solves a linear programming model which determines the proportional mix of materials from the six silos to be used so that the least amount of the most costly ingredient, limestone, is used. Then the computer adjusts the feed screws from the six silos to put this "least limestone use" solution in effect.

On-line real time feedback can also be given directly to operators working on a line. This feedback, however, need not always be computer based. For example, at Lamb Weston's huge french fried potato processing plant near American Falls, Idaho, a simple yet effective quality feedback system is used.

This plant processes about 250,000 tons of potatoes a year into french fries (primarily for McDonalds) and potato flakes (for Pringles). One specific job that many of their 1,200 employees do along a conveyor system (which carries thousands of potatoes per hour) is to cut out the "eyes" and bad spots in potatoes which have been previously peeled in a chemical solution. This has to be one of the duller jobs industry has to offer, and, as a result, minds tend to wander, "eyes" slip by, and quality slips. To keep the peelers alert, Lamb has installed a series of multicolored "traffic light" devices along the line. Quality controllers simply turn the lights to green when quality is acceptable, yellow when it begins to slip, and red when it becomes unacceptable.

CONTROL CHARTS IN SERVICE ORGANIZATIONS

Control charts of the kind we have been describing can also be used to monitor performance in many other areas besides production operations. They can be used to monitor costs, sales, absenteeism, errors in key-punching, typing, and many other clerical activities. Thus, they are useful for service organizations as well as in manufacturing.

In law enforcement, they can monitor the ratio of convictions as compared to arrests; traffic violations to accidents per day; and so on. Fleets of trucks and taxis' use of tires, gasoline, and costs of repairs can also be monitored with control chart procedures. In health care, on-line computers are given control limits to monitor a patient's critical functions such as heart beat, temperature, and respiration rates.

ACCEPTANCE SAMPLING

Acceptance sampling means accepting or rejecting entire lots of completed products on the basis of the number of defects in the sample. Inspectors are told how many pieces to inspect and how many bad items to allow: so many, or less, and the lot passes; more than that, and the lot is rejected.

Most often acceptance sampling is found in the receiving inspection department, where receiving inspectors check in the things that the company buys. Acceptance sampling is used less in fabrication or assembly operations because control charts or on-line computer systems are usually used to monitor these operations. Large lots of end products are rarely completed and *then* inspected.

Acceptance sampling is usually attribute inspection rather than variable inspection. And even more than the case of operations control charts, acceptance sampling is a matter of calculated risks because it deals with large quantities of already finished parts. There is always a chance that bad lots will be passed or that good lots will be rejected.

When there are large quantities of products, there are usually going to be at least a few defective pieces in every lot. Both buyer and seller understand this and contracts are drawn accordingly.[2] In fact, the allowable number of defects will be reflected in the price. If the buyer wants the items to have a very low percentage of defectives, he pays more than if he is less demanding.

When the products arrive at the buyer's plant, they are inspected and either accepted or rejected, depending on whether the proportion of bad items in the sample is above or below the proportion allowed. Both buyer and seller (SQC calls them the "consumer" and the "producer") take some risks. The consumer runs the risk that now and then he will accept a lot with too many defectives (the sample might have a smaller proportion of rejects than the whole lot has). The producer runs the risk that now and then a good lot will not pass inspection (if the sample happens to contain proportionally more defectives than are actually in the lot). In both of these cases the sample is, in fact, not representative, although this is not known.

Acceptance sampling does not eliminate these risks, but it does let managers decide how much risk they are willing to accept and to inspect accordingly. The more certain they want to be, the larger the samples must be (with higher inspection costs), or the fewer the number of defects are allowed in the sample before the lot is accepted.

With acceptance sampling—and unlike with control charts—users of statistical quality control do not have to make up their own tables of sample sizes and rejection numbers for their inspectors. Statisticians have developed and published sets of inspection tables which are readily available. Also, most of the calculations could be done anyway using computer packages which a company can buy or can use through a computer time-sharing service.

The published inspection tables also provide figures for several "levels" of inspection. A company's receiving inspectors inspect normally until a vendor has sent several satisfactory lots. Then the customer company reduces its inspecting and inspects only occasionally or stops entirely if the supplier becomes a "certified vendor." But, if a subsequent lot is rejected or if large numbers of defects begin showing up from certified vendors, the procedure reverts. The vendor is decertified and the receiving inspectors go to more frequent inspecting.

OPERATING CHARACTERISTIC CURVES

Every acceptance sampling plan has an "operating characteristic" (OC) curve which shows how it works. The OC curve, however, does not de-

---

[2] Actually, the buyer and seller relationship is unimportant. The problem of accepting or rejecting complete products exists regardless of whether a company buys or makes the items.

termine the plan; the plan is developed, and the curve depicts its "power" to accept good lots and reject bad lots.

The starting point of determining an acceptance plan is to determine an "objective" defective percent (or proportion).

The objective percent is the particular desired percent of bad items in the lot which the buyer will accept. The buyer does not want to accept lots with more defectives, nor does he expect lots to be much better without paying more for them.

Both buyers and sellers appreciate these points. They also know that a "plan" is one which will average out over the long run. The seller is going to deliver many lots of parts over a period of time. Some will surely be very good and contain fewer than the allowable fraction of defectives. Others will be poorer and will contain more defects than the allowable proportion.

An acceptance sampling plan is one which, based on inspecting a small sample, accepts nearly all lots which are better than the objective percent and rejects most lots which are worse. If the lots submitted are of quite varied quality, some good, some bad, the average proportion of defectives contained in all accepted lots will be close to the objective percent. In the example which follows, this objective percent is set at 2 percent, or .02, defective.

Having first decided the objective percent, the next step is to choose four other numbers. The first is called the "acceptable quality level" (AQL). In our example we set this at 1 percent defectives, or .01. The AQL is always a better quality level than the objective percent. In fact, "acceptable quality level" is a misnomer in the sense that the term refers to a considerably better quality level than the objective percent. It is so *much better* that the inspection plan is set so as to accept the AQL percent defectives in almost every case where such good lots are submitted.

Usually the plan is designed to incorporate a 5-percent risk at the AQL. This is called the producer's risk, or the α (alpha) risk. It means that lots which contain as few or fewer defectives than the AQL will be accepted about 95 percent of the time and rejected 5 percent of the time.

The third figure to be determined in the "lot tolerance percent defective" (LTPD). This is sometimes also called the "lot tolerance fraction defective" (LTFD). In our example, this was set at 3 percent defectives, or .03.

The customer (the consumer) wants the inspection plan to detect and reject almost all lots with, in this case, 3 percent defectives or more. The consumer's risk, also called the β (beta) risk, is usually set at 10 percent. This 10 percent is the fourth of the four numbers required to develop an acceptance sampling plan. This means that lots with as many as 3 percent defectives will be rejected 90 percent of the time. Still poorer lots have less chance of passing.

These four decisions, the AQL (1 percent), the alpha risk (5 percent), the LTPD (3 percent), and the beta risk (10 percent), are the constraints to the inspection plan. The objective percent is not directly used in the calculation; it is, however, behind the setting of AQL and LTPD.

From this point on, setting up the inspection plan is mathematical and is based on rather involved formulas. The end product is a set of instructions to inspectors. These instructions tell inspectors, for all possible sizes of lots, the size of the sample they should draw and how many bad items found in the sample are acceptable and how many constitute too many bad ones.

In our example, it turns out that for a lot of 10,000 or more the inspector should inspect a sample of 400 and reject all lots whose samples contain 8 or more rejects. (The plan would be expressed as $N = 10,000$, $n = 400$, $c = 7$). The "$c = 7$" means that with 7 or fewer defectives the inspector accepts the lot. But if the lot is only 1,000, we get the same quality assurance by having the inspector inspect a sample of 275 and accepting the lot if he finds no more than 5 defects. If the whole lot is 200, he should inspect 125 and accept it if he finds 2 or fewer rejects. The plan, therefore, tells the inspector, for each size lot, how big a sample to take and how good it has to be.

Figure 28–7 is this particular plan's operating characteristic curve. On

FIGURE 28–7

An operating characteristic curve

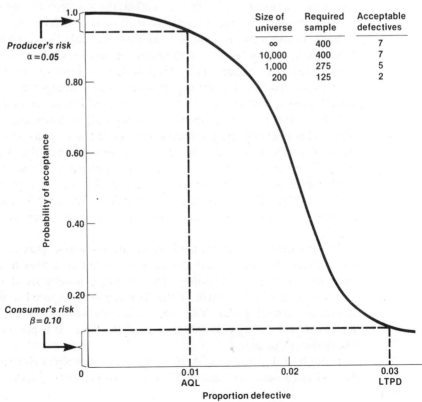

Size of universe	Required sample	Acceptable defectives
∞	400	7
10,000	400	7
1,000	275	5
200	125	2

this chart, the horizontal line at the bottom is an "if" line. *If* a lot submitted has 1, 2, 3, 4, and so on percent defectives, then we can read up to the curve and across to the left to see what the chances are that such a lot will be accepted. Lots which actually contain 1 percent defectives will pass about 95 percent of the time. Lots with actually 2 percent bad will pass about 40 percent of the time. Lots actually containing 3 percent defectives will get by only about 10 percent of the time. And lots with higher percentages of defectives will have even less chance of being accepted.

The real meaning of OC curves is more apparent when there are many successive lots of products. OC curves relate to average results covering many lots. If, over a period of time, in our example, several hundred lots of a product were submitted, and, if some lots were very good, some very bad, and some in between, then the OC curve indicates what would happen on the average.

This plan will accept lots with 1 percent bad 95 percent of the time, but, although there is no intention to do so, it will accidentally reject 5 percent of the lots submitted which are this good. It will also reject lots with up to 3 percent defects 90 percent of the time. And again, although it is unintentional, the plan will accept lots this bad 10 percent of the time.

Lots of in-between quality have the probability of acceptance as the curve shows. If the lots vary uniformly from very good to very bad, the average quality of those accepted will be a little more than 2 percent bad, which is shown as a .5 probability of acceptance.

Every acceptance inspection plan has its own operating characteristic curve, as shown in Figure 28–8. The shape of the line depends on the quality desired and the degree of certainty that this quality will be assured. The slope of the curve reflects the plan. If managers want more or less assurance, they can change any of the four original decisions. If they want more certainty, for example, they could increase the sample size and hold the acceptable number constant, or vice versa. Doing this, however, changes the whole plan, including the AQL and the LTPD. This new plan would have its own OC curve.

SINGLE, DOUBLE AND SEQUENTIAL AND CONTINUOUS SAMPLING PLANS

For very good lots or very poor lots, relatively small samples are all that are needed because the samples will contain high proportions of good or bad items; there is little doubt whether the entire lots are good enough to pass or bad enough to reject. This property can be used to advantage in SQC by first inspecting only a very small sample to see whether it is clearly good or bad. This may result, however, in many borderline cases where it is not clear whether the lot is good or bad. When this happens, it is necessary to inspect another sample and add it to the first. Having a larger sample allows the inspector to decide more certainly whether a borderline lot is good enough to pass or should be rejected.

Some SQC people, though, prefer to use just one sample and no more.

FIGURE 28–8

Family of operating characteristic curves. These curves are for four different inspection plans and show how much the change in the acceptable number of defects changes the plans.

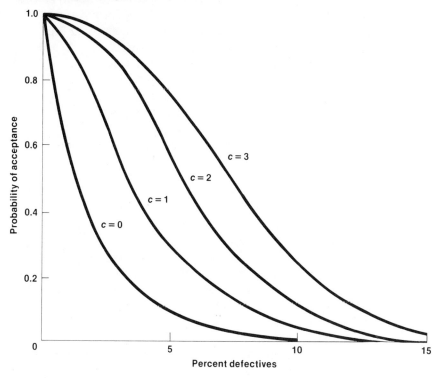

This is "single sampling." Here one and only one fairly large sample is used. After inspection, the lot is accepted or rejected. There are no more samples.

"Double sampling" begins by first drawing a smaller sample. Using this small sample, the inspector accepts or rejects all but borderline lots. With borderline lots, a second sample is drawn, inspected, and added to the first, and the accept-reject decision is again made. Figure 28–9 depicts this procedure.

"Sequential sampling" begins by drawing still smaller samples. As before, these very small samples are conclusive for very good or very bad lots, so they can be accepted or rejected right away. But there will be more doubtful cases because the very small first sample is conclusive for only very good or very bad lots. If the first sample is inconclusive, another small sample is inspected and added to the first. Putting the two samples together makes a larger-size sample, and this provides more certainty, so more of the borderline lots can be passed or rejected. But a few will still be very close to borderline lots—not yet passed or rejected. So a third sample is inspected and added to the first two. This provides more cer-

FIGURE 28–9

Single, double, and sequential sampling alternatives. These three diagrams are for essentially the same inspection objective. If numerous lots are submitted and some are inspected one way and the others a different way, the same number of acceptances and rejections would result.

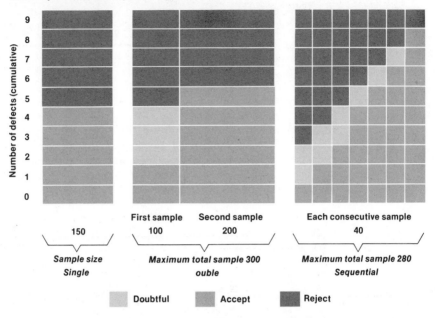

tainty and disposes of more cases. If there are still close-to-borderline lots where the sample is inconclusive, the inspector goes on to a fourth sample (or more). Figure 28–9 also shows how the successive samples work.

Another acceptance sampling procedure is "continuous" sampling. This is appropriate for assembled items which pass inspection stations or are otherwise being continuously produced by a process.

Hewlett-Packard uses such a continuous sampling plan to control the quality of their electronic products (see Figure 28–10). They inspect every fourth item. If they find even one defective unit, they inspect each of the next 30 units. If they find no defects among the 30, they go back to every fourth unit again until they find another defect, then to 30 again, and so on. Hewlett-Packard estimates that this gives them an average outgoing quality level (explained in the next section) of about 98 percent good products.

AVERAGE OUTGOING QUALITY LEVEL (AOQL)

If rejected lots were always scrapped, the average quality of products would probably be about halfway between the AQL and the LTPD, although this would also depend upon the average quality of the lots submitted. But, when bad lots of *parts* are rejected, they can be 100 percent inspected, and the lot's quality can be improved just by removing the bad

FIGURE 28–10

Hewlett-Packard's sampling inspection plan

HEWLETT–PACKARD CO. *hp* *SPECIFICATION*
ELECTRONIC TEST INSTRUMENTS

Sample Plans

Sampling of submitted products will be conducted on the following basis:

A Dodge continuous sample plan will be maintained (CSP-1) to an AOQL of 2%. Under this plan 30 consecutive products of a given type must be free of electrical defects before going on a sample plan. Once qualified for sampling, one out of each four will be inspected, and will continue until a defect or reject is found. When this occurs requalification will be required by again testing 30 products.

Example

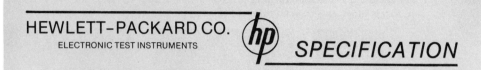

All products will be visually inspected for workmanship defects such as loose hardware, scratches, improper assembly, loose objects inside, etc. Standards covering finish defects are outlined in HP drawing A-5950-4429-1.

All documentation accompanying the instruments will be inspected for conformance.

It will generally be at the discretion of the Final QA Inspector as to what tests will be performed. He will utilize familiarity with the product to establish areas of concern. An integral part of the Final QA inspector's job is to apply a "Roving" type of inspection. This often consists of testing parameters that are not outlined in production test procedures. It is also the inspector's responsibility to pace his time and make best use of it. It is not desirable to establish restrictive procedures that prevent this.

items. This means that the quality of the lots which pass end up being quite good—and the *worse* the quality of lots first submitted, the *better* the ending quality. Figure 28–11 shows how the average outgoing quality level, the AOQL, relates to the quality of the lots submitted. If most lots

FIGURE 28–11

An AOQL curve

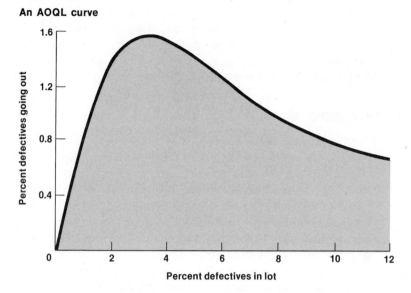

are rather bad, SQC will catch nearly all of them, and after 100 percent inspection, they will be nearly perfect. Averaging these in with other lots which passed, including the few bad lots that got through, produces an average outgoing quality level which will be better than if most lots were just good enough to pass.

Figure 28–11 probably claims a little too much, however. The true AOQL will probably not be quite this good because 100 percent inspection is not 100 percent perfect. It won't catch quite all of the defects. The true AOQL will contain a few more defectives than, theoretically, it should.

DEGREES OF DEFECTS IN ACCEPTANCE SAMPLING

Many products can have major or minor defects, or both, and at the same time. If so, the receiving inspectors may need to use two or three inspection plans at the same time and on the same sample. It may be necessary, for example, to allow no defects at all in the sample for critical or major defects. The curvature of a spring for an automobile door latch might be critical. If it curves too much, it might exert too much pressure and break and let the door swing open. If a sample contains even one major defective, the lot should probably be rejected.

Sometimes it may be desirable to watch for defects because they will jam machinery. The diameter of the head of a rivet installed by an automatic assembly machine must not be too large, or it will jam the machine. The defect is unimportant functionally; yet, it is important in keeping production moving. Again, it might be necessary to use an inspection plan which allows for virtually *no* defects in the sample.

But, where minor defects will not affect the product's operation, higher defective rates can be allowed. Perhaps a plan should be used which would accept the lot even if the sample had 10 percent minor defectives.

Thus, inspectors could be applying two or three inspection plans when they inspect a sample. The rejection number would be low for serious defects and high for minor or trivial defects.

SQC IN OPERATION

SQC may not work in practice quite the way it is supposed to. On the positive side is the extra degree of reliability from samples' being inspected thoroughly. Because they are only samples, they are usually checked more carefully, whereas inspectors on 100 percent inspection jobs often get careless. Western Electric says that sampling provides more reliable information about how many bad electrical connections there are on a switchboard with 10,000 soldered connections than does 100 percent inspection. And the United States Bureau of the Census feels that its mid-decade samples of population size are characteristically more accurate than their actual census of the entire population which occurs at the end of every decade.

Also, some 100 percent inspectors may think that they have to throw out a few products now and then, or the boss won't think that they are doing a good job.

On the negative side, particularly with acceptance sampling, SQC may end up *not* being as reliable as it is supposed to be. Acceptance sampling procedures are designed to provide average qualities—but with knowledge that an occasional good lot is rejected and an occasional bad lot gets through.

This should produce an acceptable average result. But what really happens when a lot which is actually good enough to pass is rejected? It goes back to the vendor, who checks it and finds it good enough to pass; so back the lot comes as the next regular shipment, and it probably passes this time. The result is that a good lot rarely stays rejected. The vendor cannot be criticized for doing this because he is sending lots that are of acceptable quality.

However, lots with a poor-quality level cause problems. A few of these slip through the first time; the others go back to the vendor. Some vendors are not above sending them back for a second try. Perhaps there is only one chance in four that they will pass. But one fourth of these lots got by the first time. Another one fourth of the remaining bad lots might get by if the vendor tries again. If he tries two or three times, he may get quite a bit of bad work accepted. Of course, good vendors don't do this.

Another thing (and this may happen with control charts, too, but it is more common in acceptance sampling) is the tendency for inspectors not to follow the rules. An inspector dips into a lot and finds just enough rejects in the sample to reject the lot. But he may not *reject* the lot. He may throw the sample back and take another sample, hoping this time he gets a sample that passes. Inspectors sometimes do things like this, so the result is likely to be a poorer quality than SQC should ensure.

In fairness to inspectors, it might be pointed out that it is often hard to get a representative sample. Suppose, for example, a shipment of 100,000 bolts comes in on a pallet holding 48 boxes arranged 4 boxes wide, 4 boxes deep, and 3 boxes high. It is hard for the inspector to get a random sample. To make this worse, vendors know all about this problem, and some unscrupulous ones put their substandard boxes inside and low down in the load.

Sometimes, too, parts come in metal containers and the inspector can't burrow in sideways to try to get a random sample. Vendors know about this too and put the dubious quality items largely in the center and low down.

These practical difficulties interfere with inspectors getting representative samples and, in some cases, reduce the validity of the findings of the SQC sampling plan.

REVIEW QUESTIONS

1. If statistical quality control neither makes risks nor gets rid of risks, what *does* it do? Discuss.
2. If SQC is to be used as a quality audit system, does this mean that a certain amount of faulty work is expected to pass? Explain.
3. Compare random and representative samples.
4. How are the normal curve and the standard deviation made use of in statistical quality control?
5. Why is it that books on SQC do not supply precalculated data for control charts that can be used "right now" in factory operations? Such books *do* supply precomputed numbers for acceptance sampling, so why don't they do the same for control charts?
6. Distinguish between attribute and variable inspection. Show why the distinction is important.
7. Should there be a lower control limit on a control chart for percent defectives? Why? Could such a limit ever be a minus number? Explain.
8. What is meant by "consumer's risk" and "producer's risk"?
9. A quality control plan in operation has an AQL of 5 percent. Just what does this mean to the supplier? To the purchaser?
10. When should sequential sampling be favored over single sampling? Why?
11. How can it be that the AOQL gets better as the quality produced gets worse? Explain.
12. SQC sometimes doesn't work out in practice quite the way it is supposed to. How does it work? Is what happens good? Explain.

QUESTIONS FOR DISCUSSION

1. How could statistical quality control be used to help control the quality of roof repairing jobs?

2. How can a person tell, in statistical quality control, if there has been a change in "population"? What difference would it make if there had been?

3. A specification says 4 inches ±.002 inch. The control chart shows .398 inch as the average with a standard error of .009 inch. Do these figures call for any action by anyone? Who? What action?

4. A specification calls for the dimension to be 5 inches ±.005. The control chart shows a mean of 4.998 inches and a standard error of .001 inch. What should be done about this? Suppose that the control chart showed a mean of 5 inches and a standard error of .002 inch. Should anything different be done? Why?

5. What should be done about the individual pieces outside the control limits?

6. A company had promised to ship 1,000 pieces to an important customer on the very day when something went wrong and most of the pieces had a defect which the foreman felt sure would not pass the customer's inspection. The boss "blew his top" and then ordered: "Ship them anyway! I promised to deliver today and we'll do it even if the whole shipment comes back." Discuss.

PROBLEMS

1. The quality control analyst is setting up a control chart for part A, which is to be one inch in length. The plan is to inspect a sample of four every half hour. Here are the actual measurements obtained from ten sets of four parts that were made to provide the data for the control chart:

Group	Measurement in inches			
1.	1.011	1.008	.995	.991
2.	.991	.988	.986	.989
3.	.987	.996	1.007	1.013
4.	.999	.990	1.002	.991
5.	1.001	1.008	.991	.998
6.	1.009	.990	1.008	.993
7.	1.013	.988	.996	.993
8.	.987	.994	.999	.990
9.	.995	1.001	.988	1.012
10.	1.001	.999	1.010	1.007

a. Set up control limits for this operation.

b. Suppose that we already had set up this control chart with the limits just obtained and that the above measurements were obtained by measuring a sample of four every half hour during the day. Was the operation ever out of control? When?

2. In order to set up a control chart, the following ten samples of four items were measured. These measurements are:

Sample	Measurement			
1.....................	6	15	13	6
2.....................	11	12	7	12
3.....................	9	14	7	8
4.....................	5	9	10	10
5.....................	14	13	16	14
6.....................	6	13	12	16
7.....................	9	18	8	12
8.....................	11	8	13	9
9.....................	13	15	9	5
10....................	8	10	10	9

   a. Set up a control chart for this operation.
   b. After this chart was constructed, measurements of production were made every half hour. Here are the first four sets:

Time	Measurements			
8:30..................	7	10	10	7
9:00..................	10	11	10	8
9:30..................	10	8	9	11
10:00.................	16	12	15	8

   Is the operation in control? Is there any tendency toward bad work? Show the figures.

   3. According to the control plan, eight bolts will be measured every half hour, and the machine will be stopped if it is out of adjustment. Ninety-five percent of the bolts should be within 4 inches ±.004 inches. The last set of eight showed these measurements:

4.001	3.990
3.998	4.002
4.009	3.998
3.997	4.000

   Should the machine be stopped and reset? About what percent of the bolts is likely to be beyond the limits the way the machine is now running?

   4. The Tab Typewriter Company tests the strength of the metal stampings on which key faces are mounted. Below are the test results for samples from two different suppliers. These samples were pulled apart and their tensile strength recorded.
   If Tab wants greater strength, which source should it buy from? If it wants consistency, which one? Is either difference very certain from these samples?

Source A*	Source B*
171.2	134.9
139.3	155.2
152.7	170.4
154.1	160.7
156.7	151.0
145.0	155.2
133.4	184.6
163.1	148.2
148.3	131.6
159.4	166.1

* Tensile strength in thousands of pounds per square inch.

5. Construct a control chart for percent defectives based on these data (percent defectives found in samples of 400):

Sample number	Number of defects	Sample number	Number of defects
1	2	11	3
2	0	12	0
3	8	13	5
4	5	14	6
5	8	15	7
6	4	16	1
7	4	17	5
8	2	18	8
9	9	19	2
10	2	20	1

6. What will be the average percent defectives which will be received and passed if the quality of 20 lots is the same as those listed in problem 5? In this case, use the OC curve on page 710.

SUGGESTED SUPPLEMENTARY READINGS

Grant, Eugene L., and Leavenworth, Richard S. *Statistical Quality Control.* 4th ed. New York: McGraw Hill, 1972.

Jacobs, R. M., et al. "Certification, Standards and Quality Assurance." *Quality Progress,* February 1973, pp. 23–25.

Mate, J. A. "I Buy the QC Concept." *Quality Progress,* February 1973, pp. 29–31.

appendixes

appendices

Appendix A

Discount table

Present value of $1 received annually for N years

	Percent						
	5	10	15	20	25	30	40
Today...............	1.000	1.000	1.000	1.000	1.000	1.000	1.000
Year							
1...................	.952	.909	.870	.833	.800	.769	.714
2...................	1.859	1.736	1.626	1.528	1.440	1.361	1.224
3...................	2.723	2.487	2.283	2.106	1.952	1.816	1.589
4...................	3.545	3.170	2.855	2.589	2.362	2.166	1.849
5...................	4.329	3.791	3.352	2.991	2.689	2.436	2.035
6...................	5.075	4.355	3.784	3.326	2.951	2.643	2.168
7...................	5.786	4.868	4.160	3.605	3.161	2.802	2.263
8...................	6.463	5.335	4.487	3.837	3.329	2.925	2.331
9...................	7.108	5.759	4.772	4.031	3.463	3.019	2.379
10..................	7.722	6.145	5.019	4.192	3.571	3.092	2.414
11..................	8.307	6.495	5.234	4.327	3.656	3.147	2.438
12..................	8.864	6.814	5.421	4.439	3.725	3.190	2.456
13..................	9.394	7.103	5.583	4.533	3.780	3.223	2.468
14..................	9.899	7.367	5.724	4.611	3.824	3.249	2.477
15..................	10.380	7.606	5.847	4.675	3.859	3.268	2.484
20..................	12.530	8.514	6.259	4.730	3.954	3.316	2.497
25..................	14.203	9.077	6.464	4.948	3.985	3.329	2.499
30..................	15.528	9.427	6.566	4.979	3.995	3.332	2.500
35..................	16.474	9.603	6.604	4.988	3.997	3.333	2.500
40..................	17.420	9.779	6.642	4.997	3.999	3.333	2.500

Appendix B

Discount table

Present value of $1

	Percent						
	5	10	15	20	25	30	40
Today.................	1.000	1.000	1.000	1.000	1.000	1.000	1.000
Year							
1....................	.952	.909	.870	.833	.800	.769	.714
2....................	.907	.826	.756	.694	.640	.592	.510
3....................	.864	.751	.657	.578	.512	.455	.364
4....................	.822	.683	.572	.482	.410	.350	.260
5....................	.784	.621	.497	.402	.328	.269	.186
6....................	.746	.564	.432	.335	.262	.207	.133
7....................	.711	.513	.376	.279	.210	.159	.095
8....................	.677	.466	.327	.233	.168	.123	.068
9....................	.645	.424	.284	.194	.134	.094	.048
10...................	.614	.386	.247	.161	.107	.084	.035
11...................	.585	.351	.215	.134	.086	.064	.025
12...................	.557	.319	.187	.112	.069	.049	.018
13...................	.530	.290	.163	.093	.055	.038	.013
14...................	.505	.263	.141	.078	.044	.029	.009
15...................	.481	.239	.123	.065	.035	.023	.006
20...................	.384	.149	.061	.026	.012	.005	.001
25...................	.303	.092	.030	.010	.004	.001	
30...................	.241	.057	.015	.004	.001		
35...................	.197	.040	.010	.003			
40...................	.153	.022	.004	.001			

Appendix C

Calculation of actual rate of return by interpolation

On page 85 of the text, the discussion said that it is possible to arrive at the actual rate of return on the investment in a project by using interpolation.

The problem presented there compared two alternatives, A and B. A called for one machine to be bought at a cost of $20,000. B called for two machines to be bought for a total cost of $10,000.

The analysis on page 85 showed that B should be chosen because the return from A would not be great enough to pay back the extra $10,000 investment and also earn the 20 percent return desired and used in the calculation.

To find the actual rate of return on the extra $10,000 required for A, if this alternative were to be selected, it is necessary to try different discount rates until the present value totals for A and B are equal. When they are equal, the rate of return used for discounting is the rate that the extra investment needed for project A will yield.

In the example we used 20 percent in the original comparison and found that the extra investment in A would not produce this much. We then recalculated the example, using 16, 12, and finally 8 percent before finding out how much the extra investment in A would yield. It proved to be a 9.3 percent return. If the company wants a higher rate than 9.3 percent, it should choose B and invest the extra $10,000 elsewhere. (Furthermore, we have not yet considered income taxes, which would reduce the 9.3 rate to 4.8 percent.)

The way to find the exact rate (the 9.3 percent in this case) is to try two or three trial calculations, as is illustrated in Figure C–1. Such trial calculations will reveal interest rates above and below the actual rate. The actual rate can then be found by interpolation.

FIGURE C–1

Year	Cash (outflow or inflow)	1st trial Present value at 16% of $1	of cash flows	2d trial Present value at 12% of $1	of cash flows	3d trial Present value at 8% of $1	of cash flows
0	($10,000)	1.000	($10,000)	1.000	($10,000)	1.000	($10,000)
1	2,000	.862	1,724	.893	1,786	.926	1,852
2	2,000	.741	1,482	.800	1,600	.855	1,710
3	2,000	.641	1,282	.714	1,428	.794	1,588
4	2,000	.552	1,104	.637	1,274	.735	1,470
5	2,000	.476	952	.568	1,136	.680	1,360
6	2,000	.410	820	.508	1,016	.629	1,258
7	2,000	.353	706	.452	904	.585	1,170
8	2,000	.305	610	.405	810	.541	1,082
Remaining value of project B after 8 years	2,000	.305	(610)	.405	(810)	.541	(1,082)
			−1,930		−856		+408

$$8\% + (4 \times 408 \div 1264) = \text{actual rate}$$
$$8\% + (4 \times .323) = \text{actual rate}$$
$$8\% + 1.3\% = 9.3\%$$

To work this out it is necessary to set the problem up as is done in Figure C–1, whose data columns and numbers are different from those in Figure 4–4. The cash flow column in Figure C–1 is wholly a comparison of proposal A with B. A takes $10,000 more starting cash than B, so this shows as a negative cash inflow at the beginning of year 1 (shown in Figure 4–3 as the end of year 0). A operates at a $2,000 lower cost per year than B, so it yields a comparative cash inflow every year of $2,000.

Next comes trial-and-error discounting. The inflow column was first discounted at 16 percent and then was added up. The total was −$1,930, so the project will not pay back the extra $10,000 in 8 years plus 16 percent return. It falls $1,930 short of doing this. The next trial was 12 percent, and again there was a negative number: −$856. The extra investment in A will not yield 12 percent. Then 8 percent was tried. This time there was a positive answer, +$408; so A's extra investment will yield 8 percent and more.

From here on, the actual rate of return can be found by interpolation. The present value, calculated at 8 percent, differs from the 12 percent figure by $1,264, and it differs from 8 percent by $408. So the actual rate is 408 divided by 1,264 of the 4-point spread between 8 and 12 percent. The calculation in Figure C–1 shows that this comes (pretax) to 9.3 percent.

It would probably be a good idea in capital investment calculations to use, as a discount rate, the interest rate available on other investments. Then, if a project's return is positive, it shows that the project promises to yield the usual percentage and more. And it shows how much more. If the sum is negative, the project will not yield the usual rate of return.

Appendix D

Solution to preventive repair problem*

THE equation for calculating the expected number of breakdowns B_n, where n is the policy for the number of periods that will elapse between preventative overhauls, is:

$$B_n = N \sum_1^n p_n + B_{(n-1)}p_1 + B_{(n-2)}p_2 + B_{(n-3)}p_3 + \cdots B_1 p_{(n-1)}$$

where:

N = number of machines in the group

p_n = probability of machine breakdown in period n

For example, the expected number of breakdowns if the preventative overhaul policy is monthly, is:

$$B_1 = Np_1$$
$$= 50(.05) = 2.50$$

If the policy is to overhaul every two months:

$$B_2 = N(p_1 + p_2) + B_1 p_1$$
$$= 50(.05 + .02) + 2.50(.05)$$
$$= 3.63$$

If the policy is to overhaul every three months:

$$B_3 = N(p_1 + p_2 + p_3) + B_2 p_1 + B_1 p_2$$
$$= 50(.05 + .02 + .03) + 3.63(.05) + 2.50(.02)$$
$$= 5.23$$

---

* On page 273.

In words, the above calculation says the expected number of break-downs (B_3) is the product of N, the total number of machines, times the probability that a machine will breakdown in periods 1 or 2 or 3 ($p_1 + p_2 + p_3$), plus the expected number of machines which will breakdown in period 2 (B_2) multiplied times the probability that B_2 machines will breakdown again after one period (p_1), plus the expected number of machines that will breakdown in period 1 (B_1) multiplied times the probability that these machines will breakdown again after two periods (p_2).

For a four month policy:

$$B_4 = N(p_1 + p_2 + p_3 + p_4) + B_3p_1 + B_2p_2 + B_1p_3$$
$$= 50(.14) + 5.23(.05) + 3.63(.02) + 3.50(.03)$$
$$= 7.44$$

The cost figures for each maintenance policy (preventive overhaul of every machine every month, or every two months, or every three months, and so on) are given in Figure 12–5 on page 274.

Column 3 in Figure 12–5 is calculated by dividing column 2 by column 1. Column 4 is column 3 times $700. Column 5 is the total number of machines preventatively overhauled per month times $200 per overhaul. For example,

$$(50/1)(\$200) = \$10,000$$
$$(50/2)(\$200) = 5,000$$
$$(50/3)(\$200) = 3,313$$

Total costs, column 6, is simply the sum of columns 4 and 5.

Appendix E

Areas under a normal curve

SECTION A

This table shows the percentage of area under a normal curve to the left of a specified number of standard deviations. The percentage of area under a normal curve to the right of a specified number of standard deviations is the complement of the listed percent. For example, the area to the right of -2.4 standard deviations is $100\% - 1\% = 99\%$.

Standard deviations	Per-cent	Standard deviations	Per-cent	Standard deviations	Per-cent	Standard deviations	Per-cent
-3.0	.1	-1.4	8.3	$+0.2$	57.9	$+1.7$	95.3
-2.9	.2	-1.3	9.9	$+0.3$	61.7	$+1.8$	96.2
-2.8	.3	-1.2	11.7	$+0.4$	65.4	$+1.9$	96.9
-2.7	.4	-1.1	13.8	$+0.5$	69.0	$+2.0$	97.5
-2.6	.6	-1.0	16.1	$+0.6$	72.4	$+2.1$	98.0
-2.5	.8	-0.9	18.6	$+0.7$	75.6	$+2.2$	98.4
-2.4	1.0	-0.8	21.4	$+0.8$	78.6	$+2.3$	98.7
-2.3	1.3	-0.7	24.4	$+0.9$	81.4	$+2.4$	99.0
-2.2	1.6	-0.6	27.6	$+1.0$	83.9	$+2.5$	99.2
-2.1	2.0	-0.5	31.0	$+1.1$	86.2	$+2.6$	99.4
-2.0	2.5	-0.4	34.6	$+1.2$	88.3	$+2.7$	99.6
-1.9	3.1	-0.3	38.3	$+1.3$	90.1	$+2.8$	99.7
-1.8	3.8	-0.2	42.1	$+1.4$	91.9	$+2.9$	99.8
-1.7	4.7	-0.1	46.0	$+1.5$	93.1	$+3.0$	99.9
-1.6	5.7	0.0	50.0	$+1.6$	94.3	$+3.1$	100.0
-1.5	6.9	$+0.1$	54.0				

SECTION B

This table shows the cumulative proportion of area under a normal curve from the left tail to the point indicated by the number of standard deviations above the mean. For example, at 0.0 standard deviations above the mean, the area is .500000; at 1.64 standard deviations above the mean, the area is .94950. To determine areas under the curve below the mean, use the complement of the tabular value. For example, the area under the curve to the left of the mean -1.64 standard deviations is $1.0 - .94950 = .05050$.

	.00	.01	.02	.03	.04	.05	.06	.07	.08	.09
0.0	.50000	.50399	.50798	.51197	.51595	.51994	.52392	.52790	.53188	.53586
0.1	.53983	.54380	.54776	.55172	.55567	.55962	.56356	.56749	.57142	.57535
0.2	.57926	.58317	.58706	.59095	.59483	.59871	.60257	.60642	.61026	.61409
0.3	.61791	.62172	.62552	.62930	.63307	.63683	.64058	.64431	.64803	.65173
0.4	.65542	.65910	.66276	.66640	.67003	.67364	.67724	.68082	.68439	.68793
0.5	.69146	.69497	.69847	.70194	.70540	.70884	.71226	.71566	.71904	.72240
0.6	.72575	.72907	.73237	.73536	.73891	.74215	.74537	.74857	.75175	.75490
0.7	.75804	.76115	.76424	.76730	.77035	.77337	.77637	.77935	.78230	.78524
0.8	.78814	.79103	.79389	.79673	.79955	.80234	.80511	.80785	.81057	.81327
0.9	.81594	.81859	.82121	.82381	.82639	.82894	.83147	.83398	.83646	.83891
1.0	.84134	.84375	.84614	.84849	.85083	.85314	.85543	.85769	.85993	.86214
1.1	.86433	.86650	.86864	.87076	.87286	.87493	.87698	.87900	.88100	.88298
1.2	.88493	.88686	.88877	.89065	.89251	.89435	.89617	.89796	.89973	.90147
1.3	.90320	.90490	.90658	.90824	.90988	.91149	.91309	.91466	.91621	.91774
1.4	.91924	.92073	.92220	.92364	.92507	.92647	.92785	.92922	.93056	.93189
1.5	.93319	.93448	.93574	.93699	.93822	.93943	.94062	.94179	.94295	.94408
1.6	.94520	.94630	.94738	.94845	.94950	.95053	.95154	.95254	.95352	.95449
1.7	.95543	.95637	.95728	.95818	.95907	.95994	.96080	.96164	.96246	.96327
1.8	.96407	.96485	.96562	.96638	.96712	.96784	.96856	.96926	.96995	.97062
1.9	.97128	.97193	.97257	.97320	.97381	.97441	.97500	.97558	.97615	.97670
2.0	.97725	.97784	.97831	.97882	.97932	.97982	.98030	.98077	.98124	.98169
2.1	.98214	.98257	.98300	.98341	.98382	.98422	.98461	.98500	.98537	.98574
2.2	.98610	.98645	.98679	.98713	.98745	.98778	.98809	.98840	.98870	.98899
2.3	.98928	.98956	.98983	.99010	.99036	.99061	.99086	.99111	.99134	.99158
2.4	.99180	.99202	.99224	.99245	.99266	.99286	.99305	.99324	.99343	.99361
2.5	.99379	.99396	.99413	.99430	.99446	.99461	.99477	.99492	.99506	.99520
2.6	.99534	.99547	.99560	.99573	.99585	.99598	.99609	.99621	.99632	.99643
2.7	.99653	.99664	.99674	.99683	.99693	.99702	.99711	.99720	.99728	.99736
2.8	.99744	.99752	.99760	.99767	.99774	.99781	.99788	.99795	.99801	.99807
2.9	.99813	.99819	.99825	.99831	.99836	.99841	.99846	.99851	.99856	.99861
3.0	.99865	.99869	.99874	.99878	.99882	.99886	.99899	.99893	.99896	.99900
3.1	.99903	.99906	.99910	.99913	.99916	.99918	.99921	.99924	.99926	.99929
3.2	.99931	.99934	.99936	.99938	.99940	.99942	.99944	.99946	.99948	.99950
3.3	.99952	.99953	.99955	.99957	.99958	.99960	.99961	.99962	.99964	.99965
3.4	.99966	.99968	.99969	.99970	.99971	.99972	.99973	.99974	.99975	.99976
3.5	.99977	.99978	.99978	.99979	.99980	.99981	.99981	.99982	.99983	.99983
3.6	.99984	.99985	.99985	.99986	.99986	.99987	.99987	.99988	.99988	.99989
3.7	.99989	.99990	.99990	.99990	.99991	.99991	.99992	.99992	.99992	.99992
3.8	.99993	.99993	.99993	.99994	.99994	.99994	.99994	.99995	.99995	.99995
3.9	.99995	.99995	.99996	.99996	.99996	.99996	.99996	.99996	.99997	.99997

Appendix F

Waiting line models

BASIC ASSUMPTIONS

As discussed in Chapter 26, queuing (or waiting line) models are based on rather complex mathematical and probability assumptions about how and when customers arrive to be served at a service facility; how they wait in line; who is next to be served; the population size of the customers; how long the waiting line can get before the customers will not join the line; and several other assumptions which relate to who serves and how long it takes. If these assumptions can be reasonably met, then there are a number of queuing formulas which can be used to estimate several characteristics about the situation under study—such as the average waiting time of customers; the average length of the line; the average idle time of servers, and so on.

A common assumption of many queuing models is that the probability that some number of customers $P(x)$ will arrive during some time period T is defined by the Poisson probability distribution whose equation is:

$$P(x) = \frac{e^{-\lambda T}(\lambda T)^x}{x!}$$

where λ (the Greek letter lambda) is the average arrival rate per time period $T;$ and e is the base of natural logarithms and is approximately equal to 2.718.

Although it is not necessary to use this formula to solve simple queuing problems, the calculation of a few values of $P(x)$, given values of T and λ, will describe the general shape of the Poisson probability distribution: If customers (people, machines, airplanes, and so on) arrive on the average of four per hour ($\lambda = 4$) and we are interested in the probability of zero through ten customers arriving in a one-hour time period T ($T = 1$), the calculations would be:

$$P \text{ (zero customers arriving)} = \frac{(2.718^{-4(1)}) \times (4 \times 1)^0}{0!} = .018$$

$$P\,(1) = \frac{(2.718^{-4(1)}) \times (4 \times 1)^1}{1!} = .073$$

$$P\,(2) = \frac{(2.718^{-4(1)}) \times (4 \times 1)^2}{2!} = .147$$

and so on, as shown on page 635.

Plotting these probabilities in Figure F–1 shows the general shape of the Poisson distribution, which has been found to be a common pattern in many real life arrivals of customers. Since the area under the curve has a total probability of 1.0, the total area under the curve from zero to five, for example, is the probability of five or fewer arriving per hour, on the average—which can be obtained by summing the probabilities for 0, 1, 2, 3, 4, or 5 arriving, which is 0.784.

FIGURE F–1

Poisson probability distribution

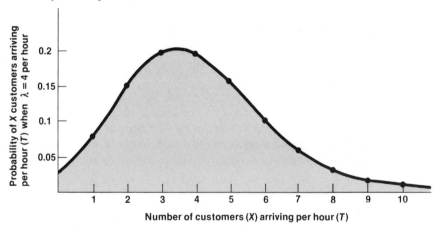

Number of customers (X) arriving per hour (T)

Likewise, the probability that a server can serve x number of customers in time period T is also assumed to be explained by the Poisson probability distribution.[1] μ simply replaces λ in the Poisson formula.

---

[1] Service *times* are assumed to be explained by the negative exponential distribution, which is the mathematical equivalent of service *rates* (average customers served per time period) being explained by the Poisson distribution. Since the queuing equations presented here require only λ and μ, this relationship will not be explored here.

In summary, the assumptions of the simplest model (Model 1) are:

Single server.

Only a single line may form.

First come, first served (the priority rule for deciding who is served next is called "queue discipline").

Large number of customers (called an "infinite calling population").

The line can get very long ("unlimited line length").

Arrival and service patterns are explained by the Poisson probability distribution, given λ and μ and time period T.

μ must be greater than λ. ($\mu > \lambda$)

Using these assumptions, the equations shown in Figure F–2 can be mathematically derived.

AUTOMOBILE REPAIR SHOP CALCULATIONS (MODEL 1)

As review, mechanics cost $10 per hour, the extra server (the stock chaser) costs $3 per hour, $\lambda = 4$, and $\mu = 10$, with the existing single server. It is estimated that μ would increase to 12 with the addition of the stock chaser. Under the existing situation, the relevant costs are simply the expected idle costs of the mechanics, which on a daily (8-hour) basis are:

$$4 \text{ per hour} \times 8 \text{ hours} \times W \times \$10$$

Where:

$$W = \frac{1}{\mu - \lambda} = \frac{1}{10 - 4} = .167$$

Thus:

$$4 \times 8 \times .167 \times \$10 = \$53.44$$

If the stock chaser is added, W is:

$$W = \frac{1}{12 - 4} = .125 \text{ hours}$$

and idle mechanics cost is reduced to:

$$4 \times 8 \times .125 \times \$10 = \$40 \text{ or a savings of } \$13.44$$

Since the stock chaser costs an extra $24 per day, and only $13.44 is expected to be saved, the stock chaser should not be hired. But, should the stock chaser be hired if a new labor contract won the mechanics a raise to $13 per hour, and, because of increased business, the average arrival rate increased to 5 per hour? Average daily idle costs would now be:

$$W = \frac{1}{10 - 5} = .2 \text{ hours}$$

and

$$5 \times 8 \times .2 \times \$13 = \$104$$

By adding the stock chaser, W falls to $\dfrac{1}{12 - 5} = .143$ hours which reduces idle mechanics cost to $74.36, a saving of $29.64.

BANK DRIVE-UP WINDOW CALCULATIONS (MODEL 2)

As we change the assumptions of Model 1, the calculations become more difficult but not impossible. Model 2 has all of the assumptions of Model 1 except that the waiting line (including the customer being served) is assumed only to be able to grow to a length of N customers. This is also called a "truncated" or "finite waiting line" model. The formulas for this model are in Figure F–3 at the end of this Appendix.

As review, the bank drive-in window can service customers at a rate of 1 every 4 minutes, on the average, or 15 per hour ($\mu = 15$). Customers arrive at an average rate of 12 per hour ($\lambda = 12$). There is only room for 3 cars, plus the car being served ($N = 4$). The bank feels it costs $1.00 each time a customer leaves and parks elsewhere because there is no space to wait. Assuming a 30-hour week, 52 weeks per year, what would be the annual value to the bank of *expanding* the waiting space by 1, 2, 3, 4, and 12 cars? The computations, which we calculated with a computer (all of which are not used in our analysis) are:

	Total number of waiting and serving spaces for cars (N)					
	4	5	6	7	8	16
L	1.563	1.868	2.142	2.387	2.605	3.608
Lq	0.861	1.139	1.396	1.628	1.836	2.813
W	0.148	0.171	0.191	0.209	0.226	0.302
Wq	0.082	0.104	0.125	0.143	0.159	0.236
P_a*	0.878	0.911	0.933	0.949	0.956	0.994
Value	—	$507	$920	$1,222	$1,444	$2,161
Cost	—	$600	$900	$1,100	$1,300	$2,900

*P_a is the proportion of potential customers which will enter the line because it is not full; $1 - P_a$ is the proportion which will "balk" and not enter the line.

Since 18,720 customers are expected to arrive annually (30 hours per week $\times$ 52 weeks $\times$ 12 per hour), we can calculate the value of the expansion alternatives as:

$$\text{Value} = \text{Current cost} - [(1 - P_a) \times 18{,}720 \times \$1]$$

For the existing situation (space for four cars),

$$\text{Current cost} = (1 - .878) \times 18{,}720 \times \$1 = \$2{,}174$$

Thus, for example, the value of adding one more space ($N = 5$) is:

$$\text{Value} = \$2{,}174 - [(1 - .911) \times 18{,}720 \times \$1] = \$507$$

This amount is the "break-even" or maximum amount that the bank should pay to add one extra space. Similarly, the other values, would be the maximum amount they would pay for adding that number of extra spaces.

A plot of "value" and this cost structure is shown in Figure 26–1 on page 638. It appears that a total of from six to nine spaces would be beneficial, with a total of eight spaces (four additional ones) probably being the best trade-off between value and cost.

FIRE EQUIPMENT DISPATCHING CALCULATIONS (MODEL 3)

Model 3 is similar to Model 1, except the service rate, μ, does not assume a Poisson probability distribution pattern. In fact, it can have any pattern as long as S, the *standard deviation,* of the service *time* can be specified. If the service *time* is constant (no variability) which is the case for many machines which have a fixed cycle, then $S = 0$.

A fire department dispatches its fire engines to fires from alarm headquarters, which is staffed around the clock by a single dispatcher. Assume all of the conditions of Model 1 hold, except that a study has been made of how long it takes the dispatcher to handle each call for service. "Service" here consists of answering the call for service (which only comes from telephones), obtaining the address of the fire, determining which fire trucks to send, and notifying the selected equipment that they should respond to the fire. The arrival rate of "calls for service" is approximated by the Poisson distribution with $\lambda = 10$ per hour, and, from the time study mentioned above, the following service times were observed from a random sample:

Observation*	Service time in minutes (X_i)
1	1
2	2
3	1.5
4	3
5	2.5
6	1.5
7	2
8	2.5
9	3
10	1
Total	20.0

* The sample should probably be larger than 10; this small sample size is used to simplify explanation.

The standard deviation of these observations is given by the equation:

$$S = \sqrt{\frac{\sum_{i=1}^{n} (\bar{X} - X_i)^2}{n - 1}}$$

where $n =$ the number of observations in the sample.

First, $\bar{X}$, the average service time, is $\frac{20.0}{10} = 2$, which translates into a

service rate (μ) of $\frac{60\text{ minutes}}{2\text{ minutes}} = 30$/hour. The standard deviation, S, is:

$$S = \sqrt{\frac{(2-1)^2 + (2-2)^2 + (2-1.5)^2 + (2-3)^2 \cdots + (2-1)^2}{10-1}}$$

$$= \sqrt{.555} = .75\text{ minutes or,}\ \frac{.75}{60} = .0125\text{ hours.}$$

In summary:

$$\lambda = 10\text{ per hour}$$
$$\mu = 30\text{ per hour}$$
$$s = .0125\text{ of an hour}$$

Utilizing the equations from Figure F–3:

$$L = .428$$
$$Lq = .095$$
$$W = .043,\text{ or 2.58 minutes}$$
$$Wq = .010,\text{ or .6 minutes or 36 seconds}$$

If $\lambda = 20$:

$$L = 1.427$$
$$Lq = .760$$
$$W = .071,\text{ or 4.26 minutes}$$
$$Wq = .038,\text{ or 2.28 minutes}$$

FARQUHAR COMPANY CALCULATIONS (MODEL 4)

This model handles the case in Figure 26–2 on page 639, the multiple channel, single phase situation where all assumptions of Model 1 apply, except that the customer at the head of the single line is served entirely by the server which is next available. The number of servers, N, must be specified, and μ is the rate for *each* server, which must be equal for all servers (channels). Common examples of this system exist at many post offices and banks. Customers wait in a single line and are served by the first available postal clerk or bank teller.

Farquhar currently has two office copiers; each located in two separate office areas. For *each* machine, the average service rate, μ, is 15 copying jobs per hour. (A job may be anywhere from one to several hundred copies.) Clerks arrive at *each* machine with material to be copied at the rate of eight per hour ($\lambda = 8$). Complaints have been made that one machine may be "swamped" while the other one is idle. One suggestion has been to move the two machines to a central area, where the clerks would wait in a single line for the first available machine. However, this would incur additional nonproductive costs for "walking time" of $.15 per order or \$2.40 per hour (.15 × 2 machines × 8 orders/hr.) for the entire company. If clerk time is valued at \$4.00 per hour, should the machines be consolidated as proposed?

First, for the machines "as is" where:

$$\lambda = 8$$
$$\mu = 15$$
$$N = 1$$

We can use Model 1 equations since this is really two independent single channel, single phase systems:

$$L = 1.143$$
$$Lq = .610$$
$$W = .143 \text{ hours}$$
$$Wq = .076 \text{ hours}$$

The *hourly* cost of the system "as is" assuming clerks are not idle when they are actually using the machine is 2 machines × 8 arrivals × .076 idle hours × \$4 per hour = \$4.86.

Putting the machines together, the parameters for Model 4 calculated from the equations in Figure F–3.

$\lambda = 16/\text{hour}$ (both groups will now arrive at the central location)
$\mu = 15$ (rate for each machine)
$N = 2$ (2 servers or channels)

And:

$$L = 1.491$$
$$Lq = .424$$
$$W = .093$$
$$Wq = .027$$

Hourly cost of the consolidation is:

(16 arrivals × .027 idle hours × \$4 per hour) + \$2.40 walking cost = \$4.13

The annualized savings, through the consolidation would be:

40 hours/week × 52 weeks × (\$4.86 − \$4.13) = \$1,539.20

MACHINE GROUP SERVICING CALCULATIONS (MODEL 5)

Model 5 is similar to Model 1's assumptions, except that the population of customers is not "infinite" or very large, but "finite," or limited. The dividing line between infinite and finite depends on the values of λ and μ, but, as the size of the finite customer population gets larger and larger, the values of L, Lq, and so on produced from Model 5 will eventually be the same as those calculated from Model 1. For this model, we must specify N, the size of the finite customer population.

For our machine servicing example, λ, the arrival rate, is for each customer in the finite calling population of 5 machines. So, $N = 5$, and λ is ¼ or .25. This says, on the average, .25 machines arrive each hour, since a "whole" machine arrives, on the average, every 4 hours. The service rate, μ, is every .5 hours or $1/.5 = 2$ per hour. We must do this arithmetic to put λ and μ into the same time unit, in this case, rates per hour. The values for this situation, which were also produced from the equations in Figure F–3, are:

$L = .832$ (the number of machines, on the average, which are in need of service or are being serviced)

$Lq = .311$ (the number of machines, on the average, which are in need of service)

$W = .799$ (the average time, about 48 minutes, that each machine spends waiting and being serviced)

$Wq = .299$ (the average time, about 18 minutes, that each machine waits to be serviced once it is ready to be served)

The relationship between Wq and W is quite logical. In the above example, $W - Wq = .5$, which is the average service time of a half hour. On the other hand, why is the difference between L and Lq not equal to 1, the machine being served? The answer is that since the probability that there are *no* machines waiting to be served or being served is always greater than zero then there can be times when the mechanic is caught up, or idle. Thus, on the average, the difference between L and Lq will always be a fraction less than 1.

FIGURE F–2

Characteristics of basic queuing models

Model	Model name	Channel/phase	Arrival rate distribution	Service rate* distribution	Calling population	Queue discipline	Other conditions which must be specified
1.	Basic	Single channel single phase	Poisson	Poisson	Unlimited	First come, first served	None
2.	Limited line length	Single channel single phase	Poisson	Poisson	Unlimited	First come, first served	Maximum length the line can be, including the one being served.
3.	Any service time distribution	Single channel single phase	Poisson	Any	Unlimited	First come, first served	The standard deviation of the service times.
4.	Multiple channel service	Multiple channel single phase	Poisson	Poisson	Unlimited	First come, first served	The number of servers or channels in parallel.
5.	Limited number of customers	Single channel single phase	Poisson	Poisson	Limited	First come, first served	Size of the calling population.

* Service *time* distribution is assumed to be negative exponential, which is equivalent to service *rates* being Poisson distributed. Additional assumptions: $\mu > \lambda$, except in Models 3 and 5. Arrivals are independent.

FIGURE F–3

Formulas for basic queuing models

Model	Solution* sequence	L — Average number waiting and being served	Lq — Average number waiting in line	W — Average time each customer spends waiting and being served	Wq — Average time each customer spends waiting in line	Special equations
1	Any	$\dfrac{\lambda}{\mu - \lambda}$	$\dfrac{\lambda^2}{\mu(\mu - \lambda)}$	$\dfrac{1}{\mu - \lambda}$	$\dfrac{\lambda}{\mu(\mu - \lambda)}$	$\rho = \dfrac{\lambda}{\mu}$
2	$\rho, L, Lq,$ W, Wq, Pa	$\dfrac{\rho}{1-\rho} - \dfrac{(N+1)\rho^{N+1}}{1-\rho^{N+1}}$	$L - 1 + \dfrac{1-\rho}{1-\rho^{N+1}}$	$\dfrac{1}{\mu(1-\rho)} - \dfrac{N\rho^N}{\mu(1-\rho^N)}$	$W - \dfrac{1}{\mu}$	$Pa = 1 - \left(\dfrac{1-\rho}{1-\rho^{N+1}}\right)\rho^N$
3	$\rho, S, Lq,$ L, W, Wq	$Lq + \rho$	$\dfrac{(\lambda^2\,S^2) + \rho^2}{2(1-\rho)}$	$\dfrac{L}{\lambda}$	$\dfrac{Lq}{\lambda}$	$S = \sqrt{\displaystyle\sum_{i=1}^{n} \dfrac{(\bar{x} - x_i)^2}{n-1}}$
4	$\rho, Po, Lq,$ L, W, Wq	$Lq + \rho$	$\dfrac{Po \cdot \rho^N \cdot \dfrac{\rho}{N}}{N!\left(1 - \dfrac{\rho}{N}\right)^2}$	$\dfrac{L}{\lambda}$	$\dfrac{Lq}{\lambda}$	$Po = \left[\displaystyle\sum_{n=0}^{N-1}\left(\dfrac{\rho^n}{n!}\right) + \dfrac{\rho^N}{N!}\dfrac{1}{1 - \dfrac{\rho}{N}}\right]^{-1}$
5	$\rho, Po, Lq,$ L, Wq, W	$Lq + 1 - Po$	$N - \dfrac{\mu + \lambda}{\lambda} \cdot (1 - Po)$	$Wq + \dfrac{1}{\mu}$	$\dfrac{1}{\mu} \cdot \dfrac{N}{1 - Po} - \left(\dfrac{\mu + \lambda}{\lambda}\right)$	$Po = \left[\displaystyle\sum_{n=0}^{N} \dfrac{N!}{(N-n)!} \cdot \rho^n\right]^{-1}$

* Some formulas require a solution from another formula. This sequence lists the order in which these formulas should be solved.

Definition of variables:

λ = the arrival rate per unit of time.

μ = the service rate per unit of time.

ρ = the utilization proportion of the service facility.

Pa = the proportion of potential customers which will enter the system (Model 2).

Po = the probability of zero arrivals during a given time period.

N = the maximum length of the waiting line, including the one being served (Model 2); For Model 5, N is the number of channels or servers.

S = formula for the standard deviation of a sample.

Appendix G

Random numbers for
Monte Carlo problems*

217	590	735	965	276	027	658	289	260	572
686	359	273	366	451	539	308	080	747	416
584	895	372	370	694	623	364	449	416	877
379	668	206	918	238	485	587	543	322	654
933	051	047	945	927	272	310	017	002	807
755	482	252	018	695	273	123	943	518	037
806	672	856	030	043	852	957	768	006	207
242	601	105	033	672	850	951	621	414	904
593	877	679	098	970	840	391	543	174	703
638	780	709	407	697	973	687	859	476	611
039	302	411	195	374	198	057	531	721	508
322	160	509	543	422	523	351	152	617	169
507	794	941	115	728	071	748	679	252	396
447	300	889	181	370	532	608	883	520	539
547	539	210	354	861	025	229	731	141	786
322	810	756	491	869	285	371	709	431	629
536	990	532	133	215	626	463	616	172	135
439	027	759	297	544	890	049	784	156	641
238	273	941	056	196	283	184	154	714	282
709	739	310	685	146	114	027	141	774	229
692	912	670	340	319	116	843	317	396	990
270	999	075	843	918	453	942	797	606	082
054	579	869	187	940	406	743	855	108	135
834	482	068	368	619	539	991	799	920	400
287	594	981	898	433	496	837	673	576	516
943	344	947	996	457	875	060	475	161	741
696	094	870	050	758	332	843	475	933	153
407	272	332	502	258	963	896	467	287	506
120	799	798	761	876	032	477	832	223	404
994	899	118	417	093	298	356	455	145	854

---

* On page 645.

Appendix H

Additional topics in linear programming

In Chapter 25 on linear programming, the text presentation was carried up to the point where an optimal solution of the problem of how many cars and station wagons to make was determined. Further uses of the data in the final simplex iteration, presented in Figure 25–8 on page 622, were omitted there and left to be presented here.

Shadow prices

The values in the simplex criteria row of the final iteration's tableau are called "shadow prices." The ones which are of particular interest are the negative ones of -245.4565 and -54.543, which belong to $X(3)$ and $X(4)$, the engine and stamping departments slack capacities.

This means, for example, that the opportunity cost of not expanding each additional unit of capacity for the engine department is $245.46. This can be calculated as follows: First, note that the final rates of substitution between $X(3)$ and $X(1)$ and $X(2)$ are $-.6363$ and 1.0909. If we could change the engine department's capacity (in terms of six-cylinder engines for two-door cars) from 9,000 to 9,001, and, ignoring for the moment the cost of doing this, we could increase our contribution. This would be possible if we shifted the use of stamping capacity. In our solution there is no $X(4)$, stamping department slack.

But, by giving up making .6363 two-doors, we could produce stampings for 1.0909 station wagons. We would be sacrificing $190.90 by producing fewer two-doors, but we would gain $436.36 by producing more station wagons, leaving a net gain of $245.46.

In Figure 25–5, this would essentially move the engine department's constraint line to the right, while maintaining the same slope. This would shift point C down and to the right. This shift in point C's location is along the stamping department's constraint line and is directly related to its rate of substitution between two-doors and wagons of .5833, which is the ratio of .6363/1.0909.

Ranging

We have just demonstrated the meaning of shadow prices. The −$245.46 is the opportunity cost for each unit we might increase the capacity of the engine department above 9,000 in terms of two-door cars. (We are still ignoring the possible cost of doing this.) Our question now is, over what *range* of increase in this capacity would the −$245.46 opportunity cost apply before we reach some other department's capacity. In linear programming this is called "ranging."

In our case, we could move the engine department's capacity constraint line over to the right (and while maintaining the same slope) to point H in Figure 25–5, and would have enough capacity to make 4,667 two-doors and 4,000 wagons. At point H we would reach the capacity of the wagon assembly department, so that beyond this point the shadow price of −$245.46 would no longer apply. The engine department's capacity at point H would have to be enough to make 4,667 two-doors and 4,000 wagons (the values at point H can be found by simultaneously solving the wagon assembly and stamping equations). This translates into capacity requirements, expressed in equivalent two-doors of:

$$4,667 + 1.5(4,000) = 10,667 \text{ two-doors}$$

Using shadow prices and ranging for decision making

Armed with the shadow price for a limited resource and the range over which it applies, the analyst can calculate the maximum amount he can afford to pay for increases in capacity. And he knows how much capacity he can add in the department without reaching some other department's capacity. Suppose that the capacity of the engine department could be increased only in the increments listed and at the hypothetical costs listed in Figure H–1. The relationships would then be:

FIGURE H–1

Capacity (in two-door terms)	*Change in capacity*	*First year cost to reach this capacity*	*Opportunity cost avoided*	*Net contribution*
9,000	0	0	0	0
9,500	500	$137,500	$122,730*	$−14,770
10,000	1,000	262,500	245,460	−17,040
10,500	1,500	362,500	368,190	5,690
10,667	1,667†	462,500	409,181	−53,318

*$245.46 × 500.
†Maximum increase before wagon assembly capacity constraint is reached.

Since the only capacity expansion level which produces a positive contribution is the expansion to 10,500, should it be carried forward? Since this solution is for one week's operations, the annual increase in contribution would come to $295,880 ($5,690 × 52 weeks). This is an excellent return on the first year cost investment of $362,500 so the expansion should be undertaken.

A similar analysis can be made with the −$54.54 shadow price for $X(4)$, the stamping department. We will not go through it here, nor will we go into the interesting problem of how to arrive at the solution if we add the two shadow prices together (−$245.46 and −$54.54 add up to −$300). Since the engine and the stamping department capacities of 9,000 and 7,000 are both in terms of two-doors, the expansion of capacity of one unit in each of these two departments will avoid an opportunity cost of $300, the unit contribution of two-doors.

Parametric sensitivity analyses

As an alternative to doing the capacity expansion analysis for the engine department by hand, most computerized simplex programs compute the range over which each shadow price applies. In addition they also allow us to perform a "parametric sensitivity analysis" of the problem. For example, recall that $X(3)$'s capacity could only be added (because of technical limitations) in increments of 500. Using parametric sensitivity analysis procedures, we simply tell the simplex program first to solve the problem with $X(3)$'s capacity at 9,000, and then to increase it to 9,500, resolve the problem, up it to 10,000, re-solve, and so on until the range of 10,667 has been reached or exceeded. At each solution point, the final tableau and objective function value would be reported so that they could be compared against the cost of capacity expansion. For problems with many variables, this procedure is essential, not only because the analyst does not have a graphic "picture" to look at, but because the calculations become unmanageable.

Similar parametric sensitivity tests can be done on other $B(I)$ values, $C(J)$ values, and even particular coefficients in the equations. For example, recall our discussion on page 616 of changing the process in the engine department so that the new ratio between six-cylinders and eight-cylinders was 1:1.25 instead of 1:1.5. Suppose we were somewhat unsure if this was exactly the new ratio between the two. But suppose that we thought the actual ratio would be somewhere between 1:1.2 and 1:1.3. We could perform a parametric sensitivity analysis on this coefficient by beginning it at 1.2, solving, and incrementing it by .01, solving again, successively, until 1.3 was reached.

This would produce 11 solutions which could then be compared to see if the "uncertainty" of this ratio made any difference on the solution mix and upon the objective function. If it didn't, then we would know that the solution is not sensitive to this factor. If it proved to be sensitive, then more analyses could be made if it is worthwhile to pin down exactly its effects on results.

COST MINIMIZATION WITH THE SIMPLEX METHOD

Cost minimization can also be done with the simplex method. We will continue using our automobile assembly problem but with certain changes. We will assume that a new process has been developed in the engine department which has changed the six-cylinder and eight-cylinder ratio from 1.5 to 1.25. And, because of reasons not associated with our problem, management has ruled that the engine and stamping departments should work at their capacity. Overtime is allowed in the stamping department (at an extra cost of $100 per two-door car or equivalent in station wagons), but overtime is not allowed in the engine department where maintenance time needs preclude overtime. The unit costs are $2,000 per two-door and $2,800 per station wagon for all automobiles produced on regular time. Overtime costs apply to all stamping department production in excess of 7,000 cars (in terms of two-doors).

The problem can now be formulated as:

Minimize:

$$F = \$2,000T + \$2,800W$$

Subject to:

$$
\begin{array}{rcl}
T & \leq & 6,000 \\
W & \leq & 4,000 \\
T + 1.25\ W & = & 9,000 \\
T + .5833W & \geq & 7,000
\end{array}
$$

We have introduced three new things in this problem which require modifications in the simplex procedure. They are: cost minimization; "=" constraints; and "≥" constraints. Minimization requires only a slight change in the procedure, while the incorporation of equality and of greater-than-or-equal-to constraints requires the addition of certain new variables and other modifications.

The major change in the procedure for cost minimization is simply to change the sign of the values in the objective function.

This means that the objective function now becomes:

Maximize:

$$F = -\$2,000T - \$2,800W$$

When we *maximize* a negative objective function, it is exactly the same as *minimizing* a positive objective function. Other than this change, *exactly the same rules* for calculating the $Z(J)$ and $C(J) - Z(J)$ rows are used. Additionally, the *same rules* for choosing the variable entering the BASIS (largest positive value rule) and the variable leaving the basis (smallest positive quotient rule) apply. An optimal (least cost) solution has been reached, as before, when all simplex criteria row values (the $C(J) - Z(J)$'s) are negative or zero. The optimal objective function value will be negative rather than positive, however, which identifies it as a cost rather than a contribution.

"Greater than" or "equal to" constraints

Cost minimization problems, however, require some constraints which are either minimum ($\geq$) or equality ($=$) constraints. If we had only maximum ($\leq$) constraints, the simplex procedure would always produce an optimal solution, which in our automobile production problem, would say to produce *zero* two-doors and *zero* wagons. While this would certainly minimize costs, it wouldn't make any practical sense. The first thing required for handling $\geq$ constraints is to add a "surplus" variable much as we added a "slack" variable to $\leq$ constraints. The second thing is to add an "artificial" variable.

The stamping department's constraint is thus transformed from an inequality to an equation as follows:

$$T + .5833W - \text{surplus} + \text{artificial} = 7,000$$

First, let us explain the use of the surplus variable. Suppose, in a solution, that $T = 5,000$ and $W = 10,000$ (assume that the artificial equals zero).

Then:

$$5,000 + .5833(10,000) - \text{surplus} + 0 = 7,000$$

And surplus equals 3,833, the amount stamping capacity is above 7,000. A surplus variable always has a coefficient of -1 in the initial tableau.

The artificial variable is used for one purpose: that is, to form the stamping department's column in the initial tableau's identity matrix and to be in the BASIS in the initial feasible solution. It has a coefficient of 1 and is required because each identity matrix column must contain a positive 1 and not a -1 as is the surplus variable's coefficient. Additionally, since the artificial variable is placed in the initial feasible BASIS, we want to insure that it is not in the BASIS in the optimal solution. We insure this by assigning the artificial variable a very large cost in the objective function. This causes the simplex procedure to regard the artificial variable to be a very costly product. And since we are minimizing costs, it will remove it (and its very large cost) from the BASIS by the time the optimal solution has been reached.[1]

---

[1] If an artificial variable is in the BASIS in the optimal solution, this means that there was not a feasible solution to start with, and the constraint to which the artificial belongs is the offending infeasibility.

Equality constraints

Equality constraints also need an artificial variable to form the identity matrix and to be in the BASIS for the initial feasible solution since they do not have a slack variable. Similarly, we also assign a very large cost to these artificial variables to assure that they will not be in the BASIS in the optimal solution.

Assigning costs to surplus and slack variables

It will be recalled that in our present problem we can work overtime in the stamping department at a cost of $100 per unit of capacity above 7,000. We can incorporate this possibility automatically into the simplex procedure just by adding this cost to the objective function for the surplus variable. Similarly, if we had wanted to assign a unit cost to idle or slack capacity, this cost could have been added to the objective function for the appropriate slack variable. (We have not done this in our example because we have assumed, perhaps unrealistically, that slack capacity has no cost.)

Summary of requirements for constraint types

Let us summarize the requirements for slack, surplus, and artificial variables, and objective function values for the three kinds of constraints:

	Description of coefficient in initial tableau		
Constraint type	*Slack*	*Surplus*	*Artificial*
Less than or equal to ($\leq$)	1		
Equality ($=$)			1
Greater than or equal to ($\geq$)		-1	1
Objective function coefficient	Cost (negative), contribution (positive), or zero, depending on the problem.	Cost, contribution, or zero, depending on the problem.	Always a large cost (negative value) whether maximizing or minimizing.

Computer solution to cost minimization problem

We put our problem on a computer which solved it as a cost minimization problem using the simplex method. Figure H–2 shows the initial and last iterations, numbers 0 and 3.

First we should note the $C(J)$ row in iteration 0. $X(5)$ and $X(7)$ are the artificial variables where we have assigned each an arbitrarily large cost of -999999. Also note the -100 cost attached to $X(6)$, the surplus variable associated with using overtime in the stamping department.

The initial BASIS values contain slacks $X(3)$ and $X(4)$, the assembly capacities for two-doors and wagons, and the two artificials $X(5)$ and $X(7)$. The first variable to enter the BASIS is $X(1)$ because its simplex criteria value is the largest positive number, and the variable it replaces is $X(3)$.

In iteration 3, and the optimal solution shown at the top of Figure H–2 calls for producing 6,000 two-door cars and 2,400 station wagons. Column $B(I)$ in iteration 3 shows us that 400 overtime hours were used in the stamping department and that there is still a slack of 1,600 in the station wagon assembly department.

$X(5)$ and $X(7)$, the two artificial variables, have left the BASIS. The objective cost value is $-\$18,759,992$ ($6,000 \times \$2,000 + 2,400 \times \$2,800 + 400 \times \$100 = \$18,760,000$). The shadow prices may be interpreted in the same way as described earlier.

FIGURE H–2

Computer solution to simplex cost minimization problem

Bibliography

Section I, Chapters 1, 2, 3, 4.

Albanese, Robert. *Management: Toward Accountability for Performance.* Homewood, Ill.: Richard D. Irwin, Inc., 1975.

APICS Certification Examination Program—Contact APICS National Office, Suite #504, Watergate Office Building, 2600 Virginia Avenue N.W., Washington, D.C. 20037.

Bittel, Lester R. *Improving Supervisory Performance.* New York: McGraw-Hill, 1976.

Gaither, N. "The Adoption of Operations Research Techniques by Manufacturing Organizations." *Decision Sciences,* October 1975, pp. 797–813.

————. "Educational Characteristics of Manufacturing Executives." *Academy of Management Journal,* December 1975, pp. 883–88.

Gellerman, Saul W. "Supervision: Substance and Style." *Harvard Business Review,* March–April 1976, pp. 89–99.

Hellriegel, Don, and Slocum, John W., Jr. *Management: A Contingency Approach.* Reading, Mass.: Addison-Wesley Publishing Co., Inc., 1974.

Lambert, Z. V., and Kniffin, Fred W. "Consumer Discontent: A Social Perspective." *California Management Review,* Fall 1975, pp. 36–44.

Laughhunn, D. J. "Capital Expenditure Programming and Some Alternative Approaches to Risk." *Management Science,* January 1971.

Meyer, R. A. "Equipment Replacement under Uncertainty." *Management Science,* July 1971.

Peters, G. A. "Consumerism: Burden or Benefit?" *Quality Progress,* January 1973, pp. 19–20.

Singhui, S. S. "Determination of a Cut-Off Rate for New Investment Decisions." *Management Advisor,* January 1972.

Smith, Robert L. "Professionalism within Production and Inventory Control." *Production and Inventory Control,* vol. 12, no. 4, 1971, pp. 41–50.

Stull, R. A. "Profiles of the Future: A View of Management to 1980." *Business Horizons,* June 1974, pp. 5–12.

Webster, Frederick D., Jr. "Does Business Misunderstand Consumerism." *Harvard Business Review,* vol. 51, no. 5, 1973, pp. 89–97.

Whitsett, D. A. "Making Sense of Management Theories." *Personnel,* May 1975, pp. 44–52.

Section II, Chapters 5, 6.

Alford, C. L., and Mason, J. B. "Generating New Product Ideas." *Journal of Advertising Research,* December 1975, pp. 27–32.

Andrews, Bryan. *Creative Product Development.* Langman, 1975.

Bender, Paul. *Design and Operation of Customer Service.* Anacom, 1976.

Fisk, George, and Chandran, Rajan. "How to Trace and Recall Products." *Harvard Business Review,* November–December 1975, pp. 90–96.

Galloway, E. C. "Evaluating R&D Performance—Keep It Simple." *Research Management,* March 1971.

Gisser, Philip. *Launching the New Industrial Product.* New York: American Management Assn., 1972.

Gray, Irwin; Bases, Albert L.; Martin, Charles H.; and Sternberg, Alexander. *Product Liability: A Management Response.* Anacom, 1976.

Hopkins, D. S. "Roles of Project Teams and Venture Groups in New Product Development." *Research Management,* January 1975, pp. 7–12.

McLaughlin, William G. *Fundamentals of Research Management.* New York: American Management Assn., 1970.

Principles and Applications of Value Engineering. Washington, D.C.: U.S. Department of Defense, 1970.

Section III, Chapters 7, 8, 9, 10, 11, 12.

Baloff, N. "Extension of the Learning Curve—Some Empirical Results." *Operations Research Quarterly,* December 1971.

Bennett, K. W. "Best Seller '72: Run, Robot, Run." *Iron Age,* December 23, 1971.

"Big Questions about Industrial Capacity." *Fortune,* January 1976, p. 104.

Blanchard, B. B., Jr., and Lowery, Edward E. *Maintainability: Principles and Practice.* New York: McGraw-Hill, 1969.

Boulden, J. B., and Buffa, E. S. "Corporate Models: On-Line Real Time Systems." *Harvard Business Review,* July–August 1970, pp. 65–83.

Burack, Elmer H. *Manpower Planning and Programming.* Boston: Allyn & Bacon, 1972.

Campbell, G. J. "Tapping Your Plant's Hidden Capacity." *Industrial World,* November 18, 1974, pp. 52–54.

Carruth, E. "Big Move to Small Towns." *Fortune,* September 1971.

"Computer Controlled Machines." *Purchasing,* April 15, 1971.

Edwards, G. A. B., and Koenigslaenger, F. "Group Technology, The Cell System, and Machine Tools. *The Production Engineer,* July–August 1973.

Geoffrion, Arthur M. "Better Distribution Planning with Computer Models." *Harvard Business Review,* July–August 1976, pp. 92–99.

Goodman, D. A. "A Sectioning Search Approach to Planning of Production and Work Force." *Decision Sciences,* October 1974, pp. 545–63.

Improving Material Handling in Small Businesses. New York: Material Handling Institute, 1969.

"Industrial Development and Plant Location." Reported annually in the October issue of *Business Management.*

Levings, G. E. "Small Computers: Big Boost for Materials Handling." *Industry Week,* January 17, 1972.

McAuley, John. "Machine Grouping for Efficient Production." *The Production Engineer,* February 1972.

Markland, R.E. "Analyzing Geographically Discrete Warehousing Networks by Computer Simulation." *Decision Sciences,* April 1973, pp. 216–36.

Morcrombe, V. J. "Straightening Out Learning Curves." *Personnel Management,* June 1970.

Oates, D. "Switching Off the Assembly Line." *International Management,* December 1974, p. 61.

Plant Engineering. Technical Publishing Co. (monthly).

"Point-of-Use Components Storage Transforms Plant Layout." *Factory,* November 1971.

Renner, E. J. "Plant Capacity: Physical or Financial?" *Management Review,* February 1976, pp. 4–14.

"Site Selection Handbook." *Industrial Development* (Annual).

Soderman, Sten. *Industrial Location Planning.* New York: Halsted Press, 1975.

Thomopoulos, N. T. "Mixed Model Line Balancing with Smoothed Station Assignments." *Management Science,* May 1970.

Vollman, Thomas E. "Capacity Planning: The Missing Link." *Production and Inventory Management,* 1st quarter 1973, pp. 61–74.

Section IV, Chapters 13, 14, 15, 16.

Annus, J. W. "Facing Today's Compensation Uncertainties." *Personnel,* January–February 1976, pp. 12–17.

Ashford, Nicholas A. *Crisis in the Workplace: Occupational Disease and Injury.* Cambridge, Mass.: M.I.T. Press, 1976.

Betz, G. M. "Interpreting OSHAs 'General Duty' Clause." *Plant Engineering,* March 4, 1976, pp. 75–78.

"Disaster in Productivity." *Fortune,* December 1974, p. 24.

Ely, D. C. "Team Building for Creativity." *Personnel Journal,* April 1975, pp. 226–27.

"The Evolution of America's Industrial Safety Movement." *Occupational Hazards,* September 1975.

Ford, Robert N. "Job Enrichment Lessons from AT&T." *Harvard Business Review,* January–February 1973, pp. 96–106.

Fringe Benefits. Washington, D.C.: Chamber of Commerce of the United States (biennially).

Gramaldi, J. V., and Simonds, R. H. *Safety Management.* 3d. ed. Homewood, Ill.: Richard D. Irwin, Inc., 1975.

Hodge, B. J., and Tellier, R. D. "Employee Reactions to the Four-Day Week." *California Management Review,* Fall 1975, pp. 25–35.

Hutton, D. T. "OSHA Citations: How to Avoid Them and What to Do about Them When You Can't." *Material Handling Engineering,* February 1975.

Neuman, John L. "Make Overhead Cuts That Last." *Harvard Business Review,* May–June 1975, pp. 116–26.

Reuter, V. G. "A New Look at Suggestion Systems." *Journal of Systems Management,* January 1976, pp. 6–15.

Saleh, S. D., and Hosek, J. "Job Involvement: Concepts and Measurements." *Academy of Management Journal,* June 1976, pp. 213–24.

Smith, H. R. "The Half-Loaf of Job Enrichment." *Personnel,* March–April 1976, pp. 24–31.

Wilson, R. M. S. *Cost Control Handbook.* New York: Holsted Press, 1975.

Wooton, L. M., and Tarter, J. L. "The Productivity Audit: A Key Tool for Executives." *MSU Business Topics,* Spring 1976, pp. 31–41.

Section V. 17, 18, 19, 20, 21, 22, 23.

Abbott, ———. "Forecasting for Inventory Control." *Proceedings, 1975 APICS Conference,* pp. 390–400.

Aggarwal, S. C., and Stafford, E. "A Heuristic Algorithm for the Flow-shop Problem with a Common Job Sequence on All Machines." *Decision Sciences,* April 1975, pp. 237–51.

Anthony, T. F., and LaFarge, R. L. "Multiple-Phase Purchasing-Production Scheduling." *Journal of Purchasing and Materials Management,* Winter 1975, pp. 15–21.

Baker, K. R. "Comparative Study of Flow-shop Algorithms." *Operations Research,* January 1975, pp. 62–73.

Berry, William L. "Lot Sizing Procedures for Requirements Planning Systems." *Production and Inventory Management,* 2d quarter 1972.

Bonsack, R. A. "Computer-based Manufacturing Planning and Control Systems." *Production and Inventory Management.* 2d quarter 1976, pp. 94–117.

Burlingame, L. J. "MRP—A Hope for the Future or a Present Reality." *Material Requirements Planning.* Chicago: American Production and Inventory Control Society, 1973, pp. 17–28.

Communication Oriented Production Information and Control System (*COPICS*). Vol. 1–8. IBM Corp., 1972.

Conlon, J. R. "Is Your Master Production Schedule Feasible?" *Production and Inventory Management,* 1st quarter 1976, pp. 57–63.

England, W. B., and Leenders, M. R. *Purchasing and Materials Management.* 6th ed. Homewood, Ill.: Richard D. Irwin, Inc., 1975.

Lamberson, L. R.; Diederick, D.; and Wuori, J. "Quantitative Vendor Evaluation." *Journal of Purchasing and Materials Management,* Spring 1975, pp. 19–28.

Lanford, H. W. *Technological Forecasting Methodologies.* New York: American Management Assn., 1972.

Mabert, V. A. "Statistical versus Sales Force—Executive Opinion Short Range Forecasts: A Time Series Analysis Case Study." *Decision Sciences,* April 1976, pp. 310–18.

May, J. G. "Linear Program for Economic Lot Sizes Using Labor Priorities." *Management Science,* November 1974, pp. 277–85.

Moskowitz, H., and Miller, J. G. "Information and Decision Systems for Production Planning." *Management Science,* November 1975, pp. 359–70.

New, C. "Job Shop Scheduling: Who Needs a Computer to Sequence Jobs?" *Production and Inventory Management,* 4th quarter 1975, pp. 38–45.

Orlicky, Joseph A.; Plossl, G. N.; and Wight, O. A. "Structuring the Bill of Materials for MRP." *Production and Inventory Management,* 4th quarter 1972.

Parsons, J. A. "In-Process Inventories under the Base-Stock Inventory Control Policy." *Journal of Systems Management,* November 1975, p. 40.

————. "Multi-Product Scheduling on a Single Machine." *Journal of Systems Management,* August 1974, pp. 43–44.

Paul, R. L. "Exercise in Finite Loading." *Journal of Systems Management,* March 1975, pp. 7–9.

Plossl, G. W., and Wright, O. W. *Material Requirements Planning by Computer.* Chicago: American Production and Inventory Control Society, 1971.

Putnam, A. O., and Everdell, R. "ROP's and MRP in Perspective." *Production and Inventory Management,* 3d quarter 1974, pp. 1–5.

Ravnick, D. A., and Fisher, A. G. "Probablistic Make-Buy Model." *Journal of Purchasing,* February 1972.

Roberts, B. J. "Vendor Rating Using Military Standards 105D." *Journal of Purchasing and Materials Management,* Winter 1975, pp. 30–33.

Schneeweiss, C. A. "Smoothing Production by Inventory—An Application of the Wiener Filtering Theory." *Management Science,* March 1971.

Shycon, Harvey N., and Sprague, Christopher R. "Put a Price Tag on Your Customer Servicing Levels." *Harvard Business Review,* July–August 1975, pp. 71–78.

Tersine, R. S. "Scientific Determination of Single-Order Quantities." *Purchasing and Materials Management,* September 1975, pp. 52–65.

Tersine, Richard J. *Materials Management and Inventory Systems.* Elsevier, North Holland, 1976.

Trippi, R. R., and Levin, D. E. "A Present Value Formulation of the Classical EOQ Problem." *Decision Sciences,* January 1974, pp. 30–35.

Wheelwright, S. C., and Makridakis, S. *Forecasting Methods for Management.* New York: John Wiley & Sons, 1973.

Section VI, Chapters 24, 25, 26.

Benson, L. A. and Sewall, R. F. "Dynamic Crashing Keeps Projects Moving." *Computer Decisions,* February 1972, pp. 14–18.

Brightman, Harvey J., and Kaczka, E. E. "A Computer Simulation Model of an Industrial Work Group." *Decision Sciences,* October 1973, pp. 471–86.

Butler, A. G., Jr. "Project Management: A Study in Organizational Conflict." *Academy of Management Journal,* March 1973, pp. 84–101.

Green, Thad B. "A Statistical Analysis of the Utilization Effectiveness of a PERT Program." *Decision Sciences,* July 1973, pp. 426–36.

Gunderman, James R., and McMurry, Frank W. "Making Project Management Work." *Journal of Systems Management,* February 1975, pp. 7–11.

Hughes, A. J., and Grawiog, D. E. *Linear Programming: An Emphasis on Decision Making.* Reading, Mass.: Addison-Wesley Publishing Co., 1973.

Maciariello, Joseph A. "Making Program Management Work." *Journal of Systems Management,* vol. 25, June 1974, pp. 8–15.

Moberly, L. E., and Wyman, F. P. "An Application of Simulation to the Comparison of Assembly Line Configurations." *Decision Sciences,* October 1973, pp. 505–16.

Plane, D. R., and Kochenberger, G. A. *Operations Research for Managerial Decisions.* Homewood, Ill.: Richard D. Irwin, Inc., 1972.

Ringer, L. J. "Statistical Theory for PERT in Which Completion Times of Activities Are Interdependent." *Management Science,* July 1971.

Strenski, J. B. "PERT Charting Public Relations." *Public Relations Journal,* February 1975, pp. 22–23.

Swanson, Lloyd A., and Pazer, Harold L. "Implications of the Underlying Assumptions of PERT." *Decision Sciences,* October 1971.

Section VII, Chapters 27, 28.

Adam, E. E., Jr. "Behavior Modification in Quality Control." *Academy of Management Journal,* December 1975, pp. 662–79.

Burnstein, Herman. *Attribute Sampling.* New York: McGraw-Hill, 1971.

Eshelman, R. H., and Pond, J. B. "Gaging and Testing." *Automotive Industries,* March 1, 1972.

Juran, Joseph M., and Gryna, Frank M. *Quality Planning and Analysis.* New York: McGraw-Hill, 1970.

Kirkpatrick, E. G. *Quality Control for Managers and Engineers.* New York: John Wiley & Sons, 1970.

Oxenfeldt, A. R. "Developing a Favorable Price—Quality Image." *Journal of Retailing,* Winter 1974–75, pp. 8–14.

Proceedings of the American Society for Testing Materials (annual).

Quality Assurance (monthly).

Wolff, P. "Quality Control: Survival of the Fittest." *Purchasing,* November 1, 1971.

Index

W–X

This book has been set in 10 and 9 point Times Roman, leaded 2 points. Section numbers and chapter titles are 24 point Vanguard Medium and section titles are 24 point Vanguard Light. Chapter numbers are 54 point Weiss Series II. The size of the maximum type page is 27 picas by 47½ picas.